Contemporary
Financial Intermediation

Dedication

To Elaine, Regina and Nate
My spiritual lenders of last resort
Stuart I. Greenbaum

To my parents, Lata and Viru
For everything that made this possible
Anjan V. Thakor

To Angela, Nuria and Mireia
The much valued counterforce in life
Arnoud W. A. Boot

Contemporary
Financial Intermediation

THIRD EDITION

Stuart I. Greenbaum
Washington University in St. Louis

Anjan V. Thakor
Washington University in St. Louis

Arnoud W. A. Boot
University of Amsterdam

ELSEVIER

AMSTERDAM • BOSTON • HEIDELBERG • LONDON • NEW YORK • OXFORD
PARIS • SAN DIEGO • SAN FRANCISCO • SINGAPORE • SYDNEY • TOKYO
Academic Press is an Imprint of Elsevier

Academic Press is an imprint of Elsevier
125, London Wall, EC2Y 5AS, UK
525 B Street, Suite 1800, San Diego, CA 92101-4495, USA
225 Wyman Street, Waltham, MA 02451, USA
The Boulevard, Langford Lane, Kidlington, Oxford OX5 1GB, UK

Notices
Knowledge and best practice in this field are constantly changing. As new research and experience broaden our understanding, changes in research methods, professional practices, or medical treatment may become necessary.

Practitioners and researchers may always rely on their own experience and knowledge in evaluating and using any information, methods, compounds, or experiments described herein. In using such information or methods they should be mindful of their own safety and the safety of others, including parties for whom they have a professional responsibility.

To the fullest extent of the law, neither the Publisher nor the authors, contributors, or editors, assume any liability for any injury and/or damage to persons or property as a matter of products liability, negligence or otherwise, or from any use or operation of any methods, products, instructions, or ideas contained in the material herein.

British Library Cataloguing-in-Publication Data
A catalogue record for this book is available from the British Library

Library of Congress Cataloging-in-Publication Data
A catalog record for this book is available from the Library of Congress

ISBN: 978-0-12-405196-6

For information on all publications
visit our website at http://store.elsevier.com

Printed and bound in the United States of America

Publisher: Nikki Levy
Acquisition Editor: J. Scott Bentley
Editorial Project Manager: Susan Ikeda
Production Project Manager: Melissa Read
Designer: Mark Rogers

Working together
to grow libraries in
developing countries

www.elsevier.com • www.bookaid.org

Abbreviated Contents

Extended Contents

Preface

In writing this book we set out to modernize the teaching of bank management at universities and collegiate schools of business. Our goal is to expand the scope of the typical bank management course by (1) covering a broader, but still selective, variety of financial institutions, and (2) explaining the *why* of intermediation, as opposed to simply *describing* institutions, regulations, and market phenomena. Our approach is unapologetically analytical, and we have tried to make analysis an appealing feature of this book. We will consider the book a success if it leads students to not only discover the endless subtlety and plasticity of financial institutions and credit market practices, but also develop an appreciation for *why* these institutions, market practices, and governmental regulations are encountered. The unifying theme is that informational considerations are at the heart of what most banks do.

The novelty of our approach lies in both the analytical orientation and our choice and sequencing of topics. We begin with the questions of why financial intermediaries exist and what they do. We believe that understanding the why of financial intermediation will prepare the readers for the inescapable volatility of the future. Regulations, institutions, and claims will change, but the functional foundations on which financial intermediaries are built will remain basically the same.

This is the third edition of this book, and we have added our good friend Arnoud Boot as a coauthor. Arnoud's input has helped us to provide a more complete treatment of global banking issues, including developments in the European Union, especially those since the global financial crisis of 2007–2009. Also the complexity of the financial system, the proliferation of linkages between institutions and financial markets, and systemic concerns warrant substantial attention. The significant changes that have occurred in global financial markets and regulation in the aftermath of this crisis made it essential to revise the second edition to reflect these changes.

PEDAGOGY

Each chapter (except the Introduction) begins with a glossary of terms that students will encounter while reading that chapter and will revisit throughout the book. Key nonbanking concepts are discussed in Chapter 1 to provide students with a clear basis on which to proceed. Within each subsequent chapter, we provide numerical examples, laying out each step from idea to solution. Each chapter ends with review questions, and many chapters include case studies to help students appreciate the power of the concepts as well as the complexities.

Moreover, because some chapters contain basic as well as more technical materials, more advanced discussions are isolated in boxes. Interesting, but inessential, information is likewise presented in isolated passages. This provides the instructor with enhanced flexibility in customizing the course.

ORGANIZATION

The book contains 18 chapters and an introductory chapter. The introductory chapter describes the motivation and background for the book, highlighting the central role of financial intermediation in economic progress. It also briefly summarizes each chapter in the book and discusses the Great Recession that followed the financial crisis of 2007–2009, linking the various chapters to the developments before, during, and after the crisis.

In Part I, Chapter 1 discusses the key concepts of information economics, game theory, market completeness, options, and other topics we use throughout the book. We recommend that these concepts, which are central to the issues encountered in subsequent chapters, be discussed when needed in the context of subsequent chapters, rather than being dealt with at the outset of the course.

In Part II, Chapters 2 and 3 examine the functions of financial intermediaries. Chapter 2 describes the variety of financial intermediation and the basic services provided by financial intermediaries. Chapter 3 sets forth the information-based theory of financial intermediation and explains how banks evolved from goldsmiths.

Part III addresses the identification and management of the major risks in banking. Chapter 4 discusses the major risks banks face, particularly those that are basic in the provision of financial services: interest rate risk, liquidity risk, and credit risk. Each risk is first discussed as an independent source of risk. Then it is recognized that in practice these risks are correlated, which calls for an integrated approach to risk management. Enterprise risk management is discussed as one such approach. Chapter 5 takes a deep dive into interest rate risk, and this risk is explained from the vantage point of the arbitrage-free term structure of interest rates (under both certainty and uncertainty). Chapter 6 focuses on liquidity risk.

The discussion of credit risk is taken up in Part IV, which focuses on the major on-blalance-sheet activities of banks. Chapter 7 analyzes credit risk and the lending decision. Credit rationing and other lending anomalies are examined in Chapter 8, which also includes a discussion of multiperiod credit contracting issues. Chapter 9 covers a few special topics in credit, including syndicated loans, loan sales, and project finance.

Part V deals with "off-balance sheet" banking. Chapter 10 discusses commercial bank contingent claims, including loan commitments, letters of credit and bankers' acceptances, interest rate swaps, and related contracts like caps, collars, and swaptions. Chapter 11 addresses securitization.

New to this edition, Parts VI and VII cover bank capital structure and the financial crises, respectively. Part VI covers the funding of the bank and has two chapters. Chapter 12 examines the economics of the deposit contract and also discusses (non-depository) "shadow banking". Chapter 13 is devoted to how a bank determines its capital structure. It also includes a discussion on some of the common myths that seem to sometimes enter into discussions of bank capital structure. This is followed by a discussion of various theories of bank capital structure. Part VII, which contains Chapter 14, discusses financial crises, with a special focus on the 2007–2009 financial crisis. The events leading up to the 2007–2009 crisis, what happened during the crisis, and the effects of the crisis and policy responses are discussed.

Bank regulation is covered in Part VIII by Chapters 15 and 16. First, we discuss how government safety nets provided to banks necessitate regulation to cope with the moral-hazard created by the safety net. We then discuss the major agencies of bank regulation in different parts of the world, including Japan and the European Union, and the various regulations they impose on banks. Considerable attention is devoted to capital regulation and the Basel accords. Liquidity regulation and restrictions on bank activities are also discussed. Then in Chapter 16, we turn to an analysis of proposals for regulatory reform. In particular, we discuss the 1991 FDIC Improvement Act, the Financial Services Modernization Act of 1999, the Dodd–Frank Wall Street Reform and Consumer Protection Act, and E.U. Regulatory and Supervisory Overhaul, the Banking Union and the de-Larosière Report. There is considerable material in these chapters that is new to this edition.

Also new to this edition, part IX deals with evolution of banks, their interaction with financial markets, and the role of financial innovation. We begin with a discussion of the link between financial development and economic growth, and follow this with an examination of the role of financial innovation in this link. Both the bright and dark sides of financial innovation are discussed. Then we move on to the interaction between banks and markets. We end with a discussion of the competitive and complementary aspects of this relationship and the role of securitization, shadow banking, and credit-rating agencies in this dynamic.

Finally, in Part X's Chapter 18, we look to the future, conjecturing about the evolution of banking in the United States and elsewhere. We discuss what we believe will be the major drivers of change: regulation, technology, and customer preference, and what this portends for banking.

We believe it will be difficult to cover the entire book in one academic quarter or even one semester. Students for whom this book is intended are not accustomed to thinking about asymmetric information and agency issues, so it takes time to become familiar with the basic concepts. We recommend that the instructor select a subset of topics, keeping in mind that it would probably require two semesters to comfortably complete the entire book. Possible course outlines are included in the Instructor's Manual.

Whatever the approach chosen by the instructor, we hope that this book provides an accessible, if intellectually challenging, rendering of contemporary banking thought. Our own experience in teaching these materials has been rewarding. We hope the same is true for others.

SUPPLEMENTARY MATERIALS

Instructor's Manual/Test Bank/Transparency Master

Initially prepared by Daniel Indro of Kent State University and revised for this edition by Johan Maharjan of Washington University in St. Louis, the Instructor's Manual includes lecture notes and outlines for each chapter, as well as answers to the end-of-chapter questions and case studies. To offer instructors more flexibility, the Instructor's Manual provides citations of recent articles that instructors can include in their class. Summaries and discussion questions are provided to help incorporate these articles for class discussion. The Test Bank offers approximately 500 questions and problems for use on exams, homework assignments, and quizzes. A set of overheads is also available for all chapters except the first one so that instructors can use these in their classroom presentation. All this material can be found online at: http://booksite.elsevier.com/9780124051966.

Acknowledgments

The third edition of *Contemporary Financial Intermediation* has benefited from the input of many colleagues and friends. In particular, we would like to thank Christy Perry and Johan Maharjan at Washington University in St. Louis for all their hard work in bringing the book to fruition. Moreover, Johan provided outstanding research assistance and editorial input, for which we are very grateful. We also thank Matej Marinč of the University of Ljubljana in Slovenia for excellent research support and other valuable feedback.

About the Authors

Stuart I. Greenbaum

Stuart Greenbaum is the former Dean and professor emeritus at the John M. Olin School of Business at Washington University in St. Louis. He is the 2006 recipient of the Lifetime Achievement Award of the Financial Intermediation Research Society. He was named the Bank of America Professor of Managerial Leadership in 2000. Before joining the Olin School in 1995, Greenbaum served for 20 years as a faculty of the Kellogg Graduate School of Management at Northwestern University where he was the Director of the Banking Research Center and the Norman Strunk Distinguished Professor of Financial Institutions. From 1988 to 1992, he served as Kellogg's Associate Dean for Academic Affairs. Before Northwestern, Greenbaum served as Chairman of the Economics Department at the University of Kentucky, and on the staffs of the Comptroller of the Currency and the Federal Reserve.

Greenbaum has served on 15 corporate boards. He also served on the Dean's Advisory Council of the Graduate Management Admission Council, and the board of AACSB International – The Association to Advance Collegiate Schools of Business, Executive Committee of the World Agricultural Forum, and on the board of the St. Louis Children's Hospital. He was thrice appointed to the Federal Savings and Loan Advisory Council, and was twice officially commended for extraordinary public service. Greenbaum has consulted for the Ewing Marion Kauffman Foundation, the Council of Higher Education of Israel, the American Bankers Association, the Bank Administration Institute, the Comptroller of the Currency, the Federal Reserve System, and the Federal Home Loan Bank System, among others. He has on numerous occasions testified before Congressional committees, as well as other legislative bodies.

Greenbaum has published two books and more than 75 articles in academic journals and other professional media. He is founding editor of the *Journal of Financial Intermediation* and has served on the editorial boards of 10 other academic journals.

Anjan V. Thakor

Anjan Thakor is John E. Simon Professor of Finance, Director of Doctoral Programs, and Director of the WFA Center for Finance and Accounting Research, Olin School of Business, Washington University in St. Louis. Prior to joining the Olin School, Thakor was The Edward J. Frey Professor of Banking and Finance at the Ross School of Business, University of Michigan, where he also served as chairman of the Finance area. He has served on the faculties of Indiana University, Northwestern University, and UCLA. He has consulted with many companies and organizations, including Whirlpool Corporation, Allision Engine Co., Bunge, Citigroup, RR Donnelley, Dana Corporation, AB-Inbev, Zenith Corporation, Lincoln National Corporation, J.P. Morgan, Landscape Structures, Inc., CIGNA, Borg-Warner Automative, Waxman Industries, Reuters, The Limited, Ryder Integrated Logistics, AT&T, CH2M Hill, Takata Corporation, Tyson Foods, Spartech, and the U.S. Department of Justice. Among many other honors, Dr. Thakor is the winner of the Reid MBA Teaching Excellence Award, Olin School of Business, 2005, and received the Outstanding Teacher in Doctoral Program award for the University of Michigan Business School, April 2003. He has published over 100 papers in leading academic journals in Finance and Economics, including *The American Economic Review*, *Review of Economic Studies*, *Journal of Economic Theory*, *The Economic Journal*, *The RAND Journal of Economics*, *The Journal of Finance*, *The Review of Financial Studies*, *The Journal of Financial Intermediation*, and *The Journal of Financial Economics*. Besides this book, he has published seven other books.

He is a founding editor of *The Journal of Financial Intermediation* and one of the founders of *The Financial Intermediation Research Society*. He is a fellow of *The Financial Theory Group*. He has served as an expert witness on numerous banking cases and testified in US federal courts on issues related to bank valuation and capital structure.

Arnoud W. A. Boot

Arnoud Boot is professor of Corporate Finance and Financial Markets at the University of Amsterdam and codirector of the Amsterdam Center for Law & Economics (ACLE). He is chairman of the Bank Council of the Dutch Central Bank (DNB), member of the Scientific Council for Government Policy (WRR) and the Advisory Scientific Committee of the European Systemic Risk Board (ESRB) in Frankfurt. Arnoud Boot is also Research Fellow at CEPR and member of the Royal Netherlands Academy of Arts and Sciences (KNAW).

Prior to his current positions, he was a faculty member of the J.L. Kellogg Graduate School of Management at Northwestern University, Bertil Danielsson Visiting Professor at the Stockholm School of Economics and Olin Fellow at Cornell University. During 2000–2001 he was a partner in the Finance and Strategy Practice at McKinsey & Co. In 2008, he was president of the European Finance Association (EFA).

In addition to his academic activities, Arnoud Boot advises extensively on ownership structure issues, particularly related to the public/private domain, and is consultant to several financial institutions and other corporations. He is also a nonexecutive director of several agencies. His research focuses on corporate finance and financial institutions. His publications have appeared in major academic journals, such as the *Journal of Finance*, *American Economic Review*, *Review of Financial Studies*, and the *Journal of Financial Intermediation*.

Introduction

Financial intermediation has been in service of civilized mankind for centuries. Financial contracts, including financial securities (e.g., shares, bonds, and derivatives), and the markets in which they are traded have mitigated and repositioned risks to their most cost-effective venues and advantageously redistributed cash flows through time. Insurance, equity, swaps, futures, and options contracts redistribute risks from those for whom they are onerous or unacceptable to those for whom they are bearable, at a price. Credit contracts transport wealth and income through time, again for a price, facilitating (dis)saving and investments. Agents can thereby consume (invest) more (less) than they earn or possess, providing a valuable flexibility thereby benefiting individuals as well as society. Financial intermediaries play an important role in this process of risk redistribution and intertemporal adjustment of consumption. Together with financial contracts, securities and markets, financial intermediaries constitute the *financial system*.

As a civilization develops economically, its financial system becomes more complex in order to serve a greater and more nuanced demand for risk management and allocation of capital. More than a few believe that we can gauge the progress of a civilization by the sophistication and complexity of a financial system. Yet, vulnerability almost inevitably accompanies complexity. Think of the evolution of tools. The sharper a scalpel, the greater the surgeon's precision, but mistakes, however infrequent, are apt to be more damaging with a sharper instrument. In the financial context, more indirect and nuanced instruments and more time efficient markets (think high frequency trading) will improve the allocation of resources, but they also make it more challenging to control, to modulate, to regulate. Complexity consequently gives rise to bubbles and crashes that impose costs in terms of social dislocations and lost output. This means the highs are higher and the lows are lower (greater fragility and volatility), even if we are better off, *on average*.

To minimize these social dislocations, the fragility of the financial system has to be kept in check. Ordinarily, we would rely on market forces to provide the necessary checks and balances to limit the fragility of the financial system. However, this requires that market participants understand how financial contracts and securities work or fail, something that may prove to be a challenge in a complex financial system. In particular, the more sophisticated agents will know more about the securities that are traded and contracts that are used in the market, and these agents may exploit the uninformed, with predictably negative societal effects. This then becomes a predicate for public intervention in financial markets, which is undertaken at a cost in order to avoid the presumably greater costs resulting from *laissez faire* where the public is too readily exploited as a result of the private information and market power of some institutions and individuals.

Understanding these issues requires one to access the body of knowledge in the financial intermediation area, a body of knowledge that has particularly grown since the 2007–2009 global crisis. This crisis is an issue we will turn to shortly. We first explain how our discussion of this body of knowledge is organized in the book.

SOME MORE ON THE ORGANIZATION OF THE CHAPTERS

Chapter 1 develops key concepts and analytical tools that are used subsequently. Chapter 2 introduces the plenitude of financial intermediaries, stressing the variety of institutions and financial services provided. This chapter describes the variety of financial needs that emerge in the typical developed economy and the responsiveness of markets in serving them. Chapter 3 turns to the economics of financial intermediation and the details of the financial system. Chapter 4 examines the risks managed by intermediaries, particularly those that are basic in the provision of financial services. Hence we encounter liquidity, market, interest rate, and credit risks. We also examine how these risks are integrated in forming a risk culture in a recent managerial innovation and need to be managed jointly, Enterprise Risk Management. Chapter 5 treats the details of interest rate risk, particularly root causes, measurement, and control. Chapter 6 tackles the details of liquidity risk.

Chapters 7, 8, and 9 constitute a more detailed examination of credit, default, or counterparty risk, which inheres in lending and reflects the core competency of commercial banks. Lending requires a searching analysis of the creditworthiness of the potential borrower followed by an appropriate design of the lending contract. Terms of the contract involve pricing of course, but this is only the beginning. Length of the loan, periodic payments of interest, fees, amortization, and the issues of collateral and covenants provide scope for endless variation in contractual design. Indeed, the loan covenants can lengthen or shorten the expected duration of the loan. So there is almost boundless scope for tailoring the terms of the loan to create value for both the lender and the borrower. After consummating the loan, there comes the all-important monitoring whereby the lender protects itself from unacceptable deterioration in the quality of the credit. If the borrower violates covenants of the loan contract or fails to make timely payments the loan will typically "accelerate" or become payable immediately. This, of course, invites a possible receivership or more likely a renegotiation, which involves yet additional banking skills. Credit management, in all of its varied manifestations, is the defining skill set of commercial banking. Specifically, Chapter 7 deals with the basics of spot lending; Chapter 8 examines how loans are priced, why credit is rationed, and how loans are restructured to reduce the probability of default; and Chapter 9 deals with loan syndications, loan sales, and project financing.

Bank loans are most often extended as an accompaniment to a bank loan commitment (or credit line), which is an option contract growing out of an ongoing bank relationship. Loan commitments are the subject of Chapter 10. Chapter 11 addresses securitization, an intermediation technology that enables a more granular distribution of risks and augments liquidity. Originally configured to transform illiquid residential mortgages into tradable securities, securitization has been used to "liquefy" cash flows as disparate as commercial leases and life insurance policies. This important financial technology enables the more efficient distribution of risk and the augmentation of liquidity for virtually any cash flow. No surprise then that it has also been subject to serious abuses.

Chapter 12 addresses the defining liability of commercial banks, the deposit contract. The bank deposit is withdrawable on demand and serves as society's means of payment or medium of exchange. It is typically government insured, sometimes implicitly, and thereby cements an inextricable dependency between government and privately owned commercial banks. This relationship has been both rancorous and symbiotic and its history is filled with irony, both tragic and comic. This chapter includes a discussion of "shadow banking," the nondepository part of the banking system that was less regulated than depository institutions, particularly before the 2007–2009 crisis, and therefore served as a sector where some financial activities were conducted to escape the regulatory taxes that would have been incurred had these activities been performed by depository institutions.

Chapter 13 asks how banks determine their liability structure or mix of debt and equity. Leverage, or equivalently paucity of bank capital (equity), can magnify the returns to shareholders yet increase the likelihood of insolvency. The financial leverage has been a source of contention between bank owners and public regulators. We discuss regulatory bank capital requirements in a later chapter.

Chapter 14 analyzes the financial crisis of 2007–2009 that precipitated the Great Recession. Banking and proximate financial markets, most especially those that financed home mortgages were central, but this calamity came to be aptly described as a perfect storm. There were many whose collective actions led to this crisis: politicians, investment bankers, mortgage bankers, central bankers, public regulators, public auditors, risk managers, credit rating agencies, fiduciaries, and more. The Great Recession was a saga of shared guilt. The lessons are many and nuanced.

Chapter 15 turns to the objectives of public regulation of the financial system. Every developed country of the world has a public regulatory infrastructure that matches the complexity of the financial system it seeks to protect from its worst excesses. We seek to tease out the commonality among these regulatory institutions, most of which are nation-based. Some of the most important are, however, essentially supranational in keeping with the spread of globalism.

Chapter 16 discusses major milestones in bank legislation and regulation. Every banking crisis seems to inspire new legislation and regulations that condition, but fail to obviate, the next crisis. While this regulatory dynamic is reminiscent of generals "fighting the last war", it nonetheless shapes banking regulation.

Chapter 17 examines the evolving boundaries between banks and financial markets. While we often think of banks and capital markets as distinct and competitive, their boundaries have become ever less fulgent as banks and markets coevolve.

Finally, Chapter 18 offers some speculative thoughts on the future of banking.

HOW THESE CONCEPTS HELP US UNDERSTAND THE GREAT RECESSION: THE 2007–2009 SUBPRIME CRISIS

The Great Recession, beginning late in 2007, was said to be the worst since the Great Depression of 1929; it is discussed extensively in Chapter 14. It followed a 20-year period often described as the Great (is the adjective overworked?) Moderation. A perfect storm is the way some have described the Great Recession. The market for residential and commercial mortgages was central to the Great Recession's severity if not to its timing. Due to a variety of factors that we will discuss later in the book, U.S. housing prices had risen, more or less uninterruptedly for decades prompting a collective overconfidence, an arrogance, expressed most concretely in an unprecedented and unsustainable relaxation of mortgage standards. A whole vocabulary developed around deterioration in credit standards. There were lo-docs and no-docs (referring to mortgage applications that did not require adequate documentation of income, employment, etc.), as well as zero-down, neg-am, etc. (referring to easy payment terms). All of these were expressions of the provision of mortgage finance to those who would previously not have qualified for home loans, certainly not in the amount offered. The liberality in credit standards inevitably led to expanded demand for home ownership and supported a seemingly ineluctable escalation in home prices. Even if buyers could ill afford to service their mortgage debt currently, the virtually certain increase in the value of their residence would provide the capital gains to assure solvency. Not only did first mortgages proliferate, second mortgages (home equity loans) grew on the basis of rising home values. Thus, the mortgage market inflated the bubble in housing, that is, until late 2007. A nationwide decline in housing prices followed, and years later we are still dealing with painfully high unemployment and underemployment and wasted potential output in the trillions of dollars, not to mention the accompaniment of polarizing social unrest. In addition to covering these issues in the context of the 2007–2009 crisis in Chapter 14, many of the concepts discussed here are discussed in the chapters leading up to Chapter 14.

Paradoxically, it appears that the very developments of the financial market that facilitated economic growth exacerbated the Great Recession. Indeed, this is the thesis of the celebrated *This Time is Different* by Reinhart and Rogoff (2009), a meticulous study of 800 years of business cycles. Important financial contracts and the many innovations in these contracts (like securitization) facilitated unprecedented financial leverage in the household, banking, and government-sponsored enterprise (so-called GSEs, especially Fannie Mae and Freddie Mac) sectors. However, there was more to the financial innovation story. Tainted mortgages were sold to, or guaranteed by, the massively overleveraged, politically influenced Fannie Mae, and Freddie Mac, or sold for resale to Wall Street's similarly overleveraged investment banks. The investment banks resold their mortgage assets to trusts that pooled the mortgages and sold claims against the cash flows generated by the mortgage pools. This added level of intermediation, called securitization, led to "tranched" financial claims typically categorized in descending order of seniority; this is discussed at great length in Chapter 11. That is, the most senior claims would be paid in full first, followed by each descending class of claims until the periodic cash flows generated by the mortgage pools either were exhausted or all tranches were contractually satisfied. These securitized claims were complex in that the underlying pools of mortgages were large and heterogeneous and the claims on the pools were structured giving rise to added subtlety and opacity. A kind of multiplicative complexity frustrated those seeking to assess the risk of mortgage-backed securities. Buyers found it prohibitively expensive to perform independent due diligence as their clients assumed had been done routinely. Rather, buyers of mortgage-backed securities became overly dependent on the rating agencies, the Moody's and Standard and Poors of the financial marketplace. But, the rating agencies themselves were operating in an environment in which historical data – which turned out to be a poor predictor of future defaults – exhibited low mortgage defaults and created a false sense of security. Moreover, some have suggested that the rating agencies were compromised by contracts that provided them with inappropriate incentives. That is, although they had reputational incentives to credibly certify the credit qualities of the issues they rated, their immediate compensation was less dependent on the accuracy of their work than on the volume of securities they evaluated. This revenue inducement led the rating agencies to compete to retain clients who paid for their services (the "issuer pays" model), and the clients quite naturally wished to maximize the certified quality of the securities they sought to sell. We discuss rating agencies in Chapters 2 and 17. The upshot of this misbegotten dynamic was that there was "ratings inflation" – the credit qualities implied by ratings seemed exaggerated, at least with the benefit of hindsight – and there were also failures of fiduciary responsibilities in the market for mortgage-backed securities. Does the "perfect storm" come into view? There is more.

The most junior and riskiest class of the tranched securitizations were commonly unrated residual claims which were difficult for the investment banks to peddle. These would reside on the balance sheet of the investment banks for prolonged periods waiting to be resecuritized into "toxic" CDOs (Collateralized Debt Obligations). CDOs were originally developed for the corporate debt market and were named as such to represent the fact that the collateral backing the securitized claims (or tranches) consisted of debt securities. However, in the years leading up to the 2007–2009 financial crisis, the rapid growth in the CDO market came from the mortgage-backed securities market, and many CDOs were created through aggregations of the detritus (junior stubs) of earlier securitizations. As indicated, the difficulty of evaluating these leveraged, riskier claims inflated the balance sheets of the banks engaged in securitization. In addition, the market became flooded with these extraordinarily opaque CDOs which also bore exaggerated quality indications from rating agencies.

The inflated balance sheets of investment banks, like Goldman Sachs and Morgan Stanley, had to be financed without the benefit of FDIC-guaranteed deposits. Hence, they harnessed the "repo" and asset-backed commercial paper markets. So doing, the investment banks borrowed from money-market mutual funds and similar institutional investors and used their risky assets as collateral. These borrowing channels came to be referred to as the "shadow banking system." They offered the investment banks a source of short-term funding that permitted them to warehouse longer-term high-risk mortgages.

However, the institutional investors providing the financing were constrained in many cases to offering short-term loans to the banks which meant that the banks were financing their mislabeled, longer-duration, risk-augmented assets with short-term liabilities. A generation of humiliated Savings and Loan managers could have explained that this kind of balance sheet mismatch was a prescription for disaster. In addition, the investment banks that were earlier leveraged six to eight times their capital account, ballooned up to 50-60 times leverage. Chapter 13 discusses leverage choices. Orders of magnitude increases in financial leverage clearly signal danger, even to the less sophisticated. Is the storm becoming clearer?

Reinhart and Rogoff (2009) major point is that economic downturns precipitated by the financial sector tend to be more severe in depth and duration. The Great Recession provided confirming evidence.

THE LEGACY OF THE GREAT RECESSION

Fair to say, the Great Recession caused an outpouring of retrospection by all manner of specialists, anointed and self-appointed: academics, management gurus, legislators and politicians of all stripes, public regulators, and bankers themselves. Turning back to recent history, people asked how Continental Illinois Bank, the country's largest commercial lender, and celebrated as one of America's five best managed businesses by Dun's Review in 1982, could be bankrupt by 1984. And how could this most prestigious banking behemoth be victimized by a minuscule shopping center bank (Penn Square Bank) in Oklahoma?

How could the entire Savings and Loan industry, comprising 4500 firms, bet its existence on an upward sloping yield curve that was widely known to flip according to volatile interest rate expectations? The industry, heavily regulated owing to its government insured deposits, has largely vanished, leaving a residue of public losses variously estimated in the hundreds of billions of dollars. Indeed, the failure of the Savings and Loan industry reoriented mortgage finance toward mortgage bankers, investment banks, and the aforementioned GSEs. That institutional reorientation, together with the spread of securitization and excess leverage, enabled the mortgage disaster central to the Great Recession.

Thus, the Great Recession can – to some extent – be traced directly to the Savings and Loan collapse of the 1980s. In their day, the Savings and Loans originated mortgages for their own balance sheet and were hence deeply concerned about the quality (credit risk) of borrowers. With their demise, mortgages were originated by mortgage banks almost entirely for resale. So these institutions were focused on volume, subject only to minimal quality standards dictated by the GSEs and Wall Street banks. Moreover, the GSEs were under Congressional pressure to expand home ownership and the Wall Street banks were reselling their mortgages via securitization to buyers preoccupied with yield and in any case unable to independently underwrite the claims and hence dependent on the compromised rating agencies.

The next watershed financial disaster came in the late 90s with the collapse of the storied hedge fund, Long Term Capital Management (LTCM). Founded in 1994 by John W. Meriwether, a legendary trader, LTCM specialized in outsized transactions with minimal investment risk. Among Meriwether's partners were Robert Merton and Myron Scholes, world-renowned academics and Nobel Prize winners. Not only was LTCM an intellectual powerhouse, it also achieved extraordinary size and leverage that accompanied worldwide acclaim. At the beginning of 1998, the year of its demise, LTCM had almost $5 billion of book value capital, assets of almost $130 billion and off-balance sheet derivative positions of $1.25 trillion in notional value. It was a largely unregulated intermediary that traded with virtually every important financial institution on the planet. It was the very essence of what today's public regulators would deem a "systemically important financial institution" warranting public oversight. Its failure was caused by a combination of many circumstances: to an evolution away from its initial low-risk investment strategies, high financial leverage, and most notably two external shocks, the 1997 East Asia financial crisis and the 1998 default on Russian government debt. These external shocks induced unprecedented correlations among various asset classes that had previously exhibited low correlations, substantially diminished the gains from portfolio diversification, and produced losses that resulted in a flight of investors and a dissipation of capital. These events prompted a shotgun bailout financed by their trading-partner banks, but cajoled by the U.S. Treasury and the Federal Reserve. The story of this spectacular collapse is well told by Roger Lowenstein (2000) in his "When Genius Failed: The Rise and Fall of Long-Term Capital Management". From our viewpoint, LTCM provides one more data point documenting both the fragility and centrality of contemporary financial arrangements, especially when instruments and trading strategies become nuanced.

It was a brief 3 years after LTCM failed that Enron failed. This was, at the time, the largest bankruptcy in history. Enron had over $100 billion in revenues in 2000, one year before its demise. Again, a paragon fell from highest repute, trading at over $90 per share in 2001 to virtual worthlessness in the same year. Here was the world's largest energy trader, led by a blue-ribbon board and executives with nonpareil credentials, utterly demolished. Its CFO was initially charged with 98 counts of fraud, money laundering, insider trading, and conspiracy. He received a sentence of 10 years without parole. The board chairman and CEO, Kenneth Lay and Jeffrey Skilling, were charged with 53 counts of bank fraud, making false statements to banks and auditors, securities and wire fraud, money laundering, conspiracy, and insider trading. Skilling was sentenced to 24 years and 4 months in prison. Lay succumbed before sentencing. Arthur Andersen, the Enron auditor, was found guilty of obstruction of justice (destroying evidence) and was put out of business. (Andersen was to be later absolved on appeal, but too late because their dissolution proved irreversible.)

The Enron scandal decimated reputations, lives, and fortunes. It was enabled in the last analysis by misrepresentation based on aggressive accounting countenanced by one of the world's leading accounting firms, a prestigious board of directors, and an ostensibly impeccable management team. The chairman of the Audit Committee was a leading academic accountant and dean of the Stanford Business School. The Chairman of the Board was a Ph.D. in economics and the Chief Financial Officer, an MBA from the Kellogg School of Management. Moreover, Enron operated in a highly regulated environment. How could all of these controls, external and internal, layered upon each other with conscious redundancy, have ignored blatant unethical, even illegal, behaviors that were ultimately exposed by less-informed journalists and securities analysts? More to our point, these transgressions were done with novel financial transactions and aggressive accounting and obscured leverage. Perhaps most notable were the so-called Special Purpose Entities (SPEs) that permitted Enron to devolve assets and liabilities into off-balance sheet entities that permitted Enron to reduce its nominal financial leverage and thereby massively understate its risk. Remarkably, this occurred only a few years before Citibank attracted unwanted notoriety for tweaking the SPE and redeploying it as a Structured Investment Vehicle (SIV). Again, its effect was to understate financial leverage. The lesson of the Enron tragedy was again the fragility of finance and the vulnerability of the less informed. The fact that Citigroup could employ SIVs so aggressively only a few short years after Enron's widely visible discrediting is doubly puzzling.

Following Enron came the still larger bankruptcy of WorldCom, then HealthSouth, Tyco, and the convulsion that led to the failure of Lehman Brothers, the shotgun sale of Bear Stearns, Merrill Lynch, Wachovia Bank, and the government recapitalization of the commercial banking system via TARP along with AIG, General Motors, and Chrysler Corporation. What is the takeaway from these all-too-quickly forgotten lessons of painful losses, both public and private? Excess leverage (inadequate capital), opaque assets, questionable accounting, inadequate controls, weak risk management, and less than steadfast leadership and illusory public regulation proved insurmountable!

George Santayana admonished that those failing to remember the past are condemned to repeat it. But, wait, there is more. In addition to a vast body of experience, there is a rich body of theory to learn from and both are offered in this textbook. Whether the student seeks to become a finance professional or a manager elsewhere, or merely an informed citizen seeking shelter in a befuddling and rapacious world of finance, this journey in learning should reduce the likelihood of being victimized. Ultimate success cannot be assured, but this learning journey will provide you with tools helpful in understanding the economic world around you and you will therefore be empowered to make better financial and political decisions.

As you embark on this journey of learning, open yourself to an appreciation for the splendid complexity arising from the irrepressible and creative innovations and adaptations of the financial system. Private-sector resilience is followed by public regulatory responses that, in turn, spur still more circumventing innovations. The endless malleability of the financial system stems from its stock in trade being nothing more substantial than the financial contract, the variation of which is limited only by the imagination of contracting parties. But almost inevitably, private sector ingenuity gives rise to occasional chicanery and the process of intermediation therefore displays the worst as well as the best in the human condition. It is the consequent drama that makes this topic so fascinating. Enjoy the illuminating journey!

REFERENCE

Reinhart, C., Rogoff, K., 2009. This time is different: eight centuries of financial folly. Princeton University Press, Princeton, NJ.

Part I

The Background

Chapter 1

Basic Concepts

"Practical men, who believe themselves to be quite exempt from any intellectual influences, are usually the slaves of some defunct economist. Madmen in authority, who hear voices in the air, are distilling their frenzy from an academic scribbler of a few years back. I am sure that the power of vested interests is vastly exaggerated compared with the gradual encroachment of ideas."

John Maynard Keynes: *The General Theory of Employment, Interest and Money,* 1947

INTRODUCTION

The modern theory of financial intermediation is based on concepts developed in financial economics. These concepts are used liberally throughout the book, so it is important to understand them well. It may not be obvious at the outset why a particular concept is needed to understand banking. For example, some may question the relevance of "market completeness" to commercial banking. Yet, this seemingly abstract concept is central to understanding financial innovation, securitization, and the off-balance sheet activities of banks. Many other concepts such as riskless arbitrage, options, market efficiency, and informational asymmetry have long shaped other subfields of finance and are transparently of great significance for a study of banking. We have thus chosen to consolidate these concepts in this chapter to provide easy reference for those who may be unfamiliar with them.

RISK PREFERENCES

To understand the economic behavior of individuals, it is convenient to think of an individual as being described by a utility function that summarizes preferences over different outcomes. For a wealth level W, let $U(W)$ represent the individual's utility of that wealth. It is reasonable to suppose that this individual always prefers more wealth to less. This is called "non-satiation" and can be expressed as $U'(W) > 0$, where the prime denotes a mathematical derivative. That is, at the margin, an additional unit of wealth always increases utility by some amount, however small.

An individual can usually be classified as being either risk neutral, risk averse, or risk preferring. An individual is considered *risk neutral* if the individual is indifferent between the certainty of receiving the mathematical expected value of a gamble and the uncertainty of the gamble itself. Since expected wealth is relevant for the risk neutral, and the variability of wealth is not, the utility function is *linear* in wealth, and the second derivative, denoted $U''(W)$, will equal zero. Letting $E(\bullet)$ denote the statistical expectation operator, we can write $U[E(W)] = EU(W)$ for a risk-neutral individual, where $U[E(W)]$ is the utility of the expected value of W and $EU(W)$ is the expected utility of W. For such an individual, changing the risk of an outcome has no effect on his well-being so long as the expected outcome is left unchanged.

The utility function of a *risk-averse* individual is *concave* in wealth, that is, $U''(W) < 0$. Such an individual prefers a certain amount to a gamble with the same expected value. *Jensen's inequality* says that

$$U[E(W)] > E[U(W)]$$

if U is (strictly) concave in W. Thus, risk-averse individuals prefer less risk to more, or equivalently, they demand a premium for being exposed to risk.

A *risk-preferring* individual prefers the riskier of two outcomes having the same expected value. The utility function of a risk-preferring individual is *convex* in wealth, that is, $U''(W) > 0$, Jensen's inequality says that

$$U[E(W)] < E[U(W)]$$

if U is (strictly) convex in W.

Despite the popularity of lotteries and parimutuel betting, it is commonly assumed that individuals are risk averse. Most of finance theory is built on this assumption. Figure 1.1 depicts the different kinds of risk preferences.

In Figure 1.2 we have drawn a picture to indicate what is going on. Consider a gamble in which an individual's wealth W can be either W_1 with probability 0.5 or W_2 with probability 0.5. If the individual is risk averse, then the individual has a concave utility function that may look like the curve AB. Now, the individual's expected wealth from the gamble is $E(W) = 0.5W_1 + 0.5W_2$,

S. I. Greenbaum, A. V. Thakor & A. W. A. Boot: Contemporary Financial Intermediation, Third edition. http://dx.doi.org/10.1016/B978-0-12-405196-6.00001-X

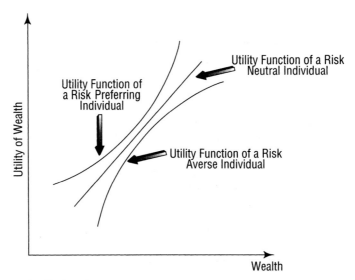

FIGURE 1.1 Three Different Types of Utility Functions.

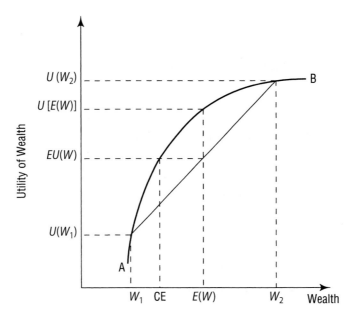

FIGURE 1.2 Risk Aversion and Certainty Equivalent.

which is precisely midway between W_1 and W_2. The utility derived from this expected wealth is given by $U[E(W)]$ on the y-axis. However, if this individual accepts the gamble itself [with an expected value of $E(W)$], then the expected utility, $EU(W)$, is midway between $U(W_1)$ and $U(W_2)$ on the y-axis, and can be read off the vertical axis as the point of intersection between the vertical line rising from the midpoint between W_1 and W_2 on the x-axis and the straight line connecting $U(W_1)$ and $U(W_2)$. Hence, as is clear from the picture, $U[E(W)] > EU(W)$. The more bowed or concave the individual's utility function, the more risk averse that individual will be and the larger will be the difference between $U[E(W)]$ and $EU(W)$.

We can also ask what sure payment we would have to offer to make this risk-averse individual indifferent between that sure payment and the gamble. Such a sure payment is known as the *certainty equivalent* of the gamble. In Figure 1.2, this certainty equivalent is denoted by CE on the x-axis. Since the individual is risk averse, the certainty equivalent of the gamble is less than the expected value. Alternatively expressed, $E(W)$–CE is the *risk premium* that the risk averse individual requires in order to participate in the gamble if his alternative is to receive CE for sure.

The concept of risk aversion is used frequently in this book. For example, we use it in Chapter 3 to discuss the role of financial intermediaries in the economy. Risk aversion is also important in understanding financial innovation, deposit insurance, and a host of other issues.

DIVERSIFICATION

We have just seen that risk-averse individuals prefer to reduce their risk. One way to reduce risk is to diversify. The basic idea behind diversification is that if you hold numerous risky assets, your return will be more predictable, but not necessarily greater. For diversification to work, it is necessary that returns on the assets in your portfolio not be perfectly and positively correlated. Indeed, if they are so correlated, the assets are identical for practical purposes so that the opportunity to diversify is defeated. Note that risk can be classified as idiosyncratic or systematic. An idiosyncratic risk is one that stems from forces specific to the asset in question, whereas systematic risk arises from the correlation of the asset's payoff to an economy-wide phenomenon such as depression. Idiosyncratic risks are diversifiable, systematic risks are not.

To see how diversification works, suppose that you hold two assets, A and B, whose returns are random variables.[1] Let the variances of these returns be σ_A^2 and σ_B^2, respectively. Suppose the returns on A and B are perfectly and positively correlated, so that $\rho_{AB} = 1$, where ρ_{AB} is the correlation coefficient between A and B. The proportions of the portfolio's value invested in A and B are y_A and y_B, respectively. Then the variance of the portfolio return is

$$\sigma_P^2 = y_A^2\sigma_A^2 + 2y_Ay_B\text{Cov(A,B)} + y_B^2\sigma_B^2 \tag{1.1}$$

where Cov(A, B) is the covariance between the returns on A and B. Then, using

$$\text{Cov(A,B)} = \rho_{AB}\sigma_A\sigma_B \tag{1.2}$$

we have

$$\sigma_P^2 = y_A^2\sigma_A^2 + 2y_Ay_B\rho_{AB}\sigma_A\sigma_B + y_B^2\sigma_B^2 \tag{1.3}$$

Since $\rho_{AB} = 1$, the right-hand side of Equation (1.3) is a perfect square, $(y_A\sigma_A + y_B\sigma_B)^2$. As long as $y_A\sigma_A + y_B\sigma_B \geq 0$, we can write Equation (1.3) as

$$\sigma_P = y_A\sigma_A + y_B\sigma_B. \tag{1.4}$$

Thus, if $\rho_{AB} = 1$, the standard deviation of the portfolio return is just the weighted average of the standard deviations of the returns on assets A and B. *Diversification therefore does not reduce portfolio risk when returns are perfectly and positively correlated.* For any general correlation coefficient ρ_{AB}, we can write the portfolio return variance as

$$\sigma_P^2 = y_A^2\sigma_A^2 + 2y_Ay_B\rho_{AB}\sigma_A\sigma_B + y_B^2\sigma_B^2. \tag{1.5}$$

Holding fixed y_A, y_B, σ_A, and σ_B, we see that $\partial\sigma_P^2 / \partial\rho_{AB} > 0$, that is, portfolio risk increases with the correlation between the returns on the component assets. At $\rho_{AB} = 0$ (uncorrelated returns),

$$\sigma_P^2 = y_A^2\sigma_A^2 + y_B^2\sigma_B^2. \tag{1.6}$$

Example 1.1

To see that diversification helps in this case, suppose $y_A = y_B = 0.5$, $\sigma_A^2 = 100$, $\sigma_B^2 = 144$. Calculate the variance of a portfolio of assets A and B, assuming first that the returns of the individual assets are perfectly positively correlated, $\rho_{AB} = 1$, and then that they are uncorrelated, $\rho_{AB} = 0$.

Solution

In the case of perfectly and positively correlated returns, $\sigma_P = 0.5(10) + 0.5(12) = 11$, or $\sigma_P^2 = 121$. With uncorrelated return, Equation (1.6) implies that $\sigma_P^2 = 0.25(100) + 0.25(144) = 61$. Thus, not only is this variance lower than with perfectly and positively correlated returns, but it is also lower than the variance on either of the components assets.

---

1. Suppose x and z are two random variables that can each take any value from $-\infty$ to $+\infty$. A random variable is one whose behavior is described by a probability density function, but its precise value is unknown. Let f(x) and g(z) be the density functions of x and z, respectively. Then, the probability that x will lie between the two numbers a and b is Pr$(a \leq x \leq b) = \int_a^b f(x)\,dx \geq 0$, and $\int_{-\infty}^{\infty} f(x)\,dx = 1$. The statistical mean (expected value) of x is E(x) $= \int_{-\infty}^{\infty} xf(x)\,dx$, its variance is $\sigma_x^2 = \int_{-\infty}^{\infty} [x - E(x)]^2 f(x)\,dx$, and the mean and variance of z are analogously defined. The covariance of x and z is Cov$(x,z) = \int_{-\infty}^{\infty}\int_{-\infty}^{\infty} [x - E(x)][z - E(z)]f(x)g(z)\,dx\,dz$ and the correlation between x and z is $\rho_{xz} = $ Cov$(x,z)/\sigma_x\sigma_z$ where σ_x and σ_z are the standard deviations (square roots of the respective variances) of x and z, respectively.

The maximum effect of diversification occurs when ρ_{AB} is at its minimum value of -1, that is, returns are perfectly negatively correlated. In this case

$$\sigma_P^2 = y_A^2\sigma_A^2 - 2y_A y_B \sigma_A \sigma_B + y_B^2 \sigma_B^2 \tag{1.7}$$

so that

$$\sigma_P = \left| y_B \sigma_B - y_A \sigma_A \right|. \tag{1.8}$$

This seems to indicate that the portfolio will have some risk, albeit lower than in the previous cases. But suppose we construct the portfolio so that the proportionate holdings of the assets are inversely related to their relative risks. That is,

$$y_A / y_B = \sigma_B / \sigma_A \tag{1.9}$$

or

$$y_A = \sigma_B y_B / \sigma_A. \tag{1.10}$$

Substituting Equation (1.10) in Equation (1.8) yields

$$\sigma_P = y_B \sigma_B - (\sigma_B y_B \sigma_A / \sigma_A) = 0$$

indicating that in this special case of perfectly negatively correlated returns, portfolio risk can be reduced to zero!

Even when assets with perfectly negatively correlated returns are unavailable, we can reduce portfolio risk by adding more assets (provided they are not perfectly positively correlated with those already in the portfolio).[2] To illustrate, suppose we have N assets available, each with returns pairwise uncorrelated with the returns of every other asset. In this case, a generalized version of Equation (1.6) is

$$\sigma_P^2 = \sum_{i=1}^{N} y_i^2 \sigma_1^2 \tag{1.11}$$

where y_i is the fraction of the portfolio value invested in asset i, where $i = 1,\ldots, N$, and σ_i^2 is the variance of asset i. Suppose we choose $y_i = 1/N$.

Then, defining σ_{max}^2 as the maximum variance among the σ_i^2 (we assume $\sigma_{max}^2 < \infty$, and permit $\sigma_i^2 = \sigma^2$ for all i in which case $\sigma_{max}^2 = \sigma^2$), Equation (1.11) becomes

$$\sigma_P^2 = \sum_{i=1}^{N} \left[\frac{1}{N} \right]^2 \sigma_i^2$$
$$\leq N \left[\frac{1}{N} \right]^2 \sigma_{max}^2$$
$$= \frac{\sigma_{max}^2}{N}.$$

As N increases, σ_P^2 diminishes, and, in the limit, as N goes to infinity, σ_P^2 goes to zero. Thus, if we have sufficiently many assets with (pairwise) uncorrelated returns, we can drive the portfolio risk to as low as we wish and make returns as predictable as desired.

An obvious question is why investors do not drive their risks to zero. First, not all risks are diversifiable. Some contingencies affect all assets alike and consequently holding more assets will not alter the underlying uncertainty. This is the notion of *force majeure* in insurance. Natural calamities such as floods and earthquakes are examples, as are losses attributed to wars. Second, as the investor increases the number of securities held in the portfolio, there are obvious costs of administration. These costs restrain diversification, but in addition numerous studies indicate that a large fraction of the potential benefits of diversification is obtained by holding a relatively small number of securities. That is, the marginal benefits of diversification decline rapidly as the number of securities increases.

Finally, cross-sectional reusability of information diminishes the incentive to diversify. We shall have more to say in Chapter 3 about information reusability since this is a major motivation for the emergence of financial intermediaries. It suffices to say that if a lender invests in learning about a customer in the steel business in order to make a loan, it will see a potential

---

2. In pointing out the "fallacy of large numbers," Samuelson (1963) shows that diversification is not necessarily preferred by risk averse individuals if one adds more wealth to the portfolio as more assets are added. The notion of diversification for portfolios of securities was introduced by Markowitz (1959).

benefit in lending to others in the steel business. The resulting concentration spreads the costs of becoming informed. Thus, we observe diversification within areas of specialization among most financial intermediaries. And when we speak of financial intermediaries processing risk, we mean that they are typically diversifying some, absorbing some, and shifting some to others.

RISKLESS ARBITRAGE

Arbitrage is the simultaneous purchase and sale of identical goods or securities that are trading at disparate prices. This opportunity for riskless profit is transitory because the exploitation of such opportunities eliminates the initial price disparities.

The term *arbitrage* is often loosely applied to situations in which objects of trade are similar, but not identical, and where the risk is thought to be small but not totally absent. Since such situations are often referred to as arbitrage, the redundant "riskless arbitrage" has emerged to describe arbitrage rather than limited risk speculation (a situation in which a profit can be had for a small risk). Thus, succinctly defined, riskless arbitrage is profit without risk and without investment. We shall later discuss "risk-controlled arbitrage" as an illustration of limited risk speculation. Consider the following illustration of riskless arbitrage.

Example 1.2

Suppose that there are two possible states of the economy next period: high (H) and low (L). Available in the capital market are two risky securities, R_1 and R_2, and a riskless bond, B. The state-contingent payoffs and current market prices of these instruments are presented in Table 1.1. Examine whether there are riskless arbitrage opportunities.

TABLE 1.1 State-Contingent Payoffs and Prices of Securities

	Payoff in State		
Security	H	L	Current Price
R_1	$100	0	$40
R_2	0	$100	$40
B	$50	$50	$43

Solution

Since you can combine R_1 and R_2 to get a payoff that is equivalent to that from B, you can see now that there is an opportunity for riskless arbitrage. If you buy one unit each of R_1 and R_2 for a total outlay of $80, you are assured of $100 next period, regardless of whether state H or L is realized. So you can sell two units of B for $86 earning a riskless profit of $6. You are obliged to pay the buyers of these two units of B a total of $100 next period, but this you can do from the cash inflows produced by the securities R_1 and R_2 that you possess. Since you can sell these two units of B before you even buy R_1 and R_2, your profit requires no investment on your part and no risk. You could of course sell an arbitrarily large number of units of B and buy the appropriate units of R_1 and R_2, giving yourself a veritable money machine. But as your purchases and sales increase in volume, it is reasonable to expect the prices of the securities to converge, thereby eliminating the opportunity for riskless arbitrage again. An important implication is that the prices of related securities cannot be determined independently of each other. This observation has provided a powerful way to price derivative securities such as options.

The notion that any capital market equilibrium should preclude riskless arbitrage has proved to be a powerful concept in many applications in finance, including financial intermediation. We will see this idea applied in other contexts, including the valuation of contingent claims such as loan commitments.

OPTIONS

An option is a contract that gives the owner the right to either buy or sell an asset at a predetermined price at some future time or over some fixed time interval. Consider an asset whose value at time $t = 1$ will be X. Viewed at $t = 0$ (the present), X is a random variable. A *call option* entitles its owner to *buy* this asset at a fixed price, P_c, at or before $t = 1$. If he does not wish to buy the asset, he can allow the option to expire unexercised. Thus, the value of the call option at $t = 1$ is

$$C(t = 1) = \begin{cases} X - P_c & \text{if } X > P_c \\ 0 & \text{if } X \leq P_c. \end{cases} \tag{1.12}$$

The theory of option pricing explains $C(t = 0)$, the value of the call option at $t = 0$. The basic idea is to construct a portfolio consisting of the underlying stock and a riskless bond in such a manner that it yields the same payoff as the option. Since there can be no riskless arbitrage in equilibrium, the prices of this portfolio should equal the price of the option. We can then price the option by using the observed prices of the stock and the bond. We will have more to say about option pricing in later chapters.

Symmetrically, a *put option* entitles the option owner to *sell* an asset at a fixed price, P_p, at or before $t = 1$. Thus, at $t = 1$ the value of the put option is

$$P(t = 1) = \begin{cases} P_p - X & \text{if } X > P_p \\ 0 & \text{if } X \leq P_p. \end{cases} \tag{1.13}$$

In addition to being a put or call, an option can be either *European* or *American*. A European option can be exercised only at some predetermined maturity date, for example, at $t = 1$ in the above discussion. An American option can be exercised any time prior to maturity. Thus, an American option never can be worth less than its European counterpart.

An important property of options that we will use frequently is *that the more volatile the value of the underlying security on which the option is written, the more valuable the option.* The following example illustrates this property.

Example 1.3

Consider a European call option with an exercise price $P_c = \$100$. At $t = 1$, X will be \$110 with probability 0.5 and \$90 with probability 0.5. For simplicity, suppose everybody is risk neutral and the discount rate is zero (so that future payoffs are valued the same as current payoffs). Then from Equation (1.12) we have

$$C(t = 1) = \begin{cases} \$10 & \text{with probability } 0.5 \\ 0 & \text{with probability } 0.5 \end{cases}$$

Thus, $C(t = 0) = 0.5(10) = \$5$. Now suppose we increase the variance of X, keeping its mean unchanged. Let X be \$150 with probability 0.5 and \$50 with probability 0.5. From Equation (1.13) we have

$$C(t = 1) = \begin{cases} \$50 & \text{with probability } 0.5 \\ 0 & \text{with probability } 0.5 \end{cases}$$

Thus, $C(t = 0) = 0.5(50) = \$25$. The call option is now five times more valuable! You should work through a similar example for put options to convince yourself that puts have the same property.

Option pricing theory[3] is used in our later discussions of the valuation of off-balance sheet claims like loan commitments, and in our analysis of deposit insurance.

MARKET EFFICIENCY

An efficient capital market is one in which every security's price equals its "true" economic value[4]. But what is true? In economics, it means a price that incorporates *all* the information available to investors at the time. In an efficient market, an *appropriately defined set of information* is fully and immediately impounded in the prices of all securities. The basic idea is that competition among investors and the resulting informational exchanges will lead to market efficiency. This implies that price changes in an efficient market must be random. If prices always reflect all relevant information, then they will change only when new information arrives. However, by definition, new information cannot be known in advance. Therefore, price changes cannot be predictable.

We speak of three forms of market efficiency, distinguished by the amount of information impounded in the price. A market is said to be *weak-form* efficient if prices impound all historical information. In a weak-form efficient market, if P_t is the price at time t, then the expected value (at time t) of the price at time $t + 1$ conditional on the price at time t, written as $E(P_{t+1}|P_t)$, is the same as $E(P_{t+1}|P_t, \ldots, P_0)$, the expected value of P_{t+1} conditional on the entire history of stock prices up until time t (that is, $P_t, \ldots, P_0$). That is,

$$E(P_{t+1} \mid P_t) = E(P_{t+1} \mid P_t, P_{t-1}, P_{t-2}, \ldots, P_0). \tag{1.14}$$

This means that you can do no better forecasting tomorrow's price P_{t+1} using the entire history of prices than you could using just today's price P_t. The reason is that weak-form efficiency implies that P_t itself should contain all the historical information contained in the sequence $\{P_{t-1}|P_{t-2}, \ldots, P_0\}$.

---

3. Option pricing theory was pioneered by Black and Scholes (1973) and Merton (1973).
4. "Market efficiency" was pioneered by Fama (1970).

Semistrong form market efficiency requires that all publicly available information be contained in the current price. Since all historical information is in the public domain, a semistrong form efficient market is always weak-form efficient. However, there may be contemporaneous information in the public domain that became available after the most recent price was determined. Thus, semistrong form efficiency is a more demanding form of efficiency than weak-form efficiency.

A market is *strong-form* efficient if prices impound *all* information, including that possessed by insiders. Few economists believe that markets are strong-form efficient. Although there is a mountain of empirical evidence accumulated over nearly two decades suggesting that markets are semistrong form efficient, recent theoretical and empirical research has shown that the market may not even be (always) weak-form efficient.[5]

If the capital market were strong-form efficient, there would be no role for financial intermediaries as information processors (unless intermediaries were crucial in making the market efficient). However, when strong-form efficiency fails to obtain, we can have different individuals primarily possessing different sorts of information. In Chapter 3, we will show that in such markets, financial intermediaries have a role to play. At many junctures in this book, we will discuss how the efficiency (or lack thereof) of markets affects the profits to be earned from financial intermediation. An example of this is financial innovation.

MARKET COMPLETENESS

The economic world we inhabit is complex and pervasively uncertain. It is often useful to think of this uncertainty in terms of the possible states of nature that can occur in the future. Each such state, call it θ, can be viewed as a possible economic outcome. For example, θ may correspond to different levels of gross domestic product. Although we do not know what θ will be tomorrow, we can assign a probability distribution over possible values of θ. For the theory, it does not matter how many values θ can take. For simplicity, suppose θ can take integer values from 1 to some arbitrary number N.

In evaluating problems of economic efficiency, an important consideration is the *number* of different *financial securities* available relative to the number of states of nature. Two financial securities are considered "different" if they do not have identical payoffs in every state. To see the implications of this, consider the following simple example.

Example 1.4

Suppose there are three states of nature and only two securities may be thought of as shares of stock issued by two different companies. The payoffs offered by these securities in the different states of nature are shown in Table 1.2.

TABLE 1.2 Example With Three States of Nature and Two Securities

	States of Nature		
	1	2	3
Security 1 payoffs	10	20	15
Security 2 payoffs	15	0	25

Consider now an individual who owns 10 percent of security 1 and 20 percent of security 2. If $\theta = 1$ occurs, his wealth will be $0.10(10) + 0.20(15) = 4$. If $\theta = 2$ occurs, his wealth will be $0.10(20) + 0.20(0) = 2$. If $\theta = 3$ occurs, his wealth will be $0.10(15) + 0.20(25) = 6.5$. Thus, the value of the individual's portfolio can be described by the vector (4, 2, 6.5), where the first element corresponds to his wealth in state 1 and so on.

While the individual can achieve the vector (4, 2, 6.5), it is easy to see that one cannot achieve the vector (2, 6.5, 9.5). It is impossible for one to find ownership fractions in the two securities that will allow one to achieve this wealth vector. The reason is that there are fewer (independent) securities than there are states of nature. If we had a third security, we could have ensured that our individual could achieve any desired income vector. Of course, in reality individuals are also constrained by their budgets. The point is simply that when there are fewer securities than there are states of nature, it is generally impossible for the individual to attain any desired future wealth rearrangement. This is ultimately a limitation on the individual's ability to insure against contingencies.

The securities depicted in our simple example are not really stocks or bonds or any of the other financial securities commonly found in the capital market. Rather, these securities are claims to income in different states of the world. We can nevertheless visualize a market where such claims are traded. We would then have a number of securities, one for each state of nature, promising to pay 1 dollar if that particular state occurred and nothing otherwise. Such securities are called *primitive state-contingent claims* or *Arrow-Debreu securities* after the economists Kenneth Arrow and Gerard Debreu, who

---

5. See Schwert (2003) and Fama and French (2008).

first studied this issue and later went on to win Nobel Prizes in Economics (Debreu, 1959). Such a market would represent an ideal way of organizing a securities exchange, since it would give individuals complete freedom (subject only to their own purchasing power limitations) in designing portfolios that deliver the desired distribution of income in different states of the world. That is, an individual can design any "homemade" security in such a market.

If there are as many Arrow-Debreu securities as there are states of nature, the market is referred to as *complete*. In a complete market, an individual can achieve any desired distribution of income, subject to the individual's budget constraint. On the other hand, if there are fewer Arrow-Debreu securities than there are states of nature, we have an *incomplete market,* which places a limitation on the ability of transactors to manage uncertainty. The conceptual beauty of a complete market is that we can examine the market prices of securities that are currently trading and determine the market price of any *new* security we may wish to introduce. We can do this without knowing the preferences of individual investors in the economy. The key is that we can use the prices of existing securities to compute the prices of the (fictitious) Arrow-Debreu securities, and then use this information to price any new security we want to introduce. Suppose that in Example 1.2, we are given the prices of securities R_1 and R_2; recall that the price of each security is $40. Moreover, R_1 pays off $100 in state H and 0 in state L, whereas R_2 pays off 0 in state H and $100 in state L. Let Pi_H and Pi_L be the prices of the Arrow-Debreu securities in states H and L, respectively. Then, the market price of security R_1 should be 100 times the price of the state H Arrow-Debreu claim, that is, $40 = 100\, Pi_H$, $Pi_H = 0.4$. Similarly, the market price of security R_2 should be 100 times the price of the state L Arrow-Debreu claim, that is, $Pi_L = 0.4$. We are now ready to price any security in this two-state economy. For example, the riskless bond in Example 1.2, which pays $50 in each state, should be priced at $50Pi_H + 50Pi_L = \$40$. A security that pays $1,000 in state H and $56 in state L should sell at $1000Pi_H + 56Pi_L = \$422.40$, and so on.

The concept of market incompleteness is used in Chapter 16 in connection with our discussion of financial innovation. Other applications can be found in chapters on off-balance sheet activities, securitization, and deposit insurance.

ASYMMETRIC INFORMATION AND SIGNALING

Economic transactions often involve people with different information. For example, the borrower usually knows more about its own investment opportunities than the lender does. Corporate insiders normally know more about the values of assets owned by their firms than shareholders. A doctor can be expected to be better informed about his or her own medical expertise than a patient.

The better-informed economic agents have a natural incentive to exploit their informational advantage. Insider trading scandals on Wall Street illustrate how those with access to privileged information can profit, despite laws aimed at preventing such activity. Of course, those who are uninformed should anticipate their informational handicap and behave accordingly. It is this interaction between the inclination of the informed to strategically manipulate and the anticipation of such manipulation by the uninformed that results in distortions away from the "first best" (the economic outcome in a setting in which all are equally well-informed).

Problems of asymmetric information were brought to the forefront when George Akerlof, who later went on to win the Nobel Prize in Economics for his contribution, sought to explain why used cars sell at such large discounts relative to the prices of new cars.[6] The following example takes some shortcuts, but conveys the intuition of Akerlof's analysis.

Example 1.5

Consider a used car market in which differences in the care with which owners use their cars lead to quality differences among cars that started out identical. It is natural to suppose that the owner of the used car knows more about its quality than potential buyers. As an example, assume that there are three possible quality levels that the used car in question can have, $q_1 > q_2 > q_3 = 0$. If the quality level is q_3, the car is a lemon. Such a car would be priced as being worthless if buyers could correctly assess its quality. If the quality is q_2, the car has a value of $5, and if the quality is q_1, the car is worth $10. Assume that all agents are risk neutral and a buyer does not want to pay more for a car than its expected worth. In a similar vein, the car owner does not wish to sell at less than what the car is worth. Suppose that each car owner knows his car's quality, but buyers only know that cars for sale can be of quality q_1, q_2, or q_3. Faced with a given car, they cannot identify its precise quality. However, they believe that there is a probability 0.4 that the quality is q_1, a probability 0.2 that it is q_2, and a probability 0.4 that it is q_3. What will happen in such a market?

Solution

If all cars are offered for sale, risk neutral buyers will compute the *expected* value of a (randomly chosen) car as $(0.4) \times \$10 + (0.2) \times \$5 + (0.4) \times 0 = \$5$. Hence, if the market is competitive, we would expect $5 to be the market clearing price. However, at this price those who own cars with quality q_1 will refuse to sell. Thus, only cars of qualities q_2 and q_3 will be offered at $5.

---

6. See Akerlof (1970).

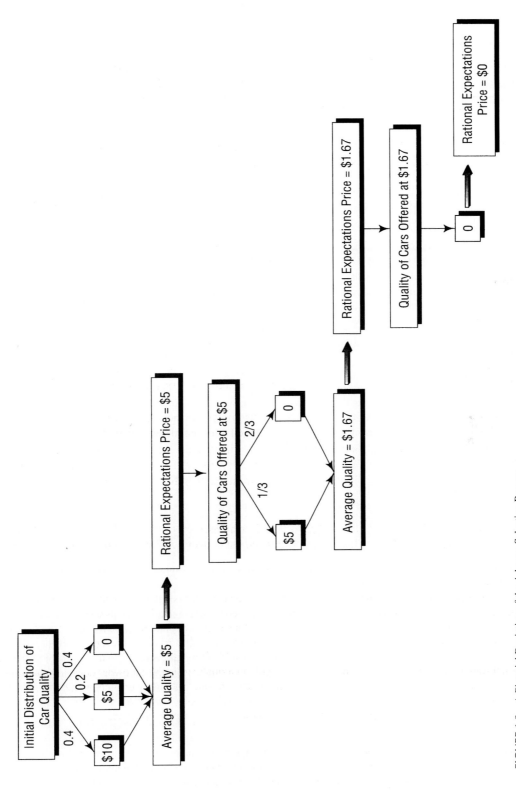

FIGURE 1.3   A Pictorial Depiction of the Adverse Selection Process.

However, buyers will anticipate this and revise their beliefs about the quality dispersion of cars in the market. They will now assume that if the selling price is $5, the probability is $0.2/(0.2 + 0.4) = 1/3$ that the quality is q, and it is $2/3$ that it is q_3. Thus, the expected value of a car drops to $(1/3)(5) + (2/3)(0) = \$1.67$. No cars will, therefore, be bought at $5 (it cannot be a market clearing price). Now if $1.67 is the price, those with cars of quality q_2 will drop out and the only cars offered for sale will be lemons. This process is called *adverse selection* and it results in the market clearing price being driven to zero. In other words, the demand for cars at any positive price is zero, and the market breaks down, as depicted in Figure 1.3. You should note a key assumption made in this example. All market participants have *rational expectations*. That is, uninformed buyers rationally anticipate what informed sellers will do at any given price and informed sellers rationally anticipate the demand buyers will have at that price. Hence, we do not need to go through a sequential process of price convergence to zero. No cars will be bought or sold.

The insight that asymmetric information can cause market failure was novel and striking. Its profound implications were quickly recognized to extend well beyond the used car market. Informational asymmetries were seen as being capable of causing markets to break down and thus possibly justify regulatory intervention by the government. Indeed, in the chapters that follow, we will examine banking regulation from this informational perspective.

However, calls for regulation based on Akerlof's analysis were too hasty. Market participants have the capability and incentives to deploy mechanisms to prevent market failure, and in any case market failure is the most extreme form of distortion created by asymmetric information. To see this in the context of our used car example, consider the following extension of that example.

Example 1.6
Suppose that cars of different qualities have different probabilities of engine failure within a given time period, and that these differences are reflected in their values of 0, $5, and $10. Suppose the failure probability is 0.1 for the q_1 quality car, 0.5 for the q_2 quality car, and 1 for the q_3 quality car. Do warranties have a role to play in this market?

Solution
To prevent market failure, the sellers of better cars must somehow distinguish themselves from the sellers of lower quality cars. One way to do this would be with warranties or guarantees. The seller of the q_1 quality car can announce that he will reimburse the buyer W_1 if his car fails, and the seller of q_2 quality car can announce that he will pay the buyer W_1 if his car fails. If buyers believe that *only* the owners of q_1 quality cars will promise a W_2 payment upon failure and that only the owners of q_2 quality cars will promise a W_2 payment upon failure, then they will make the appropriate inference and should be willing to pay prices that accurately reflect the qualities of the cars offered for sale. In order for such an indirect transfer of information to be effective, no seller should wish to mimic the strategy of a seller of a different quality car. Otherwise, buyers will eventually learn of the potential mimicry and the credibility of the signal will be destroyed.

Since the failure probability for a q_1 quality car is 0.1, the buyer should be willing to pay $10 (the intrinsic worth of a q_1 quality car) plus 0.1 times W_1, the latter being the amount he expects to collect from the seller. Thus, the equilibrium price (P_1) of a q_1 quality car should be $10 + 0.1W_1$. Similarly, if the owner of a q_2 quality car follows his equilibrium strategy, the equilibrium price (P_2) of a q_2 quality car should be $5 + 0.5W_2$. To ensure that the q_2 quality car owner will not misrepresent himself as a q_1 quality car owner, W_1 should be set to satisfy

$$10 + 0.1W_1 - 0.5W_1 \leq 5 + 0.5W_2 - 0.5W_2. \qquad (1.15)$$

The left-hand side (LHS) of Equation (1.15) is the expected payoff to a q_2 quality car owner misrepresenting himself as a q_1 quality car owner; he receives a price P_1 and has an expected outflow of $0.5W_1$ to pay the liability under the warranty. The right-hand side (RHS) of Equation (1.15) is what the q_2 quality car owner gets if he follows his nonmimic strategy; he receives a price of P_2 and has an expected cash outflow of $0.5W_2$. When someone is indifferent between telling the truth and lying, it is conventionally assumed that truth-telling will be chosen. Thus, Equation (1.15), which is referred to as an *incentive compatibility* (*IC*) *condition,* can be treated as an equality and we can solve it to obtain $W_1 = 12.5$. IC here means that the seller's incentives to maximize personal profit should be compatible with truthful representation of the car's quality.

The IC condition that ensures that the seller of lemons does not mimic the seller of q_2 quality cars can be similarly expressed as follows

$$5 + 0.5W_2 - W_2 \leq 0. \qquad (1.16)$$

Solving Equation (1.16) as an equality yields $W_2 = 10$. It is straightforward to verify that the seller of q_2 quality cars will not mimic the seller of lemons under the described conditions, that is, q_2 quality cars will be offered for sale.

You can easily verify that this scheme guarantees that the seller of lemons will not mimic the seller of q_1 quality cars and that the seller of q_1 quality cars will not mimic either the seller of q_2 quality cars or the seller of lemons.

To summarize, we have produced a simple scheme of "warranties" that prevents market failure. The seller of q_1 quality cars promises to pay the buyer $12.5 if his car fails; this enables him to sell his car for $10 + 0.1(12.5) = \$11.25$. The seller of q_2 quality cars promises to pay the buyer $10 if his car fails; this enables him to sell his car for $5 + 0.5(10) = \$10$. The lemons are withdrawn from the market.

The warranty offered here can be viewed as a *signal* of quality. A (perfectly revealing) signal is one that enables the uninformed to infer the information that the agent possessed privately *a priori*. For a signal to be useful it must be *informative,* and this requires that the signaling mechanism be incentive compatible. In turn, IC requires that the cost of signaling must be negatively correlated with quality.[7] That is, it must be less costly at the margin for a higher quality seller to emit a given signal. The higher cost of signaling serves to deter the lower quality sellers from mimicking their higher quality counterparts. In our context, you can see that a warranty of $12.50 imposes an expected liability of $1.25 on the q_1 quality seller, $6.25 on the q_2 quality seller, and $12.50 on the seller of lemons.

Note too that *in equilibrium* (i.e., when each seller maximizes expected profit) the chosen signal is *costless* for the seller emitting it. Although the q_1 quality seller promises to pay $12.50, he has only a 0.1 probability of having to pay, and since he collects $11.25 upon selling the car, his cash inflow net of the expected liability is $10. This is exactly what he would have gotten *without* issuing a warranty, if we were in a "first best" world in which the quality of each car was common knowledge. Likewise, the q_2 quality seller's net cash inflow is $5. Signals are *costless* in equilibrium. The reason for this, as you may have guessed, is that the seller is (correctly) compensated by the buyer for issuing the warranty, that is, cars with better warranties sell at higher prices. Such signals are called *nondissipative*[8] because the cost of the signal is a *transfer payment* from one party to the other, and there is no loss in the aggregate.

We can also have *dissipative* signals. To see this, suppose that instead of paying cash, the seller promises to reimburse the cost of repairing a portion of the damage. The q_1 quality seller promises complete coverage, the q_2 quality seller offers to absorb half the cost of repair, and the lemons owners choose not to participate. For every dollar it costs the seller to fix the damage, its value in terms of improved car quality is $0.80. You can now easily verify that there exists a signaling scheme similar to the one derived previously which ensures truthful signaling by each seller, assuming that the seller is willing to accept a net payoff (after dissipative signaling costs are deducted) that is less than the car's worth. The q_1 quality seller's net receipt is less than $10 and the q_2 quality seller's is less than $5. Each absorbs a signaling cost for which it is not compensated, that is, there is a net loss due to signaling.[9] For example, dividends can be a dissipative signal of future cash flows if they are personally taxed at a higher rate than capital gains (as was the case prior to the 1986 Tax Reform Act) and if external financing involves (transactions) costs that are avoided by financing with retained earnings. Later in this book, we will see other examples of dissipative signaling.

The concept of asymmetric information underlies much of what we discuss in this book, so you should expect to encounter it in more than a few of the remaining chapters.

AGENCY AND MORAL HAZARD

It has been observed that the key distinction between man and machine is *moral hazard*.[10] First introduced in the insurance literature, this term describes situations in which the incentives of principal (the employer or the owner of the property) and agent (the employee or the person renting/using the property) diverge. A rational economic agent can be expected to maximize his own expected utility,[11] and where his self-interest conflicts with the principal's, the principal will suffer. The principal must therefore design a contract that will achieve a congruence between her goals and the agent's.

Examples of moral hazard abound. Consider automobile insurance. If you have a car that you know is worth $500 and your collision insurance will pay you $1,000 if the car is completely destroyed, you may be tempted to let your car roll down the hill and collide with an immovable object. Now you may never dream of doing this, but your willingness to spend on the maintenance of brakes may be subtly affected by your insurance policy. In any case, insurance companies cannot afford to assume that ethical or reputational considerations dominate their customers' behaviors. This is one reason why we observe deductibles in insurance contracts. Coinsurance clauses are designed to share the risks and thereby bring the insured's incentives into closer alignment with those of the insurer.

Moral hazard is also common in financial contracting among claimants in a corporation. Suppose you manage a firm and your goal is to maximize shareholder wealth. If you have risky bonds outstanding, you will not always choose investments that maximize the total value of the firm. Rather, you may choose projects that maximize the value of equity at the expense of the bondholders. This can be illustrated with the following numerical example.

---

7. Michael Spence, who made this point, was awarded the Nobel Prize in Economics for his contribution to the economics of asymmetric information. See Spence (1973, 1974). A book that discusses this extensively is Bolton and Dewatripont (2005).

8. See Bhattacharya (1980).

9. If the seller is unwilling to bear the dissipative cost of signaling and the buyer will not bear it either, then a signaling equilibrium will fail to exist.

10. See Ross (1974).

11. We will refer to agents in the masculine and principals in the feminine.

Example 1.7
Consider a firm that will liquidate one period hence at time $t = 1$. There are no taxes and the firm can invest $30 in a risky venture at $t = 0$ using retained earnings. If the investment is not made, shareholders get a dividend of $100 at $t = 0$. The firm's debt requires a payment of $100 at $t = 1$, and its investment choices are described in Table 1.3.

For simplicity, assume that the discount rate is zero. What should the firm do?

TABLE 1.3 Payoffs Related to Different Investment Opportunities

	State of Nature	
Strategy	Boom (with probability 0.5)	Bust (with probability 0.5)
Total firm value at $t = 1$ if no investment made and $100 dividend paid at $t = 0$	$110	$70
Total firm value at $t = 1$ if $30 investment made and $70 dividend paid at $t = 0$	$200	$5

Solution
To analyze this problem, first compute the net present value (NPV) of each choice for the firm as a whole. If it does not invest, then its expected value is $0.5(110) + 0.5(70) = \$90$. Add to this the $100 dividend paid at $t = 0$ and we get a total firm value of $190. If it does invest, then its expected value is $0.5(200) + 0.5(5) = \$102.5$. Add to this the $70 dividend paid at $t = 0$ and we get a total firm value of $172.5. Since the total firm value is lower with the investment than without, the project has a negative NPV. The apparent choice should be to reject the investment.

Hold it for a minute, though! This decision rule is the right one only if you want to maximize total firm value. But remember that your goal is to maximize the wealth of the shareholders. If there is no investment, the shareholders get $100 dividend plus $10 ($110 debt payment) in the boom state and nothing in the bust state (limited liability, which stipulates that the liability of the shareholder does not extend beyond the assets of the firm, means that the bondholders get $70 and the shareholders get $100 + 0.5(10) = \$105$). On the other hand, if the project is accepted, they get $100 in the boom state and nothing in the bust state. Thus, the value of this strategy to the shareholder is $70 + 0.5(100) = \$120$. Clearly, the shareholders want you to invest in the project. Thus, a project with a negative NPV for the firm as a whole may be chosen in the best interest of the shareholder.

This example illustrates a moral hazard faced by bondholders. The firm, acting in the interest of the shareholders, has an incentive to undertake investments that benefit the shareholders at the expense of creditors. In this example, the expected payoff to the bondholders is $0.5(100) + 0.5(70) = \$85$ if the firm does not invest in the risky project and $0.5(100) + 0.5(5) = \$52.50$ if the firm invests in the risky project. Thus, by investing in the risky project, the shareholders reduce the wealth of the bondholders by $32.50. The shareholders themselves gain $15, so that there is a net decline in total firm value of $17.50. This is the aggregate loss due to moral hazard.

In this example, we assumed that the manager acted in the best interest of the shareholders. However, that is a questionable assumption too.[12] As an agent of the shareholders, the managers can do many things that may not be in the interest of the shareholders. For example, by inflating expenses, management can divert earnings from shareholders to management. Likewise, managers can discourage takeovers and thereby entrench themselves at the possible expense of shareholders. Managers may also select myopic and low-risk investment projects with a view toward protecting their positions and reputations.

You may have noticed that a critical assumption made in these examples is that the principal (the insurance company, the bondholders, or the shareholders) is unable to completely control the agent's behavior. If it were possible to costlessly observe the agent's actions, there would be no moral hazard. If the insurance company could precisely observe the insured, it would simply prohibit all actions detrimental to the car. It is because final outcomes do not unambiguously reveal the actions that may have influenced them that such proscriptions cannot be effectively written into contracts. Thus, for moral hazard to arise, the following must occur: (i) the agent's actions (that affect the final outcome) cannot be costlessly observed by the principal, and (ii) there is some noise (exogenous uncertainty) that masks the agent's action in the final outcome.

Of course, the principal anticipates the agent's behavior. Thus, the principal attempts to design a contract that aligns the agent's incentives with it's own. Deductibles and other coinsurance provisions in insurance contracts serve this purpose.

---

12. See Jensen and Meckling (1976) and Mirrlees (1976). James Mirrlees, a British economist, was one of the pioneers in models of moral hazard in economics, and was awarded the Nobel Prize in Economics for his contributions. Tirole (2006) provides an integrated treatise.

Bondholders address moral hazard by limiting the firm's debt (the higher the debt/equity ratio, the greater is the inclination of shareholders to choose risky projects), by requiring collateral, and by including in the debt contract covenants that restrict the borrower's actions. More on this appears in Chapter 9.

Another way to address moral hazard is to contract with the agent over extended time periods. Because of the possibility of reputational consideration, the agent may restrain self-interested behavior that is to the principal's detriment.[13] However, because lives are finite and because present consumption is usually preferred to future consumption, an agent's concern for reputation will not completely eliminate moral hazard.

It is important to understand that moral hazard is *not* the same as fraud. Most interesting cases of moral hazard do not involve illegal behavior. It is not illegal for shareholders to take on riskier projects than the bondholders would like. Nor is it illegal for a manager to invest in projects with faster paybacks than shareholders would like. Moral hazard may involve fraud, but it need not. It will almost always involve ethical considerations.

Agency and moral hazard issues, like asymmetric information, pervade much of this book. The chapters that make heaviest use of these ideas are Chapter 3 in which we discuss the role of banks and other financial intermediaries, Chapters 7 and 8 on spot lending issues, and Chapter 12 on deposit insurance.

TIME CONSISTENCY

An issue that often crops up in moral hazard and adverse selection models is *time consistency*. To illustrate, suppose an employee expends effort to produce output on behalf of a principal. This output is affected by the agent's effort as well as some exogenous uncertainty that is beyond the agent's control. Thus, by observing the output the principal cannot be sure what effort the agent has taken. Suppose the principal is risk neutral and the agent is risk averse. Further, the principal must guarantee the agent some minimum level of expected utility[14] to ensure his participation. Finally, the agent would rather work less than more. The sequence of events is as follows: the principal gives the agent a wage contract, after which the agent expends some effort, following which the exogenous uncertainty is resolved, and then the output is realized. How should the agent be compensated?

If the principal could observe the agent's effort, the answer is simple. "Optimal" risk sharing is achieved if the principal pays the agent a fixed wage conditional upon the agent expending some prespecified effort, and nothing otherwise. This risk-sharing scheme is optimal because it completely insulates the risk-averse manager from risk and imposes all of it on the risk-neutral principal. Because the effort is observable, it can be directly contracted upon. The agent will then do what the principal desires and receive a certain compensation that completely insures him against the randomness arising from the exogenous uncertainty. The principal receives the (random) output, but the randomness is costless because the principal is risk neutral.

If the agent's effort is unobservable, the above contract is unfeasible. The contract will be contingent on the only observable variable, the output. If the agent is promised a fixed wage, he avoids effort, so it is necessary to relate the wage to the output. This will motivate him to work harder to increase his share of the output. However, this approach to controlling the moral hazard has a cost. Since the agent is risk averse and his wage is uncertain, he will need to be compensated for the risk he bears. This will increase the principal's wage bill.

Now suppose that after the agent has expended his effort but before the output is realized, the principal has an opportunity to renegotiate the contract. Since the agent has already taken his effort, motivational concerns are irrelevant. The principal would be tempted to offer the agent a new wage that is fixed in amount (that is, independent of the output) and slightly less than the *expected* value of the agent's wage under the old contract. The risk-averse agent will gladly accept a slight reduction in his expected wage in order to rid himself of the income uncertainty inherent in the earlier contract. The risk-neutral principal is happy to save a little on the wage bill because the risk is a matter of indifference to it. Since both the principal and the agent are happy with this new arrangement, it's difficult to see why it would not replace the old one.

---

13. See Holmstrom (1999).

14. Because the agent is risk averse, it makes more sense to talk about a reservation expected utility than a reservation wage. To see this, suppose there was a choice between two wage contracts, W_1 and W_2, where W_1 pays $144 for sure and W_2 pays $400 with probability 0.5 and nothing with probability 0.5. Suppose we take $121 as the minimum wage a risk-neutral agent will require to work for the principal. Then, such an agent will accept either a wage contract but will prefer W_2 since it has a higher expected value. On the other hand, a risk-averse agent with a utility function over wealth (W) given by $U(w) = \sqrt{W}$ will prefer W_1 to W_2. W_1 yields him an expected utility of $EU(W_1) = \sqrt{144} = 12$ utils, whereas W_2 yields him an expected utility of $EU(W_2) = 0.5\sqrt{400} = 10$ utils. If 11 utils is the minimum level of expected utility he needs in order to accept employment, then he will work only if he is offered W_1. You can see that we cannot define a minimum expected wage for such an agent since he does not evaluate his personal satisfaction by comparing expected wages. Rather, he computes the utility he expects to derive from each alternative.

This is an example of a wage contract that is *time-inconsistent*. Although it seems like a good idea to negotiate a wage contract initially which conditions the agent's compensation on the realized output, such a contract will not work if both the agent and the principal recognize that they will subsequently want to renegotiate the effect of the contract. The possibility of renegotiating the contract destroys the incentive effect of the contract. If the agent knows that his wage ultimately will be fixed, why should he work hard? To avoid this difficulty, it is necessary to build a *time-consistency* (or renegotiation-proofness) into the contract design. Contracts must be such that both parties to the contract should not have an incentive to renegotiate them.

To see how renegotiation-proofness affects contracts, consider the example of a bank–borrower relationship. The bank desires to protect itself against the borrower's incentive to increase the riskiness of the loan. It may use loan covenants that empower it to accelerate or call off the loan if the borrower violates performance standards specified in loan covenants, often expressed in terms of financial ratios. The bank believes that this threat will induce the borrower to avoid excessive risk. However, when the bank is confronted with a violation of one or more of these covenants and threatens to accelerate the loan, the borrower offers a 50 basis point increase in the loan interest rate and offers assurances that the loan covenants will remain inviolate. The bank realizes that it can increase its reported profit by accepting the borrower's proposal and therefore withdraws its threat. To the extent that the borrower anticipates this behavior, the threat is not that the loan will be accelerated, but rather that the interest rate will be increased.

This is an example of a loan contract that is not renegotiation-proof. A renegotiation-proof loan contract would have specified interest rate penalties for minor loan covenant violations and would have included a loan acceleration provision only for violations so egregious (and informative) that the bank's best interest would call for the loan's termination regardless of possible enticements by the borrower.

Thus, contracts that are not renegotiation-proof are ultimately unsustainable. There is yet another aspect of time consistency that is unrelated to renegotiation-proofness. To illustrate, we shall use an *adverse selection* example. Suppose a bank is faced with two types of borrowers: good and bad. It cannot distinguish between good and bad borrowers *a priori*, but if it could, it would lend only to the good borrowers. Suppose the borrower incurs a cost in applying for a bank loan. Moreover, the bank can discover whether a borrower is good or bad by screening borrowers at some cost. If the bank does not screen, it charges a common interest rate from both types of borrowers and all borrowers who apply for credit. Borrowers know, however, that if the bank could distinguish among borrowers, it would lend to good borrowers exclusively. Now suppose the bank announces that it will screen all borrowers, so that it can sort out the bad borrowers and offer good borrowers a lower interest rate. Is this a time-consistent policy?

The answer is no. If borrowers believe that the bank will implement its policy, no bad borrower would apply for credit since the application cost would be wasted. However, they will anticipate this and infer that all applicants are good. But if they are all good, why incur a screening cost? Borrowers, in turn, anticipate this and realize there will be no screening, in which case *all* borrowers apply. But then it pays to screen! The result is an infinite regress and there is no equilibrium. We will have more to say about this issue in our discussion of credit rationing and bank regulation.

NASH EQUILIBRIUM

When agents transact with each other and each tries to selfishly maximize, they can be viewed as engaging in a *noncooperative game*. To describe the outcome, the concept of a *Nash equilibrium* has been proposed. Note first that by "equilibrium" we mean the attainment of some sort of a "steady state" in terms of the plans of action adopted by participants so that nobody can gain by unilaterally altering their plan of action. Before describing this equilibrium concept, notice that the outcome of the game depends on each player's actions. Moreover, each individual's actions will depend on what he thinks the adversary will do, since the final outcome is the collective resolution of individual actions. Thus, how each agent perceives the game will be played has an influence on each agent's choice of strategy and these choices determine the final outcome. To have an equilibrium, we cannot have erroneous beliefs. That is, if I take an action believing that you will do something, then you cannot do something else; if you do, the outcome cannot be an equilibrium. I would regret having made the decision and would wish to change it.

This intuitive notion is captured by the Nash equilibrium concept. Suppose there are n players engaged in a noncooperative game. Let S_i be the strategy (choice of action) of players i and let asterisks identify equilibrium strategies. Then the strategies $(S_1^*, S_2^*, \ldots, S_n^*)$ constitute a Nash equilibrium if, for every $i = 1, 2, \ldots, n$, S_i^* maximizes the personal welfare of agent i when all other agents play their equilibrium strategies. That is, suppose players 1 and 2 are engaged in a noncooperative game and strategies S_1^* and S_2^* represent a Nash equilibrium. Then, holding S_2^* fixed, player 1 cannot do better with any strategy other than S_1^*, and holding S_1^* fixed, player 2 cannot do better with any strategy other than S_2^*. We now illustrate this concept in the example below and in Figure 1.4.

Example 1.8

Suppose there are two prisoners who jointly committed a crime. There is insufficient evidence to convict either of them, unless one or both disclose information. The police, in an attempt to break their bond of silence, separately offer each the following deal. If prisoner 1 confesses and informs on prisoner 2 (who does not confess and inform on prisoner 1), then prisoner 1 will be freed. Let 4 represent the payoff equivalent to being set free after confessing. We assume that confessing and informing on his partner in crime causes the prisoner to feel a twinge of remorse, so that he enjoys 5 if he is freed without confessing. Of course, if prisoner 1 confesses and prisoner 2 does not, the latter will be convicted. Let 0 represent the payoff equivalent of being convicted. If both prisoners confess and inform, then both will be convicted, but the person who confesses and is still convicted receives a lighter sentence than one who remains silent and is convicted. Let 1 represent the payoff equivalent of being convicted despite confessing. Both prisoners know that if neither confesses, they will both be set free. What will be the Nash equilibrium in this "prisoners' dilemma"?

		Prisoner 2	
		Confess	Remain silent
Prisoner 1	Confess	1,1	4,0
	Remain silent	0,4	5,5

FIGURE 1.4   Strategic Form for Prisoners' Dilemma Game Prisoner 2.

Solution

To answer this question let us first organize the payoffs to the various strategies in a matrix (known as the "strategic form" of this game). The first number in each cell is the payoff of prisoner 1 and the second number is the payoff of prisoner 2.

There are two Nash equilibria in this game: (i) both prisoners confess, and (ii) both players remain silent. To see why (i) is a Nash equilibrium, suppose prisoner 1 conjectures that prisoner 2 will confess. Then, if prisoner 1 confesses he gets 1, and if he remains silent he gets 0. So he confesses. On the other hand, suppose prisoner 2 conjectures that prisoner 1 will confess. Then, since his decision problem is same as that of prisoner 1, he too finds that confessing is optimal. Thus, (i) is a Nash equilibrium because, in choosing his strategy, each prisoner correctly conjectures the strategy of the other prisoner. Similarly, if each prisoner believes that the other will remain silent, then it is clearly best for each to remain silent. Thus, (ii) is also a Nash equilibrium.

Multiple Nash equilibria are common. Even though the two prisoners are clearly better off remaining silent, and even though they know this, it is possible for both to confess. This is because they can collude. Which equilibrium arises depends on trust among thieves.

The concept of Nash equilibrium is used extensively in the rest of this book. In particular, you will see quite a bit of it in Chapter 3, Chapters 7 and 8, and in the discussion of bank runs and deposit insurance in Chapter 12.

REVISION OF BELIEFS AND BAYES RULE

In this section, we will discuss how a rational person would react to the arrival of new information. When a person does not know everything there is to know about something that will happen in the future, he can be viewed as formulating beliefs about what will happen. These beliefs can be described by a probability distribution. That is, as an incompletely informed person, you can say that you believe that there is some probability that outcome "a" will occur, some probability that outcome "b" will occur, and so on. Now, suppose some new information arrives. It does not inform you completely, but it adds to what you already know. The question is: how will you revise your original beliefs in the face of this new information? We illustrate this in the context of a specific example.

Example 1.9

Suppose you wish to determine the television channel on which you should watch the evening news to learn about the next day's weather. There are two main channels (say 1 and 2) that you can choose from. Your main criterion is the accuracy of the weather forecast, and you believe that the weather forecaster can be either "good" (g) or "bad" (b). Right now, you think that there is a 50-50 chance that the weather forecaster on either channel is good, that is, your (prior) belief is that the probability is 0.5 that the weather forecaster is g on either channel. You also realize that nobody is perfect, so that a good forecaster has a 0.8 chance of being right and a bad forecaster has a 0.5 chance of being right. Imagine for now that the forecasters on both channels give you "point estimates" (i.e., they will tell you whether or not it will rain tomorrow) rather than probabilistic forecasts (e.g., there is a 60% chance of rain). Suppose that the forecaster on channel 1 said last night that it would rain today and forecaster on channel 2 said that it would not. If you observe rain, how should you revise your beliefs?

Solution

Clearly, it would not be wise to suddenly change your beliefs sharply and assert that the channel 1 forecaster is good and the channel 2 forecaster is bad. So, how should you proceed?

To answer this question, we need to formalize the belief revision process. *Bayes rule* is a statistical device that provides a formula to compute how beliefs should be revised. In essence, it tells us how a rational person should compute *conditional probabilities*. Suppose $x_1, \ldots, x_n$ are the possible realizations of the random variable x and $\Pr(x_i)$ is the prior (unconditional) probability that $x = x_i$, with x_i being some value chosen from $x_1, \ldots, x_n$. Similarly, y_i is some realization of the random variable y, which conveys information about x. Then, Bayes rule says that if you observe $y = y_j$, you should infer that the probability that $x = x_i$ is given by

$$\Pr(x_i | y_j) = \frac{\Pr(y_j | x_i)\Pr(x_i)}{\sum_{i=1}^{n}\Pr(y_j | x_i)\Pr(x_i)} \tag{1.17}$$

The (unconditional) probability $\Pr(x_i)$ is known as a *prior belief* and the (conditional) probability $\Pr(x_i|y_j)$ is known as a *posterior belief*. In the context of our weather forecasting example, suppose we define

$$\Pr(\text{forecaster is good} \mid \text{he is correct}) \equiv \Pr(g \mid c)$$

$$\Pr(\text{forecaster is good} \mid \text{he is wrong}) = \Pr(g \mid w)$$

$$\Pr(\text{forecaster is bad} \mid \text{he is correct}) = \Pr(b \mid c)$$

and so on. Then,
Pr (channel 1 forecaster is good | he was correct in predicting rain)

$$= \Pr(g \mid c) = \frac{\Pr(c \mid g)\Pr(g)}{\Pr(c \mid g)\Pr(g) + \Pr(c \mid b)\Pr(b)}$$

$$= \frac{0.8 \times 0.5}{0.8 \times 0.5 + 0.5 \times 0.5} = 0.615.$$

Similarly,
Pr (channel 2 forecaster is good | he was wrong in predicting no rain)

$$= \Pr(g \mid w) = \frac{\Pr(w \mid g)\Pr(g)}{\Pr(w \mid g)\Pr(g) + \Pr(w \mid b)\Pr(b)}$$

$$= \frac{0.2 \times 0.5}{0.2 \times 0.5 + 0.5 \times 0.5}$$

$$= 0.286.$$

Thus, you now think that it is more than twice as likely that the channel 1 forecaster is good compared to the channel 2 forecaster. Of course, you can wait until the next forecast and then see which (if either) of them is right. It is important to note that the latter beliefs depend in a significant way on the prior beliefs. Thus, for example, if both forecasters predict rain tonight and it does rain tomorrow, you will *not* say that it is equally likely that they are good; you will still believe that there is a greater likelihood that the forecaster on channel 1 is good. We will see Bayes rule at work in Chapter 8.

LIQUIDITY

The liquidity of any asset has to do with the ease with which it can be converted into cash. There are three dimensions to liquidity: (i) the difference, Δ, between the maximum value of the asset (typically its value to the current owner) and its value if sold; (ii) the time it takes to sell the asset at a value acceptable to the seller, t; and (iii) the cost involved in selling the asset, c. Thus, liquidity

$$\ell = \ell(\Delta, t, c),$$

and liquidity is decreasing in Δ, t, and c. The most liquid asset thus is cash. Generally, the less dependent the value of the asset on who owns it, the greater its liquidity. Thus, assets that are uniquely tied in value to their owners have relatively low levels of liquidity. Also, assets with high levels of asymmetric information and agency problems tend to have low levels of liquidity.

SYSTEMIC RISK

Systemic risk refers to a risk that affects the whole system, and is therefore not diversifiable. It is very close in spirit and meaning to the idea of *systematic* risk, but the term "systemic risk" has typically been used to describe risks that affect the entire financial system, such as a system-wide shortage of liquidity.

Traditionally, systemic risk was viewed as being completely exogenous, that is, beyond the control of any individual financial institution. But recent events have highlighted the fact that seemingly idiosyncratic risks can spread through the system and become systemic risks due to the interconnectedness of financial institutions and markets. For example, what started as defaults in the subprime mortgage market in the United States – a market that was a relatively small fraction of the global financial system – very quickly became a global financial crisis.

DISAGREEMENT

In most of mainstream economics, it is standard to assume that two people confronted with the same information will always agree. That is, suppose two agents, A and B, have different beliefs at the outset about whether a project is worth investing in or a loan is worth taking, then the standard assumption is that it is because they have different information sets, and if both were provided exactly the same information, they would always agree. In other words, their beliefs would eventually converge.

This is an assumption of convenience, however, and the idea that all agents will eventually converge to have the same beliefs has no deep support in economics, philosophy, or logic.[15] A formal theory has been developed in which agents may continue to disagree even though they keep receiving the same information signals.[16] The idea is as follows. Suppose two agents start out with different beliefs about the value of something, and they receive signals about some underlying economic variable that can help them update their beliefs about the value of the object. Then, it can be shown that if the probability distribution of the economic variable is nonstationary (i.e., it changes over time), then the agents' beliefs may never converge. This means they will continue to disagree on the value of the object.

The notion that agents may disagree, even though they have the same objective/goal (so there are no agency problems) and access to the same information (so there are no informational asymmetries) has now begun to be applied wisely in Finance and Economics to understand a variety of phenomena[17]. We will see this in Chapter 14 on the financial crisis of 2007–2009, when we discuss how financial innovation can lead to disagreement that can trigger a crisis.

MARK-TO-MARKET ACCOUNTING

The term "MTM accounting," refers to the practice of revising the value of an asset or liability to reflect its estimated (or actual) market value rather than its book value (which reflects the historical cost of acquiring the asset minus accumulated depreciation).

Until the 1990s, financial institutions used book-value or historical-cost accounting, in accordance with Generally Accepted Accounting Principles (GAAP), and Regulatory Accounting Principles (RAP). Since the early 1990s, MTM has become a part of GAAP in the United States.

Many blamed MTM for leading to fire sales and downward price spirals during the recent crisis. The argument is that financial institutions sold assets in response to diminished capital levels as a result of losses arising from marking assets to market during a period of falling prices. These asset sales then exacerbated the price decline. More on this when we turn to the 2007–2009 financial crisis in Chapter 14.

---

15. See Kreps (1990).
16. See Kurz (1994a,b).
17. See, for example, Boot, Gopalan and Thakor (2006, 2008) in their analysis of the firm's choice between private and public ownership, and Van den Steen (2010) in a development of a new theory of the firm.

REFERENCES

Akerlof, G.A., August 1970. The market for 'lemons': Quality uncertainty and the market mechanism. Quarter. J. Econ. 488–500.

Bhattacharya, S., 1980. Nondissipative signaling structures and dividend policy. Quarter. J. Econ. 95, 1–24.

Black, F., Scholes, M., 1973. The pricing of options and corporate liabilities. J. Polit. Econ. 81, 637–654.

Bolton, P., Dewatripont, M., 2005. Contract Theory. MIT Press, Cambridge, MA.

Boot, A.W.A., Gopalan, R., Thakor, A.V., 2006. The choice between private and public ownership. J. Finan. 61, 803–836.

Boot, A.W.A., Gopalan, R., Thakor, A.V., 2008. Market liquidity, investor participation and managerial autonomy: why do firms go private? J. Finan. 63, 2013–2059.

Debreu, G., 1959. Theory of Value. Cowles Foundation Monograph 17. Yale University Press, New Haven.

Fama, E.F., 1970. Efficient capital markets: A review of theory and empirical work. J. Bus. 43, 383–417.

Fama, E.F., French, Kenneth, 2008. Dissecting anomalies. J. Financ. 63, 1653–1678.

Holmstrom, B., 1999. Managerial incentive problems – A dynamic perspective. Rev. Econ. Stud. 66, 169–182.

Jensen, M., Meckling, W., 1976. Theory of the firm: Managerial behavior, agency costs and ownership structure. J. Financ. Econ. 3, 305–360.

Kreps, D.M., 1990. A Course in Microeconomic Theory. Princeton University Press, Princeton, NJ.

Kurz, M., 1994a. On rational belief equilibria. Econ. Theory 4, 859–876.

Kurz, M., 1994b. On the structure and diversity of rational beliefs. Econ. Theory 4, 877–900.

Markowitz, H., 1959. Portfolio Selection: Efficient Diversification of Investments. Cowels Foundation Monograph 16. Yale University Press, New Haven.

Merton, R.C., 1973. Theory of rational option pricing. Bell J. Econ. Manage. Sci. 4, 41–183.

Mirrlees, J., 1976. The optimal structure of incentives and authority within an organization. Bell J. Econ. 7, 105–131.

Ross, S.A., 1974. On the economic theory of agency: The principle of similarity. Proceedings of the NERB-NSF Conference on Decision Making and Uncertainty.

Samuelson, P., 1963. Risk and uncertainty: A fallacy of large numbers. Scientia 57, 1–6.

Spence, M.A., 1973. Job market signalling. Quarter. J. Econ., 355–374.

Spence, M.A., 1974. Competitive and optimal responses to signals: An analysis of efficiency and distribution. J. Econ. Theory 7, 296–332.

Schwert, W.G., 2003. Anomalies and market efficiency. In: Constantinides, G.M., Harris, M., Stulz, R.M. (Eds.), Handbook of Economics and Finance. Elsevier Science Publishers, Amsterdam.

Tirole, J., 2006. The Theory of Corporate Finance. Princeton University Press, Princeton.

Van den Steen, E., 2010. Interpersonal authority in a theory of the firm. Am. Econ. Rev. 100, 466–490.

Part II

What is Financial Intermediation?

Chapter 2

The Nature and Variety of Financial Intermediation

"Don't it always seem to go that you don't know what you've got 'til it's gone?"

Joni Mitchell

GLOSSARY OF TERMS

Euro: Common currency adopted by many member countries of the European Union.

Yield curve: Relationship between yield to maturity and maturity on debt instruments identical in all respects except maturities (see Chapter 4).

Duration: A measure of how long an investor must wait to receive payment on a bond. For bonds that repay only principal (zero coupon bonds), duration equals maturity. For coupon-paying bonds, duration is always shorter than maturity.

Spot rate: The current yield to maturity on a bond of a given maturity.

Liquidity premium: The amount by which the yield on a bond must be grossed up to compensate investors for their inability to convert the bond into cash at a moment's notice and without loss relative to the bond's true value.

Consumer loans: Loans made to individuals and families. These are primarily installment loans.

Commercial loans: Loans made to corporations. Often referred to as Commercial and Industrial (C&I) loans.

Contingent claims: Claims that may be made in the future, contingent on the realizations of some states.

Federal funds: Funds in the interbank loan market. When a bank "sells" federal funds, it is lending (usually on an overnight basis) to another bank an amount that covers a part or all of that bank's shortfall in reserves; banks are required to keep a certain fraction of their deposits as liquid reserves.

Surplus: Proceeds from the sale of equity and securities in excess of their par value, plus retained earnings.

Cash and due: Coin and currency in the bank's vaults, reserves on deposit with the Federal Reserve and with other banks, and checks deposited by customers on which funds have not yet been collected from the paying bank.

Allowance for loan losses: An allowance made to absorb anticipated (expected) future loan losses. An allowance for loan losses is a charge against current income and it increases the bank's *loan loss reserve*. Writeoffs of existing loans reduce the bank's loan loss reserve.

Undivided profits and reserves: Part of the bank's net worth.

Gramm–Leach–Bliley Act: The 1999 act that dismantled the Glass–Steagall Act restrictions separating commercial and investment banking.

INTRODUCTION

This chapter focuses on the variety of services provided by financial intermediaries (FIs). Banks are members of an expansive industry that provides a dazzling variety of financial services. The broader financial services industry includes institutions as different as commercial banks, savings institutions, and credit unions, all of which finance their assets with deposits, and government agencies, credit-rating agencies, pension funds, loan sharks, pawnbrokers, lotteries, insurance companies, mutual funds, hedge funds, and private-equity pools. To this list we could add organized exchanges for trading stocks, futures, options, bonds and commodities, parimutuel betting institutions, credit-rating agencies, and the list can be extended almost effortlessly. Broadly speaking, these institutions can be classified into two groups: depository financial institutions and nondepository financial institutions. The former include institutions that finance themselves largely with deposits, whereas the latter fund themselves in the capital market. A subset of these nondepository institutions have come to be known as the "shadow banking system."

What all these *financial institutions* have in common is the processing of risk and its subtle complement, information. FIs produce information for two kinds of applications: (i) to match transactors like a marriage broker would, and (ii) to manage risks and transform the nature of claims as when a bank produces credit information to control a borrower's credit risk. In producing information for application (i), the intermediary acts as a *broker,* whereas in producing information for application (ii), it acts as a *qualitative asset transformer.*

S. I. Greenbaum, A. V. Thakor & A. W. A. Boot: Contemporary Financial Intermediation, Third edition. http://dx.doi.org/10.1016/B978-0-12-405196-6.00002-1

Our plan in the rest of this chapter is as follows. First we define FIs and discuss brokerage and asset-transformation services. We also provide a list of the different types of services that intermediaries provide in each of these two basic groups. Next, we provide some key statistics about FIs. Then we discuss the main types of depository intermediaries: commercial banks, thrifts (savings and loan associations (S&Ls) and mutual savings banks (MSBs)), and credit unions. The next section discusses nondepository FIs: venture capitalists, private-equity firms, finance companies, insurance companies, pension funds, mutual funds, and investment banks. We cover the role of the government next and then turn to "peripheral" FIs, including pawnbrokers and loan sharks.

WHAT ARE FINANCIAL INTERMEDIARIES?

Definition: As the name suggests, FIs are entities that intermediate between providers and users of financial capital. FIs are typically multifaceted, and their activities therefore can be understood from a variety of vantage points. For example, in contrast to nonfinancial firms, FIs hold relatively large quantities of financial claims as assets. Thus, whereas the manufacturing firm holds inventories, machines, and patents as assets, the FI holds contracts of the indebtedness of their clients as assets. Both finance their assets by selling their own debt and equity; there is no compelling distinction between FIs and others on the right-hand side of the balance sheet, except that FIs tend to be more leveraged. Here we have a balance sheet perspective on the uniqueness of financial intermediation. Whereas both FIs and other types of business finance assets with debt and equity, FIs tend to hold financial claims as assets whereas others are more committed to physical assets. In Appendix 2.1, we provide a further discussion of the balance sheets of FIs.

Why Do We Have FIs?: This is tantamount to asking: What do FIs do that could not be done without them? The answer to this for *any* firm, financial or nonfinancial, is found in the flow of goods and/or services produced by the firm. After all, a firm not only selects its assets and liabilities but also manages them so as to assure the realization of the potential cash flows. That is, the (nonhuman) assets appearing on the balance sheet are combined with various kinds of labor inputs to produce the cash flows conventionally attributed to the assets. The manufacturer reshapes, transforms, and transports various raw materials and semifinished goods into more highly refined and more advantageously located goods. The services of machines and processes recorded on the balance sheet are combined with labor services to produce an inventory of more highly refined goods.

What is the analog for the FI? How does it combine its resources to produce financial services? A facile answer is that FIs borrow on the one hand and lend on the other. But this answer is incomplete because it does not explain why we need FIs to bring borrowers and lenders together. That is, if I wanted to borrow some money, why do I simply not put an ad in the newspaper and invite people to lend to me at interest rates that I could negotiate with them? While this may seem to some like a foolish thing to do, the key is to understand why it is not (normally) done, rather than to dismiss it outright. After all, is it that different from a homeowner putting up his house "for sale by owner," rather than through a real-estate agent? Why is the selling of a house different from the selling of one's indebtedness (borrowing money)? Even in countries where there is no (explicit) deposit insurance, people deposit money in banks, which in turn lend this money to people like you and me. So, why are not those depositors willing to transact directly with prospective borrowers?

The key to understanding this issue is that we live in a world of imperfect information. People would rather deposit their money in a bank than lend it directly to a stranger because they feel they "know" the bank better. It is this line of reasoning that we wish to explore further, with emphasis on the information-based financial services produced by an FI. In borrowing and lending, the FI is joining unfamiliar, but well-suited and complementary transactors, much like the marriage broker would. The FI is also allocating credit presumably to its highest and best uses while reconfiguring the attributes of the financial claims held by its clienteles.[1] These activities are so fundamental to financial intermediation that they are accorded special labels, the former being referred to as "brokerage" whereas the latter is called "qualitative asset transformation" (QAT). Let us explain each in turn.

The Brokerage Function of FIs: Brokerage activities of FIs involve the bringing together of transactors in financial claims with complementary needs. The broker is usually compensated with a fee for performing this service. The broker's stock-in-trade is information, and its special edge in performing this service derives from special skills in interpreting subtle (i.e., not readily observable) signals, and also from the reusability of information. That is, a broker has two advantages as an information processor. First, it possesses/develops special skills in interpreting subtle (not readily observable) signals. Second, it takes advantage of cross-sectional (across customers) and intertemporal (through time) information reusability. For example, a real-estate broker typically has better information than the average home buyer or seller about supply and demand conditions in a given market and is able to reuse this information on many transactions.

---

1. FIs also engage in clearing and storage activities that are still more closely analogous to manufacturing. These asset "servicing" activities include collecting, tracking, and remitting payments on mortgages, consumer credit, and other claims, as well as traditional safekeeping.

For the broker, the matching of buyers and sellers does not involve the broker as a principal in the purchase (sale). Thus the used-car dealership typically goes beyond the broker's role in that it will *purchase* used autos for resale. If it merely identified potential buyers (sellers) for counterparties, it would then be a broker. Likewise, the marriage broker fits our description of a broker, but the typical stockbroker does not. Once a broker serves as a principal and buys (sells) the asset for eventual resale (repurchase), it accepts the risk that the market may reprice the asset, and it therefore transcends the more limited role of the matchmaker.

The broker helps resolve informational problems that exist before the two sides to the transaction enter into a contract, that is, the broker helps resolve *precontract informational asymmetry.* Moreover, the broker also helps resolve informational problems that may arise after the contract is entered into, that is, the broker helps resolve *postcontract informational asymmetry.*

Precontract Informational Asymmetry and Brokerage: Precontract information asymmetry involves two kinds of information problems: adverse selection and duplicated screening. We will discuss each in turn.

Adverse Selection and Brokerage: In transactions involving FIs, adverse selection problems abound. For example, a borrower will wish to overstate his credit worthiness to potential lenders in order to make himself look like a low-credit-risk borrower. And if the lender raises the loan interest rate in order to be compensated for the higher credit risk associated with borrowers, who misrepresent their creditworthiness, the borrowers most likely to drop out are the *low*-credit-risk borrowers who may either have better credit alternatives or be simply unwilling to borrow at the higher interest rate. Consequently, the lender is left with only the high-credit-risk borrowers.

An FI such as a bank can help deal with this adverse selection problem by performing the brokerage function of credit analysis to sort out borrowers of different credit risks. That is, in this case, the broker specializes in credit analysis or develops the skills to process/interpret various types of credit information. This allows it to intermediate between borrowers and lenders and minimize adverse selection problems.

Duplicated Screening, Information Reusability, and Brokerage: Duplicated screening refers to situations in which individuals can resolve adverse selection at a cost, but there is wasteful expenditure of costly screening resources because multiple individuals end up doing the same screening. An FI can help avoid such duplication by exploiting the power of information reusability. This can be illustrated through the example given below.

Consider 100 men and 100 women searching for the "perfect" marriage partner. In order to become fully informed, each woman will need to evaluate each of the 100 men, and likewise for each of the men. Now suppose that each such evaluation (sampling) results in a fixed cost of say, $25. Then the total cost for all participants to become fully informed would be $500,000 (i.e., $2(100 \times 100 \times 25)$). Or, if we let x represent the size of the side of a square grid (100 people in this example), and c the fixed sampling cost per unit ($25 in this example), we have the result that the total cost equals $2cx^2$.

Now enter the broker! To establish a level playing field and suppress consideration of the broker's special skills, we assume the evaluation cost per unit remains unchanged at $25. However, the broker will need to examine each of the participants only once and hence its total cost of becoming informed is $2cx$, or $5000. Assuming the information is distributed at negligible cost, the saving due to the introduction of the broker is approximated by

$$S = 2cx(x - 1),$$

or $495,000 in the example. To be sure, the broker will expect to earn a profit, but this cost is redistributive rather than dissipative (resource consuming), and potential competition can be expected to limit the profit in any case. Thus, the saving associated with having a broker increases exponentially (the square) with the size of the grid, and linearly with the sampling cost per unit. At the margin ($dS/dx = 2c[2x - 1]$), the saving increases as the size of the grid expands.

The savings, due to the broker, derive from a peculiarity of information: its use does not result in its consumption. Most goods and services are transformed into waste as a result of being used. This is not true with information, and this idiosyncrasy is the key to understanding the broker's role. If the marriage broker composes a report on a particular candidate, I can use the information without in any way compromising your ability to use the same information. The same is true for a report written by a security analyst, or for a telephone book. This extraordinary reusability of information is what makes it compelling to have a broker, and the larger the grid, the greater the potential saving associated with reusing information.

In this discussion, we did not assign the broker any special advantage or skill relative to the lay person in information evaluation. If such a relative advantage exists, then let C_b = broker's evaluation cost and C_o = others' evaluation cost, with $C_o > C_b$. Then the saving due to the broker is $S = 2x[C_o x - C_b]$, with $C_o > C_b$, and the saving attendant to using the broker grows with the gap, $C_o - C_b$. That is, higher information processing skill accentuates the broker's relative advantage.

Some Further Thoughts on the Power of Information Reusability and the Value of Brokerage: To cement our understanding of the power of information reusability, consider one more example. Think of a very large geographic grid in which each intersection represents a potential oil well. Now suppose there are many oil-drilling entrepreneurs, and further suppose that after drilling a dry hole the law requires that the landscape be restored to its initial condition. Thus, there is no way to know if a particular location has been drilled unless there is an operating well at a particular location. If a broker simply collects and disseminates information about the drilling activities of each explorer, the cost of redrilling dry holes can be eliminated. Without the broker, society will bear the unnecessary cost of searching for oil in locations known to be unproductive. This aspect of information is called *cross-sectional reusability*; the same information can be utilized across a number of different users. Information reusability also has an *intertemporal* aspect; it can be reused through time. For example, a bank that learns something about a borrower while processing its first loan application can use at least some of that information in processing future credit requests from the *same* borrower.

A second aspect of brokerage relates to the *observability* of objects of search. When the object of search is trivially observable, as in the case of a person's telephone number or the address of a dry hole, the skills of the broker are of little importance. But let us be a little more precise in explaining what we mean by "trivially observable." Think of the problem of retaining an expert to assist you in the purchase of thoroughbred horses. Suppose that you are particularly interested in three traits of candidate horses – their racing records, conformation, and blood lines. Now imagine there are numerous experts available and suppose we ask each to report on the three traits of a sample horse. We then create a frequency distribution for each trait. What would we expect to observe among these frequency distributions? Because the racing records are well-defined and a matter of public record, deviations around the mean should be negligible. Observers will not dispute how many times a particular race horse has come in first, second, and so on, no more than they would dispute its age, weight, or height.

However, breeding and conformation are a very different kettle of fish. With regard to these attributes, we would expect each agent to report a different description of the subject horse. Since the ideal against which conformation is judged is multidimensional and somewhat loosely defined, each observer's characterization will be distinctive and the consequent frequency distribution will have considerable variance. Likewise for bloodlines. The facts relating to forebears may be indisputable, but the value of particular forebears is judgmental; the choice among observers thus becomes important.

It is the subtlety, vagueness, or cost of observing the objects of search that elevates the importance of broker skills. To the extent that the objects of search are trivially observable, we should wish to employ less astute observers. If all observers produce the same description, clearly we should reserve the most astute brokers for those searches where judgments matter.

The observability issue helps us to understand the striking hierarchy of brokers in society, ranging from phone books at one extreme to marriage brokers and investment bankers at the other. Indeed, investment bankers and marriage brokers have a good deal in common in that they both address the pairing of transactors on the basis of subtle attributes. If the investment banker were limited to *pro forma* financial statements and projecting cash flows, its role and compensation would both be diminished. But presumably the investment banker addresses more complicated issues of compatibility based on corporate cultures, strategic intent, succession, operating synergies, and similar nuances. Even the placing of securities requires a knowledge of buyers and sellers and how they view counterparties as well as the many details of securities' attributes, such as sinking fund provisions, collateral, and stochastic duration considerations. This explains why the reputation of the investment banker is critically important, whereas the publisher of the Yellow Pages is virtually anonymous.

To summarize, for a given attribute, the larger the grid, the more compelling the need for the broker. For a given size grid, the less readily observable the object of search, the more important the skills and reputation of the broker.

An important aspect of brokerage is that it can be performed without processing substantial risk. Information can be purchased for resale without exposing the broker in the way QAT does. To be sure, if the broker produces information before it is sold, demand uncertainty can result in losses. But information can be presold, at least in principle. The broker also exposes its reputation whenever falsifiable representations are made in connection with its sale of information. But the risk is material only to the extent that objects of search are observable with difficulty. In principle then, brokerage services can be produced risklessly, and in any case the processing of risk is not central to the production of brokerage services. This is not the case with QAT.

Postcontract Informational Asymmetry and Brokerage: In many transactions, one party to the transaction can take actions during the course of the contractual interaction that damage the interest of the other party. The reason why such behavior is possible is that these actions are "hidden" from the injured party and cannot be directly controlled or prevented. Such informational asymmetry is associated with moral hazard, discussed in Chapter 1.

Moral hazard is quite prevalent. It is encountered in insurance, where the insured may underinvest in costly efforts to prevent adverse outcomes because the insurer absorbs the resulting loss. It is encountered in banking, where borrowers may choose excessively risky projects because the bank bears a disproportionate share of the downside risk.

The FI's special skills in monitoring attenuate moral hazard. For example, banks monitor their borrowers by periodically examining the borrower's business and its financial condition and intervening in operating strategy when necessary. Insurance companies design insurance contracts and use *ex post* pricing adjustments to deter moral hazard. Venture capitalists

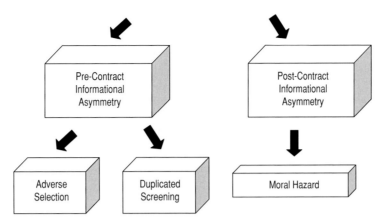

FIGURE 2.1   Key Information Problems Addressed by FIs.

use the threat of transfer of control to ensure that the entrepreneur's incentives do not stray too far from investors' desires. Thus, moral hazard provides a powerful source of economic value for the FI to emerge as a broker that can help diminish the losses due to moral hazard.

Figure 2.1 summarizes the different informational problems that create a role for the broker.

Qualitative Asset Transformation: Think of a world without intermediaries, as we did at the beginning of this discussion about the role of intermediaries. Suppose some individual wishes to borrow for the purpose of purchasing a house. The borrower must find a counterparty willing to hold a mortgage, which is a claim with a number of less desirable attributes. For example, there is no active secondary market in individual mortgages, with resultant illiquidity, and wide bid-ask spreads. The mortgage typically comes in large and irregular unit sizes. It typically has a long and uncertain duration, which is to say it may remain unredeemed for 30 years, but it can be repaid at virtually any time at the borrower's discretion and typically without prepayment penalty. Moreover, the mortgage carries with it default risk, and in the event of default, managing the collateral can be expensive. In all, the mortgage is a homely claim.

Enter the FI. It purchases the mortgage and finances the purchase with the issuance of a liability called a deposit. The deposit, in contrast to the mortgage, is almost infinitely divisible, highly liquid, and has little default risk. The FI effectively swaps deposits for mortgages, thereby modifying the claims held by its clientele. The FI is rewarded for this service with interest rate spread between deposits and mortgages.

Among the asset attributes most commonly transformed by FIs are duration (or term-to-maturity), divisibility (or unit size), liquidity, credit risk, and sometimes numeraire (currency identity). Typically, the intermediary will shorten the duration of the claims of its clients by holding assets of longer duration than its own liabilities; it will reduce the unit size of the claims of its clients by holding assets of larger unit size than its liabilities; it will enhance the liquidity of the claims of its clients by holding assets that are more illiquid than its liabilities; and it will reduce credit risk by holding assets that are more likely to default than its liabilities. By holding assets denominated in a currency other than its liabilities, it alters the numeraire of the assets of its clients.

QAT and Risk: Notice that every such asset transformation performed by the FI requires a *mismatch* with regard to that attribute on the FI's balance sheet. For example, if the duration of the FI's assets and liabilities are perfectly matched, it cannot have altered the duration of the assets of its clients. Only by absorbing the longer duration assets in exchange for shorter term liabilities can the FI reduce the duration of claims held by its customers. This is important because the mismatch on the FI's balance sheet reflects an acceptance of some type of risk, at least initially, by the FI.

If the FI holds Euro-denominated assets and US dollar-denominated liabilities, it will be exposed to variations in the dollar/Euro exchange rate. If it holds long-term assets financed with short-term liabilities, it will be exposed to interest rate risk, whereby changes in the shape and position of the yield curve will affect the FI's cash flows. Even changing the unit size of claims cannot be done without a mismatch and a consequent acceptance of risk. If the unit size of assets is larger than that of liabilities, the purchase and sale of corresponding claims cannot be perfectly synchronized and hence the FI accepts a form of inventory risk.

The case of duration transformation is particularly instructive. The yield curve is thought to be a "biased predictor' of future spot interest rates owing to a (liquidity) premium attached to long-duration claims. That is, borrowers typically prefer to borrow long term and lenders typically prefer to lend short term. This theory of the term structure of interest rates is usually associated with Sir John Hicks, a British Nobel Laureate economist. But if we introduce FIs into such a world and assume that they are indifferent to the duration of a claim, they would be able to finance the purchase of long-term assets with short-term liabilities and profit from doing so. Indeed, absent other impediments, intermediaries would continue to perform this transformation until the liquidity premium is bid down to the marginal cost of intermediating. The existence of this form of asset transformation supports the Hicksian view of the yield curve. Without a liquidity premium at the outset, there would be no incentive for the FI to perform duration transformation. If the yield curve was an unbiased predictor of future spot interest rates, there would be no profit in performing duration transformation.

Whatever the form of the QAT, a mismatched balance sheet is implied, and this in turn implies the acceptance of some form of exposure. This is the sense in which risk is integral to QAT. In managing this risk, there are basically three alternatives available to the FI. It can diversify the risk, it can shift the risk to others, or it can passively accept the exposure. The shifting of risk to others involves the use of claims such as swaps, forward contracts, futures, and options, and in principle, but rarely in practice, all of the exposure associated with the QAT can be transferred to others with the appropriate risk-shifting instruments. However, in this case the QAT reverts to brokerage. The FI has merely transferred risk among its clients, no matter how convoluted the transactions. In the case where the risk is diversifiable, presumably the FI performs this diversification on behalf of clients whose wealth is too small relative to the unit size of claims to diversify on their own. It is widely believed that this is a major rationale for mutual funds.

Although we distinguish between brokerage and asset transformation as distinct types of intermediation services, the truth is that both are performed by the same intermediaries and sometimes in combination. Take for example a duration-transforming FI that finds it is too mismatched for comfort and consequently proceeds to lengthen the duration of liabilities while simultaneously shortening the duration of its assets. In fact, it is changing the mix of its activities from more to less QAT and from less to more brokerage. In the limit, if the FI achieves a perfect duration match of its assets and liabilities, it will have become a pure broker.

Or consider an investment banker with two types of underwriting contracts, the "firm commitment" contract and the "best efforts" contract. The form involves the banker purchasing a firm's securities for resale. This is clearly a QAT contract. The banker provides the issuing firm with a *prix fixé* before the public has committed to purchase the securities. By contrast, the best efforts contract merely commits the bankers to make an honest effort to sell the securities for the best realizable price, without any further assurances. The best efforts contract commits the banker to provide brokerage services, and the banker will typically receive a fee without accepting any exposure relating to the price of the securities. Figure 2.2 lists the various services provided by FIs under brokerage and QAT. This list is suggestive, not exhaustive.

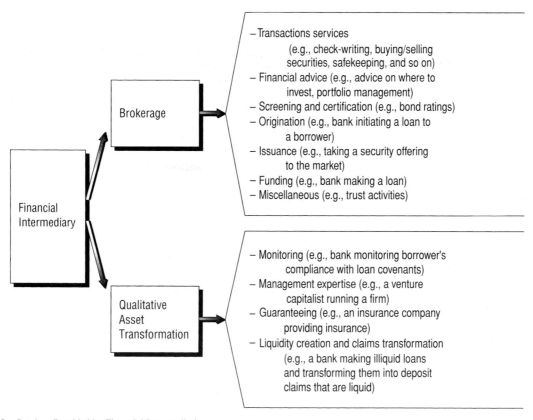

FIGURE 2.2 Services Provided by Financial Intermediaries.

THE VARIETY OF FINANCIAL INTERMEDIARIES

There are many ways to classify the many different types of FIs. In the previous section, we classified them based on the nature of the services they provide. We can also classify them based on whether or not they finance their activities with deposits.

FIs that finance (at least partly) with deposits are called deposit-type or depository FIs, whereas those that do not finance with deposits are called nondepository FIs. Jointly, depository and nondepository FIs have at their command an enormous volume of assets. Table 2.1 lists the assets of the various types of FIs, and also depicts their growth during 1980–2010. It is noteworthy that the assets of *all* types of FIs, except savings institutions, have exhibited striking growth.

The distinctions between depository and nondepository institutions have become blurred as the latter have increasingly offered products and services that compete with those of commercial banks. Consequently, individuals are increasingly turning to mutual funds rather than bank deposits for transactions and investment purposes. These developments can be seen in the data provided in Tables 2.2 and 2.3.

The shifting market shares of various institutions in the consumer loan market are reflected in the data provided in Table 2.4. Commercial banks are still the biggest players in the consumer loan market. The 10 largest commercial banks in consumer lending are shown in Table 2.5. The share of different financial institutions in total credit is shown in Figure 2.3. Having provided you with a glimpse of the market shares and sizes of the various types of institutions, we

TABLE 2.1 Total Assets of Financial Intermediaries at Year-End

Panel A: Total Assets Expressed in Billions of Dollars

Financial Intermediary	1980	1985	1990	1995	2000	2005	2008	2010
Commercial Banks	$1,704	$2,484	$3,338	$4,499	$6,709	$9,844	$14,056	$14,402
Savings Institutions	$792	$1,287	$1,323	$1,013	$1,218	$1,789	$1,524	$1,244
Life Insurance Companies	$479	$826	$1,351	$2,064	$3,136	$4,351	$4,515	$5,177
Private Pension Funds	$470	$848	$1,629	$2,899	$4,468	$5,389	$4,553	$6,080
State and Local Pension Funds	$198	$405	$730	$1,327	$2,293	$2,721	$2,325	$2,928
Finance Companies	$202	$352	$596	$705	$1,213	$1,857	$1,852	$1,595
Money Market Funds	$76	$244	$493	$741	$1,812	$2,007	$3,757	$2,755
Mutual Funds	$58	$252	$608	$1,853	$4,433	$6,049	$5,435	$7,963
Credit Unions	$69	$137	$217	$311	$441	$686	$812	$911
Financial Intermediaries' Total Assets	$4,048	$6,835	$10,285	$15,412	$25,723	$34,693	$38,829	$43,055

Panel B: Total Assets Expressed as a Fraction of Financial Intermediaries' Total Assets

Financial Intermediary	1980	1985	1990	1995	2000	2005	2008	2010
Commercial Banks	0.42	0.36	0.32	0.29	0.26	0.28	0.36	0.33
Savings Institutions	0.20	0.19	0.13	0.07	0.05	0.05	0.04	0.03
Life Insurance Companies	0.12	0.12	0.13	0.13	0.12	0.13	0.12	0.12
Private Pension Funds	0.12	0.12	0.16	0.19	0.17	0.16	0.12	0.14
State and Local Pension Funds	0.05	0.06	0.07	0.09	0.09	0.08	0.06	0.07
Finance Companies	0.05	0.05	0.06	0.05	0.05	0.05	0.05	0.04
Money Market Funds	0.02	0.04	0.05	0.05	0.07	0.06	0.10	0.06
Mutual Funds	0.01	0.04	0.06	0.12	0.17	0.17	0.14	0.18
Credit Unions	0.02	0.02	0.02	0.02	0.02	0.02	0.02	0.02
Financial Intermediaries' Total Assets	1.00	1.00	1.00	1.00	1.00	1.00	1.00	1.00

Source: U.S. Census Bureau, Statistical Abstract of the United States: 2012.

TABLE 2.2 Various Mutual Fund Statistics (in Billions of Dollars or in Percentage)

	1980[1]	1990	2000	2005	2010	2011	2012
Dollars invested in mutual funds	$134.8	$1,065.2	$6,964.7	$8,891.2	$11,831.9	$11,627.7	$13,045.3
Mutual funds share of I.R.A. market[1]	14.0%	21.8%	48.0%	46.1%	46.1%	45.2%	45.8%
Penetration of mutual funds among U.S. households	5.7%	25.1%	45.7%	44.4%	45.3%	44.1%	44.4%

[1]Mutual funds share is from the mid-1980s.
Source: Investment Company Institute 2013 Fact Book.

TABLE 2.3 U.S. Mutual Fund Industry Total Net Assets (in Billions of Dollars)

	1980[1]	1990	2000	2005	2010	2011	2012
Long-term funds							
Equity funds	$44.4	$239.5	$3,938.9	$4,886.9	$5,596.8	$5,215.3	$5,934.3
Hybrid funds		$36.2	$363.9	$609.8	$807.8	$842.8	$991.0
Bond funds	$14.0	$291.3	$816.79	$1,367.7	$2,624.1	$2,877.9	$3,426.4
Money-market funds	$76.4	$498.4	$1,845.3	$2,026.9	$2,804.0	$2,691.5	$2,693.6
Total net assets	$134.8	$1,065.2	$6,964.7	$8,891.2	$11,831.9	$11,627.4	$13,045.3
Number of funds	564	3,079	8,155	7,974	7.5	7,591	7,596

[1]All funds were reclassified in 1984 and a separate category was created for hybrid funds.
Source: Investment Company Institute 2013 Fact Book.

TABLE 2.4 Market Share of Consumer Loans (in Percentage)

	1–4 Family Mortgages						Consumer Credit					
	1990	2000	2005	2010	2011	2012	1990	2000	2005	2010	2011	2012
U.S. chartered depository institutions	42.4	34.8	33.6	30.5	30.2	30.4	52.3	35.7	35.2	46.6	45.4	44.1
Life insurance companies	7.1	3.5	2.4	2.3	2.5	2.6	–	–	–	–	–	–
Finance companies	3.02	3.6	4.5	1.8	1.6	1.4	16.8	12.7	22.3	27.9	26.3	24.6

Source: Federal Reserve Statistical Release: Flow of Funds Accounts of the U.S. 1985–1994, 1995–2004, 2005–2011, and 2012.

TABLE 2.5 Top Ten U.S. Banks Based on Total Assets in March 2013

Name	City, State	Total Assets (Billions of Dollars)	Total Deposit (Billions of Dollars)
1. JP Morgan Chase & Co.	New York (NY)	2359.2	1193.6
2. Bank of America Corp.	Charlotte (NC)	2210.0	1105.3
3. Citigroup Inc.	New York (NY)	1864.7	930.6
4. Wells Fargo & Co.	San Francisco (CA)	1423.0	1002.9
5. Bank of New York Mellon Corp.	New York (NY)	359.0	246.1
6. U.S. Bancorp	Minneapolis (MN)	353.9	249.2
7. HSBC North America Holdings Inc.	New York (NY)	318.8	114.8
8. Capital One Financial Corp.	McLean (VA)	313.0	212.5
9. PNC Financial Services Group Inc.	Pittsburgh (PA)	305.2	213.2
10. State Street Corp.	Boston (MA)	222.6	164.2

Source: SNL Financial.

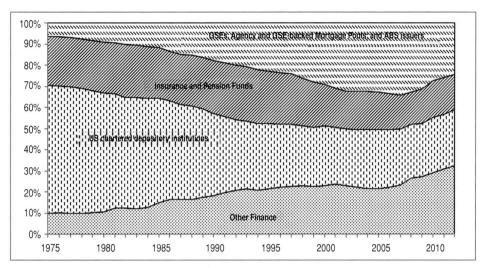

FIGURE 2.3   Share of Financial Institutions in Total Credit. *(Source: Federal Reserve Statistical Release: Flow of Funds Accounts of the U.S. 1985–1994, 1995–2004, 2005-2011, and 2012).*

now move on to a description of each of these institutions in the next section. We will also provide some international (non-US) data.

DEPOSITORY FINANCIAL INTERMEDIARIES

Depository institutions operate with high leverage, so that even a small return on total assets translates into a high return of equity. Figure 2.4 graphs the behavior through time of bank equity capital as a percentage of total assets. The figure illustrates the post-World War II upward drift in the net-worth-to-total-assets ratio through the 1960s then the long-run decline in the net-worth-to-total-asset ratio of banks until about 1980, followed by an increase in this ratio thereafter. But note these are book values and may not provide as comfortable a cushion as their levels would suggest. In Figure 2.5, we provide information on the return on assets and the return on equity at commercial banks. This figure highlights the effects

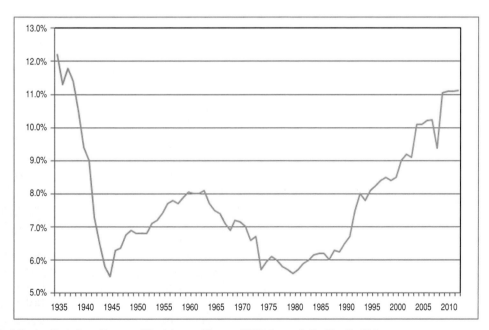

FIGURE 2.4   Bank Equity Capital as a Percent of Total Assets. *(Source: FDIC Quarterly Banking Profile).*

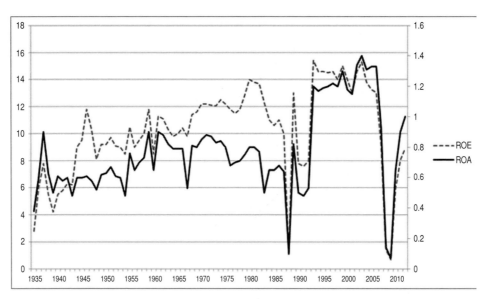

FIGURE 2.5 Commercial Bank Profitability. *(Source: FDIC Quarterly Banking Profile).*

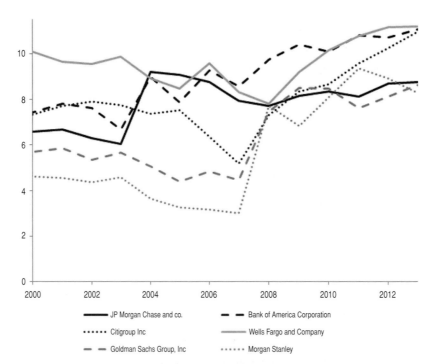

FIGURE 2.6 Total Equity to Total Assets Ratio (in %) for the Six Largest U.S. Banks. *(Source: Own computation based on Bankscope data. Largest 10 U.S. bank holding companies (see http://www.ffiec.gov/nicpubweb/nicweb/top50form.aspx)).*

leverage has on the translation from a return on assets to a return on equity. For instance, in 2004 return on assets for commercial banks was about 1.31%, whereas return on equity was 13.82%.

To highlight the problems with capitalization in banking that we have seen during the 2007–2009 financial crisis, Figure 2.6 presents the level of capital over time of the top four U.S. commercial banks and two pure investment banks; we will discuss investment banking shortly. Figure 2.7 shows the level of capital of the 10 largest European banks. And Figure 2.8 provides the average of capital ratios for the largest European and American banks. What is immediately apparent is that the European banks and the U.S. investment banks dramatically lowered their capital levels ("leverage ratios") in the

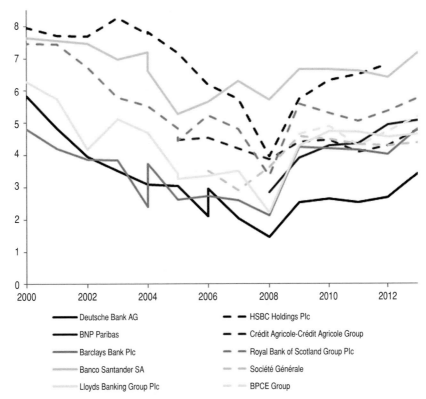

FIGURE 2.7   Total Equity to Total Assets Ratio (in %) for the Largest 10 EU Banks. *(Source: Own computation based on Bankscope data).*

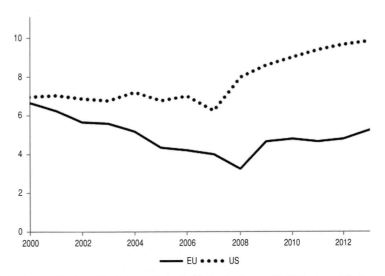

FIGURE 2.8   Comparison of the Average Equity to Total Assets Ratio (in %) for the Largest 10 EU banks and the largest 6 U.S. banks. *(Source: Own computation based on Bankscope data).*

period leading up to the financial crisis. The same applies to Citigroup, but note that Citigroup, like the European banks, was heavily involved in investment banking as well.[2] As we will discuss later, this development helped to fuel the financial crisis.

Commercial Banks

Commercial banks are widely considered the center of the financial intermediation universe because of their role in administering the community's payments, and also because commercial banks are used to transmit monetary policy impulses

---

2. The reported level of capital of European banks is not based on the same accounting treatment as that of U.S. banks. Europe follows IFRS, United States is on US GAAP. The latter produces slightly higher capitalization ratios because of more favorable GAAP netting rules.

TABLE 2.6 FDIC-insured Commercial Banks in 2012

Asset Size	Return on Assets (in Percent)	Return on Equity (in Percent)	Equity Capital (in Percent of Assets)
Less than $100 million	0.74	6.34	11.66
$100 million to $1 billion	0.87	8.13	10.64
$1 billion to $10 billion	1.19	10.10	11.72
More than $10 billion	*1.00*	*8.89*	*11.08*
Total	1.00	8.92	11.11

Source: FDIC Quarterly Banking Profile, December 2012.

originating with the central bank.[3] Their sheer size and ubiquity provide yet another basis for according commercial banks special attention.

Most commercial banks operate with considerable leverage. Table 2.6 shows that commercial banks in different size classes have a ratio of equity capital to total assets that averaged a little more than 10%. As we have seen, these levels of capital look quite high, particularly compared to the numbers we showed for the largest banks, particularly in Europe, but also those for US investment banks and commercial banks with sizable investment banking operations (see Figures 2.6 and 2.7).

The role of commercial banks in the payments system derives from their twin roles as distributor of currency (paper money and coin), and as producer and servicer of demand deposits. Currency and demand deposits are the community's principal *means of payment* and *media of exchange,* and are the major components of the money supply. Commercial banks link the central bank with the many millions of money users.

This nexus reflects on our second point, that commercial banks are central because of their role in monetary policy. The central bank seeks to stabilize economic activity by controlling the money available to support that activity. Hence, if inflation threatens, for example, the Federal Reserve will restrain the growth of money and drive up interest rates. Restricting growth of the money supply reduces the availability of bank credit to commercial banks, thereby lowering the volume of the loans they make and driving up the loan interest rates. This is the way commercial banks transmit monetary policy and fulfill their stabilizing role. We will revisit this issue in Chapter 3.

In playing this role in the conduct of monetary policy, a commercial bank acts both as a broker and as a QAT, providing all of the services listed in Figure 2.2 except management expertise. A typical commercial bank's balance sheet and its sources of revenues and expenses are shown in Tables 2.7 and 2.8, respectively.

U.S. commercial banks are regulated by the Federal Reserve System, the Office of the Comptroller of the Century (OCC), and the Federal Deposit Insurance Corporation (FDIC) at the federal level and by state banking authorities at the state level.

Commercial banks have many things in common with other depository institutions, but are distinguished by their abovementioned role in the payments system, by the diversity of their assets, and by their ownership structure. Other depositories, such as savings institutions (often called thrifts) and credit unions, have traditionally had more narrowly specialized asset portfolios – residential mortgages and consumer credit comprise the bulk of their assets, respectively, although these distinctions have been blurring and are almost irrelevant now for the most part. Commercial banks, as their name suggests, were also specialized lenders at one time, but they have evolved to the point that the largest of them holds a great variety of earning assets, including working capital, trade and term financing for businesses, residential and commercial mortgages, consumer loans, automobile loans, loans to sovereigns (governments), structured financing for corporate buyouts, and still more exotic credit instruments. In addition, commercial banks perform risk-shifting functions through their sale of standby letters of credit, swaps, and other financial guarantees. These are called "contingent claims" and have many of the attributes of ordinary insurance contracts.

The ownership structure of commercial banks is also notably different from other depository institutions. Commercial banks alone are *all* shareholder owned. Thrifts are substantially mutual, and credit unions are exclusively mutual,

---

3. Virtually every country in the world has a central bank charged with managing the money supply, acting as lender of last resort, protecting the integrity of the financial system, and other related chores. The Federal Reserve is the central bank of the United States. Counterparts in other countries include the Bank of England, the Bank of Japan, to mention a few. The European Central Bank acts as the central bank for the Eurozone; by now 19 EU member states that have adopted the Euro. Central banks are typically government owned, but the Federal Reserve has a peculiar hybrid structure reflecting a populist ambivalence toward concentrations of economic and financial power, particularly in the hands of the government. Thus, the Federal Reserve is nominally independent of government and privately owned, but as a practical matter it is neither.

TABLE 2.7 Hypothetical Balance Sheet for a U.S. Bank

Assets		
Cash and due		$125
Securities held		170
Federal funds sold		50
Loans		
Real estate	160	
Commercial and industrial	220	
Consumer	110	
All other	120	
Less unearned income:	−12	
Allowances for possible loan losses		
Total loans		598
Other assets		57
Total assets		$1000

Liabilities and Equity			
Liabilities			
Deposits			
Domestic	$661		
Foreign	119		
Total deposits		$780	
Federal funds Purchased		80	
Other liabilities		80	
Total liabilities			940
Subordinated notes and debentures			5
Equity capital			
Preferred and common stock		10	
Surplus		20	
Undivided profits and reserves		25	
Total equity capital			55
Total liabilities and equity			$1000

TABLE 2.8 Major Revenue and Expense Items for a Bank

Revenues	Expenses
–Interest on loans and marketable securities	–Interest on deposits
–Fees on loan commitments and other contingent claims	–Wages
–Fees on cash management and other transactions services	–Operating expenses, including occupancy
	–Deposit insurance premia
	–Taxes
	–Provisions for loan losses

TABLE 2.9 Composition of Noncommunity Banks Compared with Community Banks as of Year-end 2010

Noncommunity Bank Categories	Number of Organizations	Number as % of Total	Total Assets (in $ Billions)	Total Assets as % of Total	Number of Offices	Number as % of Total
Four largest banking organizations*	4	0%	5,989	45%	18,937	19%
Noncommunity banks over $100B excluding four largest	12	0.2%	2,172	16%	16,636	17%
Noncommunity banks between $10B and $100B	76	1.1%	2,430	18%	15,112	15%
Noncommunity banks between $1B and $10B	206	3%	764	6%	11,368	12%
Noncommunity banks under $1B	92	1.3%	21	0%	150	0%
Community banks	6.524	94%	1,944	15%	36,274	37%
Industry: Totals	6,914	100%	13,319	100%	98,477	100%

*These are all non-community banks.
Source: FDIC, Community Bank Study, December 2012.

that is, they are owned by their depositors (a discussion of mutual organizations appears in the next chapter). In this era of galloping globalization, it is noteworthy that American commercial banking still reflects peculiarly American concerns. Interestingly, many of these idiosyncrasies are shared by the Japanese despite profound cultural differences. This is because Japanese banking was patterned after U.S. institutions following World War II. Indeed, our financial system probably shares more in common with that of Japan than with those of our other major trading partners in Europe and the Americas.

A few of the largest banks in Europe are cooperatives, effectively member-owned banks like credit unions, yet of enormous size (e.g., Credit Agricole in France and RABO-Bank in the Netherlands). In terms of total assets, both banks would rank among the top 10 banks in the United States. Commercial banks in the United States and Japan also historically tended to be more narrowly restricted in their activities (this distinction, like so many others, has eroded substantially under the pressures of global competition) and the consequent deregulation. For examples, Germany's "universal" or "haus" banks are permitted to engage in all manners of insurance and investment banking, as well as the many activities traditionally permitted by American commercial banks. Such activities were traditionally proscribed for American commercial banks, but these restrictions have since been removed with the dismantling of the Glass–Steagall Act.

In addition to being more narrowly restricted functionally, commercial banks in the United States have also been geographically confined. Until recently, commercial banks in the United States could not operate in more than one state, with minor exceptions. Indeed, in many states, commercial banks could not operate from more than one office. This may seem quaint, but these Americanisms gave rise to over 30,000 independently chartered commercial banks at their peak, about 90 years ago. Markets were Balkanized and entry was restricted, reflecting America's populist fear of economic power concentrations, especially when such power resided in the major eastern urban centers where the country's largest financial institutions were headquartered. Also reflected in these policies (laws) was America's fear of large-scale bank failures. Recall that these practices predate federally sponsored deposit insurance, which originated in the 1930s. Populist sentiments trace back to frontier America when the West sought cheap money, manufacturers, and transport. The Eastern establishment wanted sound money and sound banks, along with market-determined prices for railroad services and manufactured goods.[4] While these sentiments now seem outdated, and deregulation in 1994 now permits interstate branching, the United States still had over 6900 banks in 2010. In Table 2.9, the banks are split up into community and noncommunity banks and various market share data are provided.

The United States has far more banks than other countries. Even with the recent trend toward consolidation, the United States retains a relatively fragmented banking market with many independent, albeit a few large ones.

Thrifts

S&Ls and MSBs, collectively referred to as thrifts, or savings institutions, are depository institutions that were specially chartered to extend residential mortgage finance. Traditionally their assets are primarily home mortgages, although their

---

4. The railroads, in particular, enjoyed market power, owing to the paucity of substitute conveyances, and this served as one basis for protracted regional conflicts.

TABLE 2.10 Key Statistics Regarding Federally Insured Savings Institutions

	1990	1995	2000	2005	2006	2008	2010
Number of institutions	2,815	2,030	1,589	1,307	1,279	1,219	1,129
Net worth to total assets	4.11%	7.84%	8.68%	11.23%	12.31%	8.93%	11.75%
Return on assets	−0.35%	0.70%	0.91%	1.19%	1.06%	−1.17%	0.70%
Return on equity	−7.65%	9.00%	11.63%	12.83%	11.18%	−13.08%	6.07%
Net income	−$3.8 billion	$5.4 billion	$8.0 billion	$16.4 billion	$15.9 billion	−$15.9 billion	$6.5 billion
Net worth	$67.5 billion	$86.1 billion	$103.6 billion	$206.4 billion	$218.0 billion	$136.9 billion	$147.4
Total assets	$1,260 billion	$1,026 billion	$1,223 billion	$1,838 billion	$1,770 billion	$1,533 billion	$1,254

Source: Office of Thrift Supervision 2010 Fact Book.

asset mix has been changing to include other assets in recent years. Thrifts have traditionally had even lower capital ratios than banks, as shown in Table 2.10, although regulation following the thrift failures in the 1980s has resulted in thrift capital ratios moving up, and actually being higher in 2004 than the average bank capital ratio (in Table 2.6).

S&Ls were chartered for the purpose of specializing in consumer savings accounts and residential mortgage loans. They came into existence to encourage thrift and to allow people to purchase homes at a time when banks were loath to finance home mortgages. They started out as small informal mutuals, and despite the fact that many have converted into stockholder-owned institutions, mutual S&Ls abound. They were regulated by the independent Federal Home Loan Bank Board (FHLBB) and insured by the Federal Savings and Loan Insurance Corporation (FSLIC). In 1989, the FHLBB was dissolved and replaced by the Office of Thrift Supervision (OTS) and Federal Reserve. The FDIC now provides federal deposit insurance for S&Ls. The financial intermediation services provided by S&Ls are similar to those provided by commercial banks, but with different emphasis.

MSBs, as their name indicates, are cooperatively owned. Like S&Ls, they too invest mostly in mortgage loans and marketable securities. They are a few hundred in number and most are located in the Northeast and the Northwest of the United States. MSBs managed to distance themselves, at least for a time, from the savings and loan crisis;[5] they were regulated by the FDIC rather than the now-defunct FHLBB and the FSLIC. The MSBs held less risky assets and operated with less financial leverage than the S&Ls, and had the good fortune to be located away from some of the worst real-estate markets of the 1980s – Texas, Oklahoma, Louisiana, and Colorado. MSBs were nevertheless damaged by the inflation-induced loss of core deposits, the consequent emergence of interest-rate risk, and the asset-quality problems of the later 1980s. Earlier proud pillars of the industry like The Bowery Savings Bank of New York and The Philadelphia Savings Fund Society were forced into humiliating restructurings, emerging as shareholder-owned shadows of their former selves.

The 1989 FIRREA (Financial Institutions and Regulatory Reform Act) legislation, which did away with the FSLIC and the Federal Home Loan Bank Board, and folded the savings and loan federal deposit insurance fund into the FDIC, further weakened the distinctions between MSBs and S&Ls.[6] As a practical matter, the distinction between MSBs and their cousins, the S&Ls, has been lost in a deluge of asset-quality problems. They are now less undifferentiated parties to the thrift industry implosion, estimated to cost taxpayers upwards of $250 billion in present value terms as of mid-1990, although subsequent estimates put the cost at around $100 billion.[7]

5. For engaging accounts of these, see Mayer (1990), and Adams (1990).

6. Although S&L deposit insurance is administered by the FDIC along with commercial bank deposit insurance, separate insurance funds are maintained. Members of FDIC, including MSBs, are insured by the Bank Insurance Fund (BIF), whereas former FSLIC members are insured by the Savings Association Insurance Fund (SAIF). Are these beltway acronyms mnemonic or ironic?

7. Loss estimates ranging from $1/4 trillion upwards were obtained by assuming long-term financing and adding in the interest cost. Described as a "bailout," the loss was merely a spectacular example of a governmental guarantee program run amok. We have many such government programs in housing, health, education, agriculture, and similar, if less spectacular fiascos have visited these programs. The Farm Credit Administration failure of the 1980s is an illustration.

The thrift fiasco was a large financial disaster. A whole industry with over thousands of firms and trillions of dollars was devastated. The industry seems to have recovered, however. Although their numbers have diminished, thrifts continue to operate successfully. Whether any will remain dedicated housing lenders for long is questionable, however. Table 2.10 provides further information on thrifts. It indicates that the financial condition of the industry is improving through time, although the numbers of thrifts have been declining through time.

In diagnosing the thrift industry collapse, some point to flaws in the deposit insurance system, particularly the failure to relate deposit insurance premiums or capital requirements to the risk assumed by the thrifts. The deposit insurance contract provided inappropriate risk-taking incentives to thrift managers. Nevertheless, for four decades, it worked like a charm. These issues will be taken up in later chapters.

Credit Unions

Like thrifts, credit unions specialize in consumer savings and are mutuals. Those forming a credit union must share *a common bond*, that is, they should be employed by the same organization. The credit union must be involved in borrowing and lending to its members. The homogeneity in borrower base facilitates the credit union's control of credit risks, but limits potential diversification. As of 2012, there were 4272 credit unions in the United States.

A credit union's liabilities consist mainly of consumer deposits, and its assets are comprised mainly of consumer loans; real-estate mortgages to members; loans to other credit unions, MSBs, and S&Ls; and government and corporate securities. Federally chartered credit unions are regulated by the National Credit Union Administration (NCUA), which also provides deposit insurance. State-chartered institutions can purchase NCUA deposit insurance as well. The services provided by a credit union include transactions services, screening, origination, monitoring, funding, guaranteeing, and liquidity creation. Like their other depository brethren, credit unions have low capital-to-total assets (stated as "reserves to assets") ratios, as shown in Table 2.11.

TABLE 2.11 Federal Credit Unions – Significant Ratios 1990–2012

	1990	1995	2000	2005	2008	2010	2011	2012
Number of institutions	8539	7329	6336	5393	4847	4589	4447	4272
Reserves to assets	4.0%	4.3%	4.5%	3.7%	3.3%	3.2%	3.2%	3.2%
Reserves and undivided earnings to assets	7.5%	10.2%	11.6%	11.3%	10.7%	10.1%	10.2%	10.4%
Reserves to loans	6.2%	6.9%	6.6%	5.6%	4.8%	5.2%	5.4%	5.5%
Loans to shares	70.4%	70.8%	78.0%	77.5%	82.8%	71.6%	68.7%	67.9%
Operating expenses to gross income	35.7%	42.3%	44.8%	58.4%	63.5%	69.8%	69.5%	69.2%
Salaries and benefits to gross income	15.0%	19.2%	20.2%	25.8%	23.9%	26.4%	28.6%	30.2%
Dividends to gross income	55.7%	42.6%	41.7%	26.0%	32.2%	19.1%	15.8%	12.9%
Yield on average assets	10.6%	8.1%	8.3%	6.8%	7.0%	5.9%	5.4%	5.2%

Source: 1995 and 2012 Annual Reports, National Credit Union Administration, Washington, DC.

INVESTMENT BANKS: KEY NONDEPOSITORY INTERMEDIARIES IN THE CAPITAL MARKET

The primary focus of this book is deposit-taking FIs, and most specially commercial banks. Investment banks, like Goldman Sachs and Morgan Stanley, specialize in the design and issuance of financial contracts. They often perform the brokerage function of bringing buyers and sellers of securities together. The key intermediation services they provide are transaction services, financial advice, screening and certification, origination, issuance, and guaranteeing. The top 20 investment banks in the United States, ranked according to their underwriting and M&A advisory fees, are listed in Table 2.12.

An investment bank is an FI that specializes in: (i) raising financial (debt and equity) capital; (ii) advising on corporate mergers and acquisitions; and related transactions; (iii) wealth management; (iv) financial and economic research;

TABLE 2.12 Bloomberg 20 Top Investment Banks

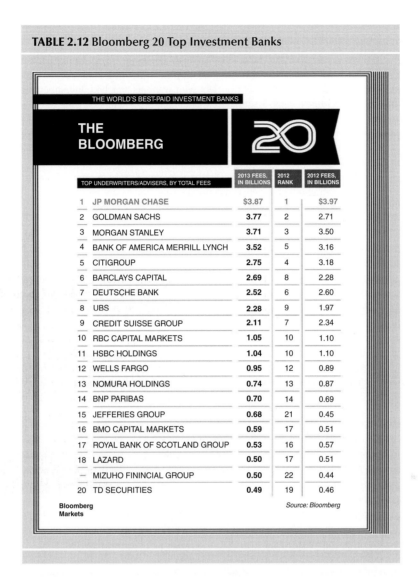

THE WORLD'S BEST-PAID INVESTMENT BANKS

THE BLOOMBERG 20

	TOP UNDERWRITERS/ADVISERS, BY TOTAL FEES	2013 FEES, IN BILLIONS	2012 RANK	2012 FEES, IN BILLIONS
1	JP MORGAN CHASE	$3.87	1	$3.97
2	GOLDMAN SACHS	3.77	2	2.71
3	MORGAN STANLEY	3.71	3	3.50
4	BANK OF AMERICA MERRILL LYNCH	3.52	5	3.16
5	CITIGROUP	2.75	4	3.18
6	BARCLAYS CAPITAL	2.69	8	2.28
7	DEUTSCHE BANK	2.52	6	2.60
8	UBS	2.28	9	1.97
9	CREDIT SUISSE GROUP	2.11	7	2.34
10	RBC CAPITAL MARKETS	1.05	10	1.10
11	HSBC HOLDINGS	1.04	10	1.10
12	WELLS FARGO	0.95	12	0.89
13	NOMURA HOLDINGS	0.74	13	0.87
14	BNP PARIBAS	0.70	14	0.69
15	JEFFERIES GROUP	0.68	21	0.45
16	BMO CAPITAL MARKETS	0.59	17	0.51
17	ROYAL BANK OF SCOTLAND GROUP	0.53	16	0.57
18	LAZARD	0.50	17	0.51
—	MIZUHO FININCIAL GROUP	0.50	22	0.44
20	TD SECURITIES	0.49	19	0.46

Bloomberg Markets

Source: Bloomberg

(v) general financial advisory services; (vi) sales and trading; and (vii) other ancillary activities such as custodial services. Most of the major Wall Street investment banks are active in a wide variety of these activities. Smaller investment banks tend to specialize more narrowly. In Box 2.1, we further expand on these activities.

SEPARATION BETWEEN INVESTMENT BANKS AND COMMERCIAL BANKS UNDONE

Legislation of the 1930s (Glass–Steagall Act) erected a wall of separation between commercial banks and investment banks. This legislation created investment banking in its singular American incarnation. No other major country, with the possible exception of Japan, had the kind of separation found in the United States. The European model is that of "universal banks" that bridge the chasm between the two forms and permit rationalization of structures dictated by the economics of the business. Glass–Steagall created two banking systems. Commercial bankers had subsidized deposits, but restricted asset choice. The investment banks were without deposit subsidies, but had great freedom on the asset side of the balance sheet, particularly with financial market linked activities (like underwriting).

The investment banks' marketing of equities complemented the commercial banks' provision of loans. At the same time, however, the investment banks sold fixed-income securities, including bonds and commercial paper – which competed directly with commercial bank loans. Similarly, the investment banks aggressively marketed money-market funds in competition with commercial banks while at the same time they brokered deposits to the banks.

BOX 2.1 Services provided by investment banks (see also United States General Accounting Office (2003)).

1. *Raising Financial Capital:* An investment bank can help a firm to finance a major investment project, acquire another company, restructure its balance sheet, expand operations, or other business purposes. Capital can include common equity, preferred equity, debt, as well as "hybrid" securities like convertible debt or debt with warrants attached. Investment banks raise capital through underwriting, private placements, venture capital, asset-based financing, and merchant banking. We briefly describe each below.
   Underwriting: Investment banks verify financial data and business claims, facilitate pricing of claims, and perform due diligence. Most offerings are "firm commitment" underwritings in which investment banks effectively purchase securities from the issuer for resale to the public. In the case of equities, they do this through Initial Public Offerings (IPOs) as well as secondary offerings. They also advise on debt issues to the public markets.
   Private Placements: As an alternative to a public offering, the banker may distribute newly issued debt or equity claims to a small number of larger, typically institutional buyers. These private placements are typically less costly to distribute because SEC registration requirements are less stringent on the supposition that the buyers are more sophisticated. Private placements are more common with debt than equity.
   Venture Capital: Investment banks also provide capital and strategic guidance to younger and smaller companies and may manage venture capital pools or even invest their own capital.
   Securitization and Asset-Based Financing: Investment banks help their clients use their existing assets to obtain additional financing without actually having to sell off these assets. The process by which this is done is called securitization, and the securities that are created in the process are called asset-backed securities. For example, a company might have (uncollected) receivables. It could then issue securities that permit the buyers of these securities to receive cash flows as these receivables are collected.
   Merchant Banking: These activities involve the investment bank committing its own capital to facilitate a variety of client transactions. That is, these are transactions involving QAT. Merchant banking transactions may include loan commitments, syndicated loans, highly leveraged transactions, bridge loans, and so on. A loan commitment is a promise by the bank to make a loan available in the future for a preidentified purpose such as an acquisition or a major project. A syndicated loan is one in which the bank is a member of a group making a loan to a borrower. A highly leveraged transaction is one in which the bank loan is part of a financing package for an acquisition or some other form of asset investment and the financing package involves a relatively high debt–equity ratio. A bridge loan is a temporary loan that serves as a bridge to more permanent future financings.
2. *Mergers and Acquisitions:* Investment banks provide a variety of services to help their clients with mergers and acquisitions: (a) due diligence; (b) valuation; and (c) other advisory and transaction services. We describe each briefly below.
   Due Diligence: When a company is considering the acquisition of another company, it needs to examine the target company's market and financial condition to ensure that it does not end up acquiring unforeseen problems or overpaying. The process by which the information relevant to this is collected and analyzed is called due diligence, and investment banks possess expertise in providing this service.
   Valuation: Any time a company is considering acquiring another company, it needs to establish the maximum price it is willing to pay. This is a blend of both the science of finance and an art form in evaluating information and making the right assumptions. Investment banks have developed expertise in valuation that they share with their clients.
   Other Advisory and Transaction Services: These include advising the client on the best type of transaction, preparing a selling memorandum, participating in negotiations, and assisting the client's board of directors with discharge of its fiduciary duties.
3. *Investment Management:* Investment banks engage in investment management primarily of two types: (a) managing funds on behalf of institutional investors; and (b) managing the assets of wealthy individuals (private banking).
4. *Research:* Investment banks conduct research on companies, financial markets, and the economy. This research is sold directly or indirectly as part of a package of services.
5. *Corporate Advisory Services:* Investment banks provide a host of advisory services to their corporate clients. These advisory services, include help with corporate reorganizations, resulting in recommendations about the sale of specific assets, the issuance of securities, and the possible negotiation of the sale of the entire company. In addition, banks offer advice relating to joint ventures, privatizations, spinoffs, tender and exchange offers, leveraged buyouts, and defense strategies against hostile takeovers.
6. *Security Sales and Trading:* Investment banks are active in the sales and trading of various securities. They banks provide sales and trading services in principally three ways: (a) market making; (b) placing new offerings; and (c) brokerage services. We describe each of these briefly below.
   Market Making: As a market maker, an investment bank promotes price stability and continuity by holding inventories of the security, with a willingness and ability to step in and redress temporary imbalances in supply and demand. For example, an investment bank may stabilize prices during an IPO.
   Placing New Offerings: Investment banks actively market new securities either as an agent or a principal.
   Brokerage Services: Investment banks also engage in sales and trading for institutions as well as individuals.
7. *Other Ancillary Activities:* This encompasses a variety of other activities like structuring transactions to manage risk. The term "structured finance" is used to refer to the mix of securities used in structuring "off-balance sheet" transactions, that is, transactions whose entire value does not show up on the clients' balance sheet. Structured financing transactions generally isolate the firm's assets and obligations in a "structure" that is apart from the main operations of the sponsor. The structure is typically called a *Special Purpose Entity* (SPE) or *Special Purpose Vehicle* (SPV). Investment banks may also offer custodial and corporate trust services.

With the dismantling of the Glass–Steagall Act and the passage of the Gramm–Leach–Bliley Act in 1999, this separation between commercial and investment banking had been eliminated. While commercial banks used the deregulation to expand in security markets' activities and occasionally acquired investment banking operations (e.g., Citi's acquisition of Salomon Brothers via its merger with Travelers[8]), the main investment banks continued to exist as stand-alone businesses. This changed during the 2007–2009 financial crisis: several investment failed and/or were driven in the hands of commercial banks (Bear Sterns, Lehman Brothers, and Merrill Lynch). Today only a few stand-alone large investment banks remain (in particular, Goldman Sachs and Morgan Stanley).

The massive failure of investment banks pointed at an inherent fragility in their activities and way of operating. Investment banks engaged increasingly in proprietary trading (i.e., trading for their own account: principal trading) and they added leverage to their balance sheet. These changes in their business model away from the typical client-oriented investment banking services were highly lucrative in the booming capital markets leading up to the financial crisis,[9] but became deadly when the market turned.

Separation of Investment Banking Activities

Because investment banks have potential access to significant amounts of proprietary information about their clients, they go to great lengths to specify to their employees rules and procedures to ensure that the bank neither trades on this proprietary information nor does it make buy/sell recommendations based on this information. That is, investment banks erect "Chinese Walls" that separate the banking part of their business from the marketing side of their business.

Investment banks are general purpose FIs largely in the service of businesses. They perform a wide range of brokerage and asset transformation services, but at base their role is to mobilize financial capital in the service of businesses and other capital users including governments and not-for-profits. Notably, investment banks do *not* provide monetary services as these are the exclusive domain of commercial banks who enjoy the use of governmentally issued liabilities and access to the Federal Reserve discount window.

OTHER NONDEPOSITORY INTERMEDIARIES

Commercial banks and investment banks are members of a vast and diverse financial services industry with overlapping markets and regulatory jurisdictions. These jurisdictional and competitive relationships condition behaviors with regard to pricing, output, attitudes toward risk, and just about every other facet of the business of financial intermediation. Therefore, we shall spend the next few pages sketching some of the more interesting members of this fascinating industry.

Venture Capitalists

Most fledgling entrepreneurs are unable to obtain bank financing. They go instead to venture capitalists. Many prominent firms, including Apple and Federal Express, began with funding from venture capitalists. Venture capitalists typically provide *both* capital and expertise that allow entrepreneurs to convert ideas into commercial ventures.

Venture capital funding is normally in the form of structured financing, including both equity and convertible debt, rather than just the loans that banks provide. The salient features of a venture capital contract are as follows:[10]

1. The entrepreneur cannot "walk away" after obtaining financing and negotiate with another financier (no *de novo* financing).
2. The entrepreneur may be relieved of control of the firm by the venture capitalist unless the firm's performance meets some minimum requirement ("performance requirement").
3. If the entrepreneur is relieved of control, he is paid a fixed amount independent of his demonstrated skill and subsequent cash flows of the firm; that is, he is bought out by the venture capitalist ("buyout" option for the venture capitalist).
4. If control remains with the entrepreneur, *both* the venture capitalist and the entrepreneur receive equity payoffs ("earnout" arrangement).

Why do venture capital contracts have these features? To understand this, consider the parties involved in these transactions. First, the entrepreneur often is either an engineer (who knows the manufacturing technology of the product to sell)

---

8. Actually this acquisition happened a few years before the passage of the Gramm–Leach–Bliley Act and was effectively "legalized" upon passage.
9. See Rhee (2010) and Morrison and Wilhelm (2007).
10. There is a large literature on venture capital. See, for example, Hellmann and Puri (2000), and Chan, Siegel, and Thakor (1990).

or a marketing expert, but he is often inexperienced in managing *all* facets of a business. Venture capitalists, while they are not necessarily intimately familiar with the production or marketing technique of the products their clients want to produce, usually have considerable management expertise and a nose for "troubleshooting" based on experience in financing and managing numerous ventures. Thus, venture capitalists possess two attributes that entrepreneurs need: financial capital and management expertise.

Typically, when the partnership between a venture capitalist and an entrepreneur commences, neither is completely sure of the entrepreneur's management ability. The initial period is one of learning for both parties. If the firm's performance were to indicate that the entrepreneur lacked sufficient management ability, it would be efficient to replace the entrepreneur with the venture capitalist to avail of the latter's managerial skills. Although such a passage of control may be the best thing for the firm, it is not obvious that the entrepreneur would be eager or even willing to relinquish control of the firm. That is, the entrepreneur's attachment to the venture he thought of and started may stand in the way of implementing the best *ex post* plan for the firm. To prevent this, both parties could agree *ex ante* to an explicit clause in the venture capital contract that allows for an orderly transfer of control. This would also benefit the entrepreneur *ex ante,* as the venture capitalist's recognition of the possibility that he can buy out the entrepreneur and take control of the firm if things go really badly will improve the terms of the initial financing received by the entrepreneur. In this regard, it is also important for the venture capitalist to have an equity claim in the firm. This not only gives the venture capitalist a more active voice in management even when the entrepreneur is in control, but also provides the venture capitalist with all the ownership incentives to invest managerial expertise in the firm and to counsel the entrepreneur.

We can now see why banks may be unwilling to lend to most entrepreneurs. Because banks do not possess managerial expertise in running young, nonfinancial firms, and also because regulation prevents them from doing so except during short, transitional periods following borrower default, the performance requirements and buyout options used by the venture capitalist are not available to the bank. Thus, if the entrepreneur turns out to be a poor manager and the business fails, the bank can do little to revive and nurture it back to success. It would simply be left holding the assets of the firm (assuming the entrepreneur defaults on his loan) as collateral of possibly dubious value. Hence, the same entrepreneur is generally more risky to the bank than to the venture capitalist.

Why do not banks hire management consultants to assist entrepreneurs in their fledgling businesses? They could. However, a management consultant would be merely an agent of the bank and thus the bank would confront *moral hazard* in motivating the consultant. A venture capitalist avoids this moral hazard by *combining* management expertise and financing into one entity. Alternatively, banks could hire the talent needed to advise entrepreneurs, as do the venture capitalists. However, because of the short-term nature of the bank's liabilities and their government guarantee, equity-type claims have traditionally been viewed as inappropriate for banks.

Banks are at less of a disadvantage relative to venture capitalists in dealing with well-established borrowers. With this more stable clientele, the bank's superior ability to access the capital markets and its ability to avail itself of deposit insurance and the discount window give it a distinct advantage. Not surprisingly, then, for firms where the manager's ability to shepherd his organization through the more vulnerable early phase is not a critical issue, bank loans tend to be preferred to venture capital. Moreover, in these cases, managers will prefer to avoid the possibility of having to relinquish control to the venture capitalist at some future time. Thus, the intermediation services provided by venture capitalists include screening and certification, funding, monitoring, management expertise, and liquidity creation and transformation.

Finance Companies

Most of the important finance companies originated as narrowly focused trade finance subsidiaries of large nonfinancial companies. Examples include General Electric Capital, General Motors Acceptance Corporation (GMAC), and FOMOCO (Ford Motor Company's finance subsidiary). Others have independent origins, including factoring specialists.[11] Finance companies lend to consumers for auto and home purchases, as well as other purposes, and to businesses for a wide range of applications. These intermediaries usually specialize in processing riskier credits, and most of their lending is done on a secured basis, that is, with collateral, unlike commercial banks that lend on both unsecured and secured bases. There are three basic types of finance companies: sales finance companies that make car and appliance loans; personal finance companies, which make small personal loans (for example, for debt consolidation); and business finance companies, which make commercial loans and leases. The intermediation services provided by these finance companies include screening, origination, funding, and claims transformation.

---

11. Factors provide working capital and/or collection services by purchasing and/or servicing the accounts receivable of nonfinancial firms. Factoring is an early form of asset-backed lending, done with or without recourse.

Finance companies typically fund themselves by selling commercial paper. Indeed, the most compelling difference between commercial banks and finance companies is in their primary sources of funding. Because the commercial banks are substantially funded by governmentally insured deposits, they are invested with a special public interest and are subject to pervasive regulation. The finance companies do not have access to subsidized funds and are not subject to regulatory restrictions, proscriptions, examinations, and supervision.

The commercial paper sold by finance companies is an unsecured general obligation of the issuer and has a fixed maturity of less than 9 months. Most often, the maturity of commercial paper is shorter than 6 months at the date of issue. Commercial paper is typically sold in large denominations and is rated by specialized credit-rating agencies. Because the paper is unsecured, issuers are usually compelled to purchase a dedicated (back-up) loan commitment in order to obtain a favorable credit rating. Back-up loan commitments are sold by commercial banks expressly for the purpose of providing the commercial paper issuer with the funds to redeem its paper in case rolling over the maturing paper proves to be infeasible. The back-up commitment from the bank ensures the commercial paper issuer's ability to redeem its paper, conditional only on the bank's performance on its loan commitment.

The commercial paper market is notoriously fragile. Macroeconomic shocks have been known to paralyze commercial paper issuance. In addition, the fortunes of a particular borrower may preclude use of the commercial paper market. Thus, the back-up loan commitments, or "back-up lines," are critically important to the lender, especially in light of the unsecured status of commercial paper.

Finance companies are an illustration of the evolution of competition between regulated and largely unregulated segments of the financial services industry. The captive finance subsidiaries, the most important players in this market segment, grew out of trade credit provided by larger, better-rated nonfinancial corporations. Having developed the expertise necessary to underwrite the credit of their customers and having established secure sources of funding, why would not one offer these financial services to the community beyond one's customer base? This is the logic that drove GMAC from the exclusive financing of its own auto sales to becoming the largest home-mortgage servicer in the United States. It is the same logic that drove Ford Motor Credit into the savings and loan business and General Electric Capital into virtually every facet of banking (with the notable exception of deposit taking), including the ownership of Kidder Peabody, a failed major investment bank in the United States.

Trade credit, the driver in this story of horizontal and vertical integration, arises moreover as the natural accompaniment to trade between parties with widely disparate access to the credit markets.[12] Consider General Electric (GE), a large and well-rated company that sells industrial equipment to smaller, less well-known companies. In periods of credit stringency, GE's customers are crowded (rationed) out of the credit market well before GE, and this reduces the demand for GE's products. In order to smooth the cyclicality of demand for its goods, GE will borrow in order to provide its customer with uninterrupted access to credit. This will stabilize and also increase the demand for GE's nonfinancial output. Enhanced revenues and decreased cost should ensue, the latter owing to more predictable production runs and smaller inventories.

Trade credit is a natural complement to trade in nonfinancial goods and services whenever traders have different degrees of access to capital markets. It illustrates a very basic attribute of banking, namely the negligible natural barriers to entry. Thus, in the absence of regulatory restrictions, one would expect to see a steady flow of new FIs entering and others departing (failing or merging) as the industry adjusts to changes in the demand for its services. Hence, those that specialize in the provision of financial services can expect competition from their own clients who enjoy the advantage of being largely unregulated, but must therefore borrow in the open market without the benefit of government subsidies.

The market share of finance companies, measured in terms of asset size, is a small fraction of that of commercial banks,[13] but this probably understates the importance of finance company competition, especially for the money-center and super regional banks that typically serve the same customers, middle-market companies, and the larger consumer markets.

Insurance Companies

Private sector life and health insurance companies manage trillions of dollars of assets. Property and casualty insurers control hundreds of billions of dollars in assets. Together, the insurers are slightly less than half the size of the commercial banking industry. As in the case of thrifts, many insurance companies are organized as mutuals (cooperatives) rather than as shareholder-owned institutions. Some key statistics pertaining to the life insurance industry in the United States are provided in Table 2.13. As is evident, life insurance firms invest the premiums they collect in a wide variety of assets, including real estate.

---

12. Although less common, there is no reason why trade credit cannot flow from buyer to seller. Wal-Mart, Costco, and Home Depot are much larger and often more creditworthy than their suppliers. One would expect these retailing giants to offer credit to reduce the likelihood of supply interruptions and to benefit from the reduced production cost their suppliers would experience as a result of regularized production and reduced inventories.

13. See the Federal Reserve's Flow of Funds Accounts.

TABLE 2.13 U.S. Life Insurance Companies-Significant Ratios 1990–2009

Item	1990	1995	2000	2002	2005	2006	2008	2009
U.S. Companies[1]	2,195	1,650	1,269	1,284	1,119	1,072	976	946
Income	402.2	528.1	811.5	734.0	779.0	883.6	940.6	781.4
Life Insurance Premiums	76.7	102.8	130.6	134.5	142.3	149.2	147.2	124.6
Annuity Considerations[2]	129.1	158.4	306.7	269.3	277.1	302.7	328.1	231.6
Health Insurance Premiums	58.3	90.0	105.6	108.7	118.3	141.2	165.0	166.2
Investment and Other	138.2	176.9	268.5	221.5	241.4	290.4	300.3	259.1
Payments under Life Insurance and Annuity Contracts	88.4	227.6	375.2	301.3	365.7	422.7	445.1	374.9
Payments under Life Insurance Beneficiaries	24.6	34.5	44.1	48.2	53.0	55.7	59.9	59.5
Surrender Values under Life Insurance[3]	18.0	19.5	27.2	32.9	39.2	38.5	58.6	48.1
Surrender Values under Annuity Contracts[3,4]	n.a	105.4	214.0	142.9	190.3	237.8	236.7	182.7
Policyholder Dividends	12.0	17.8	20.0	21.0	17.9	18.4	19.1	16.2
Annuity Payments	32.6	48.5	68.7	55.0	63.9	71.1	69.6	67.1
Matured Endowments	0.7	1.0	0.6	0.6	0.6	0.6	0.6	0.6
Other Payments	0.6	0.9	0.6	0.6	0.7	0.6	0.6	0.6
Health Insurance Benefit Payments	40.0	64.7	78.8	78.7	79.6	97.0	118.9	122.0
Assets	1,408	2,144	3,182	3,380	4482	4,823	4,648	4,959
Government Bonds	211	409	364	481	590	579	634	685
Corporate Securities	711	1,241	2,238	2,266	3,136	3,413	3,104	3,436
(Percent of Total Assets)	50	58	70	67	70	71	67	69
Bonds	583	869	1,241	1,475	1,850	1,882	1,968	2,050
Stocks	128	372	997	791	1,285	1,531	1,136	1,386
Mortgages	270	212	237	251	295	314	353	336
Real Estate	43	52	36	33	33	33	32	28
Policy Loans	63	96	102	105	110	113	122	123
Other	110	133	204	244	319	371	402	350
Interest Earned on Assets (In Percent)[5]	8.89	7.41	7.05	5.38	4.90	5.35	5.70	4.60
Obligations and Surplus Funds[6]	1,408	2,144	3,182	3,380	4,482	4,823	4,648	4,959
Policy Reserves	1,197	1,812	2,712	2,507	3,360	3,608	3,471	3,812
Annuities[7]	798	1,213	1,841	1,550	2,174	2,328	2,137	2,422
Group	516	619	960	570	758	807	716	798
Individual	282	594	881	980	1,415	1,521	1,422	1,624
Supplementary Contracts[8]	17	25	34	14	16	17	13	16
Life Insurance	349	511	742	833	1,029	1,110	1,134	1,178
Health Insurance	33	63	96	111	141	153	186	196
Liabilities for Deposit-Type Contracts[9]	18	20	21	364	456	487	454	416
Capital and Surplus	91	151	188	202	256	266	263	301

n.a. = Not Available
[1]Includes life insurance companies that sell accident and health insurance in 2000 and 2002.
[2]Excludes certain deposit-type funds from income due to codification in 2002.
[3]"Surrender values" include annuity withdrawals of funds in 2000 and 2002.
[4]Excludes payments under deposit-type contracts in 2002.
[5]Net rate.
[6]Includes other obligations not shown separately.
[7]Excludes reserves for guaranteed interest contracts in 2002.
[8]Includes(excludes) reserves for contracts with and without life contingencies in 1994 and 2000 (2002).
[9]Policyholder dividend accumulations for all years.
Source: U.S. Census Bureau, Statistical Abstract of the United States: 2009–2010.

Insurance companies hold many of the same kinds of assets found on the balance sheets of commercial banks, but insurer assets are financed for the most part with *contingent* liabilities. That is, the insurance company's liabilities become current (or terminate, in the case of annuities) upon the occurrence of some prespecified event, the timing or realization of which is inherently uncertain when the insurance contract is written. Insurance is written against a large variety of contingencies. Life insurance companies typically contract against the expiration of life or the realization of health care needs.[14] Property and casualty insurers write policies against: (i) damage or loss of physical or intellectual property, including the loss of income or extraordinary expenses associated with the property damage or loss, (ii) liability, (iii) health care needs, and (iv) surety. Surety contracts guarantee third-party contractual performance. Examples include fidelity, construction and bail bonds, and also standby letters of credit that are a mainstay of the commercial banking business. Standby letters typically guarantee the repayment of third-party debt.

For example, A might be vaguely interested in extending credit to B, but may not be entirely sure about repayment prospects. A then may request that B arrange a standby letter of credit with her bank, insurance company or other credible financial guarantor. In exchange for the payment of an appropriate insurance premium,[15] the guarantor will accept the risk of repaying A's loan to B in the event B fails to do so. This kind of financial guarantee is commonly written by commercial banks, property and casualty (multiline) insurers, and even "pure" financial guarantors (monoline insurers) who do nothing more than guarantee performance of third parties under debt contracts.

The most striking differences between banks and insurance companies are found on the liability sides of their respective balance sheets. Wherever the liabilities of banks change, often instantaneously and at the sole discretion of depositors, insurance liabilities change on the occurrence of events largely uncontrollable by the claimant. In addition, the duration of life insurance liabilities, in particular, is much longer than that of commercial bank deposit liabilities. Thus, life insurers can and do hold longer-term assets than commercial banks. This difference in duration may be the most fundamental difference between banks and life insurers (the liabilities of property and casualty insurers tend to be shorter than those of life insurers). Life insurers and pension funds are allegedly the two largest private-sector pools of long-term money.[16]

In order to distinguish insurance from the kind of risk-shifting that takes place through the purchase (sale) of a financial futures contract or an option or a "swap" contract, insurance is commonly defined as involving some application of the law of large numbers. Thus, insurance requires some pooling of risks among independent events to avail of diversification and make it easier to price such risks. It is difficult for investors to avail of such diversification themselves because of the bulky unit size of some claims. Again, a strong analogy between insurance and banking emerges: diversification enables banks to manage credit and withdrawal (interest rate) risks, and individuals' limited wealth and access to credit markets limits the potential for "homemade" diversification. The intermediation services provided by insurance companies include screening and certification, origination, funding, monitoring, guaranteeing, and claims transformation.

Pensions

Along with life insurance, private pension funds accumulate the long-term liabilities that are capable of funding the durable assets so critical to real capital accumulation. In earlier years, when bank deposits were subject to interest rate ceilings and competition was more restrained, banks and thrifts too were capable of making 7- to 10-year fixed-interest-rate business loans and even 30-year fixed-rate mortgages with acceptable levels of interest rate risk. The shortened duration of deposits, however, has rendered banks and thrifts less able to provide long-term credit. To be sure, banks and thrifts offer longer-lived loans, but the interest rates on them are typically variable. These sequences of short-term loans provide the borrower

---

14. Life and health insurance are genteel euphemisms that support marketing efforts. It is more difficult, to be sure, to sell death and illness insurance.
15. Mehr (1986) explains the origin of the term "premium" in insurance that directly links the insurance business to commercial banking: "If a Greek shipowner planned a voyage to bring cargo from a foreign land, he would borrow the necessary money by pledging his ship as collateral. The contract provided that if the ship failed to return to port intact, the lender would have no claim against the shipowner. This type of contract [called bottomry] became common throughout maritime countries . . . The interest charged on these contracts included a sum in addition to that normally charged for the loan to compensate the lender for writing insurance [accepting credit risk] to cover the safety of the voyage. This additional amount, logically, was called a premium, and to this day the consideration paid for insurance is still referred to as a premium." *Fundamentals of Insurance,* second ed., Irwin, 1986, p. 13.
16. The careful reader will note that this distinction is easily overdrawn in that policy loans can be made against nonterm life insurance policies at the owners discretion. Moreover, life insurance can "lapse" as a result of the insured's decision not to make timely insurance payments. A second nuance relates to the distinction between discretionary withdrawals of depositors and the presumably uncontrollable random events that trigger insurance claims. Most states of nature that trigger insurance claims are subject to some human influence. This ability to affect the insured contingencies is referred to as moral hazard (see Chapter 1).

with no certainty regarding future for longer-term credits, and this has elevated the importance of the pension funds and life insurance.[17]

The liabilities of defined-contribution pension funds are actuated upon retirement or death of their members, at which time the member's claim is paid out as a lump sum or used to purchase an annuity. In the case of defined-benefit plans, the retirement fund pays a prescribed annuity to the claimant upon retirement. In the time interval between contributions and the termination of the funds' liability to the claimants, the contributions are invested in a wide variety of assets, everything from real estate and other equities to Treasury debt. These investments are constrained by federal legislation (ERISA), which defines the responsibilities of pension fiduciaries. The key intermediation services provided by pension funds are guaranteeing and claims transformation. The substantial asset liability management risks in defined-benefit plans have led to a migration to defined contribution plans where there is no prescribed annuity upon retirement and the ultimate pension depends on investment returns much like in mutual funds.

Pension funds are being called upon increasingly to play a role in corporate governance as representatives of their millions of beneficiaries. Historically, the pensions have been passive investors, but issues like the composition of boards of directors, executive compensation, potential conflicts of interest of executives involved in buyouts and many other issues vitally affect current and future retirees with investments in corporate America. The problem is that the pension fund managers typically hold investments in many hundreds of corporations – indeed, many adopt consciously passive strategies of cloning the stock indexes (purchasing securities that behave like the averages) – and they are simply not staffed adequately to participate in the affairs of individual corporations. This, however, is increasingly unacceptable to pension participants and the community at large as more instances of corporate abuse are widely chronicled. It seems inevitable that the guardians of America's pension assets will be forced to become more active in corporate affairs, and this will no doubt affect corporate governance in the future.

Mutual Funds

Along with pension funds, mutual funds have been major market-share winners over the past 40 years. Essentially a post-World War II phenomenon, mutual funds (including money market funds) have risen from an inconsequential share of the intermediation market in 1950 to achieve a 6% market share in 1990, and a 25% market share in 2010 (measured based on total assets). Its significant growth can also be gleaned from the penetration of mutual funds among U.S. households, which increased from 25% in 1990 to 44% in 2012 (see Table 2.2).

Mutual funds come in two basic varieties: open- and closed-end. Closed-end funds have a preestablished number of shares and the fund's initial resources typically are not augmented with the subsequent sale of shares. A closed-end fund is typically traded as a single security on organized exchanges, for example, the New York Stock Exchange, and its shares are priced directly in the market like the shares of any other company. As a consequence, the market price of closed-end fund shares can deviate, often widely, from the liquidation value of the securities they hold. Open-end funds operate on very different rules. Their shares are continuously liquidated and augmented by a specialized management company that offers shares for cash, and cash for shares at net asset value (NAV). NAV is the estimated liquidation or market value of the fund's assets divided by the number of shares the fund has outstanding. Thus, unlike closed-end fund shares, the prices of open-end fund shares cannot deviate from the value of underlying assets.

The open-end funds have given rise to large specialized fund management companies, like Fidelity, DWS Scudder, Vanguard, and Dreyfus. Each of these manages and markets a wide range of different funds, each of which is defined in terms of specific investment objectives. These investment companies earn their keep by levying fees against the funds it manages. The funds, of course, are owned by their investors. Were you to consult the financial pages of any major newspaper, you would find a section headed mutual funds wherein you could find the NAV of any of the numerous mutual funds managed by Merrill Lynch, or any of the very large number managed by Fidelity. These larger mutual fund companies typically have tens of billions of dollars under management. The key financial intermediation services provided by mutual funds include transactions services, screening, and certification.

There is nothing terribly new about mutual funds, except their explosive growth in recent decades. There are at least three reasons for the current popularity of the funds. First, money-market mutual funds, which were introduced in the 1960s, rapidly became the instrument of choice for circumventing Regulation Q deposit interest rate ceilings. As inflation accelerated in the 1970s and market interest rates soared, the spread between these rates and deposit rates gaped ever wider. The bloated opportunity cost of holding bank deposits increased the appeal of money-market funds. The rest is history!

---

17. Likewise, the departure of banks from term lending has elevated the importance of financial futures, options, and swaps, which are risk-shifting financial contracts that permit the borrower to dispose of part of the unwanted interest rate risk of an indexed loan.

Despite the competitive disadvantage of operating without a government guarantee, the mutual funds grew spectacularly, underscoring that there are limits to what the public is willing to pay for governmental deposit insurance.

By and large, the money-market funds were managed conservatively, and some even restricted themselves to holding direct debt of the U.S. government. More commonly, the funds held negotiable large-denomination certificates of deposit of banks, commercial paper, bankers' acceptances, mortgage, and other asset-backed securities, and government agency debt. Almost all of these assets were less than 1 year to maturity, and the funds traded at a constant one dollar per share.

Moreover, the money-market funds are sustained by implicit guarantees of their managers. In at least three cases, management companies made good on asset losses in order to protect their own reputations and the viability of the money funds they managed. For example, Value Line manages a money-market fund that held the commercial paper of Integrated Resources, a company that defaulted on its debt. Rather than reflect this loss in its money-market fund, which almost certainly would have meant the fund's demise, Value Line management bought the Integrated Resources commercial paper from its money-market fund at par. Notably, there was no legal or even moral obligation to protect the fund's investors, but the action was presumably motivated by the desire to maintain and build upon Value Line's reputation in managing money-market funds. Clearly, the money-market funds offered a compelling package of substitutes for the governmental deposit guarantee. Low-risk investment strategies, combined with implicit guarantees of reputable management companies, and substantially higher yields permitted the money-market funds to ravage the bank and thrift deposit markets and enjoy meteoric growth. As we will see in Chapter 14, the low (or no) risk image got battered during the 2007–2009 financial crisis. Explicit government guarantees were needed to ensure the survival of money market mutual funds.

The second and third reasons for the recent growth of mutual funds are less dramatic, but nevertheless noteworthy. In recent decades, the public has gradually become persuaded of the improbability of consistently "beating" the stock market. A sea of research, much of it academic, has demonstrated that over most extended spans of time asset managers do less well than the widely watched stock market indices, for example, Dow Jones, and Standard and Poor's. The reasons are numerous and complex, but the facts seem plain. The widespread acceptance of this idea has had a profound effect on investment behavior, and in particular it has led to the idea that if you cannot beat the averages, you can do no better than to buy the averages. Buying the averages is known as passive investment. This is done by purchasing a portfolio of securities that behave like (clone) the averages. Since this strategy typically requires holding a substantial number of securities, it is often infeasible for smaller wealth holders, and uneconomic for most. However, mutual funds can provide such a service at low cost. Thus, the popularity of passive investment strategies provides a second reason for the recent growth of mutual funds.

Finally, the past six decades have witnessed the much-heralded globalization of financial markets. Many investors believe it is as important to diversify across economies (currencies) as it is to diversify across industries. Furthermore, diversification across economies has been massively simplified in recent decades, as regulatory and tax barriers have been dismantled. However, information about foreign investment opportunities is still relatively expensive. Hence, the mutual fund has become the instrument of choice for investing abroad. Many "country funds" are closed-end and listed on the New York Stock Exchange, but there are also many open-end funds that specialize in countries and regions of the world. To mix a metaphor, as the pie of foreign indirect investment has grown larger, the bologna of specialization among funds has been sliced ever thinner.

Hedge Funds

In contrast to most mutual funds, hedge funds are actively managed funds that pursue nontraditional investment strategies. A hedge fund is a private investment pool subject to the terms of an investment agreement between the sponsor of the fund and its investors. They take both long and short positions in a variety of instruments – equities, fixed income securities, currencies, etc. – to achieve the highest return commensurate with the fund's objectives. Although the hedge fund industry has traditionally been far less regulated than mutual funds, that gap was partially closed in 2004, when hedge funds were required to register under the Investment Advisers Act. This act allows the SEC to inspect all hedge fund advisers for approval purposes. Moreover, hedge funds are now subject to many of the same requirements as mutual fund advisers.

Differences between hedge funds and mutual funds persist, however. While mutual fund sales charges and fees are subject to regulatory limits, there are no limits on the fees hedge fund advisers can charge.

Also, mutual funds are restricted in their ability to leverage against the value of securities in their portfolio, whereas leveraging and other higher-risk investment strategies are commonplace for hedge funds. In fact, hedge funds originally came into existence to invest in equity securities and use leverage and short selling to hedge the exposure of the portfolio to stock price movements. Finally, while any investor can open a mutual fund account with $1000 or less, a minimum investment of $1 million or more is typically required to become a hedge fund investor.

CREDIT RATING AGENCIES

Credit Rating agencies (CRAs) provide a brokerage function as information processors. Typically, they provide credit ratings for a variety of debt securities: municipal bonds, corporate bonds, mortgage-backed securities (MBS), and the like. These credit ratings fall in 21 or 22 discrete categories and a rating signifies an assessment of the borrower's ability to repay its debt obligations. Ratings are on an ordinal scale. For example, S&P's highest rating is AAA and the lowest is D.

CRAs are specialists in processing information that helps to arrive at an estimate of a borrower's probability of default. In the United States and the EU, there are regulatory norms that the CRAs must abide by. One of these is that in the United States, CRAs must be approved as *nationally recognized statistical rating organizations* (NRSRO) by the SEC.

The credit rating industry is an oligopoly, with three CRAs dominating the market with about 95% share.[18] These CRAs are: Moody's, Standard and Poor's (S&P), and Fitch.

CRAs produce credit ratings based on public as well as private information, and use both quantitative models and subjective judgment, based on inputs derived from financial statements as well as assessments of management quality, the firm's competitive position, etc. These ratings are not intended to be buy/sell recommendations. Moreover, they are "coarse indicators" of credit quality, with most rating agencies using a litter over 20 ratings to describe credit qualities that lie in a continuum.[19] But ratings are enormously important nonetheless, because for many institutions, capital requirements for holding debt securities, as well as which investments are considered permissible are often based on the credit ratings given to those debt instruments.

Credit ratings are assigned to a wide variety of issuers, including corporations, municipal units, states, countries, and structured finance products created by securitization; in the case of securitized mortgages, these structured finance products are called MBS. Issuers who choose to be rated have to pay the CRAs. That is why this is called an "issuer pays" arrangement. While some issuers of debt securities have the flexibility to decide whether or not to acquire a rating, corporate issuers of bonds in the United States do *not* have this flexibility since Moody's and S&P rate *all* taxable corporate bonds, even if issuers do not pay for those ratings.

The economic rationale for CRAs to exist can be found in the theory of information brokers as diversified information producers.[20] We will discuss this in Chapter 3. Moreover, credit ratings also serve a useful coordination purpose in financial markets, as they allow agents to converge to one out of many possible equilibria.[21] Issuers can use good ratings to signal low-risk and high-quality governance, thereby reducing their cost of financing. Investors can use ratings and bond yields to determine whether to invest in those bonds at those yields.

In the subprime financial crisis of 2007–2009, CRAs were blamed for having been overly generous in assigning ratings and thus not alerting investors about the risks in their investments. However, the problems of "ratings inflation" and ratings errors seemed to be confined to the ratings assigned to structured finance products and some sovereign bonds.[22] In the case of MBS, especially those backed by subprime mortgages, the rating agencies were confronted with risks that were unlike those they had assessed previously.

THE ROLE OF THE GOVERNMENT

To this point, we have sketched the major players in the world of financial intermediation. Probably the most important intermediaries to add to this list are the vast government enterprises that routinely provide a wide variety of financial services. These would include the Old Age, Survivors and Disability Insurance, Workers' Compensation, Medicare, the housing agencies (Federal National Mortgage Corporations of FNMA or "Fannie Mae," Federal Home Loan Mortgage Corporation or FHLMC or "Freddie Mac," and the Government National Mortgage Association or GNMA or "Ginnie Mae") Farm Credit Administration, Small Business Administration, Student Loan Marketing Association (or "Sally Mae"), and flood insurance programs of the Agriculture Department. And the list goes on!

Annual payments to the federal government's Old Age, Survivors, Disability Insurance, and Medicare programs are twice the *assets* of the largest commercial bank in the United States, and about one-sixth the assets of the entire commercial banking industry. Without doubt, the U.S. government is by far the largest financial services provider in the country and arguably in the world.

---

18. See Matthies (2013).

19. Goel and Thakor (2015) provide a theory that explains why ratings coarseness makes economic sense, even though it lowers welfare.

20. See, for example, Ramakrishnan and Thakor (1984).

21. See Boot, Milbourn and Schmeits (2006), and Manso (2013).

22. See Benmelech and Duglosz (2010), for example.

FINANCIAL INTERMEDIARIES ON THE PERIPHERY

Gambling

Prominent on the periphery of the financial intermediation universe is the glamorous world of legal and illegal gambling. Some deny that gambling is a financial service, but this seems a quibble. The bookmaker is as much a broker as the trader of options and financial futures. The naysayers argue that gambling *creates* risk, whereas insurance dissipates and redistributes preexisting risk. But whether the gambling relates to a manufactured uncertainty (e.g., a horse race or roulette) or to some pre-existing natural process (e.g., the number of live pups your neighbor's dog will whelp), seems incidental. The production of uncertainty is logically separable and incidental to the gambling.

The more meaningful distinction between insurance and gambling is that the former involves the exchange of a certain cost (the premium) for *relief* from an uncertain liability, whereas the latter is the exchange of a certain cost (say the price of a lottery ticket) for an uncertain future receipt. The bookmaker would just as soon wager on tomorrow's mean temperature as on the three-digit numbers generated by tomorrow's horse races. It matters not whether the bet is hedging or speculating, nor does it matter what process generates the uncertainty.[23] The bookmaker merely fills a market niche, one usually scorned or illegal. The difference between the bookmaker and the insurance agent may well be that one is legal and the other is not, but at a deeper level the insurer sells alleviation from risk to those ill-equipped to bear it, whereas the bookmaker sells risk to those who find it welfare-improving. In this latter sense, both are brokers, and possibly qualitative asset transformers too. The bookmaker is a FI in the same sense as the insurance agent or underwriter.

Pawnbrokers

Also on the periphery we have "bankers" to the poor and the excluded (who perforce are high-risk borrowers). The major participants in these market niches are pawnbrokers and loan sharks, the former legal and the latter not usually. As of 1991, there were in the United States approximately three times as many pawnbrokers (about 6900) as S&Ls.[24] Pawn loans are typically small, say $50–$100. Most of these loans are for a few weeks, sometimes months, and all are secured with merchandise (jewelry, electronics, musical instruments, guns, and the like) with a resale value roughly twice the debt. All-in interest rates range from high to astronomical, and can be as high as 25–30% per month in states without interest rate ceilings. In 2004, it is estimated that there were 15,000 pawnbrokers in the United States.[25]

Pawnbroking is a traditional form of asset-backed (secured) lending. The lender typically prefers to be repaid rather than taking ownership and liquidating the collateral (this is because the failure to repay usually ruptures a valuable customer relationship), but the creditworthiness of the borrower is rarely at issue (the pawnbroker rarely has the information necessary to form an intelligent judgment, except perhaps in cases of longtime customers). The loan is made entirely on the basis of the borrower's collateral. Default rates between 10 and 30% are common. The intermediation services provided by pawnbrokers include origination, funding, and market completeness.

The pawnbroker industry began to stagnate in the late 1990s with the rise of payday and title lending alternatives, which are discussed below.[26]

Payday Lending

Payday lenders did not operate as a formal industry until the early 1990s. Prior to this time, most payday lenders were check cashers who made payday loans as a casual extension of their core business. By 2004, there were 12,000 payday lenders in the United States,[27] with major pawn chains having also entered the business.

Payday lenders provide unsecured short-term loans to customers. The loan arises in one of two ways. One is the traditional payday loan transaction, in which the borrower writes a postdated (or undated) personal check to a lender, the lender makes a loan equal in amount to the check minus finance charge. The lender holds the check before either depositing it, or receiving cash repayment directly from the borrower, usually on the borrower's payday. The second is

---

23. If one views the bookmaker as inherently dishonest, one might prefer to gamble on a process subject to human influence, perhaps his own (moral hazard). But such an assumption about bookmakers seems gratuitous and beside the point.

The gambling enterprise is so vast that we find it done in both the public sector (lotteries) and in the private sector. In the latter, there are legal expressions (parimutuel betting, both on- and off-track and casinos) and illegal expressions (bookmaking and the "numbers game").

24. See Caskey (1991).

25. See Fass and Francis (2004).

26. See Caskey (2003).

27. The discussion follows Barr (2004).

a variant of the traditional transaction, in which no check is written, but the borrower signs an authorization that permits the lender to debit his bank account on a future date for the amount of the loan plus the finance charge. The typical loan term is 2 weeks.

The payday lending industry has grown to approximately 12,000 firms in 31 states and DC. In 2000, payday lenders made about 65 million loans to 8–10 million households, totaling $8–$14 billion in loan value, and generating over $2 billion in revenue. The industry reports gross margins of 30–45% of revenue, with losses at 1–1.3% of receivables, and return on investment of 24%. Payday lending has increasingly become controversial particularly because of the high interest rates charged (the APR can be as high as a few hundred percent). Some states therefore have an outright prohibition of payday lending or seek to cap interest rates. Under the Dodd Frank Act – discussed in Chapters 15 and 16 – further restrictions can be expected.

Title Lenders

Title lenders are similar to payday lenders, the difference being that title lenders make secured loans rather than unsecured loans. That is, instead of holding a check or debit authorization until payday, title lenders hold collateral against the loan. Typically, $250 to $1000, and the value of the associated collateral is typically three times as much.

The title lending industry is essentially an extension of the pawnbroker industry. The two differences between them are as follows: First, a pawnbroker keeps physical possession of the collateral until the loan is repaid, whereas a title lender may permit the collateral to physically rest with the borrower during the loan term and repossess it only upon default. Second, title loans are typically larger than pawn loans. These two differences, however, are not economically important for distinguishing between these two types of lenders in terms of the brokerage and QAT functions served by them. That is, payday lenders and title lenders serve essentially the same economic functions as pawnbrokers.

Like loans extended by pawnbrokers, payday loans and loans made by title lenders tend to have very high interest rates, often exceeding 25% *per month,* for an annual percentage rate (APR) of 300%. The title loan industry originated in the southeastern United States and has spread to other states like Missouri, Illinois, and Oregon. In some states, an upper limit of 30% annual interest rate was imposed, which essentially eliminated the industry there.

Loan Sharks

Whereas the pawnbroker lives on the edge of respectability (see the splendid movie of the same title, with Rod Steiger), loan sharks live beyond the pale. Dates on loan-sharking are understandably sketchy, but these FIs play a prominent role in providing credit in support of both legal and illegal enterprises.[28] The President's Crime Commission in 1967 asserted that loan-sharking was the second most important activity of organized crime.

A definitional note will help to clarify much confusion. If by loan-sharking we mean *all* illegal lending, loan-sharking will include an amorphous hodgepodge of lenders who violate usury laws. More useful, it would seem, is to think of loan sharks as lenders who can credibly make illegal or socially unacceptable threats of violence and intimidation in connection with collections. The availability of this singular and extralegal collection technology explains why this financial service is provided by criminal elements, why interest rates on such loans tend to be high, and why their clientele are typically desperate borrowers with few alternatives. The legality of their activities aside, loan sharks serve economic functions that are similar to those of payday and title lenders. In fact, some refer to payday lenders as "legal loan sharks."

Reuter and Rubinstein describe three kinds of loans made by loan sharks. Short-term small loans of under $1000 were made on a weekly six-for-five basis. Loans of $1000 or more, called "knockdowns," would call for 12 weekly repayments of $100. A third type of loan, usually for larger amounts, called a "vig" loan, would call for weekly interest payments of 1.5–3% with the principal returned *in toto* at termination of the loan.

The same authors also describe the fairly common use of collateral, but this would seem to be an anomaly, unless the credit is to be used for illegal purposes. A properly secured loan would obviate the need for, or usefulness of extralegal intimidation. Hence, the borrower should be able to borrow from any asset-based lender such as a finance company or a pawnbroker at considerably lower interest rates than those quoted by loan sharks. However, legitimate lenders could be expected to avoid lending to felons, or for projects known to be illegal.

Apparently, a substantial fraction of the loans made by loan sharks are to bookmakers down on their luck. It would not be surprising to learn that much credit also goes to finance illicit drug and stolen goods inventories. But the less glamorous side of loan-sharking must be lending to the fringes of society without the collateral to offer a pawnbroker or finance

---

28. For a fascinating description of the business, see Reuter and Rubinstein (1982), and Haller and Alvitti (1977).

company. To these unfortunates, the loan shark offers a service that no law-abiding institution, short of a charity, can provide. Whatever the moral considerations loan sharks are nevertheless an indispensable part of the financial services industry. They are bankers to the poor, the forgotten, and to those living outside the law.

CONCLUSION

This chapter has provided a selective survey of the major and more interesting members of the financial services industry. We used our description of commercial banks and thrifts to also sketch the financial environment.

Major competitors for commercial banks and thrifts include insurance companies, finance companies, pensions, and mutual funds. The linkages among these segments, the cutting edge of competition, are described in the respective sections on each. The theme is one of commonality and similarity; differences among segments of the industry are seen as legal, artificial, and exaggerated. And of course, one can never forget the government ("… where does the gorilla sleep?") as a member of this gigantic industry.

Finally, we addressed a collection of important and often neglected FIs on the periphery of the industry. Included in this collection is the woolly world of gambling – public and private, legal and illegal – and the shadowy backwaters of pawnbroking, payday and title lending, and loan-sharking. All have their assigned roles, based on the law and technology, in processing risk and information and in allocating credit. Each serves as a broker and/or asset transformer, and the more bizarre actions associated with the criminal aspects of some of these activities are absent, each makes the market work more effectively, thereby increasing the economic pie available to be shared among all.

REVIEW QUESTIONS

1. Given below is an excerpt from a conversation. Who do you agree with? Provide a thorough discussion of the theoretical and empirical underpinnings of your opinion.
    Appleton: Absolutely! I believe that when you cut through all the bull, the essential role of banks is to act as "lot breakers" and provide simple transactions service. I can't write checks against a T-bill, so I need a bank.
    Butterworth: Alex, I couldn't disagree more. Everything that I've read suggests that banks *are* special. Your proposal would destroy a key ingredient of the process by which society allocates capital from savers to investors.
    Moderator: It looks to me like we have a *fundamental* disagreement: Why do we have banks and what do they really do?
    Appleton: What's to disagree? Ask anybody and they'll say that banks are there to borrow and lend money.
    Moderator: That's obvious, but it hardly settles the issue, does it, Alex? After all, borrowing and lending are *not* services in themselves, but rather the *visible outcomes* of banks' production of financial services. The question is: What are these less transparent financial services that banks and other financial intermediaries produce? You say that the services are purely transactional, while Beth claims they are much more.
2. Discuss what is meant by brokerage and asset transformation. What factors determine the value of brokerage services?
3. List five distinct types of financial intermediaries, explain what they do, and provide a comparison/contrast of the basic intermediation services they provide.
4. Find information on capital-to-total-assets ratios for several nonfinancial firms and compare them to those for financial firms. Why the differences?
5. From the information in Table 2.6, what can you conclude about the risk in holding a representative bank's equity compared to that in holding equity in a diversified market portfolio?

APPENDIX 2.1 MEASUREMENT DISTORTIONS AND THE BALANCE SHEET

The balance sheet perspective on financial intermediation provided in the Introduction is suggestive but stylized and therefore incomplete.

The balance sheet, for banks as well as other entities, is an accounting statement that states the values of the firm's cash flows as of some specified date. In principle, the listing of assets is exhaustive and if the valuations are done properly, the remainder or net assets constitutes a sensible (unbiased) estimate of the firm's capital or net worth. However, in practice, assets are occasionally omitted (arbitrarily valued at zero), while others are improperly valued. Indeed, the principles of valuation vary across categories of assets, so that the net worth is often difficult, if not impossible, to interpret.

For example, if reputational capital is purchased, it is carried on the balance sheet at its depreciated purchase price. Called "goodwill," this asset is usually written off according to some arbitrary schedule chosen by auditors and/or other interested parties such as governmental regulatory agents. If, on the other hand, the firm chooses to develop a reputation, as opposed to purchasing an existing one, generally accepted accounting principles will accord the reputational capital zero value. Accountants defend this inconsistent treatment with reference to their "conservatism." However, from an economist's viewpoint, the practice distorts or biases balance sheets. Moreover, in a world of costly capital and information, the incentive to develop reputation is weakened by the asymmetric accounting treatment.

Now consider earning assets such as loans and securities. The accounting convention is that assets held for "trading" purposes must be marked to market, whereas those assets held for "investment" may be carried at adjusted historical cost. If the latter assets perform unexceptionally, the assets often are carried at original cost.[29] Moreover, there is no unambiguous basis for distinguishing between trading and investment motives, so the auditors exercise their discretion. This notion of valuing assets at cost seems bizarre to those naïve enough to think of the balance sheet as a description of the firm's financial condition, but many of the investment assets are *not* traded in active markets and it is therefore difficult to value them at arbitrary points in time, like December 31 and June 30. This is a systemic rather than an aberrant problem, in the sense that the *raison d'etre* of banks is to serve as repositories for those assets without active secondary markets. This is how the bank produces liquidity! But accurate point estimates of the values of such assets are inherently difficult to come by and auditors are understandably loath to oblige, given the litigious inclinations of their disparate clienteles.

The issue of Generally Accepted Accounting Principles (GAAP) versus current (or market) value accounting has been at the forefront of the ongoing debate. However, it is difficult to know what current value accounting would mean in markets with wide bid-ask spreads. Forced to do current value accounting, the auditors might insist on interval rather than point estimates, or perhaps refuse to certify the accuracy of their estimates. Would the market then be better informed? Would managers display less pathological behavior? Perhaps! Noisy, unbiased estimates may well be superior to less noisy, but biased alternatives.

The valuation problem, it should be noted, expresses itself on both sides of the balance sheet. Core deposits, for example, are treated as investment rather than trading assets, and they are carried at par, cost, or redemption value. Thus a dollar of deposits is invariably a dollar of liability. Note, however, that when banks are sold, their deposits typically command a premium. The buyer is willing to pay (typically between 1 and 6%) for the deposits. Why? Because deposits are inexpensive as a source of funding. They embody subsidy or "rent" deriving from underpriced deposit insurance and restricted entry into banking. But then, should not the valuation of deposits reflect these rents or subsidies? Does not the failure to account for them overstate the bank's liabilities and understate its net worth? This dubious accounting practice may overstate the stability of the F.I.s net worth. This distortion gave rise to much of the "hidden" capital in banking, thought to be so important in reducing banks' appetites for risk taking.

In any case, the bank balance sheet reflects a complex mix of disparate valuation practices that confound the best efforts at interpretation. Some argue that current value accounting would do the community a disservice by adding volatility to reported financial results. The counterargument is that GAAP data knowingly mislead and compromise the integrity of the system that produces such data.

REFERENCES

Adams, J.R., 1990. The Big Fix: Inside the S&L Scandal: How an Unholy Alliance of Politics and Money Destroyed America's Banking System. Wiley, New York.

Barr, M.S., 2004. Banking the poor. Yale Law J. 21, 121–237.

Benmelech, E., Dlugozs, J., 2010. The Credit Rating Crisis, NBER.

Boot, A.W.A., Milbourn, T., Schmeits, A., 2006. Credit ratings as coordination mechanisms. Rev. Finan. Stud. 19, 81–118.

Boyd, J., Gertler, M., 1993. U.S. commercial banking: trends, cycles, and policy. NBER Macroecon. Annu. 8, 368–371.

Caskey, J., 1991. Pawnbroking in America: the economics of a forgotten credit market. J. Money Credit Bank. 23, 85–99.

Chan, Y.-S., Siegel, D., Thakor, A.V., 1990. Learning corporate control and performance requirements in venture capital contracts. Int. Econ. Rev. 31, 365–381.

Caskey, J., 2003. 'Fringe banking a decade later", Working paper.

Fass, S.M., Francis, J., 2004. Where have all the hot goods gone? The role of pawn shops. J. Res. Crime Delin. 41, 156–179.

Goel, A.M., Thakor, A.V., 2015. Information reliability and welfare: a theory of coarse credit ratings.' J. Finan. Econ. 115, 541–557.

Haller, M.H., Alvitti, J.V., 1977. Loansharking in American cities: historical analysis of a marginal enterprise. Am. J. Legal Hist. 21, 12–156.

Hellmann, T.F., Puri, M., 2000. The interaction between product market and financing strategy: the role of venture capital. Rev. Finan. Stud. 13, 959–984.

Manso, G., 2013. Feedback effects of credit ratings. J. Finan. Econ. 109, 535–549.

---

29. Loans have occasionally been written down by examiners despite unexceptional performance. This typically happens when the loan has an interest reserve account that temporarily services the credit, but the financial condition of the borrower has deteriorated to the point where its ability to service the loans after the interest reserve has been exhausted is brought into question. Hence the oxymoronic "performing nonperformers."

Matthies, A.B., 2013. Empirical research on corporate credit-ratings: a literature review, SFB 649 Discussion Paper, 2013-003.

Mayer, M., 1990. The Greatest Ever Bank Robbery: The Collapse of the Savings and Loan Industry. Charles Scribner's Sons, New York.

Mehr, R., 1986. Fundamentals of Insurance, second ed. Irwin, Homewood: Illinois.

Morrison, A., Wilhelm, W., 2007. Investment banking: past, present and future. J. Appl. Corp. Finan. 19, 8–20.

Ramakrishnan, R., Thakor, A.V., 1984. Information reliability and a theory of financial intermediation. Rev. Econ. Stud. 51, 415–432.

Reuter, P., Rubinstein, J., 1982. Illegal Gambling in New York: A Case Study in the Operation, Structure and Regulation in An Illegal Market. National Institute of Justice, Washington DC.

Rhee, R.J., 2010. The decline of investment banking: preliminary thoughts on the evolution of the industry 1996–2008. J. Bus. Technol. Law 5, 75–98.

United States General Accounting Office, 2003. Investment Banks: The Role of Firms and Their Analysts With Enron and Global Crossing, Report to the Senate Committee on Banking, Housing, and Urban Affairs and the House Committee on Financial Services.

Chapter 3

The What, How, and Why of Financial Intermediaries

"All essential knowledge relates to existence, or only such knowledge as has an essential relationship to existence is essential knowledge."

Søren Kierkegaard: *Concluding Unscientific Postscript*

GLOSSARY OF TERMS

Securitization The act of converting an untraded (debt) claim, such as a bank loan, into a traded security by issuing claims against it and selling these claims to capital market investors. Essentially, securitization is a form of direct capital market financing with the bank acting as an originator and repackager of the loan.

Fractional reserve banking A banking system in which banks must hold a specified fraction of their deposit liabilities as liquid assets.

Fiat money A form of money, the acceptance of which is mandated by law.

The market model A model that states that the return on a security can be partitioned into a fixed component (called "alpha"), plus a component which is a multiple (called "beta") of the return on the "market" portfolio, plus a mean-zero residual term.

DIDMCA The Depository Institutions Deregulation and Monetary Control Act passed in 1980. See Chapters 15 and 16 for details.

Natural monopoly In some industries, due to economies of scale, the most economically efficient industry structure is to have only a single firm that is a natural monopoly.

Capital requirements There are many types of regulatory capital requirements. One of these is what we typically think of as a capital ratio, which is how much equity the bank keeps as a fraction of total assets. This is called the "leverage ratio" (see Chapter 15). There are also risk-based capital ratios.

Portfolio restrictions Restrictions on the assets that banks can hold in their portfolios.

INTRODUCTION

As the following exchange between Levin and Sviyazhsky from Part III, Chapter 27 of Tolstoy's *Anna Karenina* indicates, most people know what banks and other financial intermediaries do.

> *"Then what's your opinion? How should a farm be managed nowadays?"*
> *"What we have to do is to raise the standard of farming even higher."*
> *"Yes, if you can afford it! It's all very well for you, but. .. I'm not going to be able to buy any Percherons."*
> *"That's what banks are for."*

As perceptive as this notion of banking is, we will need a deeper understanding of banks and other financial intermediaries in order to set the stage for the remaining chapters in this book. The simple view that banks exist to provide borrowing and lending services leaves us without answers to questions such as the following: (i) What does the financial system comprise and how does it work? (ii) Why do we need *banks* to intermediate between borrowers and lenders, that is, why do not individual borrowers and lenders transact *directly* and avoid the cost of going through banks?[1] (iii) What, if any, are the economies of scale in the production of financial services provided by banks, or, how large should banks be? (iv) Why do we regulate banks and other depository institutions so intrusively? (v) If banks need to be regulated, *how* should they be regulated? (vi) How should borrowers choose whether they should borrow from banks, or venture capitalists, or directly from the capital market?

To answer these and other questions, we need a framework that builds upon that provided in the previous chapter and illuminates the role of the financial system in promoting economic growth and the *essential* functions served by financial intermediaries. While we will not provide complete answers in this chapter to all of the questions posed above, our purpose is to provide a systematic way to think about these issues, so that we have a foundation for the discussions in subsequent

---

1. A partial answer to this question was provided in Chapter 2.

S. I. Greenbaum, A. V. Thakor & A. W. A. Boot: Contemporary Financial Intermediation, Third edition. http://dx.doi.org/10.1016/B978-0-12-405196-6.00003-3

chapters. The plan for this chapter is as follows. We begin by providing an overview of the United States financial system (which is qualitatively similar to that of most developed countries) and address the question of how the financial system functions. The focus is on the types of businesses that are involved in raising capital, and the types of financing sources available to them. This helps to provide an overall framework to understand the role that banks play in the financial system. We then provide an anecdotal discussion of how a fractional reserve banking system arises from a simple goldsmith economy. After this informal discussion, we provide a model of a bank that formalizes the goldsmith anecdote and helps us to understand the role of banks as well as the need to regulate them. These two sections provide answers to questions (i) and (iii) above, and a partial answer to question (iv). The next section introduces the fixed coefficient model (FCM) as an extension of the goldsmith anecdote and examines its implications for monetary policy. The issue of economies of scale in the production of financial intermediation services is then taken up. This provides an answer to question (ii) above. Following this, we proceed to explain how banks can make nonbank contracting more efficient, and then we review empirical evidence in support of the view that banks are special. The ownership structure of depository institutions is analyzed next. We conclude with an examination of a borrower's choice of financing source to answer question (v) above.

HOW DOES THE FINANCIAL SYSTEM WORK?

Overview

In 2007, the financial services industry accounted for 40% of total corporate profits in the United States, whereas this was 29% in 2011. In the early 1980s, it accounted for only about 10%. Statistics like this have prompted some to argue that financial services are becoming disproportionately important at the expense of other sectors of the economy, such as manufacturing and services that are obviously of tangible economic value. However, nothing could be further from the truth. Given the economic hardships we faced during the recent financial crisis, it is easy to overlook the fact that the growth in financial services over the past two decades was also accompanied by some of the most spectacular economic growth we have ever witnessed. In 1980s, the U.S. gross domestic product (GDP), the most commonly used measure of the size of the economy, stood at under $3 trillion. In 2007, when the share of total corporate profits accounted for by financial services was four times as large as in the 1980s, the GDP stood at a towering figure of $14 trillion. The U.S. financial services sector employed 5.87 million people in 2012 which is about 6% of the total private nonfarm employment. This figure is expected to grow to 12% by 2018. The wealth generated by the financial services industry contributed nearly 7.9% ($1.24 trillion) to the U.S. GDP in 2012.[2]

It was not a coincidence that the U.S. economy grew so rapidly during a time when financial services grew in importance. Financial markets, and the financial service firms that operate in those markets, channel money from savers to those with investment ideas and thus, help individuals and businesses raise capital of various sorts. The more well-developed the financial system, the better lubricated this channel, and the lower are the transaction costs and other obstacles to investment and economic growth.

Indeed, the lack of developed financial systems is one of the main roadblocks to economic growth in the former eastern-block Communist countries of Europe, such as Romania. Even within the United States, where the financial system is well developed, the primary reason for the failure of small businesses is the lack of access to funding. When small businesses do succeed and create employment and growth, an important factor in their success is access to the financing needed to support growth. The fact that the U.S. financial system is well developed and innovative has been a big boon to individuals and businesses alike, as they have been able to raise relatively low-cost capital to grow through a variety of financing sources. It has also been a significant factor in the creation of prominent new firms that have been launched in the past 25 years and have gone on to become global powerhouses. Starbucks, Yahoo, Google, and eBay are but a few examples.

The Role of the Financial System in Promoting Economic Growth[3]

A rich body of research provides ample evidence that robust financial development is followed by healthy economic growth. Much of this evidence comes from a comparison of different countries. For example, in a study of 56 developing countries, the level of financial development in 1960 was a strong predictor of economic growth over the next 30 years, after controlling for a variety of economic and political factors.[4] This section will discuss this research to develop an understanding of what the facts say and *why* they say what they say. However, before delving into that, it is useful to understand the basic economics behind *how* the financial system promotes economic growth.

---

2. United States Department of Commerce: The Financial Services Industry in the United States, http://selectusa.commerce.gov/industry-snapshots/financial-services-industry-united-states

3. The discussion in this section relies heavily on Thakor (2011).

4. See Levine (1996) and (2005).

The Conceptual Link Between the Financial System and Economic Growth: Consider a simple example to see this link. Suppose we have an economy in which there are four people who own productive resources: Mary, Peter, Paul, and Sally. Mary has some money saved in a safe at her house. Peter owns an orchard and some apple seeds with which he can plant and grow trees from which he can harvest apples. Paul has a farm where he naturally produces fertilizer. Finally, Sally owns some farm equipment that is useful for farming the land.

Unless otherwise paid upfront, neither Paul nor Sally is willing to sell any goods or services. Unfortunately, Peter does not have any money to pay either one of them now. Meanwhile, Mary is patient and would not mind lending her money in exchange for a larger future payment. However, she does not know Peter well and is concerned that he might be a crook.

Without a financial system in this community, Peter would be limited to planting whatever apple trees he can using his own seeds and labor, but without any fertilizer or farm equipment. Suppose he can plant a few trees and harvest 1000 apples a year. That then defines his economic output.

Now suppose that the economy has a financial system in place which includes a bank and financial market where financial securities are traded. As such, Peter can now go to the bank and apply for a loan that would be repaid from future sales of apples. Before the loan is approved, the bank will conduct a credit check and determine if Peter is a good credit risk. Moreover, once the loan is granted, the bank will also monitor Peter to make sure that he is not a crook who absconds with the bank loan. With the assurances provided by the bank, Mary will be willing to deposit her money in the bank in exchange for a higher payment in the future that will contain a 10% interest for her. This option of earning an interest is better than keeping the money locked up in a safe and earn zero interest. With the bank loan, Peter can now afford to buy some fertilizer from Paul and some farm equipment from Sally on a cash-on-purchase basis. He now plants more trees and each tree produces more apples, so he ends up with 20,000 apples rather than 1000. The existence of a financial market has increased the economic output of this economy. A further increase in the economic output may arise from the fact that Paul and Sally may use the money received as payment from Peter to produce more fertilizer and farm equipment. This output may have applications in other parts of the economy which further increases the economic output, and so on. See Figure 3.1.

This simple example illustrates three key channels through which the financial system contributes to economic growth:

- it increases trade and the flow of goods and services;
- it increases the rate of physical capital accumulation; and
- it increases the efficiency of combining capital and labor in production.

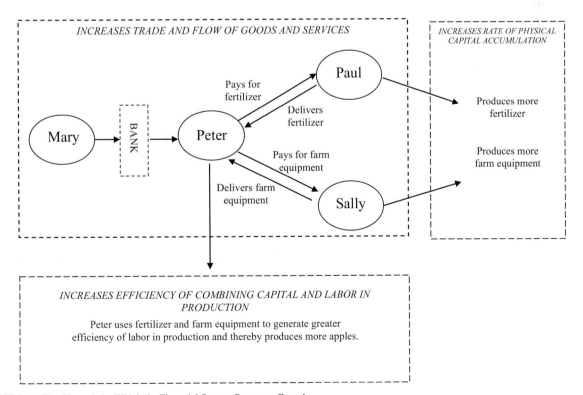

FIGURE 3.1   The Channels by Which the Financial System Promotes Growth.

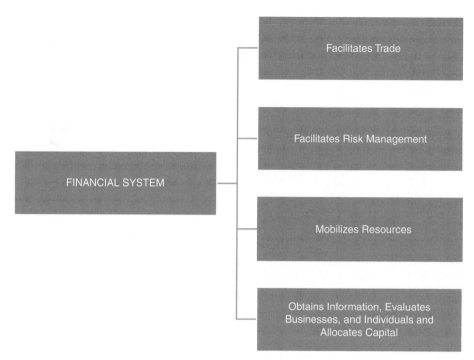

FIGURE 3.2 The Basic Services Provided by a Financial System.

The Services the Financial System Provides and How They Help Economic Growth: Figure 3.2 shows the four basic services that financial systems provide which help spur economic growth.[5]

The Financial System Facilitates Trade: In primitive economies, much of the trade was based on barter, something that Peter and Paul/Sally were unable to do in our example because Peter did not have any apples in his inventory to trade. The invention of money minimalized the need for barter trade and thereby increased commercial transactions and trade. In modern economies, it is not enough to have money to facilitate transactions – this money needs to be moved around. With the appropriate hubs and spokes for recording and clearing multilateral financial transactions, financial systems help move money from one party to the other, often across national boundaries. In their absence, companies would be greatly impeded in their ability to do business with each other, and economic growth would suffer.

The Financial System Facilitates Risk Management: An important service provided by financial systems is helping individuals and businesses improve their management of various sorts of risks. This is important for economic growth because an increase in risk reduces investment. In our example, Peter faces some risk when he buys fertilizer and farm equipment. A scarce rainfall may lead to a lean harvest and as such Peter may be unable to fully repay his bank loan. This may cause him to lose his farm to the bank. Or healthy precipitation might cause new apple orchards to come up in neighboring communities, increasing the supply of apples in the market, thus pushing down the price of apples. These risks may lead Peter to cut back on his investment in buying fertilizer and farm equipment. A financial system *prices* risk and provides mechanisms for pooling, ameliorating, and trading risk. It offers producers like Peter a way to manage risks. For instance, Peter could use the financial system to buy insurance against a poor harvest or he could hedge the apple price risk in the futures market. Investors like Mary can also benefit from the existence of the financial system by obtaining better risk management. For example, Mary may be worried about *liquidity risk* if she were to lend directly to Peter. Once the loan is made, Mary may not see any return to her investment until the apples are harvested and sold. But what if a medical emergency arises and Mary needs the money before then? In the presence of a financial system, Mary would simply withdraw her deposit from the bank when she needs it. Thus, *a financial system, by facilitating improved risk management for both borrowers and savers, spurs long-run investments that fuel economic growth.*

The Financial System Mobilizes Resources: As pointed out in our example, Mary's savings would have stayed locked up in her safe in the absence of a financial system. It took a financial system to mobilize those resources and get them to Peter who could put them to productive use. Almost 150 years ago, the famous economist Walter Bagehot described how the financial system helps to mobilizes resources and spur economic growth:[6]

---

5. This discussion is based in part on Levine (1996).
6. See Bagehot (1873), reprinted 1962, as noted by Levine (1996).

"We have entirely lost the idea that any undertaking likely to pay, and seen to be likely, can perish for want of money; yet no idea was more familiar to our ancestors, or is more common in most counties. A citizen of Long in Queen Elizabeth's time...would have thought that it was no use inventing railways (if he could have understood what a railway meant), for you would not have been able to collect the capital with which to make them. At this moment, in colonies and in all rude countries, there is no large sum of transferable money, there is not fund from which you can borrow, and out which you can make immense works."

What Bagehot was referring to was the ability of the financial system to mobilize resources that would permit the development of better technologies that lead to economic growth.

The Financial System Obtains and Processes Information and Allocates Capital: Individual savers, like Mary, may not have the resources or expertise to evaluate firms, projects, and managers before deciding whether to invest in them. On the other hand, financial intermediaries may have a cost and expertise advantage in collecting and processing such information, and then helping the capital-allocation process based on that information. This is a concept that is fleshed out later in this chapter. This, in turn, encourages investors to supply capital to these intermediaries, which channel the capital to businesses that make investments that fuel economic growth.

To see this, imagine that a friend of yours comes to you and asks for a loan to finance a new restaurant. While you have the money to lend, you are not sure that this investment is the right one for you. However, if your friend goes to the bank, the necessary information can be gathered by the bank about potential future income and the assets purchased with the loan that can be used as collateral and conduct necessary credit analysis with this information to decide whether to lend and how to structure the loan. Such expertise is part of the bank's business skill set. Knowing that banks will screen and monitor the lender before deciding whether to provide financing, you may be willing to deposit your money in the bank so that the bank can, in turn, use it to make loans.

To recapitulate, the financial system provides four key services – facilitates trade, facilitates risk management, mobilizes resources, and acquires and processes information that helps in the allocation of capital. These key services help to increase the flow of goods and services, increase the rate of physical capital accumulation, and increase the efficiency of combining capital and labor in production. As a result, there is more economic growth.

An Overview of How the Financial System Works

A well-developed financial system is a complex mosaic of institutions, markets, investors (businesses and individuals), savers, and financial contracts, which are all interconnected. See Figures 3.3, 3.4, and 3.5.

All three figures divide the financial system into three main parts: the users of capital, the investors who represent the sources of capital, and the financial intermediaries who facilitate the flow of capital from the investors to the users of capital. It is the flow of services provided by these intermediaries which represents the contribution of the financial system in linking the sources and uses of capital in a manner that enhances economic growth.

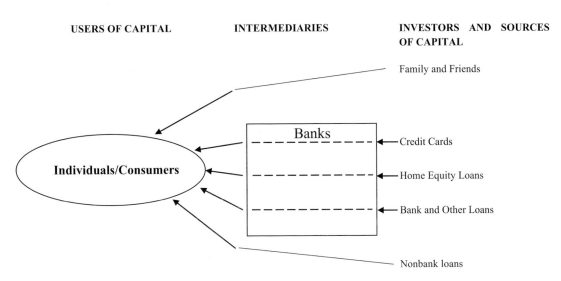

FIGURE 3.3   The U.S. Financial System: Individuals/Consumers.

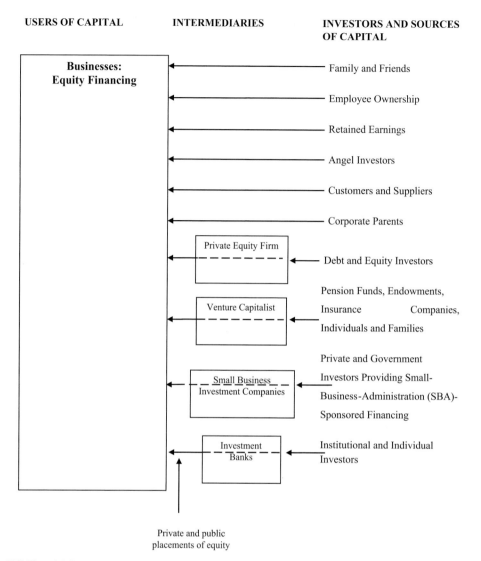

USERS OF CAPITAL   INTERMEDIARIES   INVESTORS AND SOURCES OF CAPITAL

Businesses: Equity Financing

Family and Friends

Employee Ownership

Retained Earnings

Angel Investors

Customers and Suppliers

Corporate Parents

Private Equity Firm — Debt and Equity Investors

Venture Capitalist — Pension Funds, Endowments, Insurance Companies, Individuals and Families

Small Business Investment Companies — Private and Government Investors Providing Small-Business-Administration (SBA)-Sponsored Financing

Investment Banks — Institutional and Individual Investors

Private and public placements of equity

FIGURE 3.4 The U.S. Financial System: Businesses Raising Equity Financing.

Before we can understand the role played by each part of the financial system, it is necessary to understand some key distinctions between the contracts by which financial capital is raised and the differences between individuals/consumers and businesses with respect to how these financing contracts are used.

Debt versus Equity and use by Consumers and Businesses: The financial contracts by which individuals and businesses raise capital can be broadly divided into two main groups: equity and debt. With an equity contract, a business wishing to raise capital would sell an ownership stake in the company to investors willing to provide the external financing that the business needs. In the example discussed earlier, instead of taking a bank loan, Peter could go to Mary and offer her a 30% stake in his apple business in order to raise the capital to buy fertilizer and farm equipment. The return to her investment would depend entirely on the profitability of the business. If Mary buys a 30% stake in Peter's business, then Mary is entitled to 30% of profit the business generates, assuming all profit is distributed as dividends. For instance, if Peter makes a profit of $15,000 in the first year, then Mary receives 30% of that, which is $4500. However, if the business does not make any profit, then Mary would get nothing. Moreover, Mary's investment has *no* stated maturity, which means Peter never has to return her initial investment. The only way for Mary to recoup her original investment is to sell her ownership stake to someone else.

A debt contract is similar to a bank loan – the lender is promised as repayment the original loan amount plus some interest. A debt claim has both a *stated maturity* and *priority over equity*. "Stated maturity" means that the debt contract stipulates that the lender must be fully repaid by a certain date. "Priority over equity" means that debt holders must be fully repaid before shareholders can be paid. In our earlier example, if Peter finances with a loan, he must first use all of the profit

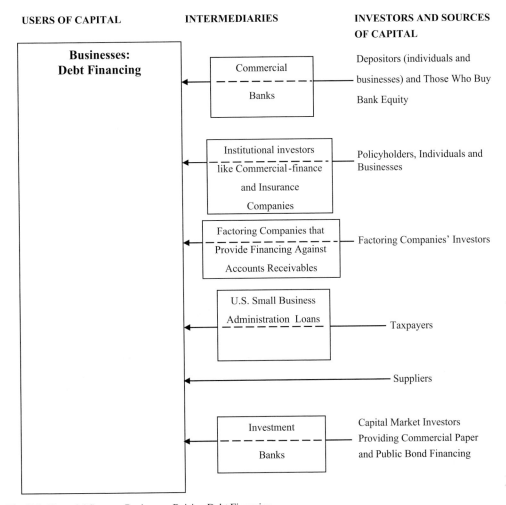

FIGURE 3.5   The U.S. Financial System: Businesses Raising Debt Financing.

from selling apples to repay the debt holder, even before he pays taxes. Only after that and paying taxes to the government can he keep what is left over as the owner of his business.

Consumers finance primarily with debt contracts.[7] There is a good reason why equity is not used in consumer financing. Since a loan taken by a consumer is essentially a financial claim by the lender on the borrower's labor income, it is relatively easy for the borrower to simply withhold the supply of this labor income – for example, by quitting work – and make the lender's claim worthless. A debt contract, with a requirement to fully repay by a certain date and penalties for failure to repay, provides better incentives for the borrower to pay off the debt claim.

Businesses finance with both debt and equity. In fact, the mix of debt and equity financing to use is an important decision for any business. The reason why equity financing is viable for businesses is that the financial system provides corporate governance to keep managerial actions roughly aligned with the interests of the financiers of the business, and businesses have powerful incentives to keep producing profits for a variety of reasons, so there are strong inherent incentives to not withhold the supply of productive inputs like labor.

Individual/Consumer Financing

Consumers can tap a variety of sources for financing, most of which is in the form of debt. See Figure 3.3.

Friends and family provide a potentially significant source of capital. These loans often have vaguely defined maturity with specific purposes. A student loan that will be repaid sometime after graduation or a car loan are some examples of such financing. Many consumers rely on these sources of financing in emergencies or for purposes for which bank loans are difficult to get.

---

7. Bank loans, home mortgages, and credit card borrowing are all forms of debt contracts.

TABLE 3.1 Consumer credit outstanding

Major Providers of Consumer Credit	Consumer Credit in $ Billions by Year				
	2006	2007	2008	2009	2010
Commercial banks, finance companies, credit unions, federal government, savings institutions, nonfinancial business	$2384.80	$2522.20	$2561.10	$2449.90	$2410.40

Source: Federal Reserve Statistical Release, February 7, 2011.

Credit card financing is a form of an unsecured debt – there is no specific collateral backing the loan. Since it is primarily used as a means of transaction financing, the issuer expects to be repaid from the borrower's income within a relatively short period of time. To encourage prompt payment, the interest rates and late-payment fees tend to be high. The viability of credit card financing rests on a well-developed financial system where banks can raise financing by securitizing their credit-card receivables and selling the claims to investors. Since an advanced financial system and a high level of trust are crucial for credit card financing to be viable, the volume of credit card finance, and hence the enormous payment-transactions convenience afforded to consumers, both decline exponentially as one moves from well-developed financial systems to less-developed financial systems.

Home equity loans are a convenient way for consumers to borrow against the price appreciation in their homes. For instance: suppose you need $50,000 and your home is worth $300,000 in the market today. You owe the bank $200,000. Then your home equity is $100,000 ($300,000 minus $200,000), and you can borrow $50,000 you need against the home equity. Of course, you will have to make additional monthly payments on this new loan once you take the loan.

Prior to the subprime financial crisis, home equity loans were a significant source of finance for many consumers. The average U.S. homeowner extracted 25–30 cents for every dollar increase in home equity during 2002–2006, and home-equity-based borrowing was equal to 2.8% of GDP every year from 2002 to 2006.[8]

Banks and other loans represent a very significant portion of the financing available to individuals. These loans include borrowing from commercial banks, finance companies, credit unions, the federal government, and so on. As of year-end 2010, consumer credit outstanding was $2.41 trillion, having grown at an annual rate of 2.5% in the fourth quarter of 2010. See Table 3.1.

Nonbank loans are provided by a wide array of lenders. Perhaps the biggest nonbank financial intermediary is the U.S. government. From Fannie Mae and Freddie Mac to Sally Mae (the Student Loan Marketing Association), the amount of credit provision that involves the U.S. government dwarfs that by any bank.

We will now turn our attention to business financing. While it is useful to create a clean separation between consumer and business financing for purposes of discussion, in practice, this dividing line is often fuzzy. In particular, many individuals will use their access to consumer financing to raise capital they need to invest in their businesses. For example, it is not uncommon for someone to charge a business purchase to his/her personal credit card, or use a home equity loan to make the investment needed to expand the business.

Business Financing: Equity

Businesses can raise equity financing from a richly diverse set of sources. See Figure 3.4.

Internal Equity Financing

Family and friends represent a very important financing source for start-up businesses. The typical family or friend investor is someone who has been successful in his/her own business and wishes to invest both to help a family member or a friend. For example, a health-care private equity firm was launched some years ago in St. Louis, MO with financial backing by family and friends because no Wall Street firm was willing to invest in a group of individuals who had operating experience in the industry but no private-equity experience. Similarly, Facebook was launched from a Harvard dorm room and eventually expanded with family and friends financing. Typically, family and friends will invest up to $100,000.

Employee ownership is yet another way firms can raise equity financing. Employee stock ownership plans (ESOPs) give employees the opportunity to become shareholders in the company. Employees may experience increased pride and

---

8. See Mian and Sufi (2010).

security as shareholders, which, in turn, may make them more productive. Employees can participate via stock purchases, by receiving a portion of their compensation as stock rather than cash, and sometimes by providing personal assets to the business. As of 2014, there are over 7000 ESOPs in place in the United States, covering 13.5 million employees (over 10% of the private-sector workforce). The total assets owned by U.S. ESOPs were estimated at over $1 trillion at the end of 2012.[9] Some of the notable majority employee-owned companies are Public Super Markets, and Lifetouch, to name a few.

Retained earnings represents a vital source of internal equity financing for businesses. A firm typically pays out a portion of profit as a dividend to its shareholders, once all its expenses, debt claims, and taxes are settled. What is then left over after the dividend payment is called retained earnings, and it augments the firm's equity. Retained earnings may be viewed as a "sacrifice" made by the shareholders in the sense that they forgo some dividends in order to build up the firm's equity. Companies generally retain 30–80% of their after-tax profit every year.

External Equity Financing

Angel financing often provides the critical first funds needed by early-stage companies that have yet to establish a track record of revenues or earnings that would enable them to attract institutional financing from venture capital firms or banks. Such financing involves raising equity from individual investors, known as "angels." These individuals look for companies with high growth prospects, sometimes have some synergies with their own businesses, and operate in an industry that the individuals have successfully worked in or are bullish about. In our earlier example, if bank loan is hard to get, Peter could turn to angel investors (typically investors who, unlike Mary, know him and something about his business) to provide the financing in exchange for an ownership stake in the business. Angel financing, however, is often quite expensive. Capital from angel investors can cost the entrepreneur anywhere from 10% to 50% of the ownership in the business. In addition, many angel investors charge a monthly management fee.

It is also possible for businesses to raise equity financing from *customers, suppliers, and sales representatives*. These parties provide financing because they may believe that the business has growth potential that may not be realized without the financial support provided by the equity input, and also that the equity position may become a profitable investment down the road. For example, IBM once invested enough in Intel to own 20% of Intel's equity. It made this investment to financially bolster Intel, a key supplier whose microprocessors were used in all IBM personal computers.

Corporate parents are yet another vital source of financing for some institutions. A holding company may provide its subsidiary with capital rather than incur the cost of raising external capital.

Intermediated Equity Capital

Apart from these nonintermediated sources of equity capital, other forms of equity capital involve financial intermediaries that help to link the sources and uses of capital. Private equity, venture capital, and investment banks, are the major players, and have been covered in the previous chapter.

BUSINESS FINANCING: DEBT
Nonmarket, Intermediated, and Direct Debt

Businesses raise large amounts of financing each year from debt from a variety of sources (See Figure 3.5). A traditionally important source of debt financing is *commercial banks*. For example, Avolon, an aircraft leasing group, announced in January 2011 that it had raised a total of $2.5 billion in debt since May 2010, with the latest coming in the form of a $465 million debt raised from a consortium of three leading U.S. banks: Wells Fargo Securities, Citi, and Morgan Stanley. Businesses use banks to obtain various forms of debt financing. This is both short-term, intermediate-term, and long-term debt financing.

As discussed in the previous chapter, *institutional lenders*, such as commercial-finance companies (e.g., GE Capital) and insurance companies, have been a major source of long-term debt financing for U.S. businesses. They make loans that may be over 10 years in maturity and thus fill a need at the longer end of the debt maturity spectrum since bank term loans are typically under 10 years in maturity.

The *factoring of accounts receivables* is another source of debt finance available to businesses. Every business that sells to customers on credit – the customer purchases the good or service but pays at a later date – generates "accounts receivables" when it makes sales. Similarly, *account payable* is a source of financing provided by the firm's suppliers. We will revisit account receivables and account payables in Chapter 5.

---

9. Source: www.esopassociation.org.

The *U.S. Small Business Administration (SBA)* provides yet another source of debt financing. The SBA offers long-term financing for purchasing fixed assets. Typically, these loans require a personal guarantee from any investor with a stake in the business exceeding 5%.

Now that we have seen how the entire financial system operates and facilitates economic growth, we will examine in depth the specific economic role that banks play and how they develop the special expertise to play that role and improve economic outcomes.

FRACTIONAL RESERVE BANKING AND THE GOLDSMITH ANECDOTE

Fractional Reserve Banking

Chapter 2 explains what financial intermediaries do. We will now continue this discussion by examining how a rudimentary bank can evolve from a goldsmith, and how this leads to a theory of fractional reserve banking. What emerges too is a theory of bank regulation. According to this theory, regulation is an almost inevitable outgrowth of fractional reserve banking.

Modern banks produce *fiat* money on the basis of *fractional reserves*. These two facts account for much of the romance, mystique, and confusion surrounding finance. Laymen have difficulty understanding that money has value solely because of its universal acceptance as money.[10]

The fractional reserve aspect of banking is similarly vexing in that it seemingly involves sleight of hand. Fractional reserve banks fund themselves with liabilities that are convertible into cash on demand, but they hold only a fraction of such liabilities in the form of cash assets. Thus there is always some probability that withdrawals will exceed the available cash.

The evolution of monetary systems from commodity money – gold, silver, or whatever – to more abstract forms of money parallels the evolution of banking systems from warehouses, or 100% reserve banks, to modern fractional reserve banks. Both follow naturally from a collective desire to use scarce resources efficiently. However, these developments have side effects as well. The substitution of fiat for commodity money concentrates enormous economic power, for good or ill, in the hands of the monetary authority. Likewise, fractional reserve banking places enormous power in the hands of individual bankers, power to jeopardize the stability of the banking system in the pursuit of personal gain.

In what follows, we shall explain the evolution of fractional reserve banking from its historical roots in warehousing.[11] The explanation is stylized and anecdotal, and is meant to stress the natural aspects of the evolutionary process as well as the essential vulnerability of fractional reserve banking systems.

The Evolution of the Primitive Goldsmith into a Bank

Think of a primitive setting in which gold is used as money – means of payment, or medium of exchange. By social convention, all debts are paid with gold and all purchases are made with gold. The system works well enough, but holding and transporting gold can be awkward. There is both a security problem and a convenience problem. The market response is to provide a warehousing service for gold. Hence the emergence of the goldsmith.

For a fee, the goldsmith provided secure storage facilities for gold. The owner of the gold would receive a warehouse receipt in exchange for her gold, with the understanding that the owner could present the receipt at her convenience to redeem the gold from the goldsmith.[12] The goldsmith's was a simple business. Similar to the furniture warehouse, the goldsmith provided safekeeping service for a fee. Simplicity itself!

Owners of gold gradually developed confidence in the goldsmith and gold flowed in and out of the goldsmith's coffers with tedious and profitable regularity. Whenever a gold owner wanted to make a purchase, she would travel to the goldsmith, withdraw the necessary gold, and take it to the market. In the market, the gold would be exchanged for the desired goods and just as routinely, the seller of the goods would return the newly acquired gold to the goldsmith in exchange for a warehouse receipt.

As these trading and payment practices became more and more pervasive, and as the goldsmith's reliability became more and more established, repeated trips to the goldsmith were recognized as wasteful. Each time a purchase was desired, the buyer would need to run to the goldsmith for gold, only to have this trip repeated by the seller, who would return the gold from whence it came.

---

10. The acceptance of money is ultimately a social convention supported by the legal system, which recognizes money as an instrument for the legal discharge of debts. This view of money serves as the basis for arguing that seigniorage rightfully belongs to the community at large and should not be appropriable by private interests.

11. A formal theory of this evolution and its implications for regulatory policies like reserve (liquidity) requirements and capital requirements in modern banking, as well as for monetary policy, can be found in Donaldson, Piacentino and Thakor (2015).

12. When transferable, it is the ownership of the receipt that governs the redemption.

Ultimately, the warehouse receipt passes from the buyer to the seller, and the only purpose served by the two trips is to test the goldsmith's integrity. But as the goldsmith's reputation for integrity grows with time and experience, the need for these trips seems increasingly unnecessary. Gradually, trade is effected with the exchange of warehouse receipts and the gold remains undisturbed in the goldsmith's vault. But the willingness to accept warehouse receipts in lieu of gold rests on the belief that the gold is available on demand. Any suspicion of the goldsmith will undermine the use of the receipts as means of payment. But so long as the goldsmith can project confidence, there is a saving to be had by avoiding the trips to and from the goldsmith.

Seen from the vantage point of the goldsmith, the growing use of receipts as means of payment means smaller flows of gold into and out of the coffers. One can imagine a time series of data points that describe the gold holdings of the smithy through time. As the use of receipts gradually replaces gold, the goldsmith's gold inventory becomes less and less volatile. In the limit, as the receipts totally displace the gold, the goldsmith's inventory remains practically unchanged through time, unless newly mined gold flows into the system, or other extraordinary occurrences take place. It gradually dawns on the goldsmith that it is not really necessary to have a unit of gold for each outstanding receipt. This idea must have come as a revelation, an epiphany. To be sure, the straitlaced would recoil at the idea of issuing more receipts than one had gold, but if no one ever withdraws the gold, then what possible harm?[13] The naughty possibility of printing extra warehouse receipts changed the world. This discovery was the banking equivalent of the Newtonian Revolution, every bit as important to banking as gravity was to physics.

Instability of the Fractional Reserve Bank

The extra receipts could not be distinguished from their more authentic counterparts and they consequently served as means of payment as readily as did the authentic (those whose issue was occasioned by a deposit of gold) receipts. The extra receipts were loaned to borrowers and earned interest. Assume that these loans are illiquid, that is, they cannot be redeemed on demand, but rather must be held to maturity in order to realize their full value. This means that the goldsmith is providing a key *liquidity transformation* service by issuing liquid claims to depositors that are backed by illiquid loans to merchants. The pedestrian goldsmith was thus transformed from a warehouse clerk into a banker! To see this, consider the following before-and-after balance sheets.

Goldsmith (Before)		Goldsmith (After)	
Gold 100 oz.	Receipts 100 oz.	Gold 100 oz. Loan 10 oz.	Receipts 110 oz.

Notice that after the goldsmith crosses the Rubicon (becomes a banker), his liabilities of 110 ounces exceed his capability to satisfy them in the unlikely event that all receipt owners should seek to convert to gold simultaneously. This potential failure is because loans are *illiquid*.

Therefore, inherent in the lending is a potential catastrophe – insolvency of the goldsmith. Of course, if the receipt owners almost never withdraw their gold, the probability of insolvency is small, perhaps very small. However, and this is critical, the risk of ruin is endogenous. That is to say, the goldsmith chooses the probability of insolvency with his choice of how many extra receipts to print, or equivalently, with his choice of how many loans to make. Each extra receipt printed and loaned earns interest and so the temptation to print receipts is limited only by the goldsmith's concern for remaining solvent. He walks the knife-edge between avarice and anxiety. Each extra receipt increases income, but at the same time increases the probability of insolvency; insolvency, of course, destroys the goldsmith's reputation and with it his ability to circulate and lend warehouse receipts.

Thus we see how the discovery of fractional reserve banking was a rite of passage, a loss of innocence. Notice, however, that conditional on the loans being repaid, the goldsmith holds assets equal to the value of his liabilities. Thus what we have here is a liquidity issue. The goldsmith can and will pay off all receipt holders, given adequate time and good loans. Nevertheless, the promise is to *pay on demand*, and this most assuredly cannot be done in *all* states of nature.

This is the essence of fractional reserve banking and its essential vulnerability. Such a system evolves quite naturally given maximizing behavior on the part of rational economic agents.

---

13. In a rational expectations equilibrium, the gold owners would anticipate this behavior of the goldsmith and adapt (redeem randomly and sufficiently frequently) to avoid being exploited by the goldsmith. But for present purposes, let us ignore this.

Regulation as a Stabilizing Influence

Left to its own devices, this kind of banking system is subject to periodic collapse. However, experience with fractional reserve banking eventually led to the discovery of a rather simple and straightforward remedy. Since the Achilles heel of the system is the illiquidity of the loans, bank runs could be averted if these assets could be liquefied. What was needed was a *bank for goldsmiths* that could lend against the collateral of a goldsmith's loans during those infrequent occasions of extraordinary redemptions. Indeed, in the nineteenth century this was achieved in the United States through commercial bank clearing houses (CBCHs), which were private arrangements between banks that agreed to put their *combined* resources (the CBCH) behind each member in times of unanticipated liquidity drains. Of course, such a bankers' bank would need virtually unlimited capacity, together with a commitment to the continuity of the system. The private arrangements did not possess such unlimited capacity, and this provided the rationale for a central bank to serve as a lender of last resort to the community of bankers. Since the central bank, which was typically government-owned, had the privilege of printing (or otherwise creating) money, the issue of limited capacity evaporated.

One more point deserves emphasis in connection with the evolution of a fractional reserve banking system with a central-bank-based lender-of-last-resort facility. In the absence of the central bank, there will always be a self-imposed limit on the volume of extra receipts printed. The fear of failure, loss of reputation, and the consequent inability to continue to lend warehouse receipts will discipline the inclination to expand lending indefinitely. Whatever this self-imposed limit, however, the introduction of the central bank acting as a lender of last resort will weaken the goldsmith's restraint. If the goldsmith knows that he can borrow against his otherwise illiquid loans, he will make more loans than if he could not use the loans as collateral. This is clear and obvious; and it is true even if the central bank charges a very high rate of interest for such emergency borrowings. Note that the interest rate for such loans is infinite in the absence of the central bank. Thus, the central bank introduces a kind of moral hazard, and this moral hazard is typically addressed by imposing cash asset reserve requirements that effectively limit the volume of a bank's lending on the basis of its cash assets. This is perhaps the most basic of prudential regulation. The point is that regulation is endogenous. It is responsive to a moral hazard arising from the introduction of the central bank as a lender-of-last-resort, which in turn is a response to a vulnerability inherent in fractional reserve banking. In turn, fractional reserve banking is a natural response to the transport costs and security concerns in a *laissez-faire* world of commodity money.

A MODEL OF BANKS AND REGULATION

That the very nature of banking necessitates regulation can also be seen in the perspective of a model in which money – rather than gold – is used as a medium of exchange. We will now develop in the box below a model that formalizes the anecdotal development of the previous section and also highlights some of the underlying informational assumptions in the analysis. The intuition is very similar to that in the earlier section.

The two-period model developed below is very simple.[14] It makes some assumptions that are not rigorously justified. Our intent is to give a broad-brush, intuitive treatment of how banks arise even in primitive economies and why it is necessary to regulate them. Before developing the model, we provide a summary of the notation used in Table 3.2

The Model: Consider an economy in which individuals are unsure of how safe their personal wealth is from theft. Thus, it pays to safeguard it. The individual can either safeguard it himself or he can pay someone else to do it. It is easy to imagine that not everybody is equally skilled in the art of safeguarding. So if you believe others are more skilled in safeguarding, you may wish to entrust safeguarding of your wealth to someone else, even though this involves paying a fee.[15] Since we will eventually reach this conclusion anyway, let us refer to you (the person who wishes to have his personal wealth safeguarded) as the depositor and the entity that safeguards your wealth as the bank. For now let us suppose there is only one depositor ($n = 1$) and only one bank ($j = 1$).

The depositor has an income of $\$y$ in each period, of which $\$c$ goes to personal consumption and $\$(y - c) = \$s$ goes to savings. These savings must be safeguarded. For now suppose there is nothing that the bank can do with this money except safeguard it. Let $\$\phi > 0$ be the fee that the bank charges to safeguard the depositor's savings. Safeguarding by the bank guarantees that the wealth will not be stolen. Also suppose that the depositor wishes to have his wealth safeguarded for only one period. Assuming that the discount rate is zero for everybody,[16] we see that the depositor's consumption at the start of the next period will be $s - \phi$ (his net

14. This model builds on features in the Diamond and Dybvig (1983) and Chari and Jagannathan (1988) models of bank runs. Papers dealing with the existence of financial intermediaries are Leland and Pyle (1977), Diamond (1984), Ramakrishnan and Thakor (1984), Millon and Thakor (1985), Boyd and Prescott (1986), Allen (1990), and Coval and Thakor (2005).
15. Naturally, this fee should be less than what it would cost you to safeguard your own wealth with the same efficacy.
16. This is a harmless assumption and can be easily dropped without affecting this analysis.

TABLE 3.2 The notation

Notation	What it Means
Y	Depositor's income in each period
C	Depositor's consumption from income in each period
S	Amount deposited in each period
ϕ	Fee charged to depositor for safekeeping of deposits
$\hat{\phi}$	Personal cost of safeguarding deposits
α	Fraction of deposits withdrawn
N	Number of depositors
M	Number of merchants
K	Merchant's cash flow
K^*	High value of merchant's cash flow when K is random
M	Loan to merchant
P	Probability of theft
R	Rate on return on bank's loan to a merchant
B	Bank's cost of monitoring merchants
U	Probability that $K = 0$, as assessed at date 0
u_1	Value of u, as per updating at date 1
u_h	High value of u_1
u_l	Low value of u_1
L	Liquidation value of merchant's investment
F	Amount depositors must spend to ensure that the bank safeguards and monitors
J	Number of banks

saving in the first period) plus \$$y$ (his income in the second period). Since the depositor is paid \$$s - \phi$ for depositing \$$s$, the interest rate on his deposit is

$$(s - \phi - s)/s = -\phi/s < 0 \tag{3.1}$$

If a negative interest rate surprises you, remember that our bank cannot make any loans and is providing the depositor a costly service. Assume for now that the bank must keep 100% reserves against deposits and that the depositor will fully withdraw at the end of the first period.

The desirability of a 100%-reserves bank: Suppose the probability of theft is p and it would cost the depositor $\hat{\phi} > \phi$ to safeguard his wealth to the extent that the probability of theft is eliminated. Thus, a necessary and sufficient condition for personal safeguarding to be optimal is that

$$s - \hat{\phi} > (1 - p)s$$
$$\text{or } \hat{\phi} < ps \tag{3.2}$$
$$\text{where } 0 < p < 1.$$

We will assume that Equation (3.2) is satisfied. Clearly, since $\phi < \hat{\phi}$, the depositor will prefer to have the bank safeguard his wealth.

Note that in stipulating that the bank charges the depositor exactly what it costs the bank to safeguard, we have assumed that there is perfect competition[17] between banks that can all safeguard s at \$$\phi$. Suppose now that $n > 1$, so that there are possibly many depositors. It would be natural to assume that there are economies of scale in safeguarding, that is, it should cost less per dollar to safeguard \$$ns$ as opposed to safeguarding \$$s$. For example, one armed guard may be able to safeguard \$100,000 just as easily as he can safeguard \$1000. Indeed, if we were to assume that the cost of safeguarding \$$ns$ is less than \$$n\phi$, the case for a large bank would be compelling, and we could even assume that $\hat{\phi} = \phi$, that is, no single individual is any more skilled than

17. For those of you well-versed in different notions of competition in economies, we have in mind Bertrand competition here.

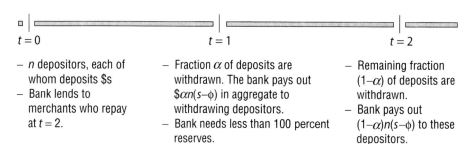

FIGURE 3.6 Sequence of Events.

another in protecting wealth. But we will assume that there are no scale economies in safeguarding. In a sense, this makes our task harder, but it helps to reduce notation.

Suppose first that all the n depositors will surely withdraw at the end of the first period. In this case, it is easy to see that the interest rate will still be $-\phi/s$. A more interesting and natural case, however, is one in which *not* all depositors will withdraw at the end of the first period. Suppose a fraction a (where $0 < \alpha < 1$) of depositors will withdraw at $t = 1$ (the end of the first period) and the remaining fraction $1 - \alpha$ will withdraw at $t = 2$ (the end of the second period). For simplicity, we assume that α is known with certainty.[18] The sequence of events is described in Figure 3.6.

A bank that borrows and lends: If the bank cannot invest any of the deposits it receives, then funds will lie idly in the bank. Note, though, that there is an opportunity to invest in this case.[19] At $t = 1$, the bank only needs to have $\$\alpha n(s - \phi)$ to meet deposit withdrawals. Suppose now that it is possible for the bank to make investments at $t = 0$, but that these investments will pay off only at $t = 2$. Let r be the rate of return to the bank on these investments.[20] We can imagine that the investments are loans to merchants who want to finance the setting up of shops, but do not have any funds of their own. Each merchant needs $\$M$, where $M > s$, so that if the merchant were to borrow directly from depositors, he would need to approach more than one depositor (in fact, he would need to approach M/s depositors). Further, there is a *moral hazard* problem in dealing with the merchant in that he has a preference for absconding with the $\$M$ he borrows rather than setting up a shop. If his actions are not monitored, he will abscond and the lender will not be paid back at all. However, at a cost of $\$b$ it is possible to monitor the merchant so that he indeed puts his borrowed funds to the stated use of setting up a shop that will generate some cash flow of $\$K > M(1 + r)$ at $t = 2$. As a start, let us suppose that $\$K$ is a sure cash flow. We will introduce uncertainty shortly.

First consider the merchant's problem if he approaches M/s depositors directly. His net expected payoff will be

$$K - M(1+r) - (bM/s) \tag{3.3}$$

since, in addition to interest, he will be charged for monitoring. Each depositor will have to individually monitor the merchant since none can rely on his cohorts to do so.[21] Now, if the merchant approaches a bank, which in turn acquires $\$M$ in deposits from M/s depositors, we will have a different outcome. The bank's monitoring cost will be $\$b$. If the bank charges the merchant exactly what it costs the bank to monitor, then the expected payoff to the merchant will be

$$K - M(1+r) - b. \tag{3.4}$$

Comparing Equations (3.3) and (3.4) we see that the merchant is clearly better off going to the bank.

Since the merchant pays the bank only at $t = 2$, the bank will have to make sure that it will have enough money at $t = 1$ to pay off depositors who withdraw then. Suppose there are m merchants (borrowers) and n depositors. Then, the bank loans out $\$mM$ and takes in $\$ns$ in deposits. Let $ns > mM$ (this will be shown to be necessary in a moment). Since $\$mM$ are loaned out, the bank does not need to worry about safeguarding that money from outright theft (it just needs to monitor the merchants it lends to). Thus, $\$(ns - mM)$ must be safeguarded. The safeguarding cost is $(ns - mM)\phi/s$, since it costs ϕ/s to safeguard $\$1$.

---

18. We will discuss later what happens if α is random.

19. Actually, even in the previous case in which all deposits are withdrawn at $t = 1$, the bank could invest at $t = 0$ in assets that pay off at $t = 1$.

20. We will not go into the details of how r is determined.

21. It is obvious that we cannot have an equilibrium in which no depositors monitor, because then it pays for at least one to monitor. To justify an individual depositor's decision to monitor, we must assume that there is some uncertainty that some depositors will not monitor (otherwise, every depositor will wish to "free ride" on the monitoring of his cohorts). One way to do this is to assume that *each* depositor believes that there is a random fraction θ of the remaining $(M/s)-1$ depositors who are simply incapable of monitoring, but no one (except those incapable depositors themselves) can identify these depositors. Thus, each of the depositors will still charge for monitoring but will not spend $\$b$. Suppose θ can be 0 with probability q_0 and 1 with probability $1 - q_0$ (when $\theta = 1$, each depositor who can monitor believes that he is pivotal in that no one else will monitor). Then, if a depositor who monitors chooses not to do so, his expected payoff will be (he always assumes that all other depositors capable of monitoring will indeed monitor) $b + q_0 s(1 + r) - s = b - (1 - q_0)s + q_0 sr$. And if he chooses to monitor, his expected payoff will be $s(1 + r) - s = sr$. Thus, it is a (Nash) equilibrium to monitor if $sr > b - (1 - q_0)s + q_0 sr$ or if $b < (1 - q_0)s(1 + r)$. Thus, if the uncertainty about incapable depositors is sufficiently large in the mind of each capable depositor (i.e., $1 - q_0$ is sufficiently high) and if the monitoring cost b is low relative to the payoff $s(1 + r)$ from successful monitoring, each capable depositor will monitor in a Nash equilibrium.

Hence, the bank promises to pay depositors

$$ns - (ns - mM)\phi/s \qquad (3.5)$$

in the aggregate if it does not pass along to the depositors any of its profits from lending to merchants. Since a fraction a of deposits is withdrawn at $t = 1$, those depositors get $\alpha[ns - (ns - mM)\phi/s]$, which you will notice is more (by an amount $(mM\phi/s)$) than what these depositors received previously. That is, the fact that part of the money is being loaned out instead of being kept in the bank's vault itself economizes on safeguarding costs. Although the loaned money must be monitored, these monitoring costs are paid by borrowers, so that depositors realize a saving in safeguarding costs.

To ensure that the bank will have sufficient funds to meet deposit withdrawals at $t = 1$, it must choose m to satisfy

$$\alpha\,[ns - (ns - mM)\,\phi/s] = ns - mM - (ns - mM) - \phi/s - mb. \qquad (3.6)$$

To understand Equation (3.6), note that the left-hand side is the amount the bank must pay out to those depositors who withdraw funds at $t = 1$. On the right-hand side, $ns–mM$ is the amount of money the bank has left over in reserves after it is through lending to the m merchants. From this it must spend an amount $(ns–mM)\phi/s$ to safeguard its reserves and an amount mb to monitor the m merchants.[22] Solving Equation (3.6), we get

$$m = (1-\alpha)ns(s - \phi) / \{M[s - (1-\alpha] + bs\} \qquad (3.7)$$

Thus, as long as the bank lends to exactly as many borrowers as stipulated in Equation (3.7), there will be no risk of withdrawals exceeding the bank's available cash reserves at $t = 1$.

Note now that the bank makes an aggregate net profit of mMr on its lending activities. This is because it is being compensated exactly for its monitoring cost by borrowers, and its safeguarding cost by deposit interest rate, although higher than $-\phi/s$ (as in the previous case when all deposits were idle), is still negative. This positive profit will attract entry by competing banks, and the resulting competition for depositors' funds will drive up the deposit interest rate. In a competitive equilibrium, each bank will earn zero profit. This will happen when the bank's profit of mMr is divided equally among the n depositors, so that each depositor gets

$$\frac{ns - [(ns - mM)\phi/s] + mMr}{ns}$$

per dollar of deposits. Thus, the deposit interest rate is now

$$\begin{aligned}&\frac{ns - [(ns - mM)\phi/s] + mMr}{ns} - 1\\ &= \frac{mMr - [(ns - mM)\phi/s]}{ns}\end{aligned} \qquad (3.8)$$

If we assume that r is high enough to ensure that the numerator in Equation (3.8) is positive, then the depositors get a positive rate of interest on their deposits.

We have taken you through a sequence of steps to show how a bank, like the goldsmith in the previous section, can develop from a simple caretaker of other people's wealth into an institution that borrows and lends money. As you must have noted, informational problems play a key role in bringing our bank to life. Banks solve two types of moral hazard problems in our simple world. First, they help to cope more efficiently with the "social" moral hazard problem of theft. Second, they also help to cope more efficiently with moral hazard in lending, which, as you know from Chapter 1, is a type of agency problem.

Do We Need to Regulate This Bank?: So far, however, there has been no need for a regulator. But that is simply because we have made numerous strong assumptions. One of them is that it is possible to monitor merchants so efficiently that they will always repay their debts fully if they are monitored. Thus, we know that a bank can repay its depositors. If it were to choose not to do so, we know for sure that the bank is at fault. A court of law with sufficiently stiff penalties on a banker who does not repay would then be sufficient to remedy this. In reality, merchants may sometimes have poor cash flows even if they do their best. That is, suppose that, viewed at $t = 0$, their cash flow K is a random variable that is 0 with probability u and K^* with probability $1 - u$. We will assume that setting up a shop is a positive net present value (NPV) exercise for the merchant, so that

$$(1-u)K^* > M(1+r). \qquad (3.9)$$

Suppose that this in itself does not affect the behavior of depositors in terms of their withdrawal policies. But at $t = 1$, depositors may learn something more about the likelihood that merchants may fail. For simplicity, assume for now that merchants have

---

22. We are assuming here that safeguarding costs are paid just after $t = 0$ and monitoring costs are paid just before $t = 1$. Note that since the merchants repay the bank only at $t = 2$ and monitoring must proceed at $t = 1$, the bank must initially pay the necessary monitoring costs and then recover these costs from borrowers at $t = 2$ through a loan interest rate that is grossed up to reflect this cost.

perfectly correlated prospects, so that they all either fail ($K = 0$) or succeed ($K = K^*$). Let us refer to the updated probability of failure that depositors assess at $t = 1$ as u_1. If there is good news, $u_1 < u$ (the probability of failure they assessed at $t = 0$) and if there is bad news, $u_1 > u$. We can think of u as the expected value of u_1 assessed by depositors at $t = 0$. Suppose u_1 can take one of two values: $u_1 = u_h$ for bad news and $u_1 = u_l$ for good news, where $u_h > u_l$. Suppose that those depositors who intended to withdraw at $t = 2$ will in fact change their minds and withdraw at $t = 1$ if they get bad news[23], that is, if $u_1 = u_h$. If they get good news, they will withdraw at $t = 2$.

The bank now faces a problem. If depositors get bad news, all depositors withdraw at $t = 1$. The bank will have insufficient funds to meet withdrawals (unless it keeps 100% reserves and does not lend to any merchants). Suppose that in this case the bank is empowered to call back all of its loans prematurely and this forces merchants to liquidate their businesses prematurely. Let L be the liquidation value of the merchant's shop at $t = 1$ (which, for simplicity, is independent of the information received by depositors at $t = 1$). Assume L is a very small number (much smaller than K^*). So, if all depositors wish to withdraw funds at $t = 1$, and if the bank proceeds to lend exactly the same amount at $t = 0$ as it did in the previous case, then there will only be $\$\alpha[ns - (ns - mM)\phi/s] + mL$ to pay depositors. Moreover, the premature liquidation of merchants' shops will be socially inefficient if L is so small that $L < (1 - u_h)K^*$. This is similar to the illiquidity problem of the goldsmith.

There is no way that the bank can prevent this unless it keeps all of its deposit funds idle, in which case it does not matter when depositors withdraw. However, this would *not* be fractional reserve banking; it would hardly be a bank as we know it. This is where a government regulator can help. Suppose it agrees to insure all deposits for the full promised payment by each bank. Then we see that those depositors who originally planned to withdraw at $t = 2$ have no reason to change their minds since the value of u_1 is now irrelevant to them; the deposit insurer has made their claims risk free! That is, this form of regulation makes banking viable when it otherwise could not have been.

This seems to be a wonderful solution and it definitely has its merits. But lest we get carried away with its virtues, let us pause and complicate things a bit more. Since banks are competitive and earn zero profits, they may wish to underspend on either safeguarding or on monitoring borrowers. Once the terms of their loan and deposit contracts are set, they could profit from spending less on safeguarding and monitoring than originally promised. This is key to the moral hazard created by introducing deposit insurance; we will discuss this in Chapters 15 and 16. In the absence of deposit insurance, depositors would not be willing to bring their money to the bank (and keep it themselves) unless they find a way to monitor the bank. Suppose that each depositor could spend a small amount of money, say $\$f$, to make sure that the bank expends the promised resources on safeguarding and monitoring. We can show, given appropriate assumptions ($\$f$ being small enough), that depositors will find it in their own best interest to do so.

Summary: Thus, one way to prevent bank runs and instability is for the government to provide deposit insurance, which is an alternative to the lender-of-last-resort (discount window) facility provided by the regulator (Central bank) in our earlier goldsmith example. But there is a fly in this ointment. When there is deposit insurance, why should any depositor care about whether the bank safeguards and monitors with the requisite vigilance? Each depositor's payoff is guaranteed and independent of the bank's actions. Hence, none will find it personally profitable to spend anything on watching over the bank to ensure that the bank expends the promised resources in safeguarding and monitoring the merchants it lends to. In other words, deposit insurance weakens or even destroys the private market discipline imposed on banks. The burden of keeping the bank in check shifts now from the market to the regulator. To achieve its objective, the regulator will have to come up with ways to dissuade the bank from exploiting the deposit insurance umbrella. In other words, the moral hazard engendered by one form of regulation, namely deposit insurance, creates the need for other forms of regulation (such as capital requirements, portfolio restrictions, and so on).

We have now completed the story we set out to tell in this section. Regulation is not just the outcome of some political agenda. It arises quite naturally from the very forces that give rise to banks. Once regulation arises to instill public confidence in banking and make banks viable entities, it creates its own moral hazards that necessitate further regulation.

THE MACROECONOMIC IMPLICATIONS OF FRACTIONAL RESERVE BANKING: THE FIXED COEFFICIENT MODEL

In this section, we examine the implications of fractional reserve banking for monetary policy. The discussion developed here formalizes some of the macroeconomic implications of the goldsmith anecdote presented earlier.

---

23. Let us not worry about why they might wish to do this. We want to give you an idea of the underlying concepts without being too rigorous. It is possible to make these ideas work more rigorously.

The Fixed Coefficient Model

The FCM is the standard textbook description of the banking firm and industry; it emphasizes the asset-transformation function of financial intermediaries. The bank's effort to maximize its profit is captured only implicitly. Consider a bank's balance sheet

Bank Balance Sheet	
R	D
M	E

where R is the reserves of the bank comprised of deposits held at the central bank, M is the bank's earning assets (loans to merchants), D is the bank's deposit liability (think of this as $n \times s$ in the context of the model in the previous section), and E is the bank's equity. We can now write the balance sheet identity for the bank as:

$$R + M = D + E. \tag{3.10}$$

Moreover,

$$R = rD, \text{ with } 0 < r \leq 1. \tag{3.11}$$

Equation (3.11) represents the fact that banks hold cash or liquid asset reserves proportional to deposits in order to insure against deposit withdrawals and/or to satisfy legal reserve requirements. The fixed coefficient, r, can be interpreted either as a legal reserve requirement or a voluntary behavioral parameter (i.e., reserves that the bank chooses to voluntarily hold). Actually, it should be interpreted as the greater of the two. In any case, the parameter relates to *liquidity or withdrawal risk*. That is, it is the bank's safeguard against a fraction (a in the context of the model in the previous section) of deposits being unexpectedly withdrawn. Next, we have

$$E = eL, \text{ with } 0 < e \leq 1. \tag{3.12}$$

Equation (3.12) represents the fact that banks hold capital reserves in some fixed proportion, e, to loans in order to protect against *insolvency or default risk*. The parameter e can be interpreted as a regulatory capital requirement and/or a voluntary behavioral parameter, or, more accurately, the greater of the two.

An Illustration of the FCM

Let us now consider the FCM in a (competitive) banking industry with zero equity ($e = 0$) where banks have only two assets (reserves held in the form of deposits at the Federal Reserve and loans to the public) and one liability (customer deposits). We shall further assume a 20% effective legal reserve requirement ($r = 0.2$). The assumption that $e = 0$ is an extreme representation of the assumption that the capital requirement is not binding.

Now suppose Bank A receives a $1000 deposit.

Bank A	
Required reserves 200	1000 deposits
Excess reserves 800	
Total reserves 1000	

Since it has excess reserves of $800 and since it earns nothing on either its required reserves or excess reserves, the bank seeks to eliminate its excess reserves by making a loan of $800:

Bank A	
Total reserves 1000	1000 deposits
Loan 800	800 deposit

The funds loaned by Bank A, although possibly initially deposited with Bank A, are soon withdrawn and deposited in another bank, say Bank B. This leaves Bank A with

Bank A	
Required reserves = total reserves 200	1000 deposits
Loans 800	

But Bank B has

Bank B

Required reserves 160 Excess reserves 640	800 deposits

and Bank B now lends away its excess reserves, so that:

Bank C

Required reserves 128 Excess reserves 512	640 deposits

The $640 loaned by Bank B is now deposited in Bank C. The process continues *ad infinitum*. At the Federal Reserve, the initial deposit would be a credit of $1000 to Bank A.

Federal Reserve

1000 deposit A

What is the offsetting asset (liability) entry?
When the $800 is withdrawn from A and deposited in B, the Federal Reserve would show

Federal Reserve

200 A 800 B

Notice that the original reserve creation (the $1000 deposit received by Bank A) spurred deposit expansion, and the deposit expansion redistributes the reserves across the banking system. However, the deposit expansion does not affect the level of reserves in the banking system. In fact, deposit expansion absorbs reserves. What this illustration of the FCM shows is that the bank's incentive to hold reserves – either voluntarily to protect against unanticipated deposit withdrawals or to satisfy a regulatory reserve requirement necessitated by the moral hazard created by the lender-of-last-resort facility – results in less lending than would be possible without reserve requirements. Moreover, it also affects the redistribution of liquidity throughout the entire banking system. This has macroeconomic implications that we explore below.

The FCM and Monetary Policy

The FCM helps us to understand the basic elements of how monetary policy works. There are three major tools of monetary policy: (i) open market operations, (ii) reserve requirement changes, and (iii) discount rate changes. These three tools are used in varying degrees to influence the stock of money and interest rates.

Open market operations are sales and purchases of government securities (Treasuries) by a special committee of the Federal Reserve. These sales and purchases affect the amount of reserves available to banks and thus, as indicated in previous subsections, the amount of lending. To see this, suppose the Fed buys $1000 in Treasury securities from the nonbank public. Then the nonbank public's balance sheet will be

Public

Bonds – $1000 Deposits of cash in Bank A + $1000	Liabilities unchanged

and Bank A's balance sheet will be

Bank A

Required reserves 200 Excess reserves 800	1000 deposits

The $800 is now available to Bank A for lending. This means that the initial open market operation of purchasing Treasuries leads to an increase in lending by banks. Another way to view this is that the government has reduced public debt (by buying back government securities) and facilitated an increase in private credit. The open market operation of selling government securities has the opposite effect.

It is obvious that a change in reserve requirements will also affect bank lending. Any increase in reserve requirements will reduce the amount of deposits available for lending, and any reduction in reserve requirements will increase the amount of deposits available for lending. Thus, when the Federal Reserve desires to implement a contractionary monetary policy (to cool down inflation, for example), it can raise reserve requirements; similarly, it can lower reserve requirements when it wishes to stimulate the economy.

Finally, the discount rate, which is the rate charged by the Fed to member banks for short-term borrowings from the Federal Reserve, also affects monetary expansion/contraction. By raising the discount rate, the Fed makes it more costly for banks to borrow and build up reserves, and therefore effectively reduces the reserves available to banks. This reduces lending. Likewise, a lowering of the discount rate facilitates increased lending.

This analysis is predicated on the "classical" assumption that the binding constraint on bank lending is the reserve requirements. If the capital requirements e [recall Equation (3.12)] were binding instead, the effects of monetary policy can be very different indeed, as we will see in Chapter 10.

LARGE FINANCIAL INTERMEDIARIES

The theories from which we borrowed some of the ideas in the previous section suggest that financial intermediaries should be of sufficient size. These arguments are based on diversification. Similar intuition applies to nondepository financial intermediaries as well. In this section, we develop this argument. We focus on the basic intuition; the mathematics can be found in Appendix 3.1. It leads to a rationale for *nondepository* financial intermediaries like investment banks, Standard & Poor's Value Line, credit rating agencies, financial newspapers, Moody's check guarantee services, portfolio managers, econometric modelers, consultants, and accounting firms.

What the theoretical research has shown is that FIs are optimally infinitely large regardless of whether they are brokers or asset transformers. That is, an FI is a "natural monopoly." This argument, which we develop below, is based on the assumption that there are no incentive or coordination problems within intermediaries. Therefore, it should be interpreted cautiously. In real-world intermediaries, there are intrafirm incentive problems that increase with the size of the intermediary. These diseconomies will dominate the diversification benefits beyond a certain size.[24]

Brokerage as a natural monopoly: Consider a broker that specializes as an information producer. One problem that the broker's customers must be concerned about is that of information reliability. This is a key issue in information production. How do these customers know that the information the broker provides is accurate and reliable? One possible way to determine this is for customers to noisily assess the reliability of the information provided by the broker, and compensating the broker more when information is judged to be more reliable. This can be done either via reputational mechanisms – attaching higher reputation for reliability to a broker whose past information has turned out to be higher quality – or by comparing the broker's information to that available from other sources.

Now, if we are dealing with a single information producer, it can be quite costly to ensure that he will use reliable information, even if we can have a noisy assessment of this reliability. This becomes a little less costly if we are dealing with a producer who is a member of a *team* of information producers because then, by producing reliable information, *each* producer benefits not only himself (by making it more likely that he will obtain higher compensation) but also the team, and a share of the team's benefits accrues to each individual producer. This is an effective mechanism as long as the team members can monitor each other to ensure that nobody gets a "free ride." As the size of the team grows, more and more independent payoffs of individual producers are being pooled together before being divided equally among the team members, so that the resulting diversification reduces the risk in each member's compensation. The risk-averse information producers are thus made better off and they demand less compensation on an expected value basis to produce information. This makes the buyers of information better off. And the benefit keeps growing as the broker gets larger. That is, brokerage is a natural monopoly.

Another economic benefit from growing large comes from *information reusability,* which was discussed in Chapter 2. When information is cross-sectionally reusable, the larger the number of information producers in the intermediary, the greater is the benefit of information reusability. The reason is that information can be reused by a greater number of information producers within the intermediary, and yet the cost of acquiring information needs to be incurred only once.

A strong implication of this analysis is that investment banks, financial newsletters, credit-rating agencies, and other information producers can benefit from growing large. A caveat is that individual members can continue to monitor (and

---

24. Millon and Thakor (1985) developed a theory of intermediation based on this tradeoff.

trust) each other as the organization grows large. If not, "free rider" problems will crop up, and it may not be beneficial to grow beyond a certain size because of the difficulty of implementing effective internal controls.

Asset transformation as a natural monopoly: Now consider an asset transformer like a bank. It borrows money from depositors and makes loans. Its advantage in being large comes from two sources.[25] First, suppose multiple depositors are needed to finance a single bank borrower and the borrower's creditworthiness has to be established through costly credit analysis. Then having a bank perform this credit analysis once conserves screening resources compared to a situation in which all the depositors engage in costly screening of the borrower. That is, a bank eliminates duplicated screening. Second, the depositors' payoff is a debt contract, it is a concave function of the bank's payoff as shown on the next page.

Because the depositors' payoff is concave, they behave as if they are risk averse. Hence, they can be made better off by reducing the risk they face, and the benefit of this is a lower interest rate on deposits. The bank can do this by diversifying its risk across many different borrowers. And, because the benefit of diversification keeps growing with size, the bank is a natural monopoly.

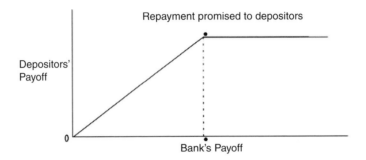

HOW BANKS CAN HELP TO MAKE NONBANK FINANCIAL CONTRACTING MORE EFFICIENT

We have spent quite some time examining the flow of services that banks and other FIs produce. These services essentially take the form of intermediating in different ways between the users and providers of capital and of reducing their costs of exchanging capital. It has been suggested that banks not only permit the capital that flows through them to be exchanged at lower cost, but they also lower the cost of capital exchange between other parties.[26]

To understand this argument, let us examine the role of bank loans in a borrowing organization's information process. It is worthwhile to draw a distinction between *inside* and *outside debt.* Inside debt is defined as a contract in which the creditor has access to information about the borrower not otherwise publicly available. The creditor may even participate in the borrower's decision process. This could be achieved, for example, by the creditor having representation on the borrower's board of directors. Bank loans are inside debt. By contrast, outside debt is defined as publicly traded debt in which the creditor depends on information about the borrower that is publicly available. Commercial paper and publicly traded corporate bonds are examples of outside debt.

Bank loans offer a special advantage in this regard. They are usually of short maturities. This means they must be periodically renewed. These renewals are accompanied by bank evaluation of the borrower's ability to meet fixed payment obligations. Thus, if the bank renews a borrower's loan, it sends a positive signal about the firm to its other creditors. Note that credibility of this signal derives from the fact that the bank "puts its money where its mouth is" when it renews the loan. Given this credible and positive signal, other higher-priority creditors find it unnecessary to expend their own resources to duplicate the bank's evaluation. Thus, bank loans help to reduce duplication in borrower evaluation by multiple creditors.[27]

Banks may also have a cost advantage in making loans to depositors. The ongoing history of a borrower as a depositor communicates valuable information to the bank about the borrower's cash-management activities. This permits the bank to assess the risks of loans to depositors and to monitor these loans at lower cost than other (competing) lenders. This consideration is particularly important in short-term loans that are rolled over because of the relatively more frequent borrower assessments. This hypothesis has empirical validity in the observation that most short-term debt is in the form of bank loans.

---

25. The discussion below is based on a model developed by Diamond (1984).

26. See Fama (1980).

27. The argument that banks can lower the contracting costs of other parties can also be found in Fama (1980). For empirical work that follows upon the study discussed in this section, see Lummer and McConnell (1989).

THE EMPIRICAL EVIDENCE: BANKS ARE SPECIAL

It turns out that there is some interesting empirical support for the theories we have presented so far. The central question of empirical interest to us is whether bank loans are unique, that is, do they provide any special service with their lending activity that is not available from other lenders? To answer this question we can examine the stock price responses to announcements of bank loans and other types of debt such as private placements of debt and public debt issues. The empirical evidence is that there is a positive and statistically significant stock price response to a borrower's acquisition of a bank loan. Further, the positive market reaction is not common to *all* private debt placements. There is, for example, a negative stock price response to debt placed privately with insurance companies. These findings seem to suggest that bank loans are unique.[28]

To examine these results let us first look at Table 3.3, which gives the distribution of announcements of different types of debt contracts for NYSE and AMEX firms.

Although there is no noticeable pattern in bank loans through time, there are two interesting observations. First, privately placed debt has been declining through time. Second, among all privately placed debt (bank loans plus other privately placed debt), bank loans dominate to the tune of 68.38%.

In Table 3.4 we provide descriptive statistics for different types of debt.

TABLE 3.3 Distributions by year of announcements of bank credit agreements, privately placed debt, and publicly placed straight debt for a random sample of 300 NYSE and AMEX-traded nonfinancial firms for the period 1974–1983

Year of Announcement	Bank Loan Agreements	Privately Placed Debt	Public Straight Debt
1974	9	4	5
1975	11	7	13
1976	7	7	8
1977	8	7	4
1978	1	8	6
1979	8	1	9
1980	11	1	10
1981	9	1	9
1982	10	1	16
1983	6	0	10
Total	80	37	90

Source: James, C., Some evidence on the uniqueness of bank loans, *Journal of Financial Economics* 19, 1987, 217–235.

TABLE 3.4 Descriptive statistics for commercial bank loans, privately placed debt, and publicly placed straight debt for a random sample of 300 NYSE and AMEX-traded nonfinancial firms for the period 1974–1983

	Type of Borrowing					
	Commercial bank loans (sample size 80)		Privately placed debt (sample size 37)		Public straight debt (sample size 90)	
Descriptive Measure	Mean	Median	Mean	Median	Mean	Median
Debt amount (millions of dollars)	72.0	35.0	32.3	25.0	106.2	75.0
Firm size (millions of dollars)	675	212	630	147	2506	1310
Debt amount/market value of common stock	0.72	0.46	0.52	0.25	0.26	0.15
Maturity of debt	5.6	6.0	15.34	15.0	17.96	20.0

Source: James, C., Some evidence on the uniqueness of bank loans, *Journal of Financial Economics* 19, 1987, 217–235.

28. See James (1987).

TABLE 3.5 Average 2-day percentage abnormal stock returns on the announcement of commercial bank loans, privately placed debt, and publicly placed straight debt offerings for a random sample of 300 NYSE and AMEX-traded nonfinancial firms for the period 1974 to 1983

Type of Event	Abnormal Stock Returns	Proportion Negative (Sample Size)
Bank loan agreement	1.93%	0.34 (80)
Privately placed debt	−0.91%	0.56 (37)
Public straight debt	−0.11%	0.56 (90)

Source: James, C., Some evidence on the uniqueness of bank loans, *Journal of Financial Economics* 19, 1987, 217–235.

As this table shows, firms using private placements and bank loans are on average smaller than firms using public offerings of debt. The average firm size in both the bank loan sample and the private placement sample is about 25% of the average firm size in the public debt sample. This evidence is consistent with the theory discussed so far. Problems of moral hazard and particularly of asymmetric information can be expected to be more severe for smaller, lesser-known firms. Hence, banks have a greater relative contribution to make in resolving these problems in such firms. Not surprisingly then, we find that bank loans are the dominant source of debt financing for small firms.

Let us now see how the stock prices of borrowing firms react to the announcements of various forms of debt. This evidence is presented in Table 3.5.

The abnormal stock return here is defined in the usual fashion as the deviation of the realized rate of return from the expected rate of return given by the market model. That is, the abnormal stock return for firm j over day t is defined as

$$R_{jt} - (\hat{\alpha}_j + \hat{\beta}_j R_{mt})$$

where R_{jt} is the rate of return of security j over day t, R_{mt} is the rate of return on the market portfolio over the same period, and $\hat{\alpha}_j$ and $\hat{\beta}_j$ are the ordinary least squares estimates of the market model parameters for firm j.

The average abnormal stock return for bank loan agreements in Table 3.4 is positive and statistically significant at the 0.01 level. In addition, two-thirds of the abnormal stock returns are positive. The negative average abnormal stock return associated with the announcement of a public offering of debt is not statistically significant.

If the positive response to bank loan agreements results from some benefit of inside debt not unique to banks, then one would expect to observe a similar response to debt that is privately placed with insurance companies. However, as Table 3.4 indicates, the response to the announcement of privately placed debt is −0.91%, which is statistically significant at the 0.10 level. Moreover, the difference between the average abnormal stock returns of bank loan agreements and privately placed debt is statistically significant at the 0.01 level.

It is possible that the differences in abnormal stock returns across different types of debt agreements could be due to systematic differences in maturity and purpose of borrowing, that is, the data may not indicate anything special about bank loans *per se*. To check this possibility, we would like to know the share price responses to the announcements of bank loans, private placements, and public debt offerings, all with the same characteristics. The evidence on this score suggests that differences in abnormal performance across these different sources of borrowing are not solely due to differences in the characteristics of the loan or differences in the characteristics of borrowers (such as size, for example). That is, the results are robust. The overall conclusion to be reached from this empirical evidence is that banks are special.

OWNERSHIP STRUCTURE OF DEPOSITORY FINANCIAL INSTITUTIONS

Depository institutions have two types of ownership forms: stocks and mutuals. Agency theory predicts that ownership form has a significant effect on the incentives and the operating efficiency of the firm. In this section, we will review the theoretical bases for this prediction and also look at some empirical evidence.

Commercial banks are exclusively stockholder-owned. Mutuals are common among insurance firms, MSBs (mutual saving banks), and S&Ls (savings and loan associations), although many mutual S&Ls have converted into stockholder-owned organizations in recent years. We will proceed as follows. First, we will examine how mutuality affects the resolution of agency and other problems. Then, we will seek an explanation for why S&Ls were dominantly mutuals and what explains the recent wave of conversions to stock ownership. Finally, we will review some relevant empirical evidence. Most of our comments apply to the United States, but we will – in concluding – also focus on Europe where mutuals (actually cooperative banks) play an important role and represent a very large segment of the financial intermediation sector.

Mutual Versus Stocks

The residual claimants in a mutual are customers. These are the policyholders of mutual life insurance companies, the depositors of MSBs, and the depositors of mutual S&Ls. For purposes of this discussion, we will limit ourselves to mutual S&Ls.

There are two key differences between a stock and mutual S&Ls. First, the owners of a stock S&L are its stockholders, whereas the owners of a mutual S&L are its depositors (and possibly its borrowers). Second, a stock S&L can increase its capital by selling common stock, whereas a mutual S&L cannot.

Consider the first difference. In a stock S&L, shareholders have a well-defined ownership right, which implies: (i) a claim to residual profits, (ii) a right to vote for the board of directors and change control of the organization, and (iii) a right to dissolve the organization. On the other hand, in a mutual S&L, the ownership rights of depositors are much weaker. As for (i), depositors in a mutual are much more like creditors than shareholders since they cannot force the mutual to pay them more than the promised interest and principal on their claims. Although in principle depositors have ownership claims to the mutual's current earnings, these claims are not transferable, and the earnings can be retained indefinitely by the institution as net worth. As for (ii), while mutual S&L depositors have voting rights, these are quite limited and are often signed over to management at the time of opening of accounts.[29] Finally, as for (iii), even though a depositor can withdraw his deposits and thereby partially liquidate the mutual fund, depositors have had little incentive to do so because of deposit insurance, especially when interest rate ceilings bounded the return to depositors.

Thus, it is imperative to distinguish between *de jure* and *de facto* ownerships in a mutual. The *de jure* ownership (legal ownership) rests with the mutual's customers. It is, however, largely vacuous. The *de facto* ownership [control of (i), (ii), and (iii)] rests with the managers and the government (which provides deposit insurance).

Of course, the inability of owners to completely control the institution – and the resulting agency problem – is encountered in stockholder-owned institutions as well. Both stock and mutual S&Ls are administered by managers whose goals may differ from the goals of the owners. However, the two types of S&Ls differ with regard to the ability of the owners to monitor managers. Stockholders have greater control over the activities of managers because control can be consolidated through the purchase of stock.[30]

Choice of Ownership Structure by S&Ls

Earlier studies viewed mutual S&Ls as either cooperatives, with depositors and borrowers working for a common goal, or benevolent associations organized to encourage saving and home ownership.[31] This view was based partly on the observation that the first S&Ls were mutuals that served smaller depositors, leaving the larger ones to commercial banks and other institutions.[32] These early community-based cooperatives, which gathered deposits from the community and offered mortgages to community members, had simple operations. The fair degree of homogeneity in mortgages made it relatively easy to assess the value of the S&L's assets based on historical data. This was just as well since the absence of a *secondary market* for residual claims meant that existing and prospective owners could not rely on the information generated by capital market trading (and pricing) to assess the value of the mutuals' assets. Whereas the simplicity of the operation of S&Ls made mutuality an acceptable ownership structure, the elimination of the classic conflict between creditors (who prefer less risk) and stockholders (who prefer more) made mutuality the *preferred* structure for many S&Ls.[33] Moreover, the simplicity of the operation of S&Ls meant that managerial expertise was not a critical element in the success of S&Ls. In the early years, therefore, the S&L industry was dominated by mutuals run by managers who were not the most talented or efficient.

---

29. This is achieved with the signing of perpetual proxies. These proxies can be revoked. However, disclosure requirements on the part of the S&L management are limited, the maximum number of votes a depositor can control is limited, there are restrictions on outside nominations to the board, and the board can eliminate a depositor's voting rights by simply redeeming his savings account. See Masulis (1987).

30. See Mester (1991) for careful empirical documentation that stock S&Ls operate with an efficient output mix, whereas mutual S&Ls operate with significant diseconomies of scope.

31. See Hester (1968) and Brigham and Pettit (1969).

32. There are also theoretical models that suggest such a role for mutuals. See Rasmusen (1988).

33. See Mayers and Smith (1986).

Over time, however, operation became more complex, and mutuals began to choose managers on the basis of expertise. Moreover, the advent of deposit insurance eliminated the agency-cost-of-debt advantage of mutuals over stocks. Since their deposits are insured, depositors are indifferent to an S&L's risk-taking behavior. The agency cost of debt was essentially absorbed by the Federal Savings and Loan Insurance Corporation (FSLIC).

Along with these developments came deregulation and an increase in competition. Mutual S&L managers have found it increasingly difficult to compete with their more efficient stockholder-owned counterparts. And their inability to augment institutional net worth through additional equity issues has made the competitive disadvantage worse. Thus, the benefits of mutuality to owners have diminished significantly. Furthermore, these increased competitive pressures mean that the probability of bankruptcy – and hence the probability of unemployment for the manager – due to inefficient behavior has increased. This means that any given level of perquisite consumption on the part of mutual managers is now more costly. Given that managers were optimally selecting their perquisites prior to deregulation, the implication is that perquisites consumption in mutuals must be *lower* after deregulation, as managers weigh the benefit of perks against the elevated probability of unemployment. Thus, the benefits of mutuality to managers have diminished as well. Combined with this is the positive incentive managers have to convert to stock ownership, since they usually benefit in the initial stock sale. The reason is that managers typically receive rights to purchase the new stock, which is usually underpriced (as in other initial public offerings). When the benefits of conversion outweigh the benefits of the new optimal (and lower) level of perquisites consumption, one would expect the S&L to convert from mutual to stock. This could explain the increased number of conversions that have been witnessed in recent years,[34] as the stockholder-ownership structure has become the preferred mode for both owners and managers.

Observations on Mutuals (Cooperative Banks) in Europe

In several European countries (e.g., France, The Netherlands, and Germany), cooperative banks play an important role, and are often part of the largest segment of the financial services industry. They often are "layered" cooperatives consisting of multiple local (member) cooperatives that "own" the central cooperative (e.g.. RABO Bank in The Netherlands, and Credit Agricole in France; the latter even has a third layer). The central cooperative may include professional services, a common treasury operation, and back-office facilities that facilitate economies of scale. Such a model may provide strong roots in local markets (via the local cooperatives), facilitating relationship banking, and simultaneously allow for scale and a matching of funding across the cooperatives.

The efficiency of such cooperatives depends very much on the culture and professionalism of the organization. Some have been highly successful and have via internal benchmarking and common practices outperformed shareholder owned banks. But this is what we would expect. Ultimately, the performance of an institution depends on many factors; ownership structure is only one of them. As stated earlier, cooperatives/mutuals might have a control vacuum that invites inefficiencies, but some may have found ways to overcome this. Recent work shows that cooperatives in some European countries have been more resilient than the banking sector in general.[35]

THE BORROWER'S CHOICE OF FINANCE SOURCE

We have seen that a borrower has access to a wide array of credit sources. How does he decide which source to approach? In Figure 3.7 below, we have sketched a hierarchy of financing sources that explains the borrower's choice based on his own attributes and the resulting demand for intermediation services.[36] The borrower's financing choice in this figure tracks a typical firm's "lifecycle."

When a firm is very young, it has two striking characteristics. First, the entrepreneur in charge may be unsure of his own management expertise, so that approaching a financial intermediary that can provide this expertise is beneficial. Second, the borrower has few tangible assets to offer as collateral. As we will see in Chapter 7, collateral is useful in controlling moral hazard whereby borrowers either stint on effort or take excessive risks. In the absence of collateral, the lender could use equity participation as a way of addressing moral hazard. Thus, it is in the borrower's interest to seek a lender who can take an equity position and thus be able to offer capital at a "reasonable" price. Both factors suggest that such firms should go to venture capitalists.

---

34. To convert from mutual to stock, the S&L must sell stock publicly through a standby rights offering to depositors and management, who are the eligible subscribers. The conversion plan must be first approved by two-thirds of the S&L's board of directors. If approved, it must be ratified by two-thirds of the depositors. Upon ratification, the stock can be offered to eligible subscribers, and if it is not fully subscribed, the unsubscribed portion must be sold to the public.

35. See Ayadi et al. (2010). Also, recent work on financial stability shows that diversity in the type of ownership structures in banking might be important, and that the presence of cooperatives may help, see Michie (2010).

36. This discussion relies to some extent on Diamond (1989) and Chan et al. (1990).

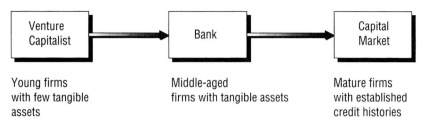

FIGURE 3.7 Hierarchy of Financing Sources.

As a firm grows and acquires tangible assets, it becomes capable of offering collateral to mitigate moral hazard. Banks, which are prohibited in the United States from taking equity positions, can now lend to such borrowers because they can offer collateral to secure their debt. Of course, all moral hazard will not be eliminated by collateral, so that there will be an important role for bank monitoring. Moreover, bank loans tend to be of short maturities, thereby generating periodic information through reassessments of the borrower. This information is reflected both in the bank's decision to renew/terminate the loan as well as in the new contract terms offered, in combination with information produced by rating agencies. This helps to reduce duplication in information production by *other* creditors of the firm, thereby diminishing overall contracting costs. The firms in this group find it better to go to banks than to venture capitalists because banks can fund their loans with insured deposits, whereas venture capitalists cannot; hence, the borrower is able to obtain a loan at a lower price.

Finally, when the firm is well-established and mature, it has a good track record for repaying its debts. This reputation can be valuable because it permits the firm to borrow at preferential rates. By taking undue asset risks, the borrower stands to lose this reputation, and thus has an incentive to limit risk-taking. Consequently, bank monitoring to combat moral hazard is less important for such borrowers, and this permits them to directly access the capital market where borrowing costs are lower; capital market access would mean that the borrower would not have to pay the bank its intermediation rents. Of course, such firms still confront problems of asymmetric information,[37] so that *nondepository* financial intermediaries such as investment banks (or credit-rating agencies) play an important role in the transfer of capital from investors to such firms. This is because they make information about firms available to investors at a lower cost than they could acquire themselves. It is interesting to note that as one moves from left to right in the financing hierarchy shown in Figure 3.7, the intermediation services provided decline and so does the cost of credit. The venture capitalist provides financing, monitoring, and management expertise; the bank provides financing and monitoring; and the capital market provides mainly financing. Of course, this discussion is not meant to suggest that these financing sources are mutually exclusive. For example, borrowers often access the capital market for commercial paper and use banks to provide loan commitments to back up these commercial paper issues.

The Role of Capital in Bank Financing

While banks are specialists in monitoring borrowers, two facts should be recognized. First, monitoring is costly, so banks need to be incented to do the monitoring. Second, there are limits to the effectiveness of bank monitoring, so there should be innate incentives for borrowers to make prudent decisions. This way, not all of the burden for ensuring such behavior falls on bank monitoring.

For the bank to have sufficiently strong incentives to monitor borrowers, it should have enough capital.[38] This is easy to see. The benefit of bank monitoring is that it increases the likelihood of the borrower repaying the loan, that is, it reduces the probability of default. Given that monitoring is costly, this benefit needs to be large enough to overcome the monitoring cost. Since borrower default creates a loan loss that is absorbed by the bank's equity capital, the higher this capital the larger is the potential loss the bank's shareholders absorb when loans default. Thus, the benefit of avoiding loan default is greater when the bank has more capital. In other words, the benefit of loan monitoring is greater when the bank has more capital. In Chapter 13, we further elaborate on a bank's choice of capital structure.

Similarly, borrowers too have stronger incentives to make value-maximizing decisions when they have more equity capital. To see this, suppose the borrower can choose one of three mutually exclusive projects: a good project (G) that maximizes the firm's value and a bad project (B$_1$) that has a present value of future cash flows that is less than the required investment (so it is a negative-NPV project) but produces some private benefits, *b* for the borrower, and another bad project

---

37. See, for example, Myers and Majluf (1984).

38. See Holmstrom and Tirole (1997) for a theory along these lines, in which shortages of capital either in banks or in borrowers lead to credit crunches.

(B_2) that also has negative NPV but produces even bigger private benefits, $B > b$, for the borrower. One can think of these private benefits as either unobservable diversions of resources from the project that the borrower could make for private gain at the bank's expense, or simply the benefit of having to work less hard to manage the project.

Now suppose bank monitoring can eliminate borrower's ability to choose project B_2, but not B_1, and that $b > 0$ is large enough that the borrower would prefer B_1 to G if the project was entirely financed with a bank loan and the borrower had no equity at stake. Then, it can be seen that if the borrower were required to invest sufficient equity in the project, it would prefer G over B_1. Anticipating this, the bank will not lend to the borrower unless the borrower puts up enough equity.

This theory has a number of important implications. One is that if borrowers do not have enough equity capital, they may be rationed. Having enough pledgeable assets to post as collateral will ameliorate this problem, so one should think of rationing as something that arises as a consequence of a combined shortage of collateral and capital. A second implication is that banks too will lend less when they have less capital. This is because insufficiently capitalized banks will not do costly monitoring, so lending will be limited to borrowers who do not need monitoring. Third, having enough capital in banks also enhances the borrower's ability to obtain financing from *other* sources, as other financiers can be assured that the bank's monitoring will result in the borrower making the right investment decisions. Fourth, when borrowers have so much capital that they would prefer G to either B_1 or B_2 even if there is no monitoring, then bank lending diminishes in importance as borrowers can directly access the capital market or other nonmonitored sources of finance. That is, bank lending is maximized at intermediate levels of firm (borrower) capital.

Blurring Distinctions between Bank Loans and Capital Market Financing: Transaction and Relationship Loans

Although in our earlier discussion, we have characterized capital market and bank financing as distinct but sometimes overlapping choices, in recent years the distinction between these two sources of financing has become increasingly blurred. For example, banks made syndicated loans in which multiple banks participate, and these loans are often traded in a manner similar to capital market trading. Banks make mortgage and credit card loans and then package them into portfolios, issue securities against these portfolios, and sell these securities in the capital market where they are traded. This is called securitization and will be discussed in more detail in Chapter 11.

Of course, banks also make loans where they add considerable unique value and the loans are not traded. Examples are small business loans where the bank–borrower relationship has value.

Research in banking has examined the difference between loans by classifying bank loans as transaction loans and relationship loans.[39] Transaction loans include loans like credit card and mortgage loans. There is little monitoring by the bank and the loans can be repackaged and traded. The bank's value added is limited mostly to its credit analysis and standardized credit analysis before credit is extended.

Relationship loans are those where the bank generates additional value by learning about the borrower through its relationship with the borrower and providing business advice. Relationship loans offer numerous other advantages related to attenuating moral hazard and private information problems. These will be discussed in Chapter 8.

Another aspect of relationship lending that has only recently begun to be explored is that it creates the potential for *differences of opinion*. For example, a bank may judge a relationship loan to be creditworthy, but its judgment may be based on a lot of "soft," nonverifiable information that is prone to multiple interpretations and disagreement. Such loans cannot readily be financed in the capital markets if investors have a different (collective) opinion about the creditworthiness of the loan. In such cases, a bank – backed by sufficient capital – can act as a "beliefs bridge" between depositors/investors and borrowers and raise deposit financing to fund the relationship loan. The bank's reputation/credibility is reliably processing soft information and this may convince depositors to extend funding they otherwise may not have. This would be another contribution of banks to relationship loans.[40] That is, the bank becomes a more stable source of funding for entrepreneurs when these entrepreneurs cannot raise market financing from investors due to disagreement or behavioral biases.

Thus, bank loans span a continuum from relationship loans at one end to transaction loans at the other. Relationship loans are the most different from capital market financing. Transaction loans are the most similar to capital market financing.

---

39. This characterization was provided by Boot and Thakor (2000). See also Rajan (1992) and Sharpe (1990) for models of relationship lending. Boot (2000) provides a review.
40. See Coval and Thakor (2005) and Song and Thakor (2007).

Shadow Banking

So far we have discussed the activities of banks and other depository institutions. But the recent subprime crisis in the United States originated in what has been called "the shadow banking system." This is the part of the financial system where short-term funding is carried out with arrangements other than deposits.[41] The shadow banking system includes institutions such as investment banks, brokerage houses, and finance companies. A lot of the collateral securing the short-term borrowing in the shadow banking system is created by securitization structures like asset-backed securities and asset-backed commercial paper. There are various investors in the market, including money market mutual funds.

A commonly used mechanism for short-term funding in the shadow banking system is the repurchase agreement (or repo). A repo is essentially a collateralized deposit. The way it works is that the borrower gives a security as collateral to the lender and borrows some amount that is a fraction x of the value of the security, with $(1 - x)\%$ being called the "haircut" on the repo. There is an interest rate paid on the borrowing and the collateral is returned to the borrower when the (short-term) loan is repaid. We will cover this in more detail in Chapter 8.

CONCLUSION

The process of financial intermediation is of central importance to the functioning of a modern economy. Some of the important conclusions to be drawn from our discussions are covered briefly below.

First, the financial system has many components that interact to foster economic growth – banks are a crucial component. Second, regulation of banks and the *raison d'etre* for the existence of banks are intertwined. Regulation is not solely the outcome of a political agenda that is separate from the reasons why banks exist. To make banking a viable business in which there is public confidence, some form of regulation is necessary. We also discussed how this regulation then becomes a component of monetary policy. Third, the incentive problems that banks and nondepository financial intermediaries resolve are such that there are natural benefits to size. Diversification can reduce incentive costs in contracting among unequally informed agents, and information reusability is greater in larger intermediaries. Hence, financial intermediaries can derive economic benefits from being large. Fourth, inside (privately placed) debt has some inherent advantages over outside (publicly traded) debt because of superior access to information about the borrower that the former provides. Bank loans are inside debt. However, even within the class of contracts qualifying as inside debt, bank loans are special. The reaction of a borrowing firm's stock price to the announcement of a bank loan agreement is more favorable on average than the stock price reaction to the announcements of other forms of inside debt. Fifth, the choice of organizational form – mutual versus stock – by a depository institution depends on the interaction between a variety of factors that include differences in the efficiency with which agency problems are resolved within mutuals as opposed to shareholder-owned institutions, the competitive environment, and the relative advantage a stockholder-owned firm has in raising capital and having complex assets priced in the capital market. This explains the initial prevalence of mutuality among thrifts and the recent trend of conversions of mutuals into stock.

Finally, there is a natural hierarchy of financing sources. In its earliest phases of development, a firm has the greatest advantage in seeking venture capital, due to the (unique) ability of the venture capitalist to assist in management. At the next stage, when early survival has been accomplished, bank loans are preferred. Although banks do not assist in management to the extent that venture capitalists do, the monitoring provided by banks is of value to firms at this stage when they are still relatively small or medium-sized. Bank monitoring helps to control incentive problems within the borrowing firm. Moreover, bank loans tend to be of short maturities, thereby generating periodic information through reassessments of the borrower. This information, as well as that produced by nondepository financial intermediaries such as credit-rating agencies, helps to reduce duplication in information production by *other* creditors of the firm, and thus reduces overall contracting costs. Moreover, large firms go directly to the capital market for outside debt. Bank monitoring is of lesser marginal value to such firms. However, such firms still confront problems of asymmetric information,[42] so that *nondepository* financial intermediaries such as investment banks (or credit-rating agencies) play an important role in the transfer of capital from investors to such firms. This is because they make information about firms available to investors at lower cost than they could acquire themselves.[43]

What are the implications of our analysis for *market efficiency*? Clearly, if the capital market were strong-form efficient even without financial intermediaries, the role for financial intermediaries would be extremely limited; they would at best provide some minor transactional services like "lot-breaking" of securities, that is, buying large denomination securities

---

41. Adrian and Ashcraft (2012) provide a review. Various alternative definitions for shadow banking system exist, see Claessens and Ratnovski (2014).
42. See Ramakrishnan and Thakor (1984) and Giammarino and Lewis (1988).
43. See, for example, Diamond (1989).

and selling smaller denomination claims against such securities to investors with wealth constraints. However, the theoretical and empirical results discussed in this chapter suggest two conclusions. First, given the pervasive problems of private information and moral hazard, it is reasonable to expect that credit markets are no more than semistrong form efficient, so that financial intermediaries have an important role to play in resolving information-based problems. Second, the informational efficiency of credit markets is *enhanced* by financial intermediaries, since they possess privileged financial information that is then learned by others who observe bank–borrower transactions.

REVIEW QUESTIONS

1. Explain how a bank evolves from a primitive goldsmith and the roles played by asymmetric information and moral hazard in this evolution.
2. Can banking ever become completely deregulated? Why or why not?
3. What do we mean by a "hierarchy of financing sources"? What determines a borrower's choice of financing source?
4. Can you shed light on the following facts and explain their possible interrelationships?
   a. Commercial paper issues by nonfinancial corporations in the United States have grown sixfold in the last 20 years.
   b. Large money center banks are turning increasingly to "middle market" borrowers (i.e., those with loan requests between $5 million and $200 million).
   c. Securitization has grown rapidly.
5. What is the difference between a "stock" and a "mutual"? Explain the differences in the resolutions of agency problems for these two types of organizations.
6. It has been said that the health of a nation's banking system is inversely related to the speed and efficiency of information flows in the economy. Explain.
7. In what way are banks "unique"? What is the empirical evidence on this issue?
8. What are the economic incentives for financial intermediaries to grow large?
9. How do banks help to make nonbank contracting more efficient?
10. Given below is an excerpt from a conversation. Comment critically on it.
    Moderator: Fine, but as long as you have fractional reserve banking, you're never going to eliminate the possibility of withdrawal risk altogether.
    Appleton: That's why you have a lender of last resort, Mike.
11. How does monetary policy affect the (short-term) growth path of an economy?
12. What are the differences between transaction and relationship loans and what is the relevance of the distinction?
13. Explain how the financial system works to promote economic growth?

APPENDIX 3.1 THE FORMAL ANALYSIS OF LARGE INTERMEDIARIES

The Model Based on Ramakrishnan and Thakor (1984): Suppose we have assets whose owners wish to attract capital. However, there is asymmetric information about the values of these assets; the owner of each asset knows more about the value than others do. As we saw in Chapter 1, this can lead to market failure if the appropriate signals are unavailable to firms. Now suppose there are some individuals who specialize in producing information about firms at a cost. Let us imagine that there are groups of individuals, with each group specializing in producing information about a particular industry or a particular firm. The cost to an individual of producing this information is $c > 0$ and each individual is risk averse, with a utility function of $U(\bullet)$ defined over monetary wealth, that is $U(\bullet)$ is increasing and strictly concave. We assume that c is a nonmonetary cost to the information producer (i.p.); it does not figure in his utility over wealth. Moreover, it is incurred only if the i.p. actually produces information about the firm he specializes in. Also, each i.p. has a minimum level of expected utility, a $\overline{U}$ that must be guaranteed by his compensation package for producing information, or he will work in an alternative occupation.

Now suppose that the firm that wishes to attract capital (or the investor who wants to decide whether he should invest in a particular asset) approaches an i.p. directly to produce information about it and release it to the market, that is, the i.p. plays the role of a rating agency. If the i.p. is just paid a fixed fee, we have a moral hazard problem in that he will avoid actually producing information, thereby saving himself the effort-related cost c. He will simply make a quick guess, collect his fee, and send the firm on its way. Investors will recognize this and the firm's price will not move. The firm will have wasted its money.

Compensation Contracts of Individual Information Producers: But suppose the firm is able to monitor the i.p. to discover something about whether he actually invested c. This monitoring produces a signal that tells the firm about the i.p.'s effort. However, this signal is noisy. Even if the i.p. invests c in information production, the signal says that he did only with probability p. With probability $1-p$, the signal is erroneous and indicates that the i.p. did not produce information. If the i.p. did not produce information, then the signal says that he did with probability q and that he did not with probability $1-q$. We assume that $p > q$, so that the signal is informative. Now let the i.p.'s compensation be as follows: pay him \$$H$ if the signal says he produced information and \$$L$ if it says he did not, with $H > L$.[44] If the i.p. does produce information, he gets an expected utility of

$$EU(\text{produce information}) = pU(H) + (1-p)U(L) - c. \tag{3.13}$$

If he does not produce information, he gets an expected utility of

$$EU(\text{does not produce information}) = qU(H) + (1-q)U(L). \tag{3.14}$$

If investors are to believe that the i.p. is credible, his compensation schedule should be incentive compatible (should induce the i.p. to invest c). That is,

$$pU(H) + (1-p)U(L) - c \geq qU(H) + (1-q)U(L). \tag{3.15}$$

It also will be necessary to make sure that the i.p. is willing to work for the firm. This requires that

$$pU(H) + (1-p)U(L) - c \geq \bar{U} \tag{3.16}$$

We can solve Equations (3.15) and (3.16) to come up with H and L. We can show that in equilibrium Equations (3.15) and (3.16) should hold as equalities, that is, treating them as equalities leads to a solution that minimizes the expected cost for each firm. To illustrate, suppose $U(x) = \sqrt{x}$ for any number x, $\bar{U} = 20$ (for simplicity), $p = 0.8$, $q = 0.2$, and $c = 10$. Solving Equations (3.15) and (3.16) as a pair of simultaneous equations with these numbers, we get $H = 10,000/9$ and $L = 10,000/36$. The i.p. earns an expected utility of exactly 20. The expected cost of information production for each firm is $0.8\,H + 0.2L = 944.44$ approximately.

The solution with an intermediary: Now suppose that there are two i.p.s, each like the i.p. in the preceding analysis, which coalesce and form a financial intermediary of two i.p.s. Each still deals with a separate firm. However, they now pool their payoffs to avail of diversification benefits. We assume that because the i.p.s are cooperating, they can costlessly observe each other's actions. This means neither i.p. has to be concerned about his partner free-riding off his effort. So now each i.p.'s compensation becomes

$2H / 2 = H$ if both signals are favorable
$(H + L) / 2$ if only one signal is favorable
$2L / 2 = L$ if both signals are unfavorable

Assuming that signals across firms are uncorrelated, the probabilities of different compensations for each i.p. are given in Table 3.6.

Note that both i.p.s will act in concert. The firms that give them compensation contracts realize that the rules of the game have changed. They must now solve the following pair of simultaneous equations.

$$p^2 U(H) + 2p(1-p)U\left(\frac{H+L}{2}\right) + (1-p)^2 U(L) - c$$
$$= q^2 U(H) + 2q(1-q)U\left(\frac{H+L}{2}\right) + (1-q)^2 U(L) \tag{3.17}$$

TABLE 3.6 Probabilities of compensations

Probability of Compensation	Compensation of Each i.p.
p^2 if both i.p.s produce information and q^2 if both do not	H
$2p(1-p)$ if both i.p.s produce information and $2q(1-q)$ if both do not	$(H + L)/2$
$(1-p)^2$ if both i.p.s produce information and $(1-q)^2$ if both do not	L

---

44. If such a compensation scheme is successful in inducing the i.p. to produce information, then it is not time consistent because everybody knows he has produced information and it is pointless to pay him less when an error-prone signal says he did not. We will ignore this problem here.

and

$$p^2 U(H) + 2p(1-p)U\left(\frac{H+L}{2}\right) + (1-p)^2 U(L) - c = \bar{U} \tag{3.18}$$

Generally, the solution to this will be different from the previous solution. Suppose, however, that firms continue to use the old contracts where $H = 10.000/9$ and $L = 10.000/36$. It can be checked in this case that Equation (3.17) is satisfied exactly and that the left-hand side of Equation (3.18) is about 20.43. That is, each i.p. in the financial intermediary enjoys a higher expected utility than he did before. Note that the expected cost of having information produced for each firm will be exactly the same as before. Thus, the formation of a financial intermediary makes i.p.s better off if firms do not alter their contracts. Of course, firms may wish to write different contracts to remove the excess utility enjoyed by the i.p.s. In this case, expected information production costs of firms are lowered.

The reason why the formation of an intermediary helps is diversification. By pooling their payoffs, the i.p.s are able to reduce individual risks. This means that they can increase their expected utility and if at least some of the benefit of this increased utility is shared with the firms they are screening, the cost of information production will also decline.

The Desirability of a Very Large Intermediary: This argument can be taken to the limit. Suppose the financial intermediary becomes infinitely large. Then, by the law of large numbers (roughly speaking) the probabilities become actual fractions. That is, if all i.p.s produce information, the intermediary knows that exactly 80% of them will get H each and 20% will get Leach. Thus, the intermediary knows that its payoff will be

$$0.8H + 0.2L$$
$$= 0.8\left(\frac{40000}{36}\right) + 0.2\left(\frac{10000}{36}\right) = 944.44$$

per i.p. with probability one. Since the financial intermediary itself can monitor its own members, it does not have to worry about moral hazard. Thus, it can promise each of its member i.p.s a *fixed* payment of 944.44, knowing that even though on any given i.p., it could receive either more or less than this amount, the random fluctuations around 944.44 will cancel out for the intermediary as a whole. Thus, each individual i.p.'s expected utility in this intermediary is $U(944.44) - 10 = 20.73$, which is higher than with the two-i.p. intermediary passes along this gain to the firms it screens, then *information production costs are lowest with a very large intermediary.*

That is, we have shown that a *diversified information broker* can lower the cost of information production and hence the cost of exchanging capital. Once again, the pivotal function served by a financial intermediary is that of providing a more efficient resolution of informational problems.

Diversification in this model is achieved by letting each i.p. within the intermediary share the risk in the compensation of every other member i.p. That is, as we add to the size of the group, each individual compensation risk is shared by an increasing number of i.p.s. Due to the risk aversion of the member i.p.s, such diversification helps to improve welfare.[45] We shall call this "diversification by sharing risks." Another type of diversification is "diversification by adding risks."[46] In this case, a single i.p. bears 100% of N independent risks, with diversification occurring as N increases. This is quite different from the first form of diversification because the total wealth of the i.p. is growing as he adds more risks. That is, instead of spreading a given amount of wealth over a larger number of independent gambles, we are spreading an increasing amount of wealth over a larger number of independent gambles. Noble laureate Paul Samuelson (1963) has called such diversification "the fallacy of large numbers," because it is not generally true that, for all risk-averse utility functions, the individual's risk aversion toward the Nth independent gamble is a decreasing function of N. In other words, while a risk-averse individual would wish to take advantage of the low number of large numbers to spread a *fixed* amount of wealth over an increasingly large number of independent gambles, he would not necessarily wish to achieve such diversification at the expense of exposing an increasing amount of his wealth to the gambles. However, there are sufficient conditions involving restrictions on utility functions that such diversification is beneficial.

---

45. An important assumption in our analysis is that the i.p.s within the intermediary can monitor each other costlessly. Millon and Thakor (1985) show that if such monitoring is impossible, then by letting i.p.s coalesce and engage in payoff-pooling, we raise information production costs. They also show, however, that if the values of firms depend on a common, systematic element, as well as on idiosyncratic factors, then information sharing within the intermediary can lead to an overall lowering of information production costs.

46. This is considered by Diamond (1984).

APPENDIX 3.2 DEFINITIONS

The Law of Large Numbers: Roughly speaking, a principle that says that if we have an infinitely large number of random variables in a sample, all of which are drawn from the same probability distribution, then the average realized value of the random variables in the sample will equal the statistical mean of the probability distribution from which they are drawn. Thus, if an individual divides his finite wealth equally across an infinitely large number of investments whose random payoffs are independent of each other, but are drawn from the same probability distribution, this individual's payoff from his investments will become (almost) *certain* and equal to the statistical mean of the probability distribution from which investment payoffs are drawn. A risk-averse individual would prefer to do this because it eliminates risk.

Event Study Methodology: A statistical approach commonly used in finance to evaluate the price impact of an event. The idea is to start with the assumption that the return on a stock can be described by the market model. Then, the next step is to estimate the values of alpha and beta by regressing the return on the stock against the return on the market for a sufficiently long time period prior to the event date and outside a two- or three-day time window around the event date. Given these estimated values, one can compute the average value of the residuals during the time window around the event date. If no new information was conveyed by the event, the average value of the residuals should be zero. If it is positive (negative), the event is interpreted as conveying good (bad) news.

REFERENCES

Adrian, T., Ashcraft, A.B., 2012. Shadow banking: a review of the literature. In: Durlauf an, S.N., Blume, L.E. (Eds.), The New Palgrave Dictionary of Economics. Palgrave MacMillan, New York, NY.

Allen, F., 1990. The market for information and the origin of financial intermediation. J. Financ. Intermed. 1, 3–30.

Ayadi, R., Llewellyn, D., Schmidt, R.H., Arbak, E., de Groen, W.P., 2010. Investigating Diversity in the Banking Sector in Europe: Key Developments, Performance and the Role of Cooperative Banks. Centre for Economic Policy Studies, Brussels.

Bagehot, W., 1873. Lombard Street. Homewood, Illinois, 1962.

Boot, A., 2000. Relationship lending: what do we know? J. Financ. Intermed. 9, 7–25.

Boot, A., Thakor, A.V., 2000. Can relationship banking survive competition? J. Financ. 55, 679–714.

Boyd, J., Prescott, E., 1986. Financial intermediary coalitions. J. Econ. Theory 38, 211–232.

Brigham, E.F., Pettit, R.R., 1969. Effects of structure on performance in the savings and loan industry. In: Friend, I. (Ed.), Study of the Savings and Loan Industry. Federal Home Loan Bank Board, Washington, DC.

Chan, Y.-S., Siegel, D., Thakor, A., 1990. Learning, corporate control and performance requirements in venture capital contracts. Int. Econ. Rev. 31, 365–381.

Chari, V.V., Jagannathan, R., 1988. Banking panics, information, and rational expectations equilibrium. J. Financ. 43, 749–761.

Claessens, S., Ratnovski, L., 2014.What is Shadow Banking?, IMF Working Paper 14/25.

Coval, J., Thakor, A.V., 2005. Financial intermediation as a beliefs-bridge between optimists and pessimists. J. Financ. Econ. 75, 535–570.

Diamond, D., 1984. Financial intermediation and delegated monitoring. Rev. Econ. Stud. 51, 393–414, LI.

Diamond, D., 1989. Reputation acquisition in debt markets. J. Polit. Econ. 97, 828–862.

Diamond, D., Dybvig, P., 1983. Bank runs, deposit insurance, and liquidity. J. Polit. Econ. 91, 401–419.

Donaldson, J., Piacentino, G., Thakor, A.V. 2015. Warehouse banking. Working Paper. Washington University in St Louis.

Fama, E., 1980. What's different about banks? J. Monetary Econ. 10, 10–19.

Giammarino, R., Lewis, T., 1988. A theory of negotiated equity financing. Rev. Financ. Studies 1, 265–288.

Hester, D.D., 1968. Stock and Mutual Associations in the Savings and Loan Industry: A Study of the Economic Implications of Conversions, Federal Home Loan Bank Board, Washington, DC.

Holmstrom, B., Tirole, J., 1997. Financial intermediation, loanable funds, and the real sector. Q. J. Econ. CX11-3, 663–691.

James, C., 1987. Some evidence on the uniqueness of bank loans. J. Financ. Econ. 19, 217–235.

Leland, H., Pyle, D., 1977. Informational asymmetries, financial structure, and financial intermediation. J. Financ. 32, 371–387.

Levine, R., 1996. Foreign banks, financial development, and economic growth. In: Claude, E., Barfield (Eds.), International Financial Markets: Harmonization versus Competition. The AEI Press, Washington, DC.

Levine, R., 2005. Finance and growth: theory and evidence. In: Aghion, P., Durlauf, S.N. (Eds.), Handbook of Economic Growth, Volume 1A, Elsevier Science, Amsterdam, pp. 865–934.

Lummer, S.L., McConnell, J.J., 1989. Further evidence on the bank lending process and the capital-market response to bank loan agreements. J. Financ. Econ. 25, 99–122.

Masulis, R.W., 1987. Changes in ownership structure conversions of mutual savings and loans to stock charter. J. Financ. Econ. 18, 29–59.

Mayers, D., Smith, Jr., C.W., 1986. Ownership structure and control: the mutualization of stock life insurance companies. J. Financ. Econ. 16, 73–98.

Mester, L.J., 1991. Agency costs among savings and loans. J. Financ. Intermed. 1, 257–278.

Mian, A., Sufi, A., 2010. Household leverage and the recession of 2007 to 2009. IMF Econ. Rev. 58, 74–117.

Michie, J., 2010. Promoting corporate financial diversity in the financial services sector. Policy Stud. 32.

Millon, M., Thakor, A., 1985. Moral hazard and information sharing: a model of financial information gathering agencies. J. Financ. 40, 1403–1422.

Myers, S., Majluf, N., 1984. Corporate financing and investment decisions when firms have information that investors do not have. J. Financ. Econ. 13, 187–221.

Rajan, R., 1992. Insiders and outsiders: the choice between informed and arm's length debt. J. Financ. 47, 1367–1400.

Ramakrishnan, R., Thakor, A., 1984. Information reliability and a theory of financial intermediation. Rev. Econ. Stud. 415–432, LI.

Rasmusen, E., 1988. Mutual banks and stock banks. J. Law Econ. 31, 395–421.

Sharpe, S., 1990. Asymmetric information, bank lending, and implicit contracts: a stylized model of customer relationships. J. Financ. 45, 1069–1087.

Song, F., Thakor, A.V., 2007. Relationship banking, fragility and the asset-liability matching problem. Rev. Financ. Stud. 20, 2129–2177.

Thakor, A., 2011. Sources of Capital and Economic Growth: Interconnected and Diverse Markets Driving U.S. Growth, monograph, *U.S. Chamber of Commerce*.

Part III

Identification and Management of Major Banking Risks

Chapter 4

Bank Risks

"You got to know when to hold 'em, know when to fold 'em. Know when to walk away and know when to run."

Kenny Rogers

GLOSSARY OF TERMS

Credit Risk The risk that a borrower will fail to satisfy the terms of their loan contract.
ERM Enterprise Risk Management, an integrative approach to risk management.
Interest Rate Risk The risk that interest rates will change, causing the value of the bank's net assets to change.
Liquidity Risk The risk that an asset holder is forced to sell at a price lesser than the value obtainable if time were not constraining.

INTRODUCTION

Risk is one of those concepts with a long history and diverse interpretations.[1] Because the future is always shrouded, risk is fundamental to all human endeavors. It is, however, central to banking. Think in terms of the "core competence" of a business, its special skill, knowledge, or repute that enables it to earn an enhanced return in the service of its clientele. Without this edge, the service becomes commoditized by competitors who bid down prices to the point where profit vanishes. This core competence imparts to the producer an advantage in managing a risk inherent in the production of a particular service or economic good. These are the *core risks* that correspond to *core competencies*. For example, General Motors and Toyota presumably possess a core competence in the manufacture of automobiles, which corresponds to a unique skill in managing risks of auto safety and the provision of reliable transportation. This is why the failure of ignition switches in General Motors vehicles and accelerator and braking systems in Toyotas cost lives and exposed both to costly risk-management failures. Reputational capital was dissipated, sales were lost, and lawsuits proliferated.

But what do we mean by risk? In the context of business, risk is the distillate of randomness in the process by which earnings are generated. This randomness may be mitigated through the application of a producer's core competencies, in which case the risk is voluntarily accepted, even sought, as a business decision; hence a "businessman's risk." Alternatively, the risk may be unavoidable, as in the case of a *force majeure* or an "act of god." In this case, the only protection may be insurance, if available, or leaving the industry. The risks in business are as varied as life itself. The businessman faces possible losses owing to flood, plague, fire, machine failure, worker alienation, sabotage, war, or capricious acts of government which destroy or appropriate property (sovereign risk). Shoe stores as well as financial intermediaries face all of these risks, but banks and other financial intermediaries specialize in financial contracting and thereby rely upon counterparties' performance under their contracts. Counterparty performance is rarely assured, but it can be improved with the application of banker skills. Hence, the mitigation, control, even avoidance, of banking risks.

This raises the question of which risks are retained by the institution and which are shifted to others via some form of insurance. Core risks, which firms manage at a profit are accompanied by ancillary risks, all the many other risks that arise in the business but for which the business possesses no special skills in processing. These ancillary risks will require management nonetheless if they are not to prove destructive. Ancillary risk will be shifted to others through various means – using capital or insurance markets, modifying operations, or *in extremis* avoiding lines of business. Not all ancillary risk is avoidable, however, if one is to remain in a particular business. A residual of ancillary risk will remain to be protected against with bank equity, but fortunately one firm's ancillary risk is likely to be another's core risk, giving rise to trade in risks that permit mitigation, enhance production and the general welfare.

Risk is central to financial intermediaries in the sense that clients see these institutions as fundamentally providing a risk-abatement service. Using our automobile example, customers are motivated by a need for safe and convenient transportation services. In contrast, financial intermediaries are asked to provide credit, liquidity, interest rate certainty, and various types of insurance all of which alleviate risks for customers. Indeed, these special financial risks define categories

---

1. Bernstein (1996) provides a fascinating history of risk. Powers (2014) indicates five distinct usages of the term.

S. I. Greenbaum, A. V. Thakor & A. W. A. Boot: Contemporary Financial Intermediation, Third edition. http://dx.doi.org/10.1016/B978-0-12-405196-6.00004-5

of intermediaries. Credit risk is the *sine qua non* of commercial banking, mortality risk defines life insurers, market (price) risk is the core competency of investment banking, and property risk is the bailiwick of casualty insurers. Liquidity is provided by any financial institution that absorbs more illiquid claims than it emits. Hence, deposits in banking are withdrawable on demand, yet are invested in illiquid loans. But liquidity is a fleeting, some say ephemeral, trait of claims that is often guaranteed, either explicitly or tacitly, by central banks through their control of the supply of legal tender, the money supply. When confronted with excess withdrawals, banks can borrow from their central banks.

Note that risk is *not* due to *variability per se,* but rather due to *uncertainty.* In an *ex post* sense, we often use the terms variability and uncertainty synonymously. However, in an *ex ante* sense, the two are quite distinct. We can have a cash flow, for example, that is known *for sure ex ante* to be 1, −100, 1,000, and 0 in years 1, 2, 3, and 4, respectively. Here we have considerable variability, but *no* risk as all cash flows are known beforehand. By contrast, a cash flow that can be either +1 or −1 with equal probability in each of the next 4 years has less variability but has risk.[2] Risk, then, is related to uncertainty or unpredictability.[3]

In the following pages, we will introduce three types of risk – credit, interest rate, and liquidity risk – that commercial banks are most noted for processing. Arguably, credit risk is core to banking and interest rate and liquidity risks are ancillary. Following the discussion of these quintessential banking risks, we will turn to the subject of managing risk from a more integrated or comprehensive viewpoint, the topic of Enterprise Risk Management, or ERM.

BASIC BANKING RISKS

Banks are no different from other firms in their exposure to core and ancillary business risks even if details differ across industries. Indeed, the specific nature of these risks define the industry. A bank's shareholders, or the shareholders of any other firm for that matter, bear risk when the firm's "assets" differ in some economically relevant way from its "liabilities."

Consider the steel fabrication company in Figure 4.1. The risk to the fabricator's shareholders arises substantially from the fact that the prices of raw and fabricated steel do not move in perfect unison. This exposes the fabricator's profit to margin fluctuations and results in risk for its shareholders. Note that this risk arises from a mismatch on the fabricator's balance sheet. Its liability (what it owes its suppliers for raw steel) differs from its assets (the present value of fabricated steel it expects to sell) because the prices of raw and fabricated steel are imperfectly correlated.

Now suppose the fabricator purchases raw steel in Japan, paying its suppliers in Japanese yen, and sells fabricated steel in the United States, receiving dollars from its customers. In this case, we see that the fabricator's balance sheet is further mismatched because of the different currencies involved. Consequently, its shareholders face currency risk (due to exchange rate variability in the yen and the dollar) in addition to the price risk they faced earlier. In general, liabilities are the present value of commitments to make payments where assets are the present value of expected receipts. Since the amount and timing of both positive and negative payments are uncertain, the net of the two gives rise to risk. Mismatches imply risks. This is a notion familiar from Chapter 2. Qualitative asset transformation involves mismatching the two sides of the balance sheet, which creates a particular form of risk.

What are the major mismatches for banks? These are described in Figure 4.2 where we see that a bank's representative assets (e.g., loans) and liabilities (e.g., demand deposits) are mismatched along three dimensions. First, the assets usually involve greater credit risk than the liabilities, that is, the bank's claim against the borrower is more likely to default than the depositor's claim against the bank. Second, the assets are usually of longer duration than the liabilities. For example, a

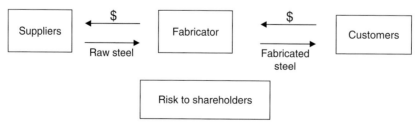

FIGURE 4.1 Risks Faced by a Domestic Steel Fabricator

---

2. For the havoc caused by not distinguishing between variability and risk, see Sprenkle and Miller (1980).

3. Another distinction is whether risk can be measured and quantified. Knightian uncertainty refers to risks where the distribution of outcomes are unknown, or cannot be specified. In cases where we know the distribution of outcomes, the outcome itself will be unknown. American Economist Frank Knight referred to this ignorance as risk as opposed to uncertainty.

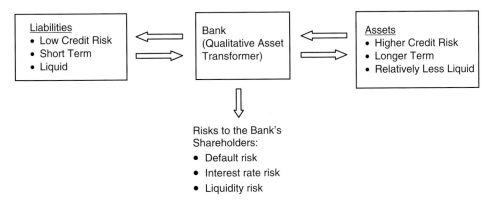

FIGURE 4.2 Major Mismatches for Banks

loan may have a 1-year maturity, whereas demand deposits are withdrawable on demand (negligible maturity). This creates interest rate risk. Third, a bank's liabilities are usually more liquid than its assets, that is, a depositor is able to withdraw funds at will, whereas the bank cannot call a performing loan at will, and the loan is unlikely to trade in an active secondary market. Hence, liquidity risk. We shall consider each of these risks in more detail as a prelude to subsequent chapters where we provide more technical detail.

CREDIT, INTEREST RATE, AND LIQUIDITY RISKS

Default, Credit, or Counterparty Risk

A party to whom you lend funds may fail to fully discharge the terms of the loan contract. For a bank, this is the risk that a borrower fails to deliver contractual payments on a timely basis. This risk is central to virtually all rental transactions, and as in the case of almost all insurance contracts, moral hazard is a key element of credit risk.

Banks can avoid credit risk by purchasing assets with little or no default risk, such as government securities or the debt of other triple-A rated borrowers. However, such a strategy will provide very little return over the bank's cost of borrowing and with other intermediation costs factored in, the bank's profit may be negative. Thus, certainty is achieved, but only at the cost of losses. The bank thus chooses assets with nontrivial default risk, and in doing so exploits its special ability (core competency) to mitigate default risk by resolving moral hazard and other informational problems. In Chapters 2 and 3, we indicated that banks enjoy a special advantage in screening and monitoring borrowers.

Cash flow variations arise from both physical and moral hazards. Banks screen borrowers in order to assess lending risk *ex ante*. This involves an analysis of the borrower's financial statements and other relevant financial and operating information. In this capacity, the bank is similar to a bond-rating agency. The bank's monitoring is designed to control moral hazard, which occurs after the loan is made. As we will see in some detail in the next chapter, the borrower is likely to have both an incentive and opportunity to take actions after a borrowing that increases the bank's risk exposure. This is why restrictive covenants are included in loan contracts. However, bank monitoring of borrower compliance with these covenants is required to control moral hazard. Thus, the efficiency with which the bank performs its basic functions is key to determining its own credit risk.

Moreover, loans are subject to management as a portfolio. A bank can further control its default risk by holding many loans with imperfectly correlated prospects and thereby diversifying. However, the bank's assessment, monitoring, and contract design skills are usually somewhat specialized leading to diversification within a limited set of industries.

Interest Rate Risk

If the firm's assets and liabilities are traded, they are subject to being revalued by the market. Any such revaluation, due to changes in either the level or structure of interest rates, is described as interest rate risk. For example, suppose a bank makes a 2-year, $1 million loan for which it charges 6% interest. It faces the choice of financing the loan with a 2-year deposit at 4% per annum, or with a 1-year deposit at 2% per annum. The former choice will result in $20,000 in interest earnings for each of the 2 years provided the loan performs as contracted. However, if the bank chooses the 1-year financing, it will earn $40,000 in year 1, but its earnings in year 2 will depend on the currently unknown 1-year interest rate prevalent a year from now. Should the 1-year rate remain unchanged, the bank will enjoy a second year of earning $40,000. And if the 1-year rate were to fall to 1%, management will do even better and record second-year earnings of $50,000. But interest rates may rise as well, as the S&L industry discovered to its chagrin in 1980–1981, and should the 1-year rate rise to, say, 6%, the bank will merely break even in year 2. This example illustrates both the essence of interest rate risk and its discretionary aspect. The risk could have been avoided with the choice of 2-year financing, assuming of course that 2-year financing was available. If not available, or if available only at a rate exceeding 6%, the bank need not have offered the borrower a 2-year, fixed-rate loan at 6%.

Indeed, the bank's cost of 2-year funds would no doubt have played a role in pricing the loan at the outset. Whatever, the bank's choice of loan pricing, it would have faced the choice of 1-year, 2-year, or *n*-year funding and that choice would, to a first approximation, determine the interest rate risk underwritten by the bank. Notably, whatever the duration (im)balance chosen by the bank, it could use derivatives to mitigate or amplify its interest rate risk. We will explore this alternative in greater detail in Chapter 5.

Another aspect of interest rate risk arises from loan prepayment uncertainty. The duration of a loan can be shortened at the borrower's discretion through premature repayment or through violation of loan contract terms, in which case the loan automatically "accelerates." Apart from defalcation, if market interest rates drop precipitously, the borrower is likely to exercise its option to refinance, in which case the loan is prepaid and a new one issued. This prepayment phenomenon makes expected duration shorter than term to maturity and it also transforms duration (im)balance into a random variable.

Liquidity Risk

The risk that an asset owner is unable to realize its full value at the time a sale is desired is the liquidity risk. In banking, the liquidity risk of a borrower is that the lender may choose *not* to renew a loan that a borrower wishes to renew. Similarly, the liquidity risk faced by a bank is that depositors may unexpectedly withdraw their deposits and the bank may be unable to replace them without impairing its net worth. This risk applies symmetrically to borrowers in their relationship to banks, as well as to banks in their relationship to depositors. Depositors are lenders to their bank. In general, liquidity risk is more than just withdrawal risk. It refers to the potential loss the seller of an asset incurs because the selling price falls below the fundamental value of the asset.

The most extreme manifestation of liquidity risk is that the asset owner is simply *unable* to sell at any positive price, that is, the only feasible selling price is zero – a kind of market failure. In credit markets, this phenomenon is known as *credit rationing,* whereby a borrower is refused credit regardless of price. We shall have more to say about credit rationing in Chapter 8, but for now it suffices to say that this phenomenon has long perplexed economists because it indicates an apparent suspension of price as the arbiter of allocations.

Liquidity risk has yet another interpretation. Asset markets vary widely in their development and level of activity. At one extreme, we have flea markets for "one-of-a-kind" items of dubious authenticity. At the other we have 24-hour around-the-world markets for currencies and government debt in which large quantities are traded at relatively low cost. More primitive and less active markets are typically characterized by large bid–ask spreads, defined as the difference between the price at which one can buy and simultaneously sell an asset at the same place. For example, you can *buy* a Treasury bill at an *ask* of $98½ and *sell* it at a *bid* of $98¼, in which case the bid–ask spread is $98½ –$98¼ = $¼. Bid–ask spreads range from small fractions of a percent of the asset's value for actively traded assets, to 6% or 7% for residential property. Still larger bid–ask spreads are evidence for infrequently traded, heterogeneous, and hard-to-value objects such as antique automobiles or works of art. Bid–ask spreads are often taken to reflect the liquidity in asset markets.

Illiquid assets are those for which "full value" is not readily realizable. That is, time and effort are required to capture the full value of an asset that is relatively illiquid.[4] Hence, a bank holding illiquid assets can find itself unable to redeem its liabilities on short notice, and the problem of managing the balance sheet against this eventuality is referred to as liquidity or cash management (cash is the asset with liquidity *par excellence*). The central bank, with its capacious lender-of-last-resort facility, was created to address those instances when the bank, having sound albeit illiquid assets, is unable to meet its withdrawals. The central bank provides other banks with crisis-avoiding liquidity by lending against illiquid but otherwise presumably sound earning assets. Indeed, the central bank was designed to socialize a portion of the bank's liquidity problem.

ENTERPRISE RISK MANAGEMENT

Earlier in this chapter, we took a first pass at explaining credit risk, interest rate risk, and liquidity risk as if they existed in distinct silos. That is how these risks are managed at many financial institutions. But in recent years, a more integrated approach to risk management has emerged. We now discuss this contemporary approach, beginning with a motivation for its adoption.

---

4. Were all assets perfectly liquid at all times in the sense that they can be sold with no delay at full value without incurring a cost, there would be no role for marketing.

The twenty-first century has become the Age of Risk Management owing to egregious business failures dating back to the 1980s. Enron, Tyco, WorldCom, Continental Illinois Bank, the Savings and Loan industry, and more recently, the Deepwater Horizon oil spill, the nuclear meltdown at Fukushima-Daiichi, and the massive failures during the 2007–2009 global financial crisis were widely diagnosed as risk-management failures. Even in cases such as Countrywide Mortgage, where venality allegedly played a role, an effective risk-management structure might have averted disaster. The commonality of risk-management deficiencies prompted an elevation of the standards of risk management that were codified in legislation (The Sarbanes-Oxley Act and Dodd-Frank Act are two American examples) and stricter public regulation in both Europe and the United States (see Office of the Comptroller of the Currency, 2014). Moreover, the credit-rating agencies, especially Standard and Poor's and Moodys, widely excoriated for their own conflicts and errors in evaluating toxic mortgage-backed securities, incorporated stricter risk management and governance standards among their assessment criteria. Various stock exchanges also added stricter governance and risk-management requirements.

Elevated risk-management standards became part of corporate governance mandating more accountability from public company boards of directors. Less than pristine but nonetheless widespread board practices became unacceptable. Boards dominated by management with the CEO serving as chairman, interlocking arrangements, backscratching practices, casual attendance, and preparation for board meetings were all common but unacceptable with the recent elevation of corporate governance standards. The growing formality, granularity, and integration of risk management became a central part of this elevation of governance standards.

Best practices in risk management came to be referred to as ERM. Put most simply, ERM unified and codified standards and practices of risk management. Earlier, risk management was common among large business organizations, but it was essentially fragmented and informal. Financial risk management involved capital budgeting and financing decisions with special attention to the debt–equity mix (financial leverage) and related decisions on hedging, diversifying, and shifting risk using the panoply of financial instruments including swaps, options, and futures. Other operating risks would be addressed elsewhere in the organization using insurance markets, hence, Errors and Omissions, Directors' and Officers', property, and life insurance. Still other operating risks were addressed by maintaining slack in the forms of inventory, inspection, and other seemingly redundant resources. Yet other bonds and guarantees would be exchanged to redistribute risks among the object organization, its customers, and its vendors. The fragmented nature of risk management within organizations was flawed in two ways. Its haphazard distribution within the organization was conducive to errors of omission and nowhere was risk integrated and pondered as a holistic challenge. Nowhere were all of the variegated exposures, mitigants, and residual risks aggregated to portray the overall risk of the business. This was the conundrum that ERM addressed.

Initially, ERM sought to summarize all material risks with a view to presenting a single-valued index to describe the total risk of the enterprise. However, it was quickly recognized that this was impractical given the extreme variety of risks and more particularly the wide differences in their measurability, especially among larger, more complex financial institutions. Financial risks are sometimes measurable unambiguously but operating risks less so. Some hazards are very destructive, but fortunately they occur only infrequently. Think of the BP Gulf of Mexico oil spill, for example. Estimated to have cost to the order of $50 Billion, but *ex ante* this exposure might easily have varied by an order of magnitude, or more. Likewise, oil spills are not uncommon, but one of the Deepwater Horizon's magnitude, and at sea, was unprecedented. Hence, its probability was *de minimis*, but difficult to evaluate with any precision. Its standard error of estimate might easily be an order of magnitude larger than its expected value! When many such risks are to be summed and compounded, errors magnify beyond the realm of practicality. This realization led ERM practitioners away from the idea that the summation of risks was merely a communication problem. Hence, the idea that ERM was to simply aggregate all business risks was superseded in favor of the more modest ambition to catalog and evaluate all material risks in order to focus on the most disastrous, the risks that threatened organizational sustainability. ERM would thereby reduce or ideally eliminate the errors of omission enabled by the fragmentation of risk management across the many venues within the organization.

ERM therefore is nothing more than a comprehensive and systematic approach to the management of material risks facing the organization. The ultimate goal is to avoid errors of omission that threaten organizational sustainability and the attendant punitive costs of receivership and reorganization, so-called bankruptcy costs. The key points in ERM are the recognition and prioritization of all material risks. Improved communication is central. Only therewith can risks be managed effectively.

Implementation of ERM varies across organizations and industries as risks vary according to environments. Thus, energy companies share a unique concern for environmental problems. Mining and construction companies tend to focus on worker safety issues. Social media issues are of particular concern to consumer-facing industries. Financial intermediaries are naturally inclined to give priority to financial risks, including credit (counterparty), liquidity, interest rate, and market risks. Global intermediaries tend to be exposed additionally to exchange rate risks.

TABLE 4.1 The OCC's Risk Taxonomy

Credit risk	Risk of borrower's failure to comply with loan contract terms (a more detailed discussion appears in Chapter 7)
Interest rate risk	Exposure to losses arising from duration imbalances on assets and liabilities (a more detailed discussion appears in Chapter 5)
Liquidity risk	Inability to realize full value on an asset owing to the need to monetize it on short notice (a more detailed discussion appears in Chapter 6)
Price risk	Risk of assets varying in market value
Operational risk	Risk of loss resulting from inadequate or failed internal processes, people and systems, or from external events
Compliance risk	Failure to adequately monitor and supervise, to ensure compliance with laws and regulations, both public and private, applicable to the organization
Strategic risk	Failure to achieve the goals of the enterprise's articulated strategy
Reputation risk	Risk of loss of brand equity or organizational credibility that jeopardizes the organization's ability to function successfully

These special concerns are reflected in the way organizations categorize their risk concerns, the taxonomy of risk. Overarching risks will often warrant a standing committee of the board of directors. Mining and airline boards may have safety committees. Consumer brands companies may have social responsibility committees. Commercial banks will have credit committees and often ALCO (Asset, Liability committees), the latter to focus on interest rate and liquidity risks.

To illustrate, the commercial bank risk taxonomy, shown in Table 4.1, is prescribed by the Office of the Comptroller of the Currency, the primary public regulator of nationally chartered banks in the United States.[5]

The above is specific to commercial banking as regulated by the OCC. Individual banks may add granularity, and banks outside the purview of the OCC may have somewhat different risk categories. Virtually all commercial banks would cover these categories in one way or another. However, once we leave the world of commercial banking, one could expect some variation in the taxonomy of risks. For example, life insurers sell annuities (protection against elongated life), life insurance (protection against premature death), and health and accident insurance (protection against debilitation). These longer-term liabilities generate cash flows that tend to fund investment-grade securities, mostly longer term debt of governments and corporations. Life insurance companies consequently process relatively little credit or counterparty risk, but have major exposure to mortality, morbidity, and longevity risk owing to their liabilities. A life insurer's major concerns would be the ability to predict life and morbidity expectancy among groups. Hence, pandemics, medical technology, and lifestyles would be major concerns. On the investment side, they are exposed to repricing in capital markets, but relatively little liquidity risk. Again, assets and liabilities are of relatively longer term and durations are better matched than among commercial banks. Life insurance company boards will be structured accordingly and Investment and Finance Committees will tend to replace the Credit and ALCO committees commonly found among commercial bank boards. Thus, public company board structures adapt to the hazards and exposures each find most threatening, quite as one might expect.

In the realm of financial intermediation, the type of risk an intermediary processes as its specialty is defining. It gives the intermediary its identity and we therefore refer to such risk as a core risk. The core risk derives from the intermediary's core competency. Thus, we have Table 4.2.

TABLE 4.2 The Core Risk is Defining

Institution	Core Risk/Competency
Commercial bank	Credit or counterparty credit risk
Investment bank	Market or price risk
Life insurer	Mortality/morbidity/longevity risk
Property/casualty insurer	Assorted physical or moral hazards

---

5. In the United States, banks are chartered both by the federal government and by the states. However, state chartered banks are regulated by the federal government via the Federal Deposit Insurance Corporation as well as the Federal Reserve System.

ERM and Tail Risks

Financial intermediaries create value by processing core risks. They possess special skills and financial capital that permit them to accept specific types of risk at lower net cost than other economic agents and they therefore profit in doing so. The commercial bank, for example, possesses special skills in designing and administering credit contracts. It can therefore offer credit at a lower cost to the borrower than can other lenders without such skills. The bank will therefore be motivated to accept as much credit risk as it can. The limits on its ability to accept credit risk inhere in its stock of specialized human capital (lending officers and other credit specialists) and financial capital. At any moment, these resources are fixed (adjustments in human and financial capital are costly, especially in the short term) and this limits the amount of credit the bank will desire to extend. Readily available inputs fix the amount of credit risk the bank can profitably absorb. To be sure, even with additional lending capacity at its disposal, the bank will not be indiscriminate in absorbing credit risk. It will choose those risks with which it is thoroughly familiar so that it can price the risk appropriately and control the risk via design and monitoring of the credit contract. It will also seek to control risk concentrations by establishing a maximum loan size according to borrower and lender circumstances and may also limit total loans according to industry and/or geography, as well as individual borrower characteristics. A key part of the bank's skills lie in discriminating among potential borrowers with a view to controlling credit losses.

The insurer possesses comparable skills, but these relate to selection, pricing, and administration of liabilities rather than assets. The life insurer chooses its mortality risk exposure with the same discriminating skill that the banks deploy with regard to borrowers. It too will expect to earn a profit on each life insurance contract it sells and will therefore wish to sell as many as possible, but it too confronts limitations imposed by the short-term fixity of human and financial capital and it needs to be mindful as well of concentrations of risk, even core risks.

In addition to the mundane management of core risk, the intermediary must be ever mindful of those special risks that are capable of overwhelming the organization, those referred to as existential or tail risks. They are existential because they threaten the organization's sustainability. They are tail risks because their impact is mercifully infrequent and therefore these hazards reside in the tail of the probability distribution. For the larger commercial bank, a protracted and severe economy-wide recession of the type realized in 1929 or 2007 illustrates such a risk. In such an event, credit risk diversification implodes as all credit risks become correlated and depositors queue up to withdraw their funds. The bank is no longer viable. In the case of the life insurers, an avian influenza pandemic could impose mortality losses, which again become correlated via contagion and could easily overwhelm its claims-paying ability jeopardizing viability. Such tail risks are the overarching concerns of ERM. Because these risks portend overwhelming outcomes – consider the Fukushima-Daiichi meltdown or the BP's Deepwater Horizon oil spill – and because their realization is so rare, they tend to be badly mispriced. They often are simply ignored.

Psychologists and behavioral economists have spent long hours pondering these tail phenomena and a rich literature on behavioral biases has been produced. We discuss some of them which are particularly relevant for understanding how individuals and institutions deal with tail risks.

Overconfidence

Overconfidence is said to be "the most robust finding in the psychology of judgment,"[6] or simply the "mother of all biases."[7] Investors and executives often resort to rules of thumb eschewing careful analysis and readily available information. Kahneman refers to this in his famous book *Thinking, fast and slow* as "fast thinking."[8] Overconfidence is also manifest in group dynamics in the literature on groupthink where it subsumes both excessive optimism and certainty regarding estimates. The resulting congenital optimism leads to underestimation of negative tail risks.

Anchoring (Focalism)

This decision-making bias stems from the undue impact of recency. Thus, a large loss suffered recently leads to overestimating the probability of a current loss and symmetrically the absence of a recent loss results in underestimation of current period exposure. In forming judgments, the decision maker is thus affected by the way in which information is presented and recency is one dimension of the presentation format. Taleb's famous book *Black Swan*, which maintains that unprecedented events tend to be underpriced, is a type of anchoring.[9] According to this hypothesis, extreme events, unless they

---

6. See DeBondt and Thaler (1995).
7. See Bazerman and Moore (2012).
8. See Kahneman (2011).
9. See Taleb (2010).

occurred recently, tend to be underestimated or even ignored. As an extreme occurrence fades into the past its probability of occurrence tends to not only be diminished, but also becomes increasingly biased toward zero.

Groupthink

Groupthink describes a particular group dynamics leading to a decision-making pathology. Occurring under widely observed conditions, groupthink can lead to a degradation of decision making whereby group members sacrifice their independence in favor of herding behavior.[10] A minority, often of one, becomes the decision maker often with impetuosity and unwarranted rectitude. A variety of groupthink symptoms could lead to overestimation of the group's power and morality, pressures toward uniformity of viewpoint and closed-mindedness. The conditions that give rise to groupthink include cohesiveness, isolation, lack of diversity, partiality of leadership, absence of procedural protocols, stress, recent failures, and moral dilemmas.

Groupthink has special relevance for tail risk because ERM ultimately devolves to boards of directors which are vulnerable to the preconditions of groupthink. Corporate boards often make a virtue of collegiality that can be readily conflated with cohesiveness. Similarly, boards are rarely paragons of diversity and their insulation from shareholders and other stakeholders has been widely chronicled in the proxy access literature as well as legislative and regulatory deliberations. Board decisions are often taken under stressful conditions and moral dilemmas are not uncommon. Decisions from the Enron board room prior to its collapses would have served well in illustrating the pathologies of group decision-making. Groupthink and its symptomatic optimism relate directly to tail risk assessments. According to this frame of thought, the probability of calamitous events is routinely underestimated by groups like public company boards or partners' committees.

Decision Biases and Discernibility

The decision biases essayed by psychologists and behavioral economists illuminate the puzzle of mispricing of negative tail risks. The common neglect of existential risks challenge our understanding, but they may nevertheless be rational given their diminutive probabilities of occurrence. However, there remains the inescapable impression that in many cases, neglect reflects errors of omission. Hence, the resort to decision biases and even fanciful metaphors like the Black Swan. One interpretation of apparent neglect is that many of these existential risks have very small probabilities, and it is difficult to distinguish indefinitely small probabilities from zero. There are many analogies in nature. For example, unaided by special instruments small particles are invisible and high-frequency sounds are inaudible. We require particle accelerators, microscopes, telescopes, hearing aids to enable perceptibility. Closer to home, high-frequency trading occurs too quickly for unaided human response. In each case, human senses are simply too coarse and sluggish to perceive certain phenomena without the aid of special instruments. Likewise, we can think of ERM, a formalized set of risk-management tools and protocols, as an instrument for heightening the perceptibility of low probability events. Let us turn now to the organizational and communicative innovations and other tools that in sum comprise the best practices of ERM.

Organizing for ERM

Implementation of ERM requires organizational adaptations with attendant costs. Adaptations are at the board and senior management levels as well as throughout staff and operating levels of the organization. Let us consider each of this triad of organizational changes.

The Board

Much of the work of the Board of Directors of a public company is performed by standing committees. Although formally advisory in large part, these committees explore issues in depth and make recommendations that the board most frequently will affirm without challenge. This is the product of a pervasive culture that is widely described as collegial. The culture is essentially cooperative and collaborative by necessity because boards tend to be severely time constrained so that when they become contentious they tend also to become inefficient or even dysfunctional. Boards therefore tend to reconfigure their membership when disputes severely inhibit decision-making. Endless time is rarely available for the tedious discovery of consensus.

---

10. The symptoms and conditions that follow are derived from Janis (1982).

Before the implementation of ERM, virtually all public company boards would have an Audit Committee, a Compensation Committee and a Nominating and Governance Committee. In addition to these three, there would be company- or industry-specific committees to reflect overarching board concerns. However, the introduction of a standing committee of the board charged with the responsibility for integrative risk management is culturally transformational. First, other committees tend to have responsibilities that are nonoverlapping, but the risk-management committee is charged with intersecting responsibilities. Its integrative responsibility forces it to monitor other committee's labors. Second, vetting business strategy is one of the few responsibilities of the board that tends *not* to be delegated to a subcommittee. It is so fundamental that it is commonly reserved to the committee of the whole. However, ERM is the functional complement to strategy. Whereas the latter seeks to discover organizational opportunities, the former explores hazards or constraints that limit opportunities. In this sense, risk management is the complement to strategy. Indeed, risk management in its integrative expression can be viewed as a facet of strategy and therefore the standing committee charged with ERM calls into question the nondelegability of the business strategy process. ERM enhances board accountability, but also subtly transforms corporate governance.

Executive Risk-Management Committee

The introduction of a standing committee of the board charged with risk management prompted the creation of an officer's risk-management committee, if only to dialog with the board on issues of organizational sustainability. When risk management was distributed among disparate operating units, operating risks might ultimately come to a Chief Operating Officer and financial risks might find their way to the Chief Financial Officer, but integration was lacking and errors of omission were too easily tolerated. Aggregation and prioritization of risks needed C-suite attention to organize, contextualize, and interpret information to be brought to the board. The board might monitor, supervise, and counsel, but execution and formulation remained a management responsibility. Thus, effective risk management requires a C-suite committee to support and complement the board's risk-management activities.

Office of the CRO

The final organizational innovation prompted by ERM is the Chief Risk Officer, along with the supporting staff. One aim of ERM is to facilitate the vertical and horizontal flow of risk information within the organization. Information is the lubricant of ERM and it falls to the CRO and staff to augment the communication of risk information. In addition to specialists and technicians, the CRO will often designate *rapporteurs* in each significant staff and operating unit within the organization. In addition to foster dialog, the CRO will have a basket of measurement and communication tools. Simulation and stress tests gauge the organization's ability to withstand various shocks, both external and internal. Shocks that might be simulated include fraud, hacking, disruptive technological advances, economy-wide economic disturbances, or *force majeure*, such as hurricanes, fires, or floods. Simulations ask whether such exigencies would threaten solvency, liquidity, or operating continuity. Thus, the CRO collects and processes risk information on an organization-wide basis for transmission to both the board and C-suite committees for their analysis and dispositive actions.

The Communication Triad

As in the case of the organizational triad, there is a corresponding triad of communication tools associated with ERM. They are the Risk Culture Statement, the Risk Register, and the Risk Appetite.

Risk Culture

Definitions of risk abound. Hence, risk management has a variety of interpretations. The Statement of Risk Culture seeks to dispel the ambiguity surrounding thought and behaviors. It seeks to promote a common understanding within the organization of terms, values, and practices regarding risk and its management. It is about getting *all* organizational members on the same page or initializing. This may seem a simple, even pedestrian, task. But in large, complex organizations where workers have disparate incentives, not to mention languages and educational preparations, fostering a common vocabulary can be a formidable challenge. Fostering shared values is a still more ambitious challenge. The content of the Statement of Risk Culture therefore normally includes a glossary of risk vocabulary, a risk taxonomy, and a statement of organizational purpose, values, and aspirations. Sometimes these are described as mission, vision, and values.

Culture is about shared values and the organization's ultimate purpose revolves around collaboration and cooperation. Large, complex organizations are constantly striving to align individuals in order to foster a common understanding and motivation. Many risk failures derive from a misalignment of values, and the purpose of the culture statement is to combat behavior that is alien to the organization. All too common rogue behavior in banking is well illustrated by the "London Whale" event at J. P. Morgan Chase, by the trading scandals at AIG involving Credit Default Swaps, at Societe Generale involving Jerome Kerviel, and at Barings Bank in Singapore involving Nick Leeson. The recent LIBOR conspiracy among banks centered in London is still another example. Such antisocial behavior has brought huge costs as well as ill-repute to the banking community. The culture statement seeks to articulate organizational fundamentals, both positive and normative, to avoid misunderstandings among members and thereby reduce the probability of behaviors that add unwanted (ancillary) risk to the organization. At the outset, a common vocabulary and framework for thinking about risk is required. Only thereafter can categoricals and calibrations be established that will set boundaries on individual's ability to accept risk on behalf of the organization. Only then can standards for supervision and monitoring of risks be effective.

Risk Register

The Risk Register records all perceived risks facing the organization. Information is collected from correspondents throughout the organization. Each operational unit and each staff unit will routinely report to the Office of the CRO on issues as perceived on the front line. Employees, customers, vendors, investors, the general public, capital providers, labor unions, environmentalists, and still other stakeholders all pose hazards and risk for the organization. All need to be monitored and those doing the monitoring need to report the emerging and material risks to the Office of the CRO so that all material risks can be and are memorialized in the Risk Register, the diary of all organizational exposures. The aim is to be comprehensive and detailed; encyclopedic.

The recording of exposures in the Risk Register will normally include a narrative describing each risk, its origin, imminence and idiosyncrasies. The narrative will normally be accompanied by calibration that estimates the gross risk (exposure) and its probability of realization, the steps taken to mitigate the risk, as well as a description of steps that might be taken to further mitigate (insurance, use of financial derivatives, and/or operational measures such as added supervision) and their costs, and finally an assessment of residual or remaining risks. The purpose is to record it all in order to minimize omission errors. This is a necessary first step toward managing material risks. Awareness is the antidote to all the decision biases and behavioral eccentricities – the groupthink, the congenital optimism, the anchoring – that predispose toward omission and even denial. Those who lead cannot claim ignorance if risks are systematically recorded and calibrated. The well-kept Risk Register will therefore compel managerial attention.

Risk Appetite

The Communication Triad is completed with the Risk Appetite, a written statement of the organization's risk preferences. The Risk Appetite is the normative counterpart to the Risk Register and is perforce the product of dialog between the board and senior management. The Risk Appetite statement is a detailed and granular interpretation of those risks that are core as well as those that are ancillary. Limitations on the acquisition of various types of risk are spelled out in detail. Those risks the organization will wish to absorb, mitigate, and minimize will be enumerated and calibrated. The Risk Appetite statement will thereby effectively configure the organization's balance sheet. Indicated also will be the sanctioned use of risk mitigants including natural hedges that give rise to basis risk (think of the life insurance company selling annuities) or financial derivatives such as swaps, options, or futures contracts, or operating measures such as added safety and security equipment or slack productive resources including inventories, back-up equipment, and extra space or diversification among vendors.

All of the available risk mitigants engender added operating costs and/or possibly new forms of exposure. Risk mitigation, like risk management more generally, is an often a subtle, nuanced process calling forth technical skills – financial, engineering, logistical, and scientific – that can challenge the mastery of both directors and managers. This knowledge void often leads to the employment of content specialists both within and outside the organization. When the need for granularity and detail confronts the limits of board and management mastery, consultants are often marshaled and the drafting of the Risk Appetite becomes an intellectual journey, an invaluable learning experience for both the board and senior management. A well-cast Risk Appetite statement not only distinguishes between core and ancillary risks, but also establishes absolute limits (tolerances) on various kinds of exposures. The Risk Appetite will likewise list those exposures that are to be avoided categorically (e.g., those that endanger customer or workers' lives). Thus, each and every variety of risk must be acknowledged along with the organization's willingness to tolerate it, given the culture, financial, and real resources of the organization. Each of the exposures enumerated will require quantification in both gross and net amounts, where mitigation intervenes. Moreover, covariation among risks must be acknowledged where these are material. Especially important can be the tendency for carefully constructed diversification to implode in times of economic stress or natural disaster. In the final analysis, the Risk Appetite is a comprehensive statement of risk preferences and tolerances which is ultimately confronted with the more positive or descriptive statement of extant risks enumerated in the Risk Register. These two statements, subordinate to the Risk Culture Statement, are counterparts and complements that shape organizational policy.

Other ERM Innovations

The Organizational and Communications Triads can be said to define ERM, but a host of more operational tools are important for characterizing and quantifying specific risks. For example, scenario planning contemplates future states of the world. Political, economic, regulatory, environmental forces are pondered and their possible impacts on the organization are examined. Likewise, war gaming considers competitive and technological drivers that may give rise to disruptive forces such as product obsolescence, severe price breaks, a fundamental shift in consumer tastes owing to successful marketing efforts of rivals. Typically, outside experts are convened for such deliberations and Delphic forums are organized to present outside-the-box thinking in preparation for the organization's uncertain future.

Simulations and stress tests represent another more quantitative tool. Mathematical models of the organization, its balance sheet, income and fund-flow statements are formulated in computer language and then perturbed, typically by altering parameters or exogenous variables, one at a time or in combination, to see how endogenous variables of special interest are affected. Monte Carlo methods are often employed so as to evaluate how random disturbances of varying likelihood will affect earnings, liquidity, capital, and other measures of organizational performance. Stress tests have become *de rigueur* for bank public regulators and management as well. These simulations ask how 1, 5, 10, and 20% credit losses might affect cash, income, and capital adequacy of the bank. Similarly, other variables such as demand deposits, investments, or fee income are perturbed to explore their implications for the key measures of bank performance. Simulations are based on mathematical models that incorporate simplifications and assumptions that are inevitably debatable. They have nevertheless proven enormously useful in guiding regulatory and management policy especially with regard to financial leverage, asset concentrations, and overall financial performance.

Dashboards are often employed as yet another tool of ERM. These are detailed displays, typically on computer screens, that track a variety of risk and performance measures in real time and therefore provide information in a readily accessible, compelling, and efficient manner. One can easily understate dashboard importance, but the assembly and presentation of disparate and complex information in a convenient real-time fashion represents a substantive advance in communication and this is a central aspect of ERM. The dashboard is an enhancement in risk discernibility for those most responsible for its management.

CONCLUSION

This chapter introduced the defining topic of risks in banking. The earlier half was devoted to an overview of the three types of risk that are fundamental to commercial banking. Credit risk, the risk that a borrower fails to fulfill the terms of a loan contract, we refer to as "core" in that it is the domain in which the bank most compellingly creates value and earns profit. In managing credit risk, the bank marshals its core competencies in attracting and screening loan applicants, designing, and administering loan contracts. These skills are quintessential in commercial banking and subsume qualifying customers, pricing, design of covenants, securing collateral, servicing payments, monitoring the borrower, enforcing terms, and renegotiating the loan when necessary.

In addition to credit risk, the bank inescapably sustains interest rate and liquidity risks. By financing illiquid loans with liquid deposits, and other short-term claims, the bank provides its customers with liquidity. The bank thereby absorbs illiquidity for which it presumably is paid a premium embedded in the spread between loan and deposit interest rates. In the normal course of business, this illiquidity is both sustainable and profitable. However, in times of financial stress, either local or more general, provision of this liquidity service exposes the bank to *en masse* withdrawals (runs) that can threaten bank viability. The central bank, a social contrivance with the ability to print money limitlessly, is designed to address this problem. However, the challenged bank typically will need appropriate collateral to borrow at the central bank, and in any case the bank's independence may be compromised if it requires central bank assistance. The liquidity service provided by the central bank is neither costless nor limitless.

Interest rate risk results from the duration of bank loans exceeding the duration of the deposits with which they are funded. The nominal term of demand deposits is obviously zero, but they do not display infinite turnover. Consequently, their effective term exceeds their nominal term. Whenever the duration (effective term) of assets differs from that of the liabilities with which they are funded, the bank is subject to gains (losses) arising from shifts or twists in the yield curve. This interest rate risk is integral to the basic lending function since the effective duration of assets and liabilities is characterized by an inescapable randomness. Interest rate risk arises from the bank's fundamental need to finance its credit extensions and both bank loans and deposits are terminated at the initiative of bank customers who are influenced by variations in market interest rates and a variety of other external events. It is the bank's inability to forecast bank runs and interest rate movements that leads us to treat these risks as ancillary. Unlike credit risks which are core and produce a regular surplus, ancillary risks evoke no special competencies and produce no regular surplus attributable to the bank. Both liquidity and interest rate risks are nevertheless integral to banking and must therefore be managed. Some would aver that since banks provide a liquidity service and earn a premium thereby, this should be considered a core service as well. But, without the central bank lender-of-last-resort facility, this service would be unsustainable. Thus, any net earnings the banks earn should be considered a transfer payment from the central bank. The liquidity service is therefore core to the central bank, and not the borrowing commercial bank.

The second part of our chapter on risk addresses ERM, a relatively recent innovation in response to spectacular business losses dating back to the mid-1980s that have been attributed to errors of omission in risk management. These oversights were ascribed to the traditional practices of risk management, particularly to their distributed, fragmented, and *ad hoc* design. Insurance was delegated to one locale, financial market hedging to another, operating decisions to yet another, and nowhere were these risks seen in their unity or totality. The traditional fragmentation of risk management encouraged neglect of interactions and other omissions.

ERM sought to correct this apparent weakness by providing a set of protocols or best practices that enhance vigilance and promote disciplined coordination in the management of all material business risks. ERM prescribes an organizational infrastructure, the Organizational Triad, comprising the standing board committee, the parallel C-suite committee, and the Office of the CRO. Each has defined responsibilities that in sum lubricate the flow of risk information within the organization and provides accountability for risk management at the very top of the organization. A corresponding Documentary Triad, including the Risk Culture Statement, the Risk Register, and the Risk Appetite, provide discipline by spelling out both perceived risks and risk preferences in both narrative and quantitative terms according to a common vocabulary. A variety of other tools are deployed to facilitate the measurement and communication of various risks, but the two triads can be said to broadly define ERM. Ultimately, ERM seeks to reduce errors of omission by facilitating the flow of risk information and localizing accountability for risk management at the pinnacle of the organization.

REVIEW QUESTIONS

1. Compare and contrast "core" and "ancillary risks."
2. What are the three major financial risks banks face?
3. What is ERM? Why is it needed?
4. What is "tail-risk"? Why have tail risks proved so difficult to manage?
5. How should ERM be organized within the bank? Explain the two triads of ERM.
6. What is risk culture and why is it fundamental?

REFERENCES

Bernstein, P.L., 1996. Against the Gods: The Remarkable Story of Risk. Wiley, New York.

Bazerman, M.H., Moore, A., 2012. Judgment in Managerial Decision Making, eighth ed. Wiley, New York.

DeBondt, W.F.M., Thaler, R., 1995. Financial decision-making in markets and firms: a behavioral perspective. Handbooks of Operations Research and Management Sciences, 9, 385–410.

Janis, I.L., 1982. Groupthink: Psychological Studies of Policy Decisions and Fiascoes, second ed. Cengage Learning, Boston, MA.

Kahneman, D., 2011. Thinking, Fast and Slow, first ed. Farrar, Straus and Giroux, New York.

Powers, M.R., 2014. Acts of God and Man: Ruminations on Risk and Insurance. Columbia Business School Publishing, New York.

Sprenkle, C.M., Miller, H.M., 1980. The precautionary demand for narrow and broad money. Economica 47, 407–421.

Taleb, N.N., 2010. The Black Swan: The Impact of the Highly Improbable, second ed. Penguin, London.

Chapter 5

Interest Rate Risk

"Bets on the directions of interest rates are like the little girl from the nursery rhyme with the curl on her forehead. When they are good, they can be very, very good, but when they are bad, as NCNB Corp. is now finding out, they can be horrid."

Kelley Holland: *American Banker,* March 20, 1990

GLOSSARY OF TERMS

Zero-coupon bonds Bonds that pay no coupon, so that the entire repayment to bondholders is at maturity.
Duration Measure of interest rate sensitivity where contrary to maturity timing of all cash flows is taken into account.
Immunization The act of insulating the institution from interest rate risk.

INTRODUCTION

In this chapter, we take a deep dive into interest rate risk. Our focus is on how it is measured and how it is managed by financial institutions. Since the concept of interest rate risk is used in conjunction with fixed-income instruments, we begin with a review of how fixed-income instruments (like loans and bonds) are valued. Then we analyze the *term structure of interest rates* and discuss how the term structure is determined under certainty and uncertainty. This is followed by a discussion of *duration* and *convexity*. These concepts are basic to the notion of interest rate risk, so it is important to understand them before we discuss interest rate risk in detail, which we do next. Selected interest rate risk-management techniques are subsequently examined. A case study is provided to illustrate some practical issues in interest rate risk management.

THE TERM STRUCTURE OF INTEREST RATES

Review of Fixed-Income Valuation

What is the current value of a $250 riskless cash flow to be received in 1 year? We solve this problem by using the principle of *riskless arbitrage.* In particular, to prevent riskless arbitrage – which is essential in an efficient capital market – the price of this riskless cash flow in equilibrium must be related to the prices of other riskless instruments. In particular, suppose we observe that a U.S. government bond that promises $100 in 1 year is currently trading at $94.56. From this, we can deduce that the implicit 1-year return on riskless instruments is 5.75% (since $94.56 [1 + 0.0575] = $100). Thus, we should be currently willing to pay $250/[1.0575] = $236.41 for the riskless promise to receive $250 in 1 year.

But what if the riskless cash flow is promised to us 2 years from now? Well, then we have to find a riskless instrument of similar maturity (2 years) and payment characteristics (the only promised payment is 2 years from now and there are no interim payments). Suppose we observe that United States government "pure-discount" bonds with a 2-year maturity that promises a $100 payment are currently trading at $88.58. Then we can deduce that the 2-year riskless yield, on an annualized basis, is given by, i_o^2, where $100 / [1 + i_o^2]^2 = $88.58. Solving this equation implies an annual two-period yield of $i_o^2 = 6.25\%$. Thus, we get Figure 5.1.

That is, even though both the year 1 and year 2 cash flows are riskless, they have different discount rates applied to them. Why?

The reason is that future one-period interest rates are expected to *increase.* In our example, we know that the 1-year riskless rate at date 0 is 5.75% and the 2-year riskless rate at date 0 is 6.25%. We can infer the 1-year riskless interest rate, i_1^1, that is expected to prevail in the future at date 1. We can solve for it as follows:

$$\$221.45 = \frac{\$250}{[1.0575][1 + i_1^1]}$$

which yields $i_1^1 = 6.75\%$. That is, the two-period rate of 6.25% is the *geometric average* of the successive one-period rates, 5.75% and 6.75%.

S. I. Greenbaum, A. V. Thakor & A. W. A. Boot: Contemporary Financial Intermediation, Third edition. http://dx.doi.org/10.1016/B978-0-12-405196-6.00005-7

	0	1	2
Cash flow		$250	$250
Discount rate		5.75%	6.25%
Present value at $t = 0$		$236.41	$221.45

FIGURE 5.1 Cash Flows and Discount Rates.

The Yield Curve

What we have seen above is that interest rates on debt instruments of different maturities are related through investors' expectations about future interest rates. A useful concept for this discussion is *yield to maturity* (YTM), which is defined as the internal rate of return that equates the present value of the future cash flows from a bond to the current market price of the bond. The annual two-period yield of $i_o^2 = 6.25\%$ that we derived above on a U.S. government bond is a YTM. The relationships among the yields on different bonds are summarized by the *term structure of interest rates.* We define the term structure of interest rates (or the yield curve) as the relationship between the YTM and the length of time to maturity for *debt instruments of identical default risk characteristics.* It is critical to equalize the default risk of the bonds whose yields we are comparing. For simplicity, we will confine our attention to bonds without default risk. Thus, the *YTM* on a bond with m periods to maturity is defined as the annualized equivalent discount rate at which the cash flows from the bond must be discounted m periods to arrive at its market price. Figures 5.2 and 5.3 show two different yield curves, each describing the yields of bonds that are identical, except in maturity. The yield curve in Figure 5.2 is for U.S. Treasuries and is upward sloping. It is the "on the run" curve, in which the *implicit* zero-coupon yield curve is interpolated from full-coupon bond prices. The yield curve in Figure 5.3 is for German

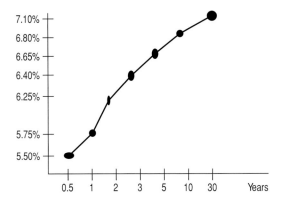

FIGURE 5.2 Risk-Free Term Structure for U.S. Treasury Securities as of July 25, 1996.

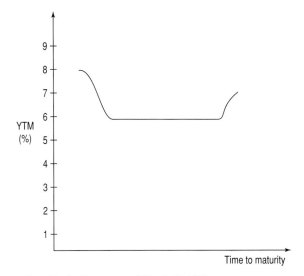

FIGURE 5.3 Yield Curve for Government Securities in Germany as of March 22, 1993.

government securities. It is cup shaped. For shorter maturities, this yield curve is "inverted," that is, the YTM decreases with maturity. For intermediate maturities, it is virtually flat, that is, the YTM is almost independent of maturity in this range. And for longer maturities, the yield curve slopes upward, that is, the YTM rises with maturity.

What determines the shape of the yield curve? For simplicity, we will examine this question first in a world of perfect certainty. Uncertainty will be dealt with subsequently. In both cases, we assume that a financial market equilibrium precludes *riskless arbitrage.*

Yield Curve Determination Under Certainty

The Basic Model

Let P_t^m and i_t^m be the price and YTM, respectively, at time t of a bond of maturity m years. We assume the unit of time is 1 year, and all bonds are traded, so that prices are available from the market. As an illustration, we will examine the yield relationship between two bonds, one with a maturity of 1 year and the other with a maturity of 2 years. For simplicity, we will assume that each is a zero-coupon (pure-discount) bond and has a face value, F, of \$1. A zero-coupon bond makes a single promised payment (often called a balloon payment) at maturity, and no payments prior to that. Now, the YTM on the 1-year bond at the present time ($t = 0$), i_0^1, is the internal rate of return that discounts the \$1 face value over one period to equal the current market price of the bond.

$$P_0^1 = \frac{F}{1+\text{YTM}} = \frac{1}{1+i_0^1}. \tag{5.1}$$

Similarly, the YTM on the 2-year bond at $t = 0$, i_0^2, is the internal rate of return that discounts the \$1 face value over two periods to equal the current market price of the bond.

$$P_0^2 = \frac{F}{(1+\text{YTM})^2} = \frac{1}{(1+i_0^2)^2}. \tag{5.2}$$

Now suppose we take \$1 today and invest it in the 2-year bond. Because it sells at $\$P_0^2$, we will be able to buy $1/P_0^2$ units of it. Then, 2 years from now (at $t = 2$), our investment will fetch us a (sure) payoff equal to the number of bonds we have bought ($1/P_0^2$) times the face value of each bond (\$1). That is, our payoff at $t = 2$ will be [using Equation (5.2)]

$$1/P_0^2 = (1+i_0^2)^2. \tag{5.3}$$

Another use of our \$1 would be to invest it in the 1 year bond right now. We will be able to buy $1/P_0^1$ units of it at $t = 1$, then our payoff will be the number of bonds we have bought ($1/P_0^1$) times the face value of each bond (\$1). That is, our payoff at $t = 1$ will be [using Equation (5.1)]

$$1/P_0^2 = (1+i_0^1). \tag{5.4}$$

What shall we do with this money at $t = 1$? Invest it, of course! Suppose we invest in another zero-coupon, \$1 face value, 1-year bond that will be issued a year from now (or equivalently, a multiyear bond with 1 year left to mature). Since we are currently in a world of certainty, we should be able to forecast the price, P_1^1, of this 1-year bond (issued 1 year from now) with perfect accuracy. With $\$(1+i_0^1)$ to invest, we should be able to buy $(1+i_0^1)/P_1^1$ units of this bond. Note that the YTM, i_1^1, of this bond is the internal rate of return that discounts the \$1 face value over one period to equal the current bond market price, and is thus

$$P_1^1 = 1/(1+i_1^1). \tag{5.5}$$

Since we have bought $(1+i_0^1)/P_1^1$ units of this bond at $t = 1$, and the face value of each unit is \$1, our payoff at $t = 2$ will be [using Equation (5.5)]

$$[(1+i_0^1)/P_1^1]\times 1 = (1+i_0^1)\,(1+i_1^1). \tag{5.6}$$

The Absence of Arbitrage and the Yield to Maturity Relationship

Equilibrium in this market requires that there be no riskless arbitrage opportunities. That is, we should not be able to do better at $t = 0$ with either the strategy of investing into the 2-year bond or investing in the 1-year bond and rolling over the proceeds into another 1-year bond. Both strategies should yield identical proceeds at $t = 2$ since we started out in each with identical \$1 investments. That is, the expressions in Equations (5.3) and (5.6) should be equal. This gives

$$(1+i_0^2)^2 = (1+i_0^1)(1+i_1^1),$$

or

$$(1+i_0^2) = \sqrt{(1+i_0^1)\,(1+i_1^1)}. \tag{5.7}$$

Thus, the (annualized) YTM on the 2-year bond should be the *geometric average* of the YTMs on two successive bonds, each of maturity 1 year. This relationship is sometimes known as the *expectations hypothesis,* because it says that the yield on a long-term bond should be based on the expectations of investors about the yields on a sequence of short-term bonds. The general form of Equation (5.7) for any arbitrary number of years, n, is

$$(1+i_0^n) = \sqrt[n]{(1+i_0^1)\,(1+i_1^1)\,(1+i_2^1)\,(1+i_3^1)\ldots(1+i_{n-1}^1)} \tag{5.8}$$

Spot Rates and Forward Rates

The future yields, i_1^1, i_2^1, i_3^1, are known as *forward* rates, whereas the current yields, $i_0^1, i_0^2, \ldots, i_0^n$, are known as *spot* rates. Note that the forward rate for any period in the future can be defined with the help of a ratio of bond prices. To see this, solve Equation (5.7) to obtain

$$i_1^1 = \frac{(1+i_0^2)^2}{(1+i_0^1)} - 1.$$

Now, substituting for $1+i_0^1$ and $1+i_0^2$ from Equations (5.1) and (5.2) respectively, we get

$$i_1^1 = \frac{P_0^1}{P_0^2} - 1.$$

Similarly, we can obtain $i_2^1 = \dfrac{P_0^2}{P_0^3} - 1$, and so on. A one-period-hence forward rate can thus be thought of as the interest rate on a one-period loan starting at some future point in time. An n-period-hence forward rate is the interest rate on an n-period loan starting at some future point in time. The general formula for the YTM on a bond of maturity n periods to be issued t periods from now (i.e., the n-periods hence forward rate for time t) is $i_t^n = \sqrt[n]{\dfrac{P_0^t}{P_0^{n+t}}} - 1$. We can see now how the shape of the yield curve is determined. If investors believe that short-term interest rates will keep rising, then $i_0^1 < i_1^1 < i_2^1 < \ldots < i_{n-1}^1$, so that $i_0^1 < i_0^2 < i_0^3 < \ldots < i_0^n$, and the yield curve will be upward sloping. On the other hand, if investors believe that short-term interest rates will keep falling, then the yield curve will be inverted, or downward sloping. Given a set of bond prices, we can compute the implied forward rates in the market as we do in the example below.

Example 5.1

Suppose there are three zero-coupon bonds that are identical in all respects except maturity. Each bond has a face value of \$10 million. One of them matures a year from now and is currently selling at \$9,523,809. The other matures 2 years from now and is currently selling at \$8,734,386. The third matures 3 years from now and is currently selling at \$7,513,148. Compute the YTM for each of the three bonds, plot the yield curve (assuming that you can interpolate smoothly), and compute the available forward rates.

Solution

We will solve this problem in two steps. First, we will use the specified bond prices to compute the various date-zero YTMs. Second, we will calculate the implied forward rates for different maturities by computing ratios of bond prices.

Step 1 Using our previous analysis, we have

$9,523,809 = 10,000,000 / (1+i_0^1)$, which gives $i_0^1 = 0.05$ or 5%.

Similarly,

$8,734,386 = 10,000,000 / (1+i_0^2)^2$, which gives $i_0^2 = 0.07$ or 7%. And,

$7,513,148 = 10,000,000 / (1+i_0^3)^3$, which gives $i_0^3 = 0.10$ or 10%.

Step 2 We will now compute the implied forward rates. The data given to us are that
$P_0^1 = \$9,523,809$, $P_0^2 = \$8,734,386$, and $P_0^3 = \$7,513,148$. Now,

$$
\begin{aligned}
i_1^1 &= \frac{P_0^1}{P_0^2} - 1 \\
&= \frac{9,523,809}{8,734,836} - 1 \\
&= 9.03809\%,
\end{aligned}
$$

and

$$
\begin{aligned}
i_2^1 &= \frac{P_0^2}{P_0^3} - 1 \\
&= \frac{8,734,836}{7,513,148} - 1 \\
&= 16.25469\%.
\end{aligned}
$$

Notice that the geometric mean of 5%, 9.03809%, and 16.25469% equals the current 3-year yield of 10%. Likewise, the geometric mean of 5% and 9.03809% equals the current 2-year yield of 7%. In addition, the geometric mean of the current 2-year yield of 7% and the 1-year rate 2 years hence of 16.25469% will equal the current 3-year-rate of 10%. Thus, all possible 3-year investment strategies should produce identical returns. Our analysis so far has proceeded under the assumption of certainty. We now introduce uncertainty about future interest rates.

THE LURE OF INTEREST RATE RISK AND ITS POTENTIAL IMPACT

As we saw in our earlier examples, yields of bonds of different maturities can be different. In Figure 5.1 we depicted a case in which the 1-year yield is 5.75% and the 2-year annual yield is 6.25%. That is, if we buy the 1-year bond at date 0 and hold it until date 1, we get a return of 5.75% and if we buy the 2-year bond at date 0 and hold it until maturity at date 2, it will give us a return of 6.25% per year. The difference in returns, 6.25% − 5.75% = 0.5%, is called the *term premium*. We may define an *m-period term premium* as the difference between the expected return on holding for one period of a bond with maturity $m + 1$ periods at the time of purchase and the return on a bond of a one-period maturity. If term premiums are positive, then longer-term bonds should have higher expected returns. In a world of certainty, the term premium reflects simply investors' expectation that future interest rates will be higher than current rates. But in a world of uncertainty – in which interest rates fluctuate randomly – the term premium has two components: one reflecting *expected* changes in future interest rates, and the other reflecting a premium demanded by risk-averse investors for bearing the risk (in holding longer maturity bonds) that future changes in interest rates will deviate from what is expected (this can be viewed as a premium for bearing interest rate risk).

The term premium is usually positive. This can be seen in Figure 5.4, which depicts the estimated 10-year term premium in the United States Treasury Bond market. This figure shows that term premiums have declined somewhat since 1990, but are highly volatile. If it does decline on average, it suggests a greater willingness on the part of investors to hold longer maturity securities. Given investor risk aversion, this may be indicative of a lower perceived macroeconomic volatility. Alternatively, risk aversion may have come down.

The term premium is usually positive and creates a strong inducement for banks to mismatch their asset and liability maturity structures. By holding assets of longer maturities than their liabilities, banks can profit from a positive term premiums. This is the lure of interest rate risk. But this is risky too, as the following example shows.

Example 5.2

Suppose a bank's only asset is a 5-year United States government zero-coupon bond that promises to pay $100 million in 5 years. Its only liability is a 1-year $100 million certificate of deposit (CD). The YTM on 1-year riskless instruments is 5.75% and on 5-year riskless instruments is 6.65%.

This bank's balance sheet in economic value terms will look like this:

Economic Value Balance Sheet (in millions)

Assets		Liabilities and Equity	
Government bond	$72.48	CD	$70.92
		Equity	$1.56
Total	$72.48	Total	$72.48

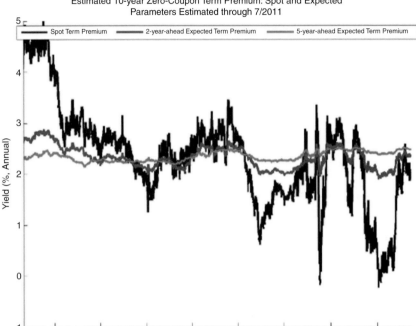

FIGURE 5.4 United States – Estimated 10-Year Term Premium in the U.S. Treasury Market, 1993–2012. *Durham (2014), More on U.S. Treasury Term Premiums: Spot and Expected Measures, Federal Reserve Bank of New York, Staff Reports, no 658, revised, May 2014. – Exhibit 1, follows page 15 in that report.*

The economic value of the government bond is $72.8 = \dfrac{\$100}{(1.0665)^5}$ whereas the economic value of the CD is $70.92 = \dfrac{\$100}{1.0575}$.

The economic value of the bank's equity is a plug and it arises from the term premium represented by the difference in the rates or return on the bank's assets and liabilities. As long as interest rates do not change, the bank will earn the term premium.

Now what happens to the value of the bank's equity if there is a parallel shift of the yield curve and all yields increase by 100 basis points (b.p.s)? The new economic value balance sheet now looks like this:

Assets		Liabilities	
Government bonds	$69.17	CD	$70.26
		Equity	–$1.09
Total	$69.17	Total	$69.17

The new economic value of the government bond is $\dfrac{\$100}{[1.0765]^5} = \$69.17$ and the new economic value of the CD is $\dfrac{\$100}{[1.0675]} = \$70.26$.

The equity value, which is a plug, is value of assets – value of liabilities = $69.17 –$70.26 = –$1.09.

So we see that even though there was only a modest and equal increase in all interest rates, the economic value of equity fell from $1.56 million to a negative $1.09 million. Why? The reason is that the long-term cash flow represented by the bank's asset has a value that is much more sensitive to interest rate changes than the short-term cash flow represented by the bank's liability. Thus, banks that are typically mismatched in a manner similar to our hypothetical bank – with assets of longer maturity than liabilities – experience a decline in their equity values when interest rates rise.

The existence of a positive term premium has profound implications for banks. On the one hand, it allows banks to profit from a maturity mismatch on their balance sheets. On the other hand, it imposes interest rate risk on banks. So, while the lure of profiting from maturity mismatching can be quite strong, the risk of mismatching can be ruinous, as many in S&Ls and Orange County, CA, found out to their chagrin.

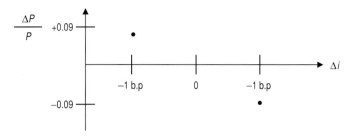

FIGURE 5.5   Price Changes for one b.p. Change in Yields.

Could the bank have hedged its shareholders against interest rate risk by matching maturities? Not necessarily. The reason is that the banks need to match the *exact timing* of their asset and liability cash flows. Shorter-term cash flows behave differently than longer-term cash flows. To hedge its shareholders against interest rate risk, the bank must understand something about how asset and liability values will change, *given* changes in market yields. That is, the bank's shareholders will be protected against interest rate movements if, *for a given change in market yields,*

Percentage Price Change in Assets = Percentage Price Change in Liabilities

or

$$\left.\frac{\Delta P_A}{P_A}\right|_{\Delta_i} = \left.\frac{\Delta P_L}{P_L}\right|_{\Delta_i} \tag{5.9}$$

where ΔP_A = change in price of asset, P_A = price of asset, ΔP_L = change in price of liability, P_L = price of liability, and Δ_i = change in interest rate.

Let us now examine the value $\left.\frac{\Delta P}{P}\right|_{\Delta_i}$.

Consider first a *flat* term structure, with $i = 10\%$ and a 10-year zero-coupon bond with \$100 par. How will the price of this bond change if yields (interest rates) change by one b.p.? (Figure 5.5).

$$P(\text{no change}) = \frac{\$100}{(1.10)^{10}} = \$38.5543$$

$$\left.\frac{\Delta P}{P}\right|_{\Delta i=+0.0001} = \frac{\$100}{(1.1001)^{10}} = \$38.5193$$

$$\left.\frac{\Delta P}{P}\right|_{\Delta i=-0.0001} = \frac{\$100}{(1.10009)^{10}} = \$38.5894$$

$$\left.\frac{\Delta P}{P}\right|_{\Delta i=+0.0001} = -0.09\%$$

$$\left.\frac{\Delta P}{P}\right|_{\Delta i=-0.0001} = 0.09\%$$

DURATION

The Inappropriateness of Maturity for Coupon-Paying Bonds

We saw that relative price change ($\Delta P/P$) is related to the yield change (Δi). A mathematical relationship between $\Delta P/P$ and Δi given by *duration,* which is related to but different from maturity. The *maturity* of a bond tells the investor how long he must wait before receiving the terminal cash flow of the bond, or alternatively when the bond will mature or be redeemed. The maturity of a bond, however, does not give the investor all the needed information about the price volatility of the bond, unless it is a zero-coupon bond. This is because bonds of the same maturity can differ in their coupon payments through time. Moreover, in addition to coupon payments, bonds often provide other cash flows before maturity, such as amortizations. A bond that makes relatively large coupon payments early or amortizes rapidly has a shorter effective maturity than a bond that makes most of its large coupon payments late in the life of the bond. The reason is that the former generates much of its total cash flow well before its actual maturity date, whereas the latter skews its cash flows closer to its actual maturity date. We should, therefore, expect different sensitivities of the prices of these bonds to changes in interest rates. Note that we are now shifting our focus from zero-coupon bonds to bonds that may or may not pay coupons. All bonds we consider in our analysis are *nonamortizing,* that is, only coupon payments are received prior to maturity, and the entire principal is paid at maturity.

Duration is the Answer

Duration, which is calibrated in the same temporal units as maturity, captures the timing of *all* cash flows generated by a bond, not just the terminal cash flow, and therefore is a more sophisticated measure.[1] The duration of a bond is defined as the weighted average of the times to arrival of *all* scheduled future payments of a bond, where the weight attached to each payment reflects the relative contribution of that payment to the value of the bond. That is, each weighting factor is the present value of that payment divided by the present value of all payments of the bond. Consider a bond with N years to maturity, coupon payments $C_1, C_2,\ldots C_N$ where C_t is the coupon paid t years from now, and a principal (balloon) payment of B_N made at maturity. Let the term structure be *flat,* with i as the annual yield for all cash flows. Then the price of the bond at $t = 0$ is the present value of future payments:

$$P = \frac{C_1}{1+i} + \frac{C_2}{(1+i)^2} + \ldots + \frac{C_N + B_N}{(1+i)^N} \tag{5.10}$$

To see how P is related to i, let us take a derivative

$$\frac{dP}{di} = \frac{-C_1}{(1+i)^2} + \left[\frac{-2C_2}{(1+i)^3}\right] + \ldots + \left[\frac{-N[C_N + B_N]}{(1+i)^{N+1}}\right]$$

or

$$dP = \frac{-di}{1+i} + \left[\frac{C_1}{1+i} + \frac{2C_2}{(1+i)^2} + \ldots + \frac{N(C_N + B_N)}{(1+i)^N}\right]$$

Dividing both sides by P gives us:

$$\frac{dP}{P} = \frac{-di}{1+i}\left[\frac{\frac{C_1}{(1+i)} + \frac{2C_2}{(1+i)^2} + \ldots + \frac{N(C_N+B_N)}{(1+i)^N}}{\frac{C_1}{(1+i)} + \frac{C_2}{(1+i)^2} + \ldots + \frac{(C_N+B_N)}{(1+i)^N}}\right]$$

We can write this as:

$$\frac{dP}{P} = \frac{-di}{(1+i)}\left[1\left\{\frac{\frac{C_1}{(1+i)}}{\frac{C_1}{[1+i]} + \frac{C_2}{[1+i]^2} + \ldots + \frac{[C_N+B_N]}{[1+i]^N}}\right\} + 2\left\{\frac{\frac{C_2}{(1+i)^2}}{\frac{C_1}{[1+i]} + \frac{C_2}{[1+i]^2} + \ldots + \frac{[C_N+B_N]}{[1+i]^N}}\right\}\right.$$
$$\left. + \ldots + N\left\{\frac{\frac{C_N+B_N}{[1+i]^N}}{\frac{C_1}{[1+i]} + \frac{C_2}{[1+i]^2} + \ldots + \frac{[C_N+B_N]}{[1+i]^N}}\right\}\right] \tag{5.11}$$

The numerator in each term represents the time of arrival, 1, 2,..., N, of a payment that is weighted by the present value of that payment. In the denominator, we have the present value of the sum of all cash flows promised by the bond, which should be its current market price, P. Define

$$w_t \equiv C_t / (1+i)^t \text{ for all } t = 1,\ 2,\ldots,N-1 \tag{5.12}$$

as the coefficient attached to the payment to be received t years from now.[2] Let $w_N \equiv (C_N + B_N)/(1 + i)^N$. Then, using Equation (5.12) and the definition of P, we can write Equation (5.11) as

$$\frac{dP}{P} = -\frac{di}{[1+i]}\left[\frac{(w_1 + 2w_2 + 3w_3 + \ldots + Nw_N)}{P}\right] \tag{5.13}$$

---

1. This concept was introduced by Macaulay (1938). Our treatment relies in part on generalizations by Fisher and Weil (1971), and Ingersoll et al. (1978).
2. Each w_t is appropriately viewed as a "maturity coefficient" rather than a "weight" because the w_t's do not add up to one. However, each w_t divided by the denominator in Equation (5.13) is a weight, that is, the $\hat{w}_t$'s in Equation (5.14) are weights.

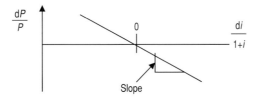

FIGURE 5.6   Duration

This equation gives the relationship between prices and yields. A fixed-income instrument's duration is its "price elasticity" and it relates percentage price changes to changes in yields. See Figure 5.6.

Duration is the negative of the slope of the relationship shown in Figure 5.6. Thus, if we know the duration of an asset, we can predict its price sensitivity to a given change in yield. We can write:

$$\frac{dP}{P} = -D\left[\frac{di}{1+i}\right]$$

where D is duration. Defining $\hat{w}_t \equiv w_t / P$, we can write:

$$D = \sum_{t=1}^{N} t\hat{w}_t. \tag{5.14}$$

Thus, Equation (5.14) says that, to arrive at the bond's duration, we compute a weighted average of the times to arrival of its different promised payments, where the weight attached to each time to arrival is equal to the present value of the cash flow associated with that time to arrival divided by the price of the bond.

We can think of the duration of a bond then as a metric for the average number of years a holder of that bond must wait before recouping his investment. For risk-assessment purposes, duration is a much more meaningful attribute of a bond than its maturity. The shorter the duration of a bond, the lower is its price volatility. Holding everything else (including the current value or price of the bond) fixed, an increase in coupon payments reduces duration, and an increase in maturity increases duration. A zero-coupon (pure discount) bond has the longest duration among bonds of the same maturity; indeed, its duration is equal to its maturity. These bonds have recently become very popular. One significant advantage that they offer is that the average annual return they offer over the maturity period (the YTM) is known with certainty (in absence of default) in advance; that is, since the cash flows they generate are at maturity, there is no reinvestment risk. With coupon bonds, the realized YTM will depend on the future interest rates at which the coupons can be reinvested. However, zero-coupon bonds are also very risky because of their longer duration and consequent higher price volatility. When interest rates are falling, the holder of a zero-coupon bond realizes a greater price appreciation than the holder of an otherwise similar coupon-paying bond. But when interest rates rise, the holder of the zero-coupon bond also experiences a greater price decline! Let us see the effect of duration at work in the following simple illustration.

Duration at Work: Some Numerical Examples

The following key points about duration are worth noting:

1. Duration is denominated in years. It is a measure of the "weighted average life" of the bond.
2. Longer maturity assets have longer durations, *ceteris paribus*.
3. For zero-coupon bonds, duration = maturity. For all other bonds, duration < maturity. Holding everything else fixed, an increase in the coupon decreases duration.
4. The duration of a floating-rate instrument ("floaters") where the coupon changes with interest rates is the time until the next repricing.

Example 5.3

Consider an interest rate environment in which the one-period annual yield is 10% and the two-period annual yield is 9.7824%, and suppose we have two riskless bonds (each with a 2-year maturity) that are identical in all respects except that one is a zero-coupon bond that matures 2 years from now and promises a balloon payment of $1109.60, where the other is a bond that will pay a coupon of $100 1 year from now and another coupon of $100 plus a balloon payment of $900 2 years from now. Compute the durations of these two bonds.

Solution

We solve this problem in three steps. First, we compute the current prices of the zero-coupon bond and the coupon-paying bond using the yield data provided. We find that both are equally priced. Second, we calculate the duration of the coupon-paying bond, which is less than that of the zero-coupon bond. Finally, in Step 3 we compute the variances of possible price changes (due to random interest rate movements) and show that the variance is higher for the zero-coupon bond.

Step 1 The discount rate for one period cash flows is 10% and the discount rate for two-period cash flows is 9.7824%. Thus the price of the zero-coupon bond is

$P_0 = 1109.6/(1.097824)^2 = \$920.64$.

Similarly, the price of the coupon bond is

$P_c = [[100/1.10] + [1000/(1.097824)^2]] = \$920.64$.

Step 2 The above calculation shows that both bonds are equally priced. The duration of the zero-coupon bond is its maturity, which is 2 years. The duration of the coupon-paying bond is

$$D = \hat{w}_1 + 2\hat{w}_1$$

where $\hat{w}_1 = [100/1.10]/920.64 = 0.09875$ and $\hat{w}_2 = [1000/(1.097284)^2]/920.64 = 0.90125$.

That is, 9.875% of the value of this bond is attributable to its first period coupon and 90.125% of its value is attributable to the sum of its second period coupon and principal. Hence, $D = 0.09875 + 2(0.90125) = 1.90125$ years.

---

5. The duration of a bank's "core deposits" is typically taken as zero.
6. The duration of a portfolio is the weighted average of the durations of all the assets in the portfolio.

Using Duration to Measure the Impact of Interest Rate Shocks on a Bank's Equity

Value

Recall that a bank's balance sheet can be expressed as

$$A = L + E$$

where A = assets, L = liabilities, and E = equity. Then, given a change in yield Δi, the balance sheet changes can be expressed as:

$$\Delta A = \Delta L + \Delta E \tag{5.14}$$

Now:

$$\frac{\Delta A}{A} = -D_A\left[\frac{\Delta i}{1+i}\right]$$

which implies

$$\Delta A = -D_A[A]\left[\frac{\Delta i}{1+i}\right] \tag{5.15}$$

Similarly,

$$\frac{\Delta L}{L} = -D_L\left[\frac{\Delta i}{1+i}\right]$$

which implies:

$$\Delta L = -D_L[L]\left[\frac{\Delta i}{1+i}\right] \tag{5.16}$$

Assuming that the yield shock to the assets is identical to the yield shock to the liabilities, we can substitute Equation (5.15) and (5.16) in Equation (5.14) to obtain:

$$\Delta E = \left[-D_A[A]\frac{\Delta i}{1+i}\right] - \left[-D_L[L]\frac{\Delta i}{1+i}\right]$$

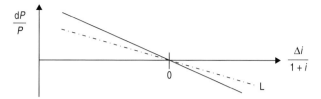

FIGURE 5.7   Asset and Liability Duration for Traditional Bank

which implies:

$$\Delta E = \left[\{-D_A[A] + D_L[L]\} \left[\frac{\Delta i}{1+i} \right] \right]$$

or

$$\Delta E = -\left[D_A - D_L \left\{ \frac{L}{A} \right\} \right] [A] \left[\frac{\Delta i}{1+i} \right] \qquad (5.17)$$

where ΔE is in dollars.

So, when market yields change, what drives the change in the bank's equity value? There are three main drivers:

1. The size of the shock $\left(\dfrac{\Delta i}{1+i} \right)$
2. The amount of the leverage the bank uses
3. The mismatch between the durations of the bank's assets and liabilities. The bank will be "immunized" when $D_A = D_L \left\{ \dfrac{L}{A} \right\}$

How does this matter to a bank or a savings institution? To address this question, note that a traditional bank or savings institution has assets of longer duration than liabilities. Thus, its durations look like those shown in Figure 5.7.

What this means is that if yields increase, the bank's equity value declines (recall Equation (5.17)), which shows that when $D_A > D_L$ and $L < A$, the term $\left[D_A - D_L \frac{L}{A} \right] > 0$, so $\Delta E < 0$ for any $\Delta i > 0$. If yields decrease, the bank's equity value increases. Thus, when a bank mismatches its balance sheet in the traditional way, it accepts interest rate risk in this way. Immunization closes the "gap."

A bank can alter its degree of immunization by changing the durations of its assets and liabilities. It can do this in two ways: on-balance sheet and off-balance sheet. On-balance sheet initiatives include making new types of loans, seeking new liabilities, and changing its capital structure. Off-balance sheet initiatives include repurchase agreements, futures, options, and swaps (we will discuss these in a later chapter).

CONVEXITY

If a bank is interested in protecting its net worth against unexpected interest rate changes, duration matching can help; matching terms to maturity cannot do this unless all investments are of the zero-coupon variety. Suppose now that a bank is immunized and yields subsequently change. Does the bank remain immunized? The answer is no. The reason is that duration is an *approximation*. In fact, it is a *linear* approximation of a *nonlinear* relationship between prices and yields. We can see this with an example.

Example 5.4

Suppose we have a 10-year zero-coupon bond that is risk free, has a par value of $1000, and is priced to yield 10%. What is its duration and how well will duration predict price changes if the yield moves up or down by 500 b.p.s?

Solution

Note that because this is a zero-coupon bond, thus maturity = duration; so the duration here is 10 years. The current price of the bond is: $\dfrac{\$1000}{(1.10)^{10}} = \$385.54$. Now consider the prices of this bond in response to a 500 (b.p.) change in the yield.

Prices	Yield Change	
	+ 500 b.p.	− 500 b.p.
Duration-predicted Price: $\frac{\Delta P}{P} = -10\left[\frac{\pm 0.05}{1.05}\right] = \pm 47.62\%$	$385:54[1 - 0.4762] = \$201.95$	$385.54[1 + 0.4762] = \$569.13$
Actual price	$\frac{\$1.000}{(1.15)^{10}} = \$247.18$	$\frac{\$1.000}{(1.05)^{10}} = \$613.19$
Error	−$45.23	−$44.78

We see then that duration *overpredicts* price declines when interest rates rise and *underpredicts* price increases when interest rates fall. Moreover, duration makes greater errors when yields rise than when they fall. This means that the duration approximation makes values look worse than they truly are when interest rates change, and this bias gets stronger as convexity increases.

Why does duration make such prediction errors? The reason is that the true relationship between price changes and yield changes is *convex,* not linear.

When we first calculated the relationship between dP and di, we took a first derivative, which gave us the slope of the function in a "local" area, that is, the slope of the curve, dP/di at di = 0. However, if we had gone further and computed the second derivative, we would have found $\frac{d^2 P}{di^2} > 0$, that is, all fixed-income securities are convex.

One implication of convexity is that duration will do a reasonable job in predicting price changes as long as interest rate changes are in the neighborhood of di = 0, that is, relatively small changes like, say, 1 b.p. But the larger the interest rate change, the more erroneous duration is in predicting price changes. See Figure 5.8 below.

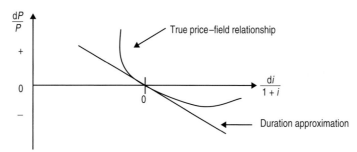

FIGURE 5.8 Price–Yield Relationship is Convex

Implications of Convexity for Fixed-Income Securities and for Banks

There are three important implications of convexity for fixed-income securities:

1. The price decline given a rate increase is *smaller* than the price increase given a rate decrease of the same absolute magnitude as the rate increase.
2. Duration changes as yields change.
3. Greater convexity implies greater errors in the predictive ability of duration.

There are two important implications of convexity for banks:

1. Duration immunization is a dynamic process since asset and liability durations change as yields change.
2. If the bank's asset portfolio is more convex than its liability portfolio, then properly done duration immunization never hurts the bank in the sense that the error associated with duration being an approximation tends to understate the value of the bank's equity.

INTEREST RATE RISK

How Interest Rate Risk Can Affect a Financial Institution's Net Worth

The successful financial institution must understand its interest rate risk and manage the *durations* of its assets and liabilities. A *pure broker* need not worry about interest rate risk because its assets and liabilities are always more or less automatically duration matched. On the other hand, the *asset transformer* is often exposed to very subtle forms of interest rate risk. Consider the following simple example. A bank is borrowing and lending funds of two maturities: short-term (1 year) and long-term (2 years), all zero-coupon. Loans consist of $40 million short term and $40 million long term, while liabilities are $60 million short term and $10 million long term.[3] All numbers are in market value terms as of October 30, 2012. Hence, the bank's balance sheet is

Bank's Balance Sheet as of October 30, 2012			
Short-term loans	$40,000,000	Short-term liabilities	$60,000,000
Long-term loans	$40,000,000	Long-term liabilities	$10,000,000
Total assets	$80,000,000	Total liabilities	$70,000,000
		Equity	$10,000,000
		Total equity and liabilities	$80,000,000

Assume that the yield curve as of October 30, 2012, is a flat solid line; Annual yields on assets and liabilities of all maturities are 10%.

Now suppose that on October 31, 2012, the yield curve shifts parallel such that all yields rise to 12%.

Each dollar of short-term assets (or liabilities) decreases in value to $0.9821428 and each dollar of long-term assets (or liabilities) decreases in value to $0.9646045. The new balance sheet in market-value terms looks as follows

Balance Sheet as of October 31, 2012			
Short-term loans	$39,285,712	Short-term liabilities	$58,928,568
Long-term loans	$38,584,180	Long-term liabilities	$9,646,046
Total assets	$77,869,892	Total liabilities	$68,574,613
		Equity	$9,295,279
		Total equity and liabilities	$77,869,892

Thus, the market value of equity falls by $704,721 or 7.047%. The shift in the term structure affects the values of *both* the assets and the liabilities, but it has unequal effects on assets and liabilities due to unequal duration. To see this, note that the duration of short-term assets is 1 year and the duration of long-term assets is 2 years. The weights attached to the short-term and long-term assets are 0.5 and 0.5. Thus, the duration of the asset portfolio is 0.5 × 1 + 0.5 × 2 = 1.5 years. Similarly, the duration of the short-term liability is 1 year and the weight attached to it is $60 million/$80 million = 0.75, while the duration of the long-term liability is 2 years and its weight is $10 million/$80 million = 0.125. Thus, the duration of the liability portfolio is (0.75 × 1 + 0.125 × 2) = 1 year.

While unequal duration is risky, it is also a service provided by an asset transformer. By funding short (acquiring short-duration liabilities), the intermediary reduces the duration of its clientele's assets, thereby earning any term premium embedded in the yield curve. One simple way to eliminate interest rate risk altogether is to *equalize* the durations of assets and liabilities at all times. But then the institution forgoes duration/maturity transformation, a potentially profitable type of asset transformation.

A Case Study in Interest Rate Risk

Banks and other depository institutions often deliberately mismatch the durations of their asset and liability portfolios to profit either from term premiums or from their own expectations (guesses) about where interest rates are headed. Depository institutions characteristically fund their longer-lived assets with shorter-term liabilities. For instance, S&Ls historically funded 30-year fixed-rate mortgages with deposits that were often subject to withdrawal on demand.[4] Similarly, commercial banks would finance 5- and 7-year fixed-rate "term" loans with demand and savings deposits, both of which could be withdrawn at a moment's notice. Such mismatches inevitably entail interest rate risk.

As an illustration, consider NCNB Corporation, a North Carolina-based banking company, which later went on to become Nations Bank and then merged with Bank of America; the bank speculated that there would be an interest rate downturn in 1990.[5] It thus lengthened the duration of its investment portfolio through 1989. At year end, the bank had a

---

3. You can easily verify that the asset and liability portfolios here have different durations.

4. Because of mortgage prepayments, 30-year fixed-rate mortgages have uncertain duration, typically of 7–12 years.

5. This discussion was reported by Kelly Holland in *American Banker,* March 20, 1990.

liability-sensitive balance sheet, largely because of its holdings of $6 billion in long-term Government National Mortgage Association (GNMA) mortgage-backed securities. As of December 31, 1989, about $1.5 billion more of NCNB's liabilities than its assets would have repriced over the next 12 months. If interest rates had fallen, NCNB would have enjoyed a huge profit. Instead, interest rates rose. As of year end 1989, the yield on 30-year GNMAs was 9.49%. By March 16, 1990, the 30-year GNMA yield was 9.95%. NCNB consequently suffered a $180 million unrealized loss in its bond portfolio. That news – plus disclosures in March 1990 that problem loans could rise by 25% in the first quarter of 1990 – sent NCNB's stock plummeting from $46 in the first week of March 1990 to $40 by March 19, 1990, a decline of 12%.[6]

The Savings and Loan Experience and Other Episodes

Another striking example of the consequences of interest rate risk is the experience of the U.S. savings and loan (S&L) industry in the 1980s. S&Ls have traditionally financed themselves with short-maturity deposits and invested in relatively long-maturity, fixed-rate mortgages. Consequently, their liabilities repriced more frequently than their assets. As long as the yield curve sloped upward, this was a profitable maturity transformation. But in the late 1970s and early 1980s, the yield curve inverted as yields rose to historic highs. S&Ls took significant losses. This dissipation of much of the industry's net worth was the triggering event that led to the decimation of the industry years later. In particular, the loss of net worth meant that these institutions had much to gain and little to lose by pursuing risky investments. This led to further losses. The financial distress of Orange County in California in the 1990s is another example of the potentially devastating effect of interest rate risk.

Why Take On Interest Rate Risk?

The immediate question is: Why do banks and S&Ls *choose* to accept such exposure? That is, we have seen that it is possible for the bank to avoid taking much of the interest rate risk it normally takes on simply by matching the durations of its assets and liabilities, so interest rate risk is largely an avoidable risk. To answer this question, we go back to the theory of the term structure of interest rates. The presence of a risk premium in the term structure invites those who are more risk tolerant than the "average" (or representative) investor to hold long-term assets and fund these assets with shorter-term liabilities. Their reward is the premium in the yield curve that reflects the greater risk aversion of the respective investor.

Why should banks and other depository institutions be more risk tolerant than others? This is an issue we will take up in later chapters, but for now it suffices to note that deposit insurance may be one reason for a preference for risk on the bank's part. Of course, not all banks will desire to take on the same amount of risk. As in the case of their borrowers, the risk-taking propensities of banks depend on their own capital levels. Banks with more capital may wish to make investments that are less risky than those desired by banks with less capital.

The upshot of this discussion is not that an asset transformer should not take interest rate risk, but rather that such risk must be carefully assessed and managed.

CONCLUSION

This chapter has examined interest rate risk and its role in the bank's overall risk exposure. Next to credit risk, this has been the most important source of risk for banks historically. Interest rate risk is linked to the term structure of interest rates. Our analysis of the term structure both under certainty and uncertainty shows how yield and maturity are related. In both the certainty and uncertainty cases, the concept of riskless arbitrage plays a key role. Further, our analysis shows that the risk in holding a bond is more appropriately assessed in terms of its duration rather than its term to maturity. The definition of duration and the examination of its relevance in measuring the price volatility of bonds indicate how coupon-paying bonds should be analyzed. We also examined the concept of convexity and measures of interest rate risk exposure.

CASE STUDY: EGGLESTON STATE BANK

Introduction

Mr. Edward Eggleston, CEO and primary stockholder of Eggleston State Bank, the bank he founded some 30 years ago in his hometown of Bloomington, OR, is worried. He has just gotten off the phone with an old friend of his, Fred Fisher. Fred had reported the difficulties he was having with his job search.

---

6. As Mr. John W. Munce, senior vice president and balance-sheet-management executive at NCNB put it, "We were postured to benefit from falling rates over a 12-month horizon. We definitely took some losses."

Fred's and Edward's life stories were remarkably similar. College roommates, they had both founded small hometown banks in the years following college and had managed to be quite successful for a number of years. But now, Fred is effectively wiped out – his bank has been closed by regulators and his fortune, invested entirely in the bank, has evaporated. Currently, he is going through the process of looking for a new job, maybe in the sort of big city he had always prided himself on avoiding.

Fred's bank had been fairly small, with $30 million in total assets, but had been consistently profitable as a small-town bank doing traditional banking – accepting deposits from individuals and small businesses in the short-term, while making long-term mortgage loans and business loans. But when state banking regulations were relaxed, allowing a branch of a major state bank to move into town, things got tighter. This competition, along with increasing volatility in interest rates and the bank's traditional mismatching of its balance sheet, led the bank into a situation with increasingly deteriorating capital, with a drop in capital over a 3-year period from $2 million to under $300,000. Finally, regulators moved in and took over the bank.

Edward Eggleston sighs, and wonders to himself whether the same thing could happen to his bank. His bank is much larger than Fred's with total assets of over $400 million (see Exhibit A). But with the rise of several regional banks with assets in billions of dollars, Edward is beginning to feel like he may face the same kinds of problems that beset Fred's bank, in the form of increased competition from larger, more sophisticated banks. He decides to meet with his executives to carefully investigate the exposure of Eggleston State Bank to interest rate risk, and to discuss the possibilities for hedging against changes in interest rates.

EXHIBIT A Eggleston State Bank

Year-End Balance Sheets (in Thousands)		
	2004	2005
Assets		
Cash & due from banks	$59,696	78,645
U.S. govt. obligation	$38,612	45,284
Other govt. obligations	$58,030	49,456
Other securities	$6,678	6,439
Loans and discounts	$250,950	290,125
Bank premises	$12,698	21,924
Other assets	$2,996	2,876
Total assets	$429,660	494,749
Liabilities		
Demand deposits	$178,668	184,694
Time deposits	$122,164	166,995
Deposits of the U.S. govt.	$10,164	3,429
Other govt. deposits	$57,190	59,805
Due to commercial banks	$7,266	12,987
Total deposits	$375,452	427,910
Other liabilities	$23,520	34,925
Total liabilities	$398,972	462,835
Capital Accounts		
Common stock	$5,838	5,630
Capital surplus	$15,008	14,472
Undivided profits	$7,952	9,828
Reserves	$1,890	1,985
Total capital accounts	$30,688	31,915
Total liabilities and capital accounts	$429,660	$494,750

EXHIBIT B Total Deposits (in millions of dollars)

	High	Low	Daily Average
	(Expected Duration 6 Months)		
2001	305	257	284
2002	323	291	301
2003	363	323	357
2004	375	307	363
2005	427	375	400

The Meeting

A week later, Edward Eggleston is sitting in his office with Carol Chipley and Douglas Date. Carol is a recent graduate of a top MBA program with strong analytical skills, hired in part to help modernize the bank's approach to risk management. Douglas, on the other hand, has risen to his current position from within the bank, primarily due to his sharp eye for detail and sound common sense.

Eggleston: O.K., gang. You both know our situation as well as I do. What I'm interested in is what options we have for action, and which you think we ought to pursue. Should we remain mismatched, or is it time for us to move into hedging?

Date: Well, as you know, Ed, I've always been skeptical about us getting involved in the latest fads in banking. After all, I don't see that we are so mismatched. Remember that article I showed you a while back, about a bank that started fooling around in the futures markets on the bad advice of a smooth-talking broker? I'm afraid that if we aren't careful, we could wind up making a big mistake. Besides, we've been here for 30 years now, steadily profitable. Why should we mess with a good system?

Chipley: I think that you are right, Douglas, when you say that we should be careful. But I think that for every story about banks losing money because a hedging program was poorly planned, we can find a dozen stories about banks that lost money, or even went under, because they weren't hedged at all. Plus, the banking environment has changed significantly in recent years. So what worked for the last 30 years might be fatal to us over the next 30 years.

Date: People are always saying that, but I don't really see what has changed. We've gotten bigger, but this is still a small-town bank. Our borrowers and our customers are mostly individuals and small to medium-sized businesses. Carol, weren't you just showing me the other day a chart showing how smooth our deposit flows have been over the past 5 years? (See Exhibit B). And the new administration seems committed to keeping Ft. Washington open, so it looks like the overall business outlook for the community is about the same as it ever was: stable and solid as a rock. This is a fairly prosperous area, after all. (See Exhibit C).

Chipley: Well, I'm not so sure that we can count on any administration keeping promises about military bases. But anyway, closing Fort Washington isn't the only risk that we face. I think that the increasingly competitive nature of banking means that world markets can affect what happens in our little town. Twenty years ago, our customers might not have worried so much about differences in interest rates; we were their hometown bank and we knew them and their business. But banking is more impersonal now, and we can't just expect our depositors to stay with us if we don't offer competitive interest rates. I think our investment and loan portfolios deserve a careful look (see Exhibits D and E).

Eggleston: Well, those are the reactions that I expected to hear from you. But I think that now is the time for some hard-boiled analysis. Let's sit down right now and come up with some likely interest rate scenarios. Then Carol can work with the figures and let us know exactly what would happen to the bank under a variety of circumstances (see Exhibit F).

The Numbers

During the meeting, the bankers came to an agreement on the following probabilities for the following scenarios:

The Assignment

Eggleston: Carol, I'd like for you to take these numbers and report back to me on some very specific questions. What exactly is the extent of our mismatching? What would happen to the bank under the various scenarios that we've talked about? What kind of hedging program, if any, should we use to protect the bank?

EXHIBIT C Market Area Economic Data Income and Housing

Annual Household Income	Percentage of Households
Under $3,000	28%
$3,000–$6,999	20%
$7,000–$14,999	30%
$15,000–$24,999	21.5%
$25,000+	0.5%
Home Ownership	
All Housing Units	30,000
Owner-occupied	51%
Rental	38%
Unoccupied	11%
Major Area Employers, Bloomington	
Ft. Washington	25,000
Lockheed	1,000
Kraft Foods	850
Bloomington College	730

EXHIBIT D Eggleston State Bank

(Investment Portfolio, Today)

Description	Par value	Coupon	Years to maturity	Book value	Bond rating
U.S Government Securities					
Bills	2,500,000	—	8 months	2,235,000	—
Notes	4,000,000	6.00	2 years	3,765,000	—
Bonds	40,000,000	7.00	25 years	39,284,000	—
Other Government Securities					
Municipal securities	50,000,000	6.00	22 years	49,456	Baa
Corporate Bonds					
Lockheed	7,000,000	12	17 Years	6,439	Aaa

EXHIBIT E Eggleston State Bank

(Loan Portfolio, Summary Report, Today)

Borrower type	Coupon	Estimated	Book value
Short-term individual (cars, and so on)	13.27	2.1	14,700,000
Short-term business	12.31	1.8	7,234,000
Medium-term business	11.45	5.3	42,300,000
Long-term business	10.4	7.9	78,766,000
Home mortgages	8.3	9.1	179,000,000

EXHIBIT F Likely Interest Rate Scenarios

(Scenario Names)	Good	Bad	Ugly
Probability	0.5	0.3	0.2
U.S. Govt. Securities			
Bills	11.00%	9.00%	12.00%
Notes	10.00%	10.00%	13.00%
Bonds	9.00%	11.00%	14.00%
Other Govt. Securities			
Municipal securities	9.25%	11.75%	15.25%
Corporate Bonds			
Lockheed	9.75%	10.75%	13.75%
Loans			
Short-term individual	13.25%	11.25%	14.25%
Short-term business	12.25%	10.25%	13.25%
Medium-term business	10.50%	10.5%	13.75%
Long-term business	9.80%	10.75%	13.75%
Home mortgages	9.00%	11.50%	14.50%

Review Questions

1. What is the term structure of interest rates?
2. Under certainty, if the term structure is determined to preclude riskless arbitrage, what is the relationship between the yields on bonds of different maturities and why?
3. What is duration and why is it a more valid metric to consider for coupon-paying bonds than maturity? What is the relation between duration and price volatility for bonds with the same maturity?
4. What is convexity? Discuss its potential usefulness in evaluating bonds.
5. Discuss the pros and cons of duration mismatching for a depository institution.
    Suppose there are three zero-coupon bonds, identical in all respects except maturity. Each bond has a face value of $1000. One of them matures a year from now and is currently selling at $855.66. Another matures 2 years from now and is currently selling at $835.33. The third matures 3 years from now and is currently selling at $775.85. Compute the YTM for each of the three bonds, plot the yield curve (assuming that you can interpolate smoothly), and compute the available forward rates.
6. The annualized YTM on a single-period pure discount bond is 12% and that on a two-period pure discount bond is 10.45%. There are two bonds. One is a two-period, pure discount bond that promises a balloon payment of $1200 at maturity. The other is a bond that will pay a coupon of $100 one period hence, and a coupon of $100 plus a balloon payment of $1000 two periods hence. Compute the duration of these bonds and their possible price changes prior to maturity.
7. Given below is an excerpt from a conversation between two people. Provide a critique.

Moderator: So, what do you people think? Will we ever really understand what happened to the American banking industry well enough to know what should be done?

Appleton: Well, I think banks and S&Ls were simply victims of the environment. We had an inverted yield curve – long rates were lower than short rates – for a while and this made it difficult for financial institutions to reap their normal profits from asset transformation; you know, I've never believed in the expectations hypothesis. It's a theoretical nicety with no practical relevance. Of course, the increased interest rate volatility didn't help. As if this wasn't enough, there was an enormous increase in competition, both domestic and international. These institutions must have felt like they were being squeezed by a powerful vise.

Moderator: By the way, Alex, I'll give you another reason not to like the expectations hypothesis – it's also wrong.

Appleton: I didn't know that. Are you sure? In any case, it's good to know you agree with me, Mike. But frankly, I'm surprised. Knowing how you and Beth feel about this, I thought I'd get more of an argument.

Moderator: Well, cheer up, Alex. My agreement with you is only partial. I agree that depository financial institutions faced a tough environment during the last 15 years or so. But I also think they could have *managed* their risks more intelligently. For example, they could have reduced the duration gaps in their asset and liability portfolios and made use of contemporary immunization techniques to hedge their interest rate risks. Like some of the investment banking houses, they could have been more innovative in brokerage activities, so that the resulting fee income would have made banks less dependent on the riskier asset transformation activities. Just look at the profits earned by some investment bankers who stripped Treasuries and sold zeros (pure discount bonds) like CATS (Certificates of Accrual of Treasury Securities) and TIGRS (Treasury Investment Growth Receipts). No, Alex! The real story runs much deeper than your "passive victims of the environment" explanation. I think banks and S&Ls *exploited* the system and ripped off taxpayers.

REFERENCES

Durham, B.J., 2014. More on U.S. Treasury Term Premiums: Spot and Expected Measures. Federal Reserve Bank of New York, Staff Reports, no 658, revised.

Fisher, I., Weil, R.L., 1971. Coping with the risk of interest rate fluctuations. J. Bus. 44, 408–431.

Holland, K., 1990. Capital: NCNB loses big bet on long-term rates. Am. Banker, 20.

Ingersoll, J.E., Skelton, J., Weil, R.L., 1978. Duration forty years later. J. Financ. Quant. Anal. 13, 627–650.

Macaulay, F., 1938. The Movements of Interest Rates, Bond Yields, and Stock Prices in the United States Since 1856. National Bureau of Economic Research, New York.

Chapter 6

Liquidity Risk

"Everything that can be counted does not necessarily count; everything that counts cannot necessarily be counted."

Albert Einstein

GLOSSARY OF TERMS

Duration Mismatching When the duration of the bank's assets is not equal to the duration of its liabilities.
Informational Frictions Includes both asymmetric information and moral hazard.
Lender of Last Resort A central bank that stands ready to provide the bank with emergency liquidity in case it is needed.
Wholesale Financing typically short-term funding coming from the interbank market or institutional investors (repos, FED funds, commercial paper, large denomination CDs, etc.); often alternative for deposits but not insured.

INTRODUCTION

The purpose of this chapter is to examine liquidity risk in some detail. We begin by discussing the sources of liquidity risk. We then turn to the interaction between liquidity and default risks. Next we discuss the interaction between liquidity and interest rate risks, and provide some formal definitions of liquidity risk.

Having established these basics, the chapter turns to how liquidity risk can be managed. In line with the Enterprise Risk Management (ERM) framework discussed in Chapter 4, a framework for the management and governance of liquidity risk is introduced. Following this, we consider various approaches for mitigating liquidity risk. These approaches include keeping liquid assets, reducing withdrawal risk in deposits, and preserving access to funding markets. Also, the role of the lender-of-last-resort in reducing liquidity risk is discussed. That discussion highlights the difficulty any lender-of-last-resort would have in distinguishing between a liquidity crisis and an insolvency crisis and hence in coming up with the appropriate policy response. In concluding, we comment on the systemic nature of liquidity risk.

WHAT, AFTER ALL, IS LIQUIDITY RISK?

There are occasions on which the bank does not have ready access to funds that it needs, and is therefore forced to incur costs. These could be the costs associated with passing up investment opportunities. Alternatively, they could be distress-financing costs. These are examples of situations in which the financial intermediary faces liquidity risk. We define *liquidity risk* as the risk of being unable to satisfy claims without impairment to its financial or reputational capital.[1]

It is important to distinguish between illiquidity and insolvency. The latter relates to a condition in which the value of the firm's liabilities exceeds the value of its assets, and hence its net worth is negative. Illiquidity can be as damaging and costly as insolvency, but it is a form of distress rooted in the (non)marketability of assets rather than in their ultimate or full value. To be sure, this may be a vacuous distinction when addressed at close range. Nevertheless, in thin markets, time and marketing efforts often are essential to the realization of asset values. Liquidating assets on short notice often results in "distress" or "fire sale" prices which are below the assets' true values in normal times. The relationship between time available for marketing and the realizable values of assets is central to the notion of liquidity

Informational frictions are at the heart of liquidity problems. To see how informational asymmetries interact with default and interest rate risks to create liquidity risk, let us imagine that you own a bank that has made loans of $1 million with a maturity of 2 years and financed them with uninsured demand deposits. As a banker, you know more about the default risk of your loans than outsiders do, that is, there is asymmetric information about loan quality. Now, suppose that 6 months down the road, $400,000 of deposits are withdrawn because your depositors suffer a "liquidity shock", that is, they have an urgent need for funds to take care of some expenditures, such as medical care of paying for college. However,

---

1. The BIS comes with a very similar definition: "Liquidity is the ability of a bank to fund increases in assets and meet obligations as they come due, without incurring unacceptable losses" (BIS, 2008).

S. I. Greenbaum, A. V. Thakor & A. W. A. Boot: Contemporary Financial Intermediation, Third edition. http://dx.doi.org/10.1016/B978-0-12-405196-6.00006-9

your existing stock of cash assets is only $100,000. This means you need to raise $300,000 to fund the deposit withdrawal. If potential depositors' perceptions about the quality of your loan portfolio are sufficiently favorable, you will not have any trouble acquitting new deposits in the amount of $300,000. But suppose that outsiders have received unfavorable information about your loans.[2] If this information is sufficiently unfavorable, new deposits may simply not be forthcoming,[3] or you might have to pay an excessively high interest rate – relative to the rate you consider "appropriate" – to attract the necessary deposits.[4] The point is this can happen even though your loans are in good shape. Your problem is that you know this, but your potential new depositors do not. This is an example of liquidity risk.

There are four points we should note about this example. First, the problem for your bank started with existing depositors experiencing their own "liquidity shock" or need for liquidity. Second, an informational asymmetry about asset quality plays a pivotal role in creating liquidity risk. If you know your loan quality is good and outsiders knew as much about your loan quality as you do, then you would be able to acquire the deposits you need at a price that you consider appropriate for the risk associated with the loan portfolio. This eliminates liquidity risk. Third, it is easy to confuse insolvency or credit risk with liquidity risk. That is, if the bank's loan quality truly deteriorated and the credit risk of the bank for (uninsured) depositors went up, the bank would be faced with insolvency risk and new deposits would not be forthcoming even if there was *no* asymmetric information about loan quality between you and your potential new depositors. An outside observer would simply see the bank unable to raise new deposits and think this was a manifestation of liquidity risk when it is really an insolvency problem.

Fourth, duration mismatching may be an important ingredient in creating liquidity risk, but it is not a necessary ingredient. To see the importance of duration mismatching, suppose your asset and liability portfolios were perfectly duration matched. Then the assets that were funded by a specific set of liabilities would pay off at the same time that the liabilities came due, and informational asymmetry about these assets that arises *after* these assets are on the bank's books would not matter. Of course, if an informational asymmetry exists about the new loans you make, then a premium reflecting this asymmetry will show up in the interest rate on the deposits raised to fund these loans. However, you can pass this premium along to your borrowers in the way you price your loans, so that your capital is not impaired.

The Interaction Between Liquidity and Default Risks

Liquidity risks and default risks are interrelated. If a sudden need for liquidity forces you to sell illiquid assets quickly, the value that is realized might be low and impair solvency in the sense that the proceeds from the sale of those assets may be insufficient to satisfy the claims of your creditors. So liquidity risk may trigger default risk. The opposite may happen too: concerns about credit risk (i.e., default risk) of existing assets may cause a freeze in funding markets, making it difficult or impossible for the institution to raise the financing it needs to invest in new loans, thereby triggering liquidity problems. What this means is that liquidity and default risks should not be looked at in isolation.

Typically, we think that a big part of liquidity risk is withdrawal risk, which stems from a bank's deposits being of shorter duration than its assets. Thus, the deposits used to finance loans come due before the loans mature, and if they are withdrawn but cannot be rolled over, we have liquidity risk.

The Interaction Between Liquidity and Interest Rate Risks

We now turn to the interaction between interest rate risk and liquidity risk. There are two ways to explain this interaction. First, suppose we have deposit interest rate ceilings. Given this ceiling, a rise in market interest rates causes withdrawals because depositors can earn higher rates elsewhere. Hence, deposit interest rate ceilings transform interest rate risk into withdrawal risk.

Another way to understand this interaction is by returning to the example we discussed in the section under interest rate risk. If the term structure receives a random shock that causes interest rates to rise, it is possible that you will experience a deposit outflow as your depositors will want to reinvest their money at the prevailing higher interest rates. You have two ways to finance these withdrawals. One way is for you to acquire new (partially insured) deposits. But this

---

2. This information may be different from what you know about your loans, that is, you may still know more than outsiders and may thus believe that your loan quality is good.

3. Indeed, it is possible that all of your existing deposits may be withdrawn. Observe that deposit insurance may mitigate this, but note banks do often depend on other (noninsured) funding sources like wholesale financing (see Huang and Ratnovski (2011), and Bouwman (2014)).

4. In fact, your willingness to pay such a high rate of interest may be viewed as a signal of poor loan quality. Then, liquidity risk can be interpreted as the likelihood of incurring this signaling cost.

may require you to pay a premium to depositors due to a possible informational asymmetry about your loan portfolio. Moreover, you must satisfy reserve and capital requirements on deposits. An alternative is to liquidate part of your asset portfolio to meet these unanticipated deposit withdrawals. You can do this by selling off marketable securities you hold or by selling off some of your loans.[5] Due to an informational asymmetry about your loans, however, you may only be able to sell your loans for less than what you think they are worth. The loss you incur as a result is also a part of liquidity risk. Although this loss is precipitated by an unfavorable move in interest rates, note again the central role played by asymmetric information. Moreover, the greater the asymmetric information, the greater the potential for loss, and hence the lower the asset's liquidity. This is why, despite an active secondary market, a corporation's common stock is not as liquid as a U.S. Treasury bill.

SOME FORMAL DEFINITIONS OF LIQUIDITY

Think of P^* as the full-value price of an asset, that is, the highest price an owner can expect to realize by liquidating one unit, provided all useful preparations are made for the sale. If the asset is sold before all useful preparations can be made, a lesser price will be realized. Call this lesser price P_i, where $i = 0, \ldots, n$ indicates the time used for marketing, and n is the time needed to realize full value. The length of time used should be thought of as the interval between a decision to sell and the time at which a sales contract is consummated.[6] Hence

$$P_n = P^*$$

and for all values of $i < n$, the realized price of the asset, P_i, is less than full value. One way to think of liquidity is in terms of

$$L_1 = \frac{P_i}{P^*}.$$

A limitation of this definition is that the liquidity of a particular asset depends on the value of i chosen. Thus, for low values of i, one asset may be more liquid than another, whereas for greater values of i, the liquidity comparison might be reversed. This impedes the consistent ranking of assets according to their liquidity. One way to mitigate, if not obviate, this problem of liquidity reversal among assets is to think in terms of an "average" value of i. Hence

$$L_2 = \frac{1}{n} \sum_{i=0}^{n} \frac{P_i}{P^*}.$$

A still more appealing approach recognizes the inherent uncertainty regarding i, the time interval between the decision to sell, and the actual sale. Thus, we can view it as a random variable with a probability distribution, $g(i)$, which stipulates the probability of each possible outcome $(i = 0, \ldots, n)$. The expected value of an asset, $E(P)$, is then defined as

$$E(P) = \sum_{i=0}^{n} g(i) P_i,$$

and this leads to a third definition of liquidity, which is

$$L_3 = \frac{E(P)}{P^*}.$$

The liquidity concept can be further generalized to account for marketing expenditures, say M. The more general view is that the realizable price of an asset depends on time, marketing expenditures, and full-value price, so that

$$P_i = f(i, M, P^*),$$

---

5. A bank can sell its loans to another bank just as a firm would sell its debt in a private placement. This practice, which is quite old, is known as "loan sales." A more recent practice is securitization, which involves the bank selling the loan, typically as a component in a portfolio of loans, directly to investors in the capital market. This is usually done through an underwriter and is a process of converting a previously untraded security into a traded security. We will have a lot more to say about this in Chapter 11.

6. The terms of the transaction are fixed at the time the sales contract is consummated, but the transfer of property takes place at the "closing," a date that may coincide with the date of the sales contract, but often occurs later.

and if $\bar{M}$ is the optimally chosen marketing expenditure,

$$E(P') = \sum_{i=0}^{n} g(i) f(i, \bar{M}, P*)$$

is the expected value of an asset, conditional to the owner's spending optimally on marketing. This leads to our fourth definition of liquidity

$$L_4 = \frac{E(P')}{P*}$$

and $M/P*$ can be thought of as a measure of the market's thinness, a measure akin to the bid–ask spread.

Note that the positive relationship between available time for marketing and marketing effort on the one hand and realizable value on the other has nothing to do with changes in supply or demand for the asset; the realizable value increases in the context of given market conditions. Time is not used to await a more favorable market, but rather to do the marketing necessitated by costly information. For a depository institution, there are many ways to reduce liquidity risk. An obvious way is to simply keep more liquid assets on hand. The other is to reduce the deposit withdrawal risk that creates liquidity risk. A third way is to rely on a lender of last resort who stands ready to replenish the bank's liquidity when needed. In what follows, we discuss each in turn.

THE MANAGEMENT OF LIQUIDITY RISK

As part of its ERM, introduced in Chapter 4, a bank needs to put in place policies and actions to control and manage liquidity risk. These include the allocation of responsibilities, formulating procedures, setting limits, and the actual measurement and management of liquidity risk. In Table 6.1, we present a framework outlined by the Bank for International Settlements (BIS).

Reducing Liquidity Risk With Liquid Assets

Think of the fractional reserve banking system described in Chapter 3. That bank can be thought of as holding two kinds of assets: cash and loans that mature in two or more periods (prior to maturity the loans are assumed to be worthless). The bank's liabilities all mature in one period, and may or may not be renewed (withdrawn). If the fraction withdrawn after one period is equal to, or smaller than, the bank's holding of cash assets, the bank will continue in business for two periods, at least. On the other hand, if withdrawals exceed the bank's holding of cash assets, that bank will be unable to honor its liabilities – it has promised all depositors immediate access even though its own capacity to satisfy claims is strictly limited by its holding cash assets.[7] Therein lies the liquidity conundrum of banking.

Notice that an important role of a bank is the provision of liquidity services, and it provides this service by mismatching its balance sheet on the liquidity attribute, that is, it holds assets that are less liquid than its liabilities. This is one form of asset transformation. The *quality* of this liquidity service provided by the bank depends on three factors: the liquidity of its loan portfolio, the cash (or liquid assets) it has on hand, and the withdrawal risk in its deposit base. By investing in more liquid loans and/or keeping more cash on hand, the bank can improve its own liquidity. However, it does so at the expense of profits. An alternative would be to seek ways to dissipate withdrawal risk, which is what we turn to next.

Reducing Liquidity Risk by Dissipating Withdrawal Risk

A depository institution can reduce the variance of its deposit flows by diversifying the sources of funding, that is, having many distinct and dissimilar depositors. This is formally demonstrated in Appendix 6.1. A diverse depositor base results in more predictable deposit flows; the improved predictability reduces the cash needed to service a deposit base to any arbitrary probabilistic standard. That is, the larger and more diverse the depositor base, the smaller the cash holding necessary to achieve any preselected probability of a stock-out (liquidity crisis). This is one way the depository institution *produces* liquidity. Nevertheless, withdrawals will sometimes exceed the institution's capacity to service them, even though this may

---

7. This is the rationale behind the standard measure of liquidity in the savings industry, which is the ratio of cash and short-term U.S. government securities and other specified securities to deposits and borrowing due within 1 year. Following the 2007–2009 financial crisis the Dodd-Frank Act (see Chapter 15) has introduced a more extensive regulation of liquidity dictating the holdings of high quality liquid assets (HQLA). The – so called – liquidity coverage ratio (LCR) became active in the United States, and similar regulation was adopted in Europe (see Chapter 15).

TABLE 6.1 BIS Principles for the Management of Liquidity Risk.

Fundamental principle for the management and supervision of liquidity risk:

Principle 1: A bank is responsible for the sound management of liquidity risk. A bank should establish a robust liquidity risk management framework that ensures it maintains sufficient liquidity, including a cushion of unencumbered, high-quality liquid assets, to withstand a range of stress events, including those involving the loss or impairment of both unsecured and secured funding sources*

Governance of liquidity risk management

Principle 2: A bank should clearly articulate a liquidity risk tolerance that is appropriate for its business strategy and its role in the financial system

Principle 3: Senior management should develop a strategy, policies, and practices to manage liquidity risk in accordance with the risk tolerance and to ensure that the bank maintains sufficient liquidity. Senior management should continuously review information on the bank's liquidity developments and report to the board of directors on a regular basis. A bank's board of directors should review and approve the strategy, policies, and practices related to the management of liquidity at least annually and ensure that senior management manages liquidity risk effectively

Principle 4: A bank should incorporate liquidity costs, benefits, and risks in the internal pricing, performance measurement, and new product approval process for all significant business activities (both on- and off-balance sheet), thereby aligning the risk-taking incentives of individual business lines with the liquidity risk exposures their activities create for the bank as a whole

Measurement and management of liquidity risk

Principle 5: A bank should have a sound process for identifying, measuring, monitoring and controlling liquidity risk. This process should include a robust framework for comprehensively projecting cash flows arising from assets, liabilities, and off-balance sheet items over an appropriate set of time horizons

Principle 6: A bank should actively monitor and control liquidity risk exposures and funding needs within and across legal entities, business lines, and currencies, taking into account legal, regulatory, and operational limitations to the transferability of liquidity

Principle 7: A bank should establish a funding strategy that provides effective diversification in the sources and tenor of funding. It should maintain an ongoing presence in its chosen funding markets and strong relationships with funds providers to promote effective diversification of funding sources. A bank should regularly gauge its capacity to raise funds quickly from each source. It should identify the main factors that affect its ability to raise funds and monitor those factors closely to ensure that estimates of fund raising capacity remain valid

Principle 8: A bank should actively manage its intraday liquidity positions and risks to meet payment and settlement obligations on a timely basis under both normal and stressed conditions and thus contribute to the smooth functioning of payment and settlement systems

Principle 9: A bank should actively manage its collateral positions, differentiating between encumbered and unencumbered assets. A bank should monitor the legal entity and physical location where collateral is held and how it may be mobilized in a timely manner

Principle 10: A bank should conduct stress tests on a regular basis for a variety of short-term and protracted institution-specific and market-wide stress scenarios (individually and in combination) to identify sources of potential liquidity strain and to ensure that current exposures remain in accordance with a bank's established liquidity risk tolerance. A bank should use stress test outcomes to adjust its liquidity risk-management strategies, policies, and positions and to develop effective contingency plans

Principle 11: A bank should have a formal contingency funding plan (CFP) that clearly sets out the strategies for addressing liquidity shortfalls in emergency situations. A CFP should outline policies to manage a range of stress environments, establish clear lines of responsibility, include clear invocation and escalation procedures, and be regularly tested and updated to ensure that it is operationally robust

Principle 12: A bank should maintain a cushion of unencumbered, high-quality liquid assets to be held as insurance against a range of liquidity stress scenarios, including those that involve the loss or impairment of unsecured and typically available secured funding sources. There should be no legal, regulatory, or operational impediment to using these assets to obtain funding

Public disclosure

Principle 13: A bank should publicly disclose information on a regular basis that enables market participants to make an informed judgment about the soundness of its liquidity risk-management framework and liquidity position

In their "Principles for sound liquidity risk management and supervision" the BIS complements this principle with the following "instruction" to supervisors: "Supervisors should assess the adequacy of both a bank's liquidity risk-management framework and its liquidity position and should take prompt action if a bank is deficient in either area in order to protect depositors and to limit potential damage to the financial system." (BIS, 2008).
Source: BIS (2008).

happen only with very small probability, and in that sense the system is imperfect. Indeed, this is the system's Achilles' heel. Bank runs are the trauma that illustrates this vulnerability of fractional reserve banking, a vulnerability caused by the illiquidity of bank assets.

Reducing Liquidity by Preserving Access to Funding Markets

The management of liquidity is referred to as the treasury function, and it is usually entrusted to the chief financial officer (CFO). It is her responsibility to "fund the bank." This requires a thorough understanding of the institution's cash flows, as well as all potential sources of liquidity. Ultimately, protection comes from maintaining diverse, capacious, and reliable sources of funding against future contingencies. This explains why the typical bank will borrow from virtually *all* reasonably priced sources. To be sure, cost will be a consideration, but opportunities to reduce short-run funding costs by concentrating on fewer funding sources are commonly avoided.

In "paying up" for funding diversity, the bank is purchasing lines of credit, and this reduces the likelihood of being rationed. It is common for funding sources to evaporate under stress; CFOs understand this only too well. Continental Illinois Bank and Trust found that holders of its large CDs (Certificates of Deposit) abandoned them in their hour of keenest need, and the high-yield bond market went into eclipse when Drexel Burnham Lambert was forced into insolvency because banks chose to withdraw their funding. And in the 2007–2009 financial crisis many commercial banks, including Northern Rock in the United Kingdom, and investment banks "discovered" that access to short-term wholesale financing could disappear overnight. The conventional protection against the trauma of being rationed is to accept the extra cost of participating in as many markets as possible, thereby diversifying funding sources. Liquidity is consciously purchased by banks as well as their borrowers, and it is the fragility of liquidity that makes this part of banking particularly challenging.

Reducing the Liquidity Risk of an Individual Bank with a Lender of Last Resort

It was long ago discovered that the liquidity of a fractional reserve banking system can be ensured with a thoroughly credible "lender of last resort" (LLR). This was the major motivation for the creation of central banks, including the Federal Reserve System. With an institution capable of creating money limitlessly, it becomes possible to support banks facing the most extraordinary deposit outflows. Provided that the banks are sound (solvent, given reasonable time to liquidate their assets), this could be done by having the central bank lend to the banks using their illiquid loans as collateral. With such a lending facility, sound but illiquid banks could be protected and financial market disruptions avoided. This argument is developed more fully in Appendix 6.2.

However, an inexpensive, readily available LLR faces the danger of inheriting the entire liquidity management problem of the banking industry. That is, the bank's incentive to hold cash assets (or even diversify its deposit base) is weakened if borrowings from the central bank are inexpensive and readily available. This is a moral hazard associated with the introduction of the LLR, and it has two implications. First, it shifts deposit seigniorage from the public to privately owned banks. Second, the LLR is also exposed to the credit risk of the bank's collateral. The moral hazard of lower, voluntarily held cash assets explains the consequent introduction of cash asset reserve requirements, and also why there are carefully administered detailed rules and informal restrictions governing access to the discount window.

Thus, legal reserve requirements and LLR pricing and availability shift at least a portion of the liquidity management problem back to the banks. Other banks, without access to an LLR facility, own the liquidity problem outright.

THE DIFFICULTY OF DISTINGUISHING BETWEEN LIQUIDITY AND INSOLVENCY RISKS AND THE LLR'S CONUNDRUM

In practice, it is not always easy to distinguish between liquidity risk and insolvency risk, as indicated earlier. This was true, for example, in the 2007–2009 subprime crisis. Financial institutions in the shadow banking system found that there was a sharp increase in the "haircuts" on the collateral used in repurchase transactions, which meant a substantial reduction in short-term liquidity. Similarly, mutual funds faced massive withdrawals by investors. These were the conditions prevailing during the 2007–2009 crisis; see Chapter 14 for more on this.

Many interpreted these conditions as a liquidity crisis. Consequently, central banks undertook massive interventions in the capital market, infusing huge amounts of liquidity. However, in reality this was an insolvency crisis, and when this was recognized, the actions of central banks (especially the Federal Reserve) turned to the kinds of initiatives needed to deal with an insolvency crisis, for example, infusing more capital into banks.

The reason why liquidity and insolvency risks are hard to distinguish in practice is simple.[8] When a bank is faced with a liquidity crisis, it means that its financiers are pressed for funds and cannot make funding available to the bank because of their own "liquidity shock." When a bank is faced with an insolvency crisis, it means it has experienced a deterioration in the quality of the assets on its balance sheet and its risk of insolvency has gone up, and as a result its financiers are unwilling to fund the bank. Since the outcome in both cases is the same – the drying up of funding for the bank – it is hard to tell what kind of crisis the bank is facing.

CONCLUSION

Liquidity risk is possibly the most important risk in banking. In their asset-transformation role, banks engage in liquidity transformation: banks typically have longer duration assets than liabilities, and offer via the liability side of the balance sheet liquidity services to their depositors. The effect is that banks might be confronted with roll-over risk and withdrawals of deposits that could cause funding gaps.

The 2007–2009 financial crisis showed the systemic nature of liquidity risk as well as its close relationship to insolvency risk. Unexpectedly high subprime mortgage defaults elevated concerns about insolvency risk, leading to funding markets breaking down, and inducing institutions to engage in asset sales caused downward price spirals, putting enormous stress on the stability of the financial system.[9] These effects related to how fundamental concerns about insolvency risk caused liquidity to shrink are discussed in Chapter 14, and the regulatory responses are covered in Chapters 15 and 16.

REVIEW QUESTIONS

1. What is liquidity risk and how is it linked to interest rate and credit risks? What is the role of asymmetric information in creating liquidity risk?
2. How can liquidity risk be managed? What are some of the impediments faced by banks in implementing an *integrated* risk-management system that managers credit risk, liquidity risk, and interest rate risk?
3. What factors lead to an increase in the bank's liquidity risk and why is it important for the economy that banks take on liquidity risk?

APPENDIX 6.1 DISSIPATION OF WITHDRAWAL RISK THROUGH DIVERSIFICATION

Suppose that a bank has n depositors, each of whom deposits $1. Each deposit is subject to withdrawal after one period, but may remain for two. Assume that the probability that a $1 deposit will be withdrawn after one period is one in ten, that is, $p = 0.1$, but whether a given deposit is actually withdrawn after one period cannot be known until that one period has passed.

Deposits are used to fund loans that pay back in full in two periods, but are worthless until they mature. (There is no secondary market in loans.) This is a harmless simplifying assumption and does not affect the argument that follows. Of course, the bank will need to hold some fraction of its assets in cash in order to satisfy its one-period withdrawals. The question is how much cash the bank should prudently hold. If the bank has $1 or $1 million of deposits, the probability of withdrawal remains fixed at 10%, and the expected withdrawal is this probability multiplied by the amount of deposits. However, if the bank has only $1 in deposits, the withdrawal inevitably will be all or nothing at all, zero or one. Indeed, the expected value of $0.10 is unattainable, and the bank's decision to hold 10 percent in cash, if feasible, is virtually pointless.

However, as the bank's depositors increase in number, assuming independence among them, the withdrawal of 10% becomes more predictable; in the limit, as depositors become more and more numerous, a 10% cash holding will "almost certainly" satisfy deposit withdrawals.

This idea is apparent from the definition of the standard deviation of a binomial distribution where n is the number of depositors and $q \equiv 1 - p$; the standard deviation of the bank's deposits will be $\sigma = \sqrt{npq}$.

Note that this measure of uncertainty varies with the square root of the *number of depositors,* and hence in the limit as the number of depositors increases to infinity, the standard deviation per dollar of deposit equals $\lim_{n \to \infty} (\sigma / n) = 0$.

This means that as the number of depositors becomes larger, the withdrawal uncertainty *per loan* diminishes, approaching zero in the limit, even though the withdrawal probability remains unchanged at $p = 0.1$. So, as the depositor population increases, the 10% withdrawal can be treated increasingly as a routine (almost fixed) cost, rather than as a potential

---

8. Farhi and Tirole (2012) provide a model in which the central bank cannot distinguish between a liquidity crisis and an insolvency crisis.
9. See Brunnermeier and Pedersen (2009).

catastrophe. The risk of ruin, the probability that withdrawals exceed the bank's cash holding, never actually becomes zero since $\sigma/n \to 0$ only in the limit. But the risk of ruin can be managed, and made indefinitely small by diversifying the bank's sources of funding.

APPENDIX 6.2 LENDER-OF-LAST-RESORT MORAL HAZARD

In a world of fiat money, value derives from an administered or artificial scarcity. That is, our money is money by fiat or legal mandate (hence legal tender) and is not convertible into gold or any other commodity at a fixed exchange rate, as in the case of commodity-backed money. The more money the government prints, or otherwise creates, the less its value, and this applies to bank deposits as well as to paper money. The administered scarcity of money also creates a monopoly profit referred to as "seigniorage." This profit on the production of money is shared by the privately owned banks and the public, via its effective ownership of the central bank. The Federal Reserve is nominally owned by member commercial banks. However, the equity in the Federal Reserve banks pays a statutorily fixed rate of return, much like a bond, whereas the residual earnings of the Federal Reserve flow back to the U.S. Treasury via a special franchise tax. Given that neither central bank nor private bank deposits pay interest (any interest rates below competitive rates will sustain the point), the distribution of seigniorage between the banks and the public (or central bank) depends on the cash asset reserves the banks choose to hold. The more reserves banks hold, the smaller will be banks' share of the seigniorage.

Since the introduction of an LLR reduces the amount of reserves the banks will desire to hold, it effectively shifts seigniorage from the public to the banks. This is the moral hazard associated with the introduction of an LLR, and it explains that one rationale for legal reserve requirements (that stipulate the minimum cash assets that banks must hold) is to restore the "appropriate" sharing of seigniorage between banks and the public.

This point is easily illustrated. Suppose we have a single commercial bank with $10 million in deposit liabilities, an amount consistent with the money supply the central bank wishes to maintain in consideration of monetary policy. There are no reserve requirements and no LLR facility. The commercial bank voluntarily holds 10% of its assets in cash against withdrawal risk. It makes no difference whether the bank's cash assets are vault cash or deposits at the central bank, so for simplicity assume that these assets are all on deposit at the Federal Reserve where they earn nothing. The commercial bank's balance sheet would then be

Commercial Bank		
Cash assets	$1 million	Deposit liability
Loans or other earning assets	*$9 million*	*$10 million*
Total assets	$10 million	Total liabilities $10 million

The Federal Reserve's balance sheet, to a first approximation, would show

Federal Reserve		
Earning assets	$1 million	Deposit liability $1 million

Note that the Federal Reserve's deposit liability corresponds to the bank's cash assets. Now suppose the Federal Reserve introduces an LLR facility. It has no reason to change the money supply, but banks now have a new source of liquidity. Hence, they will feel less need to hold nonearning cash assets. Say they cut these holdings from 10% to 5%. The bank's balance sheet now becomes

Commercial Bank		
Cash assets	$0.5 million	Deposit liability
Loans or other earning assets	*$9.5 million*	*$10 million*
Total assets	$10 million	Total liabilities $10 million

and the Federal Reserve shrinks to

Federal Reserve		
Earning assets	$0.5 million	Deposit liabilities $0.5 million

In effect, $0.5 million in earning assets have been transferred from the Federal Reserve's balance sheet to the bank's balance sheet, and this occurs as a direct consequence of the introduction of the LLR.

One could argue that if the LLR facility is properly priced, the moral hazard will be discouraged. However, note that before its introduction, the LLR interest rate was infinite, so that any finite interest rate will improve bank liquidity, and should therefore result in some reserve dissipation. As a historical matter, the LLR tends to price low for reasons that are not entirely clear. This generous pricing practice aggravates the moral hazard problem and heightens the need for legal reserve requirements.

Thus, reserve requirements control the moral hazard of the LLR, and a lowering of reserve requirements transfers deposit seigniorage from the public to the banks. Raising reserve requirements has the reverse effect. One hundred percent reserve requirements shift all deposit seigniorage to the public. This is the basis for the conventional wisdom that the reserve requirement is a tax on the banks, but one could just as easily argue that any reserve requirement less than 100 percent is a subsidy to banks. The hard question here is: To whom should the monopoly rents associated with administered money belong?

REFERENCES

BIS, 2008. Principles for Sound Liquidity Risk Management and Supervision. Basel Committee on Bank Supervision, Bank for International Settlement, Basel.

Bouwman, C., 2014. Liquidity: how banks create it and how it should be regulated. In: Berger, A.N., Molyneux, P., Wilson, J.O.S. (Eds.), The Oxford Handbook of Banking, second ed, Oxford, UK.

Brunnermeier, M.K., Pedersen, L.H., 2009. Market liquidity and funding liquidity. Rev. Finan. Stud. 22, 2201–2238.

Farhi, E., Tirole, J., 2012. Collective moral hazard, maturity mismatch, and systemic bailouts. Am. Econ. Rev. 102, 60–93.

Huang, R., Ratnovski, L., 2011. The dark side of bank wholesale funding. J. Finan. Intermed. 20, 248–263.

Part IV

"On Balance Sheet" Banking Activities

Chapter 7

Spot Lending and Credit Risk

"Neither a borrower nor a lender be; for loan oft loses itself and a friend, and borrowing dulls the edge of husbandry."

William Shakespeare

GLOSSARY OF TERMS

Loan The extension of credit via a typically untraded and illiquid debt contract.

Security A financial claim, debt, or equity, which may be traded or untraded.

COD Cash on delivery as a method of payment for goods received.

Commercial Paper Unsecured debt, offered as a short-maturity (less than 270 days) security by corporations.

T-bills, T-notes, and T-bonds Debt securities of varying maturities issued by the U.S. government through the U.S. Treasury Department; hence, "T" for Treasury.

FHLB Federal Home Loan Bank. The Federal Home Loan Bank System, headed by the Federal Home Loan Bank Board, was formerly the primary regulatory agency for savings and loan associations. The district home loan banks are now providers of financial services, including liquidity, to smaller commercial banks and thrifts.

FHLMC This stands for the Federal Home Loan Mortgage Corporation. Also known as "Freddie Mac," its basic function is to facilitate the provision of liquidity to lenders by purchasing existing mortgages from their portfolios. It finances these purchases by borrowing from the Federal Home Loan Banks, issuing GNMA-guaranteed mortgage-backed bonds, selling mortgage participation certificates on which it guarantees interest and principal, and selling guaranteed mortgage certificates.

FNMA This stands for the Federal National Mortgage Association. It is a privately owned (stockholder-owned), government-sponsored enterprise. Also known as "Fannie Mae," its basic function is to provide a secondary market in trading and securitizing home mortgages. It is the largest purchaser of residential mortgages in the United States. Its activities are similar to those of Freddie Mac, except that it faces no statutory limitations on the organizations with which it can conduct business.

GNMA This stands for the Government National Mortgage Association. This is a wholly owned, corporate instrumentality of the U.S. government, operating within the Department of Housing and Urban Development (HUD). Also referred to as "Ginnie Mae," its role is to enhance liquidity in the market for mortgages. Ginnie Mae does this in a variety of ways. For example, many mortgages carry a fixed interest rate so that when market interest rates rise, existing mortgages sell at a discount (i.e., at less than face value). Ginnie Mae issues a commitment to the mortgage seller (e.g., the originating financial institution) to purchase the mortgage at a fixed price. After acquiring the loan, Ginnie Mae sells it to "Fannie Mae" at the prevailing market price. Ginnie Mae absorbs any discount from the price paid to the seller. Another function of Ginnie Mae is to guarantee securities backed by government-insured or guaranteed mortgages. That is, Ginnie Mae provides guarantees for securitized claims against portfolios of government-insured mortgages.

S&P Stock Index Standard & Poor's composite index of 500 large-company stocks.

Incentive Compatibility A condition that requires the alignment of incentives between the agent and the principal. See Chapter 1.

C&I Loans Commercial and Industrial loans. These are loans extended to nonfinancial firms.

Nash Equilibrium A steady state attained when none of the contracting parties has an incentive to change its actions unilaterally. See Chapter 1.

HLT Highly Leveraged Transaction, which is a loan to a borrower with a very high debt/equity ratio.

Collateral An asset used to secure a loan. Failure to repay the loan completely and in time results in a transfer of the collateral to the lender.

Absolute Priority Rule A rule that prioritizes creditors' claims to a borrower's assets according to their seniorities.

GAAP Generally Accepted Accounting Principles.

Prime Rate A reference/benchmark borrowing rate posted by the bank for its better customers.

LIBOR London Interbank Offer Rate. This is the interest rate banks charge each other for short-term loans in the United Kingdom.

CD Rate The interest rate offered by banks on certificates of deposit.

Optimal Stopping Rule A statistical decision rule that tells the decision-maker when to stop a sequential sampling process and make a decision. For example, a bank may have $1 million to lend and knows that the longer it waits, the more loan applicants it can screen before deciding who to lend the money to. However, waiting is costly because of the time value of money. An optimal stopping rule in this case would specify conditions under which the bank would find it most profitable to stop screening further loan applications. Another example is determining when a bank should stop acquiring additional information about a borrower, and make a decision.

Discriminant Analysis A statistical technique used to identify the factors most useful in predicting an event. An example would be the factors useful in predicting bankruptcy.

The Glass–Steagall Act An act passed by Congress in 1933 to separate commercial and investment banking in the United States. It prohibits commercial banks from engaging in securities underwriting and other investment banking activities as well as the activities of insurance companies.

S. I. Greenbaum, A. V. Thakor & A. W. A. Boot: Contemporary Financial Intermediation, Third edition. http://dx.doi.org/10.1016/B978-0-12-405196-6.00007-0

INTRODUCTION

For many commercial bankers, lending is the heart of the business. Loans dominate asset holdings and account for a large share of revenues and costs. Lending takes place in both spot and forward credit markets. We begin here with a discussion of spot lending.

The purpose of this chapter is to explore the asset side of the bank's balance sheet. We begin in the next section with a brief review of the most prominent assets on a bank's balance sheet. The following section explains what we mean by lending, and the difference between loans and securities. We also discuss how these assets are purchased. The structure of loan agreements is discussed in a subsequent section. This is followed by a section that discusses the major informational problems in loan contracts and the importance of (perceived) loan performance for the determination of a bank's stock price. The next section examines credit analysis. Our emphasis is on the economic underpinnings of the various traditional factors considered in credit analysis. In particular, we relate these economic underpinnings to the informational problems pervasive in loan contracting. In the section that follows, we turn to sources of credit information. We consider both internal sources within the bank and external sources such as financial information agencies. In the next section, we take up analysis of borrower's financial statements. We follow it up with a section on the examination of loan covenants. Our focus is on the why of each covenant. A case study follows the concluding section.

DESCRIPTION OF BANK ASSETS

Trends in the Composition of Bank Assets

There are three basic types of assets on a bank's balance sheet: loans, marketable securities, and cash. (See Figure 7.1.) Before we discuss each of these in detail, we will briefly review recent trends in the composition of bank-asset portfolios.

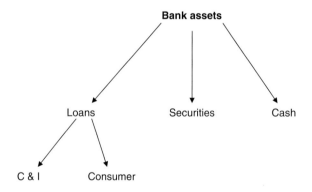

FIGURE 7.1 Spot Lending.

In Figure 7.2, we show the time-series behavior of the composition of commercial bank assets. While loans have risen slightly as a fraction of total assets in the late 1970s and 1980s, they declined slightly thereafter. Security holdings declined slightly in the late 1970s and have been relatively steady since. Cash and reserves declined quite a bit until the 2007–2009 financial crisis, but then grew substantially. A clearer picture of what has been going on emerges from Figure 7.3, which shows the time-series behavior of commercial bank loans, mortgages, and consumer loans. It is apparent that C&I loans have declined in relative importance as banks have increased their mortgage holdings.[1]

There are two main reasons for this trend. The first has to do with the changing nature of commercial lending. A bank has an advantage over the capital market in providing credit to a firm as long as banks have cheaper access to loanable funds than investors, *and/or* banks can resolve private information and moral hazard problems more effectively. Over the years, much of the deposit-related rents available to banks have eroded, thereby extinguishing virtually all of the funding advantage possessed by banks. Moreover, with the boom in financial innovation in the last two decades, a variety of

---

1. Consumer loans mainly comprise credit cards, installment loans, car loans, and other similar loans, primarily aimed at financing the needs of individual consumers and households. Mortgages are also consumer loans but typically considered a separate category within consumer loans. Most consumer loans are essentially "commodity products," with apparently little product differentiation across banks. However, this does not mean there is no room for innovation. For example, Wells Fargo gained prominence in the consumer loan market with its hybrid of a fixed-rate mortgage and an adjustable-rate loan. Moreover, the effectiveness with which credit information is processed is crucial in determining the attributes of consumers to whom these loans are made, and hence their profitability.

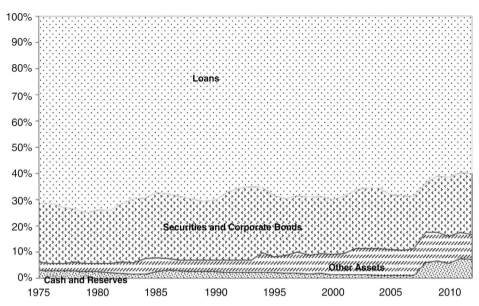

FIGURE 7.2   Composition of Commercial Bank Assets *(Source: Federal Reserve Statistical Release: Flow of Funds Accounts of the U.S. 1975–1984, 1985–1994, 1995–2004, 2005–2011, and 2012).*

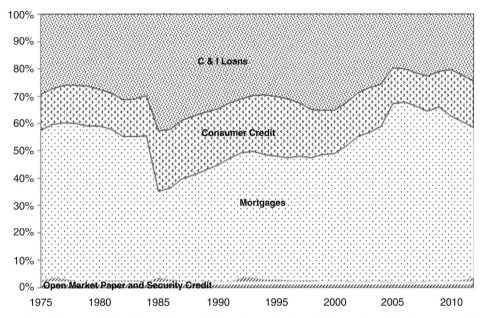

FIGURE 7.3   Composition of Commercial Bank Loans *(Source: Federal Reserve Statistical Release: Flow of Funds Accounts of the U.S. 1975–1984, 1985–1994, 1995–2004, 2005–2011, and 2012).*

new securities have been used by firms to raise funds directly from the capital market. These securities, as well as the securitization of bank-originated loans (see Chapter 11), have been designed to cope with the very problems of private information and moral hazard that banks have specialized in solving.[2] Thus, the relative advantage of banks over the capital market in providing credit to firms has diminished. With the capital market becoming a more viable source of competition in the commercial lending arena, the profitability of lending to large corporations has declined significantly for banks; hence, the relative decline in C&I lending. Nonetheless, commercial lending continues to be an important source of finance for companies and individuals, and when bank lending declines due to exogenous shocks to bank capital, small firms that rely largely on bank financing, are especially affected by this.

---

2. For example, Green (1984) shows that a convertible bond (i.e., a bond that can later be converted to stock by the bondholder) can be effective in controlling the moral hazard problem stemming from the borrowing firm's inclination to invest in risky projects to the detriment of bondholders.

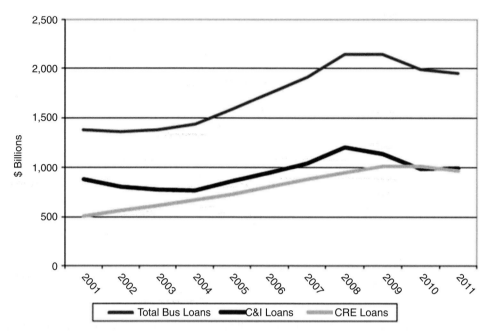

FIGURE 7.4   Commercial Bank Loans 2001–2011 *(Source: June Call Report Data, and Cole, 2012).*

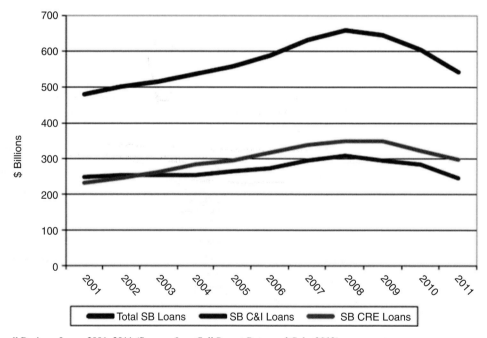

FIGURE 7.5   Small Business Loans 2001–2011 *(Source: June Call Report Data, and Cole, 2012).*

As a consequence of the financial crisis, the Federal Deposit Insurance Corporation (FDIC) closed more than 100 banks during 2009, something that had not happened since 1992. Moreover, during 2009–2011, a total of 397 banks failed. The consequences for bank lending to small businesses were severe. It has been documented that during 2008–2011, small-business lending in the United States declined by $116 billion, or almost 18% from $659 billion to only $543 billion[3] (see Figures 7.4 and 7.5).

---

3. See Cole (2012).

Types of Bank Loans

We will first discuss business loans, often referred to as C&I loans, which fall into four main categories.

1. *Transaction Loans:* A transaction loan is negotiated for a specific purchase and is tailored to the particular needs of the purchaser. The demand for these loans from a particular borrower is typically episodic and hence each loan is negotiated separately. The loan is usually secured by the asset being financed with the loan (e.g., equity in another company), and repayment is expected to come from the use of this asset.
2. *Working Capital Loans:* These loans are used by firms to finance routine day-to-day transactions. Thus, they are general purpose, short-term borrowings and are often used either to purchase current assets (like inventories) or to repay debts incurred in purchasing current assets. These loans are also usually secured by collateral such as accounts receivables or inventories.
3. *Term Loans:* These are longer maturity loans used to buy fixed assets requiring large outlays of capital. Maturities typically run from 3 to 10 years. Repayment is normally amortized because it comes out of the cash flows generated by the asset financed with the loan. Borrowings are almost always drawn down under revolving lines of credit or similar commitments.
4. *Combinations:* Working capital loans often include provisions that permit the conversion of short-term borrowings into term loans at the borrower's request.

We will now briefly review consumer loans.

1. *Consumer Loans (excluding mortgage loans):* The most important types of consumer loans are direct loans and bank credit card receivables. A *direct consumer loan* is typically financing for the purchase of durable goods such as cars, boats, or appliances, and is secured with the asset being purchased. *Bank credit card* borrowings are a form of short-term, unsecured general purpose credit. Credit cards became widely used in the mid-1960s. Credit card lending has proved to be very profitable for banks.[4] The profitability of bank credit cards stems from three sources: (i) the discount at which the bank purchases sales slips from merchants (this discount typically ranges from 2% to 6%), (ii) the interest rate charged to a card user who chooses not to remain current in payments (most cards extend an interest-free grace period based on a monthly billing cycle), and (iii) the annual membership fees charged to credit card users.[5]
2. *Mortgage Loans:* These are a specialized form of consumer and commercial lending. The purpose of a mortgage loan is to finance the acquisition or improvement of real estate. These loans are almost always secured by the real estate they finance. The three principal types of mortgage loans are: residential mortgage loans, construction loans, and commercial mortgage loans.

Until the advent of securitization, mortgage loans were illiquid assets because of the uniqueness of each property, the severity of private information problems, and the uncertain maturity of the loan due to the possibility of prepayment by the borrower. However, securitization took care of many of these impediments to the marketability of mortgages and facilitated the liquification of these instruments. This was especially true in the market for residential mortgages where Fannie Mae and Freddie Mac led the way under government auspices.

Securitization is a technology for transforming illiquid loans into traded liquid securities by separating the origination of the instrument from its funding. Typically, a financial institution such as a bank "originates" the loan, that is, it screens the applicant, designs the loan contract, and determines the pricing parameters. However, instead of using deposits to fund the loan as in the traditional case, the bank sells the loan to a special trust that assembles a portfolio of loans and funds the portfolio in the capital market, often with the advice and assistance of an investment banker. The services provided by the investment banker include the sale of claims against the loan portfolio to investors and then the maintenance of a secondary market in the securitized claims. The enormous growth in securitization in the past two to three decades is evidence of its benefits in the mortgage market. These benefits stemmed from the liquidity created by the standardization, diversification, possible subsidies provided by the government via Fannie Mae and Freddie Mac, and new contract design that accompanied securitization. Securitization is discussed in greater detail in Chapter 11.

Earlier, fixed-rate mortgages – in which the borrower's interest rate is fixed over the life of the mortgage – dominated the market. However, since the legalization of adjustable-rate mortgages (ARMs) in the 1980s there has been an explosion in the variety of mortgage designs. The terms of mortgages are as varied as the needs of borrowers and the imagination of lenders.

---

4. Except during 2009–2010 when credit losses mushroomed in the wake of financial crisis (Durkin et al. (2014)). See also Ausubel (1991).
5. Many banks waive these annual fees because of increased competition for credit card business.

Marketable Securities Held by Banks

1. *Bankers Acceptances:* These instruments arise mostly in connection with international trade. A banker's acceptance is a bank-guaranteed indebtedness of the bank's customer to a third party. This instrument usually arises as a time draft written by a firm in order to pay for some goods either in local currency or in foreign exchange. The draft is then "accepted" by the bank, that is, the bank guarantees its face value at maturity. The acceptance is then either held by the bank or sold in the secondary market and may be held by another bank. The originating bank typically charges a fee for the guarantee (acceptance) that is independent of the interest paid on the borrowing. Maturity is usually less than 6 months.

   A banker's acceptance facilitates trade between parties that operate in different legal systems with wide geographical and cultural separation. If the exporter does not know the importer well enough, it will not ship goods, even on a COD basis. However, it is likely that the importer's bank is better known and hence its willingness to guarantee payment – which serves the purpose of substituting its own credit risk for that of the importer – facilitates trade. The bank issuing the guarantee also can be expected to know more about the importer, usually a customer of the bank. Its informational advantage vis-á-vis the exporter allows the bank to earn a fee on the acceptance. Thus, bankers' acceptances are closely tied to the bank's role in providing a more efficient resolution of informational problems. For more on this, see Chapter 10.

2. *Commercial Paper:* This is unsecured debt issued on the strength of the issuer's name. It is sold on a discounted basis like Treasury bills,[6] with maturities ranging from 3 to 270 days and interest rates typically lower than prime and comparable to those on CDs and bankers acceptances. Only the best-known firms issue commercial paper because it is sold *directly* to investors, without an intermediary to resolve informational problems.

3. *U.S. Government Securities:* These are important instruments for commercial banks because of their default-free nature and the highly liquid markets in which they are traded. As we saw in Chapter 3, private information content undermines liquidity, so U.S. government securities – which embody virtually no private information – provide banks with liquidity.

   Income from all U.S. government securities is subject to federal income taxes as well as capital gains tax, but is exempt from state and local income taxes. Marketable U.S. government securities are of three types: bills, notes, and bonds. Treasury bills (T-bills) are short-term U.S. government securities (with original maturities of 91 days, 182 days, and 1 year) that, like commercial paper, are sold on a discounted basis. Treasury notes are similar to T-bills except that they have maturities not less than 1 year and not more than 7 years. Treasury bonds are issued with original maturities that often exceed 10 years, and can be as long as 30 years.

4. *U.S. Government Agency Securities:* These are certificates of indebtedness issued by agencies of the U.S. government, such as the Federal Intermediate Credit Bank, the Federal National Mortgage Association (FNMA or Fannie Mae), the Federal Home Loan Bank (FHLB), and the Government National Mortgage Association (GNMA or Ginnie Mae). They are not direct obligations of the U.S. government, and they typically trade at a small premium over Treasury debt. Income on these securities, like direct U.S. government obligations, is exempt from state and local taxes, but not from federal taxes.

5. *State and Local Securities and Municipal Bonds:* These debt instruments usually have a higher after-tax yield than Treasury and agency securities of comparable duration because of higher default risk and weaker liquidity. Their interest payments are exempt from federal income taxes as well as from home-state and local taxes. State and local government bonds can be divided into three broad categories: housing authority bonds, general obligation bonds, and revenue bonds. Housing authority bonds are issued by local housing agencies to build and administer housing. They are guaranteed by the federal government and are therefore virtually riskless. A bond is called a general obligation bond if the full faith and credit of the issuer stands behind the debt. In contrast, the interest and principal of a revenue bond is supported solely by the cash flow of a designated public project or undertaking. The revenues supporting these bonds may come from: (i) specifically dedicated taxes such as those on cigarettes, gasoline, and beer, (ii) tolls for roads, bridges, and airports, (iii) rent payments on buildings, office spaces, and the like. Typically, the bond payments are linked to the revenues produced by the project the bonds were used to finance.

6. *Other Assets:* These include vault cash and deposits at the Federal Reserve, equity in subsidiaries, physical capital like buildings, computers, and loans originated by other banks that may have been acquired by the bank as part of a loan sale or through securitization. For short periods of time, the bank may also possess a variety of other assets acquired as collateral from delinquent borrowers.

---

6. There is no explicitly stated interest rate, but the claim is sold at a price less than its face value (value at maturity), the difference implicitly defining the interest cost. Note, however, that discount yields are not directly comparable to bond yields; a translation is required to achieve comparability.

WHAT IS LENDING?

A Definition

What is a *bank loan*? Simply put, it is the purchase of an asset (the borrower's indebtedness) that is typically an illiquid and highly customized financial claim against the borrower's future cash flows. In effect, the bank is obtaining from the borrower the legal right to a prespecified portion of the borrower's future cash flows over a prespecified period of time, and paying the borrower the present value of these cash flows. The bank's claim represents the borrower's repayment obligation and the loan amount represents the present value of these future obligations, assuming no extraordinary profit for the bank.

Methods of Acquiring Loans

There are two principal methods by which banks acquire loans: through *spot market purchases* and through *forward market purchases*. In the spot market, the bank can either originate the loan and then fund it by keeping the loan on its own books, or it can purchase the loan from another intermediary that originated it. A spot loan is created when the bank extends credit to a loan applicant immediately upon approval of the application. In the forward market, the bank issues a *promise* to the applicant that it will lend in the future on prespecified terms. Such a promise is known as a *loan commitment*. The bank commits to lend to the borrower up to a certain amount in the future on terms that are prespecified and at the option of the borrower. In this case, the bank is committing to purchase a financial claim from a particular borrower at some time in the future.

We discuss these two methods of asset acquisition in separate chapters. Spot market purchases and forward lending are covered in separate subsequent chapters. This division is merely for expositional convenience. In practice, the volume of spot and forward lending are inextricably linked. The extent of spot lending by the bank depends on how many of its outstanding loan commitments sold in previous periods are exercised or taken down in the current period. In general, a higher volume of takedowns of outstanding loan commitments implies a lower volume of spot lending in the current period, although the *total* volume of lending in the current period may rise (relative to that in the previous period) because of an unexpectedly high take-down on previously made commitments. This follows from the size constraints on banks associated with financial and human capital limitations.

The Decomposition of the Lending Function

The Decomposition

The subtlety of lending transactions is often blurred in the bundling together of distinct services relating to credit transactions. The normal commercial bank loan is logically decomposable into origination (the broker), funding (the lender), servicing (the collector), and risk-processing services (the guarantor). And lending can be thought of largely as credit risk management that includes these four activities as well as the bank's credit culture. See Figure 7.6.

Origination involves the activity of initiating a loan to a borrower. It is often described as the initial solicitation of the borrower and the screening of the loan application by the bank. Origination includes credit analysis and the design of the loan contract, both of which we discuss at length later in this chapter. *Funding* is the actual extension of the loan after an affirmative decision is reached in the credit-analysis process. *Servicing* involves collecting loan repayments and keeping records. *Risk processing* involves postlending monitoring to control default risk, as well as activities designed to control the bank's interest rate risk arising from a loan duration that differs from the duration of the bank's liabilities. The *credit culture* involves the bank's organizational design, reporting arrangements, communication practices, and incentive schemes for credit officers. We will discuss credit culture later in the book. Much of our focus in this chapter and the next will be on origination (in particular, loan contract design and credit analysis) and risk processing (in particular, the control of default risk).

Industry Specialization

In the thrift industry (savings and loan associations, mutual savings banks, and the like), different institutions provide distinct credit services, which is clear evidence of institution specialization. For example, the mortgage banker originates loans and the mortgage processor services the loans. The loan is typically funded by the public (the net saver or surplus spending unit) in the form of newly purchased savings and loan deposits or mortgage-backed securities. The bulk of the credit and interest rate risk is sustained by savings and loan stockholders, the U.S. government (FDIC, NCUA, GNMA), specialized private insurers (e.g., Mortgage Guarantee Insurance Corporation), or some combination of the three (FNMA, FHLMC). In commercial banking, it is common for the bank to hold originated loans. Consequently, the origination, servicing, and

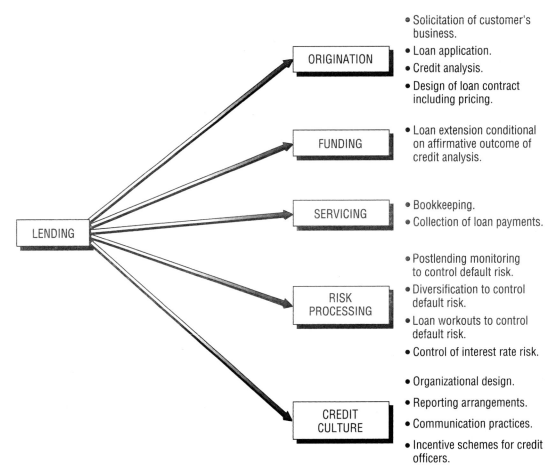

FIGURE 7.6 Decomposition of the Lending Function.

risk absorption is evidenced by an earning asset on the bank's balance sheet. The bank depositor holding a risk-free asset is funding the bank loans. The government, through the FDIC and the bank stockholders, shares the risks (uninsured depositors may sustain some exposure as well). Should the bank sell a loan, say to a closed-end mutual fund (as in the case of a savings and loan association selling mortgages to FHLMC or an investment bank for packaging into a mortgage-backed security), then the security holder would do the funding and the location of the risk would depend on the specific terms (recourse or nonrecourse) of the sale. Irrespective of the terms of the sale, however, the bank need show no earning asset on its balance sheet and virtually all the same services would have been performed and the same exposures sustained without any accounting evidence thereof. This statement requires some qualification in that if a loan is sold with recourse, the accountant will probably insist on booking the asset, but if a loan is sold without recourse and a letter of credit is issued insuring against default (the above are equivalent), the balance sheet will show no loan and the letter of credit will probably appear in a footnote to the balance sheet, but not in its body.

In fact, banking reserve and deposit insurance premiums provide banks with an incentive to sell, rather than hold, earning assets. In this way, the bank can avoid these costs.

The traditional subsidy inherent in deposits (owing to underpriced deposit insurance, Regulation Q, and entry restrictions) encouraged banks to hold earning assets whereas deposit insurance premiums, reserve, and capital requirements, along with less explicit regulatory costs, were a partial offset to the deposit subsidy. However, the deposit subsidy is rapidly disappearing, whereas many of the regulatory costs remain. Thus, we can predict that banks will de-emphasize the holding of the loans they originate, service, and guarantee. The recent emphasis on "fee income" is a reflection of this phenomenon.

LOANS VERSUS SECURITIES

In the previous discussions, we have talked about *loans* and *securities* as two distinct claims. The way we have defined loans, there is little difference between loans and debt securities, except that the latter are usually more liquid. That is, securities are traded in secondary markets, whereas loans usually are not. Loans are essentially *private* debt placements with banks. You will recall from our discussions in Chapter 4 that liquidity and marketability are interrelated. From an economic viewpoint, the distinction between loans and securities is in their *relative liquidity*.[7]

Viewed in this light, recent developments in the loan market can be seen as narrowing the distinction between loans and securities. We refer to *loan sales* and *securitization*. A loan sale, which is a fairly old practice, is simply the selling of a loan by the originating bank to an alternative funding agent, usually another bank. This can either be an *outright sale* of the loan, where the loan may have been originated by a single bank or as part of a *loan syndication*. With an outright sale, the originating bank disengages itself from the loan, that is, it makes the initial loan and then turns around and sells it to another bank, thereby removing the loan from its own balance sheet. A fee is earned for the originating service, so that the transaction leaves its mark on the originator's income statement. With an outright loan sale, the bank acts as a pure broker, although in practice almost every loan sale involves the originating bank retaining a part of the loan, so the bank is not a pure broker. Some loans are also made under syndication arrangements in which case there is *joint* origination of the loans by several banks. These loans may then be sold to others. Again, the "lead banks" in the syndicate earn fees.

Thus, loan sales enhance loan liquidity, especially if the originator maintains a secondary market. This blurs the distinction between loans and securities. A more recent practice for improving loan liquidity is securitization, which we discuss in detail in Chapter 11. Both loan sales and securitization trivialize the distinctions between loans and securities.

STRUCTURE OF LOAN AGREEMENTS

Trends in Loan Agreements

Commercial bank lending was once a fairly simple business. Most business loans were short-term, self-liquidating working capital credits, and terms were often left to informal agreements between a bank and its customers. Business lending began getting more complex in the 1930s when banks started making loans with maturities of more than a year, so-called term loans. Relations between banks and business borrowers have been growing more complex – and more formal – ever since.

Part of the push for more formality and variety in the design of agreements comes from the need for banks and borrowers to protect themselves from movements in interest rates over the credit cycle. Increases in market interest rates boost the costs to banks of funding outstanding loans and also reduce the attractiveness of existing credits. Reductions in market interest rates, on the other hand, often trigger prepayments.

Floating interest rates have been one of the most important innovations in bank lending since the advent of the term loan. Provisions for adjusting loan rates periodically give banks some protection against interest rate risk. By combining the advantages of term and short-term loans, floating rates have allowed banks to compete for a share of the business credit market – even in the face of increased competition from the commercial paper market and other nonbank credit suppliers. At the same time, floating rates have effected changes in the other terms and conditions of commercial lending. An unintended consequence has been the loss of some borrowers who switched from banks to the capital market to obtain longer-term debt with greater fixity in the borrowing rate.

Details of Loan Agreements

A loan agreement specifies the obligations of borrower and lender, makes certain warranties, and usually places certain controls and restrictions on the borrower. It states the amount to be borrowed, or *the principal*. The agreement also states *the maturity:* short-term (less than 1 year), intermediate-term (1–5 years), and long-term (greater than 5 years). *The pricing formula* is also stated. The interest rate may be a fixed or a floating rate. If the interest rate is floating, it may be "prime-plus" (e.g., the prime rate plus 1%) or "times-prime" (e.g., the prime rate times 1.05). Pricing might also be at a "transaction

---

7. From a legal standpoint, however, the distinction between a loan and a security was crucial during the Glass–Steagall Act, which prohibited commercial banks from engaging directly in securities activities. The statutory definition of a "security" is an expansive one; see Huber (1989) and Markham and Gjyshi (2014). According to the 1934 Securities Exchange Act, the term "security" means not only any stock, bond, debenture, and evidence of indebtedness, but also the "countless and variable schemes devised by those who seek the use of the money of others on the promise of profits." However, a general exception is made for situations where the *context* makes it inappropriate to treat an instrument as a security. For example, a loan participation purchased by a depository institution from another institution is not considered a security. The minimum consequence of concluding that an instrument is a security is that the antifraud provisions of the securities laws become applicable. In practice, therefore, the distinction between a loan and a security is driven largely by legal interpretation that cannot always be supported on economic grounds. With the dismantling of the Glass–Steagall Act, this distinction has become somewhat of a moot point.

rate," that is, the bank agrees *ex ante* to a fixed mark-up over a current money rate (e.g., T-bill, the negotiable CD rate, or the commercial paper rate). The agreement also states the closing fees to be paid when the loan gets funded. In a competitive situation this fee may be 0.25–0.375%, and higher in other situations. Also, a penalty or default rate of interest may be stipulated for late or early payments.

Although loan agreements usually are tailored to meet the requirements of specific situations, most contain certain standard provisions, which may be divided into three general categories: conditions precedent, warranties (also called representations), and covenants and events of default.

The "*conditions precedent*" section includes requirements that the borrower must satisfy before the bank is legally obliged to fund the loan. These conditions may include specific business transactions that must be completed or events that must have occurred. Other standard items are the opinions of counsel, certificate of no defaults, the note, and resolutions of the borrower's board of directors authorizing the transaction.

The "*warranties*" section of the loan agreement contains information and assumptions about the borrower's legal status and creditworthiness. By executing the loan agreement, the borrower attests to the accuracy and truth of the information provided as of the date of execution. Misrepresentation constitutes an event of default. Principal warranties include the following:

- A warranty that all financial statements submitted to the lender are genuine and fairly represent the financial position of the borrower (i.e., that no material adverse change has occurred).
- The borrower has a valid title to all assets.
- The borrower has complied with all federal, state, and municipal laws and is not involved in litigation.
- The borrower has filed all necessary tax returns and has paid all taxes due.
- No need for third-party consent.
- No violation of existing agreements.
- Collateral offered is owned by the borrower and is free of liens.

Covenants are a negotiated part of loan agreements. Warranties verify certain statements by the borrower at the date of execution of the loan agreement. Covenants carry forward the warranties and establish the borrower's ongoing obligation to maintain a certain status for the loan's duration. Covenants set minimum standards for a borrower's future conduct and performance and thereby accelerate the loan in the event of untoward developments. Violation of a covenant creates an *event of default* and gives the bank the right to "accelerate" the required repayment. We will have more to say about covenants in a later section of this chapter.

INFORMATIONAL PROBLEMS IN LOAN CONTRACTS AND THE IMPORTANCE OF LOAN PERFORMANCE

Informational Problems

If there were no informational problems in loans, there might not be any profits for banks in lending. At one extreme, the costless availability of information obviates the need for banks and other financial intermediaries. At the other, costly customer-specific information provides an opportunity for banks to profitably process information and facilitate lending. In general, the less transparent is the credit information about a given borrower, the greater is the bank's ability to utilize its "uniqueness" and the higher is its profit potential. Thus, the paucity of good credit information in the public domain is a thing for banks to desire.[8] Since we have already discussed the informational problems addressed by banks (Chapters 2 and 3), we will merely review these here. The first problem is that the borrower is privately informed about its own credit risk. Unless the bank can elicit at least part of this information, market failure could result (recall the discussion of Akerlof in Chapter 1). We will see shortly that *credit analysis* helps the bank reduce its informational disadvantage vis-à-vis the borrower.

The other problem in lending is *moral hazard.* When the borrower takes a loan from the bank, it becomes an agent of the bank and is in a similar relationship with the bank as the shareholders of a firm are with bondholders. This agency problem is manifested in the borrower's desire to take on additional risk to the bank's detriment, as we saw in Chapter 1. Loan contracts are therefore designed to control the borrower's risk-taking propensity. To the extent that some preference

---

8. Consider the following quote, *"Let us state a simple but often overlooked proposition: The health of a country's banking industry is inversely related to the speed and efficiency of information transfer,"* Sanford Rose, "Why Banks Make So Many Bad Loans," *American Banker*, June 19, 1990.

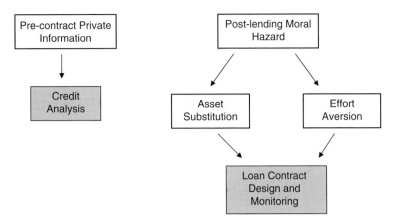

FIGURE 7.7 Information Problems in Loan Contracts.

for risk remains, the loan contract should also enable the bank to monitor the borrower and prevent actions that increase the risk of default. We will see how collateral, loan covenants, and other features of loan contracts can be structured to meet this important objective.

Figure 7.7 pictorially depicts the informational problems in loan contracts.

The Importance of Loan Performance

The bank's loan portfolio affects the financial health and viability of the bank. When bank stock prices decline, quite often most of the decline in bank stock prices is attributable to information releases about asset quality problems at banks.

Loan losses can not only mean plunging stock prices, but can also spell trouble for top management at banks. It is well known that poorer corporate performance often precipitates a higher probability of CEO turnover.[9]

Loan Portfolio Diversification as a Risk Management Tool

The performance of a bank's loan portfolio often determines its financial performance. Although diversification is often a key to managing credit losses, many banks are constrained in their diversification efforts. For example, smaller banks often feel disadvantaged in their ability to diversify their credit risk by virtue of loan size limitations and geographic insularity. Moreover, these banks prefer limiting themselves to local markets because those are the markets they are most familiar with. This specialization-induced desire to stick to what is familiar leads to credit concentrations in banks, and this is typically reflected in the incidence of financial stress in periods of recession.

Despite regulatory attempts to encourage banks to diversify – by imposing limits on the maximum amount the bank can lend to a single borrower – the effects of lack of loan portfolio diversification can be clearly seen in the performance of banks in many regions. Banks in the United States have often displayed high performance correlation with banks that are similarly geographically situated. For example, when real-estate values plunged in the 1980s in Texas, Oklahoma, and Louisiana, financial performance indicators for the banks in those states plunged as well.

It does appear, however, that the benefits of diversification have begun to more strongly influence banks' portfolio choices in the 1990s and post-2000, which coincides with the growing popularity of loan syndication, loan sales, and securitization as diversification vehicles for banks. For example, although most United States community banks conduct much of their business in their own regions, there is evidence that these banks are able to withstand local economic downturns.[10] Moreover, in contrast to their relatively poor performance in the 1980s, small banks significantly improved their performance in the 1990s.[11] Credit losses have been relatively low since. However, pressure on lending margins (in conjunction with the low interest rate environment) has suppressed profitability. Given their dependence on interest income, community banks returns have on average been lower than those of noncommunity banks. Failure rates during the 2007–2009 financial crisis were up, but community banks, especially that had remained disciplined with a diversified local lending focus, fared

---

9. See, for example, Brickley (2003).
10. See FDIC (2012) pointing to the benefits of the relationship banking model.
11. See Hall and Yeager (2002) and Bassett and Brady (2001).

relatively well. Those that shifted towards C&D (construction and development) loans were most exposed,[12] performed reasonably well over the 2007–2009 period, and overall had relatively low credit losses.

The experience of community banks during the study period appears to indicate that maintaining a stable balance between growth and earnings has been the surest path to long-term viability.

In addition, small banks have also improved their profitability and survival rates. The FDIC reported that about 1250 new community banks were established between 1992 and 2003, of which about 100 merged and about 1100 remained independent, with only four having failed. The resilience and plurality of the local U.S. banking markets may, in part, explain the better performance of the U.S. financial sector compared to that in Europe following the 2007–2009 financial crisis. The dependence of Europe on large, homogeneous, and overleveraged financial institutions (see Chapter 2) caused substantial pain.[13]

We now define terms that are routinely used in discussions of credit risk.

Interest Rate Spread: The difference between loan and deposit interest rates.

Provision for Loan Losses: A fraction of the loan principal earmarked by the bank as a buffer to absorb (expected) loan losses, and kept as part of the bank's capital.

Net Interest Spread After Provision: Interest rate spread after adjustment for taxes and subtraction of provision of loan losses.

Noninterest Income: Bank's income from activities other than lending, such as fees on cash management services, fees on contingent claims like loan commitments, letters of credit, and so on.

ROA: Bank's return on assets.

ROE: Bank's return on equity.

Nonperforming Loans/Reserves: Ratio of loans considered likely to default to the provision for loan losses.

Net Chargeoffs/Average Loans: Ratio of chargeoff of delinquent loans to the average loans extended by the bank.

Typically, interest rates are set such that interest rate spreads are higher for riskier loans. Banks also make higher provision for loan losses when the loans are riskier, and net chargeoffs/average loans also tend to be higher for such loans. Diversification can reduce the impact of losses in a particular loan class on the bank's overall net chargeoffs. Whether noninterest income, ROA, and ROE are higher or lower for riskier loans depends on the degree of competition in that particular market and cannot be unambiguously stated *a priori*.

Despite the obvious gains from diversification, why are all banks not highly diversified? There are at least four reasons. First, there is the issue of limitations on the opportunity to diversify. Many banks feel "landlocked," constrained by geography to lend in limited markets. Second, lending opportunities typically arrive sequentially and unpredictably, so that forgoing a loan because of diversification concerns may be costly because a loan that offers better diversification potential may fail to materialize later. Third, banks are often constrained by regulations that mandate serving specific communities. For example, the *Community Reinvestment Act* (CRA) requires a bank to lend to low-income borrowers in the community. This may interfere with diversification. Finally, cross-sectional reusability of information induces banks to specialize. For example, a bank that develops a special expertise in lending to auto parts manufacturers has a relative advantage in lending to this group, and it may wish to capitalize on this advantage by making such loans the focus of its loan portfolio. At best, therefore, banks tend to diversify within specialized areas of lending.

CREDIT ANALYSIS: THE FACTORS

Credit analysis examines factors that may lead to default in the repayment of a loan. The principal objective of credit analysis is to determine the ability and willingness of the borrower to repay the loan. The analysis looks at the borrower's past record (reputation) as well as its economic prospects. In most banks, this information is collected, analyzed, and stored by the credit department.

In analyzing a loan request, there are two important points to keep in mind. First, from an economic standpoint, assuming that the bank is the sole lender, it is the bank, not the borrower, that owns the asset financed with the loan. When the borrower takes a loan secured by the asset the loan is financing, it is merely purchasing a call option (as we saw in Chapter 1) from the bank. This option entitles the borrower to repurchase the asset from the bank should the value of the asset exceed the borrower's loan repayment obligation (the exercise price of the call option). The bank's loan granting decision and all of the actions it takes during the time the loan is outstanding should reflect this basic reality. Second, getting the borrower to repay the loan in today's legal environment is not always easy. Bankruptcy laws contain many provisions that

---

12. More details in the extensive community banking study of the FDIC (2012).

13. See ESRB (2014) on Europe, and Filbeck et al. (2010) on the continued strength of US community banks during the 2007–2009 financial crisis.

protect borrowers, and these often make collection of debts potentially time-consuming and costly. Hence, one of the goals of credit analysis should be to uncover the likelihood of default as accurately as cost limitations will permit.

Traditional Factors Considered in Credit Analysis

Bank credit analysts have traditionally referred to the five Cs of credit analysis: capacity, character, capital, collateral, and conditions. Since "rules of thumb" are usually the distillate of accumulated experience, they should bear a relationship to theoretical prescriptions. We therefore, interpret each of these factors in terms of the underlying economics of bank lending. The discussion that follows is summarized in Figure 7.8.

1. *Capacity*: This refers to the borrower's legal and financial capacity to borrow. The first consideration in assessing a loan request is whether the person requesting the loan is legally capable of borrowing. For example, in the case of partnerships, it is important to know whether all the signing partners have the legal authority to borrow on behalf of the partnership. In the case of corporations, the bank should check the corporate charter and bylaws to determine who has the authority to borrow on the corporation's behalf.

   Apart from legal considerations, capacity refers to the borrower's financial capability. Future cash flows are generally used to service the debt and therefore need to be carefully estimated. Evaluating borrowers' future cash flows available to service the debt is a major part of any credit analysis. Sometimes, the bank may have to demand that the borrower subordinate the claims of others to ensure that the borrower has sufficient capacity to repay the bank. An example is a small firm that has borrowed significant amounts from its major shareholders.[14]

2. *Character*: The concept of character embraces the borrower's ability to repay debts and the desire to settle all obligations within the terms of the contract. Judging character requires a careful examination of the borrower's past record in debt repayment and related behaviors. Including character in credit analysis makes sense because the better a borrower's credit reputation, the less incentive it has to default.[15] The reason is simple. Suppose a borrower knows that a single default will lead to denial of credit for a long time. The gain from defaulting is the amount the borrower does not repay the bank, but the gain from repayment is the net present value (NPV) of all the investment projects that might be

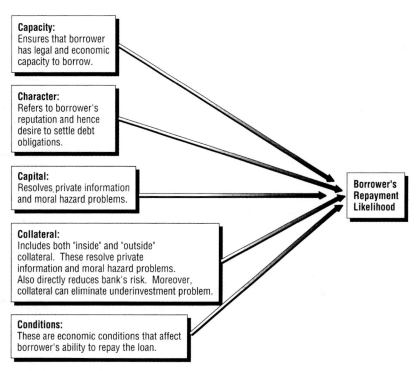

FIGURE 7.8   Pictorial Depiction of Factors Considered in Credit Analysis.

14. This is a case in which the bank may be successful in getting the borrower to subordinate the claims of earlier creditors. In general, this will be difficult as covenants on existing loans will generally prevent the borrower from taking such actions unilaterally.
15. This argument is formalized in Diamond (1989).

financed with future bank loans; defaulting on this bank loan leads to a loss of that NPV. Clearly, this NPV increases as the interest rates on future loans decline. Further, the longer the borrower keeps repaying its loans, the better its credit reputation gets and the lower its future loan interest rates.[16] Hence, when the borrower acquires a good credit reputation, it perceives a lower sequence of interest rates on its future loans than if it did not have that reputation. Consequently, the benefit of repaying the loan (or equivalently, the cost of defaulting) is greater for a borrower with a better reputation. To put it a little differently, the benefit of maintaining or building a reputation is greater the better the reputation is to start with. Hence, borrowers with better reputations (repayment records) tend to be better credit risks.

3. *Capital*: How much equity capital (as a fraction of total assets) the borrower has invested in the firm is an important factor in the assessment of that firm's credit risk. There are two effects at work here. First, a higher amount of capital lessens the moral hazard problem. Second, the higher the capital, the better is the signal sent by the firm's owners about the confidence they have in the firm's future prospects. This helps to resolve the private information problem. This is illllustrated in Example 7.1.

Example 7.1

Suppose you are a bank lending officer at the Midtown National Bank considering a loan request from Miller Manufacturing company for $1.05 million. The firm currently has $1 million in equity and its existing debt repayment obligation is $2 million. Assume that this equity is in the form of retained earnings invested in a noninterest-bearing account. The firm can invest the $1.05 million it will borrow from your bank in one of two projects (the bank cannot directly control which project the firm will invest in): A or B. Project A will yield a payoff of $2 million with probability 0.8 and $1 million with probability 0.2 at the end of the period. Project B will yield a payoff of $7 million with probability 0.2 and a payoff of zero with probability 0.8 at the end of the period. The firm's existing assets will yield a payoff of $3 million with probability 0.8 and a payoff of zero with probability 0.2 at the end of the period. The payoff on either project A or project B is statistically independent of the payoff on the firm's existing assets. These payoff distributions are common knowledge. For simplicity, there is no discounting and the bank loan you will make is subordinated to the firm's previous debt. Examine how Miller Manufacturing's behavior and the terms of lending change depending on whether or not it has the $1 million equity mentioned earlier.

Solution

We solve this problem in four steps. First, we will assume that Miller Manufacturing has $1 million in equity. Then we will analyze the firm's expected profit from choosing project A, *assuming* that the bank prices the loan believing that project A will be chosen. Second, continuing to assume that Miller has $1 million in equity, we will analyze the borrower's expected profit from choosing project B assuming that the bank prices the loan believing that project A will be chosen. These two steps are needed to determine the appropriate Nash equilibrium in this problem, that is, a situation in which the bank prices the loan believing that Miller will choose project *i* (where *i* is either A or B) and Miller indeed chooses project *i*. With $1 million in equity, the Nash equilibrium involves the bank believing that project A will be chosen. Note the key role of the informational assumption that the bank cannot observe the borrower's choice of project. The third step is to assume that Miller has no equity capital and repeat Step 1. Finally, we repeat Step 2 with the assumption that Miller has no equity capital.

Step 1

Suppose first that the firm has the $1 million in equity mentioned earlier. Let us say that you, as the lending officer, assume that Miller will choose project A. Then, the *sum* of the cash flows from the project and Miller's existing assets has the following probability distribution (Table 7.1).

Since the repayment obligation on the senior debt is $2 million, the cash flow available to service the bank loan has the following probability distribution.

TABLE 7.1 Probability Distribution of Total Cash Flows from Project A, Miller's Existing Assets and Equity

Total Cash Flow From Project A and Existing Assets (Millions of $)	Total Cash Flow With Retained Earnings Added in (Millions of $)	Probability
5	6	0.64
4	5	0.16
2	3	0.16
1	2	0.04

---

16. A better reputation leads to a lower interest rate because it becomes less likely that the borrower will default.

TABLE 7.2 Probability Distribution of Cash Flow Available to Service Bank Loan

Cash Flow Available (Millions of $)	Probability
4	0.64
3	0.16
1	0.16
0	0.04

You want to price this loan competitively because Miller has also been talking to your cross-town rival. At the same time, you do not want to lose money on this deal. From Table 7.2 you figure out that if the available cash flow is either $4 million or $3 million, Miller can fully repay the bank loan, whereas if the available cash flow is $1 million, then that is all your bank can collect. Thus, if you set the repayment obligation on your bank loan at P million, your expected collection will be

$$(0.64 + 0.16)P + (0.16)1 + (0.04)0 = 0.8P + 0.16.$$

Since we have set the discount rate at zero, this expected payoff must equal the initial loan for your bank to just break even (the farthest you can go in competing for this borrower). That is,

$$1.05 = 0.8P + 0.16,$$

which means $P = \$1.1125$ million, implying a loan interest rate of approximately 5.95%. The probability distribution of cash flows to Miller's shareholders is given in Table 7.3.

Thus, the expected value of equity if Miller invests in project A is $0.64(2.8875) + 0.16(1.8875) = \$2.15$ million.

Step 2

Now suppose that Miller were to consider investing in project B after receiving a loan priced by you under the assumption that project A would be chosen. This is the standard moral hazard problem in bank lending which we discussed earlier, since project B is riskier for you as the lender. Then, proceeding in the same way that we did for project A, we see that the probability distribution of the cash flows accruing to the firm's shareholders is as follows: $7.8875 million with probability 0.16, $4.8875 million with probability 0.04, $0.8875 million with probability 0.64, and zero with probability 0.16. Thus, the expected value of equity if the firm invests in project B is $0.16(7.8875) + 0.04(4.8875) + 0.64(0.8875) + 0.16(0) = \$2.0255$ million.

This means that Miller's shareholders prefer to invest in project A (assuming you price your loan as if project A will be selected) and you are safe in your assumption that project A will be chosen. It is, therefore, unnecessary to check what would happen if the bank were to assume that Miller will choose B. This is because there are two possibilities. Either Miller will choose A, so that it is not a Nash equilibrium for the bank to assume B will be chosen, or there is a Nash equilibrium in which Miller chooses B. But this Nash equilibrium is dominated by the one in which Miller chooses A in the sense that Miller is better off in the latter and the bank is indifferent. Thus, if your bank is to be competitive, you had better price the loan assuming that A will be chosen, since the loan price is lower in that case.

Step 3

Now we will see what would happen if Miller had no equity capital. In this case, if Miller selects project A, it has the following distribution for its total cash flow (Table 7.4).

Since the repayment obligation on senior debt is $2 million, you calculate that to service the bank loan Miller will have $3 million with probability 0.64, $2 million with probability 0.16, and nothing with probability 0.2. Following the same logic as in the case with $1 million in retained earnings, you now calculate that to permit the bank to just break even you must ask for a repayment obligation of $1.3125 million (you are assuming that Miller will invest in project A). With this, the net cash flow accruing to Miller's shareholders is $1.6875 million with probability 0.64, $0.6875 million with probability 0.16, and zero with probability 0.2. The expected value of equity is $1.19 million.

TABLE 7.3 Probability Distribution of Net (Pretax) Cash Flow Accruing to Shareholders of Miller Manufacturing

Cash Flow Available (Millions of $)	Probability
2.8875	0.64
1.8875	0.16
0	0.16
0	0.04

TABLE 7.4 Probability Distribution of Total Cash Flows from Project A and Miller's Existing Assets

Total Cash Flow (Millions of $)	Probability
5	0.64
4	0.16
2	0.16
1	0.04

Step 4

After receiving such a loan, if Miller were to decide to opt for project B instead, we can follow the same steps as before to compute the expected value of equity as $1.2175 million. Thus, Miller will choose the riskier project B, and your assumption that it will select project A is incorrect. Indeed, if you were to (correctly) assume that project B will be chosen and price the loan accordingly, Miller's incentive to choose project B would be unaltered. This means that if Miller does not have sufficient equity capital, it may opt for riskier investments than it would if it had equity capital. Since you will anticipate this as a banker, you price the loan accordingly (that is, charge an appropriately higher interest rate on the loan). It is straightforward to verify that in this example Miller is better off retaining earnings in order to convince the lender that it will choose the safer project.

Capital helps to resolve moral hazard by imposing a greater loss on the borrower for poor project outcomes. This is because capital acts as the "first line of defense" against project losses and provides a cushion of protection for the lender. Without equity capital, the borrower knows that it has a valuable call option – if the project does poorly, the lender sustains the loss (the worst the borrower can do is to get nothing), whereas if the project does well, the lender gets only its contractual payment and the borrower earns a profit. With capital, the borrower's cost of pursuing risk is increased and the value of its call option is reduced. With sufficient equity capital, the lender can align the borrower's interest perfectly with its own. Interestingly, this means that the borrower is better off.[17]

The other function of capital is as an information communicator. The entrepreneur's own contribution of equity can signal the profitability of her project. The standard argument relies on the entrepreneur being risk averse and is thus a little more complicated than an alternative line of reasoning that is developed in the example in the box below.[18]

Example 7.2

Suppose we have a firm that needs $150 to invest in a project that will yield a random payoff one period hence. The firm knows the probability distribution of the project's cash flow, but no one else does. All that others know is that the project can be type C or type D. If it is type C, then it will yield a cash flow of $300 with probability 0.8 and zero with probability of 0.2. If it is type D, the project will yield a cash flow of $600 with probability 0.5 and zero with probability 0.5. For simplicity, suppose that interest and principal payments on debt are tax deductible and that the firm can raise equity capital (it currently has negligible equity capital on its books) from those who know the firm's cash flow distribution (e.g., these may be managers who own stock). The firm currently has owners, but the book value of their equity is, for all practical purposes, zero. However, debt must be acquired in the form of a loan from a bank, which cannot tell whether the borrower has a type C or a type D project. The corporate tax rate applicable to the borrower is 30%. As a banker, how should you deal with such a borrower, assuming that the borrower is locked into either project C or project D and cannot choose its project?

Solution

The key to resolving this informational asymmetry is to use capital as a signal. As a banker, the key is for you to recognize that the riskier borrower has a greater aversion to putting up equity capital because he has a greater likelihood of losing it. So, as a banker, you can offer the borrower two choices: (i) borrow the entire $150 and repay P_D, or (ii) put up E in equity, borrow $150 – E$ and repay P_C.

We solve this problem in three steps. First, we assume that the type-D borrower opts for choice (i), the type-C borrower opts for choice (ii), and the bank earns zero expected profit on each borrower. We then solve for P_D. We also solve for P_C, but it appears as a function of E. Step 2 involves solving for E. We do this by searching for the smallest value of E that ensures that the type-D borrower does not prefer its own contract (borrowing without putting up any equity) to that of the type-C borrower (putting up E

---

17. This is because of our assumption that the pricing of bank loans is competitive, so that the greater the equity capital possessed by the borrower, the better are its credit terms. Note that this provides an incentive for borrowers to accumulate equity capital.

18. This example is in the spirit of papers in the corporate finance literature that show a firm's choice of capital structure can signal its private information about its future prospects. See Tirole (2006).

in equity). Finally, the third step is to check that, with the value of E obtained from the previous step, the type-C borrower prefers his choice to that of the type-D borrower. Steps 2 and 3 therefore confirm the assumptions made in Step 1 about the project choices of borrowers.

Step 1
Now, if borrowers self-select so that only the type-D borrower takes (i) and only the type-C borrower takes (ii), then we can proceed as follows. Given that the bank must earn zero expected profit on each contract, and the repayment probability of the type-D borrower is 0.5, P_D must equal the expected value of the bank's repayment by the high-risk borrower, that is,

$$P_D \times 0.5 = 150$$

or $P_D = \$300$, an interest rate of 100%.

Next, if only the low-risk borrower takes (ii), P_C must satisfy

$$0.8 \times P_C = 150 - E$$

or $P_C = \dfrac{150 - E}{0.8}$

Step 2
We now solve for E. Note that E must ensure that the type-D borrower does not prefer the type-C borrower's contract to his own. Although there are many values of E for which this is true, there is only one value of E for which this is true and the value of the debt tax shield for the type-C borrower is maximized. This is the value of E that is the smallest value such that the type-D borrower does not strictly prefer the type-C borrower's contract. That is, the NPV to the type-D borrower from misrepresenting [and choosing (ii)] is exactly equal to his NPV from telling the truth [and choosing (i)]. The type-D borrower's NPV from choosing (i) is

$$(600 - 300) \times 0.5 \times 0.7 = \$105$$

where 0.7 is one minus the tax rate. The type-D borrower's NPV from choosing (ii) is

$$\left(600 - \frac{150 - E}{0.8}\right) \times 0.5 \times 0.7 - E.$$

Equating the above NPV to $105 yields $E = \$70$. Thus, the repayment obligation for the type-C borrower is $\dfrac{150 - 70}{0.8} = \$100$, or an interest rate of 25%.

Step 3
You can check that the type-C borrower will strictly prefer his contract to that of the type-D borrower. His NPV from (i) is

$$(300 - 300) \times 0.8 \times 0.7 = 0,$$

and his NPV from (ii) is

$$(300 - 100) \times 0.8 \times 0.7 - 70 = \$42.$$

Thus, the bank can offer two choices:
1. Borrow the entire $150 and repay $300.
2. Put up $70 in equity, borrow $80, and repay $100.

The key here is that the bank prices each loan based on the assumption that the borrower taking a particular loan has a particular project. If the borrower does in fact have that project, then the bank earns zero expected profit. The idea is for the bank to design the loan in such a way that *incentive compatibility* is assured. In other words, no borrower has an incentive to deviate from the loan contract "intended" for it by the bank. Incentive compatibility should obtain in a *Nash equilibrium;* the bank's assumptions about the association between the borrower's project and its loan contract choice must be correct in equilibrium.

In this example, capital serves as a signal of project quality. The borrower with the less risky type-C project signals its lower risk by funding two-thirds of the required investment with equity capital. For this, it is rewarded with a lower interest rate. Despite the obvious attractiveness of this lower interest rate, the high-risk borrower is unwilling to put up the equity necessary to be granted that rate. The intuition is as follows. Due to the tax deductibility of loan interest payments, the borrower desires as large a loan as possible, *regardless* of its project characteristics. The borrower also dislikes paying interest, regardless of its project characteristics. However, a higher interest rate is less onerous when the borrower has a risky project because the likelihood of actually repaying the loan with interest is lower. To such a borrower then, the inducement of a lower interest rate in exchange for a higher capital requirement is less attractive than it is to a borrower with the safer project. It is the fact that the borrower's preferences over different capital requirement–interest rate combinations *depend* on its project characteristics that permit the bank to craft a self-selection mechanism that elicits the desired information.

It follows then that, all else remaining the same, the bank should charge an interest rate that is *inversely* related to the borrower's equity to total assets ratio. Less capitalized borrowers are more risky, not just because of the *direct effect* of capital in serving as a "first line of defense," but also because of its *indirect effect* in reducing the borrower's appetite for risk. In our examples, we imposed a zero-profit condition on the bank as a reflection of perfect competition in banking markets. This is an extreme representation of competition. In reality, banks earn profits, especially on borrowers about whom they possess credit information that is not publicly available. To the extent that banks charge higher interest rates to borrowers with lower equity positions, they may also be able to earn greater profit margins on these borrowers.[19] This can make the prospect of lending to highly leveraged (low equity) borrowers enticing for the bank, despite the higher risk involved. Indeed, such an incentive arises from the basic function of credit information production performed by banks (Chapter 3).

Banks can add highly leveraged loans to their portfolios by lending to companies that use the funds for leveraged buyouts (LBOs), acquisitions, and recapitalizations. As our earlier discussions indicate, the yields on these highly leveraged transactions (HLTs) are higher than on other commercial loans. Since these higher yields compensate the bank for higher risks, higher *expected* profits for the bank are not necessarily implied. However, in many cases these borrowers also have few alternative sources of credit, so that banks can extract higher risk-adjusted profits from these borrowers. In addition, banks usually receive fees that vary from 1% to 2% of the principal amount committed.[20] HLT loans, however, are significantly more risky than average, and involve the moral hazards discussed earlier in this section.[21] This may be one reason why there has been a recent growth in the popularity of *reverse leveraged buyouts,* whereby firms reduce their debt/equity ratios by issuing equity to retire debt acquired during LBOs. This would reduce moral hazard and benefit the firm.

4. *Collateral:* Most commercial and consumer lending is secured with collateral. Once a loan is secured by a specific asset that serves as collateral, the lender has first claim to that asset in the event of default. There are two types of collateral: "inside" and "outside." Inside collateral consists of assets owned by the firm to which the loan is extended. Examples are accounts receivables, equipment, machinery, real estate, and inventory. Even if the bank extends an unsecured loan, it would have a claim, but not necessarily first claim, against these assets. As a general creditor, however, the value of the bank's claim would be ill-defined since, in the event of bankruptcy, the bank might be one among many unsecured creditors at the mercy of the bankruptcy court. On the other hand, if one of these assets is pledged as (inside) collateral, the bank would become the primary claimant to that asset.

Outside collateral consists of assets that the bank would never have a claim to unless they were specifically designated as collateral. A good example would be personal assets of the owner of the borrowing corporation or limited partnership.

Using collateral is not costless, however. Since the borrower may undertake actions that undermine the value of the collateral to the bank, ongoing monitoring of the collateral is required. Such monitoring costs are absorbed, at least in part, by the bank. Moreover, when collateral is transferred to the bank upon default, there are liquidation costs. These include the legal costs of ownership transfer as well as the bank's costs of initially carrying and then selling off the collateral.[22] From the borrower's standpoint, use of collateral makes subsequent borrowing more expensive since fewer assets are available to general creditors on that borrowing. Despite these costs, why is collateral so widely used?

There are at least three reasons for the popularity of secured lending. We discuss each now.

a. *Risk Reduction:* An obvious reason to secure a loan is that it provides the lender greater protection against loss in the event of default. The bankruptcy code in the United States includes what is known as an "automatic stay," which freezes collection actions by creditors during bankruptcy proceedings. The idea is to provide the debtor with breathing room to put its house in order. The stay takes effect immediately upon the filing of a bankruptcy petition. However, the stay can be modified in favor of a creditor if there is "cause," including insufficient protection of the *secured* creditor's interest in that component of the debtor's property that serves as collateral. For example, suppose a bank has loaned $10 million to a firm that has just filed for reorganization under Chapter 11 of the bankruptcy code. Suppose that specific assets of the firm, currently worth $4 million, have been encumbered as inside collateral. Now, if these assets were to depreciate in value at the rate of $3000 per month, for instance, the bankruptcy court might require the firm to set aside that amount each month to adequately protect the bank's claim. Thus, securing a loan reduces the creditor's risk in the event of bankruptcy.

b. *Signaling Instrument:* Collateral can also convey valuable information to the bank. Although possible with inside collateral, the intuition comes through most clearly if one thinks of securing property as outside collateral. The logic

19. This may also be because borrowers with lower equity capital levels may be less well known and have access to fewer credit sources, so that banks can earn higher quasi-monopoly rents by producing private information about them.

20. Usually, these loans are made under loan commitments, so that the fees are commitment fees.

21. An HLT loan may not only impose a higher expected loan loss for the bank but may also involve higher loan loss volatility (see Chapter 8).

22. By regulation, banks are required to liquidate such holdings within a certain time period after acquisition, unless the collateral is a permitted bank asset holding.

is similar to that used in explaining the signaling role of equity capital. Within a class of borrowers that look equally risky to the bank even after all credit analysis is done, a borrower's willingness to offer collateral will be inversely related to its default risk on the loan.[23] The way the bank can induce a borrower to reveal its otherwise hidden risk is as follows. Suppose there are two indistinguishable borrowers, A and B. However, the bank suspects one may be riskier than the other, although it does not know which. The bank offers each borrower a choice of one contract from a pair consisting of a secured loan with an associated interest rate and an unsecured loan with a higher interest rate. Now suppose A is less risky than B. Then, A will prefer the secured loan for two reasons. First, its lower risk means that the likelihood of repaying interest is higher; hence, a lower interest rate is more appealing. Second, its lower risk means that the chance of defaulting and losing collateral to the bank is lower; hence, offering collateral is less onerous. By symmetric logic, we can see that B will prefer the unsecured loan. Getting A and B to sort themselves out like this requires, of course, that the two loan contracts offered are incentive compatible. The example in the box below shows how this can be done.

Example 7.3

Suppose that A's assets will be worth $100 for sure at the end of the period. The value of B's end-of-period assets will be $200 with probability 0.5 and zero with probability 0.5. The project (A or B) requires an investment of $30 up front and the entire amount is borrowed from the bank. The bank is unable to distinguish between A and B. Assume that the single-period riskless interest rate is 10% and everybody is risk neutral. Assume that collateral worth $1 to the borrower is worth only 90 cents to the bank. The difference of 10 cents on the dollar can be viewed as the bank's cost of taking possession of the collateral. These repossession costs have two sources. First, assets acquired from a delinquent borrower are often worth less piecemeal to the bank than they are to the borrowers as components of a productive whole. Thus, the mere act of liquidating collateral by removing it from the other assets of the firm is costly. Second, transferring control of assets from the borrower to the bank involves legal and other administrative costs. These costs are an important reason why so many bankers see the value of collateral largely in terms of its incentive effects. The problem is to determine how the bank can design a *pair* of loan contracts such that each borrower will be induced to truthfully reveal its privately known risk.

Solution

Following the intuition discussed earlier, we will need to offer borrowers two contracts: a secured loan and an unsecured loan. These contracts should be designed so that A, the safe borrower, chooses the secured loan and B, the risky borrower, chooses the unsecured loan. We solve this problem in three steps. In the first step, we solve for the interest rate on the secured loan for the bank to break even. Second, we solve for the interest rate on the unsecured loan. In the third step, we solve for the amount of collateral on the secured loan that will deter the risky borrower from preferring the secured to the unsecured loan.

Step 1

Since A will surely repay the loan, the interest rate on the secured loan, r_u, that allows the bank to just break even is the single-period riskless rate of 10%.

Step 2

On the other hand, the interest rate on the unsecured loan, r_u, should be set to satisfy the following zero profit condition for the bank

$$[0.5 \times (1 + r_u) \times 30] / [1.10] = 30 \tag{7.1}$$

The left-hand side of Equation (7.1) is the discounted present value of the bank's payoff. The promised repayment is $30(1 + r_u)$, but there is only a 0.5 probability that the bank will be repaid. Since the bank is risk neutral, it discounts at the riskless interest rate of 10%. For the bank to exactly break even, the discounted present value of its expected payoff should exactly equal the initial loan. Note that our approach is consistent with the notion that the bank owns the project and it has sold the borrower a call option on the collateral at a fixed exercise price of 30 × (1 + r_u). When the project value exceeds this exercise price, the borrower exercises the option to repurchase the project; this happens in the successful state. If the project fails, the borrower lets its option expire unexercised and the bank retains a worthless project. Solving Equation (7.1) gives 1 + r_u = 2.2. Hence, the repayment obligation on the unsecured loan is 2.2 × 30 = $66.

Step 3

Now we solve for the amount of collateral that will deter B from mimicking A and opting for the secured loan. The amount of collateral, C, that makes B indifferent between the secured and unsecured loans is the solution to the following equation

$$0.5 \times (200 - 66) = 0.5 \times (200 - 33) - 0.5 \times C. \tag{7.2}$$

---

23. See Bester (1985) and Besanko and Thakor (1987a,b) for theoretical models that demonstrate this. Empirical evidence on the signaling role of collateral is provided by Jimenez et al. (2006).

In Equation (7.2), the left-hand side is the expected value of the borrower's cash flow, net of repaying the bank, if it takes the unsecured loan. The right-hand side is the expected value of its net cash inflow if it chooses the secured loan. Note that the interest rate on the secured loan is 10% (since the bank assumes this loan will be taken by the safe borrower), so that the repayment obligation is $1.10 \times 30 = \$33$. There is a 0.5 probability that the borrower will default and lose its collateral to the bank.

Solving Equation (7.2) yields $C = \$33$. Thus, if the bank demands a collateral whose value to the borrower is at least as great as $33, only A will choose the secured loan with an interest rate of 10%. (Note that A's net expected cash flow with the secured loan is $100 - \$33 = \$67$, whereas with the unsecured loan it is $100 - \$66 = \$34$). B will choose the unsecured loan with an interest rate of 120%. The bank can thus sort its borrowers according to risk. The outcome is a Nash equilibrium; the bank's beliefs about which borrower chooses which loan is confirmed by their behaviors.

You must have noticed that the bank's collateral repossession cost had no bearing on the outcome. The reason is that the secured loan to A is *riskless*, so that A would never surrender collateral to the bank. Since the Nash equilibrium separates perfectly – each borrower revealing its type in equilibrium – and involves B choosing the unsecured loan, the bank never actually takes possession of collateral in this example. In reality, of course, few loans are riskless. With default risk in lending to A, then the bank's repossession cost would have entered the outcome since it would have affected the interest rate on the secured loan.

---

c. *Moral Hazard:* Using collateral can help resolve a variety of moral hazard problems. The three we will discuss here are: asset substitution, underinvestment, and inadequate effort supply.

Asset Substitution: Because of the option nature of the bank loan, the borrower has an incentive to choose a riskier project after obtaining the loan. In a manner similar to capital, collateral can deter such risk-taking. For present purposes, think of security offered as outside collateral. Consider the following example.

Example 7.4

Suppose Brown Bakery needs a $100 loan to finance a project that will pay off next period. Brown can choose between two projects: S (safe) and R (risky). The bank knows this but is unable to directly control the borrower's choice of project. S will yield a payoff of $300 with probability 0.9 and nothing with probability 0.1, and R will yield a payoff of $400 with probability 0.6 and nothing with probability 0.4. Everybody is risk neutral and the riskless rate is 10%. How should the bank design its loan contract so that Brown will choose the safer project? Assume once again that collateral worth $1 to Brown is worth 90 cents to the bank.

Solution

The idea is for the bank to make it in Brown's best interest to choose S. This is achieved by demanding that Brown put up sufficient collateral. Since collateral is surrendered to the bank upon default, it makes project failure costly to the borrower. Consequently, the borrower will wish to minimize the likelihood of failure by choosing S. The key assumption here is that the bank cannot *directly* control Brown's project choice. We proceed in four steps. First, we will assume that the bank offers Brown an unsecured loan, assuming that S will be chosen. We will show that this cannot be a Nash equilibrium because Brown will choose R. Second, we will let the bank assume that R will be chosen and compute the interest rate on the unsecured loan. It turns out this is a Nash equilibrium in that Brown chooses R when faced with such an unsecured loan. Third, we ask whether another Nash equilibrium is possible, say with a secured loan. We solve for the level of collateral that ensures that Brown does not (strictly) prefer R to S. We do this by equating Brown Bakery's expected profits from R and S, given a secured loan contract will indeed be acceptable to Brown Bakery and the bank. Finally, we verify that it is a Nash equilibrium for Brown to choose S.

Step 1

First suppose the bank offers Brown an unsecured loan at an interest rate r_u. If the bank assumes that Brown will choose S, then the interest rate, r_u^S, at which the bank just breaks even, is given by

$$[0.9 \times (1+r_u^S) \times 100]/[1.10] = 100. \tag{7.3}$$

Solving Equation (7.3) yields $r_u^S = 22.22\%$. Can this be a Nash equilibrium in the sense that Brown does indeed choose S? To answer this question, let us compute Brown's net expected payoffs under R and S. If Brown chooses S, its net expected payoff is

$$0.9[300 - (1.22 \times 100)] = \$160.20.$$

If it chooses R, its net expected payoff is

$$0.6(400 - 122) = \$166.8.$$

Hence, offering Brown an unsecured loan with an interest rate of 22% cannot be a Nash equilibrium since Brown will choose R instead of S, and the bank will make an expected loss on the loan since it assumed S would be chosen.

Step 2

Now suppose the bank assumes that R will be chosen. Then the interest rate, r_u^R, at which the bank just breaks even, is given by

$$[0.6 \times (1 + r_u^S) \times 100] / [1.1] = 100. \tag{7.4}$$

Solving Equation (7.4) yields $r_u^R = 83.33\%$. Now, confronted with this interest rate, if Brown chooses S, its net expected payoff is

$$0.9(300 - 183.33) = \$105.$$

If it chooses R, its net expected payoff is

$$0.6(400 - 183.33) = \$130.$$

So, Brown chooses R and this is a Nash equilibrium since the bank's belief is consistent with the borrower's behavior.

Step 3

But can we do better with *another* Nash equilibrium? Whenever we ask this question, it is natural to wonder who we are doing better for. Since the bank is assumed to earn zero expected profits in all scenarios, why should the bank care? The answer lies in competition. Recall that the zero expected profit condition is an analytical convenience. In practice we would expect the bank to earn at least a small profit. Remember too that this profit is in excess of the normal return on equity capital. Now, if the bank can design a contract that increases the borrower's expected profit without reducing the bank's, it can lure away this borrower from its competitors and build its "book" of business. Hence, competing banks should strive to give the borrower the best possible deal.

Suppose now that the bank offers Brown a secured loan instead. What you want to do as a banker is to figure out how much collateral to ask for in order to ensure that R will not be chosen. The level of collateral that leaves Brown indifferent between S and R satisfies the following equation.

$$\begin{aligned} 0.9[300 - (1 + r_s) \times 100] - 0.1C \\ = 0.6[400 - (1 + r_s) \times 100] - 0.4C, \end{aligned} \tag{7.5}$$

where r_s is the interest rate on the secured loan. We should first determine r_s. If the bank is successful in inducing Brown to choose S, then it should set r_s as follows to satisfy its zero profit condition

$$[0.9 \times (1 + r_s) \times 100 + 0.1 \times 0.9 \times C] / [1.1] = 100. \tag{7.6}$$

In Equation (7.6), note that we have used the fact that a dollar of collateral is worth only 90 cents to the bank. Solving Equation (7.6) yields

$$1 + r_s = (110 - 0.09C) / 90. \tag{7.7}$$

Substituting Equation (7.7) in Equation (7.5) and solving for C yields C = \$20,202. To avoid rounding off problems, suppose we take C = \$20.21. Then substituting this in Equation (7.7) gives us $1 + r_s = (110 - 1.8189)/90 = 1.2020$ or say $r_s = 20.21\%$ to make sure that rounding off does not leave the bank with negative expected profit.

Step 4

Now Brown's net expected payoff from choosing S is [from Equation (7.5)] \$159.79 and from choosing R it is [again from Equation (7.5)] approximately \$159.79. Hence, this is a Nash equilibrium in which Brown chooses S. Note that this equilibrium gives Brown a higher expected payoff than the previous Nash equilibrium (\$130).[24] Thus, if this borrower comes to you and says that your cross-town rival has offered an unsecured loan at 83.33% interest, you could effectively counter by offering a secured loan that requires \$20.21 of outside collateral and an interest rate of say 21%. With these terms, Brown Bakery will accept your loan and you will earn a profit.[25]

In this example, outside collateral was used since we assumed limited liability, that is, it would not be lost upon bankruptcy if it were not pledged. For somewhat different reasons, inside collateral can also deter asset substitution. By securing specific assets within the firm, creditors can ensure that these assets will not be replaced by those that increase the risk exposure of creditors. Since this reduction in asset substitution possibilities will be reflected in a better price for the firm's debt, the advantage of issuing secured debt accrues to the firm's shareholders.[26]

---

24. As noted in Chapter 1, there are often multiple Nash equilibria.

25. By this time, you may be wondering why a bank would ever make an *unsecured* loan. Note, however, that offering *both* secured and unsecured loans helps to resolve private information problems. Moreover, it is not *always* optimal to use outside collateral to resolve moral hazard. Indeed, in Example 7.4, if the payoff in the successful state for project R is \$500 instead of \$400, the best outcome is for the bank to offer an unsecured loan priced under the assumption that R will be chosen.

26. The argument that inside collateral can help in this way to resolve asset-substitution problems was made Smith and Warner (1979). See also Leitner (2006).

Underinvestment: One manifestation of the divergence of interests between the borrower and the lender is in the borrower being unwilling to invest additional funds in a project even though doing so increases the total NPV of this project.[27] The intuition is simple. Suppose you own some real estate that was financed mainly with a bank loan; this real estate is currently worth $1.5 million. You could spend an additional million dollars that would enhance the real estate's value by $1.1 million. However, suppose that the present value of your repayment obligation to the bank is $2 million. Then, although investing $1 million yields an NPV of $100,000 for the project as a whole, it is not a good idea for you, the owner/borrower. This is because you increase the present value of the cash flows accruing to you by $(1.5 + 1.1) million − $2 million = $600,000, but it costs you $1 million, that is, the investment has a *negative* NPV of $400,000 to you (the borrower), but a positive NPV of $100,000 to the borrower and lender considered jointly. The net effect is that the investment is passed up and firm value is sacrificed. This investment inefficiency arises from actions that are privately optimal for the borrowing firm's shareholders *ex post*. However, they pay a price for this *ex ante* since the lender anticipates such behavior and adjusts the terms of credit accordingly. How can we eliminate this form of moral hazard so that the *borrower* benefits *ex ante* through better credit terms?

One answer is to let the borrower *precommit* not to "underinvest" *ex post*. If the lender believes the borrower, the problem will have apparently been solved. However, such precommitment is *time inconsistent*. The lender knows that the borrower has every reason to break this promise when the opportunity presents itself. So it would be foolish for the lender to believe such a promise. Of course, loan covenants can be employed, with the lender monitoring compliance. However, as a practical matter, it is difficult to see how loan covenants could force a borrower to invest when it is disinclined to do so. This is because the lender typically does not "see" these investment opportunities unless the borrower decides to exploit them. Covenants are effective in *prohibiting* actions, but rarely succeed in forcing unobservable initiatives.

Secured debt can resolve this underinvestment problem.[28] The idea is as follows. Suppose that the firm needs additional financing to purchase an asset, and it can purchase this asset for less than its market value. Thus, the purchase is a positive NPV investment. Also suppose that the firm currently has risky unsecured debt outstanding and would not, without further incentive, purchase this asset because it would enhance the present value accruing to the firm's shareholders by less than the purchase price of the asset.

To solve this problem, suppose the firm issues new debt secured by the asset in question. Then, due to the "absolute priority" rule, the secured creditors have first claim to the asset in the event of bankruptcy, and the borrowing firm has essentially diverted (at least part of) the cash flows attributable to this asset to the new secured creditors and away from the old unsecured creditors. Since the new (secured) creditors pay a fair market value for the debt issued by the firm, the gains associated with diverting payoffs of the newly purchased asset away from the old (unsecured) creditors accrue to the borrowing firm's shareholders and increase their incentive to undertake the investment. The example in the box below illustrates how this works.

Example 7.5

Consider a firm, Johnson Supplies, that can invest $100 at the start of the period ($t = 0$) in a project that will pay off at the end of the period ($t = 1$) $400 if successful (state S_1) and zero if unsuccessful (state S_2). State S_1 occurs with probability 0.7. The initial $100 financing comes from unsecured debt issued at $t = 0$. Before the end of the period, but *after* the initial financing is raised, the firm will have an opportunity to purchase an asset (call it A) for $100. This asset will surely be worth $120 at $t = 1$. Assume that Johnson cannot be forced to purchase this asset. Compute Johnson's optimal financing strategy. Assume that everybody is risk neutral and that the riskless interest rate is 10%.

Solution

We solve this problem in six steps. First, we assume that only unsecured debt can be offered and that the date-0 unsecured creditors will assume that Johnson will purchase A when available. We then compute the interest rate on the $100 of (new) unsecured debt raised *(after* the initial financing) to purchase A. Second, we check if this can be a Nash equilibrium. We find that it is not, in that Johnson will *not* purchase A when burdened with the original unsecured debt. Third, we check if it is a Nash equilibrium for Johnson not to purchase A. That is, if the original creditors price their debt assuming that Johnson will not purchase A, will Johnson indeed not purchase A (since Johnson does not purchase A, we need not worry about the old creditors)? We find that this is a Nash equilibrium. Fourth, we introduce secured debt and compute the interest rates on the old unsecured and the new secured debt when all creditors assume that Johnson will purchase A when available. Fifth, we check if this is a Nash equilibrium. We find that it is a Nash equilibrium in that Johnson does purchase A and also wishes to issue secured debt to purchase A. Finally, in step 6, we conclude by indicating that the NPV to Johnson's shareholders is higher in the secured-debt Nash equilibrium than in the unsecured-debt Nash equilibrium when Johnson does not purchase A.

---

27. This underinvestment problem was first discussed by Myers (1977).
28. This point was made by Stulz and Johnson (1985). See also Ongena et al. (2015).

Step 1
First suppose that issuing secured debt is impossible. Thus, the $100 financing required to purchase A in the future will have to be raised with either equity or unsecured debt. Since the basic argument follows in either case, let us assume that unsecured debt will be employed. As a start, suppose the unsecured creditors at $t = 0$ (call them C_{old}) assume that Johnson will purchase A when available. Use C_{new} to label the (new) unsecured creditors who provide the $100 to buy A. Thus, at $t = 1$, the value of the firm will be $520 (in state S_1) with probability 0.7 and $120 (in state S_2) with probability 0.3. Assuming that all unsecured creditors have equal priority, C_{old} will be repaid in full in state S_1 and will receive $60 in state S_2. The payoffs to C_{new} are identical. Hence, the loan interest rates on the credits provided by C_{old} and C_{new} will also be identical. Let r_a represent this interest rate. Then, if creditors provide fairly priced debt (that is, each creditor earns zero expected profit), r_a is obtained as a solution to the following equation

$$100 = [(1+r_a) \times 100 \times 0.7 + 60 \times 0.3]/[1.1]. \tag{7.8}$$

The left-hand side of Equation (7.8) is the amount of debt financing. The right-hand side is the expected payoff to either C_{old} or C_{new}, discounted at the riskless rate of 10%. Solving Equation (7.8) yields $r_a = 31.43\%$. Thus, at $t = 1$ Johnson is obliged to repay $131.43 to C_{old} and the same amount to C_{new}.

Step 2
The first question is: Can this be a Nash equilibrium? To answer this, we must find out whether C_{old}'s assumption that Johnson will purchase A is indeed correct. Now, if Johnson purchases A, the NPV accruing to its shareholders is

$$\frac{0.7 \times (520 - 262.86)}{1.1} = \$163.63.$$

Note that Johnson's shareholders receive a positive payoff only in state S_1, and this payoff is $520($400 + $120) minus two times $131.43, where $131.43 is what Johnson owes each group of unsecured creditors. If, on the other hand, Johnson does not purchase A, then the NPV accruing to its shareholders is

$$\frac{0.7 \times (400 - 161.43)}{1.1} = \$170.91.$$

Thus, Johnson will forgo the opportunity to purchase A even though its total NPV ($120 − $100/1.1 = $18.18) to Johnson is positive. This means that it *cannot* be a Nash equilibrium for C_{old} to assume that Johnson will purchase A.

Step 3
So now suppose C_{old} assumes that Johnson will *not* purchase A. Then, the loan interest rate, r_b, is a solution to

$$[0.7 \times (1+r_b) \times 100]/[1.1] = 100 \tag{7.9}$$

Solving Equation (7.9) yields $r_b = 57.143\%$. It is simple to verify that, faced with this loan interest rate, Johnson will indeed choose *not* to purchase A. Thus, this is a Nash equilibrium, under the assumption that secured debt is impossible. The NPV accruing to Johnson's shareholders in this Nash equilibrium is given by

$$\frac{0.7 \times (400 - 157.143)}{1.1} = \$154.5.$$

Step 4
Imagine now that Johnson is free to finance A with secured debt. If Johnson chooses to do this, then the (secured) claim of C_{new} will be riskless since the minimum firm value (that prevails in state S_2) is $120 (the value of A at $t = 1$), and C_{new} have first claim to this asset. Since the riskless rate is 10%, Johnson's repayment obligation on riskless debt will be $110, and this can be covered from the value of this firm in state S_2. Now suppose C_{old} assumes that Johnson *will* purchase A when available. The loan interest rate, r_c, that C_{old} charges will then be a solution to

$$[0.7 \times (1+r_c) \times 100 + 0.3 \times 10]/[1.1] = 100, \tag{7.10}$$

where we recognize that C_{old} will be paid only $10 in state S_2 since C_{old}'s claim is subordinated to that of C_{new}. Solving Equation (7.10) gives us $r_c = 52.86\%$. Johnson's total repayment obligation, therefore, is $152.86 + $110 = $262.86.

Step 5
Is this a Nash equilibrium? Again, we consider Johnson's incentive to purchase A. If it purchases A, the NPV accruing to its shareholders is

$$\frac{0.7 \times (520 - 262.86)}{1.1} = \$163.63.$$

and if it does not purchase A, the NPV accruing to shareholders is

$$\frac{0.7 \times (400 - 152.86)}{1.1} = \$157.3.$$

Hence, Johnson will indeed purchase A (when C_{old} prices the loan assuming A will be purchased) and the conjecture of C_{old} about the firm's incentive to purchase A is supported by its behavior. To complete our verification that this is a Nash equilibrium, we must also make sure that Johnson will indeed wish to issue secured debt to purchase A. To check this, let us hold the fixed price of the loan given by C_{old}, so that the firm must repay $152.86. If Johnson issues unsecured debt to purchase A, then C_{new} will ask for a loan interest rate of 31.43% [since they solve Equation (7.8) to determine this loan interest rate], so that the NPV accruing to Johnson's shareholders is

$$\frac{0.7 \times [520 - (152.86 + 131.43)]}{1.1} = \$150.$$

Step 6

Thus, Johnson will indeed choose to finance A with secured debt. Moreover, the NPV to Johnson's shareholders in this Nash equilibrium ($163.63) exceeds that in the previous Nash equilibrium when it could only finance the purchase of A with unsecured debt ($154.5). Hence, it will *not* be in the interest of Johnson Supplies to precommit to never issue *secured* debt in the future through restrictive covenants written into its loan contract with C_{old}.

Apart from illustrating how secured debt can resolve the underinvestment problem, this example brings up an interesting point related to the design of covenants in loan contracts. It is sometimes believed that creditors wish to protect themselves against future expropriation by including loan covenants that prohibit the firm from issuing future debt that has a higher seniority claim against any subset of the firm's assets. When all is said and done, however, in a competitive market it is the *borrower* who decides what covenants to accept, since the lender can presumably adjust the price of the loan (to at least break even) depending on the covenants that the borrower is willing to accept. What our example shows is that it may be optimal for the borrower to leave itself the flexibility to avail of secured borrowing in the future in which the newly purchased assets are used as collateral, so that new creditors have the most senior claim to the assets.[29] This not only makes the borrower better off, but it even lowers the interest rate on the initial debt (C_{old} in our example). In our example, the interest rate on the loan provided by C_{old} is 57.143% when the issuance of debt of higher seniority in the future with respect to *any* asset is prohibited, and it is 52.86% when such issuance is permitted. The reason for this, of course, is that the ability to issue secured debt in the future resolves the underinvestment problem of debt.

Inadequate Effort Supply: Another moral hazard is that the borrower may expend insufficient effort in managing the firm when its assets are highly leveraged. Collateral can help to resolve this moral hazard problem, too. The following example uses outside collateral to illustrate the point.

Example 7.6

Consider an entrepreneur, Mr. David Barnes, who borrows $100 at $t = 0$ (the start of the period) and invests the loan in a project that will pay off at $t = 1$ an amount $300 in the successful state (state S_1) and nothing in the unsuccessful state (state S_2) for his start-up firm, Barnes Manufacturing. The probability of S_1 is $p(e)$, where e is Mr. Barnes' effort in managing the project. Mr. Barnes can choose one of two effort levels: high (h) or low (l). Mr. Barnes sustains a personal cost of $40 to expend h and nothing if l is chosen. Assume $p(h) = 0.8$ and $p(l) = 0.6$. Mr. Barnes has collateral available, but collateral worth $1 to him is worth 90 cents to the bank. Assume that the bank cannot observe Mr. Barnes' choice of effort. The riskless interest rate is 10%. Compute the optimal loan contract.

Solution

We want to show in this example that Mr. Barnes will work harder if the bank has loaned him $100 with a secured debt contract. We will proceed in four steps. First, we will assume that the bank is restricted to offering an unsecured loan. We show that it is not a Nash equilibrium for Mr. Barnes to choose $e = h$. Second, continuing with the unsecured debt assumption, we show that it is a Nash equilibrium for Mr. Barnes to choose $e = l$, and for the bank to price its loan accordingly. Third, we introduce collateral and solve for the amount that makes Mr. Barnes indifferent between l and h. We find that with this level of collateral it is indeed a Nash equilibrium for Mr. Barnes to choose h. Finally, in the fourth step, we check that Mr. Barnes himself is better off with secured debt, which serves as a precommitment that he will work harder.

Step 1

Suppose first that the bank restricts itself to offering an unsecured loan. If the bank assumes that Mr. Barnes will choose $e = h$, then the interest rate, r_h^u, it should charge on this unsecured loan to just break even satisfies

$$[0.8 \times (1 + r_h^u) \times 100 / [1 + 0.10] = 100, \tag{7.11}$$

---

29. Remember that in our example, C_{old} and C_{new} have equal seniority when the debt is unsecured, and C_{new} has higher seniority when it is secured. It should be noted, though, that our example does not show that it is optimal to issue new debt that has the seniormost claim against *all* of the firm's assets. Rather, the optimal new debt in the example is a prior claim against a subset of the assets and *no* claim against the remaining assets.

which yields $r_h^u = 37.5\%$. To check if this is a Nash equilibrium, we need to ask whether Mr. Barnes, faced with this loan contract, will indeed choose $e = h$. Mr. Barnes' expected payoff with $e = h$ is

$$0.8 \times (300 - 137.5) - 40 = 90,$$

whereas his expected payoff with $e = l$ is $0.6 \times (300 - 137.5) = 97.5$. Thus, this is not a Nash equilibrium since Mr. Barnes prefers $e = l$.

Step 2

It is, however, a Nash equilibrium for the bank to assume that Mr. Barnes will choose $e = l$, and price the unsecured loan accordingly. The loan interest rate, r_l^u must satisfy

$$[0.6 \times (1 + r_l^u) \times 100 / [1.10] = 100, \tag{7.12}$$

which yields $r_l^u = 83.33\%$. Mr. Barnes' expected payoff with $e = h$ is $0.8 \times (300{-}183.33) - 40 = 53.34$. His expected payoff with $e = l$ is $0.6 \times (300 - 183.33) = 70.00$. Thus, it is a Nash equilibrium for the bank to price its unsecured loan assuming that Mr. Barnes will choose $e = l$.

Step 3

Now let us see if we can do better by using collateral. Let C be the collateral that leaves Mr. Barnes indifferent between choosing l and h. Then r_l^u and C must be related by the following equation

$$[0.8 \times (1 + r_h^u) \times 100 + 0.2 \times 0.9C = 110, \tag{7.13}$$

The left-hand side of Equation (7.13) recognizes that the bank is repaid in full if the project is successful (this has probability 0.8) and only collects the collateral if the project fails (with probability 0.2). The value of the collateral to the bank is 0.9C. Solving Equation (7.13) gives

$$1 + r_h^s = 1.375 - 0.00225C. \tag{7.14}$$

Now, the amount of collateral needed to leave Mr. Barnes indifferent between l and h is given by

$$\begin{aligned} &0.8 \times [300 - 100 \times (1.375 - 0.00225C)] - 0.2C - 40 \\ &= 0.6 \times [300 - 100 \times (1.375 - 0.00225C)] - 0.4C \end{aligned} \tag{7.15}$$

Note that in Equation (7.15) we have substituted for r_h^u using Equation (7.14). Solving Equation (7.15) yields $C = \$30.61$. Using this value of C in Equation (7.14) gives $r_h^u = 30.613\%$. To have Mr. Barnes strictly prefer h, suppose we choose $C = \$30.62$. Mr. Barnes' payoff if he chooses $e = h$ is now the left-hand side of Equation (7.15) with $C = \$30.62$ and $r_h^u = 30.613\%$. It is \$89,386. If Mr. Barnes chooses $e = l$, his expected payoff is the right-hand side of Equation (7.15) and is given by \$89,384. Hence, Mr. Barnes prefers to choose h, and it is a Nash equilibrium for the bank to offer this secured loan on the assumption that Mr. Barnes will choose $e = h$.

Step 4

Note that Mr. Barnes' expected payoff in the Nash equilibrium with *unsecured* debt is \$70, whereas in the Nash equilibrium with secured debt it is \$89,384 (if Mr. Barnes chooses $e = l$) or \$89,386 (if Mr. Barnes chooses $e = h$). Thus, Mr. Barnes is better off by taking a secured loan, even though the use of collateral is dissipative.

We have discussed the various roles of collateral. The type and amount of collateral used will depend on which of these problems is dominant.[30] As mentioned earlier, using collateral can be costly, however, because of repossession costs. Additional costs are created because the quality of collateral must be appraised prior to making the loan and then monitored regularly during the life of the loan. The reason for the appraisal and monitoring is that variations in the quality of a particular type of collateral across different borrowers may be quite large. For example, when collateral consists of accounts receivable, it will be of much higher quality if it is pledged by a borrower that has receivables due from well-capitalized companies with triple A ratings than if it is pledged by a borrower with receivables due from weak credit risks. Another example is *contract receivables*,[31] whose risk increases with volatility in business cycles. The point is that all collateral is not

---

30. Empirical evidence on the relationship between collateral and borrower risk appears in Berger and Udell (1990), Boot et al. (1991), Cole et al. (2004), and Jimenez et al. (2006). These studies find that large prime borrowers are less likely to be asked to pledge collateral, whereas *observably* higher risk borrowers usually receive secured loans. (This is *not* inconsistent with our analysis that, among a group of *indistinguishable* borrowers, collateral can sort by inducing lower-risk borrowers to pledge more collateral). The finding that large, well-known borrowers are asked to pledge less collateral is also plausible since informational problems are likely to be less severe for such borrowers.

31. A "contract receivable" is an amount that a contractor is due to receive upon successful future completion of a contract. It involves chattel paper that shows the associated monetary obligations. Loans secured by contract receivables are often created when building or manufacturing contractors, dealers, or retailers need working capital.

the same, and the deployment of collateral has various costs associated with it. These costs must be traded off against the potential benefits of collateral in deciding how to use collateral in lending. We turn now to the last of the "five Cs" of credit.

5. *Conditions:* By this we mean the economic conditions that affect the borrower's ability to repay the loan. Debts are repaid from four sources: income, sale of assets, sale of stock, and borrowing from another source. All of these should be assessed in determining the desirability, price, and other terms of the loan. The borrower's ability to generate income depends on: the selling prices of its goods, costs of inputs, competition, quality of goods and services, advertising effectiveness, and quality of management. Analysis of the borrower's financial statements as well as its management should inform the bank about the borrower's ability to create income.

SOURCES OF CREDIT INFORMATION

The information used in underwriting credit is inherently costly and of uneven quality. The banker's critical skill in credit lies in assembling the most germane information at the lowest possible cost without violating legal requirements or social norms. This means identifying novel sources of information and using standard sources in clever ways. Following is a brief description of some of the standard sources of bank credit information, but we should emphasize that standard uses of standard sources is unlikely to produce anything better than average results. The clever use of credit information is a cultivated art form that distinguishes the successful lender from the pack.

Standard credit sources can be classified as: internal and external. By internal sources we mean those within the bank, and by external sources we mean all other.

Internal Sources

1. *Interview with Applicant:* The loan interview normally establishes the uses to which the borrowed funds will be put for the loan request and the conformity of the application with the bank's loan policies. For example, the bank's policy guidelines usually stipulate a minimum equity input by the borrower, so that a violation of this guideline can be discussed with the borrower, leading perhaps to a smaller loan request. The loan interview is also used to judge intangibles related to the borrower's future repayment behavior. Moreover, it also provides the loan officer with an opportunity to advise the applicant about any additional financial information that might be needed for evaluating the application.

2. *Bank's Own Records:* A bank normally maintains records of its depositors and borrowers. This source of information allows the bank to assess the borrower's past behavior.[32] For example, bank records will show the payment performance on previous loans, the balances carried in checking and savings accounts, and overdrawing patterns, if any. Even for applicants who have never been customers of the bank, the central file may contain some information if these applicants were solicited as potential customers.

External Sources

1. *Borrower's Financial Statements;* These are required of most borrowers. Audited statements are common requirements in commercial lending. Even in consumer lending, where loans are usually small, an applicant is normally asked to list what he/she owns, income and expenses, and outstanding debts.

2. *Credit Information Brokers:* Information agencies or credit bureaus systematically collect financial information on potential borrowers and make it generally available at a price (recall Chapter 3). The most widely known is *Dun & Bradstreet* (D&B), which collects information on over 3 million businesses in the United States and Canada. D&B's *Business Information Report* provides information on the type of business, nature of ownership, composite credit rating, promptness with which the firm makes payment, sales, net worth, number of employees, general condition of the firm including information about its physical facilities, customer base, balance sheet information, the usual size of the firm's deposit balances, its payments record under loan agreements, and biographical information on principals. More detailed information can be found in D&B's *Key Account Report.* In *Dun's Review,* D&B also publishes information about financial ratios for a large number of industries.

Comparative financial information can also be found in the *Annual Statement Studies* published by *Robert Morris Associates,* a professional association of professional lenders. There are numerous other surveyors of credit information, specializing in consumer, business, and even governmental borrowers.

---

32. In Chapter 3, we pointed out that this may be an important advantage of banks in granting credit.

3. *Other Banks*: Banks sometimes check with other banks that have had relationships with the loan applicant. They may also check with the firm's suppliers,[33] to learn how the firm pays its bills, and with the firm's customers to determine the quality of its products and the dependability of its service.

ANALYSIS OF FINANCIAL STATEMENTS

In evaluating the borrower's ability to service a loan, the bank will focus on the firm's internal sources for future generation of funds. These are: (i) net income, (ii) depreciation[34], (iii) reduction of accounts receivables, and (iv) reduction of inventories. To assess the potential of these cash flows, the bank examines the borrower's financial statements. However, financial statements are *noisy*. It is often necessary to work with audited statements that are months too old, along with unaudited interim statements that raise questions of authenticity. Even audited statements have their problems owing to the idiosyncracies of GAAP and the occasional lapses and professional compromises of auditors. These problems aside, financial statements value assets using nonmarket criteria such as book values, and income is distorted accordingly. Thus, financial statements should be interpreted with caution. An illustration is provided by the bursting of the stock market bubble in 2000 that was credited by some to a bond analyst raising questions about the credit worthiness of Amazon.com's debt based on accounting information not accurately reflecting cash flows for credit risk assessment purposes and concluding that Amazon's credit risk was higher than it seemed.[35]

Evaluation of the Balance Sheet

Assets

1. *Accounts Receivables: Accounts receivables* are among the shortest maturity assets on the borrower's balance sheet and are typically seen as the major source of cash flows to service short-term loans. Standard analyses focus on the sizes, sources, and aging of accounts, as well as the extent to which the accounts receivables are actively managed and diversified. As with any other risky asset portfolio, diversification lowers risk. The bank may also wish to investigate the financial attributes of those who owe money to the borrower since these speak to the quality of the borrower's receivables. Credit bureaus are especially useful in evaluating the quality of the borrower's receivables. Also, the current status or aging of receivables is a powerful indicator of their quality. For example, if a large fraction of receivables are 90 days or older and the convention is to pay in 30 days or less, the implications are transparent.

   Not all borrowers need to be screened equally carefully. Relatively low-risk borrowers who may be close to qualifying for unsecured loans often fall under a "bulk" or "blanket-assignment" lending plan. For such borrowers, the bank may require only monthly borrowing-base certificates and aging or inventory listing, without maintaining active day-to-day control over collections. In the next risk category may be customers who keep good records and have a well-diversified accounts receivables portfolio. For such borrowers, the bank may impose additional reporting requirements, including detailed assignment, collection, and aging schedules. In the highest risk category are borrowers with weak balance sheets and inadequate working capital. Here the bank requires all standard reports plus copies of shipping documents, delivery receipts, and assigned invoices against which the bank will lend. It is common for the bank to require such borrowers to remit collections directly to the bank in the form of checks "in kind." This is a way for the bank to exercise additional control. The bank might even mail invoices directly to the accounts in the borrower's accounts receivables portfolio, asking for payments to be made directly to the bank.[36]

2. *Contract Receivables:* A borrower may be a contractor who has been engaged to perform some task in the future. Official recognition of this may appear in *chattel paper* that shows the monetary obligations of the party for whom this task is being performed. These monetary obligations are called contract receivables. Chattel paper often serves as collateral for a working capital loan. Contract receivables are riskier than accounts receivables since payment is conditional on the borrower's future performance. There is consequently a *double moral hazard,* one that the borrower may not successfully complete the contracted task and the other that the third party may not pay the borrower even if the task is successfully completed.[37] Thus, greater monitoring efforts are warranted for contracts receivables.

---

33. Another source of information about a potential borrower's suppliers is the *Credit Interchange Service* of the *National Association of Credit Management.*
34. Since depreciation is not a cash outflow but is subtracted in computing net income, it should be added back to arrive at cash flow.
35. Quite often, these issues are related to a divergence of accounting income from cash flows.
36. This procedure is often referred to as handling borrowers on a "notification" basis.
37. With accounts receivables, you can see that only one of these two hazards is present.

3. *Inventory:* The age, liquidity, price stability, obsolescence, shrinkage, the adequacy of insurance coverage, the stage of processing, and the firm's method of inventory accounting are all issues in evaluating inventories.

As with any other form of collateral, the bank should be concerned about incentive effects as well as liquidation value. However, valuing partially processed inventories is difficult and a credit-analysis art form. Both raw materials and finished goods inventories are easier to value and have greater liquidity than partially processed goods. In many cases, raw material inventories have the broadest market and the lowest price volatility. As with other collateral, monitoring is crucial in that inventory stocks are constantly in flux, with potentially damaging consequences for the secured lender.

4. *Fixed Assets:* Normally, banks do not consider the sale of a fixed asset as a source of funds for loan repayment. However, surplus fixed assets can be occasional and strategic sources of cash flows. Whereas the main importance of fixed assets lies in their ability to *produce cash flows* and *not* in their resale value, business restructurings often generate surplus fixed assets whose expeditious sale can be value creating.

5. *Intangible Assets:* These include trademarks, patents, copyrights, and goodwill. These assets are normally accorded little value by a bank because of their illiquidity and measurement errors. There are, of course, exceptions, but by and large bankers apply large discounts to such assets.

6. *Amounts Due:* Banks often take a dim view of a firm's management if the firm's assets include amounts due from officers and employees. Amounts due create the suspicion of internal fraud and nepotism.

Liabilities and Net Worth

1. *Accounts Payable:* The borrower's accounts payable should speak volumes to its bank. If the borrower does not pay its trade creditors timely, why should the bank expect to be treated differently? The bank should ascertain whether payables are in the form of notes since this may indicate that the firm has been denied trade credit. The bank should be similarly alarmed if the borrower has been asked by its suppliers for cash-on-delivery (COD) terms. In case the borrower owes money to its own shareholders or officers, the bank should demand explanation and may ask that such liabilities be subordinated to any bank loan. The bank should also review the amounts accrued for taxes and other expenses.

2. *Long-Term Liabilities:* These consist of term loans, debentures, notes, mortgage loans, and other liabilities with maturities exceeding 1 year. The bank should be concerned with the *nature* and *maturity of* these obligations and the provisions that have been made for meeting the required payments. Their covenants may also be important for the bank considering a loan request. In particular, it is important to know whether the outstanding debt is secured and if so, which assets have already been pledged as collateral.

3. *Net Worth:* The importance of equity capital to credit analysis is transparent, given our earlier discussions. However, *accounting* net worth is a particularly treacherous account because it is fraught with measurement errors. This item is the residual of assets and liabilities, with each asset and liability independently evaluated *with error*. Hence, the net worth compounds all of the errors embedded in the underlying accounts. If all assets and liabilities could be evaluated at market, the net worth should be the economic value of equity claims. However, with accounting distortions and other measurement errors, accounting net worth can be a hard-to-interpret residual.

4. *Contingent Liabilities:* These are important because of their potential to become *actual* liabilities. If they do, they could seriously impair the debt-servicing capability of the borrower. Assessing the relevant probabilities and exposures may call for considerable information and sophistication. Moreover, such liabilities do not always appear in the body of the borrower's balance sheet. Even when footnote disclosures reveal the borrower's exposure (maximum liability), the present value of the liability depends also on the unspecified contingencies and probabilities.

The Income Statement

Income statement analysis complements balance sheet analysis. Bankers tend to emphasize the balance sheet in evaluating short-term loans, but devote greater attention to the income statement for longer-maturity loans. Recall that the balance sheet measures *stocks,* whereas the income statement measures *flows.* Hence, by looking at past and present income statements, the bank should be able to learn something about the degree of stability in the borrower's cash flows. Of course, in determining cash flow trends, the bank should be careful to note possible changes in the borrower's accounting practices can obfuscate.

The bank will often use both the balance sheet and the income statement in its *ratio analysis.* Key financial ratios convey information about the firm's liquidity, stability, profitability, and cash flow prospects.

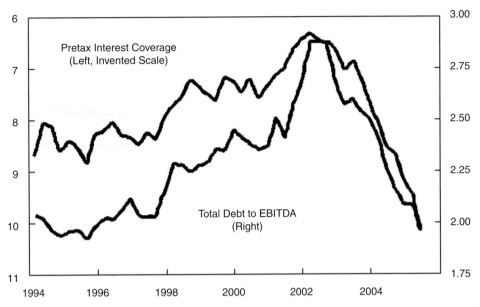

FIGURE 7.9   United States – Measures of Corporate Financial Performance for Investment Grade Corporate Borrowers (Ratio), 1994–2005 (*Source:* Citigroup.) *Note:* Pretax interest coverage is net income from continuing operations before taxes divided by reported gross interest expense. Data are for industrial credits within the Citigroup BIG Credit Index.

Basically, there are four types of ratios: liquidity, activity (or turnover), profitability, and financial leverage.

1. Two measures of liquidity are commonly used: current ratio = current assets/current liabilities, quick ratio (or acid test ratio) = $\dfrac{\text{current assets} - \text{inventories}}{\text{current liabilities}}$.

   a. By "current" we mean a duration of less than 1 year.
2. Activity ratios include the following:
   a. Inventory turnover ratio = sales/inventory.
   b. Average collection period (in days) = receivables/sales per day.
   c. Total assets turnover = sales/total assets.
   d. Fixed asset turnover = sales/net fixed assets.
3. There are also numerous profitability ratios. These include:
   a. Profit margin on sales = net profit after taxes/sales.
   b. Return on total assets = net profit after taxes/total assets.
   c. Return on net worth = net profit after taxes/net worth.
4. The leverage ratio is defined as total debt/total assets.

Perhaps the two most important leverage ratios used by lenders are: pretax interest coverage and total debt to EBIT-DA.[38] Pretax interest coverage is defined as net income from continuing operations before taxes divided by reported gross interest expense. EBITDA is earnings before interest, taxes, depreciation and amortization. Figure 7.9 shows the behavior of these ratios through time for investmentgrade U.S. corporate borrowers. It shows that the credit risk of these borrowers has been declining since 2002.

It is worth emphasizing that these ratios are usually expressed in terms of accounting values. Since bankers evaluate these ratios against peers, it is useful to remember that different firms may use different accounting methods. We provide a case at the end of this chapter that calls for ratio analysis as part of the credit evaluation process.

LOAN COVENANTS

Covenants are special clauses designed to protect the bank and prohibit the borrower from taking actions that could adversely affect the likelihood of repayment. By agreeing to loan covenants that limit its actions, the borrower precommits to eschewing strategies that might expropriate wealth from the lender. The effect is to reduce the moral hazard faced by the lender and

---

38. See Sufi (2009), who empirically shows the importance of total debt/EBITDA.

improve the terms of the loan agreement for the borrower. That is, loan covenants reduce the agency costs of debt and thereby benefit the borrower *ex ante,* and also the lender. Indeed, covenants make possible loans that would not otherwise be made at all. There is, of course, a limit to how restrictive a set of covenants the borrower will wish to accept. Restrictive covenants can make the loan reasonably safe for the lender but may deprive the borrower of valuable investment options and strategies.[39]

Loan covenants normally depend on the financial condition of the borrower, its investment opportunities, the track record of its management, and the lending philosophy of the bank. Covenants are commonly classified into four kinds: affirmative covenants, restrictive clauses, negative covenants, and default provisions.

Affirmative Covenants

These are obligations imposed on the borrower. A commonly used covenant in this group is a requirement that the bank be periodically furnished with financial statements. The purpose, of course, is to permit the bank to keep track of the borrower's financial condition and enable preventive steps to be taken if trouble is indicated.

Another example is a requirement that the borrower maintain a minimum level of working capital. Banks will occasionally require the borrower to maintain a management acceptable to the bank. If management should change due to resignation, death, or other causes, the bank must approve the replacement.

Restrictive Clauses

These are designed to impose limits on the borrower's actions. A commonly used restrictive clause is one that limits the amount of dividends the borrower can pay its shareholders. The economic rationale for this covenant is transparent. A major concern for any creditor is the borrower's inclination to divert liquidity and net worth to shareholders rather than keep it within the firm to protect creditors.

It is also common for the bank to restrict salaries, bonuses, and advances to employees of the firm, as well as to limit specific types of investments such as purchases of fixed assets. The economic rationale for restrictions on investments is to protect creditors against asset substitutions that may reduce the value of the firm's debt. By purchasing a fixed asset, for example, the bank may be replacing cash on its balance sheet with an asset that will produce risky cash flows; this may increase the risk exposure of creditors.

Negative Covenants

While restrictive covenants limit certain actions, negative covenants prohibit them outright, absent the bank's consent. A common negative covenant is the *negative pledge clause,* usually found in unsecured loans. It prohibits the borrower from pledging any of its assets as security to other lenders. While the negative pledge clause is more common in unsecured loans, it is also encountered in secured loans. The banker may want to include this clause even though the bank's claim is protected with collateral because if the borrower defaults, the value of the collateral may be substantially diminished. In this case, the bankruptcy law stipulates that for that portion of the bank's claim in excess of the value of the collateral, the bank has the same status as a general (unsecured) creditor. So the fewer the assets of the firm that are pledged for other loans, the greater is the share available to the bank in the event of bankruptcy.

There may also be prohibitions regarding mergers, consolidations, and sales of assets. The reason for this is that these developments can alter the firm's risk profile, possibly to the creditor's detriment. It is also common for the bank to prohibit borrowers from making loans to others or guaranteeing the debts or other performances of others. Again, the economic rationale is clear. If the borrower were to do these things, it would assume additional credit risk on its account. By prohibiting such actions, the bank protects its own claim.

Default Provisions

These are intended to make the entire loan immediately due and payable under certain conditions. Ordinarily, even though the bank has covenants that are intended to govern the borrower's behavior, violation need not automatically empower the

---

39. There may be circumstances in which restrictive loan covenants could perversely increase the likelihood of default by precluding actions the borrower could have taken to make both the bank and itself better off. For example, the purchase of new equipment by the borrower may be prohibited and yet the borrower's cash flows could be improved to such an extent by this purchase that the lender would be better off *ex post* if this covenant were relaxed. In such instances, the lender has an obvious incentive to renegotiate and relax the covenant (see Berlin and Mester, 1992). However, if the lender is unsure of the borrower's motive for renegotiating and therefore uncertain of its potential benefit to the lender, it may refuse to renegotiate.

bank to call the loan as long as scheduled payments are being made. However, some covenants will include an *acceleration clause* that specifies *events of default.* Effectively, violation of a covenant leading to any of the events of default automatically places the loan in default and full payment becomes due immediately. This permits the bank to take more timely actions than would be possible if it had to wait until a payment was missed. Acceleration clauses are often triggered by the following:

- Failure to make timely payments.
- Inaccuracy in representations and warranties.
- Violation of covenants.
- Bankruptcy, liquidation and/or appointment of a receiver.
- Entry of a judgment in excess of a specified amount.
- Impairment of collateral, invalidity of a guarantee and/or security agreement.
- Failure to pay other indebtedness when due or to perform under related agreements
  - Cross default.
  - Cross acceleration.
- Change of management or ownership.
- Expropriation of assets.

Any of the above may be considered an event of default, in which case the loan is accelerated and will lead to either renegotiation or default. In some cases, the loan agreement provides the borrower a period of time, referred to as a cure or grace period, to correct its default. If cured, the bank is then required to continue the loan. In the case where the default is not cured, the bank may terminate the lending relationship. The bank may also set off the borrower's deposits against its obligation to repay the loan and exercise its right to foreclose on collateral and even force the borrower into receivership. The cross-default provision gives the bank the right to declare an event of default when the borrower is in default on another obligation. Though banks rarely exercise the right to accelerate loan repayment, having this right substantially strengthens a lender's position.

Other Parameters of the Loan Agreement

Loan agreements have many provisions other than amount and price that must be negotiated between the bank and the borrower. Some of the more important parameters of the loan agreement are:

- A *take-down schedule:* a time table for withdrawing funds from the bank.
- An *installment schedule:* a time table for repaying the interest, other charges, and principal.
- A *compensating balance requirement:* an obligation by the borrower to maintain deposits at the lending bank. (This requirement is usually stated in terms of the *average* deposit balance but may include minima as well.)
- A *prepayment provision:* a possible penalty for repaying a loan earlier than required.

The loan agreement also may contain provisions especially tailored to a specific situation. For example:

- The borrower agrees to sell, within the next 12 months, at public auction, or by any other commercially reasonable means, a commercial property owned by the borrower located at the corner of Oak and Spring Streets in Center City.
- The borrower agrees, within 180 days, to divest himself of his interest in a partnership known as Branson Truck Lines, and to apply any and all proceeds from the sale thereof to this loan.
- The borrower agrees to obtain, as soon as possible, and to assign to the bank, $100,000 of term life insurance.

It is worth keeping in mind that covenants, no matter how elaborate, can never anticipate all contingencies and prevent all disasters. For example, a borrower could have adequate liquidity as measured by its stock of working capital, and yet its actual liquidity position may be very poor because its accounts receivables portfolio is concentrated in a few high-credit-risk accounts. No loan covenants can replace vigilant and ongoing monitoring by the bank.

CONCLUSION

In this chapter we have examined the bank's spot-lending decision. We have seen that a loan typically is an illiquid debt contract, without an active secondary market. The distinction between bank loans and traded bonds is significant on two grounds. First, trading tends to narrow informational gaps between borrowers and lenders, so that bank loans usually have less known about them than corporate bonds. Second, banks perform valuable screening services that overcome private information problems and postlending monitoring that resolves moral hazard problems. Thus, we should expect banks to lend to borrowers about whom less is known *a priori* and to those who have a rich set of investment opportunities so that moral hazard is a concern. This suggests a way to think about which borrowers approach banks and which go to the capital market (recall Chapter 3).

We have also discussed the design of loan contracts by banks in light of the informational problems they face. We have devoted considerable attention to the role of collateral and capital in overcoming these informational problems in traditional credit analysis.

Banks use a variety of internal and external information sources in order to perform the credit analysis needed to effectively screen borrowers. We have discussed these sources to highlight the potential impact of information availability on the bank's credit decision and its loan contract design. We hope that our discussions in this chapter have convinced you that the bank's lending decision is a complex one and expertise in credit analysis, loan contract design, and postlending monitoring is a valuable resource. Hence, the uniqueness of a bank (recall Chapters 2 and 3). However, even the best experts cannot *always* effectively overcome informational problems in loan contracting. Sometimes these problems are insurmountable, and sometimes new information arrives that makes a previously negotiated loan contract inefficient. How banks deal with such situations is the subject of the next chapter.

CASE STUDY: INDIANA BUILDING SUPPLIES, INC.

The date is January 15, 2001. Alex Brown, vice president of the First National Bank of Bloomington (FNBB), was approached by Peter Willis, one of his loan officers who recently completed his training program at the bank after graduating with an MBA from a leading business school. Peter has been concerned about the financial ratios of one of FNBB's borrowers, Indiana Building Supplies, Inc. (IBS). The bank has installed a new software package to assist in its credit analysis, and this package monitors existing borrowers, alerting the bank to possible problems. This software package has indicated deterioration in some key financial ratios of IBS and has Peter worried about the likelihood that IBS will be able to repay the $473,000 it owes to FNBB by the due date of December 26, 2006.

Peter told Alex that he had run a special computer analysis on IBS about a month back and had noticed that some of the key financial ratios of the firm were trending downward. Peter based his assessment of IBS's ratios on the data provided in Tables 7.5 and 7.6. Not only were these ratios below the averages for the building supplies industry, but they were also at

TABLE 7.5 Indiana Building Supplies, Inc. Balance Sheet Year Ended December 31

	2000	2003	2004	2005
Cash	$100,000	120,000	90,000	70,000
Accounts receivable	400,000	480,000	600,000	600,000
Inventory	500,000	550,000	800,000	900,000
Total Current Assets	$1,000,000	1,150,000	1,490,000	1,570,000
Land and building	100,000	90,000	217,000	221,000
Machinery	150,000	260,000	202,000	179,000
Other fixed assets	85,000	66,000	27,000	15,000
Total Assets	1,335,000	1,566,000	1,936,000	1,985,000
Notes payable, bank	47,000	53,000	110,000	473,000
Accounts and notes payable	156,000	171,500	233,800	319,000
Accruals	82,000	350,500	252,200	34,300
Total Current Liabilities	285,000	575,000	596,000	826,300
Mortgage	50,000	40,000	36,000	33,000
Common stock	900,000	900,000	1,150,000*	867,000**
Retained earnings	100,000	51,000	154,000	258,700
Total Liability and Equity	1,335,000	1,566,000	1,936,000	1,985,000

*The company issued common stock in 2004.
**In 2005 the company repurchased some stock, citing the unusually low market price of its stock.

TABLE 7.6 Indiana Building Supplies, Inc. Income Statement

	2000	2003	2004	2005
Net sales	$5,000,000	4,400,000	$5,600,000	$4,500,000
Cost of goods sold	4,000,200	3,400,000	4,500,000	3,500,000
Gross operating profit	$ 999,800	$1,000,000	$1,100,000	$1,000,000
General administration, selling, and interest expenses	521,467	582,000	849,667	519,000
Depreciation	80,000	105,000	80,000	72,000
Miscellaneous	65,000	93,000	77,000	71,500
Net income before taxes	333,333	220,000	93,333	337,500
Taxes (40%)	133,333	88,000	37,333	135,000
Net income	$ 200,000	$ 132,000	$ 56,000	$ 202,500

variance with the stipulations in the loan covenants negotiated between IBS and FNBB. Table 7.7 shows industry averages as well as loan covenant stipulations for key financial ratios for IBS. After his financial analysis, Peter contacted Bob Clemens, president of IBS, by phone and followed up with a letter providing details justifying his concerns. Clemens replied with a brief letter in which he conceded that some of the financial ratios had dipped below the levels specified in the loan covenants, but that there was no cause for alarm since the financial health of IBS was generally sound. Clemens pointed to the remarkable improvement in the firm's profit margin in 2005 relative to 2003 and 2004, and the fact that his return on net worth in 2005 was significantly above the industry average. When Peter called Clemens after receiving his reply, he explained to him that he was still concerned about the violations of ratio requirements in the covenants and wanted Clemens to send him data on the prices that IBS was charging customers for its finished goods. He also asked for (unaudited) quarterly financial statements on IBS.

Clemens seemed somewhat irritated by this request and reminded Peter that IBS had banked with FNBB for a long time and that Peter's predecessor had never been so picky with IBS even when it experienced substantially lower profit margins in 2003 and 2004. Nevertheless, he sent Peter the information he requested. When Peter analyzed this information, he found that IBS was charging higher prices than many of its competitors, especially those outside Indiana. Moreover, its quick ratio, current ratio, and its inventory turnover ratio all exhibited greater variations from quarter to quarter than the industry averages for these ratios.

IBS is a company that sells lumber products and a wide range of other building supplies in central and southern Indiana as well as in parts of Ohio and Missouri. The company's seasonal working capital needs as well as small capital equipment purchases have been financed primarily by loans from FNBB. IBS caters to basically two kinds of customers: local customers in

TABLE 7.7 Indiana Building Supplies, Inc.

	Ratios Specified in Loan Covenants	Industry Averages for 2005
Quick ratio	≥ 17	1.6
Current ratio	≥ 2.5	2.5
Inventory turnover ratio	≥ 9.00	8.5
Average collection period	NA	37 days
Fixed-asset turnover	NA	13.3
Total asset turnover	NA	3.00
Return on total assets	NA	9.5%
Return on net worth	NA	15%
Debt ratio	≤ 38%	31%
Profit margin on sales	NA	3%

Notes: These figures are based on year-end figures taken from balance sheets and income statements of representative firms in the industry. These figures have been roughly constant for the past 5 years.

southern and central Indiana and those elsewhere. Demand from the Indiana customers is somewhat erratic, but because of their strong desire to purchase from local suppliers and IBS's long-standing reputation, their demand is less sensitive to price increases than the demand of the other customers. In the past, whenever costs of raw materials have escalated, Clemens has personally visited many of his local customers and explained to them that he needed to increase his prices to keep pace with rising costs. These efforts have been successful in convincing the Indiana customers not to switch to other suppliers. Clemens has been far less successful in passing along such price increases to other customers. They usually seem to be able to locate alternative sources of supply when IBS increases its prices.

Recently, David Klinghoffer, the chief financial officer (CFO) of IBS, has been urging Clemens to confine attention to IBS's "loyal" Indiana customers, and thereby reduce the marketing costs involved in reaching out-of-state customers. In the past, Clemens was reluctant to embrace this strategy because of the erratic nature of demand from Indiana customers. When IBS was price competitive, it could always count on a predictable level of demand from its Ohio and Missouri customers. Increased competition and higher costs, however, seriously damaged IBS's profit margins in 2003 and 2004 and persuaded Clemens to raise prices in 2005 to improve profitability. Klinghoffer, who had also been advocating higher prices, pointed out to Clemens with great delight that their strategy had been a smashing success and the firm had been more profitable in 2005 than it had ever been since 2000. Thus, both Klinghoffer and Clemens were dismayed by what they viewed as "senseless pestering" by Peter Willis.

The matter has now come before Alex Brown. Peter has pointed out to Alex that FNBB has an "acceleration clause" in its loan contract that empowers it to force IBS to repay its entire loan to FNBB immediately because of the violations of covenants. Alex was hesitant to do that and decided to call Clemens. When Alex advised him of the seriousness of the situation and the possibility that the bank would insist on immediate repayment of the entire loan unless some corrective action was taken, Clemens said it was likely that IBS would need an additional 1-year loan of about $200,000 (preferably at a 10% interest rate) to cover the amount payable on a note that was due to another creditor in a few weeks. He also requested FNBB to advise him regarding specific steps that the bank wanted IBS to take.

After hanging up the phone with Clemens, Alex asked Peter to bring him a detailed financial analysis of IBS, along with the specific reasons why Peter was so concerned. He also asked Peter to evaluate whether IBS's request for additional credit should be approved and to recommend specific steps IBS should be asked to take if the existing loan is not accelerated and new credit is granted. Alex wants Peter to pay particular attention to the fact that the "bottom line" *does* seem to indicate that IBS has done well in 2005, which makes Peter's worry somewhat anomalous.

Questions

Imagine that you are Peter Willis. Prepare a comprehensive ratio analysis for IBS. Should the bank call back the entire loan now? Why or why not? Should FNBB be worried or is Peter just overreacting? Is it possible for IBS to generate enough cash by year-end 2006 to make full repayment to FNBB? How valid are comparisons of IBS's financial ratios to the industry average?

REVIEW QUESTIONS

1. What are the different types of assets on a bank's balance sheet?
2. What is a "bank loan"? What are the different ways in which a bank can acquire loans?
3. Discuss the similarities and differences between loans and securities.
4. What are the major informational problems in loan contracts?
5. What is the purpose of credit analysis? Compare and contrast capital budgeting within a nonfinancial firm with credit analysis within a bank.
6. What are "the 5 Cs of credit"? What do we mean by a borrower's "character" and why is it important?
7. Can you explain intuitively why capital can resolve asset substitution moral hazard?
8. Discuss intuitively how capital can help the bank to resolve "adverse selection" problems. It would be useful to start out by explaining first what we mean by "adverse selection," and why it is a problem for the bank. Can you relate this role of capital in a bank loan contract to a venture capitalist's insistence on a minimum equity capital input by an entrepreneur seeking venture capital?
9. Please address the following questions:
   a. What is a reverse LBO?
   b. What are the main reasons why customers of banks become higher-quality credits after reverse LBOs?
   c. Why are we observing such a large increase in reverse LBOs now?

10. What is the extent of secured lending among C&I loans? What are the two main types of collateral?

11. What are the costs of collateral? Why is "outside" collateral so popular despite these costs?

12. What is "underinvestment moral hazard"? Explain the intuition underlying the claim that collateral can attenuate this moral hazard. What are the implications of this for the design of bank loan covenants?

13. What is a "contract receivable"? Why is it usually more risky than an "accounts receivable"?

14. What are the main sources of credit information for banks in conducting credit analysis?

15. What is the role of ratio analysis in credit assessment? What are its limitations?

16. Overheard was the following conversation between two friends:

Tom: I find it offensive that a bank would tell me what to do and what not to do when it makes me a loan. After all, I own the asset I'll buy with the loan because I have an *equity* stake in it. The bank is only lending me the money.

Jack: That's nonsense, Tom! When you buy an asset with a bank loan, it's the *bank* that owns the asset, and don't you forget it. What do *you* think? Explain your answer.

17. What are "affirmative covenants," "restrictive clauses," "negative covenants," and "default provisions"? Discuss the role of each in the design of credit contracts.

18. What are "expert systems" and what are banks attempting to achieve with them as part of credit analysis?

19. Consider a firm that has a bank loan outstanding that requires the firm to repay $900 one period hence. The firm has $300 in retained earnings that can either be paid out as a dividend to the firm's shareholders or invested in a project that will yield a single cash flow one period hence. The firm has a choice of investing in a safe project S, or a risky project R. The safe project will yield $1000 for sure one period hence, whereas the risky project will yield $2000 with probability 0.4 and nothing with probability 0.6. Assume that everybody is risk neutral and that the discount rate is zero. Which project has the higher *total* NPV for the firm? Which project will the firm choose, assuming that decisions are made to maximize shareholder wealth?

20. You are a bank loan officer. ABC Corporation has requested a $2.1 million loan. The corporation has $2 million in retained earnings and an existing debt obligation that calls for a repayment of $4 million one period hence. The firm has existing assets that will be worth $6 million with probability 0.7 and nothing with probability 0.3 one period hence. These are the future values of the assets in place if the firm does not make any investment at present. The firm also has the choice of investing in one of two mutually exclusive projects (A or B). Project A will yield $4 million with probability 0.7 and $2 million with probability 0.3 one period hence. Its cash flows are uncorrelated with (and in addition to) those from the assets in place. Project B will yield $13 million with probability 0.2 and nothing with probability 0.8. Its cash flows are also uncorrelated with those from the assets in place. Assume that everybody is risk neutral and that there is no discounting. Moreover, ABC's existing debt has seniority over any new bank loan. Compute ABC's project choice and your pricing of the bank loan in two cases: (i) ABC has $2 million in retained earnings that will be kept within the firm for one period, (ii) ABC has already announced that the retained earnings will be paid out as dividends right now and hence unavailable to augment ABC's cash flows one period hence. Assume that your bank's cost of funds is zero and the bank is competitive (prices the loan to earn zero expected profit).

21. Consider a firm that needs $350 to invest in a project that will yield a single cash flow one period hence. The firm knows the probability distribution of this cash flow, but no one else does. As a banker you only know that the firm is either low risk (L) or high risk (H). If it is L, then it will yield $500 with probability 0.8 and nothing with probability 0.2 one period hence. If it is H, it will yield $1500 with probability 0.6 and nothing with probability 0.4 one period hence. The firm itself knows whether it is H or L. Assume that both the principal and interest repayments on any debt are tax deductible. The corporate tax rate applicable to this firm is 0.2. There is no equity capital on the firm's books at present, but it would raise equity if needed. The firm is locked into being either L or H, but as a banker you cannot tell which type it is. Assume everybody is risk neutral and that the discount rate (and the bank's cost of funds) is zero. Also, your bank is competitive (prices loans to earn zero expected profit). Construct a scheme consisting of two different loan contracts (one requiring the borrower to finance the project partly with equity capital and the other requiring no equity) such that the firm will truthfully reveal its private information by its choice of loan contract.

22. Consider a firm that can invest $250 right now, at $t = 0$, in a project that will yield a single cash flow one period hence, at $t = 1$. This $250 investment will be raised by issuing unsecured debt at $t = 0$. The project will yield $500 with probability 0.8 and nothing with probability 0.2 at $t = 1$. Immediately after the initial investment but before the end of the period (say at $t = 1/2$), the firm can purchase another asset, call it A, for $250 also. If purchased, A will yield a sure payoff of $300 at $t = 1$. Those who lend the firm money at $t = 0$ cannot observe at $t = 1/2$ whether the firm had this investment opportunity. Everybody is risk neutral and the riskless rate is 12%. If you are the banker the firm has approached for a $250 loan at $t = 0$, compute the price of your loan in two cases: (i) the firm can finance the acquisition of asset A with unsecured debt or not at all, and (ii) the firm can finance the acquisition of asset A with debt secured by the asset in question. Assume that in case (i), your bank (the initial lender) will have the same seniority as the new (unsecured) creditors who supply funds to purchase A. Your bank is competitive in loan pricing.

23. Given below is an excerpt from a conversation. Critique it.

a. *Butterworth:* I'll let that pass because I want to address your question, Mike. You know over 70% of business loans are secured, and collateral has some really beneficial incentive effects from the bank's standpoint. Moreover, it permits the bank to engage in creative loan-contract design that helps to resolve some thorny informational problems. It also leads to improved bank monitoring of borrowers, which is a key function associated with both secured and unsecured lending. To make a really long story short, I think that business lending is a key component of banks' activities. If regulation discourages this, then I think we'll have seriously weakened the financial intermediation process.

b. *Moderator:* If the role of banks in business lending were to diminish, what sort of losses to society do you foresee, Beth?

c. *Butterworth:* That's my favorite topic, Mike, so we could be here all night if I get going. But just briefly, I think that in the process of originating these loans, designing loan contracts, structuring covenants, including the crafting of collateral requirements, monitoring, and the restructuring of loans for borrowers in financial distress, banks have developed considerable expertise. It would be a shame if the financial system evolved in such a way that these skills would need to be relearned by others.

24. What is the "lending function" and how can it be decomposed? What is the usefulness of the decomposition?

REFERENCES

Ausubel, L., 1991. The failure of competition in the credit card market. Am. Econ. Rev. 81, 50–81.

Bassett, W.F., Brady, T.F., 2001. The economic performance of small banks, 1985–2000. Fed. Reser. Bull., 719–728.

Berger, A.N., Udell, G.F., 1990. Collateral, loan quality, and bank risk. J. Monetary Econ. 25, 21–42.

Berlin, M., Mester, L., 1992. Debt covenants and renegotiation. J. Financ. Intermed. 2, 95–133.

Besanko, D., Thakor, A.V., 1987a. Competitive equilibria in the credit market under asymmetric information. J. Econ. Theory 42, 167–182.

Bensako, D., Thakor, A.V., 1987b. Collateral and rationing: sorting equilibria in monopolistic and competitive credit markets. Int. Econ. Rev. 28, 671–689.

Bester, H., 1985. Screening vs. rationing in credit markets with imperfect information. Am. Econ. Rev. 75, 850–855.

Boot, A., Thakor, A.V., Udell, G.F., 1991. Secured lending and default risk: equilibrium analysis and monetary policy implications. Econ. J. 101, 458–472.

Brickley, J., 2003. Empirical research on CEO turnover and firm-performance: a discussion. J. Account. Econ. 36, 227–233.

Cole, R. A., 2012. How Did the Financial Crisis Affect Small Business Lending in the United States?, SBA working paper, www.sba.gov/advocacy.

Cole, R.A., Goldberg, L.G., White, L.J., 2004. Cookie cutter vs. character: the micro structure of small business lending by large and small banks. J. Financ. Quant. Anal. 39, 227–251.

Diamond, D., 1989. Reputation acquisition in debt markets. J. Polit. Econ. 97, 828–862.

Durkin, T.A., Elliehausen, G., Staten, M.E., Zywicki, T.J., 2014. Consumer Credit and the American Economy. Oxford University Press, Oxford, UK.

ESRB, 2014. Is Europe Overbanked? Report of the Advisory Scientific Committee, European Systemic Risk Board, No. 4.

FDIC, 2012. FDIC Community Banking Study.

Filbeck, G., Preece, D., Woessner, S., Burgess, S., 2010. Community banks and deposit market share growth. Int. J. Bank Marketing 28, 252–266.

Green, R., 1984. Investment incentives, debt, and warrants. J. Financ. Econ. 13, 115–136.

Hall, J., Yeager, T.J., 2002. Does 'relationships banking' protect small banks from economic downturns? Regional Economist, Federal Reserve Bank of St. Louis.

Huber, S.K., 1989. Bank Officer's Handbook of Government Regulation, third ed. Gorham & Lamont, Warren, Boston, MA.

Jimenez, G., Salas, V., Saurina, J., 2006. The determinants of collateral. J. Financ. Econ. 81, 255–281.

Leitner, Y., 2006. Using collateral to secure loans. Bus. Rev. Fed. Reserve Bank Philadelphia Q2, 9–16.

Markham, J.W., Gjyshi, R., 2014. Research Handbook on Securities Regulation in the United States. Edward Elgar Publishing, Northampton, MA, USA.

Myers, S., 1977. Determinants of corporate borrowing. J. Financ. Econ. 5, 147–175.

Ongena, S., Cerqueiro, G., Roszbach, K., 2015. Collateralization, bank loan rates, and monitoring. J. Finan. forthcoming. doi: 10.1111/jofi.12214.

Rose, S., June 19, 1990. Why banks make so many bad loans. American Banker.

Smith, C.W., Warner, J.B., 1979. On financial contracting: an analysis of bond covenants. J. Financ. Econ. 7, 117–161.

Stulz, R.M., Johnson, H., 1985. An analysis of secured debt. J. Financ. Econ. 14, 501–522.

Sufi, A., 2009. The real effects of debt certification: evidence from the introduction of bank loan ratings. Rev. Financ. Stud. 22, 1659–1691.

Tirole, J., 2006. The Theory of Corporate Finance. Princeton University Press, Princeton.

Chapter 8

Further Issues in Bank Lending

"A banker is a fellow who lends you his umbrella when the sun is shining and wants it back the minute it begins to rain."

Mark Twain

GLOSSARY OF TERMS

Discount Window A facility, often referred to as lender of last resort, where banks can borrow short term from the Federal Reserve to meet their liquidity needs, normally using Treasury securities as collateral. The interest rate charged for these advances, a tool of monetary policy, is called the "discount rate."

Open Market Operations Purchases and sales of government securities by the Federal Reserve to adjust the legal reserves available to banks to support their deposit liabilities. Sales of government securities to banks reduce the reserves available to banks, and purchases of government securities from banks increase these reserves. This is a tool of monetary policy.

Interest Elasticity of Investment Measure of the sensitivity of demand for investment funds by corporations to changes in interest rates (their borrowing rates).

Monetary Policy The Central Bank's (Federal Reserve's) policy with regard to the money supply and interest rates.

Reserve Requirement The fraction of bank's deposits and other (short-term) funding sources that must be kept as liquid assets, either as cash in vault, or as deposit with the Federal Reserve.

CD A certificate of deposit. This is a time deposit with a stated maturity and interest rate. It may be negotiable (marketable) or nonnegotiable (nonmarketable).

Consol Bond A bond with an infinite maturity, that is, one that promises a perpetual coupon stream and has no principal repayment.

Credit Crunch Precipitous reduction in the availability of credit.

INTRODUCTION

In Chapter 7 we examined informational problems in lending and how these problems are addressed through the design of loan contracts. In this chapter, we continue our discussion of loan transactions and extend it to cover a variety of issues such as the initial pricing of loans and adjustments in contractual terms that take place after the loan is made. While Chapter 7 was concerned mainly with static issues in lending, this chapter is concerned mainly with dynamic issues. We begin the next section with a discussion of how profit margins are assessed and how loans are priced. In the section that follows, we examine the reason for possible price rigidities in loan contracts and credit rationing. The bank's optimal lending process is described in the next section. We then explore the economic incentives for banks and borrowers to develop long-term relationships. This is followed with a discussion of loan default and restructuring. A case study is presented to help illustrate the concepts.

LOAN PRICING AND PROFIT MARGINS: GENERAL REMARKS

In this section, we discuss how banks assess the profitability of loans and how these are priced. We begin our discussion with an analysis of the assessment of profit margins. This is followed by a discussion of benchmark lending rates, after which we discuss compensating balances. We conclude the section with an analysis of the link between default risk and bank profit margins.

Assessing Profit Margins

To assess the profit margin of a loan, a bank should first determine its sources of income from lending. These are (a) the interest on the loan, (b) noninterest fee income on the loan, and (c) income from fees charged for services the borrower

S. I. Greenbaum, A. V. Thakor & A. W. A. Boot: Contemporary Financial Intermediation, Third edition. http://dx.doi.org/10.1016/B978-0-12-405196-6.00008-2

purchases due to the lending relationship. As for (b), there are many sources of noninterest fee income. These include closing fees (charged for concluding the loan agreement), loan-servicing fees, and commitment fees (fees charged for making credit lines or loan commitments available).[1] As for (c), borrowers may purchase a variety of services from banks due to the lending relationship. These include cash-management services and trust services, for example. If the purchase of these services can be linked to the taking of the loan, then the net profit from the sales of these services by the bank should be attributed to the loan.

After assessing the income from the loan, the bank should compute the expenses incurred to generate that income. These expenses include processing costs, salaries, postage, advertising and other marketing expenses, occupancy expenses, and other loan-servicing costs. Finally, the bank should compute the costs of funding the loan. These costs include the cost of demand and time deposit and nondeposit funds supporting the loan, as well as the costs of servicing deposits. Having assessed income expenses and costs, the bank can calculate its profit on the loan as shown in Table 8.1.

Benchmark or Reference Lending Rates

Our previous discussion of profit margins did not explain how a particular loan interest rate itself should be determined. In practice, banks set the interest rates on loans by relating them to a benchmark or reference interest rate. A commonly used reference rate is the *prime interest rate*.[2] Traditionally, the prime rate was the interest rate posted by the bank for short and intermediate maturity loans for its most creditworthy customers, usually corporations with "blue-chip" credit ratings.

Nowadays, the bank's most creditworthy customers pay less than the prime. The prime is an administered rate loosely linked to market interest rates, and it tends to be more sluggish than market rates.

Determining the prime rate is one of the many decisions a bank makes in the process of managing its balance sheet. Whereas each bank sets its own prime lending rate, the behavior of competing financial institutions is a major influence. In addition, three major categories of market interest rates provide the principal inputs in the prime-rates setting process: (a) the rates on nonloan bank assets, (b) rates on bank-acquired liabilities, and (c) rates on corporate debt claims that are close substitutes for bank loans. Also, the term structure of interest rates, bankers' expectations of future interest rates, the expected growth in deposits, and the expected growth in loan rates are important in setting the prime.

Many of the bank's loan rates are indexed to the prime rate, either additively as in "prime plus" (i.e., prime plus 1%) or multiplicatively as in "prime times" (i.e., prime 1.05). Thus, a decision to alter the prime rate involves adjustments in a bank's entire schedule of business loan rates. This means that a bank must consider expected demand for all types of loans in determining its prime rate.

Later in this chapter we will discuss the bank–customer relationship, a particularly important topic in view of the growing emphasis on *relationship banking*. For now, it suffices to note that "customer relationships" are arrangements whereby a bank provides a variety of services to long-established customers, and these relationships must also be considered in setting the prime rate. Customers are typically risk averse and hence dislike frequent and unpredictable adjustments in their borrowing rates. Thus, in order to foster customer relationships, the bank may wish to smooth the prime rate in relation to market interest rate movements. The usual customer relationship includes two features that are particularly relevant to prime rate determination – compensating balance requirements and loan commitments. We will deal with loan commitments in the next chapter. Compensating balances are dealt with next.

TABLE 8.1 The Profit Equation

Income	Expenses	COST of Funds = Profit
Loan interest	Loan-processing costs	Cost of demand deposits
Noninterest fee income	Salaries	Cost of time deposits
Income from bank services	Postage	Cost of nondeposit funds
	Advertising and marketing occupancy costs	Servicing costs

1. See Berg et al. (2015). They provide evidence that 80% of loans to the U.S. publicly traded firms contain fees.
2. Another reference lending rate is the London Interbank Offer Rate (LIBOR), which is the virtually risk-free rate on short-term borrowing between banks in the London credit market. The Fed Funds rate is the analog in the U.S. market.

Compensating Balances

Increased competition in banking in recent years has reduced the use of "compensating balances." Nevertheless, some banks still require minimum average deposit balances (known as compensating balances) as partial compensation for bank loans and other bank services. The bank's compensation results from not paying interest (or paying below-market interest) on compensating balances.

Compensating balances frequently are used with loan commitments or lines of credit. They can be viewed as raising the effective loan rate. Although compensating balances requirements are usually stated as percentages of the dollar amounts of credit lines, many arrangements require the deposit of additional balances when credit lines are activated or used. Nominal loan rates are quoted in terms of the loan principal. If a borrower must use a part of the loan to meet compensating balances requirements, the effective loan rate on the funds available for the borrower's use will exceed the stated rate because the borrower is paying loan interest on funds committed to remain in his deposit account. This means that a bank can increase effective loan rates by simply increasing compensating balance requirements and leaving its prime rate unchanged. In other words, given the fact that the prime rate affects the bank's entire schedule of lending rates, the bank may respond to changes in market interest rates by leaving the prime unchanged but changing nonprice loan terms – maturities, collateral requirements, or compensating balance requirements – so that effective lending rates can be *selectively altered*.

The Relationship Between Lending Profit and Default Risk

How should a bank set the interest rate on a loan? In the previous chapter, we made the simplifying assumption that each loan is priced to yield zero expected profit to the bank. As mentioned earlier, this is a representation of perfect competition among lenders. Such prices should only be viewed as minimal, however, since loan markets are imperfectly competitive. Thus, loans will be priced so that banks earn profits. The question is: How should the price of the loan be related to its riskiness? We will show that, because of agency problems, banks may price loans so that riskier borrowers are charged less than safer borrowers on a *risk-adjusted* basis.

Example 8.1

To examine this issue, imagine that banks can charge any borrower 150 basis points above the interest rate at which the bank would break even (in an expected value sense) on that borrower. This is a simple way to recognize the inertia induced by transactions costs or switching costs. That is, the bank can charge a borrower 1.5% above its breakeven rate before the customer will consider switching to another bank. By assumption, the bank's own borrowing cost is the riskless interest rate. Now suppose the bank has two types of borrowers who are observationally separable. One is a low-risk borrower, Safeway, Inc., and the other is a high-risk borrower, Gamble Brothers. Although the bank can distinguish between these two types, it cannot directly control what the borrower does with the bank loan. Each borrower has the choice of investing in one of two mutually exclusive, single-period projects: S and R, each of which requires a $100 investment. The cash flow probability distributions of these projects are given in Table 8.2 ("w.p." means "with probability").

Compute the bank's expected profit on each borrower.

Solution

We solve this problem in three steps. First, we examine Safeway, Inc. and ask what project the bank would like Safeway to choose. It turns out the answer is S. We then solve for the interest rate the bank can charge that will induce Safeway to choose S. Second, we examine Gamble Brothers. If the bank assumes that this borrower will choose R, then the breakeven interest rate is so high that the borrower declines the loan. We solve for the interest rate that induces Gamble Brothers to choose S. Finally, in Step 3 we compute the bank's expected profit on each borrower, and find that this profit is higher on Safeway. Note that one key assumption

---

TABLE 8.2 Probability Distribution of Project Cash

Borrower Type	Cash Flow Distribution for S	Cash Flow Distribution for R
Low risk (Safeway, Inc.)	$150 for sure	$153 w.p. 0.9 and zero w.p. 0.1
High risk (Gamble Brothers) The riskless interest rate is 5%.	$150 w.p. 0.8 and zero w.p. 0.2	$161 w.p. 0.5 and zero w.p. 0.5

here is that the bank is unable to directly control the borrower's project choice, so that it must attempt to influence it through its loan pricing. Another key assumption is that the markup over the breakeven interest rate that the bank can charge is constant across borrowers.

Step 1

Consider first Safeway, Inc. If the bank assumes that this borrower will choose S, then its breakeven loan interest rate is 5%. Since it can charge another 1.5% without losing this borrower, it can post a loan interest rate of 6.5%. We can see that if the bank charges this interest rate, Safeway's net expected payoff is

1. 150–106.5 = $43.5 if project S is chosen and
2. 0.9(153–106.5) = $41.85 if project R is chosen.

Thus, the bank's assumption about Safeway's project choice is validated. Note that since the markup over the breakeven interest rate is fixed, the bank's expected profit is higher the lower is the riskiness of the project that the borrower chooses. Thus, it is in the bank's interest to ensure through its loan pricing policy that the borrower chooses S rather than R. In the case of Safeway then, the bank can charge an interest rate of 6.5%.

Step 2

Consider now Gamble Brothers. If the bank assumes that this borrower will select R, then it must set the repayment obligation on the loan at $210 to break even (i.e., note that [($210 × 0.5)/1.05] = $100). But Gamble Brothers would not take a loan at those terms. If the bank assumes that Gamble Brothers will choose S, then its breakdown interest rate is 31.25% (i.e., [($131.25 × 0.8)/1.05] = $100). We can verify that as long as the interest rate is no more than 31.67%, Gamble Brothers will prefer S to R. Thus, let us say that the bank will charge 31.67%.

Step 3

We can now compute the bank's net expected profit on each borrower. On Safeway, Inc., the bank earns a net profit of $1.5 or 1.5%. On Gamble Brothers, the bank's net expected profit is ($131.66 − $131.25) × 0.8 = $0.328. That is, the bank earns a higher expected profit on the low-risk borrower than on the high-risk borrower, even though it charges the latter a higher loan interest rate.

The example illustrates the pricing difficulties associated with high-risk borrowers: charging higher interest rates might be counterproductive if it invites moral hazard.

The intuition is as follows. A high-risk borrower has riskier projects than a low-risk borrower and therefore the bank's breakeven interest rate on such borrowers is higher, that is, high-risk borrowers must be charged a relatively high interest rate even *before* the bank's profit margin is considered. Further, because their probability of repaying the loan is lower, such borrowers must be charged a higher *nominal* interest rate premium over the breakeven rate for the bank to earn a *given* profit. However, as our example shows, the higher the interest rate charged by the bank, the greater is the borrower's desire to switch to a riskier project. This is a general result. It is intuitive because a high repayment obligation means that even if the project succeeds, the borrower's net payoff after repaying the bank is relatively low, and perhaps even negative. This makes it more attractive for the borrower to gamble on projects that yield larger payoffs if they are successful but have lower success probabilities. The bank rationally anticipates such behavior by the borrower. It realizes that to earn the same expected profit on the high-risk borrower that it does on the low-risk borrower, it will have to charge the high-risk borrower such a high interest rate that the borrower would be induced to choose greater risk than the bank would like. In other words, the bank has less room to earn profits on the high-risk borrower because increases in interest rates discourage such borrowers from choosing the desired relatively safe investments.

The management implication is obvious. Banks may wish to refocus their attention on the low-risk, low-spread borrowers. Deposit insurance has distorted these incentives and induced banks to pursue riskier investments than would otherwise be optimal. Moreover, to the extent that riskier borrowers are less well known, the intermediation rents that banks can earn from servicing these borrowers may also be greater. This too creates incentives for banks to pursue riskier borrowers. It turns out that the incentive effects of interest rates influence the *overall* allocation of credit, not just the pricing of loans. This is an issue we examine in the section on credit rationing.

The Mathematics of Loan Pricing

Having provided the basic background for loan pricing, we now develop the mathematics behind how loan processes are determined. It turns out that bank loan pricing has a close relationship to the principles of capital budgeting used by non-financial firms.

The Basic Components in the Loan Pricing Equation

The bank would like to set the price of the loan so as to have NPV $\geq$ 0 to the bank. To ensure NPV $\geq$ 0, the expected loan revenues must exceed the bank's "cost of funds" plus the "institutional costs" of making the loan, that is.

Expected loan interest revenue:

$\geq$ Institutional cost of loan

+ [amount of debt financing in the loan $\times$ cost of debt]

+ [amount of equity financing in the loan $\times$ cost of equity].

Since expected loan revenue:

= [loan interest rate $\times$ size of loan] – expected loss on the loan,

we can write:

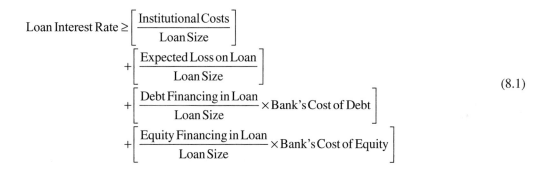

$$\text{Loan Interest Rate} \geq \left[\frac{\text{Institutional Costs}}{\text{Loan Size}} \right] + \left[\frac{\text{Expected Loss on Loan}}{\text{Loan Size}} \right] + \left[\frac{\text{Debt Financing in Loan}}{\text{Loan Size}} \times \text{Bank's Cost of Debt} \right] + \left[\frac{\text{Equity Financing in Loan}}{\text{Loan Size}} \times \text{Bank's Cost of Equity} \right] \tag{8.1}$$

Institutional Costs

The institutional costs of making a loan are the direct cost of monitoring the loan and the collateral, the direct costs of screening the applicant, and the allocated overhead costs. Included in the allocated overhead costs are the costs of using property, plant, and equipment, and the costs of regulation and management.

There are various empirical estimates of institutional costs that are available for United States banks. Older studies by Oliver, Wyman & Company, and McKinsey & Company suggested that costs could run as high as 250 basis points. Of course, this cost will vary depending on the size of the bank, the market in which it operates, the existing regulations, and the type of loan.

Expected Loss on a Loan

The formula for this is:

Bank's expected loss on a loan = probability of default $\times$ the expected loss *given* default.

Figure 8.1 shows how each component of the expected loss on a loan behaves as a function of the value of the borrower's asset given that the borrowing is secured with the project financed by the loan.

In practice, banks often use a "recovery rate" of 30%, implying an expected loss given a default of 70%. The average probability of default for midmarket lending might be around 1.2%.

Many banks now use the borrower's credit rating to estimate probabilities (this is also consistent with the approach in the Basel II Capital Requirements that we will discuss in a later chapter). Moody's KMV, a division of Moody's Corporation, estimates ranges of default probabilities based on credit ratings as follows:

AAA/Aaa = 0.02%–0.03%

AA/Aa = 0.03%–0.10%

A = 0.10%–0.24%

BBB/Baa = 0.24%–0.58%

BB/Ba = 0.58%–1.19%

The Capital Structure Supporting a Loan

Just like a nonfinancial firm finances its assets with a mixture of debt and equity, so does a bank finance its loan with a mixture of debt and equity. How does a bank determine the mix?

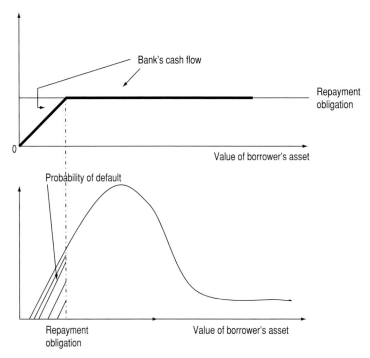

FIGURE 8.1 The Bank's Expected Loss on a Loan.

Here we use a well-known result from corporate finance, namely that firms with more volatile cash flows and higher assets betas (greater systematic risk) use more equity in their capital structures. Similarly, a bank will use more equity capital in its financing of a loan that has higher potential for cash flow volatility and thus higher risk. In practice, a bank will create numerous loan categories and decide which category a particular loan belongs to. Each loan category will have a hypothetical capital structure, and categories associated with more risk will have more capital allocated to them.

The Required Rate of Return on the Bank's Debt and Equity Capital

The pretax cost of the bank's debt is simply the average cost of all of the bank's debt. This includes the costs of various types of insured and uninsured deposits, the cost of various forms of nondeposit short-term borrowings like advances, and the cost of subordinated debt. Then:

$$\text{Cost of debt} = \text{average pretax cost of debt} \times [1 - T] \tag{8.2}$$

where T is the bank's effective tax rate.

What determines the cost of the bank's equity capital? This is the minimum expected rate of return that the bank's shareholders demand, given the risk in their investment. Now bank assets are unique because they are primarily *debt claims*. This means that the bank's payoff on a loan is fixed *unless* default occurs. In computing the risk of default, the bank must assess the default risk of a single asset as well as the default risk that a single asset adds to a diversified portfolio.

Default Risk of a Single Loan

Suppose a bank is considering lending to a firm. If it makes the loan, the firm will have approximately $75 million of debt due in one year and an expected market value of assets of $150 million in one year. The standard deviation of the firm's assets is assumed to be 17%. (See Figure 8.2)

What Figure 8.2 gives is a single number representing the probability of default. It is what is *expected*. It does not tell us the bank's actual losses, which are random variables with probabilities associated with them. Thus, we need to characterize the *distribution* of losses as well. For each loan in the portfolio, we can characterize the probability of losses using: (i) the mean loss (expected loss) and (ii) the loss volatility.

To see this with an example, suppose a bank has made a loan to a farm on an island where it rains on one side or the other in a given year, but never on both sides. The probability of rain on any given side is 0.5. Assume that the loan repayment is

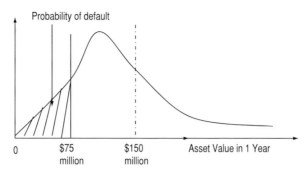

FIGURE 8.2   Distribution of Firm's Asset Value.

$1 million and the loss given default is 100%. In this case, the bank's expected loss = 0.5×$1 million = $0.5 million. The loan loss volatility = standard deviation of loan loss:

$$\sqrt{0.5[\$1\,\text{million} - \$0.5\,\text{million}]^2 + 0.5[0 - \$0.5\,\text{million}]^2} = \$0.5\,\text{million}.$$

Default Risk of a Loan Portfolio

Now let us consider the effect of forming loan portfolios. Just as with expected returns, the expected loss of a loan portfolio is the weighted average of the individual expected loan losses, adjusted to take into account portfolio diversification effects. To see how diversification affects the loan loss volatility of the portfolio, suppose that the bank now makes two loans, one to a farm on one side of the island and another to a farm on the other side. Assume each loan is $0.5 million, so the total amount loaned out is $1 million. What now is the distribution of losses in the loan portfolio?

Note first that the bank's expected loan loss is still $0.5 million (the sum of the expected loan losses on the two loans, each of which is 0.5×$0.5 million = $0.25 million). The loss volatility on each loan is

$$\sqrt{0.5[\$0.5\,\text{million} - \$0.25\,\text{million}]^2 + 0.5[0 - \$0.25\,\text{million}]^2} = \$0.25\,\text{million}.$$

Recognizing that each loan has a weight of 0.5 in the portfolio and that the two loans are perfectly negatively correlated, we can use Equation (1.7) to obtain the portfolio loan loss volatility as:

$$\sqrt{(0.5)^2(\$0.25\,\text{million})^2 + (0.5)^2\,(\$0.25\,\text{million})^2 - 2(0.5)(0.5)(\$0.25\,\text{million})(\$0.25\,\text{million})]} = 0$$

Thus, portfolio diversification eliminates loan loss volatility in this case.

This means that the amount of equity capital supporting a loan depends on the characteristics of the portfolio that the loan belongs to. When the bank adds a loan to an existing portfolio, it computes the impact of this additional loan on the loan loss volatility of the portfolio in order to compute the incremental loss volatility due to the loan and consequently the equity capital needed to support the loan.

Distribution of Portfolio Losses

The distribution of portfolio losses is *not* normal. In practice, the distribution is very skewed. As Figure 8.3 shows, there is a high probability of "small" (less than expected) losses, and a small (but positive) probability of extremely large losses.

In Figure 8.3, curve A represents the distribution of portfolio losses when the portfolio is not very well diversified. The variance of losses and, hence, the loan loss volatility is quite high. Moreover, the distribution is skewed in that mean lies to the right of the peak of the distribution, that is, there is a relatively high probability of losses that are smaller than the expected loss. As the portfolio becomes better diversified, we move to Curve B, which as a distribution diversification makes the distribution with a lower loan loss volatility. Further diversification makes the distribution look like Curve C, which is beginning to concentrate most of the high-probability outcomes around the mean or the expected loss. In the limit, as the portfolio becomes perfectly diversified, as in the case of the portfolio of loans to the two firms considered earlier, the distribution collapses to a single point represented by the expected loss, that is, all loan loss volatility is eliminated.

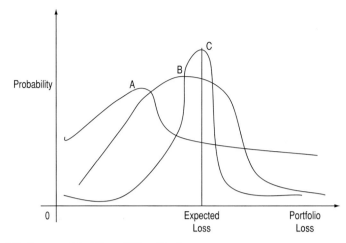

FIGURE 8.3 Distribution of Portfolio Losses and the Effect of Diversification.

Recap and Summary

Once the bank has estimated the equity capital to be committed to a loan, it can use Equation (8.1) to determine the minimum loan interest rate.[3] The actual interest rate will depend on market conditions; the greater the bank's monopoly power in a given market, the greater will be the (positive) spread between the loan interest rate and the minimum rate given by Equation (8.1). A summary of the loan interest rate determination is given in Figure 8.4.

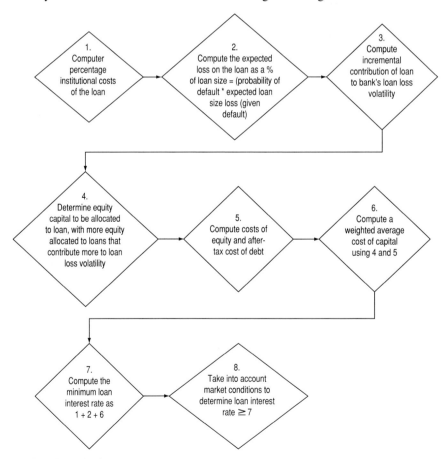

FIGURE 8.4 Loan Interest Rate Determination.

3. The equity cost of capital used in Equation (8.1) can either be just the bank's overall equity cost of capital or it can be a loan-specific cost of capital, adjusted to account for the riskiness of the loan relative to the whole bank. The latter is the appropriate approach, particularly when the loan has risk characteristics that differ from those of the bank's existing asset portfolio.

Some of the important additional considerations are that loan commitments should be included in the analysis. Moreover, it should be recognized that covenants in the loan contract reduce the risk of a new loan, highly "concentrated" (say in a particular industry as loans to firms of similar size) portfolios should require more capital.

CREDIT RATIONING

Credit rationing is defined as a situation in which a lender refuses to extend credit to a borrower at the price *posted by the lender* for that borrower class. Credit rationing is *not* a phenomenon whereby a potential borrower refuses to accept credit because the price is "unfair" or too high. The essential point is that credit is denied at a price selected by the lender itself. Even if the borrower offers a higher interest rate than that asked for by the lender, a loan is refused by the lender.

Credit rationing is a puzzling practice.[4] When credit is rationed, there is an unsatisfied demand for credit at the price posted by the bank, that is, credit demand exceeds supply at that price. Conventional economic theory, or just plain common sense, suggests that the bank could increase its profits by increasing the price of credit. If the supply function for credit is upward sloping and the demand function is downward sloping, as shown in Figure 8.5, then this should bring about the usual equilibrium in which demand and supply are equated. Since the bank is supplying more credit and at a higher price, its profit should be greater. Thus it seems irrational for profit-maximizing banks to ration credit.[5] Is it?

While it is conceivable that banks forgo profitable lending opportunities, it seems implausible. We thus ask whether it is rational for a profit-maximizing bank to ration credit.

Why Should We Be Interested in Credit Rationing?

It is believed that a fall in the money supply restricts spending. This could happen even if the fall in the money supply caused only a small increase in interest rates, or if spending is not curtailed by an interest rate increase. The reason is that a fall in the money supply would leave banks with less to lend, forcing them to reduce their lending, even if customers did not reduce their loan demand. Thus, spending was viewed as being constrained by the availability of credit to banks, and this credit was allocated to customers through nonprice means such as credit rationing. This argument, popularly known as the "availability doctrine," suggested an alternative transmission channel for monetary policy that was based in an important way on the monetary policy argument.

There are two reasons why we should be interested in studying credit rationing in connection with monetary policy. First, with credit rationing, monetary policy can be effective in influencing aggregate investment by corporations even with

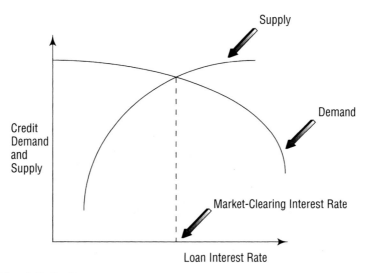

FIGURE 8.5 The Demand and Supply for Credit.

---

4. Included in credit rationing is the practice of "redlining," which involves the lender refusing to extend the credit based on considerations of race, gender, and so on. This is illegal and is not the focus of our discussion. See Cohen-Cole (2011) for some empirical evidence on location-based discrimination in consumer credit issuance.
5. Samuelson (1952) was the first to suggest this.

little variation in interest rates. That is, if the Federal Reserve feels that inflationary pressures need to be abated by curtailing spending, it could cause a slowdown of the economy without major changes in interest rates. This could be achieved by reducing the liquidity of banks, which in turn could lead to reduced bank lending due to credit rationing, even if investment demand by corporations was unchanged. Thus, the effectiveness of monetary policy would have *not* been empirically documented. An important implication of this is that in the presence of credit rationing, the monetary policy options of inducing increased interest rates through a higher discount window borrowing rate and of reducing the amount of credit available through open market operations (bond sales) are not necessarily equivalent. Credit can be reduced even if investment demand is insensitive to monetary policy manipulations.

Second, it has been empirically found that a more stringent monetary policy does not affect all borrowers equally. Thus, if credit rationing is better understood with respect to the identities of those who are rationed, we may be able to better predict the effects of a restrictive monetary policy.[6]

Why Is There Credit Rationing?

In order to understand why a profit-maximizing bank might ration credit, we need to examine the conditions under which it would not be optimal for the bank to increase its loan interest rate when faced with excess demand for credit. It is difficult to see why banks would do this if they had as much information as the borrower. If the bank was perfectly informed, it could always set an appropriate risk-adjusted price and lend accordingly.

However, in a world of asymmetric information, credit rationing can be an optimal strategy for a profit-maximizing bank. The explanation turns upon two types of information hurdles.[7] First, a bank may not be able to distinguish perfectly between borrowers with different credit risks, even after it has analyzed each borrower's financial information. This is called the *precontract private information* problem. Even if the bank knows the *average* riskiness of borrowers within a given risk classification, it may not be able to identify individual risks [recall the Akerlof, 1970 discussion in Chapter 1]. The bank will, therefore, charge a common price to all within the risk class, so that some borrowers are subsidizing others. A second problem is that the bank may not be able to completely control the borrower's actions. The borrower may thus be able to increase project risk, either through its choice of projects or through its expenditure of effort, without detection by the bank.

Now imagine that a loan interest rate is announced by the bank for a particular risk class, and at that interest rate there is an excess demand for loans by borrowers in that risk class. What would happen if the bank chose to increase the loan interest rate? One possibility is *adverse selection*. Safer borrowers within the given risk classification may be unwilling to borrow at the higher interest rate, so that the mix of borrowers within the pool becomes riskier. If this happens, the bank's expected profit could actually be *lower* at the higher interest rate; we provide a simple numerical example below to illustrate. A second possibility is that an increase in the loan interest rate could *worsen* the moral hazard problem. That is, those borrowers within the pool who have some latitude in their investment decisions may choose riskier projects at the higher loan interest rate. This again could mean a lower expected profit for the bank at the higher loan interest rate. Thus, the bank may conclude that increasing the loan interest rate is not worthwhile since its expected profit is maximized at an interest rate at which credit demand exceeds supply.[8] Figure 8.6 depicts this graphically.

We now provide numerical examples to illustrate these concepts. We will first focus on the *adverse selection* problem, ignoring moral hazard for the moment.

Example 8.2

Suppose that you are the loan officer for the Midtown Community Bank and you know that within a particular risk class, there are two types of borrowers: low-risk borrowers and high-risk borrowers. However, you cannot distinguish between them.

You believe that the probability that a randomly chosen borrower is low risk is 0.5 and that the borrower is high risk is 0.5. There are 1000 potential loan applications of each type within this risk class. Each applicant would like a loan of $100. The low-risk borrower will invest this loan in a project that lasts for one period hence will yield $130 with probability 0.9 and nothing with probability 0.1. The high-risk borrower will invest the loan in a project that will yield $135 with probability 0.8 and nothing

---

6. Early evidence on rationing is provided by Jaffee and Modigliani (1969). Jiménez et al. (2012, 2014) show that tighter monetary policy reduces lending from weak banks and this is specially pronounced for risky firms. See also Chong et al. (2013) for evidence from China on credit constraints of small and medium enterprises.

7. What follows is an adaptation of the work of Stiglitz and Weiss (1981).

8. That is, suppose r is the loan interest rate, C is the bank's per dollar cost of funds, and θ is the repayment probability. Then the bank's expected return per dollar loaned is $\rho = [1 + r] \theta - C$. The point is that θ cannot be taken as being unaffected by r. As r is raised, θ falls. Assuming that θ is a decreasing and concave function of r (that is, $\partial\theta/\partial r < 0$, $\partial^2\theta/\partial r^2 < 0$), we see that the function $\rho(r) = [1 + r] \theta(r) - C$ attains a unique maximum with respect to r.

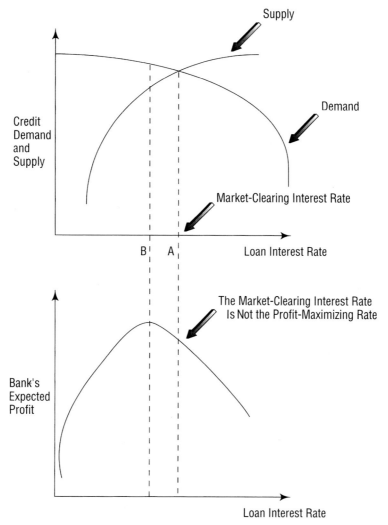

FIGURE 8.6   Credit Rationing.

with probability 0.2 one period hence. Midtown Community Bank is a monopolist with respect to these borrowers.[9] Assuming that the only pricing instrument available is the loan interest rate, how should you price a loan to a borrower in this risk class so as to maximize the bank's expected profit? You have only $100,000 available to lend and the junior lending officer who reports to you has advised you that 2000 loan applications were received when it was announced that the bank would charge an interest rate of 29%. The current riskless rate is 5%. Assume that a borrower must have at least 1 dollar of net profit in the successful state in order to apply for a bank loan,[10] and that there is universal risk neutrality.

Solution

This example shows how informational considerations can impart rigidity to the bank's loan interest rate. To show this, we proceed in three steps. First, we will compute Midtown Community Bank's expected profit if it charges a rate of interest of 29% and is forced to randomly ration half its loan applicants (because all potential borrowers apply). Second, we calculate Midtown's expected profit if it charges a rate higher than 29%. In this case, the low-risk borrowers drop out, so that the bank lends only to the high-risk borrowers. Finally, in the third step, we compare the bank's expected profits from the first two steps and show that Midtown Community Bank's expected profit is maximized by setting the loan interest rate at 29% and randomly rationing half its credit applicants. The key to this finding is that the bank cannot distinguish between the low- and high-risk borrowers.

---

9. We could generalize this example to one in which there are numerous imperfectly competitive banks.

10. This assumption is meant to create a strict incentive for the borrower to apply for a bank loan. In its absence, we could have a situation in which the borrower is indifferent between applying and not applying, and then we would need to assume that an application is made in that case.

Step 1

Clearly, if you charge an interest rate of 29%, you will have to ration credit since you can lend only $100,000 to this group of borrowers and the demand is for $200,000. Now, the *maximum* interest rate that your bank can charge without losing the low-risk borrowers is 29%. At this interest rate, the net profit of the low-risk borrower in the successful state is

$$130 - 129 = \$1,$$

because the repayment obligation is $129. Clearly, the high-risk borrowers will also choose to apply at this interest rate since the net profit of such a borrower in the successful state is

$$135 - 129 = \$6.$$

The total expected profit of Midtown Community Bank, if it lends at an interest rate of 29%, is

$$\frac{(0.5 \times 0.9 \times \$129 + 0.5 \times 0.8 \times \$129) \times 100,000}{1.05} \tag{8.3}$$
$$= \$4428.57$$

The expression in Equation (8.3) can be understood as follows. There is a 0.5 probability that the borrower is low risk, in which case the bank gets repaid $129 with probability 0.9. Similarly, there is a 0.5 probability that the borrower is high risk, in which case the bank gets repaid $129 with probability 0.8. This explains the term in the parentheses of the numerator in Equation (8.3). This is multiplied by 1000 since the bank can make 1000 such loans. We discount at the riskless rate of 5% since the bank is risk neutral. The initial outlay of $100,000 is finally subtracted to arrive at the bank's expected profit.

Step 2

Since there is unsatisfied loan demand at the 29% interest rate – half the loan applicants are turned down – it is natural to ask if Midtown can earn a higher expected profit by increasing the loan interest rate.[11]

Clearly, if you raise the loan interest rate above 29%, the low-risk borrowers will not wish to borrow. Since only the high-risk borrowers remain, you might as well raise the loan interest rate all the way up to 34%, the maximum you can charge the high-risk borrowers before they too drop out. We refer to 34% as a *market clearing* interest rate since at this level, loan demand equals loan supply.[12]

Midtown Community Bank's total expected profit at this interest rate is

$$\frac{0.8 \times \$134 \times 1,000}{1.05} - \$100,000 \tag{8.4}$$
$$= \$2,095.24$$

Note that Equation (8.4) recognizes that the bank knows that only the high-risk borrowers will apply.

Step 3

It is clear now that the bank earns a greater profit by charging 29% and rationing half its loan applicants rather than raising the loan interest rate to a market clearing 34%. This illustrates how adverse selection may cause a profit-maximizing bank to ration credit. Raising interest rates in the face of excess demand may drive away the best customers and leave the bank worse off.

We now turn to an illustration of the *moral hazard effect.*

Example 8.3

Suppose Midtown Community Bank has received a loan application at $t = 0$ from a firm that currently has no assets except for an investment opportunity available one period hence, at $t = 1$. The customer has stipulated that the loan must be made available at $t = 0$ or not at all. The investment outlay required at $t = 1$ is $I_1 = \$100$, of which $55 will come from a bank loan. The firm will make its decision on whether or not to invest at $t = 1$. The firm currently has some securities outstanding. If the investment is made at $t = 1$, it will yield $\$\tilde{y}$ per year perpetually, beginning at $t = 2$. Although $\tilde{y}$ is not known now, it will be known at $t = 1$. There are five possible states of the world at $t = 1$, as shown in Table 8.3.

Thus, if state 1 is realized at $t = 1$, the project will pay $15 per year perpetually beginning $t = 2$.

Assume that the riskless rate is 10% and the corporate tax rate is zero. Assuming that $55 of I_1 will be financed with a loan, and the rest will come from the firm's retained earnings, compute Midtown's expected return as a function of the promised loan interest rate. Assume that I_1 is a perpetual loan (a consol) with interest payable at the end of each period, beginning at the end of the first period, that is, at $t = 2$.

---

11. As the ensuing discussion will make clearer, the loan demand curve in this example is downward sloping in the loan interest rate.
12. Since there are 1000 high-risk loan applicants and each demands a $100 loan, loan demand will be $100,000.

TABLE 8.3 Probability Distribution of $\tilde{y}$

State	Probability	$\tilde{y}$
1	0.05	$15
2	0.05	$16
3	0.30	$17
4	0.40	$18
5	0.20	$19

Solution

The basic idea conveyed by this example is that it does not benefit the bank to keep increasing the loan interest rate because, beyond some point, an increase discourages the borrower from investing when the bank would prefer to proceed with the project. We solve this problem in three steps. First, we provide a framework for linking the bank's *actual* annual interest payment on the loan as a function of the *promised* interest payment. Second, we calculate the interest payment the bank can *expect* to receive each period for different values of the promised loan interest rate. Finally, in Step 3 we conclude that the bank's expected return is maximized at an "interior" loan interest rate, so that if loan demand exceeds loan supply at this rate, the bank will ration credit rather than raise the loan interest rate further.

Step 1

Since at $t = 1$ all uncertainty is resolved, we can view 10% as the appropriate discount rate in determining whether or not to undertake the investment at $t = 1$. That is, I_1 will be made at $t = 1$ if the value of the perpetuity at $t = 1$ exceeds the investment outlay, that is, if and only if $\tilde{y}_s / 0.10 \geq I_1$, where $\tilde{y}_s$ is the share of $\tilde{y}$ accruing to the borrower. Because $I_1 = 100$, we need $\tilde{y}_s = 10$. If the investment is undertaken, then $\tilde{y}_s = \tilde{y} -$ interest on the $55 loan. Note that the borrower follows this rule because at the time it has to make the investment (at $t = 1$), it already has the money loaned by the bank, and hence treats it as its own retained earnings.

Let r be the actual annual interest payment on the risky bank loan (viewed at $t = 0$, r is a random variable), assuming a perpetual loan with interest payable every period, beginning at $t = 2$. Let r be the *promised* annual interest payment on any debt outstanding at $t = 0$, where r is promised to begin at $t = 2$.

Note that the bank loan is risky only when viewed at $t = 0$. As mentioned earlier, it becomes riskless at $t = 1$. At $t = 1$ then, the value of the bank's loan is the value of a riskless consol bond with an annual coupon equal to the interest payment the bank knows it will receive perpetually, that is, the value of the bank's loan $= \dfrac{\text{interest payment}}{0.10}$. For example, at $t = 0$ the promised interest payment to the bank may be $17, but at $t = 0$ we do not know whether this promise can be kept. But suppose at $t = 1$, state 3 is realized. Then, if the firm adopts the project, the promise can be kept for sure, and the $t = 1$ value of the loan is $17/0.10 = $170. Alternatively, if state 2 occurs, the promise will not be kept; the bank will receive only $16 per year perpetually if the project is adopted. Thus, the time 1 value of the loan is $16/0.10 = $160.

Step 2

Now the expected returns to Midtown with different loan interest payments (choice of investment made at $t = 1$) are given in Table 8.4.

TABLE 8.4 Expected Returns to Bank

Promised Loan Interest $\tilde{r}$	Minimal Level of $\tilde{y}$ for Investment I_1, to be Made by Borrowing Firm's Shareholders	Probability (at $t = 0$) that Investment I_1 Will be Made	Expected Interest Payment on Bank Loan (view at $t = 0$)
≤$5	$15	1.00	$\tilde{r}$
$6	16	0.95	$5.70
$7	17	0.90	6.30
$8	18	0.60	4.80
$9	19	0.20	1.80
$10	20	0.00	0

In this table, the fourth column is obtained by multiplying each promised payment in the first column by the corresponding probability in the third column. The numbers in the third column are obtained by examining the second column and Table 8.3. The smallest possible $\tilde{y}$ value in Table 8.3 is \$15, so that the probability of observing a $\tilde{y}$ greater than or equal to \$15 is 1.00. Similarly, from Table 8.3 we see that the probability of obtaining a $\tilde{y}$ at least as great as \$16 is the probability that the state that will occur is either 2, 3, 4, or 5; this probability is 0.95. The rest of the numbers follow similarly.

Step 3

The above table shows that Midtown Community Bank's expected return *peaks* at a promised loan interest of \$7. Note that the present value of the bank loan at $\tilde{r} = \$7$ is 6.3/0.10 = \$63, which exceeds the loan amount of \$55; hence, Midtown will be willing to lend. Thus, if the loan demand exceeds the loan supply at that rate, Midtown will be unwilling to extend more credit even if the borrower offers a higher interest rate. Credit rationing occurs here because of moral hazard. However, this moral hazard is a little different from that discussed earlier, wherein the borrower increased the bank's default risk by switching to a risky project from a safe project. Here the borrower prefers not to invest in a project that would have enhanced the bank's expected return; underinvestment is the problem here.

Bank Capital and Credit Rationing

A bank's capital position also may affect its decision to ration credit since different categories of loans have different capital requirements. Consider a bank that has the necessary deposits but would need to raise additional capital to satisfy a loan request. The additional cost of raising this capital, relative to that of raising money from other sources, will then be a charge against the bank's profit from making the loan. If this additional cost is sufficiently high, the bank may prefer to invest the available deposits in marketable securities rather than in loans. Many allege that this is what happened in 1990–1992 and led to a *credit crunch* in the United States despite monetary policy initiatives aimed at reviving the economy.[13]

Another reason why there may be a link between a bank's capital and credit rationing is that there is a relationship between the bank's capital and its incentive to monitor that we discussed in Chapter 3.[14] A bank with insufficient capital may not monitor the borrower at a cost. Consequently, the economic value of a bank loan diminishes with a decrease in capital, and a bank with sufficiently low capital will view the default probability of the (unmonitored) loan as being so high that it does not view the loan as worth making.

There is empirical evidence of (nonprice) quality credit rationing. For example, subprime mortgage borrowers cannot get mortgages without a sufficient equity input (down payment).[15] Consistent with the theories,[16] there is also evidence that when banks experience negative shocks to their capital positions, they tend to reduce their lending, which may be interpreted either as a reduced demand for bank loans or as banks simply lending less (possibly due to credit rationing that goes up when bank capital declines). In general, it is very difficult to tell whether reduced bank lending is due to supply or demand effects. However, some research has been able to separately identify supply effects.

One such study took advantage of a "natural experiment" involving the U.S. branches of Japanese banks to identify the relationship between the shocks to bank capital and bank loan supply.[17] During 1989–1992, the Japanese stock market declined precipitously. As a result, many Japanese banks found that their capital ratios dropped below the 8% minimum required by Basel I. This, in turn, led the U.S. branches of these Japanese banks to reduce their lending. A 1% decline in the capital ratio of the Japanese parent led to a 6% decline in lending at the brank. Thus, this research shows that when banks experience a decrease in their capital ratios, they tend to cut back on their lending.[18]

We have so far assumed that the bank and the borrower have a one-period relationship. As pointed out earlier, when the bank and the borrower contract with each other over many time periods, it is sometimes possible to reduce informational problems. Indeed, this is one reason to have long-term bank–borrower relationships.[19]

13. Thakor (1996) develops a theoretical model that makes precisely this point, and also provides supporting empirical evidence. The model assumes that the additional cost of capital associated with raising capital is exogenously given, and does not provide an endogenous justification for this cost.
14. Recall that this argument is based on the theory developed by Holmstrom and Tirole (1997).
15. See Chomsisengphet and Pennington-Cross (2004). This too is consistent with the Holmstrom and Tirole (1997) theory.
16. See Holmstrom and Tirole (1997) and Mehran and Thakor (2011).
17. See Peek and Rosengren (1997). Peek and Rosengren (2013) review the evidence on the importance of the bank lending channel for the transmission of monetary policy.
18. There is a substantial evidence that well capitalized banks better weathered through the global financial crisis and needed to cut back on lending less than undercapitalized banks (see Berger and Bouwman, 2013, Gambacorta and Marques-Ibanez, 2011, and Košak et al., 2015).
19. What may help too to is to include collateral in the loan contract. This discourages moral hazard and could mitigate adverse selection. Cerqueiro et al. (2014) point to the role of collateral in the design of the lending contracts. They show that declining values of collateral can push banks to increase interest rates on credit and tighten credit if information problems cannot be mitigated.

THE SPOT-LENDING DECISION

We now turn to the bank's lending decision in light of the possibility of credit rationing. To understand this, we should begin by noting that credit analysis, which is an integral part of the lending decision, is not a binary (0 or 1) process whereby the bank either conducts credit analysis or not. It should more appropriately be viewed as a continuum; the bank can perform credit analysis to varying degrees of detail.

The more elaborate the analysis, the more costly it is for the bank. The point to note is that the degree of elaboration is a matter of choice for the bank and represents an important element of the spot-lending decision-making process.

The bank must determine its spot-lending policy under uncertainty about both the quantity and the quality of loan demand, and within its own capacity constraints. These constraints include limits on screening and monitoring resources. Consequently, the bank may be unable to accommodate more than a predetermined level of aggregate lending without significantly sacrificing loan quality. Loan quality deterioration may imply an unacceptable elevation in the likelihood of ruin for the bank. This means that the first step in lending policy may be for the bank to establish an upper bound, say $\bar{L}$, on the bank's aggregate lending for a given period, say $(0, T)$.[20] Loan applicants arriving after the bank has reached its loan maximum are presumably rejected indiscriminately, and we refer to this phenomenon as *rationing in the large*. Before reaching its loan maximum, the bank does not ration indiscriminately. Rather, it recognizes applicant attributes and rejects only the less desirable. This phenomenon is referred to as *rationing in the small*.[21] The decision to ration an applicant in the small is predicated on the outcome of the bank's credit analysis and its lending prior to the applicant's arrival, as we shall see subsequently.

Consider now a bank that extends $1 credit to each randomly arriving customer over a fixed planning period $(0, T)$. If a loan applicant arrives at time t, where $0 \leq t \leq T$, the bank conducts credit analysis to estimate the borrower's repayment probability θ, takes into account cumulative loans made to date, say L_t, and the remaining time until the end of the bank's planning horizon, $T-t$. The bank's spot-lending decision can be viewed as an *optimal stopping problem*, that is, the bank must decide when to stop conducting credit analysis and make a decision on whether to grant or deny credit to the applicant based on the available information. Figure 8.7 depicts this decision-making process in a flow chart format.

It is worth noting that at each step, the bank is really making two decisions: (i) whether to acquire and/or process more information about the borrower at additional cost or stop the information acquisition/processing, and (ii) conditional on having decided not to process any more information, whether to extend credit or deny it. Note that these two decisions are made *simultaneously* at each step, rather than sequentially. Moreover, these decisions are affected by L_t and $T-t$. The larger the L_t – the smaller is $\bar{L} - L_t$ – the more stringent will be the bank's credit standard (i.e., the higher will the estimated θ have to be for the applicant to be granted credit), holding everything else constant. The bank becomes more selective because it has less money to allocate to applicants arriving after t. For similar reasons, the smaller is $T-t$, the more stringent is the bank's credit standard, holding everything else constant. Another important observation is that the *size* of the flow chart (i.e., the number of steps) in Figure 8.7 is *not* predetermined. Rather, it depends on the information revealed by the credit analysis at each step, as well as L_t and $T-t$. Sometimes, the flow chart will have only one step. Based on a preliminary (and possibly cursory) examination of the borrower, the bank may decide to terminate the credit analysis process and either deny credit or grant it. We would expect this to happen in the case of borrowers who are very familiar to the bank either because of their previous credit history or because they belong to some group that contains members with similar default attributes that are relatively well known to the bank. For example, the bank may extend credit to IBM or deny credit to a highly leveraged firm in a risky industry without significant investment in credit analysis in either case. Thus, both intertemporal and cross-sectional reusability of credit information will affect the spot-lending decision flow chart. In addition to information about the borrower, L_t and $T-t$ will also affect the size of the flow chart for reasons similar to those mentioned earlier. For example, if $L-L_t$ is large and $T-t$ is small, the flow chart may shrink in size as the bank eases its credit standards and grants loans based on favorable results from initial credit analysis.

The amount of information possessed by the bank at the outset about the borrower also has other effects. The bank might charge the borrower a higher interest rate than the breakeven rate that could be charged *given* the bank's information. This is because the bank has better information about the borrower than competing banks do, so it knows that its pricing policy will not cause the borrower to go to a competing lender. It is referred to as the hold-up problem.[22] For example, suppose the information possessed by competing banks indicates that a borrower's default probability is 0.08. Based on its own information, the incumbent bank knows that it is 0.065. Then the incumbent may charge the borrower a rate commensurate

---

20. In the simplest formulation, this capacity constant, $\bar{L}$, can be thought of as a fixed number of dollars, but a more sophisticated formulation might have this capacity a convex and increasing function of the opportunities the bank perceives.

21. Some refer to "rationing in the large" as a borrower being shut out of the bank credit market entirely and "rationing in the small" as loan rejection by an individual bank. Our usage differs.

22. See Rajan (1992).

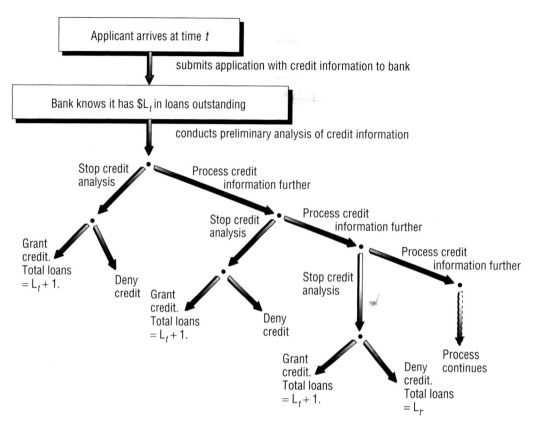

FIGURE 8.7   Flow Chart of the Spot-Lending Decision.

with a default-probability of 0.08, thereby earning a positive expected profit due to its informational advantage. We discuss this aspect of bank–customer relationships further in the next section.

Note that the flow chart explains how the bank makes decisions regarding rationing in the small. Once $L_t = \overline{L}$, *all* loan applicants are rationed in the large without any credit analysis.

Some implications of this lending policy perspective are discussed as follows:

- An increase in L will decrease aggregate rationing. This does not mean, however, that each loan applicant will necessarily face a reduced likelihood of rationing. The reason is that the bank will follow a less selective policy from the outset, so that the loans granted by time t will probably be larger. However, it is true that, holding L_t *fixed*, the bank implements a more lax credit standard at time t when a larger L is chosen at the outset.
- The effect of $\overline{L}$ on the probability of a *stockout* – the bank exhausts its inventory of loanable funds – at time t is ambiguous. This is because a higher $\overline{L}$ increases the lending capacity on the one hand and leads to more lax credit standards on the other. The first effect diminished the stockout probability and the second effect increases it.

LONG-TERM BANK–BORROWER RELATIONSHIPS

In this section, we discuss some of the benefits of long-term banking relationships. This will build on our own discussion of relationship lending in Chapter 3. One benefit is that moral hazard may be reduced. The other is that private information problems can be dealt with more effectively because of information reusability. As we will illustrate in the ensuing discussion, this has potential implications for the design of loan contracts as well as for credit rationing.

Long-Term Relationships and Moral Hazard

When a borrower knows that it may need to borrow in the future, it may limit actions in the current period which would impose losses on the bank. The borrower trades off the current benefits from exploiting the bank against the future costs of poorer credit terms or credit rationing due to these current actions. To see this, consider the following example given in the box below.

Example 8.4

Consider a borrower, Kiddie Toys, Inc., that can choose between two projects, S and R. Project S yields $150 with probability 0.8 and zero with probability 0.2, whereas project R yields $162 with probability 0.5 and nothing with probability 0.5. The bank's cost of funds is equal to the riskless interest rate of 5%. As a banker, you cannot control your borrower's project choice directly because you cannot observe this choice. You are restricted to making unsecured loans. Assume universal risk neutrality. Moreover, you can charge Kiddie Toys not more than 150 basis points above your breakeven interest rate or it will switch to another bank. Compute the expected payoffs to Kiddie Toys and the bank under the following scenarios: (i) the bank and the borrower can contract with each other over only one period, and (ii) the bank and the borrower can contract over two time periods. In case (i), Kiddie Toys will request a single loan of $100, and in case (ii), Kiddie Toys will need a sequence of two $100 loans, with the ability to choose between S and R in each period.

Solution

We proceed in four steps. First, we show that in scenario (i) the bank denies credit to Kiddie Toys at any interest rate because it fails to break even regardless of the project chosen by Kiddie Toys. Second, we consider scenario (ii) and show that, by contracting over two periods, it *is* possible for the bank to induce Kiddie Toys to choose S in the second period. For a fixed second-period interest rate that guarantees S will be chosen in the second period, we solve for the maximum interest rate the bank can charge in the first period such that Kiddie Toys will choose S in that period, given that the bank will lend in the second period only if the first-period loan is repaid. Third, given the second-period interest rate in Step 2, we solve for the first-period interest rate needed to permit the bank to break even across its two-period horizon. Finally, in Step 4 we allow the bank to set its first-period interest rate 150 basis points above its breakeven interest rate. We check that Kiddie Toys will choose S in *both* periods and compute the expected profits of the bank and Kiddie Toys.

Step 1

Consider case (i) first. Suppose the bank assumes that Kiddie Toys will choose project R. Then it must set the borrower's repayment obligation at $105/0.5 = $210 in order to break even in expected value terms. Given this, Kiddie Toys chooses not to borrow. If the bank assumes that Kiddie Toys will choose S, then it must set its repayment obligation at $105/0.8 = $131.25 (an interest rate of 31.25%) in order to break even, again in an expected value sense. However, at this interest rate, the expected payoff to Kiddie Toys from choosing S is $0.8(150 - 131.25) = \$15.00$, whereas from choosing R it is $0.5(162 - 131.25) = \$15.375$. So the bank's belief about the borrower's project choice is contradicted, and it cannot be a Nash equilibrium for the bank to set the loan interest rate at 31.25%. Indeed, the maximum interest rate, i_{max}, that the bank can charge such that Kiddie Toys does not strictly prefer R to S is given by the following equation:

$$0.8[150 - (1 + i_{max})100] = 0.5[162 - (1 + i_{max})100].$$

Solving this equation yields i_{max} = 30%. However, at 30%, the bank fails to break even, regardless of the project chosen by Kiddie Toys. Hence, no credit will be extended to the borrower at any interest rate, that is, we have an extreme form of credit rationing. The expected payoff to the bank as well as to the borrower is zero.

Step 2

Now consider scenario (ii). Suppose that as a banker you tell Kiddie Toys: "I'll give you a first-period loan of $100 at an interest rate of i_1, and a second-period loan of $100 at an interest rate of i_2, conditional on your repaying the first-period loan. If you default on the first-period loan, then you will not get any second-period credit."

With such a contract, suppose we set i_2 = 30%. Then we know that the borrower will choose S in the second period. Given this second-period loan interest rate, let i^*_{max} be the maximum value of i_1 such that Kiddie Toys will prefer to invest in S in the first period. Thus, i^*_{max} is the solution to the following equation.

$$0.8\{[150 - (1 + i^*_{max})100] + 0.8 \times [150 - 130]\}$$
$$= 0.5\{[162 - (1 + i^*_{max})100] + 0.8 \times [150 - 130]\}. \tag{8.5}$$

Note that in Equation (8.5), on the left-hand side we have written Kiddie Toys' expected payoff over two periods from choosing S in the first period, given that S will be chosen in the second period. On the right-hand side, we have written Kiddie Toys' expected payoff over two periods from choosing R in the first period, given that S will be chosen in the second period. In each case, we have recognized that second-period credit will be forthcoming only if the first-period project succeeds and the first-period bank loan is repaid; this is done by letting Kiddie Toys' second-period payoff be zero if its first-period project fails and Kiddie Toys consequently defaults on the first-period loan. Solving Equation (8.5) yields i^*_{max} = 46%.

Step 3

Given a second-period interest rate of 30%, let I_1 be the first-period interest rate that the bank needs to charge to break even; remember that at 30%, the bank is making an expected loss on the second period loan. Now, $\hat{i}_1$ is the solution to the following equation:

$$[0.8(1 + \hat{i}_1) \times 100 - 105] + 0.8[0.8 \times 130 - 105] = 0 \tag{8.6}$$

In Equation (8.6), the term $0.8(1+\hat{i}_1)\times100-105$ is the bank's expected profit on the first-period loan and $0.8 \times 130 - 105$ is its expected profit (which is negative) on the second-period loan. The latter is multiplied with 0.8 (the probability of repayment on the first-period loan) since the second-period loan is made only if the first-period loan is repaid. Solving Equation (8.6) gives $\hat{i}_1 = 32.25\%$. Note that now the bank is breaking even across two periods rather than in each period.

Step 4

If we assume that on its two-period transaction, the bank can charge 150 basis points above its breakeven rate without losing Kiddie Toys to another bank, then i_1 will be set at 33.75% (which is 32.25% + 1.5%). Kiddie Toys will now choose S in each period. The bank's expected profit over its two-period relationship is given by

$$0.8(1+i_1)\times100-105+0.8(0.8\times130-105)$$
$$=0.8\times133.75-105+0.8(0.8\times130-105)$$
$$=\$1.20.$$

The expected payoff to Kiddie Toys is given by

$$0.8(150-133.75)+0.8[0.8(150-130)]$$
$$=\$25.08.$$

As this example illustrates, both the bank and the borrower are better off with a long-term relationship. We go from a situation in which no credit is extended in a single-period relationship to one in which the bank and the borrower negotiate a two-period contract that permits each party to earn a positive expected payoff. The intuition for this improvement is as follows. In the single-period case, it is impossible for the borrower to produce non-negative expected profit for the bank if it chooses project R, and it is impossible for the bank to induce the borrower to choose project S at an interest rate that permits the bank to break even, assuming that the borrower chooses S. So, no credit is extended. In the two-period case, the bank can commit to a second-period loan at a lower interest rate than it would take for to guarantee that the borrower will choose S in the second period. The bank can recoup this expected loss on the second-period loan by elevating the interest rate on the first-period loan appropriately. This high first-period interest rate will not induce the borrower to choose R in the first period because the borrower is promised a *subsidized* second-period loan only if it repays its first-period loan. This means that the borrower now perceives a *greater cost* to taking risk in the first period than it does in a one-period setting. This creates sufficient room for the desired first-period loan interest rate adjustment by the bank without risking a switch to project R by the borrower.

To recapitulate, a multiperiod relationship with the borrower can mitigate moral hazard.[23] It is less likely that the borrower will exploit the bank when it knows that it must deal with the same bank again. This creates an incentive for bank–borrower relationships.

Three points are worth noting. First, it is important for the bank to offer the borrower a *binding* two-period contract. Since the bank anticipates a loss on its second-period loan, it would prefer not to extend this loan once the second period has arrived. Hence, it is important that a binding contract be negotiated at the outset. Second, as usual, the borrower is free to seek credit elsewhere after the first period. However, no bank will be willing to extend credit to the borrower in a one-period setting, and the incumbent bank is extending a *subsidized* second-period loan. Hence, the borrower will prefer to remain with the same bank for the second period. Finally, it is *time consistent* for the bank to deny the borrower second-period credit, conditional on first-period default, in accordance with the terms of the two-period contract. This is because the bank loses money if it lends in the second period, and will thus do so only if it is bound to do so.

Long-Term Relationships and Private Information

One important advantage of a long-term relationship is that the bank learns about the borrower through time. This lessens the extent to which the borrower is privately informed relative to the bank, and hence improves credit allocations. In other words, the longer a borrower contracts with a bank, the better will be the credit terms it receives. As the borrower keeps repaying the bank, it keeps building an ever-improving track record that enables it to obtain better credit terms through time.[24] We can see this with the following illustration.

---

23. Mitigation of moral hazard through long-term bank-borrower relationships has been examined by Boot and Thakor (1994). See Bhattacharya and Thakor (1993), and Freixas and Rochet (2008) for discussions of the literature. Ioannidou and Ongena (2010) provide empirical evidence on the importance of bank–borrower relationships.
24. See Diamond (1989).

Example 8.5

Suppose The Midtown Community Bank is faced with two types of borrowers that it cannot distinguish, G and B. The type-G borrower wishes to borrow $100 to invest in a single-period project that yields $135 with probability 0.9 and zero with probability 0.1 at the end of the period. The type-B borrower wishes to borrow the same amount in a project that yields $150 with probability 0.4 and zero with probability 0.6 at the end of the period.[25] If the borrower comes to the bank for a loan in the second period, it will be to finance exactly the same kind of project as in the first period. Assume that The Midtown Community Bank is perfectly competitive and there is universal risk neutrality. Compute the borrower's interest rates on its first- and second-period loans. Midtown's cost of funds is 5%, the riskless rate. Assume that the bank's *prior belief is* that there is a 0.8 probability that the borrower is of type G and a 0.2 probability that it is of type B.

Solution

The basic idea is to examine how the bank learns about the borrower through time and how this learning affects the terms of credit. We proceed in four steps. First, we solve for the first-period interest rate that is the same for all borrowers since Midtown cannot distinguish among borrowers. Second, we solve for the breakeven second-period interest rate, conditional on first-period project success and loan repayment by the borrower. Repayment of the first-period loan leads Midtown to revise upward its belief that the borrower is of type G. Hence, the second-period interest rate in this case is lower than the first-period interest rate. Third, we solve for the breakeven second-period interest rate, conditional on first-period project failure and default. This default leads Midtown to revise downward its belief that the borrower is of type B. This interest rate consequently turns out to be so high that no borrower wishes to take a second-period loan at that rate. Finally, in Step 4 we discuss how the first- and second-period rates might actually be determined by Midtown, and the effect of the relative bargaining powers of Midtown and the borrower on this rate.

Step 1

Since The Midtown Community Bank is pooling these two types of borrowers, its breakeven loan interest rate in the first period will reflect the *average* success probability. Let the probability represent the bank's prior belief that the borrower is of type G and let p represent the success probability of a type G borrower. Also let q represent the success probability of a type-B borrower. Then, the average success probability assessed by the bank is given by

$$\gamma p + (1-\gamma)q = 0.8 \times 0.9 + 0.2 \times 0.4 = 0.8.$$

Hence, the first-period loan interest rate at which the bank breaks even is

$$(1.05/0.8) - 1 = 0.3125 \text{ or } 31.25\%.$$

Step 2

Now, suppose the borrower repays his first-period loan. Then how should Midtown revise its beliefs about the borrower's type? To answer this question, one needs to use *Bayes rule,* which, as we saw in Chapter 1, says that

$$\Pr(x_i \mid y_i) = \frac{\Pr(y_i \mid x_i)\Pr(x_i)}{\sum_{i=1}^{n}\Pr(y_i \mid x_i)\Pr(x_i)} \qquad (8.7)$$

where $x_1, \ldots, x_n$ are the possible realizations of the random variable x and $\Pr(x_i)$ is the prior probability that $x = x_i$, with x_i being some value chosen from $x_1, \ldots, x_n$. Similarly, y_j is some realization of y. In our context, application of Bayes rule means that
Pr(borrower is type G|project succeeds) = Pr(G|S)

$$= \frac{\Pr(S|G)\Pr(G)}{\Pr(S|G)\Pr(G) + \Pr(S|B)\Pr(B)} \qquad (8.8)$$

$$= \frac{p\gamma}{p\gamma + q(1-\gamma)}.$$

Using Equation (8.8), we see that if there is repayment of the first-period loan, then the bank believes that the probability that the borrower is of type G is given by:

$$\Pr(G \mid S) = \frac{0.9 \times 0.8}{0.9 \times 0.8 + 0.4 \times 0.2}$$
$$= 0.90.$$

Hence, the average second-period success probability is given by:

$$0.9 \times p + 0.1 \times q = 0.9 \times 0.1 + 0.4 = 0.85.$$

25. If the two types of borrowers wished to borrow different amounts and the bank knew which type wanted to borrow how much, the bank would be able to distinguish one type from the other.

The breakeven interest rate of the bank on the second-period loan, conditional on first-period success, is given by 1.05/0.85–1 = 23.53%.

Step 3
Note that if there is nonrepayment of the first-period loan due to project failure, then Midtown assesses the probability of the borrower being of type G as (in the equation below, "F" denotes failure)

$$Pr(G|F) = \frac{Pr(F|G)Pr(G)}{Pr(F|G)Pr(G) + Pr(F|B)Pr(B)}$$
$$= \frac{(1-p)\gamma}{(1-p)\gamma + (1-q)(1-\gamma)}$$
$$= \frac{0.1 \times 0.8}{0.1 \times 0.8 + 0.6 \times 0.2}$$
$$= 0.4.$$

The bank assesses the *average* success probability for this kind of borrower as

$$0.4 \times p + 0.6 \times q = 0.4 \times 0.9 + 0.6 \times 0.4 = 0.6.$$

Thus, the bank's breakeven interest rate is (1.05/0.6)–1 = 75%. But at this rate, neither type would wish to borrow. This means that a borrower who defaults on his first-period loan is effectively denied second-period credit.

Step 4
If the borrower's first-period repayment behavior is freely observable by other banks, then the competitive Midtown Community Bank will charge interest rates of 31.25% and 23.53% on the first- and second-period loans, respectively. Thus, the loan interest rate declines through time for a borrower who repays his loans. At the other extreme, if competing banks are completely uninformed about the borrower's repayment behavior, then Midtown could charge up to 31.25% on the second-period loan and thus make a profit on its second-period loan. Anticipation of this profit could induce Midtown to compete by lowering its first-period loan interest rate below 31.25%.[26] Of course, this might strengthen the bargaining power of the borrower who repays his first-period loan. Having paid a lower than breakeven interest on its first-period loan, he knows that the bank need only charge 23.53% on the second-period loan to break even on *that* loan. Of course, the borrower had agreed to pay more, but now that promise is "water under the bridge," and (at some cost in terms of his reputation) the borrower could force Midtown to recontract. The interest rate on the second-period loan may end up somewhere between 23.53% and 31.25%, with the exact interest rate depending on the bargaining strengths of Midtown and the borrower.

In practice, other competing banks do learn something about the borrower, but typically not as much as the incumbent bank. Therefore, through time an *informational surplus* is created in the bank–borrower relationship that could benefit both the incumbent bank and the borrower. Some have argued that this informational surplus could also be socially wasteful. The point is that the incumbent bank's informational advantage could result in its extracting monopoly rents by charging excessively high loan interest rates. This means that the borrower's share of its own project profit is diminished. The borrower's marginal return to working hard to enhance project profits is thereby reduced, and the borrower curtails its effort input. Thus, projects pay off less on average.

LOAN RESTRUCTURING AND DEFAULT

We have so far presented a simplified view of the default process: If the borrower has insufficient cash flow from its project, it defaults. However, as our discussion of bank–borrower relationships has indicated, there is gain from the relationship between the bank and the borrower. Thus, even if we ignore the legal and administrative costs of bankruptcy, the termination of the bank–borrower relationship through default (leading to bankruptcy) is usually costly. The costs to the borrower are transparent. But the bank suffers a cost as well, since a loan default diminishes bank capital. This means that the bank as well as the borrower would be interested in staving off default if possible. This is a major impetus for the widely observed restructuring of bank loans.

There has been extensive research on the issue of default and renegotiation. The basic insights of this research are that the *design* of the debt contract has a lot to do with borrower's incentive to default and the lender's incentive to be willing to

---

26. These issues are analyzed by Sharpe (1990).

renegotiate. Moreover this research has also examined the conditions under which debt contract themselves are the efficient financial contract given the possibility of default and renegotiation.[27]

Types of Financial Distress

Loan restructuring becomes necessary when the borrower is in financial distress. For expositional ease we will classify financial distress into three degrees of severity: mild, moderate, and severe.

(a) Mild Financial Distress: Mild distress is a situation in which the borrower faces the prospect of temporarily insufficient cash flows to service its outstanding debt obligations, but the economic value of the firm comfortably exceeds its repayment obligations. Thus, the borrower faces a temporary cash flow shortfall, rather than insolvency. If forced, the firm could, at some cost, overcome its cash flow deficiency and meet its scheduled debt repayment. Examples are: delaying some investment plans, selling selected assets, or issuing new equity. However, such adjustments could diminish the firm's economic value. A less costly alternative may be to approach the lenders with a request to restructure the firm's debt. Lenders, such as banks, may be willing to accommodate such requests for two reasons. First, it signals flexibility on the bank's part and thus improves its reputation in the credit market. Second, to the extent that such an accommodation minimizes borrower value dissipation, the bank may be better off in the long run. Indeed, it can claim for itself a part of the saving achieved by the debt restructuring.

The usual approach to restructuring such loans stretches out the loan's maturity and reduces current interest payments in exchange for an increase in future interest payments. We will discuss two cases of such loan restructurings.

Case 1: Revlon:[28] In 1986, Revlon was acquired by Ronald Perelman, a well-known corporate acquirer, and made a wholly owned subsidiary of Perelman's MacAndrew and Forbes Holdings, Inc. This acquisition was a highly leveraged transaction (HLT), financed with loans from Chemical Bank, Chase Manhattan, Citicorp, and Manufacturers Hanover. An HLT is a loan to a borrower whose debt-to-equity ratio is inordinately high relative to its peers. In particular, it is defined as financing for a buyout, acquisition, or recapitalization that pushes the borrower's liabilities-to-assets ratio to more than 75%, or a loan that doubles the company's liabilities and its leverage ratio reaches 50%. Revlon had a good record for meeting its financial obligations, and until 1989 it did not appear to be in any danger. However, two events resulted in a mild crisis. First, intense regulatory scrutiny of HLTs in 1990, combined with a deteriorating market for subordinated debt that banks used to augment their capital, caused Revlon's lenders to rethink their position with regard to such loans. The banks decided that they did not want the Revlon loans on their books. They thus designed a refinancing package of four term loans totaling $1.25 billion and a $550 million revolving credit facility, and offered these for sale to other lenders. Second, even though Revlon had generally performed well since the Perelman acquisition, many were concerned about its future because of increased competition from Procter & Gamble Company, which had recently acquired Faberge and Elizabeth Arden.

Moody's Investors Service downgraded Revlon's debt rating in January 1990 and noted that industry consolidation "could make maintenance of market shares more difficult and put additional pressure on cash flows." These developments made Revlon's potential creditors nervous.

The refinancing package offered by the original four banks included loans with 4-year maturities, that is, they would come due in 1994. However, $365 million in Revlon's senior debt would mature in 1995, so banks that bought the refinancing package could find it difficult to help Revlon obtain refinancing in 1994 to repay the 4-year loans. Many potential creditors did not want to deal with a situation in which a subordinated tranche was paid off just before senior lenders were paid. There was additional concern about the refinancing of a $500 million to $600 million balloon (principal) payment that would need to be made in 1994.

These difficulties led the four original banks to revise the terms of the deal they were offering to the market. These revisions took the form of structural and pricing adjustments. They were, however, not expected to affect the cost of the loan for Revlon. Rather, any changes in fees or pricing were expected to come out of the pockets of the four banks that underwrote the entire package and would be stuck with any portion of the loan they could not sell.

This case illustrates some of the difficulties that banks face in restructuring a borrower's debt even when the borrower is in relatively good financial condition. Indeed, Revlon even indicated that asset sales in the next few years were likely and that the resulting cash flows would provide the necessary cushion for complete debt service.

---

27. See Hart and Moore (1998). They show that debt contracts are optimal when projects exhibit constant returns to scale and cash flows and asset liquidation value are positively correlated.
28. News about Revlon was reported by Lipin (1990a).

Case 2: Zale Corporation:[29] A Dallas-based jewelry retailer, Zale Corporation, was purchased by Peoples' Jewelers Limited, Toronto, and Swiss-based Swarovski International Holdings AG in late 1986. As in the case of Revlon, the acquisition was financed with considerable debt, making it a HLT. The bank loans used to finance the acquisition were short term. In 1990, Zale was faced with the prospect of repaying these loans. In years past, these loans probably would have been rolled over, with Zale financing its repayment with a high-yield bond issue. However, disarray in the junk-bond market meant that this type of financing was out of the question. Since Zale was not in a position to repay its bank loans without significant impairment to its asset value, it preferred restructuring of its $300 million in acquisition-related debt.

Zale was provided with a restructured $300 million loan commitment maturing in May 1993. This commitment involved unsecured loans, but with the banks being at the same level of seniority as much of the company's high yield from its parents.

Zale illustrates the kinds of steps that borrowers and banks are willing to take to avoid costly default and formal bankruptcy.

(b) Moderate Financial Distress: This is a situation in which default is imminent without debt restructuring. Given the *existing* debt repayment obligations, the economic value of the firm's assets is less than its repayment obligations. However, it is possible that if creditors agree to restructure the debt, the firm could produce sufficient future cash flows so that the *economic value* of the firm's assets would exceed the value of restructured debt, which in turn would exceed the current value of the firm's debt. In this case, the creditor's forbearance is a bet on a change in the company's fortunes. Thus, both the firm's shareholders and its creditors could benefit from the restructuring. The following example illustrates this possibility.

Example 8.6

Marvelous Computers, Inc. currently owes its creditors $120. It is run by an entrepreneur, Mr. Bill Doors, who could manage the firm for one period at a personal cost of $5. Mr. Doors has a unique ability to manage Marvelous Computers; under his stewardship the firm's assets one period from now will be worth $125 with probability 0.9 and $100 with probability 0.1. Under any other management, the firm will be worth $90 for sure, which is its current liquidation value. Assume that the riskless rate is zero and that there is universal risk neutrality. Analyze the possible strategies for the creditors.

Solution

There are basically two strategies for the creditors, so that we solve this problem in two steps. First, we analyze what would happen if the creditors insisted on debt repayment on existing terms. Second, we analyze what would happen if the creditors agree to a restructuring that involves a reduction in Mr. Doors' debt obligation. We find that reducing the face value of the debt increases its economic value to creditors. Hence, restructuring is the preferred strategy.

Step 1

If creditors insist on debt repayment on existing terms, it is clear that Mr. Doors will prefer to default. This is because his payoff conditional on default is zero, whereas if he continues for one more period, his expected payoff is

$$0.9(125 - 120) + 0.1(0) - 5 = -\$0.5,$$

given that the debt obligation must be settled first before Mr. Doors collects anything. Since Mr. Doors' equity in the firm is worth only $4.50 and the *personal* cost to him of operating the firm is $5, he computes a payoff of −$0.50 to managing Marvelous Computers for another period. The creditors' payoff if Marvelous Computers defaults is the liquidation value of the firm, $90.

Step 2

But now suppose creditors agree to a restructuring whereby the debt repayment obligation of Marvelous Computers is reduced to $119. Mr. Doors' expected payoff from operating Marvelous Computers for another period is then

$$0.9(125 - 119) + 0.1(0) - 5 = \$0.4,$$

compared to zero in default. Hence, the restructuring provides Mr. Doors with the incentive to continue to operate Marvelous Computers. The value of the debt (the expected payoff to creditors) now becomes

$$0.9 \times 119 + 0.1 \times 100 = \$117.10.$$

Thus, by *reducing* the *face value* of debt by $1, creditors can *increase* its *economic value* by $27.10!

---

29. News about Zale was reported by Lipin (1990b).

We will now see a case of a company in moderate financial distress.

Case 3: The Trump Organization: This company owned and operated a number of hotels (such as the Trump Plaza Hotel) and casinos (such as the Taj Mahal Hotel and Casino), and had over $2 billion in debt in 1990. On Friday, June 15, 1990, the Trump organization failed to make a $30 million interest payment to bondholders of Trump's Castle Casino, leaving Mr. Trump 10 to 30 thirty days to avoid bankruptcy. Banks, which were major lenders, proposed to postpone some interest payments and provide additional debt financing to enable the Trump organization to avoid bankruptcy.

The four major lenders were the banking units of Citicorp, Chase Manhattan, Bankers Trust, and Manufacturers Hanover. However, there were over 100 additional banks with smaller loans to the Trump organization, and there were also bonds outstanding. The Trump organization's crisis in June 1990, which led to the missed payment, necessitated negotiations between Mr. Trump and the four big banks. Although the banks were nervous about Trump's cash situation, they probably viewed it as prudent not to force Trump property and sell it to repay the notes. The banks faced a dilemma. On the one hand, they wanted the Trump organization to conserve cash by missing some interest payments on the bank loans as well as on the bonds. On the other hand, they did not want the company to be forced into default by bondholders who could then force a liquidation to collect amounts owed to them. Bondholders had first liens on three of Mr. Trump's properties through first mortgage bonds: the Trump Taj Mahal, Trump Castle Funding, and Trump Plaza Funding.

This was a classic situation in which default seemed imminent without debt restructuring, and yet it seemed to be in the interest of major lenders to forestall default. Indeed, at that time, most of the major lenders seemed confident that their loans to the Trump organization would be sound if default could be avoided.[30] Not surprisingly, the eventual outcome of the negotiations between the Trump organization and its major lenders was that some 80 banks agreed on Tuesday, June 26, 1990, to lend the company an additional $65 million to avoid bankruptcy. The banks also agreed to defer interest payments on $850 million of their $2 billion of outstanding loans.[31]

(c) Severe Financial Distress: This is defined as a situation in which the borrower actually defaults on some debt obligation. A debt-restructuring plan may be worked out to preclude formal bankruptcy proceedings. In some cases, the borrower may actually announce its intention to file for reorganization under Chapter 11, and a subset of the lenders may agree to restructure the debt so that a portion of the debt can be repaid and a more efficient reorganization plan can be implemented than one that would be possible if *all* the lenders had to be accommodated. Such a reorganization plan may either be achieved outside of bankruptcy or during bankruptcy proceedings. There are numerous examples of companies that have announced bankruptcies during 2004–2005 but continued operating as they reorganized, such as many airlines (e.g., Northwest) as well as companies in the automotive industry (e.g., Delphi). We have already shown that avoiding formal bankruptcy may benefit both the lender and the borrower, but this may not always happen. We will now provide a simple example to show how it may be beneficial for some lenders to help the borrower pay off some of the debt in order to achieve a more efficient reorganization plan.

Example 8.7
Consider Marvelous Computers managed by Mr. Bill Doors. The firm has two kinds of debt outstanding: senior debt under which it owes $100 to bondholders, and a subordinated bank loan that requires a repayment of $1,000. The assets of Marvelous Computers have a current liquidation value of $200, but if the firm continues to operate, it will be worth $1,100 with probability 0.9 and zero with probability 0.1 one period hence. To manage the firm for an additional period, Mr. Doors incurs a personal cost of $5. Mr. Doors has declared that he wishes to file for bankruptcy and has contacted both the bank and the bondholders' trustee. The bondholders wish to liquidate the firm immediately. What should the bank do? Assume universal risk neutrality and a risk-free interest rate of zero. Mr. Doors owns all of the firm's equity.

Solution
We solve this problem in two steps. First, we compute the expected payoffs to all the concerned parties from continuation and liquidation. Second, we examine how the most efficient plan could be implemented. In this example, this is achieved by having the bank buy out the senior debt.

Step 1
It is easy to see why the bondholders prefer immediate liquidation: since the liquidation value of Marvelous Computers is $200 and they have seniority, they stand to collect $100, the full amount owed to them. On the other hand, with continuation they

---

30. Lipin and Goodwin (1990) quote an official in the New York office of a major Japanese bank as saying: "We are concerned, but we are still confident with [Mr. Trump's] situation" as far as the developer's ability to make interest payments on his bank debt. They also quote an official with a European bank that was a colender on a $220 million facility for the Trump Palace as saying, "From a financial point of view, I have no problem with the deal."
31. This was reported by Horowitz and Goodwin (1990).

receive $100 with probability 0.9 and nothing with probability 0.1, that is, the expected value of their claim is $90. From the bank's perspective, however, the expected payoff is $0.9 \times (1,100-100) = \$900$ if the firm is continued, and $100 if the firm is liquidated immediately. Mr. Doors also prefers bankruptcy since as a shareholder he collects nothing if Marvelous Computers continues, but the personal cost of continuation is $5.

Step 2

To ensure that the most efficient investment plan is chosen during bankruptcy, the bank can buy out the senior debt for $100. Moreover, the bank could agree to restructure the loan so that Mr. Doors owes only $1,090, instead of $1,100. Now, the continuation plan will be acceptable to all parties since Mr. Doors' expected payoff is

$$0.9 \times (1,100 - 1,090) - 5 = \$4,$$

the senior bondholders' payoff is $100, and the bank's expected payoff is

$$0.9 \times 1,090 - 100 = \$881.$$

We will now discuss two cases of severe financial distress.

Case 4: West Point Acquisition Company: This company was the vehicle for Mr. William Farley's acquisition of a number of companies. On March 31, 1990, West Point Acquisition Company defaulted on the payment of $796 million in principal and interest to a bank group led by Bankers Trust and Wells Fargo & Company. The loan was made to finance the acquisition of West Point-Pepperell, Inc. Earlier, Mr. Farley had obtained a 4-year extension of a separate $1 billion bridge loan to West Point-Pepperell for operating purposes and this was also due on March 31.[32] West Point-Pepperell also had $900 million in outstanding junk bonds.

The banks that loaned West Point Acquisition the money had anticipated the default and had been trying to reach an agreement about how to restructure the loan. It also was reported that the banks wanted to avoid bankruptcy proceedings, but wanted Mr. Farley to reach an agreement with the public holders of the West Point-Pepperell high-yield bonds. Mr. Farley had reportedly offered bondholders a significant equity stake in West Point-Pepperell in exchange for a postponement in interest payments on the debt for up to 3 years.

Bankers Trust and Wells Fargo were also the lead banks on the $1 billion bridge loan, although the composition of the bank group differed from that of the acquisition loan. Apart from the 4-year extension, the bridge loan was restructured with a $165 million *increase* in the amount of credit and a *reduction* in the loan interest rate from prime plus 2.5% to prime plus 1.5%. This illustrates that lenders may be willing to reduce the actual repayment obligation to increase the *expected* payoff to them.

Case 5: Ames Department Stores, Inc.: On Thursday, April 27, 1990, Ames Department Stores, Inc. announced that it had sought protection from its creditors in the federal bankruptcy court by filing for reorganization under Chapter 11 of the Bankruptcy Code.[33] In 1988, Citibank led a bank group that provided $900 million in financing for the purchase of the Zayre department store chain. Hurt by an industry downturn, Ames was in technical default on the $900 million credit agreement and was trying to negotiate a second waiver from the Citibank-led group. Ames said that it filed under Chapter 11 after talks broke down. The basic problem for Ames was apparently the stoppage of shipments to Ames by suppliers who were concerned about the company's cash flow crisis.

At the time of bankruptcy, Ames said that Chemical Bank had agreed to provide it with $250 million of *debtor-in-possession (DIP)* financing. The loan was to be used to repay vendors and fund operations while the company attempted to formulate a reorganization plan. The agreement on DIP financing between Ames and Chemical was, however, subject to court approval. Citibank was also reported to be interested in getting the business. In the box below, we provide further details on DIP financing.

---

32. See Goodwin and Lipin (1990a). A *bridge loan* is typically made by a commercial or investment bank to provide interim financing for a takeover. A lender must support a bridge loan with capital. It is part of what has come to be known as "merchant banking," which refers to banks taking financial positions in corporate control activity (i.e., takeovers and acquisitions).

33. See Goodwin and Lipin (1990b).

Notes on Debtor-in-Possession [DIP] Financing[34]

What exactly are DIP loans, and why have they grown so popular? We discuss these issues here.

Firms filing for bankruptcy often face even greater pressures *after* filing for protection under the bankruptcy laws. These pressures stemmed from suppliers and customers shunning the bankrupt firm because of liquidity concerns. To overcome these difficulties, the 1978 Federal Bankruptcy Code set unified standards for how a debtor could obtain new working capital so that vendors, suppliers, and customers would continue with the company during bankruptcy. The debtor company is protected by freezing both its assets and its liabilities, including working capital bank lines. In place of the corporation, a new legal entity – the debtor-in-possession – is created. The 1978 Bankruptcy Code provides incentives for lenders to make *new* debt financing available to the bankrupt firm. It does so by providing a "super priority" lien that gives such a lender a very senior claim on the borrower's cash flow. This claim stands just behind normal administrative expenses but before existing credits, including senior debt. The lien also provides for the loan to mature or be repaid before the debtor emerges from bankruptcy. Some of the key features of DIP loans are as follows:

1. The DIP lender has claim to any assets not already backing other credits. If assets are insufficient to cover the DIP lender's claim, the DIP lender can make a prior claim on assets already pledged to existing creditors and use them as collateral for the new loan.
2. Most DIP loans are made as part of loan commitments. Commitment fees range from 2.5% to 4% of the line and loan interest rates from 1.5% to 2.5% over prime. In addition, there are usually syndication fees.
3. Even if the debtor is forced to liquidate while in bankruptcy, the DIP lender is the first to be repaid.

DIP financing is said to have originated in 1984 when Chemical Bank set up a unit to market DIP financing as a new product. The operation began to blossom in 1987 when Texaco, Inc. filed for Chapter 11 protection after losing a $10 billion lawsuit to Pennzoil Company, and turned to Chemical with a $2 billion DIP loan request that was eventually scaled back to $750 million.

Since its inception, the market for DIP lending has become fiercely competitive, but it can also be quite profitable for banks.[35] The United States Supreme Court, in its 2004 decision in *Till v. SCS Credit Corporation*, 1245. Ct. 1951, noted the existence of a free market for lenders advertising financing for Chapter 11 debtors-in-possession. The statutory framework governing DIP loans is Section 364 of Title 11 of the U.S. Bankruptcy Code.

This case illustrates how lenders may be willing to provide *additional* financing to a borrower unable to repay its existing debt. The reason is as follows. Often a company's cash flow can be impaired by perceptions on the part of its customers, supplier, and possibly creditors that it is in financial distress. In Ames' case, business was disrupted because suppliers stopped shipments. In such cases, it may pay for a bank to either restructure or to infuse additional credit to help the borrower overcome its liquidity shortfall even after the borrower has filed for bankruptcy.

The Coordination Problem in Creditor Coalitions

We have shown how debt restructuring can benefit both the lender and a borrower in financial distress. In most cases, however, the borrower either has borrowed from many lenders or the original lender has sold some pieces of the loan to others. As a result, most debt-restructuring plans involve *coalitions* of lenders. This often creates *coordination problems*. It is difficult to ensure that a restructuring plan will be accepted by all creditors, because creditors often have divergent interests. In Example 8.7, we saw how disagreement between two creditors often blocks a restructuring. In that example, it was possible to resolve the conflict by having the junior debt claimant (the bank) buy out the senior debt claimant (the bondholders). However, in practice, efficient resolutions are not always that easy, as the following discussion illustrates.

In the Trump organization case discussed earlier, there were approximately 100 banks involved. Some were "participants" – banks without *direct* relationships with the Trump organization. These banks had purchased loans from the original lenders, referred to as "assignees." When a debt-restructuring plan has to be voted on, the assignees cannot vote until they go back and convince the participants. In the Trump case, this persuasion process was protracted and difficult. Many participants apparently asked to be bought out by the assignees. However, the assignees feared that "everyone would want out."[36] And in many cases, "letting a participant out" may be tantamount to providing a free put option. This is illustrated in the following example.

---

34. See Lipin (1991).
35. See Rosenthal (2005) for an extensive discussion.
36. See Goodwin and Lipin (1990a).

Example 8.8

Having survived earlier travails, Marvelous Computers finds itself in trouble again. It now has three types of debt: a bank loan with the highest priority, senior debt owned by bondholders with the next highest priority, and junior debt owned by bondholders with the lowest priority. The repayment obligations of Marvelous Computers one period hence include the bank loan of $250, senior bonds of $45, and junior bonds of $45. Mr. Doors has announced his intention to declare Marvelous Computers bankrupt. At this stage, creditors must choose one of two mutually exclusive restructuring plans: plan A under which the value of Marvelous Computers next period will be $290 with probability 0.6 and $125 with probability 0.4, or plan B under which the value of Marvelous Computers next period will be $340 with probability 1/3 and $25 with probability 2/3. If you are the bank's representative, which plan would you prefer and what sort of coordination problems would you expect? Assume universal risk neutrality and a zero discount rate.

Solution

We proceed in two steps. First, we calculate the expected payoffs to the various parties from the different plans under the assumption that the absolute priority rule will be strictly observed. Second, we examine the bank's strategies with respect to securing the compliance of junior bondholders to the adoption of the plan preferred by the bank, and discuss the coordination problems that may be encountered.

Step 1

We can readily compute the expected payoffs to the various parties under the assumption that absolute priority rules will be strictly observed. These expected payoffs are given below.

To understand how these expected payoffs are determined, consider for example the bank's expected payoff under Plan A. With probability 0.6, it is repaid in full ($250) and with probability 0.4, it receives $125; the expected value is $0.6 \times 250 + 0.4 \times 125 = \$200$ (Table 8.5).

TABLE 8.5 Expected Payoffs to Different Claimants

Claimant	Expected Payoff under Plan A	Expected Payoff under Plan B
Bank loan	$200	$100
Senior bonds	$24	$15
Junior bonds	0	$15
Equity (Mr. Doors)	0	0

Step 2

Clearly, your bank prefers plan A. Senior bondholders also prefer plan A. However, junior bondholders prefer plan B and will have to be bought out to secure their compliance. Unfortunately for your bank, they *may* insist on being bought out at par rather than at the economic value of their bonds. In this case, your bank and the senior bondholders must pay them $45. In essence, you have given them a free put option with an exercise price of $45! Your bank may find it optimal to pay the $45 since it still leaves you with a *net* expected payoff of $155, which exceeds your expected payoff from plan B. Worse still for your bank, however, senior bondholders may attempt to "free ride" and insist that you buy them out in order to implement plan A. Even though they lose $9 with plan B relative to plan A, they may figure that you have even more to lose with plan B. If your bank buys them out at $45, then they too have been given a free put option. The senior bondholders recognize that even if you buy them out, your net expected payoff with plan A is $110, which exceeds that from plan B.

Renegotiation of Debt Contracts and the Borrower's Choice of Financing Source

We have seen how important renegotiating debt contracts can be to firms in financial difficulty. Moreover, given potential coordination problems in lender coalitions, the degree of renegotiability of debt covenants and other contract features will depend on how many creditors there are and who these creditors happen to be. Debt placed privately with a small number of large investors or a single bank loan may be much easier to renegotiate than public debt. Indeed, widely dispersed debt can significantly raise the costs of renegotiation.[37] This suggests that the borrower should take into account the possibility of future renegotiation of contract terms in choosing its source of credit.[38]

---

37. See Hart and Moore (1998) for an analysis of optimal debt contracts and renegotiation of the debt contract following default.
38. See Berlin and Mester (1992) and Bolton and Scharfstein (1996). Brunner and Krahnen (2008) and Guiso and Minetti (2010) provide empirical evidence. See also the fundamental contribution of Aghion and Bolton (1992).

It has been shown that the value of the option to renegotiate debt contracts – the difference in the borrower's net expected profit under a contract when renegotiation is possible and when it is impossible – is high when the firm's ex ante creditworthiness is low. The intuition is that agency problems between shareholders and creditors are likely to be more severe among less creditworthy firms, so that the initial debt covenants to restrict the firm's actions are likely to be relatively restrictive.[39] While restrictive covenants control agency problems, they also reduce the firm's flexibility to pursue profitable investments. Consequently, the importance of renegotiation is elevated for such a firm. This implies that firms with low credit ratings are more likely to negotiate debt contracts with more stringent covenants, but with creditors who are more likely to relax these covenants selectively when they seem inefficient in light of new information. Thus, we would expect firms with poorer credit ratings to take bank loans of privately placed debt and to also accept harsher covenants.

Alternative Intermediation Opportunities Created by Financial Distress

One of the reasons why banks might wish to divest loans involving firms in financial distress is that such loans may be classified as risky or nonperforming and thus require more bank capital. Banks may sell these loans to other (possibly nonbank) financial intermediaries that operate under less stringent constraints. An opportunity for financial intermediation is thus created as assets are brokered to those who can hold them more efficiently.

Observe that in these structural distress situations the traditional intermediation role of banks has little value. Continuation is unlikely. The objective is no longer to engage in relationship banking, but rather to maximize the collection on the outstanding distressed debt. This is a more brutal activity that other types of intermediaries may specialize in. Indeed, sometimes, so-called vulture funds are established which invest in the debt of financially troubled companies to play precisely this role.

CONCLUSION

This chapter has focused on a variety of issues related to loan pricing, credit rationing, bank–customer relationships, and loan default and restructuring. In an environment in which information "decays" rapidly and new information arrives almost continuously, flexibility is important. Being able to *renegotiate* covenants and other contractual parameters in debt contracts in light of new information becomes essential. Such renegotiation can add value for both the creditor and the borrower.

Banks have an inherent advantage over capital market financing when it comes to loan workouts and renegotiation of debt contracts. This advantage derives from the bank's position as a "monolithic" lender, whereas capital market financing typically involves many disparate bondholders whose behavior is difficult to coordinate; coordination among creditors is vital to the success of any renegotiation effort. Thus, borrowers who find the option to renegotiate their debt contracts valuable are likely to gravitate to banks for credit. In an intensely competitive environment in which borrower-specific information is volatile, banks would do well to capitalize on their comparative advantage by negotiating restrictive covenants to control agency problems, but also remain flexible enough to accommodate postlending renegotiations of these covenants.

CASE STUDY: ZEUS STEEL, INC.[40]

Robert Feldon started Zeus Steel, Inc. in December of 1993. He had been a salesman for a large steel fabricator, Seminole Steel Company, prior to forming his own steel fabricating operation. In Mr. Feldon's opinion, Zeus Steel occupies a special position in the local market. Zeus buys "secondary" steel that has been rejected as top grade or "prime" by the steel mills because it is flawed in some way. Because of his long relationship with several suppliers, Mr. Feldon has been very successful in purchasing secondary steel at as much as 33% under the going rate for prime steel. Zeus' customers have no objection to using secondary steel either because Zeus removes the flaws (flattens the steel) or because the flaws are only cosmetic (small amounts of rust). The company's primary sources of supply are steel mills, insurance companies (who sell damaged steel that they have insured during ocean shipment), and steel brokers. Often the most difficult time for Zeus is when the steel market is strong and secondary steel becomes very difficult to obtain at a discount. As a fabricator, Zeus buys the raw steel and cuts it to order into smaller strips with one of its 10 shearing machines.

---

39. Empirical support is provided by Blackwell and Kidwell (1988). Dichev and Skinner (2002) show that violations of loan covenants are common (in approximately 30% of loans). See also Berlin and Mester (1992) and Demiroglu and James (2010).
40. Written by Gregory F. Udell, then at New York University. We thank Greg for providing us with this case.

Feldon started Zeus with $150,000 of his own money. He purchased a 35-year-old 30,000-square-foot building (with a new overhead crane) for $60,000 in cash plus $240,000 to be paid over a 10-year period ($2,000 per month plus interest at 8%); he bought at auction 10 used shearing machines for $100,000, of which he borrowed $50,000 from the First National Bank (FNB). The remainder of his investment plus a $50,000 line of credit from FNB was used for working capital.

Robert Feldon, who still owns 100% of Zeus Steel, has reached a critical juncture in his relationship with the First National Bank. Phillip Reiling, his old loan officer, has just taken a position at another bank, while his new loan officer, Mike Dickens (MD), has been a commercial loan officer for only 6 months (since his promotion from the credit department). These excerpts from the "credit memoranda" portion of Zeus' credit file reveal the tenuous nature of the banking relationship:

Credit Memoranda

1/30/99 MD

I visited Zeus Steel and met Robert Feldon for the first time. Feldon informed me that he was not at all pleased with his relationship with FNB. According to Feldon, Phillip Reiling had been a good friend but was not always responsive to Zeus' banking requirements. Feldon had warned Reiling of Zeus' credit needs many months ago, but nevertheless the $200,000 increase in the line of credit approved last November was treated as a last-minute "crisis." Feldon emphasized that the current $500,000 limit on the line of credit was "strangling" Zeus.

I was given a tour of the plant and was impressed with the level of activity. It seemed as though every square inch of space was being used, much of it to store raw steel. Feldon was quite proud of the fact that he had been able to buy $300,000 of "water logged" coil last month at a bargain rate of $.11 a pound; he apparently already has orders for more than half of that steel.

I told Feldon we'd be more than glad to consider an increase in the Zeus line of credit upon receipt of the 12-31-98 financial statements. Feldon indicated that statements would show an even better year than 1997.

2/26/99 MD

Received urgent phone call from Bob Feldon who indicated that he was about to purchase three new machines for $200,000. He wants FNB to finance the equipment. I suggested lunch on Friday. Feldon agreed to bring an accounts receivable and an accounts payable aging, year-end statements, and a new personal statement. Ken Heyden, Bob's accountant, will join us for lunch.

2/28/99 MD

Received a new Dunn & Bradstreet report that revealed some slowness in the trade. Earlier D&B's showed Zeus paying its bill either "discount" or "prompt."

3/2/99 MD

Entertained Bob Feldon for lunch to discuss his request for an increase in the Zeus line and also equipment financing. Also present at the lunch were Ken Heyden and John Garner, head of FNB's Metropolitan Division. Feldon was quite pleased with Zeus' 1998 performance. Much of the increase in sales was due to the acquisition of two new accounts, Archer Manufacturing and Hiawatha Motor Homes. Archer manufactures industrial tool boxes and related accessories that it sells primarily to the construction industry. Hiawatha is in the recreational vehicle business (also a manufacturer). In both cases it was understood that in order to obtain the business, Zeus would have to carry its receivables 60–75 days during peak season.

In looking at the statements, we pointed out that it looked as though Zeus was slow in the trade (accounts payable of $1,225,000). Feldon emphasized that with a larger line of credit, Zeus could return to payable its bills in 45 days. Ken Heyden pointed out that his projections indicated that a $750,000 line of credit would be appropriate.

We asked Feldon about the decrease in profit during 1998 and he responded that he just took more out in salary and that his inventory was "understated" for tax purposes. When we expressed concern over the high salary, he said defensively: "You've got my personal guarantee, don't you?"

Feldon reiterated the urgency of his request. The new shearing machines (two 48-inch and one 60-inch) were critical to servicing the two new accounts. We mentioned that we would probably require that the line be secured by accounts receivable and inventory and that FNB normally requires audited financial statements (to which Feldon only half-jokingly responded. "Ken will charge me another $10,000 for that!"). It appeared that relations were strained.

3/6/99 MD

Contracted three of Zeus' suppliers to check credit. Youngstown and Inland Steel reported that Zeus had been a longtime customer with a good credit experience. Seminole reported that it feels very confident about Feldon but they had experienced slowness up to 60–75 days in the Zeus account.

3/7/99 MD

Balance in the Zeus accounts for 1998 were:
Average Collected Balance – $55,000
Average Fee Balance – $17,000

The following meeting took place between John Garner and Dickens on Friday, March 6, 1999, in Garner's office.

Garner: Mike, I'm concerned about Zeus Steel. I know Feldon was irritable and a bit defensive with us last week; but I think he has a right to be. Frankly, this account suffered from neglect under Reiling who took Zeus for granted, keeping Feldon happy with a low interest rate. We might not be able to do everything the way Bob wants, but I believe an honest effort on our part will save the account. After all, there aren't many companies that have grown as dramatically as Zeus. Plus, I've got a lot of respect for Ken Heyden and all the business he's sent our way.

Dickens: A couple of things concern me though. Feldon has taken a lot of money out of Zeus in salary, which has resulted in undercapitalization. With the additional debt he's asking for, I think the ratios will look quite different. I'm also concerned about the company's rapid expansion – I think it may have been at the expense of a sound financial statement.

Garner: We could always bring in a finance company to take the accounts receivable and the inventory as collateral. We could then participate in their line of credit and make the equipment loans ourselves. However, as you know, this is an expensive option for Feldon – the rate on the line will probably jump to 4% over prime even with a 50% participation on our part. But honestly, I think there are better solutions that are less likely to lose the Zeus business. Zeus has a good profit record and still has a very respectable debt/net worth ratio compared to many of our other local borrowers.

Dickens: We've got to act fast – Feldon needs an answer by Monday and I know he's also talking to Midtown Bank.

Garner: As I see it, our options are: (1) increase the line of credit short of $750,000 on an unsecured basis and approve the equipment loans in accordance with FNB loan policy (75% of the purchase price and amortized over three years); (2) approve the full $750,000, but take the A/R and inventory as collateral;[41] (3) approve the equipment loan but get a commercial finance company to do the lien of credit (and buy a participation in that line).

Mike, the choice is yours. You present to the loan committee on Monday morning what you feel is our best offer. If you come up with some other alternative, that's great. All I ask is that you provide the loan committee with a detailed financial analysis in support of your recommendation.

Question: Can you help out Mike Dickens with a financial analysis of Zeus and prepare a recommendation for how the bank should proceed?

Financial Statements						
(ZEUS STEEL, INC.)						
(Prepared without audit by Kenneth Heyden & Company)						
Balance Sheet (000's omitted)						
Assets		12/31/96		12/31/97		12/31/98
Cash		$30		$68		$24
Accounts Receivable – Net		150		342		698
Inventories (LIFO)		110		326		1,006
Other Current Assets		6		8		12
Total Current Assets		296		744		1,740
Property, Plant, & Equipment	422		440		490	
Less Accumulated Depreciation	90	332	136	304	188	302
Total Assets		$628		$1,048		$2,042
Liabilities & Net Worth						
Accounts Payable		$60		$202		$768
Notes Payable – FNB		40		150		500
Current Maturities						
First National Bank		10		10		0
Mortgage		24		24		24
Other Current Liabilities		6		8		26
Total Current Liabilities		140		394		1,318
Long-Term Debt						
First National Bank		10		0		0
Mortgage		144		120		96
Total Debt		294		514		1,414
Common Stock		150		150		150
Retained Earnings		184		384		478
Total Liabilities & Net Worth		$628		$1,048		$2042

---

41. FNB does not have an asset-based loan department; therefore, if it takes the accounts receivable and inventory as collateral, it must do so without full collateral monitoring.

Income Statement (000's omitted)

Sales	$1,500	$2,600	$4,300
Cost of Goods Sold			
Beginning Inventory	90	110	326
Purchases	800	1,610	3,494
Direct Labor	250	274	425
Manufacturing Expenses	54	82	199
Ending Inventory	*110*	*326*	*1,006*
Gross Profit	416	850	862
Operating Expenses			
Officer's Salary (Feldon)	100	158	242
Commissions	90	210	290
Office Salaries	30	52	58
Depreciation	42	46	52
Provision for Bad Debts	2	2	24
Miscellaneous	*10*	*16*	*22*
Net Operating Profit	142	366	174
Interest Expense	*18*	*24*	*38*
Net Profit Before Tax	124	342	136
Taxes	*38*	*142*	*42*
Net Profit After Tax	$86	$200	$94

Projected Income Statement (Zeus Steel, Inc.)

	For the 3 Months Ended			
	3/31/99	6/30/99	9/30/99	12/31/99
Sales	$1,400	$1,800	$1,400	$1,400
Gross Profit	350	450	350	350
Operating Expenses	250	320	250	250
Net Operating Profit	100	130	100	100

	Days			
Account Receivable Aging 2/23/99 (Zeus Steel, Inc.)	0–30	31–60	61–90	Over 90
Archer Manufacturing Co.	$79,000	$80,000	$17,000	$
Able Tools Co., Inc.	46,000	52,000		
Centennial Steel Co.	12,000	6,000		
Diversey Products	52,000	38,000	22,000	26,000
Steven's Locker	58,000	48,000		
Hiawatha Motor Homes	76,000	72,000	12,000	
Seminole Steel Co.	42,000	34,000		
Smith Manufacturing Co.	8,000	22,000		
CPN Fabricating	24,000			
Cooper Heating & Cooling	18,000	26,000		
Schiller Manufacturing	30,000	36,000		
Mid-America Products	8,000	10,000	2,000	10,000
Other Accounts (under $10,000)	*22,000*	*54,000*	*6,000*	*2,000*
Total	$475,000	$478,000	$59,000	$38,000

Total Accounts Receivable: $1,050,000

Accounts Payable Aging 2/23/99 (Zeus Steel, Inc.)

Youngstown Steel	$236,000	$72,000	$	$
Seminole Steel Co.	79,000	109,000	40,000	
Inland Steel	101,000	39,000		
Atlantic Underwriters	62,000	107,000	28,000	
Independent Insurance Co.		44,000	30,000	
Robert Cunningham & Co.	57,000	83,000	19,000	
Star Steel	14,000	36,000		
Other Accounts	*23,000*	*27,000*	*19,000*	
Total	$572,000	$517,000	$136,000	$-0-

Total Accounts Payable: $1,225,000

Personal Financial Statement 2/23/99 (Robert Feldon)

Assets		Liabilities & Net Worth	
Cash	$20,000	Notes Payable	$12,000
Marketable Securities (M/V)	270,000	Credit Cards	2,000
Zeus Steel, Inc. (M/V)	2,500,000	Mortgages	
Real Estate (M/V)		Residence	84,000
Residence	300,000	Condominium	75,000
Condominium	220,000		
Personal Property (M/V)	150,000	Net Worth	3,287,000
Total Assets	$3,460,000	Total Liab. & Net Worth	$3,460,000

LOAN REPORT NUMBER:	1067	*DATE:* 11/19/98
NAME:	Zeus Steel, Inc.	
BUSINESS:	Metal Fabricating	
STARTED:	1993	
PRINCIPALS:	Robert Feldon	
CUSTOMER SINCE:	1993	
OFFICER CONTACT:	PR	
REQUEST:	$500,000 unsecured line of credit (increase from $300,000)	
PURPOSE:	Working capital	
SOURCE OF REPAYMENT:	Collection of Receivables	
DATE:	Prime plus $\frac{1}{2}$% (floating)	
	Compensating balances will be 15% of the line	

AVERAGE BALANCE:

	1997	1996	1995
Average Collected	$91,000	$73,000	$46,000
Average Free	60,000	49,000	31,000

AFFILIATED LOANS:	Auto Loan to R. Feldon –$6,325
HIGH CREDIT:	$300,000
PRESENT LIABILITY:	$300,000
MONTHS OUT OF DEBT	
(LAST 12 MONTHS)	None
GUARANTORS:	Robert Feldon (Net Worth $629,000)
COLLATERAL:	Unsecured
COMMENTS:	
DATE OF NEXT REVIEW:	3/31/99

INDUSTRY AVERAGES*

Assets Size	1 mm–10 mm	All
Balance Sheet		
Assets	%	%
Cash & Equivalents	7.2	7.2
Accounts Receivable	25.1	25.9
Inventory	28.1	25.4
Other Current	1.5	1.5
Total Current	61.9	60.0
Fixed Assets (Net)	29.8	31.6
Other Noncurrent	8.3	8.4
Total	100.0	100.0
Liabilities & Net Worth		
Notes Payable Short-Term	8.2	7.1
Current Maturity-L/T Debt	3.4	3.8
Accounts & Notes Payable – Trade	16.1	16.2
Accrued Expenses	6.9	7.7
Other Current	2.6	3.1
Total Current	37.2	37.9
Long-Term Debt	11.7	13.4
All Other Noncurrent	1.5	1.6
Net Worth	49.6	47.1
Total	100.0	100.0

Income Data			%	%
Net Sales			100.0	100.0
Cost of Sales			78.6	76.9
Gross Profit			21.4	23.1
Operating Expenses			14.2	16.4
Operating Profits			7.3	6.7
All Other Expenses (Net)			0.6	0.7
Profit Before Taxes			6.7	6.0
Ratios				
Current			1.7	1.7
Quick			0.9	0.9
Sales/Receivables			9.0	8.9
Cost of Sales/Inventory			6.5	7.2
Cash Flow/Current Maturity			3.8	3.6
Debt/Worth			1.0	1.1
ROE (Before Taxes)			27.6	26.7
ROA (Before Taxes)			12.9	10.8
Sales/Total Assets			2.2	2.2

Source: Robert Morris Statement Studies 1998 (Metal Stampings).

ZEUS STEEL, INC. Financial Analysis				
Probability	1996	1997	1998	Industry (1 mm–10 mm)
Profit	$86,000.00	$200,000.00	$94,000.00	
Salary	$100,000.00	$158,000.00	$242,000.00	
ROA (Before Taxes)	19.7	32.6	6.6	12.9
ROE (Before Taxes)	37.1	64.0	21.6	27.6
Gross Margin	27.7	32.7	20.0	21.4
Liquidity				
Quick Ratio	1.33	1.06	.56	0.9
Current Ratio	2.11	1.89	1.32	1.7
Turnover				
Accounts Receivable (Days)				
End of Period	36.5	48.0	59.2	41
Average		34.5	44.1	
Inventory				
End of Period	37.0	67.9	106.8	56
Average		45.5	70.7	
Accounts Payable (Days)				
End of Period	27.4	45.8	80.2	
Average		29.7	50.7	
Leverage				
Debt/Worth Ratio	0.88	0.96	2.25	1.0

REVIEW QUESTIONS

1. Suppose a firm has no assets at $t = 0$, except an option to acquire an investment opportunity at $t = 1$ for $500 million. The outlay required for this investment will be raised entirely through a bank loan. There are no taxes and everybody is risk neutral. The investment opportunity, if undertaken, will yield a payoff of X per year perpetually, beginning at $t = 2$. However, what X will be is *not* known *now*. This knowledge will become available only at $t = 1$. Right now, we can only describe the possible values of X (at $t = 1$) by the following probability distribution.

State	Probability	X in millions of dollars
1	0.05	100
2	0.10	150
3	0.15	180
4	0.20	200
5	0.25	210
6	0.25	220

ABC, Inc.

The riskless rate (single-period) is 10%. Draw a graph that shows the relationship between the *current* market value of a perpetual (risky) bank loan for this form and the *promised* interest rate on this loan, which must be paid every year forever, and begins at $t = 2$.

2. What is credit rationing? Why would it ever be rational for a profit-maximizing bank to ration credit?

3. What are the three main types of financial distress? Why would lenders be willing to restructure debt when the borrower is experiencing mild financial distress? What kinds of accommodations are lenders usually willing to make?

4. What sort of restructuring are lenders willing to engage in when the firm is experiencing moderate financial distress and why?

5. What sort of incentives do lenders have to restructure debt when there is severe financial distress and why?

6. What is a "bridge loan" and how is it related to "merchant banking"?

7. What is DIP financing and why might it be advantageous to existing creditors?

8. Discuss the kinds of coordination problems that can come up in loan workouts and how they might be solved.

9. You are a banker and are confronted with a pool of loan applicants, each of whom can be either low risk or high risk. There are 600 low-risk applicants and 400 high-risk applicants and each applicant is applying for a $100 loan. A low-risk borrower will invest the $100 loan in a project that will yield $150 with probability 0.8 and nothing with probability 0.2 one period hence. A high-risk borrower will invest the $100 loan in a project that will yield $155 with probability 0.7 and nothing with probability 0.3 one period hence. You know that 60% of the applicant pool is low risk and 40% is high risk, but you cannot tell whether a specific borrower is low risk or high risk. You are a monopolist banker and have $50,000 available to lend. Everybody is risk neutral. The current riskless rate is 8%. Each borrower must be allowed to retain a profit of at least $5 in the successful state in order to be induced to apply for a bank loan. You have just learned that 1,000 loan applications have been received after you announced a 45% loan interest rate. You can satisfy only 500. What should be your optimal (profit-maximizing) loan interest rate? Should it be 45% (at which you must ration half the loan applicants) or a higher interest rate at which there is no rationing?

10. Imagine this is January 1, 2002. You are head of the loan department at the High Growth Bank of Los Angeles. Mr. Alex Walker, the founder and CEO of ABC, Inc., a small manufacturing firm, comes to you with a request for a loan that his company will need no later than March 1, 2002. He has indicated that the company will repay the loan February 28, 2003, with principal and interest. ABC's balance sheet and income statement are given below.

ABC, Inc.
Balance Sheet
Year Ended December 31, 2001

Cash	$50,000
Accounts Receivable	250,000
Due from Mr. Walker	40,000
Inventory	*800,000*
Total Current Assets	$1,140,000
Land and Building	$100,000
Machinery	100,000
Other Fixed Assets	*15,000*
Total Assets	*$1,355,000*
Notes Payable, Bank	$200,000
Accounts and Notes Payable	300,000
Notes Payable, Assorted Suppliers	100,000
Accruals	*50,000*
Total Current Liabilities	$650,000
Mortgage	550,000
Common Stock	300,000
Retained Earnings	*355,000*
Total Liabilities and Equity	*$1,355,000*

ABC, Inc. Income Statement Year Ended 2001	
Net Sales	$3,650,000
Costs of Goods Sold	2,650,000
Gross Operating Profit	$1,000,000
General Administrative and Selling Expenses	400,000
Depreciation	20,000
Miscellaneous	200,000
Net Income Before Taxes	$380,000
Taxes (40%)	152,000
Net Income	$228,000

In addition to the above information, you have the following ratios, which are averages of the industry to which ABC belongs.

Current ratio	3.0
Inventory turnover ratio	10.0
Average collection ratio	25 days
Fixed-asset turnover ratio	20%
Debt ratio	30%

An important consideration in this loan request is whether or not ABC can internally generate the funds needed to repay the loan by conforming more closely to industry averages. The loan request is for $650,000. You have not determined the loan interest rate yet, but the current annual borrowing rate for this customer is 10%. Your expectation is that ABC's borrowing rate over the next few months will stay at about 10%. Should you make this loan? If you decide to make the loan, present a qualitative analysis of this loan request and make a summary statement of the necessary loan covenants. There should be at least one affirmative covenant, one negative covenant, and one restrictive clause. You are required to present a brief summary of additional information that could have improved your analysis. (Be specific.)

11. Consider a borrower that can choose between two projects, S and R, each of which will pay off a random amount one period hence. Project S will yield $250 with probability 0.9 and zero with probability 0.1 one period hence. Project R will yield $350 with probability 0.4 and nothing with probability 0.6 one period hence. The bank's cost of funds is equal to the riskless interest rate of 10%. As a banker, you cannot control your borrower's project choice directly because you assume universal risk neutrality. Moreover, you can charge this borrower 200 basis points above your breakeven interest rate before the borrower switches to another bank. Compute the expected payoffs of the borrower and the bank under the following two scenarios: (i) the bank and the borrower can contract with each other over only one period and the borrower will request a single loan of $150, and (ii) the borrower will need a sequence of two $150 loans, with the ability to choose between S and R in each period. What should be the choice of the contracting horizon?

12. Consider a firm managed by an entrepreneur. The firm has two kinds of debt outstanding: senior debt under which it owes $150 to bondholders, and a subordinated bank loan that requires a repayment of $1,250. The firm's assets have a current liquidation value of $400, but if the firm continues to operate, it will be worth $1,400 with probability 0.8 and zero with probability 0.2 one period hence. To manage the firm for an additional period, the entrepreneur incurs a personal cost of $25. The entrepreneur has declared that he wishes to file for bankruptcy and has contacted both the bank and the bondholder's trustee. The bondholders wish to liquidate the firm immediately. What should the bank do? Assume universal risk neutrality and a risk-free (discount) rate of zero. The entrepreneur owns all of the firm's equity.

13. Consider a firm that has three types of debt: a bank loan with the highest priority, senior debt owned by bondholders with the next highest priority, and junior debt owned by bondholders with the lowest priority. The firm's repayment obligations one period hence include the bank loan of $150, senior bonds of $60, and junior bonds of $50. The firm has announced its intention to declare bankruptcy. At this stage, creditors must choose one of two mutually exclusive restructuring plans: plan A under which the value of the firm next period will be $180 with probability 0.5 and zero with probability 0.5, and plan B under which the value of the firm next period will be $260 with probability 0.4 and $20 with probability 0.6. If you are the bank's representative, which plan would you prefer and what sort of coordination problems would you expect? How would you attempt to overcome these problems? Assume universal risk neutrality and a zero discount rate.

14. The following is an excerpt from a conversation. Critique it.

Appleton: If banks don't do it, someone else will.

Butterworth: I'm sure that's true, but the question is one of comparative advantage and deadweight losses, that is, reinventing the wheel. For instance, take the example of DIP (Debtor-in-Possession) financing. There's nothing in the law that says only banks can provide it but banks are the biggest players in that market. It's not a mere coincidence.

Moderator: I guess it's not surprising that the DIP financing market has grown so much, given the debt binge of American corporations in the last decade. I personally find the whole debt-restructuring process, and particularly the role of banks in it, quite fascinating. But I do find it ironic that banks are engaged in this at a time when borrowers are complaining about credit rationing by banks.

Appleton: I think this concern with credit rationing is overdone. First of all, I don't really believe banks ration credit, and if they did, it would be irrational. I'm not in the habit of worrying about why someone may want to smoke a $5 bill! Moreover, a borrower who is rational could always go elsewhere. But honestly, I have yet to see a convincing study that shows that banks ration credit.

Moderator: Come now, Alex! Do we need a convincing empirical study substantiating every little truth?

Butterworth: Please don't answer that, Alex. The fact of the matter is that it *is* possible to explain credit rationing as a rational practice. And this view that a rationed borrower can go "somewhere else" is not surprising coming from you Alex, since you don't believe banks are special anyway.

15. Describe the bank's spot-lending process, with particular emphasis on the roles of information-processing-capacity constraints and randomness in loan demand.

REFERENCES

Aghion, P., Bolton, P., 1992. An incomplete contracts approach to financial contracting. Rev. Econ. Stud. 59, 473–494.

Akerlof, G.A., 1970. The market for 'lemons': quality uncertainty and the market mechanism. Q. J. Econ. 84, 488–500.

Berg, T., Saunders, A., Steffen, S., 2015. The total costs of corporate borrowing in the loan market: Don't ignore the fees. J. Financ. (forthcoming).

Berger, A.N., Bouwman, C.H.S., 2013. How does capital affect bank performance during financial crises? J. Financ. Econ. 109, 146–176.

Berlin, M., Mester, L.J., 1992. Debt covenants and renegotiation. J. Financ. Intermed. 2, 95–133.

Bhattacharya, S., Thakor, A.V., October 1993. Contemporary banking theory. J. Financ. Intermed. 3, 2–50.

Blackwell, D.W., Kidwell, D.S., 1988. An investigation of cost differences between public sales and private placements of debt. J. Financ. Econ. 22, 253–278.

Bolton S P., Scharfstein, D.S., 1996. Optimal debt structure and the number of Cr. J. Polit. Econ. 104, 1–25.

Boot, A.W.A., Thakor, A.V., 1994. Moral hazard and secured lending in an infinitely repeated credit market game. Int. Econ. Rev. 35, 899–920.

Brunner, A., Krahnen, J.P., 2008. Multiple lenders and corporate distress: evidence on debt restructuring. Rev. Econ. Stud. 75, 415–442.

Cerqueiro, G., Ongena, S., Roszbach, S., 2014. Collateralization, bank loan rates and monitoring. J. Financ. (forthcoming).

Chomsisengphet, S., Pennington-Cross, A., 2004. Borrower Cost and Credit Rationing in the Subprime Mortgage Market. Working Paper, Office of Federal Housing Enterprise and Oversight, February 2004.

Chong, T.T.-L., Lu, L., Ongena, S., 2013. Does banking competition alleviate or worsen credit constraints faced by small and medium enterprises? Evidence from China. J. Bank. Financ. 37, 3412–3424.

Cohen-Cole, E., 2011. Credit card redlining. Rev. Econ. Stat. 93, 700–713.

Demiroglu, C., James, C.M., 2010. The information content of bank loan covenants. Rev. Financ. Stud. 23, 3700–3737.

Diamond, Do., 1989. Reputation acquisition in debt markets. J. Polit. Econ. 97, 828–862.

Dichev, I.D., Skinner, D.J., 2002. Large-sample evidence on the debt covenant hypothesis. J. Account. Res. 40, 1091–1123.

Freixas, X., Rochet, J.-C., 2008. The Microeconomics of Banking, Second ed. MIT Press.

Gambacorta, L., Marques-Ibanez, D., 2011. The bank lending channel: lessons from the crisis. Econ. Pol. 26, 135–182.

Goodwin, W., Lipin, S., April 3, 1990a. Four main banks hold bag on Trump loan payments. American Banker.

Goodwin, W., Lipin, S., April 27, 1990b. Chemical to provide debtor-in-possession financing for AMES stores. American Banker.

Guiso, L., Minetti, R., 2010. The structure of multiple credit relationships: evidence from U.S. firms. J. Money, Credit Banking 426, 1037–1071.

Hart, O., Moore S J., 1998. Default and renegotiation: a dynamic model of debt. Q. J. Econ. 113, 1–41.

Holmstrom, B., Tirole, J., 1997. Financial intermediation, loanable funds, and the real sector. Q. J. Econ. XII-3, 663–691.

Horowitz, J., Goodwin, W., June 28, 1990. Hanover: Trump loans among nonperformers. American Banker.

Ioannidou, V., Ongena, S., 2010. Time for a change: loan conditions and bank behavior when firms switch. J. Financ. 65, 1847–1878.

Jaffee, D., Modigliani, F., 1969. A theory and test of credit rationing. Am. Econ. Rev. 59, 850–872.

Jiménez, G., José-Luis Peydró, S.O., Saurina, J., 2012. Credit supply and monetary policy: identifying the bank balance-sheet channel with loan applications. Am. Econ. Rev. 102, 2301–2326.

Jiménez, G., José-Luis Peydró, S.O., Saurina, J., 2014. Hazardous times for monetary policy: what do twenty-three million bank loans say about the effects of monetary policy on credit risk-taking? Econometrica 82, 463–505.

Košak, M., Igor Lončarski, S.L., Marinč, M., 2015. Quality of bank capital and bank lending behavior during the global financial crisis. Int. Rev. Financ. Anal. 37, 168–183.

Lipin, S., May 29, 1990a. Agent banks forced to restructure Revlon loan. American Banker.

Lipin, S., June 29, 1990b. Junk bond ills force recasting of Zale loans. American Banker.

Lipin, S., February 20, 1991. Bankruptcy law made DIP loan appealing. American Banker.

Lipin, S., Goodwin, W., June 6, 1990. Trump's banks balked at a call for cash, forcing negotiations. American Banker.

Mehran, H., Thakor, A.V., 2011. Bank capital and value in the cross-section. Rev. Financ. Stud. 24, 1019–1067.

Peek, J., Rosengren, E.S., 1997. The international transmission of financial shocks: the case of Japan. Am. Econ. Rev. 87, 496–505.

Peek, J., Rosengren. E.S., 2013. The Role of Banks in the Transmission of Monetary Policy, Federal Reserve Bank of Boston. Public Policy Discussion Papers No. 13-5.

Rajan, R., 1992. Insiders and outsiders: the choice between informed and arm's-length debt. J. Financ. 47, 1367–1400.

Rosenthal, T.L., 2005. Debtor-in-possession financing: opportunities, risks and rewards. Secured Lender 8, 82.

Samuelson, P.A., 1952. Statement in "Monetary Policy and Management of the Public Debt: Hearings Before the Subcommittee on General Audit Control and Debt Management." Joint Committee on the Economic Report, 2nd Congress and Session.

Sharpe, S., 1990. Asymmetric information, bank lending, and implicit contracts: a stylized model of customer relationships. J. Financ. Econ. 45, 1069–1087.

Stiglitz, J.E., Weiss, A., 1981. Credit rationing in markets with imperfect information. Am. Econ. Rev. 71, 393–410.

Thakor, A.V., 1996. Capital requirements, monetary policy and aggregate bank lending: theory and empirical evidence. J. Financ. 51, 279–324.

Chapter 9

Special Topics in Credit: Syndicated Loans, Loan Sales, and Project Finance

"The apparently private and technical theme of corporate financing leads us step by step to the heart of major problems of national policy… We are dealing here with serious and far-reaching matters which deserve our undivided attention."

Hans J. Mast, Crédit Suisse

GLOSSARY OF TERMS

Syndicated Loan A loan in which multiple lenders participate.
Loan Sale A sale of an existing loan, or part of it.
Project Finance Financing provided for large projects that are separately incorporated from the sponsoring firm.

INTRODUCTION

In the previous two chapters, we examined a variety of issues related to bank lending. There are, however, three important topics that we did not cover. These are syndicated lending, loan sales, and project finance. Syndicated lending occurs when multiple lenders participate in making a single large loan. There is a lead lender, typically a commercial bank, in the syndicate that originates the loan and the other lenders participate by providing varying amounts of the loan. A variant of syndicated lending is *loan sales*, which we will also discuss. Project financing occurs when the sponsoring firm for a project decides to incorporate the project as a stand-alone entity outside the firm and seeks financing that has a direct claim on the project cash flows rather than the cash flows of the sponsoring firm. In this chapter, we will describe these practices and explain the underlying economic forces at work that make these practices efficient in some circumstances.

SYNDICATED LENDING

In this section, we first discuss what a syndicated loan is and the economic functions syndication serves. We then discuss the syndicated loan market, both in domestic and international lending.[1]

What Is Syndicated Lending?

A syndicated loan is a credit granted by a group of lenders, typically banks, to a borrower. Every lender has a *separate* claim on the borrower, even though there is a single loan agreement. There is typically an originating bank (or group of originating banks) that conducts the credit analysis prior to granting the loan and also negotiates the pricing structure of the loan. These originating banks, called the senior syndicate members, are appointed by the borrower and provide the key financial intermediation services of resolving precontract informational asymmetries and designing the loan contract. The others in the syndicate, called the junior banks, provide a portion of the funding. The numbers and identities of the juniors vary depending on the size, complexity, and pricing of the loan, as well as the borrower's willingness to expand its banking relationships.

Why do we observe syndicated lending? One of the main reasons is the need for the senior lenders to diversify their credit risk exposure. By inviting banks to participate, the seniors can avoid excessive exposure to a single borrower, while still earning a fee for their origination expertise, including contract design, pricing, and distribution services. That is, loan syndication is a way for the bank to solve an inherent tension between the benefits of specialization and the benefits of diversification.

---

1. See Dennis and Mullineaux (2000), Gadanecz (2004), and Allen (1990) for reviews of the syndicated lending market.

S. I. Greenbaum, A. V. Thakor & A. W. A. Boot: Contemporary Financial Intermediation, Third edition. http://dx.doi.org/10.1016/B978-0-12-405196-6.00009-4

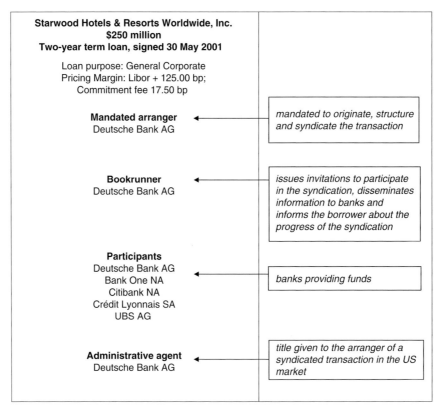

FIGURE 9.1 Example of a Simple Syndicate Structure: Starwood. *(Source: Dealogic and Gadanecz (2004)).*

For the junior lenders in the syndicate, syndication enables participation without the costs of origination expertise. That is, these banks can diversify their loan portfolio by adding credits that they lack the expertise to originate themselves. Moreover, it exposes the junior bank to the borrower, and therefore creates the possibility of a future relationship that is deeper and more profitable for the bank.

An example of a syndicated loan structure is provided in Figure 9.1. This syndicated loan took the form of a loan commitment (a topic discussed in greater depth in the next chapter) from a syndicate of banks to Starwood Hotels and Resorts Worldwide, Inc. in 2001. In this syndication, Deutsche Bank AG is the senior bank in the syndicate and Bank One NA, Citibank NA, Credit Lyonnais SA, and UBS AG are the juniors.

The Market for Syndicated Loans

Syndicated lending has been very popular in United States domestic lending for many decades. However, since the 1970s, the practice has become an important part of the international lending as well.

In the international market, loan syndications first developed as a sovereign lending business. In fact, just prior to the sovereign default by Mexico in 1982, most of the developing countries' debt consisted of syndicated loans. The repayment difficulties experienced by Mexico and other sovereign borrowers in the 1980s resulted in the restructuring of Mexican debt into Brady bonds in 1989.[2] As a consequence, emerging-market borrowers gravitated toward bond financing, causing a shrinkage in syndicated lending. A revival of syndicated lending occurred in the early 1990s, and syndicated lending became the biggest corporate finance market in the United States, as well as the largest source of underwriting revenue for lenders.[3] More recently, the 2007–2009 financial crisis has suppressed this market considerably.

---

2. A Brady bond is a U.S. dollar-denominated bond issued by an emerging market country, and collateralized by U.S. Treasury zero-coupon bonds. These bonds arose from efforts in the 1980s to reduce the debt burdens of less-developed countries that were prone to default. The bonds were named after U.S. Treasury Secretary Nicholas Brady, who helped international monetary organizations institute the debt-reduction program.

3. See Madan et al. (1999).

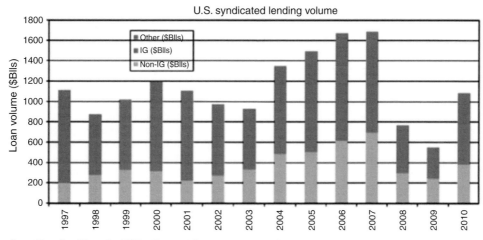

FIGURE 9.2   Syndicated Lending Since the 1997s. *(Source: ThomsonReuters LPC, and Smith et al. (2010)).*

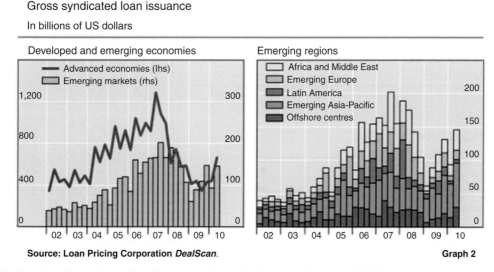

FIGURE 9.3   Syndicated Lending by Nationality of Borrower. *(Source: DealScan, and Chui et al., (2010)).*

Figure 9.2 shows the growth of syndicated lending in the United States.

By the beginning of the 1990s, banks operating in the syndication loan market had begun applying more sophisticated risk-management techniques, making more effective use of covenants and bond-pricing models. A secondary market for loan sales also began to develop as well, which began to attract nonbank financial firms like pension funds and insurance firms. Many banks began to view syndicated lending as a way to gain investment banking business. Moreover, borrowers from emerging markets began to find syndicated loans an attractive alternative and complement to other financing sources. Figure 9.3 shows syndicated lending activity in different regions around the world.

Commercial banks dominate the syndicated lending market, although investment banks became more active over time. Syndicated loans are also being increasingly traded on secondary markets, facilitated by the standardization of documentation for loan trading and its positive effect on syndicated-loan liquidity.[4]

Participants in the secondary market include: (i) market makers, (ii) active traders, and (iii) occasional sellers/investors. The market-makers are usually large commercial and investment banks. They take positions, commit capital, and create liquidity. Active traders are mainly investment and commercial banks, specialized distressed-debt traders and

---

4. The professional bodies responsible for initialing such standardization are the Loan Market Association (in Europe), the Asia Pacific Loan Market Association, and the U.S.-based Loan Syndication and Trading Association (LSTA).

institutional investors, called vulture funds, which trade distressed debt. Less active traders include insurance companies and nonfinancial corporations. Finally, there are also occasional participants who are either buyers or sellers of syndicated loans.[5]

The Brady Plan

The Brady Plan, first announced by U.S. Treasury Secretary Nicholas F. Brady in March 1989, was designed to address the debt crisis of the 1980s, which plagued some developing countries. The debt crisis began in 1982, when a number of countries, primarily in Latin America, confronted by high interest rates and low commodity prices, were on the verge of defaulting on their commercial bank loans. This caused credit flows to these countries to dry up, leading to economic stagnation.

The Brady Plan evolved in response to this crisis. Its main features were: (1) bank creditors would grant debt relief in exchange for greater assurance of collectability in the form of principal and interest collateral; (2) debt relief would be linked to some assurance of economic reform and (3) the resulting debt would be easier to trade, to allow creditors greater ability to diversify risk.

Because rescheduling occurred on a case-by-case basis, each Brady issue is unique, but most Brady restructurings included for the lenders a choice between exchanging their loans for either par bonds or discount bonds. Both par and discount bonds were 30-year collateralized bonds. Par bonds represent an exchange of loans for bonds of equal face amount, with a fixed, below-market rate of interest, permitting long-term debt service reduction through concessionary interest terms. Discount bonds represent an exchange of loans for a lesser amount of face value in bonds (generally a 30–50% discount), allowing for immediate debt reduction, with a market-based floating rate of interest. The principal of both par and discount bonds was secured at final maturity by a pledge of zero-coupon U.S. Treasury securities denominated in dollars. A portion of the interest payable on par and discount bonds (generally from 12 to 24 months coverage) was also secured by the pledge of high-grade investment securities.

The Brady Plan was successful in many respects. First, it allowed the participating countries to negotiate substantial reductions in their debt service obligations. Second, it helped commercial banks to diversify sovereign risk. Third, it encouraged many developing countries to adopt and pursue ambitious economic reforms. Finally, it has enabled many developing countries to regain access to international capital markets.

The Pricing of Syndicated Loans

Syndicated lending, in terms of the closeness of the relationship between the bank and the borrower, is somewhere between a relationship loan and a transaction loan (see Chapter 7).

The senior bank in the syndicate has a relationship with the borrower and thus, there are aspects of relationship lending that are embedded in a syndicated loan. However, the junior lenders in the syndicate are essentially making transaction loans.

The pricing structure of a syndicated loan resembles that of a loan commitment. A variety of fees are charged, as shown in Table 9.1.

In addition to the fees and the spread between the lending rate and the lender's cost of funds, various mechanisms are used to control risk exposure. These include guarantees, collateral, and covenants.

Banks have traditionally sold loans to other banks. Over time the volume has increased substantially.[6] An increasing number of banks are becoming involved in loan sales as buyers and sellers. Banks commonly employ asset sales specialists. Moreover, the number of banks selling loans through syndication has increased, and unlike traditional loan sales, an increasing number of loans (about 60%) are now being sold to buyers *outside* the U.S. correspondent banking network, mainly to foreign banks, other intermediaries, and nonfinancial firms. Maturities of loans sold range from 1 day to 2 years, with roughly 80% having maturities of 90 days or less.

What Is a Loan Sale?

A loan sale is similar to a loan syndication in that the originating bank is able to ensure that part of the funding for the loan comes from other lenders. There are two kinds of commercial loan sales: loan strips and loan participations. A loan strip

---

5. Banks may have a competitive advantage in the syndicated loan market via liquidity risk management. Gatev and Strahan (2009) point to the liquidity-providing role that banks play. Thakor (2005) develops a theory in which banks sell loan commitments as insurance against future credit rationing, that is, these are assurances of continued access to future liquidity for borrowers. See also Kashyap et al. (2002) and Pennacchi (2006). Nonbanking institutions are sporadically gaining position in loan syndicates (Lim et al., 2014). Funding though also comes from institutional investors (see Loan Syndications and Trading Association (2010)).

6. See Gadanecz (2004), Demsetz (2000), Gorton and Haubrich (1990), Gorton and Pennacchi (1995), and Pavel and Phillis (1987).

TABLE 9.1 Structure of Fees in a Syndicated Loan

Fee	Type	Remarks
Arrangement fee	Front-end	Also called *praecipium*. Received and retained by the lead arrangers in return for putting the deal together
Legal fee	Front-end	Remuneration of the legal adviser
Underwriting fee	Front-end	Price of the commitment to obtain financing during the first level of syndication
Participation fee	Front-end	Received by the senior participants
Facility fee	Per annum	Payable to banks in return for providing the facility, whether it is used or not
Commitment fee	Per annum, charged on undrawn part	Paid as long as the facility is not used, to compensate the lender for tying up the capital corresponding to the commitment
Utilization fee	Per annum, charged on drawn part	Boosts the lender's yield; enables the borrower to announce a lower spread to the market than what is actually being paid, as the utilization fee does not always need to be publicized
Agency fee	Per annum	Remuneration of the agent bank's services
Conduit fee	Front-end	Remuneration of the *conduit bank**
Prepayment fee	One-off if prepayment	Penalty for prepayment

*The institution through which payments are channeled with a view to avoiding payment of withholding tax. One important consideration for borrowers consenting to their loans being traded on the secondary market is avoiding withholding tax in the country where the acquirer of the loan is domiciled.
Source: Gadanecz (2004), Table 1.

is a short-term share of a long-term loan. When the strip comes due at the end of a given period (say 5, 30, or 60 days), the selling bank must repay the strip holder the contractual amount. In essence, funding has dried up for the loan at that point in time. To continue funding the loan, the originating bank must resell the strip for another period or provide funding itself.

A loan sale without recourse removes the loan from the seller's books and thus does not require reserves or capital to be held against it. In the 2007–2009 financial crisis, substantial grey areas were discovered where recourse arrangements (via guarantees and other assurances) continued to expose the original seller to the risks that many had assumed had been shed by the seller. These issues are not new. For example, it had been argued earlier that strips could expose banks to refunding risk. In January 1988, FASB determined that loan strips could be recorded as sales if: (i) the buyer of the strip assumes the full risk of loss, and (ii) the lender has no contractual obligation to repurchase the loan strip. The banking committee of the American Institute of Certified Public Accounts announced that it would treat a strip as a sale if, at the strip's maturity the original lender can refuse to lend because either: (i) the borrower violates a covenant in the loan contract, or (ii) a material adverse change (MAC) in the borrower's financial condition is discovered. Note that (ii) is the same as the standard MAC clause in loan commitments.

Loan Participation

Like syndicated lending, loan participation is a multilender financing arrangement. It differs from a loan strip in that it is an outright sale of a loan. Participations are loans where the lead lender ("Lead") sells a participation in a loan to one or more participation lenders.[7] The Lead continues to manage the loan on behalf of the participants. The relationship among the lenders is typically formalized in a participation agreement, which stipulates that the participant receives an undivided interest in the loan. The sale of the loan to participants typically occurs after the loan documentation has been executed by the Lead and the borrower. Unlike a syndicated loan, the participants do not contract directly with the borrower. The Lead negotiates the loan terms with the borrower, receives all the payments from the borrower, and collateral is maintained by the Lead in its own name. Participants make advances to the Lead, and these take the form of purchases of participation interests.

The advantage of being a participant rather than being a junior lender in a syndication is that the lender does not need a separate contract with the borrower and can deal solely with the Lead. Thus, a participation is very much like a pure transaction loan or capital market investment. The advantages of being a junior lender in a syndicate rather than a participant are twofold. One is that the junior lender does not have to worry about the additional risk that the Lead may become insolvent.

---

7. See Franks (2005) for a discussion.

The other is that the junior lender in a syndicate can hope to develop a relationship with the borrower, something that is less likely for a participant.

From the standpoint of the Lead, one advantage of a loan participation relative to a syndication is that it retains exclusive control over its relationship with the borrower and does not invite potential future competition for relationship lending from the junior lender in the syndicate. The advantage of a syndication for the senior lender is that, because the juniors have direct relationships with the borrowers, the senior lender can free up its own capital in an amount of credit extended by the junior lenders.

Choice Between Loan Syndication and Loan Sales

The syndicated loan market and the market for loan participations have developed because they offer distinct economic advantages for borrowers as well as lenders. For the borrowers, syndicated and participation loans offer some of the advantages of relationship borrowing along with some of the advantages of transaction borrowing (such as liquidity and hence a lower borrowing cost). For the senior lenders, loan syndication permits exploitation of their origination expertise in resolving precontract informational asymmetries and negotiating pricing terms, while also enables them to diversify their credit risk exposure. The same is true for the Lead in a participation loan. For junior lenders, the benefits of loan syndication include the ability to diversify into sectors in which they lack origination expertise and to possibly develop a relationship with the borrower which could be deepened in the future. For participants, the benefit of loan participation lies in the ability to diversify into credits where they lack relationship and/or origination expertise.

Moral Hazard and Reputation in Loan Sales and Syndicated Lending

In loan sales and syndicated lending, screening and monitoring of borrowers continues to be important. So very much in the spirit of the "banks are special" discussion in Chapter 3, banks need to have sufficient incentives to invest in screening and monitoring borrowers. However, since the lead bank in a syndicate has only a portion of the loan on its books, its incentives to engage in costly credit screening and monitoring of its loans are weaker than when the whole loan stays on its books. The same is true in loan sales. So, how can participating lenders be reassured that the lead bank will do adequate screening to ensure that only creditworthy borrowers are receiving loans?

One mechanism for this is reputation. Syndicated lending is a *repeated game*, with a great deal of reciprocity. A lead bank in one syndicate may later get invited to be a participant bank in another, or it may end up approaching the same participant banks to join a subsequent syndicate in which it is again the lead bank. If a bank establishes a poor reputation by making syndicated loans that default more than expected, it may have trouble finding participants in later deals, or it may have to take larger positions in those deals to reassure its syndicate partners that there was proper due diligence before the loan was originated.[8]

There is empirical evidence of such reputational effects in the syndicated market. In a study of the effect of large-scale bankruptcies among the borrowers of lead arrangers in loan syndicates, it was documented that such lead arrangers – who had demonstrably made poor loans that subsequently defaulted – suffered reputational damage and were less likely to subsequently syndicate loans. If they did succeed in subsequently syndicating loans, they were compelled to retain larger fractions of the loans and were less likely to attract other lenders to participate.[9]

PROJECT FINANCE

In this section, we first define project finance, the economic functions it serves, and why it has grown so much recently. We then examine the characteristics of the project financing market.

What Is Project Finance?

Project financing is a technique for financing large-scale infrastructure projects, including those in the natural-resource sectors, like energy and mining. Project financing is different in many respects from conventional financing. With project finance, the firm or public sponsor wishes to invest in a large project, and this is achieved by incorporating the project separately

8. This is also relevant in the context of securitization of syndicated loans, and the need for retention by the originator (see Altman (2012)). Sufi (2007) shows that lead banks retain a larger portion of syndicated loans when the borrower requires more intensive monitoring. We will discuss this in a later chapter on securitization (Chapter 11).
9. See Gopalan et al. (2011).

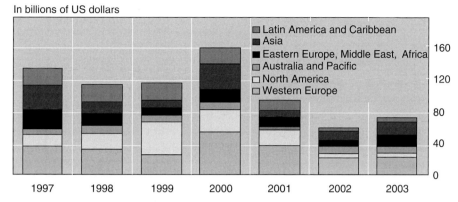

FIGURE 9.4   Project Finance Global Lending by Region. *Note:* The Amounts Shown Refer to New Bank Loan Commitments for Project Finance by Year and Region. *(Source: Dealogic ProjectWare database, and Sorge (2004)).*

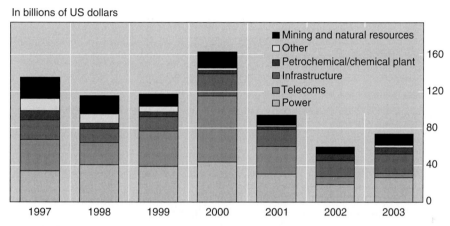

FIGURE 9.5   Project Finance Global Lending by Sector. *Note:* The Amounts Shown Refer to New Bank Loan Commitments for Project Finance by Year and Region. *(Source: Dealogic ProjectWare database, and Sorge (2004)).*

as an independent entity and seeking financing that represents a claim only on the cash flows of the projects. Typically, the sponsor, possibly with other sponsors like investment banks, invests some equity and then finances the rest of the project with debt that is typically *nonrecourse* to the sponsor. Nonrecourse debt means that the lenders have a claim only against the cash flows of the project and not against any other cash flows of the sponsor. The financing mix for the project typically involves a relatively high proportion of debt.

Why is project financing used? There are numerous reasons. First, because the cash flows of the project are *not* commingled with those of the sponsor, it is easier for lenders to resolve precontract informational asymmetries. This lowers information processing costs for the lender and therefore benefits the borrower. Second, the absence of cash flow commingling also means that the asset-substitution moral hazard is reduced. This not only lowers the borrower's cost of capital for financing the project, but also permits higher degrees of leverage to be used, generating a higher debt tax shield. Third, because multiple lenders are involved, the financing structure also has the risk-sharing advantages of syndicated lending. Finally, given the nonrecourse nature of the debt financing for the project, the sponsor does not expose itself to the risk of financial distress in case the project experiences difficulties. This is particularly important for large projects.

There are two reasons why project financing is not used for all projects. First, fixed costs are incurred in establishing a *special-purpose entity* (SPE) to incorporate the project independently. Second, the success of the project typically depends on the joint efforts of many different parties, so there are coordination costs. Project financing is attractive only when its benefits exceed these costs. Although project financing is a venerable practice, it has become an increasingly globalized business since the 1990s. In part this is due to the growing trend to privatize and deregulate many industries around the world.[10]

The trend in global project financing based on geography is shown in Figure 9.4 and by sector in Figure 9.5. The significant growth between 1998 and 2000 was in part due to the reallocation of global investors; portfolios from

---

10. For a theoretical insights on project financing see Shah and Thakor (1987). See also Sorge (2004) and Esty (2004).

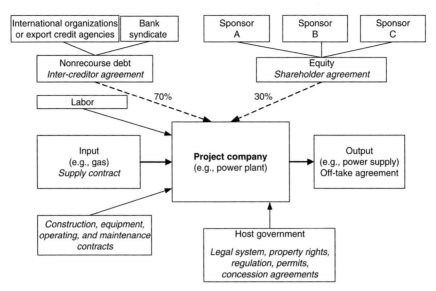

FIGURE 9.6 Typical Project Finance Structure. *Note:* A Typical Project Company is Financed with Limited or Nonrecourse (70%) and Sponsors' Equity (30%). It Buys Labor, Equipment and Other Inputs in Order to Produce a Tangible Output (Energy, Infrastructure, etc.). The Host Government Provides the Legal Framework Necessary for the Project to Operate. *(Source: Adapted from Esty, 2004, and Sorge, 2004).*

developing to industrialized economies following the East Asian crisis of 1998–1999 and new project financing investments in Europe and North America. After 2000, there was a global decline due to general economic slowdown in the early 2000s. Not reported in Figure 9.4 and Figure 9.5 is the fact that there was strong growth after 2004 which mirrored the direction of the syndicated loan market in Figure 9.2 (meaning strong growth before the 2007–2009 financial crisis, and lower levels later).

The long-term outlook for project financing is quite bullish. Future demand for infrastructure financing in developing as well as in industrialized countries is likely to grow faster than GDP.[11]

A typical project financing structure is the nexus of multiple contracting relationships as shown in Figure 9.6.

Hybrid structures that combine features of conventional financing and project financing are also being developed. With these structures, the debt financing provided to the project is still nonrecourse to the sponsor, but the idiosyncratic risk of the project is diversified away by lenders who finance *portfolios* of projects rather than single ventures. Moreover, some hybrid structures also involve partnerships between private companies and host governments with private financiers assuming construction and operating risks and host governments taking on market risks.

There are two interesting recent developments in the project finance market. One is the growing popularity of various forms of credit protection such as political risk guarantees, credit derivatives, and a variety of new insurance products that help financiers manage various risks. Second, project finance loans are also increasingly being securitized. This will add considerable liquidity to this market and lower borrowing costs for sponsors.

With such developments, the market for project finance could well begin to become more integrated with other financial markets. Figure 9.7 shows different financial arrangements available for infrastructure investments.

To summarize, project financing has grown in response to two market forces: (i) the need for borrowers to be able to obtain financing that is exclusively tied to the characteristics of the project and divorced from the sponsor's other cash flows, so as to reduce informational and agency costs, and permit higher leverage; and (ii) the need for lenders to reduce their credit risk exposure by breaking up the loan for a large project into smaller pieces that are financed by numerous lenders, with the possibility of "private–public partnerships" that involve participation by the local government. Project financing is an example of collaboration between commercial projects and investment projects to provide a variety of brokerage and qualitative asset-transformation services, such as resolution of precontract informational asymmetries, reduction of agency costs, and designing the loan contract so as to permit the borrower to obtain more leverage than would be otherwise possible.

---

11. See for example the OECD study by Della Croce and Gatti (2014).

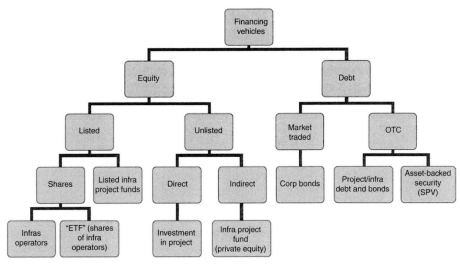

Source: Della Croce and Sharma (2014).

FIGURE 9.7   Different Channels for Infrastructure Investments.

CONCLUSION

In this chapter, we examined three special topics in lending: syndicated lending, loan sales, and project financing. One element that connects them is that project financing usually involves loan syndication as well. Loan syndication creates a loan that combines features of a relationship loan and a transaction loan, whereas project financing permits borrowers to undertake large infrastructure projects with significantly higher leverage than would be otherwise possible and with potential for risk sharing with governmental entities. Both syndicated lending and project financing involve loan commitments by lenders, a topic we will turn to in the next chapter.

REVIEW QUESTIONS

1. What is syndicated lending and what economic functions does it serve?
2. Why is a syndicated loan like a relationship loan and why is it like a transaction loan?
3. What roles do senior and junior lenders play in a syndicated loan?
4. What is project finance and what economic functions does it serve?
5. Why is leverage typically higher in project-financed ventures than in conventional financing?
6. Why is project financing typically used only for very large projects?
7. Why would securitization emerge in project financing? What are the parallels between this and the development of secondary market trading for syndicated loans?

REFERENCES

Allen, T., 1990. Developments in the International Syndicated Loan Market in the 1980s. Q. Bull. Bank England 30, 71–77.

Altman, A., 2012. Hide that syndicated junk in the closet! A case for credit risk retention in the CLO market. Chicago-Kent Law Rev. 87, 935–963.

Loan Syndications and Trading Association, presentation on the syndicated loan market, see http://www.cftc.gov/ucm/groups/public/@swaps/documents/ dfsubmission/dfsubmission_021711_535_0.pdf 2010.

Chui, M.K.F., Domanski, D., Kugler, P., Shek, J., 2010. The collapse of international bank finance during the crisis: evidence from syndicated loan markets. BIS Q. Rev.

Della Croce, R., Sharma, R., 2014. Pooling of Institutional Investors Capital, Selected Case Studies in Unlisted Equity Infrastructure. OECD Working Papers on Finance, Insurance and Private Pensions, No. 38, OECD.

Della Croce, R., Gatti, S., 2014. Financing infrastructure: international trends. OECD J.: Financ. Market Trends, 123–138.

Demsetz, R.S., 2000. Bank loan sales: A new look at the motivations for secondary market activity. J. Financ. Res. 23, 197–222.

Dennis, S.A., Mullineaux, D.J., 2000. Syndicated loans. J. Financ. Intermed. 9, 404–426.

Esty, B., 2004. Why study large projects? an introduction to research in project finance. Eur. Financ. Manag. 10, 213–224.

Franks, M.E., 2005. To participate or syndicate? That is the lender's question. Second Lender.

Gadanecz, B., 2004. The syndicated loan market: structure, development and implications. BIS Q. Rev. 75–89.

Gatev, E., Strahan, P.E., 2009. Liquidity risk and syndicate structure. J. Financ. Econ. 93, 490–504.

Gopalan, R., Nanda, V., Yerramilli, V., 2011. Does poor performance damage the reputation of financial intermediaries? Evidence from the loan syndication market. J. Finance 66 (6), 2083–2120.

Gorton, G.B., Haubrich, J.G., 1990. The loan sales market. In: George Kaufman (Ed.), Research in Financial Services 2, 85–135.

Gorton, G., Pennacchi, G., 1995. Banks and loan sales: marketing nonmarketable assets. J. Monetary Econ. 35, 389–411.

Kashyap, A.K., Rajan, R., Stein, J.C., 2002. Banks as liquidity providers: an explanation for the coexistence of lending and deposit-taking. J. Financ. 57, 33–74.

Lim, J., Minton, B.A., Weisbach, M.S., 2014. Syndicated loan spreads and the composition of the syndicate. J. Financ. Econ. 111, 45–69.

Madan, R., Sobhani, R., Horowitz, K., 1999. "Syndicated Lending", PianeWebber Equity Research Report.

Pavel, C., Phillis, D., 1987. "To sell or not to sell: loan sales by commercial banks," mimeo, Federal Reserve Bank of Chicago.

Pennacchi, G., 2006. Deposit insurance, bank regulation and financial system risks. J. Monetary Econ. 53, 1–30.

Shah, S., Thakor, A.V., 1987. Optimal capital structure and project financing. J. Econ. Theory 42, 209–243.

Sorge, M., 2004. The nature of credit risk in project finance. BIS Q. Rev., 91–102.

Sufi, A., 2007. Information asymmetry and financing arrangements: Evidence from syndicated loans. J. Financ. 62, 629–668.

Thakor, A., 2005. Do loan commitments cause overlending? J. Money, Credit Banking 37, 1067–1100.

Part V

Off the Bank's Balance Sheet

Chapter 10

Off-Balance Sheet Banking and Contingent Claims Products

"Has the attention paid to simple capital-asset ratios driven risks off balance sheet, and is off balance sheet also out of mind?"

Paul Volcker, *Chairman of the Board of Governors of the Federal Reserve system,*
in an address to the American Bankers Association, October 1985

GLOSSARY OF TERMS

Cost of Funds The effective rate paid by the bank to fund its assets. Source of funds include retail deposits, large-denomination certificates of deposit (CDs), senior and junior debt, preferred stock, and common stock.

Sunk Cost A cost that has already been incurred and cannot be recovered. Such a cost is irrelevant to a current decision because no matter what the decision, the sunk cost is not affected.

LIBOR London Interbank Offer Rate. This is the rate banks charge each other for short-term loans (usually overnight). It is a benchmark interest rate used by banks worldwide.

T-bill Rate Discount rate on short-maturity debt obligation issued by the U.S. Treasury.

Basis Point One hundredth of 1%.

Liability Management The management of the bank's sources of funding (see Chapter 12).

Derivative A financial contract, also called a contingent claim, whose value depends on the values of one or more of the underlying assets or indices of asset values. For example, Treasury-bill futures derive their value from movements in the T-bill rate. Bank regulators and banks themselves refer to derivatives more narrowly as contracts, such as forwards, futures, swaps, and options, whose primary purpose is not to borrow and lend but rather to transfer risks associated with fluctuations in asset and liability values.

Initial Public Offering A public stock offering that converts a privately held firm into a publicly held corporation.

INTRODUCTION

Once negligible in amount, and therefore worthy of no more than passing mention in banking texts, *off-balance sheet (OBS) items* of banks now amount to trillions of dollars in the United States. They include *contingent claims* that represent a variety of exposures across markets and credit risks – standby letters of credit (L/Cs), interest rate and currency swaps, note issuance facilities (NIF), options, foreign currencies, fixed- and variable-rate loan commitments, and futures and forward contracts on everything from Treasury bills to gold. Loan commitments are among the largest components of the OBS items of banks. Also, when added together, OBS items exceed the total recorded assets of most large banks. This is a little misleading, however, since only some contingent claims impose a (contingent) liability on the bank, and this *contingent liability* is only a fraction of the nominal amount of its outstanding contingent claims. Nonetheless, these data highlight the enormous importance of OBS items in the current banking environment. The enormous growth in contingent claims of banks has coincided with an explosion in the growth of exchange-traded contingent claims like options and futures. Figure 10.1 depicts the global growth of exchange-traded options and futures.

In this chapter, we focus on "OBS banking." OBS banking refers to transactions that do not appear on the bank's balance sheet, except possibly as footnotes. OBS items can be divided into two groups: option-like contingent claims and nonoption contingent claims. Table 10.1 shows the various items within each group. Any contingent claim involves a *commitment* on the part of the bank. According to *Webster's* dictionary, a "commitment" is a promise to do something in the future. An option-like contingent claim is a *promise* by the bank to settle in the future at prespecified terms and at the *option* of the holder of the commitment. Thus, an option-like contingent claim imposes a contingent liability on the bank (the seller) and endows the buyer of the commitment with an option. In a competitive market for contingent claims, the bank should be paid a fee at the time the contingent claim is sold which equals the value of the option contained in that claim. Nonoption contingent claims may also involve fees for the bank, but they do not necessarily impose a contingent liability on the bank because there is a symmetry in the obligations of the bank and the customer. Thus, even though there is a future

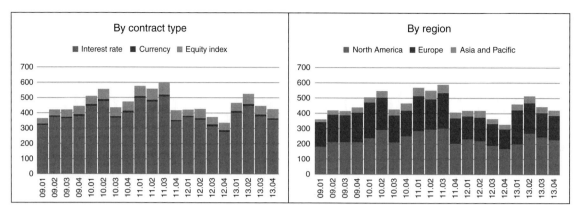

FIGURE 10.1 Volume of Exchange-Traded Futures and Options. The x axis indicates years and quarters (year.quarter). The y axis indicates volumes in trillions of dollars. *(Source: BIS Quarterly Review detailed Statistical Annex – June 2009, 2010, 2011, 2012, and 2013).*

TABLE 10.1 Off-balance Sheet Items

Item Classification	Item
Option-like contingent claims	1) Loan commitments and guarantees
	2) Options
	3) Standby letters of credit
Nonoption contingent claims	1) Interest rate swaps excluding those involving options
	2) Foreign currency transactions involving future settlement
	3) Futures and forward contracts

contingency that determines the settlement of the contract, it need not give the customer an option. For example, a forward or futures contract is a nonoption contingent claim.

OBS banking started growing explosively in the 1970s and 1980s partly because it was during this period that interest rates and foreign-exchange rates became increasingly volatile. This increased volatility in financial and foreign-exchange markets and created a strong demand from corporations for financial risk-management services. Banks found it profitable to provide these services. Thus, German companies that once borrowed only in D-marks but derived income in other currencies from their foreign operations were now helped by banks to control their foreign-exchange risk. Similarly, technology-intensive firms for whom unpredictable short-term revenues imposed severe constraints on research and development (R&D) budgets, approached banks that provided products designed to hedge overseas income and plan R&D over longer periods. The growth of OBS banking was a natural outgrowth of banks seeking to offer risk-management services.

A bank's customer faces two main types of risks. The first is business risk. It may be routine, such as that arising from unpredictable shifts in demand for the firm's output. Or it may be strategic, such as that faced by a defense firm faced with lower demand for arms following the end of the Cold War. The second type of risk is financial. For example, this is the risk of being rationed in the credit market, and the risk of abrupt random movements in interest rates, commodity prices, or currencies. This is where banks enter. They offer loan commitments that can simultaneously guarantee credit availability and interest rate insurance. And banks can offer a variety of derivatives to hedge unpredictable price movements in volatile markets.

While derivatives and other OBS items have been around for a long time,[1] they became widely used only when risk escalated sufficiently. Initially, banks were not involved in the action. Futures and options were offered mainly by organized exchanges such as the Chicago Mercantile Exchange (CME) and the Chicago Board of Trade (part of the CME Group since 2007) before banks became heavily involved. These were standard contracts for hedging price risk of commodities and later financial claims. However, when corporations wanted products tailored to their specific needs, they turned to banks for those products. This demand led to a variety of custom-tailored contracts such as loan commitments, forward contracts, and swaps.

Banks were interested in custom-designing contingent claims for their clients not only to strengthen customer relationships, but also because sales of contingent claims have proved to be a source of fee income. There are two popularly cited

---

1. For example, in existence are certificates dating back to 1863, when London bankers, working for the Confederate States of America, raised a dual-currency loan with a coupon linked to future cotton prices.

advantages of OBS banking. First, since OBS banking does not involve deposit funding, cash-asset reserves are not needed, and the implicit tax of reserve requirements is avoided. Second, in the past, banks were not required to maintain capital against OBS contingencies, although they have been required to do so since the adoption of the guidelines associated with the first Basel Capital Accord in 1987.[2]

In the previous three chapters we discussed the spot lending activities of banks. Our focus in this chapter is on *forward* markets. The rest of the chapter is organized as follows. In the next section we describe loan commitments. Economic rationales for the use of loan commitments are provided in the section that follows. Issues related to the valuation (pricing) of loan commitments are examined next. This is followed by a discussion of the differences between exchange-traded put options and loan commitments, and a discussion of the impact of loan commitments on the monetary policy. Then, in the next two sections we explain two other contingent claims: L/Cs and interest rate swaps. The issues of risks for banks offering contingent claims are taken up subsequently. The regulatory aspects of contingent claims are taken up next. This is followed by the conclusion of the chapter. A case study is provided to illustrate some of the issues facing a bank that sells contingent claims.

LOAN COMMITMENTS: A DESCRIPTION

Definition and Pricing Structure

A loan commitment is a promise to lend up to a prespecified amount to a prespecified customer at prespecified terms. Such a promise is tenable for a prespecified time period (not to be confused with the maturity of the loan). The terms usually specify how the interest rate on the loan will be computed, the maturity of the loan, and the use to which borrowed funds will be put. The bank's compensation for selling the commitment comes in a variety of forms, used in various combinations. It can take the form of a *commitment fee* that is expressed as a percentage of the total commitment and paid up front by the borrower when the commitment is negotiated. It can also take the form of a *usage fee* that is levied on the unused portion of the credit line (e.g., 25–50 basis points per year). Quite often, commitment and usage fees are employed simultaneously. Also frequently used are *servicing fees* on the borrowed amount to cover the bank's transactions costs, and *compensating balance requirements* that are deposit balances the borrower must keep with the bank during the period of their commitment relationship. These balances are computed as fractions of the total commitment and the bank pays below-market interest rates on these balances.

Table 10.2 gives a detailed description of an actual loan commitment contract. This contract illustrates an innovation in loan commitments, namely offering the customer a choice among rate bases. In this case, Blockbuster Entertainment can borrow at the prime rate, the LIBOR plus 0.5%, or the CD rate plus 0.625%. The choice increases the customer's flexibility and therefore enhances the commitment's value.

TABLE 10.2 Key Terms of a Loan Commitment Contract

Blockbuster Entertainment	
Amount	$200,000,000
Maturity	48 Months
Beginning	8-31-1990
Lender	Security Pacific
Use	General Corporate Purposes
Fee Structure	
Commitment fee	0
Annual servicing fee	12.5 basis points
Usage fee	12.5 basis points
Cancellation fee	0
Take-Down Interest Rate Alternatives	
Prime	
LIBOR + 50 basis points	
CD + 62.5 basis points	

---

2. Also called Basel I Accord. See for a history: BIS (2014).

Uses of Loan Commitments

Most business loans are made under loan commitments. The latest statistics are that 77% of new commercial loans in an average U.S. bank's portfolio are made under loan commitments, with only 23% being spot loans, and 46% of banks make *no* spot loans at all.[3] Loans made under commitments include construction and land-development loans, as well as loans to finance leveraged buyouts (LBOs) and mergers and acquisitions (M&A). Loan commitments also include backup lines of credit on commercial paper (the bank agrees to lend to the customer as an alternative to issuing paper) and NIF (in which the bank agrees to buy the short-term notes of a borrower if the latter is unable to sell them in the markets).

Kinds of Loan Commitments

In addition to use, loan commitments can be classified according to the nature of the interest rate insurance provided to the customer.

Commitments vary in the extent to which they provide interest rate insurance to the borrower. A *fixed-rate* loan commitment gives the customer the right to borrow at an interest rate that is known in advance and hence eliminates all interest rate and availability uncertainty. The more popular *variable-rate* (or fixed formula) loan commitment does not hold the borrowing rate fixed. Rather, it determines the rate according to a formula that involves some index rate. Two common formulas are: additive and multiplicative. The additive version of the variable-rate loan commitment stipulates a borrowing rate that is an index rate at the time of takedown plus a fixed add-on. The less frequently used multiplicative version stipulates a borrowing rate that is an index rate at the time of takedown multiplied by a specified constant. Commonly used index rates are the prime rate, the CD rate, the LIBOR, and the commercial paper rate. Customers may also be offered a choice of formula within a given commitment, for example, prime plus 10 basis points or 1.1 times the CD rate at the time of the borrowing.

Relative to a fixed-rate commitment, a variable-rate commitment does not provide the customer protection against stochastic fluctuations in the index rate. However, as long as there is an element of *fixity* in the borrowing rate, the commitment will have some insurance value to the customer. In the prime-plus commitment, the add-on is held fixed. The customer is thus insured against its add-on being increased due to a possible increase in its credit risk during the commitment period. Likewise, in the prime-times commitment, the multiple is held fixed. In both cases, the customer's commitment borrowing rate at the time of commitment takedown may be lower than the spot rate it would have faced in the absence of the commitment.

Although a loan commitment obliges a bank to lend at a rate below the borrower's spot rate, the bank usually has some latitude in determining whether or not to honor a commitment, even in the case of the most formal agreement. This latitude arises from the adoption of a "general nervous clause" or a "material adverse change" (MAC) clause, which is standard in virtually all loan commitment contracts. This clause allows the bank to dissolve the commitment if the customer's financial condition has "materially" deteriorated between the time the commitment was issued and the time the customer can exercise it. What constitutes material deterioration can, of course, become a legal issue should the denied customer decide to challenge the bank's assessment through litigation. This clause does, however, introduce an element of discretion into the loan commitment contract.

A Summary

We can depict a loan commitment contract as in Figure 10.2. It should be clear by now that a loan commitment is a contingent claim. The contract's contingency hinges upon the interest rate applicable to the specific borrower at the time of commitment takedown. If the spot rate is higher than the commitment rate, the customer will exercise the commitment and the bank will suffer a loss, if only an opportunity loss. If the spot rate is exceeded by the commitment rate, the customer will let the commitment expire unused and borrow instead in the spot market.[4] Thus, the bank has an obligation and the customer has an option. The bank has a loss in those states of nature in which the customer will exercise the commitment, and this loss is contingent on the occurrence of those states of nature.

---

3. See Huang (2010).

4. A usage fee alters this simple decision rule. In its presence, the customer will access the spot market only if the *effective* cost of spot borrowing – and that includes the price the customer must pay for not using the line – is lower than the commitment borrowing rate.

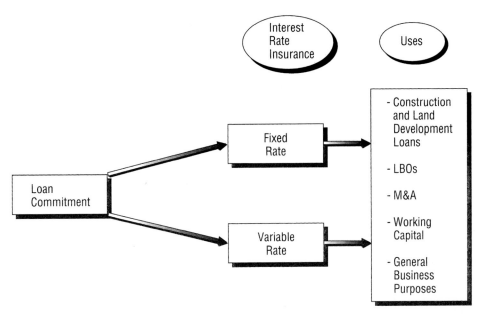

FIGURE 10.2   Depiction of Loan Commitment Classification.

RATIONALE FOR LOAN COMMITMENTS

In this section, we offer several explanations for the growing importance of commitments.

Supply-Side Explanations

The supply-side explanations for loan commitments attempt to shed light on the popularity of loan commitments by examining the incentives that banks (the suppliers of loan commitments) have to sell the contracts.

Regulatory Taxes

Some believe that loan commitments have been popular because they permit banks to generate fee revenue while keeping only minimal additional capital to support the loan commitments.[5] Moreover, until the commitment is actually taken down, there is no loan, which means no funding has actually taken place. Consequently, the bank needs no deposits until commitment takedown, which implies that reserve requirements[6] do not affect the commitment until that time. In fact, if the bank is interested only in generating the fee income related to the loan commitment, it could sell the commitment and avoid funding the (potential) loan under the commitment altogether. This could be achieved by selling the loan to another bank if and when the customer decides to exercise the commitment. Similarly, the bank could securitize the loan.

Contractual Discretion and Reputation

Another supply-side explanation for the growth in contingent claims relies upon the notion that banks face a trade-off between financial and reputational capital. Simply put, it says that since contingent claims are promises to deliver something in the future, but invariably involve "escape clauses" that introduce contractual discretion and permit the bank to not honor its promises under "extenuating" circumstances, issuing such claims gives the bank improved ability to manage its overall portfolio of *financial* and reputational capital.[7] Consider a bank that has built up a reputation for honoring its contingent

---

5. Under the Basel I Capital Accord of 1987, banks were required, for the first time, to hold capital against loan commitments, but only if the commitment maturity exceeded one year. This led to a proliferation of 364-day commitments. Under Basel III, a loan commitment of one-year or less maturity will be assessed a credit conversion factor of 20%, and those with maturity exceeding one year will be assessed a credit conversion factor of 50%.

6. Banks are required to hold "reserves" against their deposit liabilities (see Chapter 2). Various assets qualify as legal reserves, including cash in vault, deposits with the Federal Reserve, and so on. These reserve requirements vary depending on the nature of the bank's deposit liability. We will have more to say about this in later chapters.

7. This explanation is based on the theory of Boot et al. (1993).

claims even in circumstances where provisions in the terms of its contract with the other party would give it the latitude not to. For example, a bank may have agreed to a $100 million credit line at 10% interest to a customer whose spot borrowing rate at the time of commitment takedown is 15% and whose financial condition at that time is sufficiently murky to enable the bank to invoke the MAC clause and deny credit. Yet a bank with sufficient financial capital may permit the customer to exercise the commitment because this allows the bank to build up its reputational capital. Such reputational capital is of value since it enables the bank to sell *future* contingent claims at higher prices. Now suppose a bank that has accumulated quite a bit of such reputational capital but finds financial capital in scarce supply is faced with the same decision. Such a bank may well decide to invoke the MAC clause and not honor the commitment. This will result in some depreciation of its reputational capital, but it will conserve scarce financial capital. Thus, the decision to not honor the commitment can be seen as an optimal trade-off by the bank between its reputational and financial capital, and it is essentially an act of *liquefying* its reputational capital; note that, unlike the bank's financial capital, its reputational capital cannot (with good reason) be *directly* traded. In a later section, we discuss a Security Pacific interest rate swap deal where contractual discretion is employed to write down reputational capital.

You should note that the ability to introduce discretion into a contract is predicated on the contract involving the promise of *future* delivery, as a contingent claim does. Moreover, discretion in the loan commitment contract is beneficial because it permits the bank to trade off liquid against illiquid assets.

Demand Forecasting

By participating in the loan commitment market, the bank can obtain valuable information about future loan demand. The reason is that customers will purchase commitments for amounts that are related to their expected future borrowing needs. This permits the bank to plan its funding and other activities accordingly. The question we turn to next is why customers would demand loan commitments.

Scope Efficiencies in the Sale of Loan Commitments for Deposit-Financed Banks

Banks are financed to a large extent with demand deposits, so they have access to a large amount of cash. While some of this is loaned out, banks need to keep substantial liquidity on hand to meet deposit withdrawals, which can occur at a moment's notice. Once this liquidity is on hand, there are scope economies from being able to use this liquidity to allow borrowers to borrow under loan commitments. That is, cash assets on the bank's balance sheet serve *two* purposes: backing up loan commitments and also having liquidity on hand to meet deposit withdrawals.[8]

Demand-Side Explanations

Demand-side explanations focus on the benefits of loan commitments to the purchaser. Many benefits have been identified, five of which are discussed below.

Risk-Sharing Considerations[9]

As discussed in Chapter 4, banks sometimes mismatch their balance sheets in order to profit from the term premiums in the term structure of interest rates. That is but one way for banks to increase expected profits by taking on interest rate risk. Loan commitments provide another. When a bank sells a fixed-rate loan commitment, it accepts the interest rate risk that the customer would otherwise bear if it were to borrow in the spot market for credit. The customer should, of course, be willing to compensate the bank for taking this risk, and this compensation should be reflected in the price paid for the loan commitment.

Borrowers who are more risk averse than the bank should be willing to pay the bank for taking interest rate risk on their behalf. In other words, the risk premium demanded by the bank for bearing interest rate risk will be lower than that demanded by the customer for bearing the same risk if the latter is more risk averse than the former. Such a disparity in risk preferences makes trade possible between the bank and the customer, involving the bank selling the borrower a loan

---

8. Kashyap et al. (2002) proposed this theory. See also Gatev and Strahan (2006) and Gatev et al. (2009). During pronounced crises, however, borrowers can massively draw on unused credit lines which can build up liquidity risk in banks leading to a sharp decline in lending (Millon Cornett et al. (2011), and Acharya and Mora (2015)).

9. Loan commitment demand based on optimal risk-sharing considerations was first formally proposed by Campbell (1978). Also see Holmstrom and Tirole (1993) and Jiménez et al. (2009).

commitment that reduces uncertainty regarding the customer's future borrowing cost. With a variable-rate loan commitment, the bank still bears some interest rate risk but less than with a fixed-rate commitment. In essence, with a fixed-rate commitment the bank bears both the risk of changes in the index rate as well as of changes in the borrower's credit risk premium, whereas with a variable-rate commitment the bank bears only the latter risk. In either case, the risk-averse borrower is transferring (some) interest rate risk to the bank, and to the extent that the bank is willing to participate at a price that is acceptable to the borrower, we have an explanation for why loan commitments are demanded by the bank's customers.[10]

Moral Hazard

One drawback of the previous explanation is that many loan commitment customers are large, publicly owned firms with numerous shareholders. From the portfolio theory we know that even risk-averse shareholders should be indifferent to firm-specific (idiosyncratic) risk because they can diversify it away. Moreover, it is not clear why shareholders of nonbank firms should collectively demand a higher premium for bearing systematic risk than the bank's shareholders do.[11] So we would like to know if there will be a demand for loan commitments even when the bank's customers are not motivated by the desire to purchase insurance against interest rate risk.

One possibility is that loan commitments are effective in deterring *moral hazard*. The source of the moral hazard may be an incentive on the borrower's part to undersupply productive effort (relative to the case in which the borrower self-finances) or switch projects (in an undetected manner) to the bank's detriment. The intuition is as follows. We know from our discussions in Chapter 8 that the loan interest rate is distortionary in the sense that the higher this rate, the lower is the net return accruing to the borrower, and hence the greater is the borrower's incentive to reduce effort and/or switch to a riskier project. The consequences can be costly – the borrower may either need to post collateral or in extreme circumstances the bank may ration credit. A loan commitment provides a means for the bank to circumvent the distortionary effect of the loan interest rate without relying on more costly alternatives. This can be achieved by lowering the interest rate on the loan to a level sufficient to eliminate (or significantly diminish) moral hazard. This will generally mean that the bank will suffer an expected loss on the loan made under the commitment. This loss can be recouped through the commitment fee paid by the borrower at the time the commitment is made. The key is that the customer views the commitment fee as a sunk cost after it is paid, and hence the commitment fee does not affect either the level of effort or choice of project. In this way, the loan commitment helps to overcome moral hazard. The following example illustrates the point.

Example 10.1

Suppose the management of Knight Apparel Company knows at $t = 0$ that it will have available at $t = 1$ an opportunity to invest $100 in a risky project that will pay off at $t = 2$. Knight Apparel knows that it will be able to invest in one of two mutually exclusive projects, S or R, each requiring a $100 investment. If Knight Apparel invests in S at $t = 1$, the project will pay off $150 with probability 0.9 and zero with probability 0.1 at $t = 2$. If Knight Apparel invests in R at $t = 1$, the project will pay off $158 with probability 0.7 and zero with probability 0.3 at $t = 2$. Knight Apparel's project choice is not observable to the bank from which it seeks to borrow the $100.

The riskless, single-period interest rate at $t = 0$ is 10%. It is not known at $t = 0$ what the riskless, single-period interest rate at $t = 1$ will be, but it is common knowledge that this rate will be 5% with probability 0.5 or 15% with probability 0.5. Assume universal risk neutrality and that Knight Apparel has no assets other than the project on which you (as the lender) can have any claim. Figure 10.3 depicts these data.

Suppose you are Knight Apparel's banker and you know that Knight has two choices: (i) It can wait until $t = 1$ and then borrow in the spot market or (ii) it can purchase a loan commitment that will permit it to borrow at predetermined rates at $t = 1$. What advice would you give Knight Apparel? Assume a competitive loan market in which banks earn zero expected profits.

Solution

We solve this problem in six steps. First, we consider alternative (i) and show that it is a Nash equilibrium for Knight Apparel to choose S at $t = 1$ if the spot riskless rate then is 5%. Second, we continue with alternative (i) and show that this Nash equilibrium

---

10. Acharya et al. (2013) argue that banks provide liquidity to firms by pooling their idiosyncratic risks. Consequently, firms opt for credit lines especially if they are exposed to idiosyncratic risk rather than aggregate risk. Almeida et al. (2011) argue that firms secure high liquidity positions through credit lines for acquisition purposes.

11. Ignore for the time being the *risk-seeking* incentives provided to the bank's shareholders by the bank's access to a lender-of-last-resort facility and deposit insurance. We wish to focus for now on the possible economic motives for loan commitments, *abstracting* from the facilitating influence of regulation.

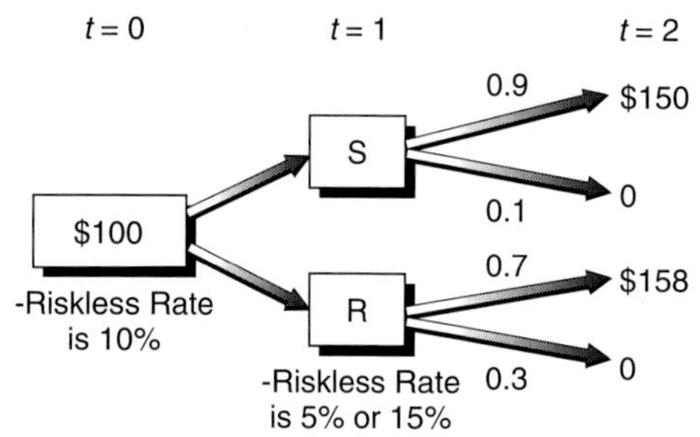

FIGURE 10.3   Investment Opportunities for Knight Apparel.

fails to exist if the spot riskless rate at $t = 1$ is 15%. The reason is that the high interest rate diverts "too much" of Knight Apparel's cash flow into repaying the bank loan, so that the borrower prefers to gamble on the riskier investment R which, despite its lower success probability, gives Knight Apparel a higher *net* payoff in the successful state. The bank must therefore price the loan under the assumption that R will be chosen. But then the interest rate is so high that Knight Apparel declines the loan. Third, we point out that passing up the investment opportunity in the high-interest-rate state is socially wasteful because S has a positive total NPV even when the riskless rate is 15%. Fourth, we consider alternative (ii), and design a loan commitment contract that induces Knight Apparel to invest in S regardless of the spot riskless rate. Fifth, we solve for the commitment fee so that the bank can earn (at least) zero expected profit on the loan and the loan commitment taken together. Finally, in Step 6 we calculate the *net* benefit of the loan commitment to Knight Apparel and show that it is positive.

Step 1

Consider alternative (i). Suppose the interest rate at $t = 1$ is 5% and you assume that Knight Apparel will choose S. Then the interest rate, i_s, that you should charge the borrower in order to just break even on the loan is obtained as a solution to the following equation:

$$0.9 \times (1 + i_s) = 1.05 \tag{10.1}$$

where 0.9 is the probability that you will be repaid by Knight Apparel. Solving Equation (10.1) gives $i_s = 16.67\%$. If Knight Apparel chooses S, its expected payoff at $t = 2$ is

$$0.9 \times (150 - 116.67) = \$30 \text{ approximately.}$$

On the other hand, if Knight Apparel chooses R, its expected payoff at $t = 2$ is

$$0.7 \times (158 - 116.67) = \$28.93.$$

Thus, Knight Apparel will prefer S to R, and it is a Nash equilibrium for you to offer a $100 loan at 16.67%.[12]

Step 2

Now suppose the interest rate at $t = 1$ is 15%. If you assume that Knight Apparel will choose S, then you should charge an interest rate, i'_s, that solves the following equation

$$0.9 \times (1 + i'_s) = 1.15 \tag{10.2}$$

Solving Equation (10.2) yields $i'_s = 27.78\%$. If Knight Apparel does indeed choose S, its expected payoff at $t = 2$ will be

$$0.9 \times (150 - 127.78) = \$20 \text{ approximately.}$$

On the other hand, if Knight Apparel chooses R, its expected payoff at $t = 2$ will be

$$0.7 \times (158 - 127.78) = \$21.15.$$

Clearly, Knight Apparel will prefer R to S, and it is *not* a Nash equilibrium for you to offer the loan at 27.78%. But suppose you assume that Knight Apparel will choose R. Then, the interest rate, i'_R, that you should charge solves

$$0.7(1 + i'_R) = 1.15,$$

---

12. Note that this Nash equilibrium is not unique. If you assume that the borrower will choose R, then the loan interest rate you should charge is the solution to $0.7(1 + i_s) = 1.05$, which yields $i_R = 50\%$. Now the borrower's expected payoff at $t = 2$ form choosing S is zero and its expected payoff at $t = 2$ from choosing R is $0.7(158 - 150) = \$5.6$. Thus, the borrower strictly prefers R to S, and it is also a Nash equilibrium for you to offer the loan at 50%. However, the Nash equilibrium we have focused on (i.e., one involving a 16.67% interest rate) is strictly preferred by the borrower (lower interest rate and strictly higher expected rate) and you, as the lender, are indifferent because you make zero expected profit in each Nash equilibrium. Thus, competition among banks will ensure that the Nash equilibrium involving the 16.67% loan interest rate will prevail.

which yields $i_R' = 64.29\%$. However, at this interest rate Knight Apparel will not borrow since its repayment obligation would exceed the maximum cash flow of the project.

Step 3

What this implies is that if Knight Apparel can only borrow in the spot market, it will invest only if the risklesss rate at $t = 1$ is 5%. If the rate is 15%, Knight Apparel will pass up its investment opportunity. This is a distortion in the following sense. Even when the riskless interest rate is 15%, project S has a positive total NPV, even though its NPV to Knight Apparel's shareholders is not positive. If Knight Apparel could somehow convince a bank that it would choose S if given a loan, the bank would be willing to extend the loan at terms that would enable the bank to break even and leave Knight Apparel with a positive NPV. However, credible communication from Knight Apparel to the bank may not always be possible (we have assumed that it is not), and if it is not, the bank must anticipate that Knight Apparel will act in its own best interest. The consequence is a bank loan that Knight is unwilling to accept, and a social waste represented by the foregone positive NPV of project S.

Step 4

We will now show that a loan commitment, negotiated at $t = 0$, can avoid this moral-hazard-induced loss. Suppose that under arrangement (ii), you offer to lend Knight Apparel $100 (if Knight Apparel wishes to take the loan) at $t = 1$ at an interest rate of 16.67%, regardless of the spot riskless rate at that time. This is a fixed-rate loan commitment. As our analysis so far has indicated, Knight Apparel will opt for S under these terms, so that your bank will break even on the loan if the riskless rate at $t = 1$ is 5%. Of course, if the riskless rate is 15%, you will lose money on the risky loan since you should be charging an interest rate of 27.78% in that case.[13] To recoup this loss, you should charge Knight Apparel a commitment fee at $t = 0$. What should this commitment fee be?

Step 5

To answer this question, note that your bank's loss, in terms of the amount that should be repaid in the successful state minus the amount that is actually repaid in the successful state, is

$$\$127.78 - \$116.67 = \$11.11.$$

The bank suffers this loss at $t = 2$ only if Knight Apparel's project succeeds (the bank also suffers a loss if Knight Apparel's project fails, but in that state the bank recovers nothing in either case), and the probability of success is 0.9. Hence, the bank's expected loss is

$$0.9 \times \$11.11 = \$9.999.$$

Since the probability of the 15% interest rate is 0.5 and we must discount from $t = 2$ back to $t = 1$ (at 15%) and from $t = 1$ back to $t = 0$ (at the 10% riskless rate prevailing at $t = 0$), we have the following present value at $t = 0$ of the bank's expected loss at $t = 2$

Thus, the commitment fee that the bank should charge Knight Apparel is $3.95, given a zero expected profit on the loan *and* the loan commitment. It is important to note that Knight Apparel pays the commitment fee at $t = 0$, so that when it confronts its project choice at $t = 1$ it treats this fee as a sunk cost and its project choice is not affected by it.

Step 6

We can compute the overall benefit from the loan commitment by comparing Knight Apparel's NPV under arrangements (i) and (ii). Under (i), since borrowing only takes place when the spot riskless rate at $t = 1$ is 5%, Knight Apparel's NPV is

$$\frac{0.5 \times \$30.00}{1.05 \times 1.10} = \$12.99$$

where you will recall that $30 is Knight Apparel's net expected payoff at $t = 2$ when it chooses S and is obliged to repay the bank $116.67 (an interest rate of 16.67%). Under (ii), the expected NPV is

$$\underbrace{\frac{0.5 \times \$30.00}{1.05 \times 1.10}}_{\substack{\text{(riskless rate at} \\ t = 1 \text{ is 5 percent)} \\ = \$20.90}} + \underbrace{\frac{0.5 \times \$30.00}{1.05 \times 1.10}}_{\substack{\text{(riskless rate at} \\ t = 1 \text{ is 5\%)}}} - \underbrace{\$3.95}_{\text{(commitment fee)}}$$

Thus, Knight Apparel experiences a *net* gain of $7.91 (which is $20.90–$12.99) by purchasing the loan commitment. Note that this improvement is the net of the commitment fee.

In this example, the loan commitment was useful in overcoming the moral hazard created by the possibility of undetected asset substitution by the borrower. A similar argument works for "effort aversion" moral hazard, and it suggests that

---

13. Note that the 27.78% interest rate is the correct breakeven rate for banks when the borrower chooses S. This assumption is validated now since the borrower will assuredly choose S when faced with a borrowing rate of 16.67%.

loan commitments add value for borrowers; this observation has empirical support in that firms that purchase bank loan commitments experience abnormally positive stock price reactions upon announcing these purchases.[14] The conclusion is that borrowers may demand loan commitments because they are able to borrow on better terms under commitments than they could in the spot market. Banks are able to provide better terms because loan commitments avoid some of the moral hazard problems that plague spot loans.

Liquidity Guarantee for Other Creditors

When a firm purchases a loan commitment, suppliers of inputs to the firm know that the firm will have access to liquidity equal to the amount of the commitment. This may reassure suppliers that the firm will have the funds necessary to service its debt obligations to them. Consequently, these suppliers may be willing to provide inputs to the firm on better terms than in the absence of the loan commitment. The result would be an overall lowering of the firm's cost of debt, which would benefit the firm's *shareholders*. This intuition can be seen in the following example.

Example 10.2

Suppose Northwestern Business Machines (NBM) has the opportunity to invest $100 at $t = 1$ in a project that will yield a random payoff at $t = 2$. At $t = 0$ the firm is uncertain about the probability distribution of the random payoff of the project; this distribution depends on a state of nature, call it θ, that will be revealed privately (i.e., it is not known to the creditors) to the management of NBM at $t = 1$ prior to making its decision of whether to invest in the project. At $t = 0$, all that NBM knows is that there is a 0.5 probability that $\theta = G$ (the "good" state), in which case the project will pay off $200 with probability 0.9 and zero with probability 0.1. If the bad state occurs, the project will pay off $130 with probability 0.9 and zero with probability 0.1.

At $t = 0$, NBM needs to buy $20 of raw materials and other inputs if it is to proceed with the project at $t = 1$. The suppliers have agreed to provide trade credit so that the $20 plus the agreed upon interest can be paid at $t = 2$.

The riskless interest rate that will prevail from $t = 1$ to $t = 2$ is 5%, and this is known to all at $t = 0$. Assume that the time that will elapse from $t = 0$ to $t = 1$ is so short that discounting can be ignored. Also assume that NBM's chief executive officer (CEO) will sustain a nonpecuniary cost (say the cost of personal effort) in initiating the project, and the pecuniary present-value equivalent of this cost is 1 dollar. All of the data for this problem are shown in Figure 10.4.

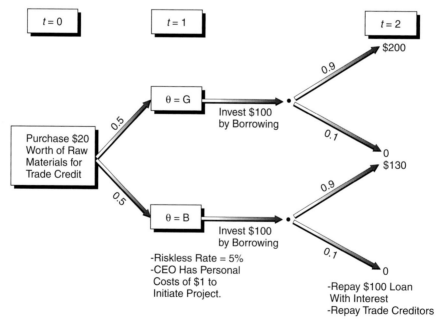

FIGURE 10.4   Investment Opportunities for Northwestern Business Machines.

---

14. See Shockley and Thakor (1997). Boot et al. (1987) provide a theory of loan commitments based on the argument that they help overcome moral hazard problems.

Compute the terms of trade credit as well as the NPV to NBM (net of the CEO's personal cost) if it: (i) borrows the $100 in the spot credit market after learning θ, and (ii) purchases a loan commitment at $t = 0$ (prior to knowing θ) that would entitle it to borrow the $100 at $t = 1$.

Assume that the bank as well as trade creditors provide credit at competitive terms, and that everybody is risk neutral.

Solution
We solve this problem in five steps. First, we consider the spot credit alternative. We show that if suppliers price their trade credit to NBM at $t = 0$ assuming that NBM will undertake the project at $t = 1$ regardless of θ, then the project is undertaken only if $\theta = G$. Second, we argue that this suggests that the only Nash equilibrium is for trade creditors to believe that NBM will undertake the project at $t = 1$ if $\theta = G$ and not otherwise. We verify in the second step that this is indeed a Nash equilibrium. Third, we consider the loan commitment alternative. We show that there exists a fixed-rate loan commitment that induces NBM to invest at $t = 1$ regardless of θ. Fourth, we verify that this commitment is part of a Nash equilibrium by checking that NBM will indeed prefer to purchase a loan commitment at $t = 0$ as opposed to borrowing in the spot market at $t = 1$. Finally, in Step 5 we show that the loan commitment makes NBM better off ex ante because it lowers NBM's overall cost of credit. It achieves this by eliminating an underinvestment problem that results in trade credit being available to NBM at a lower cost than with spot borrowing.

Step 1
Let us first consider the spot credit alternative. Since the project has a success probability of 0.9 (regardless of θ) and the riskless rate is 5%, we know from Example 10.1 that the competitive loan interest rate is 16.67%. Thus, the repayment obligation of the $100 spot loan will be $116.67. If the trade creditors assume that NBM will invest in the project regardless of θ, then the interest rate on trade credit should also be 16.67%, that is, the firm's repayment obligation should be $20 \times 1.1667 = \$23.33$. The total repayment obligation is then $116.67 + \$23.33 = \$140$. But then if $\theta = B$, its NPV is

$$\frac{0.9(0)}{1.05} - \$1 = -\$1$$

where we have subtracted the decision maker's personal cost of $1 in computing the NPV. Note that the zero in the numerator of the first term in the left-hand side of the above equation reflects limited liability (without which the zero would be replaced by 130 – 140 = –$10). Thus, the firm will *not* undertake the project if it observes $\theta = B$. If $\theta = G$ is observed at $t = 1$, then the firm's NPV is

$$\frac{0.9(\$250 - \$140)}{1.05} - 1 = \$50.43$$

so that the project will be undertaken.

Step 2
This means that it cannot be a Nash equilibrium for the trade creditors or the bank to believe that NBM will undertake the project regardless of θ. Suppose they assume that the project will be undertaken only if $\theta = G$. Then, since the probability of the project being undertaken is only 0.5, the interest rate i_t charged for trade credit (with spot borrowing of the $100 investment) must satisfy

$$0.5 \times 0.9 \times (1 + i_t) = 1.05,$$

which yields $i_t = 133.33\%$. NBM's repayment obligation to the trade creditors is therefore $20 \times 2.3333 = \$46.67$. Its total repayment obligation now becomes $116.67 + \$46.67 = \$163.34$. If $\theta = G$ occurs, NBM's NPV is

$$\frac{0.9(\$200 - \$163.34)}{1.05} - 1 = \$30.42,$$

so that the project will be undertaken in that state. However, the project will not be undertaken if $\theta = B$. Hence, the beliefs of the trade creditors about NBM's future behavior are consistent (rationalized by NBM's behavior), and it is a Nash equilibrium for them to offer trade credit at an interest rate of 133.33%. Note that the NPV to NBM from the spot borrowing alternative, computed at $t = 0$ (prior to the realization of θ) is $0.5 \times 30.42 = \$15.21$, since the firm knows that it will invest only if $\theta = G$.

Step 3
Now consider the loan commitment alternative. Suppose NBM can obtain a loan commitment at $t = 0$ to borrow $100 at 5% (the current riskless rate) at $t = 1$. Thus, its repayment obligation to the bank, if it borrows under the commitment, will be $105. Since the repayment obligation that permits the bank to just break even is $116.67, the bank's loss is $116.67 – \$105 = \$11.67$, and so the commitment fee (using the logic employed in Example 10.1) should be $\frac{0.9 \times 11.67}{1.05} = \$10.00$. Will the firm now invest in the project if $\theta = B$ at $t = 1$? To answer this, calculate NBM's NPV as $\frac{0.9(\$130 - \$105 - \$23.33)}{1.05} - 1 = \$0.43$, so that the firm will undertake the investment.

Note that we have assumed here that trade creditors believe that NBM will undertake the project regardless of θ, if it has purchased this loan commitment at $t = 0$. As our analysis indicates, this assumption is warranted.

Step 4

To verify that we have a Nash equilibrium with the loan commitment, we also need to check that NBM will prefer to purchase the loan commitment at $t = 0$ as opposed to borrowing in the spot credit market.

The NPV for NBM, assessed at $t = 0$, is

$$\frac{0.5[0.9 \times (\$200 - \$105 - \$23.33)]}{1.05} + \frac{0.5[0.9 \times (\$130 - \$105 - \$23.33)]}{1.05} - 10 - 1 = \$20.43.$$

Since this exceeds NBM's NPV with spot borrowing (\$15.21), we have a Nash equilibrium with NBM purchasing a loan commitment at $t = 0$ to borrow \$100 at 5%, and suppliers extending trade credit at 16.67%.

In this case, the loan commitment reduces the firm's overall cost of credit. Recall from Chapter 7 that collateral solved an underinvestment problem. Here the loan commitment serves a similar purpose.[15]

Step 5

The underinvestment problem arises because the project has a positive NPV to NBM (and a positive total NPV) in state $\theta = B$ only if the project's cost is just the \$100 investment. In this case, the *total* NPV of the project is

$$\frac{0.9 \times \$130}{1.05} - \$100 - \$1 = \$10.43,$$

so that the loan commitment helps to avoid a real underinvestment problem. This conclusion is appropriate if we view the \$20 worth of raw materials as a purchase that NBM would make even if the project were not available, that is, the raw materials do not add to the cost of the project. But if we interpret that \$20 as adding to the cost of the project (i.e., these raw materials would not be purchased if the project were unavailable), then the total NPV of the project is

$$\frac{0.9 \times \$130}{1.05} - \$100 - \$20 - \$1 = -\$9.57.$$

In this case the project is *socially inefficient* in the $\theta = B$ state, so that the loan commitment (which still results in the project being undertaken when $\theta = B$) does *not* resolve an underinvestment problem in the usual sense.[16] Indeed, it ends up inducing an *overinvestment*[3] by NBM that makes it better off *ex ante*.[17] In this case, the role played by the loan commitment[18] is quite different from that played by collateral in our discussions in Chapter 7.

Borrowers often use loan commitments as an assurance to other creditors. For example, commercial paper borrowers routinely purchase dedicated bank loan commitments explicitly to back up commercial paper issues.

Protection Against Future Credit Rationing

A borrower's future access to credit is threatened by three possibilities: (1) deterioration in its own credit rating, (2) deterioration in the general market availability of credit, and (3) changes in bank-specific factors that diminish the bank's ability to provide credit. A loan commitment may protect the buyer against the first two possibilities. Of course, the MAC clause in the loan commitment contract limits the usefulness of the commitment as insurance against rationing, but the empirical evidence suggests that loan commitments are nevertheless considered valuable.[19]

Surveys of borrowers indicate that the most frequently mentioned reasons given for commitments are "general convenience and minimizing loan arrangement costs," and "protection against general credit crunches." The next most frequently mentioned reasons were to "ensure credit access against a creditworthiness deterioration" and "to lock in a fixed markup over a reference interest rate."[20]

---

15. Berkovitch and Greenbaum (1990) have suggested that a loan commitment can eliminate underinvestment. The example presented above captures their intuition.

16. To reiterate, by an "underinvestment problem" we mean a situation in which the firm passes up a project with positive total NPV.

17. That is, the firm invests in the project when its total NPV is negative. It does so because the NPV to its own shareholders is positive.

18. In both this illustration as well as in Example 10.1, we have assumed that the firm has the liquidity to pay the commitment fee on its loan commitment. Why would the firm not want to use this liquidity to provide equity to the project instead and thereby reduce its total borrowing? Boot et al. (1987) examine this issue and show that the borrower is *strictly better off* using its liquidity to pay the commitment fee rather than using it as equity in conjunction with a spot loan.

19. See Sofianos et al. (1990) and Almeida et al. (2014). Thakor (2005) develops a theoretical model that explains how loan commitments can protect borrowers against credit rationing despite the presence of the MAC clause.

20. See Avery and Berger (1991).

Reducing Market Incompleteness

When the capital market is *incomplete* (recall our discussion in Chapter 1), investors and firms lack all of the risk-sharing opportunities they desire. Thus, if the market is incomplete and the loan commitment produces a payoff stream for the borrower that cannot be replicated by linear combinations of existing securities (as, e.g., in Example 10.1), then the availability of a loan commitment reduces market incompleteness. Since investors now have access to expanded risk-sharing opportunities because they can invest in firms that purchase loan commitments (as well as those that do not), these investors may be made better off by the availability of loan commitments. In other words, there may be a demand from investors for payoff patterns that can only be produced by firms that purchase loan commitments.

WHO IS ABLE TO BORROW UNDER BANK LOAN COMMITMENTS?

Not all firms have access to loan commitments, even though loan commitments represent a valuable source of liquidity for all firms. It appears that loan commitments are available primarily to firms that maintain high cash flow. In contrast, firms with low operating cash flow cannot count upon loan commitments as a source of liquidity, so they tend to rely more on their own cash reserves in managing their liquidity.[21] A reason for this is that banks use financial covenants with loan commitments, and firms must maintain high cash flow in order to remain compliant with these covenants.

In addition to the issue of who is able to borrow under commitments, there is also the question of whether a borrower who purchases a loan commitment is actually able to borrow under the commitment. Because of the MAC clause associated with commitments, banks can refuse to honor their commitments when honoring is financially too expensive, as explained earlier. During the financial crisis of 2007–2009, when liquidity was scarce, it turns out that many banks did not honor their commitments. Overall, however, credit lines still helped mitigate the negative effect of the financial crisis on corporate spending.[22]

PRICING OF LOAN COMMITMENTS

The Model

The Analogy Between Loan Commitments and Options

We develop an approach for pricing loan commitments, based on the observation that their payoff structure resembles that of a common stock put option.[23] As discussed in Chapter 1, a put option is the right to sell a security (the deliverable) at a fixed price during some fixed time interval, or at some fixed future date. The major components of this contract are the:

1. identity of the deliverable,
2. option price,
3. strike price, and
4. exercise date or period.

For example, $500 might be paid for the right to put (sell) 100 shares of General Motors common stock at $50 per share (or $5000) at any time over the next six months. The option price is $500, the strike price is $50 per share, the deliverable is 100 shares of General Motors common stock, and the exercise dates are all dates extending over the next six months. The "writer" of the option accepts the $500 option price in exchange for the responsibility to purchase 100 shares of GM stock for $5000 at the discretion of the option buyer at any time during the next six months. (Some options are exercisable only at the end of the term, rather than at any time during the term.)

Now consider the bank loan commitment. The loan commitment buyer pays a commitment fee (option price) for the right to put (sell) a security to the bank at a prespecified price over some pre-established time interval. The security is the commitment owner's IOU (debt) and the strike price is the face (par) value of the loan, that is, the dollar amount of the borrowing. The time interval is the life of the commitment. Hence, in selling loan commitments, banks are writing put options

---

21. This was documented by Sufi (2009). In a cross-country analysis, Lins et al. (2010) find that firms employ credit lines to take advantage of business opportunities in good times, but hold cash to hedge against cash flow shocks in bad times. Yun (2009) shows that firms use credit lines rather than hold cash if a takeover threat is present.

22. For empirical evidence related to banks' reluctance to honor loan commitments, see Huang (2010). Credit constrained firms drew down on credit lines due to the fear that banks might limit their borrowing in the future (Campello et al. (2010)). See also Ivashina and Scharfstein (2010), and Campello et al. (2011).

23. Thakor et al. (1981) were the first to note this analogy and develop a model to value/price loan commitments using an option pricing approach.

where the underlying deliverable is the debt instrument of the commitment buyer. The commitment buyer will take down the commitment (exercise the put option) if the value of its debt instrument on the exercise date is less than the committed loan amount (the strike price). The difference between the loan amount and the debt instrument value at the time of commitment exercise represents the customer's gain from exercising the commitment, and the present value of this gain at the time of commitment purchase should be the commitment fee or price the customer is willing to pay.

The Model

Suppose we wish to value a loan commitment issued at $t = 0$ that would allow the purchaser to borrow $\$F$ (the face value of the loan or strike price of the put option) at $t = 1$ at some predetermined interest rate i_c. The maturity of the loan will be one period, that is, it will mature at $t = 2$, and the loan (if taken) will be free of default risk. Assume that the current one-period riskfree rate is i_0. Assume that the one-period yield on the borrower's debt at $t = 1$ will either be $i_1^+ > i_0$ or $i_1^- < i_0$.

The probability of i_1^+ is p and the probability of i_1^- is $1-p$. Assume $i_1^+ > i_c > i_1^-$. Everybody is risk neutral. What is the value of this fixed-rate commitment?

Solution

At $t = 1$, suppose the spot yield on the borrower's debt is i_1^-. Then it is clear that the borrower has no incentive to take down the loan commitment since cheaper credit is available in the spot market. But if the spot yield is i_1^+, then the borrower will take down the commitment since the commitment rate is $i_c < i_1^+$ The value of the borrower's debt at $t = 1$ in this state is:

$$\frac{F[1+i_c]}{[1+i_1^+]} \tag{10.3}$$

where $F[1 + i_c]$ is the borrower's future repayment obligation at $t = 2$, which is discounted back to $t = 1$ at the spot yield i_1^+. Note that the borrower is receiving $\$F$ from the bank when it takes down the loan, and in exchange the bank is receiving a debt security worth the amount given by (10.3). That is, the borrower is selling the bank a debt security worth $F[1+i_c]/[1+i_1^+]$ for $\$F$ when it exercises its loan commitment put option. The gain to the borrower from exercising the put option is:

$$F - \frac{F[1+i_c]}{[1+i_1^+]} \tag{10.4}$$

The value of the loan commitment to the borrower at $t = 0$ is then:

$$\frac{p\left\{F - \frac{F[1+i_c]}{[1+i_1^+]}\right\}}{[1+i_0]}$$

where the expression in Equation (10.4) is multiplied with the probability of the yield i_1^+ and is discounted back to $t = 0$ at the riskless rate i_0 (since everybody is risk neutral).

We have so far discussed the valuation of fixed-rate loan commitments. Variable-rate commitments can be valued similarly. The add-on to the index rate in the variable-rate commitment would be held fixed. However, this add-on is a premium charged by the bank for the customer's default risk in excess of that reflected in the index rate. Thus, the customer will exercise the commitment whenever the fixed add-on is smaller than the add-on the customer would be charged in the spot market. Once again, we have a put option purchased by the commitment buyer. The difference is that with a fixed-rate commitment the customer is purchasing protection against an increase in its total borrowing cost (which includes an increase in the index rate as well as in the add-on reflecting borrower-specific risk), whereas with a variable-rate commitment the customer is purchasing protection only against an increase in the add-on due to a decline in its own credit rating.

Empirical Predictions of Valuation Model

The valuation model developed above suggests that borrowers purchase loan commitments to lock in borrowing rates. Hence, more commitments should be exercised when borrowers experience an increase in their cost of spot-market borrowing.

There is abundant anecdotal evidence to support this prediction. For example, in 1990, Travelers Corporation, a (then independent) Hartford-based insurance company, drew down a substantial portion of its $1.075 billion credit line after the major rating agencies downgraded its credit rating (and thereby increased its cost of borrowing in the spot credit market). It was reported that the company sought to ensure liquidity and assure its access to short-term funding after boosting loan-loss reserves by $650 million.[18]

Another testable prediction of the valuation model is that the cost of loan commitments should increase as the volatility (future uncertainty) of the customer's spot borrowing rate increases. This prediction follows immediately from the well-known property of put options that they increase in value as uncertainty in the future value of the underlying asset increases.

THE DIFFERENCES BETWEEN LOAN COMMITMENTS AND PUT OPTIONS

While there is a striking similarity between a common stock put option and a bank loan commitment, there are also important differences. Four key differences are as follows:

1. An exchange-traded put option is a binding contract – the option seller is legally liable for the contractual payment if the option is exercised. By contrast, due to the MAC clause, a bank loan commitment is a discretionary contract.
2. An exchange-traded option is a *transferable* contract, whereas a loan commitment is not. That is, if firm A buys a loan commitment from a bank, it cannot sell this commitment to firm B – loan commitments are not transferable. The commitment owner may of course exercise the commitment and lend the proceeds to firm B, but this is yet a different transaction.
3. Loan commitment pricing differs from that of exchange-traded options. For example, a loan commitment may include a usage fee that is an increasing function of the unused portion of the line. This is inconsistent with the option pricing formulation. One way to understand usage fees is in the context of the earlier explanation that banks may offer loan commitments because they provide information about future loan demand. Deviations of actual takedowns from expected takedowns under commitments represent prediction errors that may be costly to the lender. For example, if the lender incurs a cost of preparation (funding) to make the expected loan and therefore finds it costly to invest the planned funds in something other than the loan, then the lender's cost increases with the *error* in takedown prediction. Assessing a fee on the unused portion of the commitment is a way to induce the customer to provide the lender more accurate information about future loan demand.
4. A put option is either exercised in full, or not at all. Loan commitments typically do not exhibit such takedown behavior. Loan takedowns, F^*, are usually only some fraction of F, the face value of the commitment. There are two possible explanations for this partial takedown phenomenon:
   a. The customer lacks the "need" for all of the funds that can be borrowed under the commitment.
   b. The customer has a long-term relationship with the bank and seeks to foster good relations by not fully exploiting windfalls.

Consider (i) first. Its reasonableness depends on the customer's access to nonnegative NPV investment opportunities. If the customer's financial leverage is unrestricted and it has unlimited investment opportunities that yield nonnegative NPVs, then we can expect its demand for funds to be highly elastic to its borrowing rate, and the commitment is likely to be exercised in full or not at all, as implied by the option valuation model. However, positive-NPV investment opportunities are typically limited. Moreover, their ability/willingness to borrow under the commitment may be constrained by capital structure considerations, including restrictions imposed by covenants in outstanding debt contracts. In this case, loan demand will be imperfectly elastic to interest rates, and partial takedowns would then be possible. This is illustrated in Figure 10.5.

When the customer's spot borrowing rate is i^* and its commitment rate is i_c, its loan demand is F^*, which is less than the credit line F. The bank's loan supply function under the commitment is a vertical line, indicating that the bank is willing to lend any amount up to F at i_c under the commitment. With a spot borrowing rate of i, the loan supply function *may* look like that indicated in the graph. This function says that the bank is willing to lend any amount up to some number (possibly) exceeding F, at a rate of i^*, and that the amount the bank is willing to lend may not increase for relatively small increases in the interest rate beyond i^*; for sufficiently higher rates, the bank may be willing to lend more.

Now consider (ii). A customer's takedown behavior may be seen as influencing the future pricing or availability of bank services. This link presupposes some cost to the borrower of changing banks or incomplete exchange of information among banks. For example, information reusability will give the incumbent bank an advantage over competing banks with respect to information about the customer. This could enable the incumbent to offer credit at better terms than competitors could,

---

18. Lipin (1990) reported: "The move by Travelers is not expected to be an isolated event. More corporations will seek to maintain liquidity in a precarious economic environment, lenders say. In addition, the bank lines have become more attractive due to rising rates and other problems in the commercial paper market."

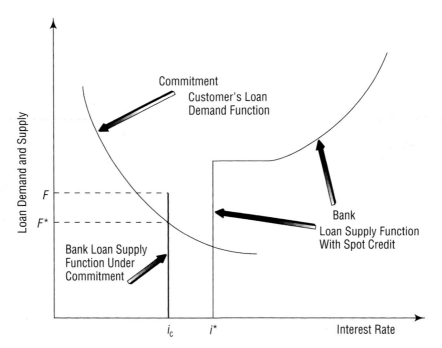

FIGURE 10.5   Partial Takedown With Imperfectly Elastic Loan Demand.

thereby making it costly for the customer to switch to another bank. Now, since the customer's exercise of the commitment imposes a loss on the bank, it is reasonable to expect the bank to adjust its loan commitment pricing based on observed takedowns. For example, if the customer develops a reputation with the bank for taking down no more than 50% of its line of credit, the bank will begin to price the loan commitment taking that into account. This will yield a lower commitment price than if the customer took down 100% of the previous commitment. Alternatively, the bank will raise the commitment price if it expected the customer to take down 30% of the previous commitment and it actually took down 50%. Of course, one could argue that the customer should *explicitly* reduce the size of the commitment if it does not plan to use all of it. However, the customer may still request a larger commitment than it needs under *normal* circumstances because of the possibility that an unexpectedly large credit need may arise in the future. But to the extent that the bank perceives that the probability of that happening is low, the price of the commitment will be lowered by the customer's previous partial takedowns. This phenomenon is similar to an automobile owner choosing *not* to file some auto collision claims with his insurance company due to the (adverse) learning the insurance company engages in when a claim is filed. In Table 10.3 we summarize the similarities and differences between loan commitments and put options.

TABLE 10.3 Similarities and Differences Between Loan Commitments and Put Options

	Put Option	Loan Commitment
Similarities	1. Deliverable or underlying security	1. Customer's indebtedness (IOU)
	2. Option price	2. Commitment fee
	3. Strike price	3. Size of the loan commitment (*F*)
	4. Exercise date	4. Date commitment can be taken down
Differences	1. Binding contract	1. Discretionary contract
	2. Transferable (tradeable) contract	2. Nontransferable contract
	3. No usage fee	3. Usage fee
	4. Exercised either in full or not at all	4. Often partially exercised

LOAN COMMITMENTS AND MONETARY POLICY

Regulators conduct monetary policy by altering the quantity of credit or money supply and its *price* (interest rates). Loan commitments are a source of slippage in the Fed's ability to conduct monetary policy.[24] The reason is that once a commitment is sold, the amount of lending is determined by the customer's demand for funds at the prespecified interest rate. Now suppose the Fed wishes to implement a *contractionary* monetary policy. Using open market operations, the Fed would sell securities and drive up interest rates. While the higher interest rates reduce the demand for *spot* credit, they make borrowing under prearranged loan commitments more attractive and thereby increase takedowns.[25] Total bank lending may thus actually *expand* in the short-run in response to a contractionary monetary policy. This short-run perversity is likely to be reversed eventually as banks adjust by reducing the volume of their loan commitments in subsequent periods. Nevertheless, the growth of loan commitments can increase money market turbulence and frustrate monetary policy efforts.

OTHER CONTINGENT CLAIMS: LETTERS OF CREDIT

Loan commitments are not the only contingent claims that have registered striking growth in recent years. In this section, we discuss two others that have grown impressively, commercial and standby L/Cs.

Commercial Letters of Credit and Bankers Acceptances

Commercial L/Cs are used to facilitate trade, most commonly international, and are one of the oldest of banking contracts. In a typical transaction involving an L/C, the exporter has limited knowledge of the importer's ability to pay and limited ability to enforce contracts across national boundaries. The exporter therefore asks the importer to arrange for its bank to issue an L/C guaranteeing payment to the exporter upon presentation of the appropriate shipping documents. The exporter obtains the bill of lading and other shipping documents when goods are loaded on the ship for export. The L/C is a promise by the importer's bank to pay the exporter, given the necessary shipping documents. Thus, as the third party to the transaction, the bank substitutes its own creditworthiness for that of the importer and thereby reduces the default risk confronting the exporter.

When the exporter presents the necessary documents to the paying bank, it receives either a *sight draft* (immediate payment) or a *time draft* promising payment at some future date. In the latter case, the resulting instrument becomes a *bankers acceptance,* which is marketable and usually quite liquid. Thus, a bankers acceptance can be viewed as an outcome of a commercial L/C. Any draft "accepted" by a bank in the performance of its obligation under a commercial L/C is a bankers acceptance.[26]

In other words, a commercial letter of credit is essentially a *performance guarantee.* It can be defined as a promise to endorse or "accept" a time draft conditional on prespecified terms being satisfied. The act of accepting the time draft implies that, from the exporter's viewpoint, the bank's promise to repay replaces that of the debtor, and this creates a negotiable security. Consequently, the bank bears the risk that the debtor (importer) may default. Figure 10.6 depicts the steps leading to the creation of Banker's Acceptances. For simplicity, we have included only the importer's bank. Sometimes the exporter's bank is also involved as an intermediary between the exporter and the importer's bank, and time drafts may be accepted by both banks, giving rise to "two-name paper."

If the importer's (or buyer's) bank accepts a time draft and thereby creates a bankers acceptance, it has two choices. It can either hold the acceptance or it can sell it in the secondary market. If it decides to hold the acceptance, it ends up funding the credit (it has essentially extended a loan to the importer), so that the act of acceptance is automatic. However, if the acceptance is sold in the secondary market, the *holder* of the acceptance will provide funding, but the bank *guarantees* payment.

Standby Letters of Credit

A *standby letter of credit* also guarantees the performance of an "account party," usually in a commercial or financial transaction, but it does not necessarily involve a funding transaction. A standby L/C issued by the "second party's" (the buyer or

---

24. See Duca and Vanhoose (1990).
25. This is because an increase in market interest rates increases the cost of spot borrowing for the bank's customers, whereas the commitment rate either stays the same (under fixed-rate commitments) or rises less (under variable-rate commitments).
26. See Carmichael and Graham (2012).

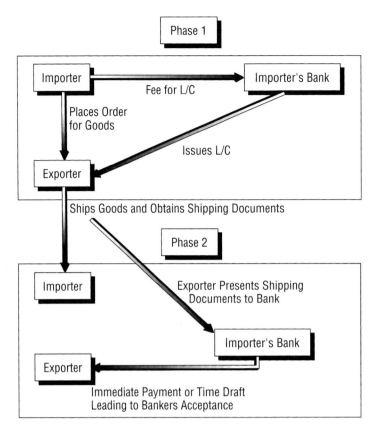

FIGURE 10.6 The Letter of Credit, Banker's Acceptance Nexus.

debtor or the party that owes some sort of performance to the "first party") bank obligates that bank to compensate the first party (the seller or the creditor or the party that is owed) in the event of a performance failure. The second party would then be liable to its bank for the disbursements the bank made under the L/C. From this perspective, standby and commercial L/Cs are similar. However, with a commercial L/C the issuing bank usually advances payment and is repaid by its customer, whereas with a standby L/C the bank makes payment only if its customer fails to fulfill a contractual obligation. Consequently, the bankers acceptances associated with commercial L/Cs have no counterpart among standby L/Cs.

Standby L/Cs are often used in international trade to facilitate transactions in which the seller has insufficient knowledge of the buyer's creditworthiness. Of course, the seller must still rely on the buyer's bank to "make good" on its promise, which is why there is often a second bank – typically the seller's – that augments the issuing bank's guarantee with its own. Such L/Cs are known as *confirmed letters of credit.*

Standby L/Cs are also used to guarantee performance in contracts involving greater variety and complexity than the simple international trade contract described above. Through standby L/Cs, banks now operate in areas that were once the exclusive domain of bonding, title, and insurance companies. For example, suppose a builder promises to deliver a completed building by a prespecified date or face a predetermined penalty. The buyer could ask the builder to obtain a standby L/C to guarantee the contract. Thus, if the builder fails to keep its promise, the buyer can collect the penalty amount from the bank that issued the L/C. The builder would then be responsible to pay its bank the penalty amount disbursed earlier by the bank. In banking, standby L/Cs are used as credit enhancements for securitizations and backups for commercial paper when the market gets skittish, that is, they replace loan commitments, thereby avoiding the risk of the MAC clause.

The Option-Like Feature of Standby Letters of Credit

Standby L/Cs can also be viewed as *put options,* like loan commitments. In the case of a loan commitment, the customer purchases an option to sell to the bank a security (the customer's indebtedness) that may be of less value at the time of exercise than the exercise or strike price (the amount loaned to the customer). In the case of a standby L/C, the bank agrees to purchase from the creditor a claim (the debtor's indebtedness) at par, contingent on the failure of the primary debtor to "perform," that is, to honor the claim. That is, the "first party" (the creditor) has the option to "put" the primary debtor's debt claim to the bank when nonperformance by the debtor renders the value of its debt claim less than par. In exchange for writing the option, the bank collects a fee. The option feature of a standby L/C implies that a bank that issues this instrument is conveying to the buyer a contingent claim and imposing on itself a contingent liability. The latter becomes an actual liability if the primary debtor fails to perform under the stipulations of a contract.

One important difference between loan commitments and standby L/Cs as put options is in the random processes influencing the market values of the underlying claims in the two cases and in the consequent trigger mechanisms giving rise to exercise. In the case of a loan commitment, an increase in the customer's spot borrowing rate, above the commitment. In the case of standby L/Cs, nonperformance by the debtor depresses the value of the claim below the strike price (the guaranteed value of the claim), prompting exercise of the option. Another important difference lies in enforceability. Unlike the loan commitment, the standby L/C does not have a MAC clause and is therefore more rigidly binding.

OTHER CONTINGENT CLAIMS: SWAPS

What Are Swaps?

A *swap* is an agreement between two parties to exchange their exposure to a specific risk. The trade often involves an intermediary acting as either principal or broker.[27] Thus, for example, a swap is a tool for managing various types of risk. Basically an interest rate swap involves exchanging interest payments on notional securities with different prospects such as duration or the method by which interest payments are determined. For example, suppose a firm has a floating-rate liability and a fixed-rate asset. Such a firm will suffer losses if interest rates rise sharply. Now suppose another firm has a fixed-rate liability and a floating-rate asset. This firm will suffer losses if interest rates fall sharply. These two firms could arrange a swap to exchange their interest payments and thereby reduce their exposures to interest rate risk.

Interest rate swaps were first used in the Eurobond market during 1981. Large international banks, which lend mostly on a floating-rate basis, were the first to use swaps in which they exchanged the fixed-rate interest obligations on their liabilities for lower-cost floating-rate interest payments on equivalent notional amounts of claims. The swap market migrated to the United States in 1982 when the first domestic swap took place between Sallie Mae (Student Loan Marketing Association) and the ITT Financial Corporation. Since then this market has experienced explosive growth, and is now worth trillions of dollars of notional claims.

A typical swap involves the exchange of a fixed for a floating rate over an agreed amount (notional amount) for a specific period; the floating rate is typically indexed to the LIBOR, the prime, or the T-bill rate.

How a Swap Works?

Suppose we have two firms. Firm A is a bank with $150 million of loans that promise a floating interest rate of prime plus 25 basis points, financed with $150 million of 10-year bonds promising fixed 10% interest rate. Firm B is an S&L with $150 million of fixed-rate mortgages financed with short-term MMFs (money market funds) and CDs with interest rates indexed to the T-bill rate. Each institution is exposed to interest rate risk that it wishes to hedge.

We could now arrange a $150 million, 10-year interest rate swap between the bank and the S&L. The swap may be structured as follows. The S&L agrees to pay the bank a fixed rate of 10% per year on $150 million, for 10 years. In return, the bank agrees to make the S&L a floating-rate payment at 2.5 basis points above prime, on a $150 million principal. In this way the bank and the S&L have effectively exchanged their liabilities. Each has now hedged its interest rate exposure since the fixed-rate liability more closely matches the S&L's fixed-rate assets, whereas the floating-rate liability more closely matches the bank's floating-rate assets. Figure 10.7 depicts this arrangement.

Early on, swap transactions normally involved an intermediary functioning as a broker – typically a commercial bank or an investment banker.

More recently, intermediaries have performed more like asset transformers, effectively providing guarantees to both parties to a swap transaction. For example, if the bank in the above transaction defaults, the intermediary would collect the fixed 10% from the S&L and make payments to it at 25 basis points above prime. Thus, *it would assume the role of the bank* until it can find an appropriate firm to replace the departed bank. And to the extent that it may not have the bank's

---

27. See Hull (2011) and Gyntelberg and Upper (2013).

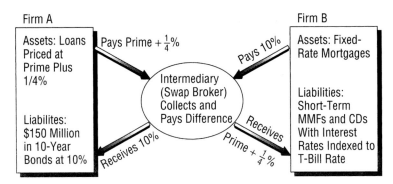

FIGURE 10.7 An Example of an Interest Rate Swap.

balance sheet, the swap broker would expose itself to interest rate risk. For example, if interest rates were to rise sharply, the intermediary would lose.[28]

Traditionally the most common type of swap was the one described in our example, namely that involving a dollar fixed-rate loan swapped for a dollar floating-rate loan. Such a swap is called a "plain vanilla" swap. Recently, however, different types of swaps have proliferated. One is a floating-to-floating swap where parties agree to swap floating rates based on different index rates. For example, a bank whose assets are floating-rate loans at prime plus 20 basis points and whose liabilities are floating-rate CDs at LIBOR minus 40 basis points may wish to swap the interest payments on its liabilities with those of an institution that has the interest rate on its liabilities indexed to the prime rate. Such swaps are known as *basis swaps*.

Another popular swap involves currencies. For example, a bank may have foreign loans financed by domestic deposits, so that the interest payments on its loans may be denominated in Japanese yen, while the interest payments on its deposits may be denominated in dollars. Such a bank might wish to swap its yen-denominated payments for dollar-denominated payments (perhaps with a Japanese bank that has dollar-denominated loans financed by yen-denominated deposits raised in Japan).

There are two common types of currency swaps: traditional *fixed/fixed currency swaps* and *cross-currency interest rate swaps*. A fixed/fixed currency swap involves fixed interest rates in each currency. Principal may or may not be exchanged. If principal is exchanged, this kind of swap transforms a fixed coupon bond denominated in one currency into a fixed coupon bond in another currency. With a cross-currency interest rate swap one exchanges a fixed payments stream for a floating payment stream, as well as payments in different currencies. These contracts are occasionally combined in a single transaction, and sometimes the currency and interest rate components are separated. There are other variations as well. For example, there are swaps in which the two parties exchange yields on assets of different maturities (or currency denominations), rather than interest payments on liabilities. The point is that a swap can be tailor-made to suit the needs of the swapping parties, so that the potential variety of swaps is almost limitless. Some of these are discussed in the next subsection.

Swaps and Swap-Related Innovations

(a) Interest Rate Swap Variations: Some variations on the basic interest rate swaps are listed below.

- *Amortizing Swap:* This is a swap in which the notional principal amount diminishes over the life of the swap in a specified manner. This may be done so that payments match the expected cash flows of a financing project or the prepayment schedule of a mortgage.
- *Indexed Amortization Swap:* This is an amortizing swap in which the amortization of the notional principal depends on the stochastic value of some index like say the 3-month LIBOR.
- *Forward Swap:* This is a swap that does not begin until a designated future date. The fixed rate in the swap is linked to spot market rates, and the swap must be executed on the prespecified date.

---

28. Because swap transactions are intermediated like this, there is "counterparty risk," arising from the fact that one of the parties to the swap contract will back out of the contract, and the intermediating swap broker may fail to step in and replace the defaulting party. In the crisis of 2007–2009, one of the reasons why the Federal Reserve assisted in the "rescue" of Bear Stearns via its acquisition by J.P. Morgan Chase is that it was a counterparty and swap broker in trillions of dollars in swap contracts, and the Federal Reserve was unsure of what would happen to the finance market if these swap contracts came undone. For further description of the failure mechanics of investment banks, see Duffie (2010).

- *Step Up/Down:* This is a swap in which the fixed-rate payments level varies, either increasing or decreasing over some portion of the swap term. For example, the fixed rate in the swap might be set below the market for the first 2 years, with an above-market rate for the remainder of the term.

(b) Swaps Involving Asset Payoffs Other Than Interest Rates

- *Commodity Swaps*: In a commodity swap, the contracting parties agree to exchange payments based on the value of a particular physical commodity, for example, gold, oil, or silver. One party pays a fixed price for the commodity and receives the spot price of the commodity at some future date. This relatively new contract that may appeal to commodity fund managers is generally short (2–3 years), but maturities up to 7 years are available.
- *Indexed Returns Swaps*: In this swap, one of the payments is linked to the total return of a market portfolio, like the S&P 500. This return can be exchanged for a payment stream based on either a fixed rate, such as the current T-bill rate (for a specific maturity) plus 30 basis points, or some floating rate (e.g., the LIBOR). An interesting type of indexed return swap is a *foreign indexed swap,* which is designed to capture the relative performances of security types (e.g., U.S. equities vs. Japanese equities). For example, suppose an investor owns a 5-year U.S. floating-rate note yielding LIBOR plus 50 basis points. This investor wants to invest in Japanese government bonds, but cannot trade the securities directly and wants to manage the foreign-exchange risk. He can enter into a swap whereby he receives the dollar equivalent of the monthly returns on the Japanese bond and pays LIBOR, giving him a total return equal to the Japanese bond return plus 50 basis points.
- *Mortgage Swaps:* This is a swap that replicates all or a portion of the return characteristics of mortgage securities. In the most basic structure, a mortgage yield is exchanged for a floating-rate return, and the notional balance on which the payments are based is amortized according to either a specified schedule or the actual prepayment experience of the underlying pool of mortgages. The most recent innovation in this class is an *indexed amortization swap* in which a fixed-rate payment is exchanged for a floating-rate payment, but the notional balance amortizes according to a schedule that depends on the movements in the yield of a prespecified security. For example, if the yield on the security falls by somewhere between 50 and 100 basis points, then the balance will amortize by 7% over the next period.

(c) Derivative Securities Based on Swaps

- *Swaptions*: With a swaption, one of the contracting parties has the option to allow an existing swap to be terminated or extended. These contracts are also called *cancelable, callable,* or *putable swaps,* and they can either be American or European in their options characteristics. Thus, a swaption is basically an option on a swap. Suppose two parties, A and B, enter into a contract in which A sells a *call swaption* to B. Then, at the exercise date, B can choose whether or not to exercise the option. If B exercise his option, he enters into a swap to receive, say, a fixed-rate payment in exchange for a floating-rate payment. These payment terms are all prespecified, as in a regular swap. The only difference is that one of the two parties has the legal right to decide whether or not to execute the swap at a future date.
- *Caps*: A *cap* is a swap contract in which the interest payments themselves have option characteristics. That is, the exercise (strike) price is set at particular interest rate levels. For example, suppose party A goes to a swap broker and buys a cap based on the 3-month LIBOR from a "cap writer" (party B), who represents the other party to the contract. Party A pays a premium (the price of the options) to the swap broker who subtracts his fee and passes along the remainder to party B. Now, party B is obliged to periodically (on each reset date) pay party A an amount equal to:

$$\text{notional principal} \times \max\{0, \text{3-month spot LIBOR} - \text{strike rate}\},$$

where max (x, y) means the greater of x and y. Suppose the strike rate is 10%. Then if the 3-month spot LIBOR is 12%, party B must pay party A an amount equal to 2% of the notional principal, whereas if the 3-month spot LIBOR is 9%, party B pays nothing on the reset date. Thus, a cap is simply a sequence of consecutive expiration options. These options can be viewed as call options on the specified interest rate or put options on the underlying security. When rates rise, the security's price falls and the option becomes more valuable. As with a standard common stock option, the value of a cap (and hence the initial option premium) increases as the interest rate rises.

The cap market has developed numerous derivatives and customizations. Some of these are:

- *Floors:* Here party B pays party A an amount equal to notional principal $\times \max\{0, \text{strike rate} - \text{spot market rate on a specific security}\}$ on the date of exercise (reset date) of the periodic option.
- *Collars:* Here party B pays A an amount equal to notional principal $\times [\{0, (\text{spot rate} - \text{cap strike rate})\} - \max\{0,(\text{floor strike rate} - \text{spot rate})\}]$. That is, A is buying a cap from B and simultaneously selling a floor to B.

Suppose the cap strike rate is 15% and the floor strike rate is 10%. Then if the spot rate on the chosen security is 17%, the spot rate minus the cap strike rate is 2%, so party A receives 2% of the notional principal. If the spot rate is 9%, then the floor strike rate minus the spot rate is 1%, and party A receives 1% of the notional principal. If the spot rate falls between the cap and floor strike rates (say at 12%), then party A receives nothing.

Advantages and Disadvantages of a Swap as a Hedging Instrument

Since a swap is an instrument to hedge interest rate risk, it is natural to ask how it compares with other ways of hedging interest rate risk. We now compare swaps with two alternatives: interest rate futures and debt refinancing.

Swap Versus Interest Rate Futures

What is a Futures Contract?

An interest rate futures contract is an exchange-based contract (as opposed to over-the-counter) to buy or sell a particular financial asset (such as a T-bill) for a specific price at a prespecified date in the future.

Before we can compare swap with a futures contract, you should be aware of how a futures contract can be used to hedge. Consider an S&L with long-term fixed-rate mortgages as assets and short-term CDs as liabilities. Suppose this S&L were to short (sell) a CD futures contract, that is, it could promise to deliver (sell) at a *fixed* price. Then, if interest rates rise in the future, the market value of the CD falls and thus the S&L receives a cash inflow equal to the (positive) difference between the fixed delivery price and the market value of the CD.[29] On the other hand, if interest rates fall and the market value of the CD rises as a result, the S&L will experience a loss. Thus, the gain to the S&L if rates rise is offset by the loss if rates fall. In this way, the S&L's interest rate exposure is hedged.

Advantage of a Swap Over a Futures Contract

Interest rate futures are *standardized* contracts with specific delivery dates and specific types of instruments.[30] Thus if you wish to hedge the interest rate risk on a financial claim that is not one of the deliverable instruments on which futures contracts are written, you must choose a futures contract on a deliverable that most closely resembles the claim you wish to hedge. Since the resemblance will be imperfect, you will bear *cross-hedging* risk. Moreover, even if the resemblance were perfect, you would bear *basis risk* (the risk that the relation between the spot and futures prices will change randomly). The major advantage of a swap contract over a futures contract is that a swap can be tailored to suit the customer's need because it is not a standardized contract. Thus, better interest rate hedging is often possible with a swap than with a futures contract. Note, however, that swaps are increasingly becoming more standardized and hence similar to futures contracts, but with longer hedging periods.

Disadvantages of a Swap

(i) Imperfect standardization means that it is not always easy to find a counterparty to the desired swap transaction. That is, futures contracts are more liquid than swaps contracts. (ii) Related to (i), the highly customer-specific nature of swaps means that *search costs* may be significant in some transactions. These costs will be passed on to the swapping parties by the swap broker, in the form of a higher fee. Thus, customers face higher transactions costs with swaps than with futures. (iii) There is a greater risk of nonperformance (default) with a swaps contract than with a futures contract. This is because the exchange guarantees execution with a futures contract, whereas with a swap one party could be left in the cold if the other party reneges and there is no (backup) guarantee by the swap broker. If there is a backup guarantee by the swap broker, then the swap broker plays the role of a clearinghouse. But even in this case, there is the possibility of nonperformance by the swap broker. Following the 2007–2009 financial crisis, there have been various legislative initiatives aimed at reducing counterparty risk by enforcing standardization and requiring clearing and settlement via Central Counter Parties (CCPs).

Swaps Versus Refinancing

How do you Hedge Risk by Refinancing?

One simple way for a firm to adjust its interest rate exposure is to *directly* refinance. That is, suppose a firm has fixed-rate liabilities and desires floating-rate liabilities. It could simply repurchase its fixed-rate liabilities, financing the repurchase by issuing floating-rate liabilities. Why is this simple approach not always preferred to swaps and futures?

---

29. These are not the S&L's own CDs, but rather a standardized contract. The S&L would not actually buy the CD, but just receive cash settlement.

30. Deliverables in interest rate futures are: T-bills, T-notes, T-bonds, bank and Eurodollar CDs, sterling CDs and gilts, and Ginnie Maes.

Advantages of a Swap Over Debt Refinancing

(i) Swaps avoid many of the transactions costs encountered with debt refinancing, such as legal fees, advertising, and regulatory restrictions. This is because a swap is *not* considered *new* borrowing or a public offering. Rather, it is only regarded as an exchange of interest payments on existing liabilities. (ii) Swaps also avoid many disclosure requirements of new financing because they are not considered new borrowing. This may be of importance to firms that wish to protect the confidentiality of strategic information. (iii) Many firms with low credit ratings pay a higher differential on fixed-rate debt, relative to floating-rate debt, than higher quality firms do. Such low-quality firms may wish to borrow in the floating-rate market and then swap these floating-rate liabilities for fixed-rate liabilities, perhaps avoiding some of the credit risk premium they would need to pay on newly issued debt. Thus, an important reason for the emergence of interest rate swaps (given the availability of direct debt refinancing) may well be that the search costs and credit evaluation costs encountered in nonintermediated (public debt market) transactions can be effectively lowered by financial intermediaries (swap brokers) who specialize in mitigating such informational frictions.

OTHER CONTINGENT CLAIMS: CREDIT DERIVATIVES

An important development in the contingent-claims markets that banks are involved in is *credit derivatives,* a market that barely existed until 1997, but is now trillions of dollars in magnitude. The basic idea behind a credit derivative is simple. A lender essentially purchases from a third party a put option on the borrower's debt, which entitles the lender to "put" the debt, if its value is impaired due to, say, default, to the third party. This way the lender purchases insurance against credit risk. Banks have been active players on both sides of this market, both as purchasers of credit risk insurance and as sellers of this insurance.

Figure 10.8 shows the explosive growth of the credit derivatives market from 1996 through 2010.[31] Moreover, with the spread of securitization to the credit-derivatives market, there is *pooling* and tranching of diverse credit risks. This enables idiosyncratic shocks to individual credit risks to be diversified away and risks to be spread out over many market participants. In principle, this could offer benefits. However, the 2007–2009 financial crisis has exposed the downside of this development in terms of elevating some types of risks; see Chapter 14 on the financial crisis.

The development of the credit derivatives market has been facilitated by the growing standardization of credit-derivatives contracts, and the creation of indices that offer hedges against pools of U.S. as well as non-U.S. corporate credits, such as European and Japanese corporate credits. While initial credit derivatives were simple credit default swaps involving single companies, much of the recent growth has been via pooling together of numerous credits and then tranching as in other forms of securitization (see the next chapter). Securitization has also invited significant institutional participation in this market. It is estimated that a large percentage of the trading volume in credit derivatives is accounted for by hedge funds (discussed earlier in the book).

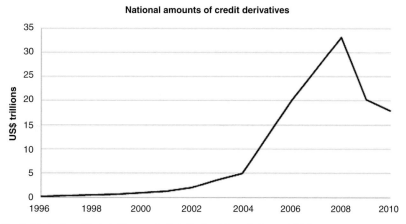

FIGURE 10.8   Growth in Credit-Derivatives Market. *(Source: British Bankers' Association and BIS).*

---

31. For the use of credit derivatives in banking, see also Minton et al. (2009), Hirtle (2009), and Stulz (2010).

RISKS FOR BANKS IN CONTINGENT CLAIMS

An Overview of Risks

With the enormous growth in the contingent claims products offered by banks, there has been growing concern that their balance sheets grossly underestimate their risks. The reasons for concern are twofold. First, because contingent claims have not required reserves or capital to support them, it has been quite tempting for banks to sell these claims in large volume, so that the OBS risk for any individual bank can become substantial. If the bank is lucky, it earns its fee revenues from sales of these claims, without suffering the adverse consequences of risk. But if things go sour, the bank could experience capital impairment, which in turn could provide further incentives for it to take risk because of the (put option) nature of deposit insurance. Of course, under the BIS capital guidelines, banks are now required to hold capital against OBS claims, so that their attractiveness to banks may decline somewhat. Second, contingent claims often create interlocking relationships across banks that could strengthen the *contingent effect* of bank failures.

We can now address the risks in individual contingent claims.

Risks in Loan Commitments

Regulators regard loan commitments as the second-riskiest contingent claim, just behind standby L/Cs, which are discussed below. A bank faces three types of risks in loan commitments: (i) the risk that it may have to lend at a lower-than-spot-market margin or even a negative margin due to fixity in the commitment rate, (ii) the risk that it may be forced to lend to higher-risk customers than its spot market, given the pool, that is, borrowers it would not have loaned to in the spot market, given the conditions at the time of commitment takedown, and (iii) the risk that it may have to fund commitment when its own liquidity is low and costly to replenish. Each of these risks is discussed below.

1. *The Risk of Lending at Low Margins:* One risk in loan commitments is that the bank may be compelled to grant loans at interest rates that either reduce profits relative to spot lending opportunities, or result in direct losses. This risk is lower per dollar of commitment with variable-rate commitments, but is present nonetheless. For example, the commitment may permit the customer to borrow at prime plus 1%. The bank cannot be assured, however, that the customer's creditworthiness will not deteriorate between the time the commitment is issued and the time that it is exercised. A customer who is "prime plus one" when the prime is 10% is likely to be riskier than "prime plus one" when the prime climbs to 20%. The creditworthiness of a borrower can be expected to vary inversely with market interest rates since higher interest rates will usually absorb a greater fraction of the borrowing firm's cash flows. Thus, even under a variable-rate commitment the bank is exposed to the risk of earning a lower interest rate on commitment loans than it would if the same funds were invested in spot loans with the same credit risk.

   The prime-times contract addresses this linkage between the prime and the customer's add-on. This contract imposes opportunity costs of the type described above only when the customer's appropriate add-on rises by more than the percent indicated in the commitment. Although the prime-times contract imposes some risk on the bank, the bank's exposure per dollar under this contract is less than for the prime-plus contract. This is because customer add-ons for spot borrowing tend to increase exponentially (as in 2, 4, 8, 16. . .) with increase in the prime rate, rather than proportionally (as in 2, 4, 8. . .) as in the prime-times commitment contract.

   Even if the customer's creditworthiness does not vary with market interest rates, the bank faces a risk with loan commitments due to sluggishness in the prime rate.[32] This sluggishness means that the bank's funding cost is only imperfectly correlated with the prime, so that as the bank's funding cost changes with movements in market interest rates, the bank will need to adjust the add-on (or multiple) to the prime that it charges the borrower. In a variable-rate commitment this add-on (multiple) is held fixed, so that as interest rates rise, the add-on (multiple) the bank should charge to break even grows larger and larger than the commitment add-on (multiple). At sufficiently high prime rates, the bank's spread between the commitment rate and its cost of funds may well invert and become negative. Of course, the reverse is true when rates are falling, but there is an asymmetry due to the option nature of the commitment since the customer will simply let the commitment expire unexercised. This is a risk that the bank does not face with spot lending because it can always adjust the add-on to the prime to reflect the prime's sluggishness in responding to market interest rate movements.

---

32. Recall the discussion in Chapter 8 of the sluggishness in the prime relative to market interest rates.

2. *The Risk of Being Forced to Lend to Excessively Risky Customers:* Loan commitments also may expose banks indirectly to increased *credit risk.* The relationship between interest rate and credit risks is manifested in two ways. First, as interest rates increase and become more volatile, the economic value of the cash flows generated by the customer's investments may become smaller and more uncertain. That is, when inflation increases, the percentage spread between nominal and real interest rates is likely to widen more than the percentage spread between nominal and real cash flows. Thus, under both fixed- and variable-rate commitments, high and volatile interest rates can expose the bank to increased credit risk. Second, high and volatile interest rates can increase credit risk through an asset substitution effect (recall the credit rationing discussion in Chapter 8) that is more likely with variable-rate commitments. The customer can be expected to adapt to a higher borrowing rate by choosing investment projects with higher expected payoffs, and these usually would have been rationed in the spot market. Note that this risk is different from that discussed under (i) in that the risk there is that the bank's profit margin on "acceptable" borrowers – those it would not have rationed in the spot market – may become too low, and the risk here is that the bank may have to lend to "unacceptable" borrowers. This risk is obviously absent in spot lending.

   Of course, the MAC clause is supposed to enable the bank to extricate itself from a commitment to a borrower whose financial condition has deteriorated significantly. The safety provided by this clause may be limited, however, due to the bank's reputation-driven reluctance to invoke the MAC.[33]

3. *The Risk of Funding Commitments in Low-Liquidity Periods:* There are two reasons why a bank may find itself liquidity constrained. One is that there may be a marketwide decline in liquidity. The other is that there may be bank-specific problems that cause familiar sources of liquidity to become substantially more expensive or even dry up. In either case, commitments become costlier to fund, a risk that is not encountered with spot lending.

Risks in Letters of Credit

Commercial L/Cs are used for routine trade transactions and carry with them credit risk, whereas standby L/Cs are mainly financial guarantees under which, in exchange for fees, banks guarantee a variety of financial obligations of borrowers to specified third parties. These pledges include credit enhancement facilities to municipal borrowers, commercial paper issuers, and those involved in securitizations. Banks consider these guarantees risky because they are irrevocable and are activated by borrower financial distress.

   There are three basic types of risks faced by banks in L/Cs: (i) credit risk, (ii) documentation risk, and (iii) political risk. We discuss each in turn.

Credit Risk

Commercial and standby L/Cs differ in that the bank pays on performance with commercial L/Cs and on nonperformance with standby L/Cs. This difference is not that significant for the bank's risk exposure, however, since it is not the ability of the debtor to perform the stipulated task that determines the bank's risk. Rather, the bank's risk in both cases turns on the debtor's reimbursement of the bank. Thus, one risk the bank faces with either a commercial or a standby L/C is *routine credit risk.* Bankers have recognized the similarity between the risks faced in normal lending and in issuing L/Cs. Although L/Cs are originated in a number of "nontraditional" divisions within the bank, such as municipal or corporate finance divisions, bankers say they apply the same credit screening procedures to standby L/Cs that they apply to their loans.

   It is often claimed that standby L/Cs are more risky than commercial L/Cs. One reason for this claim is that standby L/Cs pay on nonperformance, whereas commercial L/Cs pay on performance. As noted above, this distinction is not that significant for assessing the bank's risk exposure across the two L/Cs. Another reason why standbys are considered riskier than commercial L/Cs is that the latter routinely generate collateral in the form of goods in storage or transit (". . . commercial L/Cs are self-liquidating"), whereas standbys may be unsecured. However, collateral does not always accompany commercial L/Cs, and standby L/Cs are not always unsecured. Furthermore, financial distress often accompanies a decline in the value of the customer's collateral, so that collateral may offer the bank only limited protection in the case of L/Cs.

   It is true, nonetheless, that regulators and banks consider standby L/Cs as the riskiest of all the contingent claims offered by banks. One reason may be that standby L/Cs are used to cover almost any contingency, whereas commercial L/Cs are used for routine trade transactions. Thus, standby L/Cs may be riskier simply because they cover a variety of contingencies.

---

33. See Boot et al. (1993).

Documentation Risk

Documentation presents another source of risk in commercial L/Cs. Although this risk is routinely accepted by banks, a Federal Reserve survey found that in approximately 35% of the cases examined, documentation *failed* to conform to the requirements of the L/C. Improper documentation can invalidate a contract and prompt the buyer to refuse to accept delivery. In this case, the bank will be forced to find a buyer on its own, or to take possession of the goods.

Political Risk

U.S. exporters are sometimes unfamiliar with the foreign bank issuing an L/C. They may also be concerned about the political climate in the importer's country. The exporter may, in these cases, obtain a confirmation from a U.S. bank that is then obliged to make payment if the drawee is unable to do so. The confirming (American) bank faces two risks. One is that the issuing (foreign) bank will default, and the other is the political risk of exchange controls.

Risks in Interest Rate Swaps

Although swaps aggregate to trillions of dollars, this figure is the sum of the principal amounts involved in the deals. In fact, only the interest rate streams are at risk since each issuer retains its obligation for its own principal. Moreover, as swap brokers, the liabilities of banks are quite limited. There are two types of risks in swaps: (i) counterparty risk and (ii) legal risks. We discuss each now.

Counterparty Risk

The biggest risk for the bank is that one of the swap partners will be unable to make its interest payments. The bank then has to either assume the interest payments for the defaulting party or replace the defaulting party; this is essentially an exposure to interest rate risk. As an overall assessment, however, swaps appear to be the least risky of the three major contingent claims that we have discussed.

Legal Risks

There may be significant *hidden* legal risks in swaps that have only recently begun to surface. For example, there have been cases in which a failed bank launched court proceedings against a solvent counterparty bank over a swap, claiming that the counterparty should have honored the swap contract even after the failed bank declared bankruptcy. This was done despite the fact that the terms of the contract allowed for "limited two-way payments," under which if one party defaulted, the other was *not* liable for any payments under the contracts. (These are in contrast to "full two-way payment" contracts, under which both parties are obligated to make full payments under the swap contract even if one party defaults on other obligations. Solvent counterparty banks often make good on their liabilities (despite *no* contractual obligation to do so) because of reputational concerns and nervousness about whether their lack of contractual obligations would hold up in court if they refused to perform. This event vividly illustrates the manner in which a bank can use the contractual discretion in a contingent claim to (optimally) write down its reputational capital in order to conserve financial capital. It also shows that this trade-off is bank specific, since different banks have different reputations and different levels of financial capital.

REGULATORY ISSUES

The *Basel Accord* (Basel 1) reached under the auspices of the *Bank for International Settlements* (BIS) in 1987, stipulated a new set of *capital guidelines* under which loan commitments with maturities under 1 year were not subject to capital requirements, whereas longer-maturity commitments had a 4% capital requirement (which is half the capital requirement against most loans). Moreover, a commitment that the bank can unconditionally cancel without cause and for which it conducts an annual credit review (to decide whether it should be continued) was regarded as having a maturity under 1 year. Standby L/Cs or other types of bank guarantees are also subject to capital requirements. The capital requirement against standby L/Cs is 8%.

Under the "standardized approach" of Basel III, off-balance-sheet-items will be converted into "credit exposure equivalents" through the use of "credit conversion factors" (CCFs).[34] Commitments with an original maturity of up

---

34. See *Minimum Capital Requirements* – Bank for International Settlements www.bis.org/publ/bcbs128b.pdf.

to one year will receive a CCF of 20%, which means the capital to be allocated to it by the bank would be 20% of the capital that would need to be allocated to the loan under the commitment. Commitments with maturities exceeding one year will receive a CCF of 50%. Any commitments that are unconditionally cancellable at any time by the bank without prior notice, or that effectively provide automatic cancellation due to a deterioration in a borrower's creditworthiness, will receive 0% CCF. Standby L/Cs and acceptance will receive a CCF of 100%, as will sale and repurchase agreements (repos).

OBS items continue to be free of cash-asset *reserve requirements.* Thus, a bank need not hold cash-asset reserves against a loan commitment until the customer exercises it, at which stage the amount taken down is a loan. If the bank funds this loan with deposits, then it must hold reserves against these deposits. But if the bank chooses to sell the loan or securitize it (see Chapter 11), it can avoid the reserve requirement.

The *accounting treatment* of contingent claims is another issue. Although many contingent claims impose contingent liabilities on banks, these liabilities do not appear on the balance sheet, except as footnotes. On the other hand, the fee collected by the bank is recognized on the income statement, albeit on the basis of an amortization schedule that requires recognition over the life of the contingency. Since the cash generated by the fee income augments the book value of the bank's assets, whereas the (offsetting) contingent liability does not increase the book value of the bank's liabilities, the sale of contingent claims permits a bank to artificially inflate the book value of its net worth. Moreover, since the fees collected and the contingent liabilities imposed can be expected to be larger during periods of greater interest rate volatility, the inflation of book net worth will be greater when interest rates are more volatile. This would not be the case if the liability diminishes at the pace the income is recognized, but this seems unlikely.

CONCLUSION

In this chapter, we have reviewed the theory of commercial bank contingent claims and have commented upon their magnitude and growth. Loan commitments and L/Cs are an outgrowth of commercial bank lending in much the same way that agricultural futures markets are an outgrowth of grain trade. By the late nineteenth century, commercial banks had adopted the practice of informally assuring renewal of the short-term notes of their customers. It was a short step from such agreements to more formalized commitments. The emergence of loan commitments of the types observed today can be traced back to the early 1920s. That period marked a shift in attitude within the banking community from the "real bills" doctrine,[35] focusing on short-term self-liquidating commercial loans, to the "shiftability" theory of funds management. The latter finds liquidity in a wider variety of bank claims, providing the basis for an increased willingness by bankers to precommit loans. Forward lending quickly developed into an integral part of commercial banking.

The emergence of liability management in the 1960s along with the tight credit conditions of 1966 and 1969 increased loan commitment activity. Tight credit conditions induced borrowers to seek more loan commitment and the advent of liability management provided banks with new means of raising the funds required to meet this demand. The late 1960s and 1970s were characterized by interest rates that were both higher and more volatile. Increasing inflation led to greater loan demand and periodic credit crunches increased the demand for credit lines. Banks became less willing to offer fixed-rate commitments in the face of highly unpredictable interest rates and thus, many began to "float" the prime (the prime rate changed 40 times in 1980 as opposed to 23 times in the 13 years from August 1955 to December 1968) and offer variable-rate commitments that provided little or no protection against changes in the prime. Moreover, the increased interest rate volatility was accompanied by elevated volatility in the capital market and the foreign-exchange market. This made risk management critical for the customers of banks, and banks provided this service through a host of new derivatives and other contingent claims.

We have also discussed how recent changes in regulation have led to the imposition of capital requirements on contingent claims. These regulatory changes mean that the supply-side incentives for commercial bank contingent claims have been weakened somewhat. Despite this, we expect contingent claims to continue to grow in importance in the future.

---

35. The main point of the "real bills" doctrine was the idea that a sufficient condition for desirable monetary policy is that all banks, including the central bank, restrict their lending to "nonspeculative" loans secured by "real" collateral, that is, inventories and other tangible assets. The legislation that established the Federal Reserve System was influenced by this doctrine. A criticism of this doctrine is that it leads to a procyclical monetary policy since the Federal Reserve makes more credit available to banks in "good times" when they have sufficient eligible collateral and less in "bad times" when they have fewer assets to serve as eligible collateral. Consequently, monetary policy exaggerates and exacerbates the business cycle.

CASE STUDY: YOUNGSTOWN BANK

Introduction

John Standard has been the CEO of Youngstown Bank since the summer of 1998. Before taking this position, he had been a vice president of operations for Interbank, a large regional bank. One of the primary reasons that he was hired by Youngstown Bank was his experience with a large operating department. At the time, Youngstown Bank had been going through some difficulties related to inefficient operating procedures, and Mr. Standard had acquired a reputation at Interbank for strong motivational and organizational skills. His management of Youngstown has been almost flawless, and the institutional culture of the bank takes great pride in the fact that the bank is a very "tight ship."

Youngstown Bank has been in business in Youngstown, Arizona, since 1910. When John Standard was brought in as CEO in 1998, the stock price was at 4½, down from a high of 10. The previous CEO was the son of the founder, and he had resisted the replacement of legacy systems with more modern information processing infrastructure, allowing the operating departments to languish in mediocrity. Prior to Mr. Standard's arrival, people barely even knew what the bank's policies were on loans! The only kinds of products Youngstown Bank offered were simple fixed-rate loans. John Standard changed all that. He put together a set of standard procedures for loans and loan commitments, and attempted to tailor the bank's policies to the risk and liquidity needs of its customers. And the stock price responded; by the end of 1999, Youngstown Bank's stock price had doubled to $9, and continued to rise through 2000.

But starting in 2001, the bank's stock price has been languishing. Even though the bank's basic structure has not changed and profitability is good, the stock price has simply not moved upward over time, although the stock prices of some competing banks have moved up significantly. The major shareholders in the bank aren't too upset yet, but there have been a few grumblings. Standard realizes that there could be major trouble down the line unless he can find a way to get the share price up. He decides to call in his chief financial officer (CFO), Bryan Shelton, to discuss the stock price situation.

The Initial Meeting

Standard: Come on in, Bryan, and have a seat. Let's get right down to business here. I'm worried about our stock price performance lately. You've been with Youngstown Bank for three years now – what was the stock price when you got here?

Shelton: It was right around 37, I think.

Standard: Well, it is just over 40 now. We closed at 40 ¼ yesterday. That's only 3 dollars in 3 years! What is going on? I don't understand it. Why is our stock price so low? Take a look at how our market-to-book ratio compares with that of our competitors. It is in the dirt! (See Exhibit A). Why?

Shelton: That's a good question. Considering how precisely we control everything, and considering that our profits and cash flows are still looking good, I don't know of any reason why the stock should be down. I'm tempted to just say that the market is failing to recognize our value. Maybe they'll come around when we post good numbers again next quarter.

Standard: Well, you might be right, but I'm uncomfortable. Maybe the market is reacting to something that we don't know about. I think we should look into this some more, and try to get to the bottom of it.

[*The meeting ends on that note, and Mr. Shelton says that he will look into the matter carefully and report back. He agrees that they should meet a week later to discuss the issue again.*]

The Second Meeting

Shelton: Well, I've looked into this some more, and frankly I'm still puzzled. Take a look at these numbers. Our current balance sheet looks good, and compares very favorably with the way it looked during 2000, the heyday of our stock price rise (see Exhibit B). Our key rations look just fine, too, compared to 2000 (see Exhibit C). Moreover, we also seem to be doing well relative to industry averages (see Exhibit D).

Standard: This all looks great, just like I thought it would. Look at this one. (*He points at Exhibit D.*) Our return on assets is great. So what do you think?

Shelton: Well, one of the people I had helping me to put these numbers together for you suggested that we might want to think about our loan commitments, which don't appear on our balance sheet. Maybe those are dragging our stock price down.

Standard: That doesn't make sense. Our policies on loan commitments haven't changed, have they? What kind of data do you have on those?

Shelton: Well, take a look at these. (*He pulls out Exhibits E and F.*) These show the history of interest rates and the fees that we charge for loan commitments. I checked on the kinds of borrowers who've been buying these commitments, and the quality of the borrowers seems to be in line with our history. To tell you the truth, I'm still struggling with what all this stuff means. I don't see that anything has changed anywhere. But our stock price. . .

Standard: Well, all I can tell you is keep working on it. See if you can find anything here that will help explain why our stock price is low. Is there something that we've overlooked? Is the bank in some danger that we've failed to realize?

[*Again, the meeting ends and they agree to meet in a week. This time, Standard has some specific questions to which he wants answers. Shelton plans to go over everything carefully, looking for some explanation for the poor performance of the stock price, an explanation that takes into account all the facts about the bank's situation.*]

The Numbers

Exhibit A
YOUNGSTOWN BANK, INC.
Market-to-Book Ratio
Comparison to Industry

Year	Youngstown	BancFirst	Industry
1991	0.51	1.21	1.18
1992	1.00	1.11	1.08
1993	1.43	1.23	1.13
1994	1.47	1.32	1.21
1995	1.60	1.43	1.31
1996	2.13	1.87	1.53
1997	1.35	1.41	1.41
1998	1.18	1.11	1.20
1999	1.35	1.32	1.27
2000	1.41	1.31	1.34
2001	1.21	1.40	1.47
2002	0.95	1.65	1.53
2003	0.81	1.89	1.66
2004	0.78	1.86	1.63

Exhibit B
YOUNGSTOWN BANK, INC.
Year-End Balance Sheets (in Thousands of Dollars)

	2000	2005
Assets		
Cash & Due	125,000	129,000
Marketable Securities	200,000	400,000
Loans:		
Real Estate	190,000	385,000
Commercial and Industrial	315,500	744,000
Consumer	140,500	153,742
All Other	131,400	142,300
Less Unearned Income:		
Allowances for Possible Loan Losses	1,316	1,500
Total Loans	776,084	1,423,542
Other Assets	78,000	150,000
Total Assets	1,179,084	2,102,542
Liabilities and Equity		
Liabilities:		
Deposits	1,000,020	1,775,420
Federal Funds Purchased	75,000	102,000
Other Liabilities	63,000	90,000
Total Liabilities	1,138,020	1,967,420
Equity Capital:		
Preferred and Common Stock	11,000	35,122
Surplus	14,064	42,000
Undivided Profits and Reserves	16,000	58,000
Total Equity Capital	41,064	135,122
Total Liabilities and Equity	1,179,084	2,102,542

Note: Volume of outstanding loan commitments in 2000 was $1,000,500 and 2005 was $4,320,000.

Exhibit C

YOUNGSTOWN BANK, INC.

Comparison of Performance for 2000 and 2005

	2000	2005
Net Income (in thousands of dollars)	8,607	16,820
Return on Assets (in percentage)	0.73	0.80
Total Liabilities to Total Assets	0.97	0.94
Total Liabilities to Common Equity	27.71	14.56

Exhibit D

Various Industry Ratios for 2005

(Averages for Similarly Sized Banks)

	Youngstown	Average
Return on Assets	0.8	0.6
Total Liabilities to Total Assets	0.94	0.97
Total Liabilities to Common Equity	14.56	21.3

Exhibit E

Interest Rate History

(Annualized Interest Rates in Percentage)

	Jan	Feb	Mar	Apr	May	Jun	Jul	Aug	Sep	Oct	Nov	Dec
1991	7.95	8.00	8.00	8.00	8.27	8.63	9.00	9.01	9.41	9.94	10.94	11.55
1992	11.75	11.75	11.75	11.75	11.75	11.65	11.54	11.91	12.90	14.39	14.55	15.30
1993	15.25	15.63	18.31	17.77	15.57	12.63	11.48	11.69	12.23	14.79	16.06	17.10
1994	20.16	19.43	18.05	17.15	19.61	20.03	20.39	20.50	20.06	18.45	16.84	16.75
1995	15.75	16.56	16.50	16.50	15.5	15.50	14.26	14.39	13.50	12.52	11.85	11.50
1996	11.16	10.98	10.50	10.50	10.5	10.50	10.50	10.89	11.00	11.00	11.00	11.00
1997	11.00	11.00	11.21	11.93	12.39	12.60	13.00	13.00	12.97	12.58	11.77	11.06
1998	10.61	10.50	10.50	10.50	10.31	9.78	9.50	9.50	9.50	9.50	9.50	9.50
1999	9.50	9.50	9.10	8.83	8.50	8.50	8.16	7.90	7.50	7.50	7.50	7.50
2000	7.50	7.50	7.50	7.75	8.14	8.25	8.25	8.25	8.70	9.07	8.78	8.75
2001	8.75	8.51	8.50	8.50	8.84	9.00	9.29	9.84	10.00	10.00	10.05	10.50
2002	9.80	9.10	8.20	7.80	7.20	6.30	5.32	5.01	7.73	5.21	5.09	8.30
2003	9.20	8.30	7.40	7.10	6.20	5.50	5.10	4.80	4.50	6.20	9.10	8.10
2004	6.10	3.00	3.00	3.00	4.00	6.83	9.23	9.30	10.20	8.50	7.43	8.91

Exhibit F

Loan Commitment Prices

(Average in Basis Points)

	Commitment Fee	Annual Servicing Fee	Usage Fee
1994	12.5	12.5	25.0
1995	12.0	12.0	25.0
1996	12.0	12.0	25.0
1997	12.5	12.0	22.5
1998	12.5	12.5	22.5
1999	12.5	12.5	21.5
2000	12.5	12.5	22.5
2001	12.5	12.5	25.0
2002	12.0	12.5	25.0
2003	12.5	12.5	25.0
2004	14.0	12.5	27.5

The Assignment

Mr. Standard gives Mr. Shelton these specific questions:

1. Is the lack of upward movement in the stock price evidence of market irrationality or overreaction, or is something else going on?
2. What should the bank do? What strategies should the bank pursue? What, if any, are the major dangers faced by the bank?

REVIEW QUESTIONS

1. What is an OBS contingent claim, and what are the major types of contingent claims observed today?
2. Define a loan commitment and briefly discuss the different types of loan commitments.
3. Provide discussion of the supply-and-demand-side motivations for loan commitments.
4. It has been claimed that a bank loan commitment has an isomorphic correspondence with a common stock put option. How valid is this claim?
5. Discuss a commercial L/C, a standby L/C, and a bankers acceptance.
6. What is an interest rate swap and how does it work?
7. What is the role of a swap broker in an interest rate swap transaction?
8. Discuss three variations of the "plain vanilla" swap.
9. What are swaptions, caps, collars, and floors?
10. What are the advantages and disadvantages of an interest rate swap relative to a futures contract as a hedging instrument?
11. What is the advantage of a swap over direct financing for hedging interest rate risk?
12. Discuss the risks faced by commercial banks in loan commitments, L/Cs, and interest rate swaps.
13. Suppose a borrower knows at $t = 0$ that it will have available at $t = 1$ an opportunity to invest $175 in a risky project that will pay off at $t = 2$. The borrower knows that it will be able to invest in one of two mutually exclusive projects, S or R, each requiring a $175 investment. If the borrower invests in S at $t = 1$, the project will yield a gross payoff of $310 with probability 0.8 and zero with probability 0.2 at $t = 2$. If the borrower invests in R at $t = 1$, the project will yield a gross payoff of $330 with probability 0.6 and zero with probability 0.4 at $t = 2$. The borrower's project choice is not observable to the bank.

    The riskless, single-period interest rate at $t = 0$ is 12%. It is not known at $t = 0$ what the riskless, single-period interest rate at $t = 1$ will be, but it is common knowledge that this rate will be 8 percent (with probability 0.6) or 15% (with probability 0.4). Assume universal risk neutrality and that the borrower has no assets other than the project on which you (as the lender) can have any claim.

    Suppose you are this borrower's banker and both you and the borrower recognize that this borrower has two choices: (i) it can either do nothing at $t = 0$ and simply plan to borrow in the spot market at the interest rate prevailing for it at $t = 1$, or (ii) it can negotiate at $t = 0$ with you (or some other bank) for a loan commitment that will permit it to borrow at predetermined terms at $t = 1$. What advice should you give this borrower? Assume a competitive loan market in which each bank is constrained to earn zero expected profit.

14. The following is an excerpt from a conversation. Critique it.

    Appleton: That's simple, Mike. The BIS stipulations are *minimum* levels, whereas the Treasury proposal gives banks choices above the BIS minima. What bothers me about the BIS guidelines, though, is that they also require banks to hold capital against *off-balance sheet items.* When these items get on the balance sheet, there is another capital requirement against them, so aren't we in a sense double counting?

    Butterworth: Not really, because there is not simultaneity involved. I think that with a trillion dollars in outstanding loan commitments alone, the issue of the contingent liability exposure of American banks is something that we just have to come to grips with. The way that RAP (Regulatory Accounting Principles) and GAAP (Generally Accepted Accounting Principles) have dealt with these contingent liabilities has been deplorable. I strongly believe depository institutions should be made to recognize these liabilities *on* their balance sheets, not merely in footnotes.

    Appleton: Beth, I think you are getting a bit carried away. Nobody has any idea how these contingent liabilities should be valued, so how do you quantify your exposure?

    Butterworth: Speak for yourself, Alex. There *are* valuation models available, although I will admit they are far from perfect. But even noisy information is better than none.

15. Critique the following excerpt from a conversation.

    Moderator: Hold it there people. Remember, I cannot be here forever. I thought we were discussing banking reform and deposit insurance. Does all this talk about off-balance sheet activities have anything to do with deposit insurance?

Butterworth: That is a good question, Mike. I honestly do not know, but my guess is that contingent liabilities represent a hidden liability for the deposit insurance fund. The more contingent liabilities the bank has, the more risk there is in the banking system.

Appleton: As both of you know, I believe that off-balance sheet activities are the future of banking, so Beth's views on this trouble me. Perhaps she has some evidence to support her claim?

Butterworth: No, Alex I do not. But I will research the matter.

REFERENCES

Acharya, V.V., Almeida, H., Campello, M., 2013. Aggregate risk and the choice between cash and lines of credit. J. Financ. 68, 2059–2116.

Acharya, V.V., Mora, N., 2015. A crisis of banks as liquidity providers. J. Financ. 70, 1–43.

Almeida, H., Murillo, C., Igor, C., Weisbach, M.S., 2014. Corporate liquidity management: A conceptual framework and survey. Ann. Rev. Financ. Econ. 6, 135–162.

Almeida, H., Campello, M., Hackbarth, D., 2011. Liquidity mergers. J. Financ. Econ. 102, 526–558.

Avery, R.B., Berger, A.N., 1991. Loan commitments and bank risk exposure. J. Bank. Financ. 15, 173–192.

Berkovitch, E., Greenbaum, S.I., 1990. The loan commitment as an optimal financing contract. J. Quant. Anal. 26, 83–95.

BIS, 2014. A Brief History of the Basel Committee. Bank for International Settlements (BIS), October.

Boot, A.W.A., Greenbaum, S.I., Thakor, A.V., 1993. Reputation and discretion in financial contracting. Am. Econ. Rev. 83, 1165–1183.

Boot, A., Thakor, A.V., Udell, G.F., 1987. Competition, risk neutrality and loan commitments. J. Bank. Financ. 11, 449–471.

Campbell, T.S., 1978. A model of the market for lines of credit. J. Financ. 33, 231–244.

Campello, M., Giambona, E., Graham, J.R., Harvey, C.R., 2011. Liquidity management and corporate investment during a financial crisis. Rev. Financ. Studies 24, 1944–1979.

Campello, M., Graham, J.R., Harvey, C.R., 2010. The real effects of financial constraints: Evidence from a financial crisis. J. Financ. Econ. 97, 470–487.

Carmichael, D.R., Graham, L., 2012. Accountants' Handbook, Volume Two, Special Industries and Special Topics, Twelfth ed. Wiley Hoboken, New Jersey.

Duca, J., Vanhoose, D.D., 1990. Loan commitments and optimal monetary policy. J. Money Credit Banking 22, 178–194.

Duffie, D., 2010. The failure mechanics of dealer banks. J. Econ. Perspect. 24, 51–72.

Gatev, E., Schuermann, T., Strahan, P., 2009. Managing bank liquidity risk: How deposit-loan synergies vary with market conditions. Rev. Financ. Stud. 22, 995–1020.

Gatev, E., Strahan, P., 2006. Banks' advantage in hedging liquidity risk: theory and evidence from the commercial paper market. J. Financ. 61, 867–892.

Gyntelberg, J., Upper, C., December 2013. The OTC interest derivatives market in 2013. BIS Q. Rev. 69–82.

Hirtle, B., 2009. Credit derivatives and bank credit supply. J. Financ. Intermed. 18, 125–150.

Holmstrom, B., Tirole, J., 1993. Market liquidity and performance monitoring. J. Polit. Econ..

Huang, R., 2010. 'How Committed are Bank Lines of Credit? Experiences in the Subprime Mortgage Crisis," Working Paper No. 10-25, Research Department, Federal Reserve Bank of Philadelphia.

Hull, J.C., 2011. Options, Futures, and Other Derivatives, Eighth ed. Prentice Hall.

Ivashina, V., Scharfstein, D., 2010. Bank lending during the financial crisis of 2008. J. Financ. Econ. 97, 319–338.

Jiménez, G., Lopez, J.A., Saurina, J., 2009. Empirical analysis of corporate credit lines. Rev. Financ. Studies 22 , 5069–5098.

Kashyap, A., Rajan, R., Stein, J.C., 2002. Banks as liquidity providers: An explanation for the co-existence of lending and deposit taking. J. Financ. 57, 407–438.

Lins, K.V., Servaes, H., Tufano, P., 2010. What drives corporate liquidity? An international survey of cash holdings and lines of credit. J. Financ. Econ. 98, 160–176.

Lipin, S., November 7 1990. Banks Fear Corporations Will Tap Lines of Credit. American Banker.

Millon Cornett, M., McNutt, J.J., Strahan, P.E., Tehranian, H., 2011. Liquidity risk management and credit supply in the financial crisis. J. Financ. Econ. 101, 297–312.

Minton, B.A., Stulz, R., Williamson, R., 2009. How much do banks use credit derivatives to hedge loans? J. Financ. Services Res. 35, 1–31.

Shockley, R., Thakor, A.V., 1997. Bank loan commitments: Data, theory and tests. J. Money Credit Banking 29, 517–534.

Sofianos, G., Wachtel, P., Melnik, A., 1990. Loan commitments and monetary policy. J. Bank. Financ. 14, 677–689.

Stulz, R.M., 2010. Credit default swaps and the credit crisis. J. Econ. Perspect. 24, 73–92.

Sufi, A., 2009. Bank credit lines in corporate finance: An empirical analysis. Rev. Financ. Stud. 22, 1057–1088.

Thakor, A.V., 2005. Do loan commitments cause overlending? J. Money Credit Banking 37, 1067–1100.

Thakor, A., Hong, H., Greenbaum, S., 1981. Bank loan commitments and interest rate volatility. J. Bank. Financ. 5, 497–510.

Yun, H., 2009. The choice of corporate liquidity and corporate governance. Rev. Financ. Stud. 22, 1447–1475.

Chapter 11

Securitization

"Robert M. Greer is apartment hunting, even though he doesn't need a place to live. What the Lones Lang Wooton managing director is seeking is the best apartment buildings for inclusion in a securitized mortgage portfolio."

American Banker, October 2, 1990

GLOSSARY OF TERMS

GNMA Government National Mortgage Association (see Chapter 7).

FNMA Federal National Mortgage Association (see Chapter 7).

FHLMC Federal Home Loan Mortgage Corporation or "Freddie Mac" (see Chapter 7).

FHA Federal Housing Administration is a federal agency within the HUD Department. The FHA makes no loans, but it operates a variety of loan insurance and subsidy programs designed for low-income housing to help stabilize that segment of the home mortgage market.

Implicit Contract A term used in economics to designate an implicit understanding between parties about future behavior. There is *no* explicit contract, nor is the promise necessarily legally binding.

GMAC General Motors Acceptance Corporation is a finance company that is a subsidiary of General Motors Corporation.

BB, A-1 Ratings Ratings given to bonds by private agencies that specialize in evaluating credit risks. Companies usually pay these agencies to have their bonds rated. The ratings are then publicized and have an impact on the yield of the rated bonds. Generally, the higher the alphabet, the poorer the credit risk, that is, an A rating is better than a B rating, and an AA rating is better than an A rating.

INTRODUCTION

Banking used to be a simple business. A bank borrowed money and loaned to others at a spread over cost. The borrowing and lending activities were reflected on the bank's balance sheet.[1] But now banks are as likely to do this business "off-balance sheet" as "on." Chapter 10 discussed some off-balance sheet activities of banks, including loan commitments. We continue that discussion with an examination of securitization and loan sales.

Let us start with a loan commitment. When a bank provides ("sells") a loan commitment, it needs to provide funding only if the customer exercises the commitment. If a "takedown" occurs, the loan appears on the balance sheet. But the bank can avoid funding, even at this stage, by selling the loan to another bank (a loan sale) or by securitizing it. Securitization involves combining the loan with others of similar characteristics, creating credit-enhanced claims against the cash flows of this portfolio, and then selling these claims to investors.[2]

The practice of loan sales by banks, which we covered in Chapter 9, is quite old; it goes all the way back to 1880. Securitization, by contrast, is more recent, dating back to 1970 when the Government National Mortgage Association ("Ginnie Mae," or GNMA) developed the GNMA *pass-through,* a mortgage-backed security collateralized by Federal Housing Administration (FHA) and Veterans Administration (VA) single-family mortgage loans. Thus, the S&L industry has been involved in securitization for over 40 years. Banks, on the other hand, are relative newcomers to this market. Although in 1977 Bank of America issued the first private-sector pass-through, which was backed by conventional mortgages, the securitizing of various types of bank loans did not begin until 1985.

Securitization is of growing importance in the U.S. economy. As of April 2011, the amount of securitized assets had risen to $11 trillion, an amount that exceeded all marketable U.S. Treasury securities.[3] The European volume is approximately 20–25% of that in the United States, but showed a much higher growth rate before the 2007–2009 financial crisis; see Figure 11.1, which also shows the volume of securitization relative to GDP.

The origins of securitization can be traced to familiar lending practices such as factoring and secured lending, and the market subsequently evolved to the securitization of pools of home mortgages. Nonmortgage asset securitization began in March 1985 when Sperry Lease Financial Corporation floated a $192.5 million public offering. These pass-through

---

1. No wonder Walter Bagehot, an economist, said, "The business of banking ought to be simple; if it is hard, it is wrong." [Bagehot (1873)].

2. For good reviews of securitization, we recommend Pavel (1989) and Fishman and Kendall (2000).

3. See Gorton and Metrick (2013).

S. I. Greenbaum, A. V. Thakor & A. W. A. Boot: Contemporary Financial Intermediation, Third edition. http://dx.doi.org/10.1016/B978-0-12-405196-6.00011-2

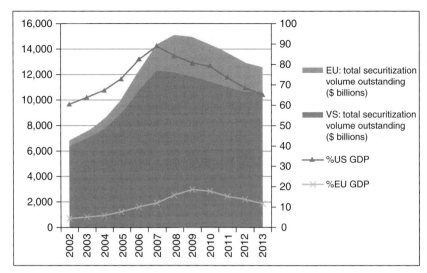

FIGURE 11.1 Total Outstanding Securitized Assets US vs. EU (and as % of GDP). Bron: SIFMA.

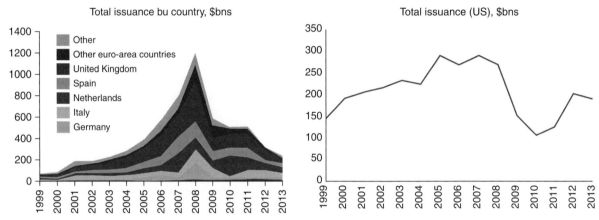

FIGURE 11.2 New Issuance in the EU and US ABS Market, 1999–2013. *(Source: Altomonte and Bussoli (2014), based on SIFMA data).*

securities (which represent direct ownership claims against the securitized portfolio) were secured by a pool of lease receivables originated by Sperry Corporation, now Unisys Corporation. Letters of credit from Union Bank of Switzerland (now part of UBS) facilitated a triple-A debt rating for the issue.

The securitization market is often referred to as the Asset-Backed Securities (ABS) market. The stated maturities in the ABS market usually do not exceed 6 years and average lives have ranged from 6 months to 5 years. Most of the market is concentrated in the 18-to-36-month period. The securitization market has increased dramatically, both in the United States and abroad. Figure 11.2 provides information on the annual ABS issuance in the United States and Europe.[4] Securitization is also important in Asia and Latin America.[5]

Currently, a wide range of assets are securitized. Examples are: automobile loans and leases, credit card receivables, commercial truck loans, and boat loans. Private issuers include commercial banks, finance subsidiaries of industrial companies, and savings institutions. See Table 11.1 for data on different types of securitized assets in the United States.

An initial obstacle to securitization in the United States was uncertainty about whether the Glass–Steagall Act problems on underwriting or distribution of corporate securities also prohibited securitization. However, in the mid-1980s, the Office of the Comptroller of the Currency (OCC) ruled that national banks could sell interests in pools of loans. A court of appeals upheld the OCC's position and ruled against the Securities Industries Association (SIA). The court ruled that sale of ABS was not limited by Glass–Steagall because these instruments were "not securities but investments in

---

4. Note the numbers for the United States (contrary to those in Figure 11.1) do not include the "agency" MBS securities market, that is, the trillions of US$ MBS securities issued by government-sponsored enterprises such as Fannie Mae or Freddie Mac. And note, Europe does typically not have "agency" securitized assets, hence Figures 11.1 and 11.2 are consistent with each other for reported European volumes. See also Altomonte and Bussoli (2014).

5. See Gyntelberg and Remolona (2006), and Scatigna and Tovar (2007).

TABLE 11.1 Asset-Backed Securities Outstanding by Major Types of Credit 1995–2012

	1995	1996	1997	1998	1999	2000	2001	2002	2003	2004	2005	2006	2007	2008	2009	2010	2011	2012
Total amount outstanding	260.9	373.8	519.6	653.6	959.6	1092.9	1238.8	1388.1	1513.9	1824.4	2126.7	2726.0	2972.2	2624.3	2347.7	2053.3	1834.3	1701.1
Automobile	52.8	66.7	79.4	88.5	109.4	140.5	167.0	187.6	191.5	177.3	195.9	196.2	181.2	141.5	128.4	117.4	118.4	143.3
% of Total	20.2%	17.8%	15.3%	13.5%	11.4%	12.9%	13.5%	13.5%	12.6%	9.7%	9.2%	7.2%	6.1%	5.4%	5.5%	5.7%	6.5%	8.4%
Credit card	129.9	167.1	191.0	199.6	213.8	236.8	265.9	293.3	303.5	297.5	287.2	291.5	324.4	315.6	300.3	216.9	164.1	127.9
% of Total	49.8%	44.7%	36.7%	30.5%	22.3%	21.7%	21.5%	21.1%	20.0%	16.3%	13.5%	10.7%	10.9%	12.0%	12.8%	10.6%	8.9%	7.5%
Home equity	34.3	60.6	105.7	146.6	338.0	352.6	388.6	452.9	497.7	711.5	843.2	1085.3	1040.2	834.3	679.9	594.2	522.0	469.4
% of Total	13.2%	16.2%	20.3%	22.4%	35.2%	32.3%	31.4%	32.6%	32.9%	39.0%	39.6%	39.8%	35.0%	31.8%	29.0%	28.9%	28.5%	27.6%
Manufactured housing	16.1	22.1	28.6	37.4	47.9	52.4	51.7	47.9	39.3	34.1	29.4	25.6	22.6	20.3	18.0	16.5	14.7	13.2
% of total	6.2%	5.9%	5.5%	5.7%	5.0%	4.8%	4.2%	3.4%	2.6%	1.9%	1.4%	0.9%	0.8%	0.8%	0.8%	0.8%	0.8%	0.8%
Student loan	6.5	14.3	25.9	31.5	36.4	44.7	48.1	58.7	87.8	122.5	159.6	200.6	229.6	237.9	239.5	240.6	234.6	234.1
% of total	2.5%	3.8%	5.0%	4.8%	3.8%	4.1%	3.9%	4.2%	5.8%	6.7%	7.5%	7.4%	7.7%	9.1%	10.2%	11.7%	12.8%	13.8%
Equipment leases	8.5	14.3	16.8	20.7	23.8	28.1	26.5	21.5	22.7	24.0	26.2	29.0	28.3	18.6	15.9	13.1	13.9	18.6
% of total	3.3%	3.8%	3.2%	3.2%	2.5%	2.6%	2.1%	1.5%	1.5%	1.3%	1.2%	1.1%	1.0%	0.7%	0.7%	0.6%	0.8%	1.1%
Other*	12.7	28.7	72.4	129.2	190.3	237.8	291.0	326.2	371.3	457.6	585.1	897.9	1145.9	1056.2	965.8	854.7	766.6	694.6
% of total	4.9%	7.7%	13.9%	19.8%	19.8%	21.8%	23.5%	23.5%	24.5%	25.1%	27.5%	32.9%	38.6%	40.2%	41.1%	41.6%	41.8%	40.8%

*"Other" includes CDOs.
Source: The Securities Industry and Financial Markets Association.

the underlying loans." The Supreme Court later refused to hear an appeal by the SIA, thereby establishing the right of national banks to securitize.[6]

In the rest of this chapter, we cover a fairly wide range of topics pertaining to loan sales and securitization. In the next section, we explain securitization and loan sales as natural outcomes of the desire to capture some of the gains from decomposing the traditional lending function. Then we describe the different ways in which securitization is achieved. This is followed by an examination of the economics of securitization in greater detail. Accounting and regulatory issues are examined in the next section. After this we explore the strategic issues faced by banks participating in the ABS market. Loan sales are examined subsequently, and this is followed by the concluding section. A case study is provided to illustrate the strategic securitization issues facing banks.

PRELIMINARY REMARKS ON THE ECONOMIC MOTIVATION FOR SECURITIZATION AND LOAN SALES

Decomposition of the Lending Function

Lending can be decomposed into at least four basic operations: (a) origination (including underwriting), (b) guaranteeing, (c) servicing, and (d) funding. This decomposition was long obscured by the *modus operandi* of financial institutions, which unified these operations. But there is nothing immutable about this unification. For example, suppose a bank were to specialize in the processing of interest rate and credit risk, along with the provision of brokerage services. It could restrict itself to writing letters of credit and loan commitments, avoiding deposits and earning assets altogether.

So why were these lending functions combined in the first place and why are they being decomposed now? The reasons are twofold: funding advantages due to the regulatory environment and information technology. Let us consider each in turn.

The Traditional Benefits of Funding Loans

In earlier times, depository institutions enjoyed an advantage in funding, and they consequently developed the expertise needed to originate and underwrite assets including loans. The funding advantage was a consequence of regulation: deposit interest rate ceilings, underpriced governmental deposit insurance, entry restrictions, and various tax advantages – particularly those related to loan-loss reserves, mutuality, and housing. The resulting rents were shared among depositors, borrowers, and owners/managers of banks and thrifts. This system, introduced in the 1930s following more than a decade of socially disruptive bank failures, was based on an *implicit contract* between depositors, owners/managers of banks and thrifts, and the government. Depositors agreed to accept a below-market return for their funds in exchange for a government guarantee; the guarantee (deposit insurance) transformed bank and thrift liabilities into contingent claims against the U.S. government. Bankers agreed to accept regulation and supervision in exchange for a subsidy that lowered the cost and extended the duration of deposits. The government accepted a residual exposure (on behalf of the taxpayers) under the deposit guarantee in exchange for the political gains from stability in the banking system.

The Erosion of Funding Benefits and the Incentives for Securitization and Loan Sales

The implicit contract between depositors, depository institutions, and the government remained intact until the inflation of the 1970s increased the opportunity cost of deposit holding from something on the order of 100 basis points to 400, 500, or even 600 basis points. This caused depositors to turn to higher-yielding money-market funds. The implicit contract began to unravel.

The trend continued with the legislatively mandated dismantling of deposit interest rate ceilings in the 1980s. As deposit interest rates rose, deposit rents of banks and thrifts eroded. In addition, entry barriers into banking began to crumble, tax preferences began to vanish, and the price of deposit insurance increased and capital requirements were raised. In varying degrees, all of these changes diminished the rents available to banks and the advantages that they enjoyed in funding loans with deposits. However, the originating, monitoring, and servicing skills that they had developed earlier remained intact. This provided the first impetus for banks and thrifts to originate and underwrite loans, but not to fund them, that is, to either sell or securitize loans.

A second impetus for loan sales and securitization was provided by advances in information technology. A successful loan sale requires that the buyer (usually another financial institution) be able to assess the payoff attributes of the loan,

---

6. See Huber (1992).

which in turn is facilitated by good information. This is even more critical for securitization in cases where the buyers are investors as opposed to financial institutions. Improvements in information processing technology have made it easier for investors to rate assets, and therefore reduce informational gaps between investors and the originators of loans (banks). Moreover, information technology has been the key to the servicing and monitoring provided by financial institutions, especially with stripped cash flows. This has facilitated securitization.[7] This argument can be seen quite clearly in the (somewhat oversimplified) numerical example given below.

Example 11.1

Suppose the North American Bank has originated a portfolio of loans. North American knows that the aggregate payoff on this portfolio will be $100 with probability 0.9 and $30 with probability 0.1. Call this portfolio A. Investors, however, are unable to distinguish between this portfolio and another loan portfolio, call it B, that has an aggregate payoff of $100 with probability 0.7 and $30 with probability 0.3. Investors believe that there is a 0.5 probability that the portfolio is A, and an equal probability that it is B. There is universal risk neutrality.

The cost to the bank of communicating the "true" value of its loan portfolio is $11; this can be viewed simply as a charge against the revenue from the sale of the loan portfolio. Think of this as a signaling cost (Chapter 1) that declines with advances in information technology because these advances enable firms to resort to lower-cost signaling mechanisms. Also, North American's net profit from loan origination and servicing is 1% of the value of the securitized loan portfolio, whereas if the loans are kept on the books and funded by the bank, the bank's net profit is 2% of the "true" value of the loan portfolio minus a fixed cost of 99 cents associated with funding (this could represent, for instance, the sum total of regulatory taxes and administrative costs). Will North American prefer to securitize or fund its loan portfolio? Does your answer change if the communication cost drops from $11 to $2?

Solution

We will solve this problem in three steps. First, we will show that if North American decides to sell/securitize its loan portfolio, it will prefer to do so *without* communicating information to investors since the cost of communication exceeds the benefits of revelation. Having shown that securitization without communication dominates securitization with communication, in Step 2 we show that North American prefers to fund the loan rather than securitize it without communication. Finally, in Step 3 we show that North American prefers to securitize with communication if the communication cost drops from $11 to $2.

Step 1

First, we compute the value of the "pooled" portfolio, that is, the price at which the bank can sell or securitize the portfolio without any information communication. Given risk neutrality, the bank offering portfolio A will be able to sell it for the average of the values of portfolios A and B, that is, at

$$\underset{\text{(expected value of loan portfolio A)}}{0.5[0.9 \times 100 + 0.1 \times 30]} \quad + \quad \underset{\text{(expected value of loan portfolio B)}}{0.5[0.7 \times 100 + 0.3 \times 30]}$$

$$= 0.5[93] + 0.5[79] = \$86.$$

Then, it is apparent that it does not pay for North American to reveal its true portfolio quality to investors, since its net payoff from doing so is $93 (the privately known value of its loan portfolio) minus $11 (the cost of information communication), which equals $82, whereas the "pooling value" of its loan portfolio is $86. Thus, securitization without communication dominates securitization with communication.

Step 2

You can see now that if North American securitizes its portfolio without communication, its net profit is 86 cents (1% of $86). But if it funds the loans, its net profit is $0.02 \times \$93 - 0.99 = 87$ cents. Thus, the bank will prefer *not* to securitize when the cost of communicating the true value of its loan portfolio to investors is $11. Combining steps 1 and 2 shows that funding the loan is North American's optimal strategy.

Step 3

If the communication cost drops to $2, North American's net profit from communicating and securitizing is $0.01 \times \$[93 - 2] = 91$ cents. This exceeds both the net profit from funding the loans as well as the net profit from securitizing without communication, and shows how improvements in information processing technology that reduce the costs of communicating financial information – can spur securitization.

A more complete discussion of this phenomenon appears in a later section.

---

7. See Greenbaum and Thakor (1987) for a discussion of securitization that assigns a role to information processing costs. Boot and Thakor (1993) explain securitization on the grounds that pooling a large number of securities in a portfolio diversifies away idiosyncratic information about individual securities, reducing the burden on investors to produce that information, and then tranching the cash flows from the portfolio to create multiple (debt) securities permits the creation of information-sensitive securities that encourage investors to engage in costly information production about the securities. See also Kareken (1987) and Fishman and Kendall (2000). An examination of the effects of asset securitization appears in Thomas (2001).

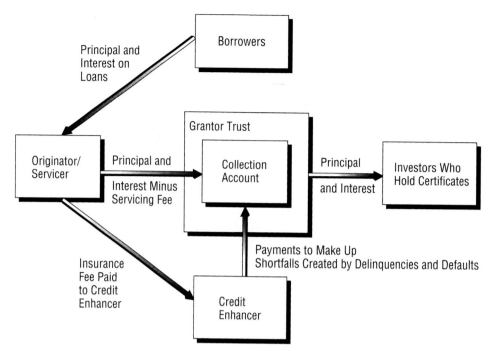

FIGURE 11.3 Cash-Flow Schematic for a Static Pass-Through.

DIFFERENT TYPES OF SECURITIZATION CONTRACTS

Loan-backed securities are collateralized by residential, multifamily, and commercial mortgage loans, automobile loans, credit card receivables, Small Business Administration loans, computer and truck leases, loans for mobile homes, and various finance receivables. There are three basic types of ABS, each of which evolved from the secondary mortgage market.

Pass-Throughs

The first type of loan-backed security is a *pass-through,* which represents *direct ownership* in a portfolio of mortgage loans that share similar maturity, interest rate, and quality characteristics. The portfolio is placed in a grantor trust and certificates of ownership are sold directly to investors; each certificate represents a claim against the entire loan portfolio. The loan originator (say a bank or a thrift) services the portfolio and collects interest and principal on the loans, although sometimes origination and servicing are provided by different institutions. The servicer deducts a fee from the collected proceeds and passes the difference along to the investors; hence the name "pass-through." Ownership of the loans (mortgages) rests with the certificate holders. Thus, pass-throughs do not appear on the originator's balance sheet. There are two structures used with pass-throughs: static pool and dynamic pool. Each is discussed below.

Static Pool Pass-Throughs

The term "static" here refers to the nature of the pool of loans against which claims are sold to investors; this pool is fixed. The trust in which the loans are held is tax free at the trust level. Taxes are levied at the *beneficiary* level. Most pass-through securities provide for monthly payments of principal and interest. Figure 11.3 shows a schematic for a typical static pass-through structure.[8] The payments made by borrowers are paid into a separate interest-bearing account maintained in the trust department of an insured bank (the trustee) in the name of the trustee. This account is known as the *collection account.* Payments into this account are applied first to pay a monthly servicing fee. On each payment date, the trustee passes along the monthly payments of principal and interest to investors. The servicer is responsible for paying the trustee's fee.

There is usually *credit enhancement* of the loan portfolio. This enhancement is provided by posting "excess" collateral and/or through an *insurance bond* purchased by the originator. The protection covers some proportion of the underlying assets at the date of issue. For example, suppose there is 15% credit enhancement with an insurance bond. The credit enhancer

---

8. The ensuing is based in part on Pavel (1989).

is then responsible for loan defaults up to that percentage of the value of the securitized loan portfolio.[9] In effect, the credit enhancer purchases the defaulted contracts. With a credit enhancement, the guarantor trust is entitled to payments from the credit enhancer to cover the losses of the loan portfolio due to defaults up to the specified coverage.

The most common type of static pass-through is the Ginnie Mae, which is a mortgage-backed security collateralized by FHA-VA mortgages. The GNMA, a direct agency of the federal government, acts as a credit enhancer, guaranteeing timely payment of principal and interest. Thus, these pass-throughs are virtually free of default risk for investors. A highly developed secondary market ensures liquidity for these instruments. The federal Home Loan Mortgage Corporation (Freddie Mac), an indirect agency of the federal government, developed a similar pass-through security in 1971, called the "participation certificate" (PC). The Federal National Mortgage Association (FNMA, or Fannie Mae) developed the mortgage-backed security (MBS) in 1981. Both the PC and the MBS are backed by portfolios of uninsured and privately insured mortgage loans. Monthly interest and full repayment of principal on PCs are guaranteed by Freddie Mac, but the timing of principal payments is not.

Private sector pass-throughs are less common than these federal agency issues. In 1977, Bank of America issued the first private sector pass-through. These securities were backed by conventional mortgages, and private mortgage insurance was purchased to cover the entire pool of loans rather than each individual loan. Since the insurance covered the loan portfolio as a whole, diversification available to the insurance company meant lower insurance cost than if individual loans, representing a subset of the portfolio, had been insured.

Dynamic Pool Pass-Through Structure

"Dynamic" refers to the pool of loans against which claims are sold to investors. The debt obligations included in the pool are usually *short term,* so that they turn over, implying changes in the composition of the loan portfolio. This structure, also known as a "revolving structure," involves a pool of loans with an average life that is *shorter* than the stated maturities of claims issued against the pool. When a loan within the pool matures, the proceeds are reinvested for a fixed period of time (the "revolving period"). During the revolving period (the duration of which can be structured to satisfy desired asset considerations), only interest is paid to the certificate holders. All principal repayments are reinvested to maintain the original principal amount. Principal amortization begins at the end of the revolving period, usually on a pass-through basis. This design is most often used with credit card receivables (e.g., JCP Master Credit Card Trust for JC Penney credit card receivables and Sears Credit Account Trust for Sears credit card receivables) where repayment periods are uncertain and can be very brief, frustrating the desire of investors to remain invested for some minimum period.

Asset-Backed Bonds

The second type of ABS is the asset-backed bond (ABB). Like the static pass-through, the ABB is collateralized by a portfolio of loans. The main difference is that in the case of an ABB, the originator sells the assets to a *wholly owned subsidiary* created for the sole purpose of securitizing the assets. Consequently, the *assets remain on the originator's (consolidated) balance sheet.* That is, instead of selling the assets to a trust that subsequently sells claims against the assets to investors, the subsidiary itself issues claims (general obligation notes) to investors. These claims are secured solely by the assets of the subsidiary and any credit enhancement obtained for the purpose. Figure 11.4 depicts the cash-flow structure of an ABB. As the figure indicates, the finance company, which is a wholly owned subsidiary of the originator, issues certificates/notes to investors, usually through an investment bank that underwrites the issue. The revenues collected by the finance company from principal and interest payments are transferred to a trustee. These revenues are added to cash contributions made by a credit enhancer and then disbursements are made to investors by the trustee.

An important difference between a pass-through and an ABB is that the cash flows from the pool of assets that serve as collateral are *not* dedicated to the payments of principal and interest on ABBs. The maturity on an ABB is usually prespecified (normally 5–12 years) and interest is generally paid semiannually.

ABBs are usually *overcollateralized.* The norm is to evaluate the collateral quarterly, and to augment it if the value falls below an amount stated in the bond indenture. The reasons for overcollateralizing are twofold.

1. Overcollateralization, like other forms of credit enhancement, increases safety for investors and therefore reduces the required yield on the ABB. This benefits the originator because any proceeds beyond what is needed to service the principal and interest on the ABB accrue to the originator but are used to augment the value of the collateral pool. Thus, the

---

9. The level of credit enhancement is typically determined by the credit-rating agency as the minimum that is required in order to assign to the loan portfolio the credit desired by the issuer.

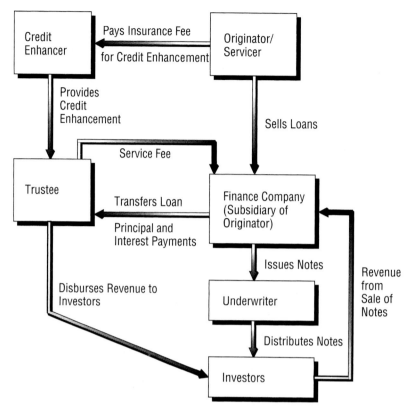

FIGURE 11.4 Cash-Flow Schematic for an Asset-Backed Bond.

overcollateralization is a particular form of *reinvestment* of the proceeds collected by the originator from the pool of assets. By reinvesting to increase the collateral, the originator reduces the risk faced by investors in the same way that a borrower reduces a lender's risk by using project cash flows to purchase additional collateral rather than using the cash flows to increase dividends to shareholders. That is, overcollateralization improves the overall outcome by diminishing a form of *moral hazard*. Other forms of credit enhancement, such as an insurance bond, also diminish moral hazard, but work a little differently. For example, with an insurance bond, the firm providing the bond would be expected to monitor the originator to ensure sufficiently high asset quality.

2. Excess collateral also protects investors against decreases in the market value of the collateral between valuation dates. This is a simple *risk-sharing* argument. If the originator is more risk tolerant than individual investors – perhaps because of a superior ability to hedge risks – then the originator provides investors a form of value-fluctuation insurance in exchange for a lower yield on the ABB. In this sense, overcollateralization is no different from any other form of credit enhancement.

ABBs have been used by both public and private entities, but private issues dominate. Major private issuers are savings and loan associations and mutual savings banks. The ABB market, however, is much smaller than the market for pass-throughs (about 5% of the market for pass-throughs). One reason for this may be that an ABB stays on the originator's books. Thus, a financial institution must hold both reserves and capital against an ABB.

Pay-Throughs

The third type of ABS is the *pay-through bond*. This security combines features of the pass-through and the ABB. Its similarity to the ABB is that the pay-through appears on the originator's balance sheet as debt. Its similarity to the pass-through is that cash flows from the pool of assets used as collateral are dedicated to servicing the bonds.

CMO

In June 1983, Freddie Mac issued a pay-through bond called a *Collateralized Mortgage Obligation* (CMO). Each CMO issue was divided into three "tranches" (maturity classes), and each class received semiannual interest payments. The

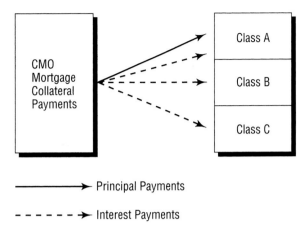

FIGURE 11.5 Cash-Flow Schematic for a CMO (for the First Five Years).

tranches, however, were strictly prioritized for the receipt of scheduled principal payments and repayments. That is, Class A bondholders received the first installments of principal payments, and any prepayments, until Class A bonds were paid off. After Class A bondholders were paid off, Class B bondholders began to receive principal payments and repayments. Class B bondholders have to be completely paid off before Class C bondholders could. Class A bondholders were repaid within 5 years of the offering date, Class B bonds will be repaid within 12 years, and Class C bonds within 20 years. Figure 11.4 provides a cash-flow diagram for a CMO for the first five years or until tranche A is repaid.

Under the structure in Figure 11.5, Class A would receive interest plus all of the principal payments passed through from the underlying mortgages until it is entirely paid off (which is estimated to take no more than five years), while Classes B and C receive only interest. While there is still variability in the rate of repayment due to the randomness in prepayment rates, the CMO structure reduces this variability by "serializing" cash flows this way. That is, CMO-holders receive a kind of "call protection." They can be reasonably confident that their bonds will not prepay (be called) prematurely.

CMOs facilitate the management of *prepayment risk*. Routinely borne by financial institutions, this risk arises from the fact that borrowers tend to *prepay* their debts when interest rates fall because they can refinance at lower rates. This is especially true for long-term mortgages that have no prepayment penalties. Thus, the financial institution does not fully benefit from the decline in its cost of funds relative to the rates on its longer-maturity assets. On the other hand, when interest rates rise, the institution's cost of funds rises but its asset returns do not, as borrowers hold on to their low-interest-rate mortgages. By investing in a CMO tranche with a sufficiently long effective maturity (say Class C in Figure 11.5), the institution can reduce its exposure to prepayment risk.

A wide variety of CMOs are available. They range from three maturity classes to more than six. Most, however, have four tranches, which include three "regular" maturity classes and a "residual" class, called the "Z class." The first three classes are paid interest at the stated rates, starting with the issue date. The Z class is basically an accrual bond in which earned interest accrues to the principal and is compound while the other classes earn interest. After the first three classes are paid off, the Z class receives regular principal and interest payments along with accrued interest.

CMOs can be used by financial institutions to facilitate asset/liability management. For example, suppose an S&L has 30-year fixed-rate mortgages financed with liabilities of shorter maturities. Such an institution could reduce the maturity mismatching on its balance sheet by swapping its mortgages for the shorter tranches of CMOs.

Both public and private sector firms participate in the CMO market. Issuers include investment banks, federal agencies, builders, and thrift institutions, among others. The issuance of a CMO is *not* an asset sale because the debt obligation stays on the originator's books. This structure was adopted to comply with tax regulations that stated that a trust could not qualify for *grantor trust status* if it issued multiclass claims that divide the cash flows in a *not prorata* fashion, as a CMO does; recall that this "tax problem" does not arise with pass-throughs because certificate holders do receive the cash flows in a prorata fashion. Thus, a CMO had to tolerate the "inefficiency" of keeping the collateral assets on the originator's balance sheet rather than selling these to a trust. This resulted in another tax disadvantage, namely that due to regulatory taxes like reserve and capital requirements and deposit insurance premiums. This limited the use of CMOs.

REMICs

The Tax Reform Act (TRA) of 1986 authorized REMICs (Real Estate Mortgage Investment Conduits). The main difference between a CMO and a REMIC is in the *tax treatment.* REMICs can qualify as *asset sales* for *tax purposes* if the following conditions are satisfied.

1. A REMIC must contain at least one regular class and no more than one residual class.
2. The collateral of a REMIC must consist of "qualified mortgages" or "permitted investments." Qualified mortgages include single and multifamily residential mortgage loans and commercial mortgages as well as mortgage-backed securities. Permitted investments include short-term interest-bearing securities used only for reinvesting monthly cash flows prior to their scheduled transfer to bondholders, investments to fund operating expenses of the REMIC, and properties acquired through foreclosure.

Securitization Innovations

New types of securitization contracts continue to proliferate for three main reasons. First, lower interest rates have made the prepayment options in mortgages more valuable to investors, who have become more sophisticated in dealing with prepayment risk. Thus, new securities that facilitate the management of prepayment risk have been created.

Second, investors who are relatively uninformed about the probability distributions of future payoffs on various securities will find themselves at a disadvantage in dealing with investors who are better informed. The uninformed will therefore demand relatively information-insensitive securities that would enable them to trade without being expropriated. The cash-flow stripping that accompanies securitization often creates information-insensitive securities by partitioning the cash flows of a composite, information-sensitive security in such a way that the senior-most security is a nearly riskless bond that would appeal to uninformed investors.[10]

Third, innovations in securitization and cash-flow stripping have also facilitated the creation of securities that appeal to informed investors. A given security with some private-information content can always be stripped into two securities, one of which is more information sensitive (has a greater private-information content) than the original security. Those who have the ability to acquire information at a cost will find that the return on their investment in information is greater with the more information-sensitive security. Thus, more of these investors will become informed, and there will be a greater demand from these investors, which in turn will elevate the price at which the security trades, and hence the issue's revenue.[11] A similar argument can be made for other attributes of the original security, which can be altered through cash-flow stripping to appeal to specific clienteles of investors. For example, investors may have different cash-flow preferences due to tax considerations and risk attitudes. Then, stripping a security into components permits the issuer to cater more effectively to the desires of these clienteles than issuing only a single class of pass-throughs would permit. Translated into dollars, this means higher revenue for the issuer. Investors desire a low prepayment rate even when interest rates are falling. Investors who want a discount mortgage security with higher prepayment can purchase a P/O ("principal-only" security).

Stripped Securities

The *stripped mortgage security* (the "strip") involves two classes of pass-through securities that receive different portions of principal and interest from the same pool of mortgage loans. For example, a pool of mortgage loans with an average APR of 8% might be split into a "premium" security with a 12% coupon and a "discount" security with a 4% coupon. When this process of "stripping" is taken to its logical extreme, it creates interest-only (I/O) and principal-only (P/O) securities. This is known as an I/O–P/O *strip.* Holders of the I/O strip receive primarily interest payments from the securitized pool, whereas the holders of the P/O strip receive nearly all of the principal payments.

Strips offer advantages to issuers as well as to investors. The advantages to investors are based on the clientele's argument presented earlier. That is, some investors may prefer information-insensitive securities, others may prefer information-sensitive securities, and yet others may desire a specific cash-flow pattern due to tax considerations. Strips can satisfy these different demands.

A financial institution can also use I/O–P/O strips for hedging against interest-rate risk. I/Os are useful in hedging fixed-rate mortgage loans and other fixed-income assets. An increase in interest rates causes a decline in the value of the I/O as with other fixed-income assets. However, the higher interest rates will slow down prepayments. This will generate

---

10. Gorton and Pennacchi (1990) have proposed this explanation as a way to understand the preponderance of diversified baskets of securities, riskless CDs, and other information-insensitive assets.
11. This intuition is provided by Boot and Thakor (1993).

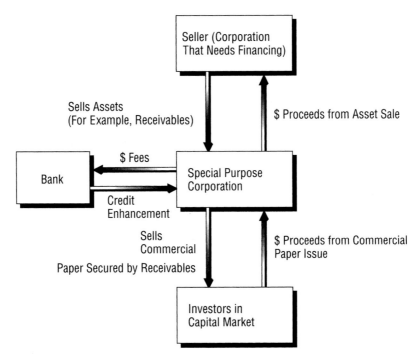

FIGURE 11.6 A Typical ABCP Program.

higher-than-expected cash flows for the holders of the I/O strips, and will thereby increase the value of the I/O. In most interest-rate scenarios, an increase in interest rates will cause prepayments to fall sufficiently to create an *inverse relationship* between the value of the I/O strips and the prices of the bank's other fixed-income assets. This provides hedging.

A financial institution can use P/O strips to hedge its fixed-income liabilities. A decrease in interest rates increases the value of a P/O strip because the discount rate for computing the present value of future principal payments has decreased. Moreover, prepayments go up, accelerating the cash flows accruing to the holders of the P/O strips, further increasing the value of that strip. Thus, the value of a P/O is inversely related to the values of fixed-income liabilities, and hedging is possible.

Asset-Backed Commercial Paper (ABCP)

ABCP is commercial paper secured by designated corporate assets, typically receivables. The term ABCP is almost oxymoronic since commercial paper is understood to be the traded, short-term *unsecured* debt of corporations. The maturity is typically 90–180 days. Figure 11.6 illustrates how an ABCP program works.[12]

A bank establishes a "special purpose corporation" (SPC). The SPC purchases credit card receivables or other assets from a corporation (the seller) in need of funding. To finance this purchase, the SPC issues commercial paper that is secured by the assets purchased by the SPC. The bank provides credit enhancement enabling the SPC to obtain a high credit rating for the commercial paper, typically through overcollateralization and/or a standby letter of credit. This credit enhancement enables the SPC to obtain a high credit rating for the commercial paper.

The ABCP market, which came into existence in 1983, has expanded rapidly, growing to a multibillion-dollar market within a decade. Fitch Investors Service reports that, in mid-1993, 175 ABCP programs were in operation, representing $75 billion in outstanding commercial paper and $150 billion in commitments. By the end of 2006, ABCP outstanding in the United States had grown to $1.1 trillion, larger than the amount of unsecured (non-asset-backed) commercial paper outstanding and a significant portion of the "shadow banking system" in the United States.[13] Global banks like Societe Generale (France), Deutsche Bank (Germany), Barclays Bank (United Kingdom), UBS (Switzerland), Sumitomo Mitsui Banking Corporation (Japan), and Canadian Imperial Bank of Commerce (Canada) were big players in this market. Following the financial crisis during which the ABCP market was under enormous stress and fell out of favor with many, outstanding volume dropped below $400 billion by 2010, and by the end of 2014 to slightly over $200 billion.[14] The boom

---

12. This discussion is based in part on Cutler and Sveen (1993) and Kraus (1993).
13. See Covitz et al. (2013).
14. For these numbers see Bank of America Global Capital Management, *Asset-Backed Commercial Paper: A Primer*, February, 2011; and Federal Reserve Bank of St. Louis, Economic Research, January 2015, http://research.stlouisfed.org/fred2/series/ABCOMP.

in the ABCP market is seen as one of the contributors to the 2007–2009 financial crisis. ABCP was used to fund off balance sheet special purpose vehicles (and conduits), and considered fragile as it supported long-term (and often opaque) assets that were typically financed with very short-maturity liabilities.[15] We will discuss this more in Chapter 14.

For now, it is still interesting to ask why had ABCP grown so much in popularity in the precrisis years? We will examine both the demand and supply sides. On the demand side, ABCP offers some firms lower cost funding than either "regular" (unsecured) commercial paper or a bank loan. Regular commercial paper may either be unavailable or too costly because of the high cost of moral hazard owing to the unsecured nature of the paper (recall Chapters 7 and 8). A bank loan may be too costly because of capital and reserve requirements. One reason why ABCP lowers the firm's funding cost is the credit enhancement provided by the bank. Not only does this directly lower the investor's risk in holding the paper, but it also signals the bank's involvement in monitoring the borrower[16] and is certification that the borrower is creditworthy. Thus, the basic screening and monitoring services provided by the bank play a key role in the ABCP market.

On the supply side, the risk-based Basel II (see Chapter 15) capital rules increased the benefits of ABCP to banks. If the bank were to extend a loan to the borrower, it would not only need to keep reserves against the deposit used to fund the loan, it would also need to set aside substantial capital (under Basel I, this was 8%). With an ABCP, the bank would need to keep capital equal to say 8% of only the credit enhancement (typically a fraction of the total borrowing). For example, a $1 billion bank loan would need $80 million in bank capital, but with an ABCP program, a bank might issue a letter of credit equal to only 10% of the total amount, so that only $8 million in capital would have to be set aside.[17] Thus, as with other off-balance sheet products, banks are able to earn fee income without posting as much capital as with conventional funding.

As already noted, the financial crisis of 2007–2009 took its toll on the ABCP market. While ABCP had become popular for regulatory arbitrage, the off balance sheet structures often did not reduce the risk for the issuing bank. Via liquidity guarantees much of the risk would come back to haunt the banks. In the summer of 2007, ABCP outstanding began a precipitous decline. The trigger had to do with growing concerns about the default risks of subprime and other mortgages.[18]

The collapse of the ABCP market also created problems for money market mutual funds (MMFs) that invest trillions of dollars on behalf of individuals, pension funds, municipalities, businesses, and others. These investments are close substitutes for bank deposits from the standpoint of investors. Many MMFs invested in ABCP, and met the withdrawal demands of their investors by selling ABCP in a liquid market, prior to 2007. Because liquidity was drained out of this market during the financial crisis, it was difficult for MMFs to meet the withdrawal demands of their investors. To help MMFs cope with this problem and to preclude further downward pressure on ABCP prices due to fire sales of these securities by MMFs, the Federal Reserve established the Asset-Backed Commercial Paper Money Market Mutual Fund Liquidity Facility (AMLF).[19]

The AMLF was created by the Federal Reserve under the authority of Section 13(3) of the Federal Reserve Act, which permitted the Board, in unusual circumstances to authorize Federal Reserve Banks to extend credit to individuals, partnerships and corporations. Under the AMLF program, the Federal Reserve provided *nonrecourse loans* to U.S. depository institutions, U.S. bank holding companies, and the U.S. branches and agencies of foreign banks. These loans were fully collateralized by the ABCP purchased by the AMLF borrower. These institutions that received the loans used them to purchase eligible ABCP from MMFs, so the MMFs were the institutions that were the primary intended beneficiaries of the AMLF.

The AMLF facility was administered by the Federal Reserve Bank of Boston, which was allowed to make AMLF loans to eligible borrowers in all 12 Federal Reserve districts. The facility was announced on September 19, 2008, and closed on February 1, 2010.

The AMLF program is a good example of how government liquidity-provision intervention can help in markets that are experiencing serious liquidity shortages or breakdown either due to temporarily distorted beliefs that cause overreactions to adverse events or due to informational asymmetries.[20] Whether a liquidity crunch was the main problem during the subprime crisis is another issue altogether, and one that we will visit in a later chapter on the financial crisis of 2007–2009.

---

15. See Acharya and Schnabl (2010) and Covitz et al. (2013).
16. The credit enhancement strengthens the bank's incentive to monitor the borrower because the bank has more to lose if the borrower defaults.
17. Noting the disadvantage of funding, Mr. Joseph Rizzi, vice president for structured finance at ABN AMRO in Chicago in 1993, said, "Pricing for credit has deteriorated, and the Bank for International Settlements capital rules make no distinction between lending to a triple-A company and a hot dog stand" (Kraus (1993)).
18. See Acharya and Schnabl (2010) and Covitz et al. (2013).
19. See Board of Governors of the Federal Reserve System (Board (1988)): http://www.federalreserve.gov/newsevents/reform_amlf_htm[8/10/2013].
20. Tirole (2012) shows how government intervention can be designed to reduce adverse selection in asset markets, so that the market can rebound.

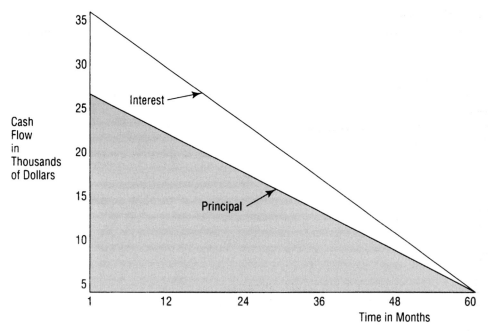

FIGURE 11.7 Cash-Flow Breakdown for CAR (Assuming an Absolute Prepayment Rate of 1.3%). *(Source: Monahan, Maureen, An Investor's Guide to Asset-Backed Securities, Shearson Lehman Hutton, Inc., March 1989).*

Securitization of Other Assets: CARS, CARDS, Intellectual Property, and So On

Auto Loans

Securitization of automobile loans began in 1985, and from 1985 to 1987, it was the largest sector of the ABS market.[21] By 2005, auto-loan securitization had reached almost $220 billion. The securitization of auto loans is actually the securitization of retail installment sales contracts that are backed by autos and light trucks. The maximum maturity of the loan is 60 months and the loans pay principal and interest on a monthly basis. These loans are packaged and sold as loan-backed securities called *Certificates of Automobile Receivables,* or "CARS," in keeping with Wall Street's penchant for catchy acronyms. They are usually *pass-through* securities, with both the principal and interest passed on directly to the certificate holders. However, the pay-through structure has also been used (e.g., by GMAC).

CARS usually involve a higher servicing fee than mortgage-backed securities because an auto loan requires more monitoring. Moreover, the value of the collateral (the car) tends to depreciate somewhat unpredictably through time, compared to the value of a home. Nevertheless, auto loans are readily securitizable because they have predictable default rates, as well as reasonably stable prepayment rates.

In the securitized auto-loan market, prepayment speed is usually indicated by the "absolute prepayment rate." This rate represents the percentage of the original loans that are expected to prepay every month. For example, a 2% rate means that 2% of the original number of the loans in the pool can be expected to prepay every month. The prepayment speed is estimated prior to the offering of the CAR and is a key factor in its pricing. Figure 11.7 gives an example of the cash-flow characteristics of a CAR over its life.

Credit Cards

Securitization of credit-card receivables began in April 1986 when Salomon Brothers privately placed $50 million of pass-through backed by a pool of Bank One credit-card receivables. These securities were called *Certificates of Amortizing Revolving Debts* or "CARDS." The original CARDS had a stated maturity of 5 years. For the first 18 months, only interest payments were passed through to investors. Principal payments received during this time by the grantor trust were used to purchase additional receivables. Investors began to receive principal payments after the first 18 months. These CARDS were not guaranteed by a third party. Bank One provided credit enhancement through excess collateral by establishing a

---

21. The first public offering of securitized auto loans was in March 1985. Salomon Brothers offered $60 million of pass-throughs backed by auto loans that were originated and serviced by Marine Midland Bank. A private insurer insured the pool, and a trust was established to hold the underlying loans. See Monahan (1989).

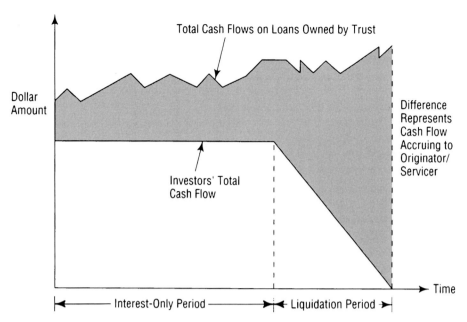

FIGURE 11.8 Pool Cash Flow for CARDS. *(Source: Monahan, Maureen, An Investor's Guide to Asset-Backed Securities, Shearson Lehman Hutton, Inc., March 1989).*

reserve fund equal to twice the historical default rate on credit-card debt. The bank also retained a 30% interest in the credit-card pool and recouped whatever was left in the reserve fund after covering defaults. This "reserve fund" concept has been applied to securitizations of assets other than credit cards, such as CARS.

Following the Bank One experiment, other banks entered the market. For instance, the Republic Bank of Delaware offered a dynamic version of CARDS with a revolving/pass-through security in January 1987. CARDS overtook CARS in 1988 as issuers like Citicorp and Sears entered the market for the first time. By 2005, the volume of credit-card securitizations had reached about $357 billion.

Outstanding balances on credit cards tend to pay down quickly. This is why CARDS often have a "lock out" or "call-protection" period (such as the 18-month period for the Bank One CARDS) during which only interest is paid to investors. The principal is reinvested in new receivables. Amortization of principal and interest begins after the lockout period. The length of the amortization period depends on the characteristics of the credit-card pool, but this is not difficult to estimate because monthly repayments rates are predictable. Figure 11.8 illustrates the cash-flow structure and suggests why an originator/servicer might be interested in CARDS.

The credit-card pass-through structure has undergone many refinements. For example, a *bullet principal payment* structure has been adopted whereby investors receive their entire principal in one lump sum at maturity. Prior to that they receive periodic interest payments exclusively. This provides investors against prepayment risk and early amortization.[22]

Other Tangible Assets

Loans guaranteed by the Small Business Administration (SBA), computer leases, and various types of trade credit have also been securitized. Securities backed by lease receivables[23] and trade credit are similar to mortgage-backed bonds. Commercial paper or corporate bonds are collateralized by lease or trade credit receivables, and the receivables remain on the issuer's balance sheet. Sometimes the issuer sells the receivables to a subsidiary that issues debt collateralized by these receivables.

---

22. An example of the bullet structure is Citibank's National Credit Card Trust 1989-1. The certificates were backed by VISA and MasterCard receivables and rated AAA/Aaa. The lockout period was 24 months, and in the 12-month period following this, prepayments were reinvested in order to meet principal and interest requirements. Union Bank of Switzerland provided both a maturity guarantee for up to 46% of the principal amount and a 12% L/C to cover potential credit risk.

23. The securitization of computer leases was first done by Comdisco in 1985, when it sold $35 million in 4½-year bonds backed by computer leases. In March 1985, Sperry Corporation followed with a $192.5 million issue of 6-year notes backed by computer leases, and in September 1985, Sperry issued another $145.8 million in debt collateralized by computer leases.

Finance leases have also been securitized. A finance lease operates over most of the leased asset's useful life. Finance leases either cannot be canceled, or if they are cancelable they require the lessee to reimburse the lessor for any losses that may be incurred as a result of the cancellation.

Still other assets that have been securitized include junk bonds, leveraged buyouts, loans for manufactured homes, and commercial loans. Other than trade receivables, securitized commercial loans include loans for employee stock option plans (ESOPS), and leveraged buyout loans.[24]

Securitization is now viewed as a vehicle that can be used for almost any asset. Among "nontraditional" assets that have been securitized are unsold airline seats, song royalties, proceeds from tobacco litigation (being securitized by various states), and natural resources like unsold oil and natural gas. The accounting statute governing securitization in the United States is FAS 140.

Securitization of Intangibles Like Intellectual Property

In all of the previous cases of securitization that we have discussed, what was being securitized was essentially a tangible asset. However, conceptually there is no reason why securitization cannot be extended to intangible assets like intellectual property. After all, an important goal of securitization is to enable the borrower to raise cash *now* against the present value of future cash flows, rather than waiting for the future cash flows to materialize. Thus, as long as an intangible asset has the potential to generate future cash flows, one ought to be able to securitize it. And that is precisely what has happened in recent years. The intangible assets that have been securitized include: trademarks, brand names, product designs, corporate name and logo, manufacturing technology, databases and patents.[25] In most cases, the firms involved were seeking financing from additional sources, since they had exhausted debt financing from traditional sources, lacked sufficient inventories to procure additional inventory-backed financing, and real estate was encumbered.

GOING BEYOND PRELIMINARY REMARKS ON ECONOMIC MOTIVATION: THE "WHY," "WHAT," AND "HOW MUCH IS ENOUGH" OF SECURITIZATION

Why?

Our purpose in this section is to examine in more detail the economics of securitization.

The Supply Side of Securitization: Issuer's Prospective Costs: The primary costs of securitization to the issuer are administrative in nature. They include legal fees, investment banking fees, and rating agencies' fees. Other costs include the costs of communicating information to investors and the cost of credit enhancement.

Issuer's Prospective Benefits: The numerous potential benefits to the issuer include management of interest rate, increased liquidity, and diversification of funding sources. In addition, securitization enables the originator to focus on the origination, servicing, and monitoring of loans and to avoid certain taxes and regulatory costs.

1. *Management of Interest-Rate Risk:* By securitizing some of its assets, a bank or a thrift may be able to better manage the interest-rate risk. For example, consider an S&L that holds residential mortgages with an average stated maturity of 27.5 years and mostly fixed rate. On the other hand, 65% of the typical S&L's liabilities are time and savings deposits that mature in less than a year. This enormous maturity mismatch creates substantial interest-rate risk for the S&L. To reduce this exposure, the S&L could securitize a pool of mortgages using the pass-through method. This would take these assets off its books and shorten the average maturity of its assets, while still allowing the S&L to service the loans and earn the servicing fee.

   Another form of interest-rate risk is prepayment risk, which can also be reduced by securitizing. It can replace the mortgages in its portfolio with pass-throughs and CMOs. This helps the S&L to diversify. Moreover, the CMO helps protect against prepayment risk.

   The S&L could also attempt to lengthen the average maturity of its liabilities, which would further reduce the gap in maturities of its assets and liabilities. It can do this by issuing mortgage-backed bonds and pay-throughs. The mortgage loans remain on the S&L's balance sheet but the average maturity of the S&L's liabilities is effectively increased since a mortgage-backed bond has an average maturity of about 5–12 years. Of course, the S&L can hedge its exposure through other, more conventional, means such as swaps, options, and futures. But in terms of both transactions costs and overall effectiveness, securitization *may* be a superior alternative in many instances.

---

24. Pilgrim Group, Inc., a mutual fund company based in Los Angeles, securitized commercial loans in 1988 when it began to sell shares in a fund that invests in collateralized bank loans made by a money center and large regional banks to domestic companies.
25. See Anson (2005), and Martin and Drews (2005). This is clearly not an exhaustive list.

2. *Increased Liquidity:* Securitization can improve the issuer's liquidity. The obvious reason is that assets that were untraded prior to securitization are traded in active secondary markets after securitization; thus, the issuer holds more liquid assets even if it retains any portion of the securitized portfolio. While the observation itself is correct, it is not terribly insightful. As our discussion of liquidity in Chapter 6 indicated, an asset is liquid if it can be sold quickly without much of a loss relative to its "true" value. This, in turn, rules out a large gap in the information the seller has about the asset's future prospects and the information a potential buyer has about those prospects. Now, active trading improves an asset's liquidity because it provides profit incentives for potential buyers to produce information about the asset. The information is then partly transmitted to others (who may be uninformed) through trading volume, prices, and related parameters.[26] Thus, trading increases the availability of information about the asset in the public domain and hence improves liquidity.

However, before an asset can be introduced for trading at a price that does not impose large *initial* losses on the seller, it must have some measure of liquidity, that is, the informational gap between the buyer and the seller should not be too large. Securitization achieves this initial measure of liquidity in two important ways. First, third-party credit enhancement reduces the effect of informational asymmetries between the issuer and investors. Credit enhancement works like a (partial) standby letter of credit in that it *substitutes* a portion of the credit risk of the asset pool with the credit risk of the credit enhancer. If investors have a better knowledge of the credit enhancer (who is likely to have an established reputation) than of the securitized pool of assets, then the relevant informational asymmetry is reduced. Sometimes there is an outright letter of credit provided by a credit enhancer, in which case the informational asymmetry is reduced further.

A second way in which securitization improves liquidity *even prior to trading* is through the pooling of a large number of assets and the subsequent partitioning of portfolio cash flows. To see this, think of a CMO with various tranches, each having its own priority status. The importance of the issuer's private information about the future portfolio returns diminishes as one moves further up the priority ladder.[27] That is, private information is less important for the first tranche (i.e., the bond with the first claim against portfolio cash flows) than it is for the portfolio as a whole. Thus, by splitting up the portfolio into tranches, the issuer essentially *distributes* the total private information related to the portfolio across the different tranches in a particular way. This in itself does *not* necessarily reduce the total information asymmetry. But it does make the high-priority tranches more liquid (less informationally sensitive) than the portfolio as a whole. The issuer can choose to retain its claim against the most information-sensitive (and least liquid), lowest-priority portion of the portfolio cash flow, and sell off the rest. The issuer needs to fund only the retained portion of the portfolio. The rest is liquefied and securitized.[28] The following illustration clarifies this point.

Example 11.2

Suppose the North American Bank has two loans, each of which is due to be repaid one period hence. The cash flows are independent and identically distributed random variables. Each loan will repay $100 to the bank with probability 0.9 and $50 with probability 0.1. However, while North American knows this, prospective investors cannot distinguish this bank's loan portfolio from that of the Southside City Bank, which has the same number of loans, but each of its loans will repay $100 with probability 0.6 and $50 with probability 0.4. The prior belief of investors is that there is a 0.5 probability that North American has the higher-valued portfolio and a 0.5 probability that it has the lower-valued portfolio. Suppose that North American wishes to securitize these loans, and knows that if it does so without credit enhancement, the cost of communicating the true value of its loans to investors is 5% of the true value. The data for this problem are depicted in Figure 11.9. Explore North American's securitization alternatives. Assuming that a credit enhancer is available and that the credit enhancer could (at negligible cost) determine the true value of North American's loan portfolio, what sort of credit enhancement should North American purchase? Assume investors are risk neutral and that the discount rate is zero.

Solution

We solve this problem in four steps. First, we show that if the North American Bank securitizes its loan portfolio as a single security (i.e., without cash-flow stripping or creating tranches), it will prefer securitization with communication (investors learn the true value of its loan portfolio) to securitization without communication (in which case investors set a pooling price of the

---

26. See Grossman (1981).

27. This point has been made by Boot and Thakor (1993). Subrahmanyam (1991) makes a somewhat different observation that is also germane. He notes that there is a sort of "information diversification" at work when one assembles portfolios of securities, that is, there is less of a private information problem about an entire portfolio than there is with respect to individual securities in the portfolio. This suggests one more way in which securitization improves liquidity.

28. This may lead to lower funding costs. Nadauld and Weisbach (2012) point at a 18bp reduction in lending rates provided by securitization. Loutskina and Strahan (2009) and Loutskina (2011) show that the additional liquidity that securitization provides may encourage banks to engage in (illiquid) bank lending (and reduces the effect of the lender condition on credit supply).

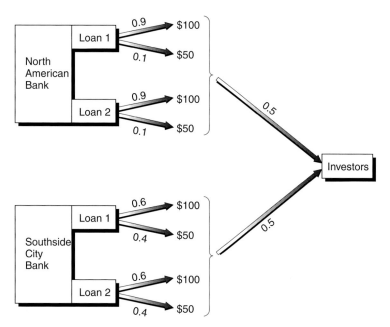

FIGURE 11.9 North American Bank's Loan Portfolio.

loan portfolio). Second, we examine the benefits of securitizing by creating two tranches represented by two particular classes of bondholders. We show that this cash-flow partitioning benefits North American by increasing its expected revenues relative to the securitization considered in step 1. Third, we stipulate a specific form of credit enhancement. Finally, in Step 4, we examine the net benefit of credit enhancement to North American and find that it is positive. Indeed, the loan portfolio is made perfectly liquid by credit enhancement. While credit enhancement by a party that knows North American's portfolio better than investors will always help, it helps to the maximum extent possible here due to the assumption that the credit enhancer can discover the *true* value of North American's loan portfolio at negligible cost.

Step 1

If North American does not communicate any information to investors, the market value of its securitized loan portfolio will be the average value assessed by investors:

{2	×	0.5	×	[0.9 × 100 + 0.1 × 50]}
↑		↑		↑
Total number of loans		Probability that loan portfolio is high-valued		Expected value of high-valued loan portfolio
+{2	×	0.5	×	[0.6 × 100 + 0.4 × 50]}
↑		↑		↑
Total number of loans		Probability that loan portfolio is low-valued		Expected value of low-valued loan portfolio

= $175.

Now, North American knows privately that its loan portfolio is worth

$$2[0.9 \times 100 + 0.1 \times 50] = \$190.$$

Thus, if it wishes to communicate its private information to investors, it will cost North American 0.05 × 190 = $9.5. It will then be able to sell its portfolio for $190 and its net payoff will be $190 − $9.5 = $180.5. This means that North American will prefer securitization with communication to securitization without.

Step 2

Consider next the following securitization alternative. North American can create two classes of bondholders in a "senior-subordinated structure" or a "juniorsenior structure." Class A bondholders, who receive the first tranche, are entitled to $100 in the aggregate. After they are paid off, Class B bondholders are entitled to receive $100 or the residual cash flow, whichever is smaller. Now, since the Class A bondholders will receive $100 for sure, regardless of whether the loan portfolio is high-valued or low-valued (note that the lowest payoff on either portfolio is $50), there is no need for the bank to communicate information to these bondholders. The price at which this portfolio can be sold is $100. Since the Class B bondholders are entitled to receive a maximum of $100, and the maximum total payoff on the loan portfolio is $200, it is apparent that these bondholders are essentially residual claimants who receive all of the cash flow remaining after the Class A bondholders are paid off. Thus, the true value of the Class B bonds must be equal to the total value of the loan portfolio minus the aggregate value of the Class A bonds, or $190 – $100 = $90. Since the market value of the total loan portfolio is $175 and the market value of the Class A bonds is $100, the market value of the Class B bonds should be $175 – $100 = $75. If North American now chooses to communicate the true value of Class B bonds to investors, it will be able to sell these bonds for $90, but the communication cost to the bank will be $0.05 \times 90 = $4.5. Thus, its net payoff on securitizing this way will be

$$\$100 + \$90 - \$4.5 = \$185.5.$$

North American's net revenue is higher when it uses securitization to partition the total cash flow from the loan portfolio into two classes with different "information sensitivities."

Step 3
Now consider credit enhancement. The best way to structure the credit enhancement is to ask the credit enhancer to pay the Class B bondholders the difference between the promised amount of $100 and the actual residual cash flow after the Class A tranche is paid off. Ignoring the possibility of default by the credit enhancer, this guarantees that Class B bondholders will receive $100 for sure, regardless of the quality of the securitized loan portfolio. Thus, no information communication by the bank is necessary. The question is: How much will North American have to pay the credit enhancer, assuming that the credit enhancement is competitively priced?

Step 4
To answer this question, suppose we label the two loans in the portfolio as 1 and 2. Then, there are four possible "states": (i) both loans 1 and 2 pay off $100 each (the probability of this is $0.9 \times 0.9 = 0.81$), (ii) loan 1 pays off $100 and loan 2 pays off $50 (the probability of this is $0.9 \times 0.1 = 0.09$), (iii) loan 1 pays off $50 and loan 2 pays off $100 (the probability of this is $0.1 \times 0.9 = 0.09$), and (iv) both loans pay off $50 each (the probability of this is $0.1 \times 0.1 = 0.01$). Now, in state (i), the credit enhancer has no liability since the total portfolio cash flow of $200 is enough to fully satisfy the claims of both classes of bondholders. In states (ii) and (iii), the total portfolio cash flow is $150, so that only $50 is available to pay off Class B bondholders after Class A bondholders are satisfied. In each of these states, the credit enhancer's liability is $50, and the total probability of these two states [i.e., the probability that *either* state (ii) or state (iii) will occur] is $0.09 + 0.09 = 0.18$. In state (iv), the total portfolio cash flow is $100, so that the credit enhancer's liability is 100. Hence, the expected value of the credit enhancer's liability is $0.18 \times \$50 + 0.01 \times \$100 = \$10$. In a competitive market (with a zero discount rate and risk neutrality), this is what North American will have to pay for the credit enhancement. Thus, North American's net payoff will be

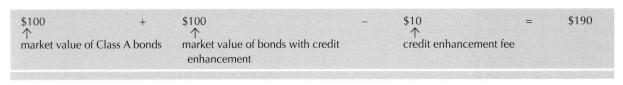

The loan portfolio has been made "perfectly" liquid!

3. *Diversification of Funding Sources*: Securitization provides originators with a way of raising financing from sources other than their traditional sources. For example, for a bank the traditional sources of funding are deposits, federal funds, subordinated debt, preferred stock and equity, all of which are essentially claims on the bank's entire asset portfolio. By segregating some assets into a pool to be securitized, the bank is able to diversify its funding sources beyond its traditional sources. This is important for any bank CFO.

4. *Enables Focus on Origination, Servicing, and Monitoring:* You will recall from our discussions in Chapter 3 that the key economic functions of financial intermediaries are related to the resolution of informational problems. One advantage of securitization is that it enables the bank to focus on the origination, servicing, and monitoring of loans, three activities that the bank can generally perform more efficiently than others because of specialization. When a bank or S&L originates a loan, it provides a valuable screening service – the bank's willingness to make the loan tells other interested but less-informed parties something about the borrower that they did not know before. This can reduce the borrower's cost of credit from other (nonbank) sources. Loan servicing is a transactional service that the bank may be able to provide at lower cost because of its specialization in handling numerous other similar transactions. And of course, monitoring of borrowers is one of the fundamental intermediation services that banks provide. By securitizing its loans, a bank can focus on these three activities without actually funding the loans. Absent regulatory help, it is not clear that banks have any special advantage in funding anyway. On the negative side, securitization might complicate loan renegotiations.[29]

---

29. Piskorski et al. (2010) point at higher foreclosure rates for securitized mortgages. Similarly, Agarwal et al. (2011) find challenges to renegotiation following securitization.

5. *Facilitates the Avoidance of "Adverse Selection" Costs:* Typically, a bank has a portfolio of assets with differing degrees of information sensitivity. Even if the market prices the portfolio correctly, it is quite possible that some of the assets are overvalued by the market and some are undervalued. Now consider a bank faced with the prospect of funding some new loans about which there is very little informational asymmetry, that is, the bank's assessment of the value of this new loan portfolio is roughly equivalent to that of the market. But suppose that the bank on the whole is undervalued. If this bank goes out and raises capital (that consists, in part, of uninsured deposits and equity) to fund these new loans in the conventional (nonsecuritization) manner, it will have to pay an "adverse selection cost" in the sense that the bank's cost of funding will be higher than it would be if investors had the same information about all of the bank's assets as the bank's managers themselves. This happens because investors who provide funding for these new loans are purchasing claims against the bank's *entire* asset portfolio. That is, these factors may account for the bank's disadvantage in funding loans.

Instead of going the conventional route, suppose the bank decides to securitize these loans. Now investors who provide the necessary capital are purchasing claims only against the new assets. Thus, if there is little informational asymmetry about these assets, there will be virtually no "adverse selection" cost.[30] An example is provided by Gelco Corporation, a truck-leasing company with a BB credit rating from Standard & Poor's. Its commercial paper, backed by high-quality leases, was rated A-1. The firm saved about 80 basis points in borrowing costs by securitizing its lease receivables.[31] This illustrates how a firm can take advantage of its marginal cost of funds on all its assets. The intuition here is similar to that for another fairly well-established practice known as "project financing," which involves a corporation establishing a legally distinct subsidiary to finance a new project. See the discussion in Chapter 9.

A key element of the benefit of avoiding adverse selection costs is that securitization through SPCs often achieves "bankruptcy remoteness" of the securitized assets from the borrowing firm. That is, the claims of lenders who provide financing to the SPC *cannot* subsequently be diluted by the claims of Debtor-in-Possession lenders to the sponsoring firm should the sponsor file for bankruptcy. However, this bankruptcy remoteness protection for the SPC investors is not perfect and can be undermined in legal proceedings. We would then expect that the greater the legal risk of bankruptcy remoteness being undermined by the courts, the higher will be the interest rates demanded by the SPC investors.[32]

6. *Avoidance of Intermediation Taxes:* Because securitization permits a depository institution to raise funds directly from investors rather than from depositors, it helps the institution to avoid "intermediation taxes" (or regulatory taxes) like reserve and capital requirements and deposit insurance premiums. This benefit is obvious in the case of a pass-through because the relevant assets are removed from the institution's balance sheet, thereby eliminating the need to hold capital against those assets. Moreover, since the proceeds from the sale of the pass-throughs are not deposits, no reserve requirements or deposit-insurance premiums are involved.

There is a more subtle interaction between regulatory taxes and the institution's choice of which assets to securitize. Many regulatory taxes, like reserve requirements, have traditionally been *flat* taxes in that they do not depend on the riskiness of the asset involved. That is, there is "pooling" of these taxes across the spectrum of asset risks, and the actual taxes correspond to some sort of average. Thus, the low-risk assets (which should have lower-than-average taxes) "subsidize" the high-risk assets (which should have higher-than-average taxes). A bank can lessen the impact of these taxes by securitizing its low-risk assets and leaving only the high-risk assets on its books. This way it would have higher-than-average risk assets on its books, but it would only pay taxes that correspond to average risk.

The Demand Side of Securitization: Investor's Perspective: Having discussed why financial institutions and other firms might wish to securitize assets, we now turn to why investors might wish to hold these assets. One way for investors to invest in a bank's assets (e.g., loans) is to purchase bank equity. Relative to that alternative, purchasing securitized claims offers a number of possible advantages, two of which are discussed below.

1. *Reduction in Market Incompleteness:* These are two ways in which securitization helps to reduce market incompleteness. First, it improves the *quality* of assets that investors can hold and thereby increases the quality spectrum of available assets. Second, it provides a greater *variety* of cash-flow streams that investors can hold. Consider the quality issue first. The claims that an institution offers investors via securitization are often of higher credit quality than the institution itself. This is due to two reasons. First, as we have discussed earlier, there are incentives for the institution to securitize both lower risk and less information-sensitive assets. Second, credit enhancement improves the quality of the asset pool

---

30. Ignore signaling complications created by the possibility that the market may revalue the bank's existing assets when the bank decides to securitize its new loans. This would occur because the market recognized that part of the bank's incentive to securitize the new assets comes from its own private knowledge about its existing assets.
31. See Shapiro (1985).
32. This is what Ayotte and Gaon (2006) find in their empirical tests.

being securitized. Thus, it is not surprising that most of the asset-backed market is triple-A or double-A rated. Securitization provides investors with access to higher credit quality claims than available otherwise.

Now consider the cash-flow variety issue. Because securitization combines pooling, cash-flow partitioning, and credit enhancement, it does *not* produce merely a linear combination of existing payoff vectors (recall the discussion of market completeness in Chapter 1). Rather, it produces claims that were previously unavailable to investors through linear combinations of existing claims. Moreover, even in the case of claims that could have been "home-manufactured" by investors who were willing to combine available securities, securitization provides a less-expensive alternative in terms of transactions costs. For example, ABS have limited prepayment risk, so the effective maturity of the security is relatively insensitive to market yields. This means that for a given decline in yield, these "positive" convexity and limited prepayment features may not be available in the same configurations to investors in nonsecuritized alternatives. Thus, securitization helps to reduce financial market incompleteness.

2. *Liquidity:* Because of the size of the ABS market and the active trading involved, investors are assured that they are buying a liquid claim. Securitization may be viewed as an alternative technology (to traditional funding) for producing liquidity.[33]

What? Securitization With Recourse Versus Deposits and Risk Sharing

The concept of recourse is key to understanding what securitization does for both the originator and the investor. When securitization is without recourse, the investor has a claim only against the pool of assets that have been securitized. He has no claim to any other assets of the originator. On the other hand, securitization with recourse closely resembles traditional balance sheet lending. The purchaser of a security with recourse has the option of trading the claim for a general bank claim like that of an uninsured depositor should the purchased asset default. If the bank fails, the investor has the option of keeping the securitized asset.

In this subsection, we will discuss securitization with recourse. It turns out that the securitization benefits are similar to those created by multiclass securities, in which sequential claims are issued against the same collateral pool. Basically, better risk sharing is achieved, since the most risk-averse investors can be sold the most senior claims. Under current law, banks are not allowed to issue multiclass or senior deposit claims against their balance sheet assets. That is, deposit claims cannot be prioritized. Hence, from the bank's perspective, a valuable opportunity to cater to "preference clienteles" among its potential depositor base is lost. However, securitization with recourse gives the bank an opportunity to profit from selectively catering to depositors with different degrees of risk aversion. Uninsured depositors can switch to a contract that gives them a *senior* claim on a part of the bank's asset portfolio (i.e., the securitized asset). A loan-backed security with a bank guarantee attached (securitization with recourse) is like a large CD with the addition of a senior keeping the securitized security rather than waiting in line with other depositors to obtain his share of the bank's *other* assets. In a capital market in which people have different degrees of risk aversion, we would expect the more risk-averse investors to buy these securitized claims, and their less risk-averse cohorts to bear more risk. Thus, securitization achieves better risk sharing than the standard deposit contract. This intuition is formalized in the model developed in the box below.[34]

The model: Consider a bank that needs to raise $d to finance its first-period investment, which returns $A($\theta$) at the end of the period, where θ is a possible future state of nature. Suppose that the bank must raise d_i in FDIC-insured deposits, d_u in uninsured deposits, and d_e in equity where $d_i + d_u + d_e = d$. Insured deposits carry an interest rate of r_f (these deposits are riskless), which is the riskless rate. We assume that the FDIC and the bank's shareholders are risk neutral. There is a single, representative uninsured depositor who is risk averse and has a utility function, $U(w)$, over wealth, which is increasing and concave, that is, $U' > 0$, $U'' < 0$ (recall the discussion of risk-aversion in Chapter 1). The alternative to uninsured deposits is to invest in the risk-free asset, which carries an interest rate of r_f.

Let $B be the repayment promised to the uninsured depositor and $D(\theta)$ the state-contingent payment actually received by them at the end of the period. To induce them to invest in uninsured deposits, it must be true that

$$\sum_{\theta=1}^{N} p(\theta)U(D(\theta)) \geq U\{[1+r_f]d_u \tag{11.1}$$

where the possible future states are $\theta = 1, \ldots, N$, and $p(\theta)$ is the probability of state θ. The inequality in Equation (11.1) says that the expected utility of the uninsured depositor from investing in these deposits can be no less than his utility from receiving a sure payoff by investing in the risk-free asset.

---

33. But, as we saw earlier, liquidity can dry up even in markets in which securitized claims are traded if investors begin to have serious doubts about the creditworthiness of the underlying assets, as we witnessed in the ABCP market in 2007. See Covitz, Lang and Suarez (2013).
34. The model is based on Benveniste and Berger (1987).

Now $[1 + r_f]d_i$ is the amount promised by the bank to the insured depositors, and $D(\theta)$ is the amount for uninsured depositors. If $A(\theta) \geq [1 + r_f]d_i + B$, the bank is solvent and the insured depositors receive $[1 + r_f]d_i$ from the bank. If $A(\theta) < [1 + r_f]d_i + B$, the bank fails. The insured depositors still receive $[1 + r_f]d_i$, but only a portion of it comes from the bank. The FDIC covers the rest. This is a situation in which the FDIC takes over the bank, pays off $[1 + r_f]d_i$ to the insured depositors, and then shares the remaining assets of the bank *proportionately* with the uninsured depositors.[35] The proportions are determined by the relative contributions of insured and uninsured deposits to the total *deposit base*. That is, whenever there is insolvency (i.e., $A(\theta) < [1 + r_f]d_i + B$), the amount collected by the uninsured depositors is

$$D(\theta) = \left[\frac{B}{B + [1 + r_f]d_i}\right] A(\theta) \tag{11.2}$$

and the amount collected by the FDIC is

$$F(\theta) = \left[\frac{[1 + r_f]d_i}{B + [1 + r_f]d_i}\right] A(\theta). \tag{11.3}$$

We can now write down each party's payoff at the end of the first period. First, the insured depositors receive $[1 + r_f]d_i$ regardless of θ. Second, the uninsured depositors receive

$$D(\theta) = \begin{cases} B & \text{if } A(\theta) \geq B + [1 + r_f]d_i \\ A(\theta)/[B + [1 + r_f]d_i] & \text{otherwise.} \end{cases} \tag{11.4}$$

The bank's shareholders receive (at the end of the period)

$$S(\theta) = \begin{cases} A(\theta) - B - [1 + r_f]d_i & \text{if } A(\theta) \geq B + [1 + r_f]d_i \\ 0 & \text{otherwise.} \end{cases} \tag{11.5}$$

The FDIC receives (at the end of the period)

$$F(\theta) = \begin{cases} 0 & \text{if } A(\theta) \geq B + [1 + r_f]d_i \\ -[1 + r_f]d_i + \left[\frac{[1 + r_f]d_i}{B + [1 + r_f]d_i}\right] A(\theta) & \text{otherwise.} \end{cases} \tag{11.6}$$

Note that the lower term in Equation (11.6) applies when $A(\theta) < B + [1 + r_f]d_i$, so that

$$-[1 + r_f]d_i + \left[\frac{[1 + r_f]d_i}{B + [1 + r_f]d_i}\right] A(\theta) < 0.$$

Thus, the *end-of-period* cash flow to the FDIC is always zero or less.

At the start of the period, the bank's shareholders pay a deposit insurance premium to the FDIC. We assume that this premium is risk insensitive and fairly priced. Let p denote this premium. To write down this premium, let us rank-order the states θ in increasing order of $A(\theta)$, so that $A(1) < A(2) < \ldots < A(N)$. Let $\theta = m$ be the state such that $A(\theta) \geq B + [1 + r_f]d_i$ for all $\theta > m$ and $A(\theta) < B + [1 + r_f]d_i$ for all $\theta < m$. Then, the expected value of Equation (11.6) is

$$\pi = \frac{1}{[1 + r_f]} \sum_{\theta=1}^{m} p(\theta) \left\{ [1 + r_f]d_i - \left[\frac{[1 + r_f]d_i}{B + [1 + r_f]d_i}\right] A(\theta) \right\}. \tag{11.7}$$

That is, the deposit insurance premium is equal to the discounted present value of the FDIC's liability.

The question is: What is the NPV of the bank's shareholders' investment? This is seen to be

$$\text{NPV} = \frac{1}{[1 + r_E]} E[S(\theta)] - \pi - d_e \tag{11.8}$$

where $E(\bullet)$ means "expected value" and $S(\theta)$ is given by Equation (11.5). Now note how B and d_u are linked. Using Equations (11.1) and (11.4) we see that they are linked as follows.

$$\sum_{\theta=1}^{m} p(\theta) U \left\{ \left[\frac{B}{B + [1 + r_f]d_i}\right] A(\theta) \right\} + \sum_{\theta=m+1}^{N} p(\theta) U(B) = U\{[1 + r_f]d_u\}. \tag{11.9}$$

---

35. Under current law, senior claims are not permitted on the balance sheets of banks. Thus, when a bank fails, the FDIC pays the insured depositors in full and shares the assets of the bank proportionately with the uninsured claimants in a manner similar to that indicated in the development below.

The left-hand side (LHS) of Equation (11.9) is the uninsured depositor's expected utility from investing in that deposit; this is obtained directly from Equation (11.4). We are using Equation (11.1) as an equality here because the bank, whose objective is to maximize the wealth of its shareholders, will pay the *minimum* amount required to attract funds from the uninsured depositor.

It is clear now that the higher d_u is, the higher B will have to be to satisfy Equation (11.9). Raising B has two effects. One is that it increases the amount collected by the uninsured depositor when the bank is solvent. The other is that it increases the uninsured depositor's proportional share of the bank's assets in insolvency.

For any fixed d_u, B must also increase as the uninsured depositor becomes more risk averse. This is because he demands a higher risk premium, or a higher expected value for his risky payoff. Of course, as B increases, $S(\theta)$ decreases, so that the bank's shareholders become worse off as the uninsured depositor becomes more risk averse [see Equation (11.8)]. This provides a strong motivation for securitization with recourse because of the possibility of reducing the risk borne by the uninsured depositor. We will now see how this is achieved.

To incorporate securitization into this model, let us partition the bank's assets into two portfolios – a balance sheet portfolio, A_b, and an off-balance sheet portfolio, A_o. The loans in A_b are funded with insured deposits and equity, which add up to $d_i + d_e$ dollars. The loans in A_o are funded with securitized bonds that fetch the bank \$$d_u$. These two portfolios combined give the same payoff as before, that is,

$$A(\theta) = A_b(\theta) + A_o(\theta). \tag{11.10}$$

We assume that the bank continues to service the loans' securities. In doing so, the bank directs receipts of loan payments to the depositors. The key feature of this new arrangement, however, is that the receipts from $A_o(\theta)$ are committed to repay the securitized bonds first. Only after these bonds are fully paid off can the revenues be directed elsewhere. That is, the securitized bondholder has a senior claim on the payment stream $A_o(\theta)$. Adding the option of securitized bond gives the holder additional protection by allowing him to change his claim to that of a balance sheet liability if the revenues from $A_o(\theta)$ are inadequate. In this case, he exercises his claim just like an uninsured depositor, as $A_o(\theta)$ and $A_b(\theta)$ are pooled together. Thus, when the securitized bondholder exercises his recourse option, he is limited to a prorata claim on the total portfolio $A(\theta)$. Let B^* be the amount promised to the securitized bond.

The securitized bondholder thus receives

$$
\begin{aligned}
& B^* \text{ if } A(\theta) \geq B + [1+r_f]d_i \\
& B^* \text{ if } A(\theta) \geq B + [1+r_f]d_i \text{ and } A_o(\theta) \geq B \\
D^*(\theta) = & \left[\frac{B^*}{B^* + [1+r_f]d_i} \right] A(\theta) \text{ otherwise.}
\end{aligned}
$$

This payoff structure is illustrated in the figure below. We have defined $\theta = n$ as the state in which $B^* = A_o(\theta)$.

In Figure 11.10, we have assumed, for comparability, that $B^* = B$, that is, the promised repayment amount is the same for uninsured deposits and the securitized bond. In that case it is clear that securitization gives the uninsured depositor a higher payoff for the same repayment amount. This higher amount comes from the additional-option feature embedded in the securitization contract. In the context of our model, what is held fixed across the securitization and no-securitization alternatives is not the promised repayment, but the initial amount raised from uninsured creditors, which is d_u. When d_u is held fixed, we have $B^* < B$.

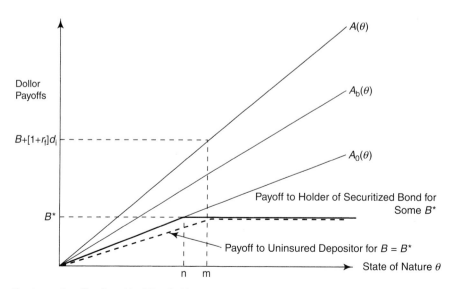

FIGURE 11.10   State-Contingent Payoff to Securitized Bondholder.

Rather than formally prove that securitization with recourse improves the wealth of the bank's shareholders, we will provide a numerical example to make the point. The basic intuition is simply that both the FDIC and the bank's shareholder are risk neutral and hence "better able" to absorb risk than the risk-averse uninsured depositor. Securitization with recourse transfers some risk away from the uninsured depositor to these parties, thereby improving risk sharing. The effect is to reduce the amount that the bank's shareholders must promise to repay the uninsured creditor, which increases the expected value of the shareholders' claim. It also increases the riskiness of their claim, but they do not care about that because they are risk neutral.

Example 11.3

The North American Bank needs to raise $50 in financing at the beginning of the period to finance an investment that will yield a random payoff at the end of the period. This payoff has the following probability distribution.

State θ	1	2	3	4
Payoff $A(\theta)$	$0	$50	$100	$150
Probability $p(\theta)$	0.25	0.25	0.25	0.25

The single-period riskless interest rate is 0.10. The bank must raise $30 in FDIC-insured deposits, $15 in uninsured deposits (with or without securitization) and $5 in equity. North American's shareholders and the FDIC are risk neutral. The uninsured depositor is risk averse with utility $U(w) = \sqrt{w}$ for wealth $w \geq 0$. Compute the NPV to North American's shareholders when: (i) they finance conventionally using deposits and (ii) when they issue a securitized bond that has a preferred claim on a specially designated asset portfolio that represents 60% of the payoff on $A(\theta)$ in any state.

Solution

We solve this problem in six steps. First, we consider conventional deposit financing and solve for B, the repayment that must be promised to the uninsured depositors in order to raise $15 from them. We do this by using Equation (11.9). Second, we solve for the insurance premium, π, using Equation (11.7). Third, we compute the NPV to North American's shareholders. Fourth, we consider the alternative of issuing a securitized bond and solve for B^*, the amount promised to the securitized bond. Fifth, we solve for the insurance premium in this case. Finally, in Step 6 we solve for the NPV accruing to North American's shareholders with securitization, which is higher than the NPV accruing to them with conventional deposit financing.

Step 1

Let us consider (i) first. Note that $d_i = 30$, $d_u = 15$, $d_e = 5$, and $r_f = 0.10$. Since the claim of insured depositors is riskless, the interest rate on these deposits should be the riskless rate, 10%. Thus, North American's repayment obligation to these depositors is $d_i[1 + r_f] = 30[1.1] = \$33$. The bank's total repayment obligation to its creditors is $33 + B$. To solve for B, we need to *conjecture* about its value first, so that we can identify the states in which North American is solvent and those in which it is not. Suppose we conjecture that $50 < 33 + B < 100$. Then North American will be insolvent in States 1 and 2, and solvent in States 3 and 4. We now solve for B using Equation (11.9):

$$\underset{\downarrow}{\text{expected utility payoffs in States 1 and 2}} \qquad \underset{\downarrow}{\text{expected utility payoffs in States 3 and 4}}$$

$$0.25\sqrt{\left[\frac{B}{B+33}\right] \times 50} \qquad + \qquad 0.5\sqrt{B} = \sqrt{1.1 \times 15}.$$

Solving this equation gives $B = \$32$, approximately. This means our conjecture is valid and that $B + 33 = \$65$.

Step 2

Next we solve for the insurance premium using Equation (11.7).

$$\pi = \frac{1}{1.1}\left\{0.25 \times 33 + 0.25\left[33 - \left(\frac{33}{65} \times 50\right)\right]\right\} = \$9.23.$$

Step 3

Further, since North American's shareholders receive something only in the solvency States (3 and 4), the expected value of the payoff for shareholders is

$$E[S(\theta)] = 0.25[100 - 65] + 0.25[150 - 65] = \$30.$$

Thus, the NPV of North American's shareholders is given by Equation (11.8) as

$$NPV = \frac{30}{1.1} - 9.23 - 5 = \$13.04.$$

Step 4

Now consider (ii). With securitization, the payoff stream of the total asset portfolio is split up as follows (Tables 11.2).

TABLE 11.2 Payoff Distributions for Portfolios

State	1	2	3	4
Payoff $A(\theta)$	0	50	100	150
Payoff to securitized bond$_f$ A_0 (θ)	0	30	60	90
Payoff from on-balance sheet asset$_f$ A_b (θ)	0	20	40	60

Now, suppose we conjecture that $50 < B^* + 33 < 100$ and that $B^* \leq \$30$. Then, state 1 is the only state in which the holder of the securitized bond gets less than the amount promised. Thus, B^* is obtained by solving the following equation.

$$0.75 \times \sqrt{B^*} = \sqrt{1.1 \times 15} = 4.062.$$

↑
cumulative
probability
of states
2, 3, and 4.

which yields $B^* = \$29.33$.

Step 5

We can now solve for the deposit insurance premium, which is

$$\pi = \frac{1}{[1+r_f]}\left\{p(1)[1+r_f]d_i + p(2)\left[[1+r_f]d_i - \left\{A_b(2) + A_0(2) - B^*\right\}\right]\right\}.$$

Note that the FDIC is liable for payments only in States 1 and 2. In State 1, it is liable for the entire repayment promised to the insured depositors, whereas in State 2, it is liable for that amount minus what it collects on the balance sheet asset, A_b (2), and whatever is left over on the off-balance sheet asset after the securitized bondholder is paid, A_o (2) – B^*. Thus,

$$\pi = \left\{\frac{1}{[1+r_f]}\ \{0.25 \times 33\ +\ 0.25\ [33\ -\ \{20\ +\ (30-29.33)\}]\}\right\}$$

$$= \$10.30$$

Step 6

Now, $B^* + [1 + r_f]d_i = 29.33 + 33 = \$62.33$. Thus, $E[S(\theta)] = 0.25[100 - 62.33] + 0.25[150 - 62.33] = \$31.34$. This means

$$\text{NPV} = \frac{31.34}{1.1} - 10.30 - 5 = \$13.19.$$

Thus, in this example securitization results in a 1.16% increase in the NPV accruing to the North American Bank's shareholders, and this gain is due to the differing risk preferences of uninsured depositors and the banks and their insurer.

How Much Securitization?

Given the proliferation in ABS and the spread of securitization to even intangible assets, an obvious question might be: Can and should everything be securitized? The answer is no, and there are three main factors that explain why there are still assets that have not been securitized.[36] These are discussed below.

1. *Ease of Standardization:* First, for an asset to be profitably securitized, it should be relatively easy to "standardize." That is, its contract features should make it a component of a relatively homogeneous portfolio of other similar assets. Mortgage loans are an excellent example. Mortgage contracts are standardized and their cash-flow patterns are, on average, quite predictable. This was not always the case. Indeed, the possibility of securitization prompted the standardization. Loans with special contract features (such as, HLT loans and some types of LBO loans secured partly by personal collateral of managers) are difficult to standardize and hence would be difficult to securitize, although we have already

---

36. See Caouette (1990).

witnessed the securitization of LBO loans. The reason for the desirability of contractual homogeneity is related to transactions and information-processing costs. When a large number of individual loans are pooled, the investor only has to evaluate the portfolio return. This creates both "informational diversification" and "statistical risk diversification," so that the portfolio cash flows are more predictable and less sensitive to the peculiarities of the individual assets. This eases the originator's/issuer's problem of designing specific securities based on the total portfolio cash flow. Moreover, it makes it easier for investors to evaluate the values of the securitized assets. This attracts a larger number of investors and improves the liquidity of the market for the securitized assets.

This is not to say that more heterogeneous and information-sensitive assets, which are more difficult to standardize, cannot be securitized. Rather, such assets would require greater credit enhancements to be securitized; the limiting case is that of "full-recourse" securitization. When the assets that comprise the portfolio are very dissimilar and difficult to standardize, the portfolio cash flows become quite sensitive to the actual choice of securities that make up the portfolio. More credit enhancement would be needed for such a portfolio, and beyond some point, it may not be worthwhile for the originator to purchase the required credit enhancement. Thus, standardization can be viewed as conserving the originator's capital in that a high credit rating can be obtained for the portfolio with *less* credit enhancement. Without the appropriate credit enhancement, the rating agencies and investors have to study individual securities in the portfolio more. To see this more clearly, consider the following example.

Example 11.4

Suppose there are three possible assets from which the North American Bank can choose two to securitize. Call these assets a, b, and c. The assets are quite similar and their cash-flow distributions are as described below. The probability of "success" for asset i is p_i. Compute the probability distributions of the various portfolio combinations. How important would it be for an investor to know precisely which two assets were in the securitized portfolio? Would your answer change if asset c were replaced by asset d, which has a cash flow that is uniformly distributed over [0, 1000] (Figure 11.11)?

Solution

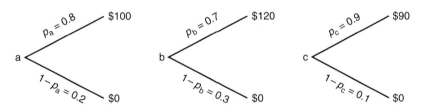

FIGURE 11.11 Probability Distributions of Assets a, b, and c.

We will solve this problem in two steps. First, we will compute probability distributions for the three possible portfolio combinations – ab, ac, and bc – and conclude that they are pretty similar. Second, we will show that replacing c by d would make a significant difference in that the investor will now need to know the portfolio composition.

Step 1

Now, if North American were to choose assets a and b, the total portfolio cash-flow distribution would be: 0 with probability 0.06 (which is $[1 - p_a] \times [1 - p_b]$), 220 with probability 0.56 (which is $p_a \times p_b$), 100 with probability 0.24 (which is $p_a \times [1 - p_b]$), and 120 with probability 0.14 (which is $[1 - p_a] \times p_b$). The expected value would be 164. If the issuer were to assemble the portfolio with assets a and c, the probability distribution would be: 0 with probability 0.03, 210 with probability 0.27. The expected value would be 161. Similarly, if the portfolio consisted of b and c, the probability distribution would be: 0 with probability 0.03, 210 with probability 0.63, 120 with probability 0.07, and 90 with probability 0.27. The expected value would be 165. The portfolio payoffs are summarized in Table 11.3.

TABLE 11.3 Probability Distributions of Various Portfolios

State/Portfolio	Low Cash Flow and Probability	Medium Cash Flow and Probability	Above-Medium Cash Flow and Probability	High Cash Flow and Probability	Expected Value
a and b	0 w.p. 0.06	100 w.p. 0.24	120 w.p.0.14	220 w.p.0.56	164
a and c	0 w.p. 0.02	90 w.p. 0.18	100 w.p.0.08	190 w.p.0.72	161
b and c	0 w.p. 0.03	90 w.p. 0.27	120 w.p.0.07	210 w.p.0.63	165

Clearly, if you were an investor deciding whether to buy a piece of the portfolio, it would not be terribly important to know the precise composition of that portfolio. All the portfolios have similar expected values and each portfolio has a low probability of a low cash-flow realization, a high probability of a high cash-flow realization and intermediate probabilities for the medium and above-medium cash flows.

Step 2

Now imagine that c is replaced by asset d, which has a cash flow that is uniformly distributed over [0,1000]. It is now easy to see that it will be quite important for the investor to know which assets are in the portfolio. For example, a combination of a and d has an expected value of $580 (the expected value of a is $80 and the expected value of d is $500), whereas a combination of a and b has an expected value of $164. And if the portfolio cash flows are partitioned, it will be even more important for the junior claimants to know the portfolio composition. This is why homogeneous pools of assets are easier to securitize.

---

2. *Extent of Private Information:* Another important consideration is the extent of private information about the asset. If the loan originator has substantial information about the loan that others do not have, then information communication costs might deter securitization. This point is related to homogeneity in that information-sensitive assets are more difficult to standardize. But, even if the loan portfolio is homogeneous, it may be costly to securitize if each loan in the portfolio is steeped in private information possessed by the originator. Truly "opaque" assets are usually difficult to sell at anywhere close to their true value. Consequently, steep discounts may be needed to entice investors to buy assets they do not fully understand. It may not benefit the originator to securitize such assets. For example, it would be difficult to securitize and sell in the United States a portfolio of consumer loans made by a local bank in Nigeria, particularly if reliable statistics on historical repayment patterns were unavailable. By contrast, U.S. credit-card receivables are relatively easy to securitize in the United States. There is only cursory initial screening of credit-card applicants, so there is not much that the lender knows that others do not know. Moreover, the contract itself is fairly standardized, and repayment patterns of *portfolios* of credit cards are quite predictable. A similar argument holds for consumer mortgages. Screening procedures for determining who gets a mortgage loan are standardized, so that once a person is given a mortgage contract, she falls in a pool about which the original lender knows little more than the rating agencies and investors.

   One important implication of how private information affects assets chosen for securitization is that the quality of the assets on the balance sheets of banks may deteriorate. The assets that are securitized are typically more liquid. Assets that stay on the books are likely to be less liquid and have other problems as well.[37] The bank may prefer to keep these lower-quality assets on its books because it may be able to sell them only at steep discounts relative to their "true" values, which may be privately known only to the bank. Since there is often an inverse relationship between liquidity and risk, the bank's portfolio risk *may* increase due to securitization. Mitigating this concern is the fact that banks can diversify by buying securitized claims against loans originated by others.

   Of course, as information technology advances, the costs of processing and communicating financial information decline. This makes securitization less costly. The obvious implication is that securitization can be expected to grow in scope and volume.

3. *Moral Hazard:* With traditional lending, the original lender combines origination, underwriting, funding, and servicing of the loan. The lender then has an incentive to monitor the loan. As we saw in Chapter 3, monitoring is an important activity of banks. With securitization, however, origination and funding are separated. This weakens the originator's incentive to monitor the loans in the securitized portfolio.[38] The reason is that monitoring is costly to the originator, and the benefits of the monitoring – an improvement in the cash flows from the securitized portfolio – accrue to the investors who have purchased the securities, not to the originator. In this context, the traditional bank can be seen as a solution to the moral hazard that can accompany loan decomposition. An obvious solution is to shift some of the credit risk back to the originator by employing securitization with partial recourse. This places the exposure with the party responsible for the monitoring, and hence reduces moral hazard.

---

37. Greenbaum and Thakor (1987) show formally that, under certain conditions, banks will securitize higher-quality (lower default risk) assets and retain on their balance sheets assets of lower quality. Agarwal, Chang and Yavas (2012) show empirically that banks hold on to higher-default risk loans (adverse selection and perceived monitoring needs might prevent the securitization of these assets). However, they do find higher prepayment risk in securitized loans.

38. This reasoning appears in Gorton and Pennachi (1990). Mester (1992) provides empirical evidence that it is less costly for a bank to monitor a loan it has originated itself than to monitor a loan it has purchased.

However, recourse raises other accounting/regulatory problems. Recall that one strong incentive to securitize comes from capital and reserve requirements, deposit insurance premiums, and other costs, which add an estimated 125 basis points to the funding costs of deposit-takers. If loans are securitized with recourse, they are not usually removed from the books, and hence none of the regulatory costs are avoided. However, the originator can utilize alternatives to recourse as a way to deal with moral hazard without keeping the loans on its books. Senior/subordinated structures, overcollateralization, and third-party guarantees can all provide credit enhancement to attenuate moral hazard.

Credit enhancement deals with moral hazard in two ways. First, it directly improves the credit quality of the securitized asset, so that investors are less affected by the quality of underwriting and monitoring provided by the originator. Second, it creates an incentive for the credit enhancer to *monitor the originator* to ensure that the originator is underwriting and monitoring the loans in the securitized portfolio. We can expect the credit enhancer to be specialized in monitoring and thus monitor the originator more efficiently than individual investors can. Moreover, just as a bank saves on monitoring costs by centralizing the monitoring activity and thereby avoiding *duplication of efforts* (Chapter 3), a credit enhancer can save on monitoring costs that would otherwise be greater because of duplicated monitoring by individual investors. There are, however, natural limits to the gains from credit enhancement since the marginal effectiveness of the credit enhancer's monitoring will expectedly decline with more monitoring (diminishing returns to scale). This will be reflected in the fee charged to the originator by the credit enhancer. Depending on the nature of the asset (in particular, the sensitivity of its cash flow to monitoring by the originator) and the level of credit enhancement sought, a point may be reached beyond which further credit enhancement is not justified from the originator's standpoint. And there may well be assets that are better for the originator to fund with deposits than to securitize and credit enhance up to the optimal limit, because of moral hazard.

Some types of commercial and industrial (C&I) loans are unlikely candidates for securitization, although we anticipate this to be a shrinking list. Loans whose values are highly dependent on lender monitoring are usually subject to a great deal of moral hazard, as we have seen in Chapters 7 and 8. Such loans are difficult to securitize because the required credit enhancement would be too costly. Put differently, unpredictability in the quality of monitoring provided by the originating lender may lead to a lot of unpredictability in the cash flows generated by such loans. We would expect, on moral hazard grounds, that such loans would be securitized infrequently. This is what we observe. However, despite this, we expect few, if any, C&I loans to not be securitized in the future.

Although things like credit enhancement and recourse can attenuate the basic moral hazard involved in securitization, it is still interesting to ask whether the incentives of banks are, in practice, affected by the knowledge that a loan that the bank is originating will subsequently be securitized. An empirical investigation of this using data on securitized subprime mortgages addressed this question.[39] In the mortgage market, a rule of thumb used by investors is the FICO score of the mortgage borrower. Loans made to borrowers that fall just above a cut-off FICO score of 620 have a higher unconditional likelihood of being securitized than loans that fall just below 620. While one might imagine that a loan with a FICO score of 619 has about the same (or slightly higher) credit risk than a loan with a FICO score of 621, the evidence shows that low-documentation loans that are originated at a FICO score just above the threshold of 620 tend to default within two years of origination at a rate that is *higher* than the rate at which loans just below the FICO score of 620.

An important reason is that the loans with FICO scores of 620+ have greater liquidity for the originator than those with FICO scores of 620−. This additional liquidity works through two channels, both of which tend to weaken the lender's screening incentives: the securitization rate and the time it takes to securitize the loan. As for the securitization rate, a 620+ loan is 10% more likely to be securitized than a 620− loan. As for the time it takes to securitize, an accepted 620−, low-documentation, subprime loan stays on the lender's balance sheet for almost two months longer than an accepted 620+ loan. The impact of the weakened screening incentives is large – the portfolio of low-documentation non-agency loans with greater ease of securitization – along the two dimensions described above – defaults at a 20% higher rate than a similar-risk portfolio with lesser ease of securitization.

These empirical findings have the striking implication that the credit screening incentives of mortgage loan originator seem to be affected by whether the loan will be securitized. When an originator knows that a loan is more likely to be held on its books rather than being securitized, it tends to screen the borrower more carefully before making the loan.

STRATEGIC ISSUES FOR A FINANCIAL INSTITUTION INVOLVED IN SECURITIZATION

Securitization is technology for liquefying claims and diversifying funding sources management by banks and other financial institutions. Its enormous growth is only one of the indicators of an ongoing revolution of ideas in the capital markets.

---

39. See Keys, Mukherjee, Sern and Vig (2010).

transferred from one bank to the other without material qualitative transformation. Third, most loan sales are made without explicit recourse to the seller. Moreover, unlike securitization, there are usually no guarantees, insurance, or any other type of explicit credit enhancement, although the portion of the loan retained by the originator functions somewhat like credit enhancement in attenuating moral hazard. Thus, a loan sale usually removes the loan permanently from the seller's balance sheet.

One striking difference between loan sales and securitization is that with a loan sale to another bank, the asset stays within the banking industry, whereas with securitization, it is converted into a capital market investment. However, loan sales and securitization provide a bank with similar advantages in terms of strategic choices. The bank's ability to specialize in originating, servicing, and monitoring loans to borrowers in specific regions and from specific industries can be put to profitable use without compromising diversification objectives, when the bank designs and implements a comprehensive loan sales and asset-securitization program.[42]

CONCLUSION

The adverse impact of the 2007–2009 financial crisis on some securitization markets has been quite severe. The ABCP market has more or less come to a standstill. However, securitization is a technology that can have distinct benefits when executed appropriately. It promotes diversification benefits and lowers funding costs. Given the significant benefits, the trend toward securitization is likely to continue in the absence of a substantial decrease in the relative cost of traditional funding for banks and thrifts. Banks' relative funding advantages of the past were based on deposit interest rate ceilings, discounting and advances, deposit insurance and the tax system, and regulated entry into banking. It is unlikely that these advantages will return, particularly in light of the significantly higher regulatory costs and regulatory uncertainty faced by banks now. Thus, securitization is likely to grow, as long as workable solutions to the moral hazard problem can be developed. If these solutions involve some form of recourse on the part of the originator, then they will need to satisfy accountants, regulators, and the contracting parties.

Securitization has been at the heart of the development of the shadow banking system. Shadow banks are defined as "financial entities other than regulated depository institutions (commercial banks, thrifts, and credit unions) that serve as intermediaries to channel savings into investments,"[43] and such "channeling" occurs through securitization. The key players in the shadow banking system are ABS, ABCP conduits, repurchase agreements (repos), and MMFs.

CASE STUDY: LONE STAR BANK

Introduction

Lone Star Bank is a relatively small but rapidly growing regional bank based in Palo Alto, California. In recent years, the bank has specialized in loans to small personal computer manufacturers. Historically, these customers have been mostly located in and around the Palo Alto and surrounding "Silicon Valley" area, but in the past few years, the bank has pursued similar business in other high-tech growth communities. Although the bank is not as large as some of its competitors, it has generated a strong reputation as a bank that understands the computer industry.

John Langston, Chief Executive Officer (CEO) of Lone Star, believes that growth in the personal computer industry will continue to be substantial. The bank would like to parlay its current reputation and expertise into a much larger presence, but faces two major constraints. First, keeping up with the fast growth of the industry will require the bank to deal with difficult funding issues, since the base of deposits available to the bank is limited by a variety of regulations and competitive considerations. In particular, leverage-ratio constraints would require the bank to raise additional capital to support a larger deposit base, and this is considered a costly alternative. Second, the bank must maintain a fairly continuous presence in the market for strategic reasons. A loss in market share could allow competitors to develop equally strong reputations for understanding the business.

With these considerations in mind, Langston calls Lana Tanner and Hugh Akston, executive vice presidents, into his office to discuss his concerns about the bank's loan pricing policies.

The Initial Meeting

Langston: You both know our situation. Since we've been doing these computer company loans, we've had great success. We saw an opportunity that other banks didn't understand. But I'm concerned about a couple of things. First, our business

---

42. One can however not exclude that monitoring incentives may suffer, see Parlour and Plantin (2008).
43. See Bernanke (2010).

loan portfolio is getting to be really heavily concentrated in the computer industry. (See *Exhibit* A.) Second, I'm worried that our success in lending to this segment might mean that we aren't pricing these loans correctly. Our return on assets has been slipping a bit lately (*see Exhibit B*), and I think we may be pricing our loans too cheaply.

Tanner: Well, the obvious thing to do would be to try to diversify by going into some other markets. But we can't forget the fiasco we had a couple of years back, when we thought we would expand heavily into real estate development loans. (*See Exhibit C.*)

Langston: (*He groans.*) Ugh, that's for sure. We took a hit on that one. I think we've learned a lesson there. We should stick to what we are good at.

Akston: Well, the next thing to look at would be the sale of some of our assets. By transferring some of the funding of loans elsewhere, we would concentrate on what we do best: identifying and monitoring successful firms. That way, we could stay in this industry segment while simultaneously diversifying our portfolio. I've talked to some other banks about doing some loan sales.

Langston: Great! Does that look promising?

Akston: Unfortunately, it really doesn't. Most of the companies we deal with are fairly small, as you know. The fact that all of these companies are producing a product that is something like a commodity to the end-user means that slight differences in technology or costs can make all the difference in the world to company profitability. We've got our team of computer wizards who are on top of all that. Ironically, though, the same knowledge advantage that has allowed us to beat the bigger banks in this market makes them too scared to buy loans from us directly. They don't think that they can tell the good borrowers from the bad ones as well as we can. And they are afraid that we would pawn off our losers on them. The bottom line is that we would have to either sell the loans for a lot less than they are really worth, or else provide a lot of credit enhancement. (See *Exhibit* D.)

Langsten: Well, I want the two of you to check into this in detail, particularly the possibility of securitizing some of our loan portfolio. Find out what our options are, and get back to me next week.

[*The meeting ends. Lana Tanner and Hugh Akston start working on the options available to the bank. Tanner will look into various kinds of securitization markets, while Akston will check into accounting and regulatory concerns.*]

The Second Meeting

Langsten: Well, Lana, you were going to look into the possibility of more direct securitization. Do you think we could package several of our loans into a pool for sale as asset-backed bonds?

Tanner: Unfortunately, even though the companies we lend to produce very similar products for sale, they vary widely in financial structure, costs, and so forth. For example, Gell Microsystems has a long-term contract with Sintel to buy memory chips at present prices. So if Washington imposes tariffs on Japanese chips, thus raising the overall cost of memory chips, Gell will benefit. Other companies have a variety of long-term or short-term contracts with other parts of the industry, including some really complicated software licensing arrangements. Quite simply put, these companies are not very homogeneous. (See *Exhibit* E.) About the only thing they have in common is their industry and the fact that they do a significant portion of their sales through business lease agreements.

Langston: So what's the bottom line?

Tanner: Well, we could try to package some of our loans to these companies, but the very different payoffs between these firms would mean that investors would have to know a lot about which firms were in the pool. The Wall Street people I talked to seemed to think that we would lose a lot of basis points in trying to sell these things, or else that we would have to overcollateralize or buy insurance bonds.

Langston: Well, it seems that we are caught between a rock and a hard place. On the one hand, we have the ability to identify and monitor good loan situations better than anyone else can. But this very advantage makes it difficult for us to get these loans off of our books.

Akston: Also, there's a factor that we haven't talked about yet. As you mentioned, we are really heavily concentrated in one relatively narrow industry. Additionally, the personal computer industry has historically been very sensitive to macroeconomic changes. When the economy turns sour, individuals and businesses can easily postpone the purchase of a new computer. That means that all of the companies we fund probably have highly correlated patterns of default. Many of our individual customers work in the computer business, too, so that default patterns on our consumer loans are also correlated with the computer industry. If we securitize with recourse, we really haven't diversified ourselves against an overall change in the computer business climate. A downturn would only be temporary, and we've weathered them before, but if we don't get some real diversification, we will be much more leveraged with respect to this particular risk – and we might lose strategic market share to better-diversified banks during a tight squeeze.

Langston: Ouch! Well, this is tough. Hugh, tell me what you found out.

Akston: Well, one thing is clear. Unless we are willing to sell these loans at huge discounts, we will have to retain a significant amount of recourse. What that means is that, for RAP purposes especially, we will have a hard time getting this stuff off our books.

Langston: O.K. Well, here's what I'd like the two of you to do. We've discussed a lot of different options for the bank, but it is time to act. I'd like you to work together and systematically examine each of the options we've mentioned as well as any others you can think of. Report back to me what the pros and cons are of each approach, and give me your final recommendation about which policy would be best for us.

The Assignment

Present the pros and cons of each approach mentioned in the case, being sure to cover the issues of fundamental importance. Try to think creatively about alternative solutions to come up with something potentially better for the bank.

Exhibit A
Lone Star Bank's Business Loan Portfolio by Industry

	2000	2001	2002	2003	2004	2005
Construction	23%	28%	35%	38%	27%	23%
Computer manufacturing	32%	38%	43%	47%	52%	55%
Retail stores	17%	18%	12%	10%	13%	12%
Distributors	5%	5%	4%	4%	5%	4%
Other	23%	11%	6%	1%	3%	6%

Exhibit B
Lone Star Bank
Profitability Measures

	2000	2001	2002	2003	2004	2005
Return on assets	0.900	0.875	0.000	0.834	0.752	0.654
Return on equity	11.2	11.0	0.0	9.4	8.7	6.32
Gross margin	54.8	54.2	50.1	54.5	53.0	51.2

Exhibit C
Lone Star Bank
Construction/Real Estate Development Loans

	2000	2001	2002	2003	2004	2005
Volume (millions)	46.0	61.6	84.7	101.1	82.6	80.9
Loan losses (percent)	0.9	1.1	2.1	3.4	1.9	1.1
Estimated net return	0.02	0.01	−0.02	−0.02	0.00	0.01

Exhibit D
Estimated Loan Sale Values

Estimated values based on a static pass-through $20 million face value pool. Market values are based on an average of estimates obtained from investment bankers contacted.

True value (NPV of estimated future cash flows):	$17,200,000
Loan sale without recourse (no credit enhancements):	$16,100,000
Loan sale with full recourse:	$17,200,000
Loan sale without recourse (with credit enhancements with a cost of $700,000):	$17,100,000

		Exhibit E			
		Customer Profiles			
Company name	Sales	Employees (Millions of dollars)	*D/A*	ROA	*P/E*
Gell Microsystems	523	2100	0.40	0.21	23
Encore Systems	215	1450	0.80	0.19	*
Southgate Comp. Systems	207	934	0.67	0.23	31
Texlon	185	1200	0.32	0.13	18
ZEON	127	600	0.87	0.29	42

Note: D/A is debt/total assets in book value terms. ROA is return on assets. *P/E* is the ratio of stock price to reported earnings.
*Not publicly traded.

REVIEW QUESTIONS

1. What are the similarities and the differences between loan sales and securitization?
2. What are the four basic components of a lending transaction? Why were these unified in the first place and why are they being decomposed now through securitization?
3. Discuss pass-through (both static and dynamic pool), ABBs, and pay-through, with particular focus on the differences between these contracts.
4. What are CMOs and REMICs?
5. Why are pass-throughs more popular than pay-throughs, and why are REMICs now replacing pass-throughs?
6. What are I/O – P/O strips and how can they be used to hedge interest-rate risk?
7. What are the supply- and demand-side forces stimulating securitization?
8. What is asset-backed commercial paper? Why has it become popular? Why don't corporations avoid banks and directly issue secured commercial paper?
9. Are there any "natural" limits to securitization? What are these? What sort of assets are most likely to be securitized and what assets are likely to be securitized?
10. Explain how a financial institution can use securitization as a tactical tool for balance sheet management and pricing, and as a strategic weapon for market penetration and diversification.
11. What does the anticipated future growth of securitization portend for the viability of banks and the ability of the Fed to control monetary aggregates?
12. Suppose bank A has two loans, each of which is due to be repaid one period hence and whose cash flows are independent and identically distributed random variables. Each loan will repay $250 to the bank with probability 0.8 and $125 with probability 0.2. However, while bank A knows this, prospective investors cannot distinguish this bank's loan portfolio from that of bank B that has the same number of loans, but each of its loans will repay $250 with probability 0.5 and $125 with probability 0.5. The prior belief of investors is that there is a 0.4 probability that bank A has the higher-valued portfolio and 0.6 probability that it has the lower-valued portfolio. Suppose that bank A wishes to securitize these loans, and it knows that if it does so without credit enhancement, the cost of communicating the true value of its loans to investors is 8% of the true value. Explore bank A's securitization alternatives. Assuming that a credit enhancer is available and that the credit enhancer could (at negligible cost) determine the true value of the loan portfolio, what sort of credit enhancement should bank A purchase? Assume everybody is risk neutral and that the discount rate is zero.
13. Given below is a conversation. Critique it.

    Moderator: O.K.! That's one for you, Alex. But I don't understand one thing. If banks are allowed to invest only in very safe assets, what happens to all of the assets that banks currently fund?

    Appleton: No big deal. These can be shifted to the capital market or funded with uninsured deposits.

    Moderator: But is such disintermediation or reintermediation necessarily a good thing?

    Appleton: I don't see why not. Banks are already securitizing many of their assets, from credit-card receivables to mortgages. What I'm suggesting is only a natural extension of that process.

    Butterworth: Sure, but there are natural limits to securitization. Besides, even with securitization, the bank acts as an originator. What you're proposing, Alex, is based, I think, on the premise that there is really nothing special about banks.

REFERENCES

Acharya, V., Schnabl, P., 2010. Do global banks spread global imbalances; asset-backed commercial paper during the financial crisis of 2007–2009. IMF Econ. Rev. 58, 37–73.

Agarwal, S., Amromin, G., Ben-David, I., Chomsisengphet, S., Evanoff, D., 2011. The role of securitization in mortgage renegotiation. J. Financ. Econ. 102, 559–578.

Agarwal, S., Chang, Y., Yavas, A., 2012. Adverse selection in mortgage securitization. J. Financ. Econ. 105, 640–660.

Altomonte, C., Bussoli, P., 2014. Asset-backed securities: the key to unlocking Europe's credit markets? Breughel Policy Contribution.

Anson, W., 2005. Intangible assets: a new source of security and securitization. Secured Lender.

Ayotte, K.M., Gaon, S., 2006. Asset-backed securities: costs and benefits of 'bankruptcy remoteness. Working Paper, Columbia University Business School.

Bagehot, W., 1873. Lombard Street: A Description of the Money Market. Kegan Paul, Trench, Trubner & Co., London.

Benveniste, L.M., Berger, A.N., 1987. Securitization with recourse: an instrument that offers uninsured bank depositors sequential claim. J. Bank. Financ. 11, 403–424.

Bernanke, B.S., 2010. Causes of the recent financial and economic crisis. Statement Before the Financial Crisis, Inquiry Commission, Washington, DC.

Board of Governors of the Federal Reserve System, 1988. Annual Statistical Digest.

Boot, A.W.A., Thakor, A.V., 1993. Security design. J. Financ. 48, 1349–1378.

Boyd, J., Smith, B.D., 1993, Intermediation and the equilibrium allocation of investment capital: implications for economic development. Working Paper, Federal Reserve Bank of Minneapolis.

Caouette, J.B., 1990. As the capital markets unbundle, what will the future bring? Special supplement on asset securitization, American Banker.

Covitz, D., Lang, N., Suarez, G., 2013. The evolution of a financial crisis. J. Financ. 68, 815–848.

Cutler, S., Sveen, P., 1993 Asset-backed commercial paper. Guide to International Commercial Paper, pp. 5–12.

Fishman, M., Kendall, L., July 2000. A Primer on Securitization. The MIT Press, Cambridge, MA.

Gorton, G., Metrick, A., 2013. Securitization. George, Constantinides, Milton, Harris, Rene, Stulz (Eds.), Handbook of the Economics of Finance, Volume 2, Elsevier, pp. 1–7, part A, Amsterdam, The Netherlands.

Gorton, G., Pennacchi, G., 1990. Financial intermediaries and liquidity creation. J. Financ. 45, 49–72.

Greenbaum, S.I., Thakor, A.V., 1987. Bank funding modes: Securitization versus deposits. J. Bank. Financ. 11, 379–402.

Grossman, S.J., 1981. An introduction to the theory of rational expectations under asymmetric information. Rev. Econ. Stud. 48, 541–559.

Gyntelberg, J., Remolona, E.M., 2006. Securitisation in Asia and the Pacific: implications for liquidity and credit risks. BIS Q. Rev. 65–75.

Huber, S.K., 1992. Bank Officer's Handbook of Government Regulation, Warren Gorham Lamont, Cumulative Supplement No. 2.

Kareken, J.H., 1987. The emergence and regulation of contingent commitment banking. J. Bank. Financ. 11, 359–378.

Keys, B., Mukherjee, T., Seru, A., Vig, V., 2010. Did securitization lead to lax screening? Q. J. Econ. 125, 307–362.

Kraus, J.R., Capital rules spur foreign banks into asset-backed commercial paper, American Banker, May 20, 1993.

Loutskina, E., 2011. The role of securitization in bank liquidity and funding management. J. Financ. Econ. 100, 663–684.

Loutskina, E., Strahan, P., 2009. Securitization and the declining impact of bank finance on loan supply: evidence from mortgage originations. J. Financ. 64, 861–889.

Martin, D., Drews, D.C., Intellectual Property: Collateral for Securitization or Lending, The Secured Lender, July–August 2005.

Mester, L.J., 1992. Traditional and nontraditional banking: an information-theoretic approach. J. Bank. Financ. 16, 545–566.

Monahan, M., 1989. An Investor's Guide to Asset-Backed Securities. Shearson Lehman Hutton, Inc, New York, NY.

Nadauld, T., Weisbach, M., 2012. Did securitization affect the cost of corporate debt? J. Financ. Econ. 105, 332–352.

Parlour, C., Plantin, G., 2008. Loan sales and relationship banking. J. Financ. 63, 1291–1314.

Pavel, C.A., 1989. Securitization. Probus Publishing, Chicago.

Piskorski, T., Seru, A., Vig, V., 2010. Securitization and distressed loan renegotiation: evidence from the subprime mortgage crisis. J. Financ. Econ. 97, 369–397.

Scatigna, M., Tovar, C.E., September 2007. Securitisation in Latin America. BIS Q. Rev., 71–82.

Shapiro, H.D., 1985. The securitization of practically everything. Institutional Investor 19, 201.

Subrahmanyam, A., 1991. A theory of trading in stock index futures. Rev. Financ. Stud. 4, 17–52.

Thomas, H., 2001. The effects of asset securitization on seller claimants. J. Financ. Intermed. 10, 306–330.

Tirole, J., 2012. Overcoming adverse selection: how public intervention can restore market functioning. Am. Econ. Rev. 102, 29–59.

Part VI

The Funding of the Bank

Chapter 12

The Deposit Contract, Deposit Insurance, and Shadow Banking

"As to guaranteeing bank deposits, the minute the government starts to do that... the government runs into a probable loss. We do not wish to make the United States government liable for the mistakes and errors of individual banks, and put a premium on unsound banking in the future."

Franklin Delano Roosevelt, in his first press conference as President of the United States

GLOSSARY OF TERMS

Charter Value The economic value of a bank to its owners (the shareholders). It can be viewed as the net present value of the profits expected to accrue to the shareholders over the life of the bank.

Anticompetitive Restrictions Restrictions aimed at limiting competition in the banking industry.

Price Elasticity of Demand A measure of the responsiveness of market demand to changes in price.

Junk Bonds Very high (default) risk bonds issued by corporations. These bonds have low credit ratings and carry high yields.

Capital Asset Pricing Model A model describing how risk is priced in the capital market. In particular, it predicts a linear relationship between the expected return on a security and its systematic risk factor (defined as "beta," the ratio of the covariance of the return on the security with that of the market to the variance of the market return).

INTRODUCTION

In earlier chapters, we focused on the asset side of the balance sheet for depository institutions. We now shift to the liability side. Although depository institutions have a wide variety of liabilities, in this chapter we will concentrate on different types of deposits, since this source of funding dominates for depository institutions and we will turn to capital in the next chapter. After covering depository institutions, we will discuss how institutions fund themselves in the shadow-banking system.

In the United States, the terms "bank deposits" and "deposit insurance" are almost inseparable. Yet, it is essential to distinguish the issues raised by the deposit contract *per se* from those related to deposit insurance. Thus, we will first discuss the deposit contract without the insurance aspect. We will then discuss "liability management", which is the process of managing the bank's net interest margin, that is, the difference between the asset revenues and the liability costs, expressed as a fraction of total assets. This will be followed by an analysis of deposit insurance. Having previously discussed the uninsured deposit contract, we will be able to see how governmental deposit insurance alters the deposit contract, and the behaviors of deposit takers.

We doubt that anyone remains to be convinced about the importance of deposit insurance-related issues. The increasing frequency of financial crises and the economic disruptions they have caused seem to reinforce the need for safety nets that reassure savers that they need not worry about the safety of the money they deposit in banks. This is because if they were worried, they would be more prone to take their money out at the first sign of trouble, which would then make the whole system vulnerable to runs on banks caused by rumors and unsubstantiated innuendos. Nonetheless, deposit insurance is not without its detractors. The main criticism is that the safety net it provides creates a moral hazard because depositors have little incentive to take the trouble to exert market discipline on the bank if it is taking excessive risk or making other imprudent choices. Many have blamed deposit insurance and greed for the S&L crisis and the widespread banking failures of the 1980s.[1] While this seems to be accepted, it is more difficult to explain why we have deposit insurance, and in particular, why we have the kind of deposit contract that seems to make federal insurance desirable. Discussions of these issues figure prominently in this chapter. What is unfortunate is that the S&L crisis was, to a great extent, avoidable, and the regulatory reforms that followed the crisis made sense well before the crisis occurred. As early as 1977, academic publications made the point that federally insured depository institutions had powerful incentives to take asset risk that was excessive from a

---

1. According to the 1993 *Economic Report of the President*, the S&L industry lost between $100 billion to $160 billion.

S. I. Greenbaum, A. V. Thakor & A. W. A. Boot: Contemporary Financial Intermediation, Third edition. http://dx.doi.org/10.1016/B978-0-12-405196-6.00012-4

social welfare standpoint, and that capital regulation, as it existed then, by itself was incapable of controlling these incentives, so that a fundamental reform of regulation was necessary.

Some might argue, however, that our historical experience (particularly since the advent of federal deposit insurance, following the Great Depression) did not prepare us for the systemic shocks like the S&L crisis. In the post-1933 period, extremely low bank failure rates made banking a rather unusual industry. So another puzzle is: Why the rash of failures did not occur prior to the 1980s? It turns out that the empirical and theoretical research on which this chapter is based provides valuable insights into the timing of the recent difficulties, and leads us to conclude that, despite our comfortable post-Depression experience, we should have foreseen many of the things that happened.

The regulatory reforms put in place after the S&L crisis of the 1980s, especially those dealing with capital requirements for depository institutions and regulatory forbearance, have served the purpose of increasing the safety and soundness of the depository banking industry fairly well, at least for the smaller institutions that were at the center of the S&L crisis. However, since 2000, massive consolidation in the banking sector and the explosive growth of the shadow-banking system, due in no small measure to the burgeoning popularity of securitization of a growing number of assets, were creating all sorts of risks that banking regulators seemed unprepared for.[2] Also very fragile funding structures and high leverage became prevalent.[3] A major part of this lack of regulatory oversight had to do with the fact that most of the shadow-banking institutions – brokerage house, money market mutual funds, investment banks, asset-backed securities conduits and the like – are not depository institutions and hence not covered by deposit insurance and banking supervisors, but under the purview of the Securities and Exchange Commission (SEC). However, the subprime crisis of 2007–2009 originated in the United States in the shadow-banking sector. Many of the institutions that became financially distressed as a result of the crisis – like AIG and Bear Sterns – were interconnected with many other institutions – including depository institutions – through swap contracts and other arrangements, and the opaqueness of these institutions and their arrangements meant that regulatory bodies like the Federal Reserve and the Treasury Department could not determine with certainty the consequences of allowing them to fail. Further complicating matters, ever-expanding bank holding companies were increasingly conducting shadow banking activities. Thus, even though these were not necessarily deposit-insured institutions, the Federal Reserve stepped in with unprecedented forms of assistance to forestall the failures of many of these institutions. These events will be discussed in greater depth in Chapter 14, which is devoted to the 2007–2009 financial crisis, but for now we note that the crisis was a rude awakening in that we have now come to appreciate that institutions can not only be too big to fail, but also "too interconnected to fail," and that systemic risk is not just some exogenous shock that comes out of thin air, but rather a consequence of the incentives built into the system, and the responses of individual institutions to those incentives.

The rest of this chapter is organized as follows. In the next section, we discuss the deposit contract. After that, we take up liability management and how it has been affected by interest-rate deregulation and deposit insurance. Then we discuss deposit insurance. We examine the arguments for and against deposit insurance, including the ability of governmentally provided deposit insurance to ward off runs on banks and panics. Issues related to the risk-sensitive pricing of deposit insurance are also examined, as is an analysis of the empirical evidence on the importance of moral hazard in federally insured depository institutions. The empirical evidence also provides insights into the timing of problems with deposit insurance. We then discuss the 1980s deposit insurance debacle in the United States, and developments that have occurred since then. We conclude with a discussion of funding in the shadow banking – nondepository institutions – sector.

THE DEPOSIT CONTRACT

The Nature of the Deposit Contract

Deposit contracts either have *defined maturities* like certificates of deposit (CDs), or are *withdrawable on demand*. We will focus on demand deposits, the quintessential banking liability. A demand deposit is created when an individual or firm deposits money in an account from which this money can be withdrawn at a moment's notice, that is, on demand.

The demand deposit contract has four important features:

- It is a debt contract.
- Its maturity is infinitesimal and it can be rolled over indefinitely.
- It is not traded in a secondary market.
- It is governed by a "sequential service" constraint.

---

2. For example, a huge market in credit default swaps (CDS) – essentially an insurance policy against default on a debt instrument – emerged and developed with little regulatory oversight.

3. See for example the *Federal Reserve Bank of New York Economic Policy Review*, Special Issue: The Stability of Funding Models (2014), and Yorulmazer (2014) in particular. In Chapter 2 we pointed out the high leverage in investment banking operations.

Debt Contract

Because the deposit is a debt contract, the depositor in an uninsured bank confronts the same asset-substitution moral hazard in dealing with the bank as the bank does in dealing with its borrowers (recall Chapters 7 and 8). That is, when a bank creates a deposit, it is simply borrowing from the depositor.

Maturity

The maturity is such that the depositor is promised the ability to withdraw at any time without penalty, that is, the depositor can sell the bank's liability back to the bank at par. Thus, a demand deposit is virtually as liquid as currency. The key difference is that currency carries no default risk, whereas an uninsured bank could default and not be able to fully satisfy withdrawal demands. Indeed, throughout *this* section we will assume that there is no deposit insurance, so that we can focus on the characteristics of the deposit contract itself.

Nontraded Contract

The fact that demand deposits are not traded in a secondary market implies that the depositor's payoff does not depend directly on how information about the bank is processed by other market participants, that is, the depositor does not face market price risk. Unlike a person who plans to sell a traded security in the market at the (random) price prevailing at a future date, a demand depositor knows precisely (in nominal terms) how much she will receive at *any* future point in time when she withdraws from her account, subject to the condition that the bank is solvent.

This last condition is not always satisfied, however. In fact, if things were believed to be going badly for the bank, we would expect the suspicious depositors to rush to the bank to withdraw their deposits. If you arrive late, it is possible that in paying off the earlier depositors the bank will have run out of money by the time you get there. In this case, absent deposit insurance, the maximum amount you can withdraw would be less than you had anticipated. In this sense, your payoff depends on what other depositors believe about the bank, just as it does with any traded debt contract that you liquidate prior to maturity.

The Sequential Service Constraint

This dependence of your payoff on the actions of other depositors occurs because the deposit contract satisfies a sequential service constraint (SSC). Hence, when a depositor seeks to withdraw, the amount the bank pays depends only on what was promised and on his place in the queue of depositors wishing to withdraw. In particular, the depositor's payoff cannot depend on any information that the bank may have about depositors in the queue behind that depositor. Thus, the bank pays depositors on a "first come, first served" basis. To see this, consider a bank that has $5 in equity, and $95 in interest-free deposits acquired from 95 depositors (each of whom deposited $1). The bank's $100 of assets consist of $20 in cash, and loans that are currently worth $80 if held to maturity. But if the loans are prematurely liquidated, they are worth only $27.50. Thus, the current (premature) liquidation value of the bank is $47.50. Now imagine that some depositors rush to withdraw their money. Others hear about this and become suspicious about the bank's assets. There is now a full-scale bank run. You are the 48th depositor in a queue of 95 when the bank's doors open in the morning. As the branch manager walks in, she counts the number of people in the queue and sees that every depositor is there to withdraw. Despite this, the SSC dictates that the bank cannot use this information in determining how much the first-in-line depositor should be paid. In this case, the manager is forced to call the outstanding loans, that is, liquidate them to collect $27.50. The first 47 depositors will each receive $1. You will receive $0.50, and all those behind you will go home empty-handed. One might argue that a more equitable approach would have been to give each of the 95 waiting depositors $0.50. But the SSC precludes that.

The nature of the deposit contract is worth examining for two reasons. First, when *all* of the bank's liabilities are uninsured, these features have significant implications for the disciplining of bank management. This suggests that the details of the demand deposit contract are probably not an outcome of chance; they serve a purpose. Second, when deposits are insured, some of these features of the demand deposit contract *encourage* bank runs, thus increasing the liability of the deposit insurer.

The Demand Deposit Contract and Economic Incentives

The Effects of Nontradability and the Debt-Like Nature of Deposits

Consider first that demandable debt is not traded and that it is a debt contract. The analysis in Chapters 7 and 8 implies that the depository institution in this case has an incentive to increase asset risk to the detriment of the depositors. That is, the institution's managers have an incentive to invest in risky loans that transfer wealth from depositors to shareholders. Similarly, depositors face a moral hazard in that the institution has an incentive to shirk in monitoring the borrowers to whom it has extended loans. This too adversely affects the depositors' expected payoff. A third form of moral hazard is fraud. Deposits are essentially "someone else's" money, and managers may be tempted to appropriate some of that money for themselves. While these pathologies have been attributed to federal deposit insurance, they were encountered even prior to the adoption of deposit insurance,[4] and our theory predicts that incentives for managerial fraud exist even with (non-traded) deposits that are uninsured. That the deposit contract is not traded aggravates the moral hazard problem because the discipline imposed by market pricing is absent.

The Effect of Maturity

It turns out, however, that the other two features of the demand deposit contract – its infinitesimal maturity and the SSC – help to attenuate these different types of moral hazard. In developing the intuition below,[5] we first consider the effect of the undefined maturity.

Suppose that there are numerous individuals who demand deposit accounts at a bank. It is natural to expect that some of these depositors are particularly skilled in analyzing the bank's financial health, whereas others are less able. Let us suppose that these skilled depositors keep a watchful eye on the bank's managers because they recognize that moral hazard could diminish their expected payoff. Now, imagine that a few of these vigilant depositors discover that the bank's risky loans are not doing well. Default on many of these loans is likely. Moreover, these depositors discover that the bank has extended numerous loans to close friends of the top managers; this raises suspicion of fraud. What should these informed depositors do? Since they have information that the bank is in peril and may default on its deposit obligations, their best bet is to withdraw their funds as quickly as possible.

When these informed depositors withdraw their funds from the bank, there are two possibilities. One is that the uninformed depositors do not react. In this case, the total outflow of funds from the bank will depend on the size of the deposit holdings of the informed depositors. If their holdings are large enough, the bank will be compelled to attract new deposits. The second possibility is that some or all of the uninformed depositors observe the withdrawals of the informed depositors and decide to follow suit. In this case, there is a bank run. In either case, the bank will need to attract new deposits to replace withdrawals, or liquidate. Liquidation will involve either the calling back of loans, with the associated disruptions in the productive activities of borrowers, or loan sales to other banks. The alternative of attracting new deposits will be difficult, for obvious reasons. Prospective depositors will see the large deposit withdrawals and will be reluctant to entrust their money to the bank. And even if some deposit money flows in, the bank will need to pay higher interest rates on these deposits. Thus, deposit withdrawals by the informed depositors are likely to be costly to the bank. The anticipation of incurring these costs could deter the bank's managers from risky investments, and from shirking on the monitoring of borrowers. It could also reduce the temptation to defraud the depositors.

The Role of the SSC

This argument suggests that the demandable nature of deposits helps to keep the bank management on its toes. There is a slight hitch in this disciplining process, however. If a depositor can rely on other depositors to monitor the bank, then all that such a depositor has to do is to keep an eye on the informed depositors. There is no need for the "free-riding" depositor to expend personal resources to monitor the bank. This can subvert depositor monitoring. The reason is that *every* depositor may think that others will do the necessary monitoring, and in that case, no one monitors! This is where the SSC comes into play. Because a depositor's expected payoff is greater if he is at the front of the queue than if he is at the rear, he recognizes that by playing a "follow the leader" strategy, his expected payoff is lower than if he monitors himself. This strengthens each individual depositor's incentive to monitor. These ideas are made concrete in the example developed in the box below.

An Illustration of the Incentive Effects of the [Uninsured] Deposit Contract

Example 12.1

Consider a bank that receives a $1 deposit at $t = 0$ from each of 105 different depositors. It invests $10 of shareholders' equity in the bank and lends $110, keeping $5 as cash reserves. Out of the 105 depositors, there are 30 depositors (called type-D_1 depositors) who are capable of monitoring the bank's management; the remaining depositors (called type-D_2 depositors) keep their money in the bank simply for transactions and safekeeping purposes. The cost of monitoring the bank for an individual type-D_1 depositor is $0.01 per period.

The bank has two mutually exclusive investment opportunities. Project (or loan) A pays $200 with probability 0.7 and zero with probability 0.3 at $t = 1$. Project B pays $150 with probability 0.9 and $112 with probability 0.1 at $t = 1$. If the bank chooses one of these projects, the probability that the bank will actually end up with that project is 0.9. With probability 0.1, the bank will

---

4. See Calomiris and Kahn (1991).

5. This intuition is based on Calomiris and Kahn (1991). See also Diamond and Rajan (2001) and Jacklin and Bhattacharya (1988).

have inadvertently chosen the other project. Thus, we assume that the bank may make errors in project choice.[6] By monitoring the bank, a type-D_1 depositor can discover the bank's true project choice at some point in time intermediate between $t = 0$ and $t = 1$, say at $t = 1/2$. These depositors can, if they desire, force liquidation of the bank by withdrawing their deposits at $t = 1/2$, and the threat of this liquidation provides a disincentive to the bank to choose the risky project. Note that the bank's projects or loans mature at $t = 1$. If they are liquidated at $t = 1/2$, they are worth only $25 to the bank. Under the terms of the deposit contract, the bank promises to pay a 12% interest (conditional on the bank having the financial capacity to do so) if deposit withdrawal occurs at $t = 1$, and no interest if withdrawal occurs before that. Thus, a depositor is entitled to $1.12 if she withdraws at $t = 1$, and $1 if she withdraws at $t = 1/2$. The risk-free discount rate is zero and all agents are risk neutral.

All the type-D_2 depositors plan to withdraw at $t = 1$, but each is subject to a random liquidity-motivated desire to withdraw at $t = 1/2$. To simplify, we will assume that even though no one knows in advance which (type-D_2) depositors will wish to withdraw at $t = 1/2$, the *fraction* of those who will wish to withdraw is known to be 5/75. That is, five type-D_2 depositors will wish to withdraw at $t = 1/2$. Assume that the bank's managers make decisions in the best interests of their shareholders. Compute the equilibrium strategies of the bank and its depositors.

Solution
It is useful to summarize the strategies available to the bank and the different types of depositors before we begin to analyze the solution. These are listed in Table 12.1.

TABLE 12.1 Strategies of Participants

Agent	Strategies		
Bank	Choose project A at $t = 0$	Choose project B at $t = 0$	
Type-D_1 depositors	Monitor and decide whether or not to withdraw at $t = 1/2$ based upon result of monitoring	Do not monitor and withdraw at $t = 1$	Do not monitor and withdraw at $t = 1/2$
Liquidity-motivated Type-D_2 depositors	Withdraw at $t = 1/2$	Withdraw at $t = 1/2$	
Other (Patient) Type-D_2 depositors	Withdraw at $t = 1$	Withdraw at $t = 1$	

We will solve this problem in four steps. First, we analyze the bank's project choice in the case in which the type-D_1 depositors do not monitor and the bank knows that there is no monitoring. We show that the bank chooses project A in this case. Second, we show that our assumption in Step 1 is invalid because it cannot be a Nash equilibrium for no type-D_1 depositors to monitor. Next, we wish to examine if it is a Nash equilibrium for all the type-D_1 depositors to monitor. We do this in two steps. In Step 3, we show that the bank chooses project B if it believes that all the type-D_1 depositors will monitor. Then in Step 4, we examine the strategy of a type-D_1 depositor when he knows that all the other type-D1 depositors will monitor and the bank has opted for project B. We show that this type-D_1 depositor *will* wish to monitor. This verifies that it is indeed a Nash equilibrium for all the type-D_1 depositors to monitor.

The key assumption in this example is that the bank's project choice cannot be contracted upon because not all depositors can observe it. If this were not the case, there would be no role for depositor monitoring.

Step 1
We will first analyze the outcome in which the type-D_1 depositors do *not* monitor the bank. Given that the bank knows that there is no monitoring, which project will it prefer? If it chooses project A and if this choice is error-free, the expected payoff of its shareholders is

$$0.7 \times [200 - 112] = \$61.6,$$

Probability of success — Total payoff — Bank's repayment to its depositors

and if it chooses project B and this choice is error-free, the expected payoff is

$$0.9 \times [150 - 112] + 0.1 \times [112 - 112] = \$3$$

Probability of high payoff — High payoff on project B — Bank's repayment to depositors — Probability of low payoff — Low payoff on project B — Repayment to depositors

---

6. This feature ensures that the type-D_1 depositors do monitor the bank in equilibrium. The reason is that the threat of depositor monitoring will, in equilibrium, cause the bank to choose the project desired by the depositors. If this choice were error-free, depositors would anticipate that the bank will make the desired project choice and therefore perceive no need to monitor. But then the bank, in turn, should anticipate the behavior of the depositors and decide to invest in the project preferred by its own shareholders. And so on and on! The point is that we have a time consistency problem that leads to there being no equilibrium. However, as our solution will make clear this problem can be avoided when the bank's project choice is error-prone.

When project choice is error-prone, the expected payoff of the bank's shareholders when project A is chosen is

$$0.9 \times \$61.6 + 0.1 \times \$34.2 = \$58.86,$$

and their expected payoff when project B is chosen is

$$0.9 \times \$34.2 + 0.1 \times \$61.6 = \$36.94.$$

Thus, if there is no monitoring, the bank will choose project A.

Step 2

The question now is: Can it be a Nash equilibrium for *no* type-D_1 depositor to monitor? This is equivalent to asking whether it is in the best interest of every individual type-D_1 depositor not to monitor when she knows that no other type-D_1 depositors are monitoring. Suppose you are one of those type-D_1 depositors. If you do not monitor, your expected payoff is

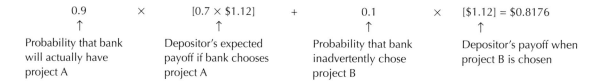

Now, if you do monitor, and discover that the bank chose project A, what should you do? If you do nothing (i.e., you do not withdraw your deposit), your expected payoff at $t = 1$ is

$$0.7 \times \$1.12 - \$0.01 = \$0.774.$$
$$\uparrow$$
$$\text{your monitoring cost}$$

If you withdraw, you know that the bank will be forced to liquidate its asset portfolio since it has only \$5 in cash reserves and there are five type-D_2 depositors who will withdraw at $t = 1/2$ for liquidity purposes. Liquidation will fetch \$25, so that the bank will have a total of \$30 to disburse. You are sure to receive your \$1 at $t = 1/2$. Thus, your payoff will be

$$\$1 - \$0.01 = \$0.99.$$

This means that if you monitor and discover that project A has been chosen, you should demand to withdraw your deposit at $t = 1/2$. On the other hand, if you find that project B was chosen, your payoff is

$$\$1.12 - \$0.01 = \$1.11$$

if you wait until $t = 1$ to withdraw, and it is \$0.99 if you withdraw at $t = 1/2$. Hence, it is better for you to wait until $t = 1$ (remember that your *time value* of money between $t = 1/2$ and $t = 1$ is zero). We can now compute the overall expected payoff to you from monitoring. This payoff is

$$0.9 \times \$0.99 + 0.1 \times \$1.11 = \$1.002$$

↑	↑
Probability that you will discover project A was chosen and will therefore withdraw at $t = 1/2$	Probability that you will discover that project B was chosen and will therefore withdraw at $t = 1$

Clearly, this payoff exceeds your payoff if you do not monitor (\$0.8176). This proves that you have an incentive to monitor when others do not, which means that it cannot be a Nash equilibrium for nobody to monitor.

Step 3

Let us now examine if it is a Nash equilibrium for all the type-D_1 depositors to monitor. We begin by noting that if the bank believes that all these depositors will monitor, then it is in the bank's best interest to choose project B. This is verified below.

If the bank chooses project A, then there is only a 0.1 probability that project B will be inadvertently chosen. That is, there is a 0.9 probability that the bank will be liquidated at $t = 1/2$. Thus, the expected payoff of the bank's shareholders from opting for project A is

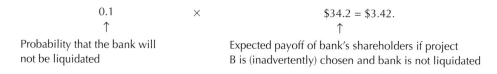

If the bank opts for project B, then there is only a 0.1 probability that the bank will be liquidated at $t = 1/2$ (this is the probability that project A will be erroneously picked). Thus, the expected payoff of the bank's shareholders from opting for project B will be

$$0.9 \times \$34.2 = \$30.78.$$

Clearly, the shareholders are better off opting for project B.

Step 4
The next step is to examine the strategy of a type-D_1 depositor when he knows that all the other type-D_1 depositors will monitor and the bank has opted for project B. If you are that depositor and you monitor, your payoff (at $t = 1$) is $1.12 if you discover at $t = 1/2$ that the bank indeed chose project B. But if you discover that project A was chosen, then you will want to withdraw your deposit. The problem now is a little different from the previous case. You realize that if you discover that project A was chosen, so will the 29 other type-D_1 depositors. When added to the five liquidity-motivated type-D_2 depositors, this means that the line of those who wish to withdraw at $t = 1/2$ will be 35 depositors long. But the bank has only $30 upon liquidation, and hence can only satisfy the first 30 depositors. Assuming that each person who goes to the bank will have an equal probability of being one of the first 30, the probability is 30/35 that you will be one of the first 30 withdrawers.[7] In this case, your *expected* payoff is only $\frac{30}{35} \times \$1 = \$0.8571$, since you get nothing if you are not one of the first 30 in line. Thus, your overall expected payoff from monitoring is given by

$$0.9 \times \$1.12 + 0.1 \times \$0.8571 - \$0.01 = \$1.0837.$$
$$\uparrow$$
$$\text{Monitoring cost}$$

If you decide not to monitor, then you are behaving like a type-D_2 depositor. Your expected payoff will be $1.12 if the other type-$D_1$ depositors discover that project B was chosen (the probability of this is 0.9), and it will be zero if they discover that project A was chosen and decide to liquidate the bank at $t = 1/2$ (the probability of this is 0.1). Hence, your overall expected payoff from not monitoring is

$$0.9 \times \$1.12 = \$1.008.$$

Another possible strategy is for you to behave like a liquidity-motivated type-D_2 depositor and withdraw your deposit at $t = 1/2$ *without* monitoring. In this case, you recognize that there is a 0.9 probability that the other type-D_1 depositors will not withdraw and a 0.1 probability that they will. If the other type-D1 depositors do not withdraw, there are only six depositors in all (including you) who wish to withdraw at $t = 1/2$. The bank will be forced to liquidate, and you will receive your $1 for sure. If the other type-D_1 depositors withdraw, the bank will also liquidate, and you will have a 30/35 chance of getting your $1. Thus, your expected payoff from withdrawing without monitoring is

$$0.9 \times 1 \times \$1 + 0.1 \times \frac{30}{35} \times \$1 = \$0.9086.$$

Comparing the three payoffs ($1.0837, $1.008, and $0.9086), we see that your best strategy is to monitor. Hence, it is a Nash equilibrium for all the type-D_1 depositors to monitor the bank, and for the bank to choose project B.

Although we worked out this numerical example explicitly for the case of asset-substitution moral hazard, the intuition for managerial fraud is similar. In either case, the demandable nature of deposits puts pressure on bank management to not deviate too far from the desires of the depositors, and the SSC lends credibility to the depositors' threat to monitor to ensure "proper" bank behavior by creating a situation in which all vigilant depositors wish to monitor. Thus, these specific features of the deposit contract play an important role in aligning the incentives of the contracting parties in an uninsured bank. This leads naturally to the question of deposit insurance. Before we get to that, however, we discuss liability management in a bank.

LIABILITY MANAGEMENT

We have so far discussed the economics of the deposit contract. The use of the deposit contract is an integral component of what is called *liability management*.

---

7. By the SSC, this is the probability that you will receive your $1.

What Is Liability Management?

Depository institutions pay particular attention to their *net-interest margin* (NIM), which is the difference between the yield on assets and the interest cost of liabilities, expressed as a fraction of total assets. Liability management refers to the institution's strategies for maintaining the continuity and cost effectiveness of funding assets.

There are three main (interrelated) issues in liability management. The first is *diversification,* which refers to choosing among funding sources so as to avoid over-dependence on a particular source. A second choice involves the *mix* of liabilities. Depository institutions raise funds using a variety of deposits,[8] each of which represents a specific contractual form that is a strategic choice. The third choice is about liability *maturity structure,* which determines the bank's interest-rate risk exposure for a given asset maturity structure. We discuss each issue briefly in what follows.

Diversification

Diversifying funding sources reduces liquidity risk (recall Chapter 6). Borrowing and lending in the federal funds market, borrowing at the discount window, dealing with repurchase agreements, and utilizing large CDs, brokered deposits, and Eurodollar deposits are techniques that banks use to diversify. Borrowing in the fed funds market and at the discount window is usually short term; most fed funds transactions are *overnight loans,* although the number of *term fed funds* transactions, with maturities in weeks, has increased recently. For longer-maturity liabilities, banks rely on a variety of deposits. Prominent among these are *negotiable CDs,* called *jumbos,* which are actively traded large-denomination time deposits with market-determined interest rates, a minimum maturity of one week, and denominations exceeding $100,000. Most negotiable CDs are issued directly to customers, although some large institutions issue them to brokers, who then sell them to other investors. Deposits marketed this way are called *brokered deposits.*

Large banks also use *Eurodollar deposits,* which are time deposits denominated in dollars but held in banks outside the United States, including foreign branches of U.S. banks. Eurodeposits are created in many ways. Perhaps the simplest way is when an American transfers money on deposit in a U.S. bank to a bank in another country. These deposits remain in dollars. Eurodeposits are subject to the Federal Reserve's cash-asset reserve requirements, and are not protected by U.S. deposit insurance.

Banks also raise funds by using *repurchase agreements* or "repos." A repo is the sale of a marketable security, with the agreement to repurchase it at a specified future date. That is, it is a loan secured by a marketable security. As long as the securities pledged against repos are U.S. government or government agency securities, repos are not subject to reserve requirements. Repos range in maturity from overnight to a month or more. Since repos involve collateral, they are not considered deposits and hence are not covered by deposit insurance.

Banks use a variety of other funding sources, such as subordinated debt as well as securitization and loan sales. Securitization also facilitates diversification of the bank's loan portfolio. Moreover, bank holding companies can issue commercial paper.

Liability Mix

Bank liabilities can be divided into two categories: products and investment instruments.[9] A product entitles the purchaser to a financial claim as well as to some bank services. That is, it is a contract that bundles monetary and possibly nonmonetary payoffs. An example is a checking account on which the bank pays interest and provides transactions services. For corporations, other services include cash management at possibly subsidized prices. Thus, purchasers of product-based deposits, called "customers", receive both explicit and implicit interest, and the demand for such deposits depends both on the explicit interest as well as on the value depositors attach to the bank's services.[10] Because many of these services are demanded by retail depositors, deposits tend to be small (below the *de jure* deposit insurance coverage limit of $250,000 per account). Moreover, customers prefer to have the payoffs on their contracts as insensitive as possible to the fortunes of the intermediary itself. For example, a life insurance policy provides its beneficiaries with a specified cash payment conditional on the death of the insured. That function is less efficiently performed if the contract calls

---

8. We ignore for now nondeposit sources of funding, such as wholesale funding.

9. See Merton (1993). He argues that in financial institutions, there is a commingling of products and investment instruments. Examples are life insurance policies and some types of deposit contracts. Merton and Thakor (2015) point out that many financial intermediaries raise financing from investors (who purchase investment instruments) and customers (who purchase products). They explain that the efficient arrangement is for customers to be insulated from the credit risk of the intermediary, but investors to be exposed to it.

10. These services are often valued very highly by depositors. Song and Thakor (2007) develop a theoretical model in which banks earn rents on core (retail) deposits and use these deposits to finance relationship loans.

instead for the death benefit to be conditioned on the financial condition of the insurance company as well as on the death of the insured.[11] Consequently, an increase in the policyholder's risk due to a decline in the insurance company's financial condition may require a greater reduction in the insurance premium than would be actuarially fair. It may, therefore, pay for the insurance company to reduce the policyholder's risk as much as possible. In the case of banks, this may explain why product-based deposits are typically fully insured.

Investment instruments, on the other hand, are simply financial claims, similar to the liabilities of nonfinancial firms. The bank provides no transactions or other services to the claimholder, so the design of these contracts involves the same risk-return tradeoffs faced by nonfinancial firms. An example of an investment instrument is a brokered CD. Deposit contracts that are investment instruments tend to be purchased by institutions, are relatively large in denominations, and include uninsured deposits. Their prices are usually determined through secondary-market trading.

One of the bank's liability-management choices is the appropriate mix of product-based deposits and investment instruments. Because of the relative insensitivity of their values to the bank's riskiness, product-based deposits do not involve much monitoring of bank management by depositors. Investment instruments, on the other hand, have values that are sensitive to the bank's riskiness, and it pays for the holders of these claims to monitor the bank. The bank is, therefore, subject to greater market discipline with these deposits. From the standpoint of the bank's management, there may be a desire to reduce the bank's reliance on such deposits in order to limit market discipline. Of course, doing so may sacrifice diversification in funding sources, with the attendant liquidity risk that may eventually result in a loss of control for management. The bank's shareholders, on the other hand, would like sufficient reliance on investment instruments to ensure the desired level of market discipline. This suggests a liability-management agency problem between shareholders and managers of banks.

The Duration Structure

Given its asset duration structure, the bank's choice of liability duration structure will determine its interest-rate risk. Given long-duration assets, choosing a matching long duration on the liability side will minimize interest-rate risk. However, given a bank's added value in providing particular assets and liabilities (based on its customers' needs), banks typically end up with liabilities of shorter duration than assets.

Banks often resolve this tension by using derivatives (Chapter 10). The better-managed banks purchase the most beneficial assets and liabilities and then use options, futures, and swaps to achieve the desired degree of immunization against interest-rate risk.

DEPOSIT INSURANCE

The Rationale for Deposit Insurance: A Historical Perspective

The Need for Deposit Insurance

If the demand deposit contract discussed earlier works well in disciplining bank management, why do we need deposit insurance? The reasons are many. Not all make perfect sense in today's environment, but we will get to that later. For now, let us simply note that an uninsured (demand) deposit contract can be quite disruptive. In a sense, it can lead to *overdisciplining* of banks. This can be seen as follows. In the previous section, we assumed for simplicity that the vigilant depositors could discover the bank's project choice without error. In reality, this discovery is likely to be error-prone. It is then possible that the bank is forced to liquidate assets even when its project choice is congruent with the preferences of depositors. This is socially wasteful *ex post*.

In addition, systematic elements in the risk profiles of the asset portfolios of banks may give rise to a *contagion effect* among banks. That is, when one bank fails, depositors suspect that the failure may be due to systematic risk elements that pervade the asset portfolios of *all* banks in that geographical area, and this may lead to spreading bank runs. Since it often takes a long time for the precise reasons for a bank's failure to become public, the contagion effect may be encountered even when the failure of a particular bank is due to idiosyncratic factors such as poor management. Indeed, this is the rationale for the "too big to fail" doctrine, which leads the government to rescue sufficiently large banks from failure.

Both of these problems are reduced with deposit insurance. When a government agency insures a bank's deposits, it guarantees that the depositors will receive their promised payment, regardless of the bank's financial condition. This makes it unnecessary for depositors to monitor the bank, and it lessens the likelihood of runs on individual banks or on groups of banks.

---

11. Merton (1993) suggests that an Arrow–Debreu economy (see the discussion of market incompleteness in Chapter 1) illustrates this point. A complete set of such securities provides a Pareto-efficient allocation of resources. But efficiency would be lost if the payoffs on such securities were also contingent on the issuer's financial condition (see also Merton (1989), and Merton and Thakor (2015)).

Historical Background

Federal deposit insurance came into existence in the United States with the enactment of the Banking Act of 1933, and the creation of the Federal Deposit Insurance Corporation (FDIC) to insure bank deposits. The insurance system was extended the following year to S&Ls with the creation of the Federal Savings and Loan Insurance Corporation (FSLIC), which insured S&L shares (deposits). In 1971, deposit insurance was also made available to credit unions.[12] All of this was inspired by the Great Depression and the massive runs on banks that forced President Roosevelt to declare a "banking holiday" in March of 1933. The banking panics of the Great Depression were not new, however. There were as many as seven panics from 1866 to 1934. We will use the term "bank run" (in the singular) to denote a situation in which depositors at a *single* bank wish to exchange their deposits for currency, and the term "banking panic" to denote a situation in which depositors at many banks wish to exchange their deposits for currency.

Before federal deposit insurance, panics were often addressed by *suspending convertibility* of deposits into cash. Under this approach, the bank was simply closed to depositors who wished to withdraw their money. By giving the banks "breathing room" during which "mass hysteria" had a chance to die down, more information about the financial condition of the bank could be released. Unless this information confirmed the worst fears of depositors, they could be persuaded to refrain from withdrawing their money when the suspension was lifted. Suspension amounted to default on the deposit contract and was a violation of banking law. Nevertheless, five out of the seven panics referred to previously involved suspension of convertibility (those in 1873, 1890, 1893, 1907, and 1914).[13]

Another method that was used during banking panics was the *issuance of clearinghouse loan certificates*. These arose from *Commercial-Bank Clearinghouses* (CBCHs), private-market arrangements among banks that served some of the functions of a central bank. Initially a CBCH was formed to facilitate check clearing. Prior to the formation of the New York CBCH in 1853, for example, commercial banks collected checks by a process of daily exchange and settlement with each other. The clearinghouse centralized the settlement process by permitting exchange to be made with the clearinghouse alone. However, as it evolved, the clearinghouse was able to provide additional information-based services such as *certification* (based on a minimum capital requirement needed to become a member of the clearinghouse) and *monitoring* (based on periodic audits) of its member banks. Members who failed to satisfy CBCH regulations were disciplined with fines or expulsions. This economized on individual monitoring costs that depositors would have had to incur in the absence of a clearinghouse.

One way for a bank to reduce the likelihood of a run is to reduce the depositors' concern about the bank's assets. The clearinghouse loan certificate, first issued during the panic of 1857, was an attempt to do this. A policy committee of the CBCH first authorized the issuance of loan certificates. Whenever a member bank had insufficient cash to satisfy deposit withdrawals, it could apply to the CBCH loan committee for certificates. Borrowing banks were charged interest rates varying from 6% to 7% and were required to present acceptable collateral. These certificates, which typically had maturities of 1 to 3 months, could be used by the bank in place of currency. Depositors were willing to accept the loan certificates in exchange for demand deposits because the loan certificates were claims on the CBCH, rather than on the individual bank. Thus, depositors obtained some insurance (diversification benefits) against individual bank failure. This meant that when there was a run on a bank, the bank could either pay off depositors in loan certificates (thereby exchanging claims against its own assets for claims against the CBCH), or it could raise new deposits from depositors who would be sold loan certificates. The bank would then use the proceeds to pay off the older depositors. In this way, the problem of bank-specific risk arising from informational asymmetries was resolved through a private system of coinsurance among banks.

Despite the efforts of the CBCHs to restrain member banks, they could not eliminate *all* moral hazard. Besides, there was the possibility of the CBCH itself being corrupted. Thus, there remained a role for monitoring by depositors. This, in turn, led to occasional runs on banks.

Reasons for Federal Deposit Insurance

Even though private arrangements can diminish the likelihood of bank runs, there are two reasons why they cannot eliminate them. First, even though a private arrangement like the CBCH provides depositors with some diversification, this diversification is limited by the size of the group of member banks. Size limitations may arise from transportation or information costs. Moreover, as the group grows larger, the cost to the CBCH of cheating by an individual bank diminishes, and the CBCH's incentive to monitor its members is weakened. This may be one reason why a large number of new clearinghouses sprang up within a 10-year period following the establishment of the New York CBCH in 1853, rather than a single "mega" clearinghouse emerging. A second weakness of private arrangements is that depositors can never be completely sure of the integrity of the arrangement. Thus, there was still some incentive for depositors to monitor the CBCH. In turn, this implies that panics could not be avoided.

---

12. Legally, a credit union does not accept deposits but issues shares in the credit union to its members. In reality, credit union shares are so similar to deposits that we will not distinguish between them.

13. See Gorton (1988).

The establishment of the Federal Reserve System in 1914 was partly in response to the inadequacy of private arrangements in performing key central bank functions. Nevertheless, the Fed could not prevent the banking panics of the Great Depression, and this eventually led to the establishment of federal deposit insurance. Two of the arguments for federal deposit insurance are discussed below.

1. *Money Supply: the Macroeconomic Argument:* At a macroeconomic level, deposit insurance acts as a stabilizer by preventing reductions in the stock of money through bank failures. Since commercial banks are the main providers of the nation's money stock, large-scale uninsured failures of commercial banks would reduce the national money supply. Deposit insurance helps to prevent this in two ways: (a) it replaces deposits that would otherwise be lost, and (b) it discourages banking panics by preserving public confidence.

   The reason why deposit insurance has to be *federal* is the credibility of the federal government in its promise to meet all contractual payments. Because of its virtually unlimited authority to raise revenues through taxation, the federal government can meet payout commitments that may be far in excess of the deposit insurance fund. This taxation may be explicit (the government can simply raise taxes) or implicit (the government can print more money to repay depositors, thereby taxing by reducing the real value of each unit of money).

2. *Improving Consumer Welfare: the Microeconomic Argument:* We have already noted the incentive of individual depositors to monitor the bank. This results in costly duplication of monitoring. In the numerical illustration of the previous section, the equilibrium involves all 30 vigilant depositors monitoring the bank even though monitoring by just one depositor would suffice. There are two ways in which federal deposit insurance helps to reduce overall monitoring costs. First, because a government agency (the federal insurer) is insuring deposits, the need of insured depositors to monitor is either eliminated (when deposit insurance is complete) or diminished (when deposit insurance is incomplete). Moreover, since the federal insurer must itself monitor banks, even uninsured depositors perceive a much smaller need to monitor. In other words, most of the monitoring burden is shifted from individual depositors to the federal insurer. This eliminates much of the duplicated monitoring encountered with uninsured deposits, *without* any residual monitoring incentives as with the private CBCH arrangement. Second, a federal deposit insurer can be expected to specialize in monitoring insured banks because it must deal with a large number of them. Thus, even apart from reducing duplication, there may be a direct reduction in monitoring costs. For example, in our numerical illustration, instead of monitoring costing 1 cent per audit, it might cost 3/4 cent per audit.

The overall effect of reduced monitoring costs will be to increase the *effective* interest rates on deposits,[14] but this benefit of deposit insurance may be offset by a host of implementation problems that we have yet to address.

Banking Runs and Panics: Theories and the Empirical Evidence

Although the idea that deposit insurance can eliminate bank runs is an old one, research in the last decade has provided a clearer understanding of *why* bank runs and banking panics occur. In light of the recent S&L and banking turmoil, linked by many to federal deposit insurance, alternative arrangements deserve careful consideration. This subsection offers a perspective that should be useful in thinking about these issues.

When informational imperfections interfere with the functioning of a market, governmental intervention may be warranted. An example is Akerlof's lemons problem in the used car market (recall Chapter 1); "lemons laws" protect used car buyers in many states. Another example is the Federal Aviation Authority's regulation of airline safety and the Federal Drug Administration's regulation of the medicinal drug market. In these markets, it is very costly for consumers to let the market provide the necessary disciplining of providers. Similarly, if banking panics disrupt the productive sector of the economy, federal deposit insurance may be warranted if it is effective in reducing the likelihood of panics. The two main theories discussed below explain *how* deposit insurance can prevent runs and panics.

1. *The "Sunspots" Theory of Bank Runs:* This theory maintains that bank runs are triggered by completely random events like "sunspots."[15] Suppose that we live in a two-period world with three points in time: $t = 0, 1, 2$. Individuals are risk averse. At $t = 0$, individuals have endowments of wealth that they wish to invest in projects. Each project requires a $1 investment at $t = 1$, pays off $R for sure at $t = 2$ if not liquidated earlier, and has positive NPV, that is, each offers a rate of return sufficiently higher than the riskless rate (which is zero) if continued until $t = 2$. Let $R > \$1$. However, if the project is liquidated prematurely at $t = 1$, then there is a loss of productive efficiency and the project pays off only $1.

---

14. To see this, imagine that in the previous numerical illustration, depositors can be assured that the bank will choose project B, and the total monitoring cost to ensure this choice is only 3/4 cent.

15. See Noyes (1909) and Gibbons (1968). Bryant (1980) and Diamond and Dybvig (1983) provide more contemporary treatments. The discussion below is based on Diamond and Dybvig (1983). The empirical evidence indicates that bank runs are not sunspots-like phenomena, but are typically triggered by insolvency concerns that depositors have about banks (see Gorton (1988). We discuss this in more detail later.

At $t = 0$, individuals are unsure of their future preferences for the timing of their consumption. At $t = 1$, they receive a "preference shock" and learn whether they are about to die or will live another period. If they are about to die, they want to withdraw the money they have invested and consume it immediately at $t = 1$. If they learn that they will live, then they want to leave their money in the projects and consume R at $t = 2$. For the population as a whole, a (random) fraction, f, of individuals are "diers" at $t = 1$ and a fraction, $1 - f$, are "livers."[16]

What would happen without a bank? Well, if you discover at $t = 1$ that you are a dier, you will liquidate your investment and consume \$1. Call the first-period consumption C_1^D, that is, $C_1^D = 1$, and your second-period consumption, $C_2^D = 0$. If you discover that you are a "liver," then you will choose to consume nothing at $t = 1$ (i.e., $C_1^L = 0$) and you will consume an amount $C_2^L = R$ at $t = 2$. Thus, the *nonbank outcome* is the pair $\{C_1^D = 1, C_2^D = 0\}$ or the pair $\{C_1^L = 0, C_2^L = R\}$, depending on the individual's type. Is this the best outcome from the standpoint of an individual at $t = 0$? The answer is obviously no! Since you are a *risk-averse* individual, you would like some insurance at $t = 0$ against a random future shock to your own preference for consumption. This is where a bank can help.

The basic idea is as follows. To provide risk-averse individuals insurance against preference shocks, a bank can arise to promise those withdrawing at $t = 1$ a little more than \$1 and those withdrawing at $t = 2$ a little less than R, still ensuring that the promised payoff at $t = 2$ exceeds that at $t = 1$. Since $R > 1$, this is simply a temporal redistribution of the individual's wealth from a state of nature in which wealth is relatively high to one in which it is relatively low, that is, a classic insurance scheme. Compare this to a capital market that also redistributes temporally, but involves no insurance aspect. As long as the bank has a reasonably good idea of how many individuals will withdraw on average at $t = 1$ (this is similar to insurance companies estimating likely outcomes based on actuarial tables), it can structure the deposit contract in such a way that a known fraction of projects are liquidated at $t = 1$ to pay off the withdrawers. Note that more projects will need to be liquidated than there are withdrawers because each depositor is promised more than \$1 and the liquidation value of each project at $t = 1$ is \$1. Hence, those waiting until $t = 2$ will receive less than R. This is a nice arrangement because the $t = 2$ payoff exceeds the $t = 1$ payoff, so if a depositor can "afford" to wait until $t = 2$, he will. Thus, one possible outcome is that only the diers withdraw at $t = 1$ and all the livers wait until $t = 2$. All depositors are better off than they would be without a bank because they have received some insurance at $t = 0$ against unpredictable future changes in their preferences.

The fly in this ointment, however, is that the entire scheme rests delicately on the assumption that none of the livers withdraws at $t = 1$. But what if a liver believes that others like him might "panic" and withdraw at $t = 1$? If this belief is justified, it would be foolish for him to be the only patient depositor since the bank will have to liquidate *all* its projects at $t = 1$ and there will be nothing left to disburse at $t = 2$. So he will attempt to withdraw at $t = 1$ as well. In other words, the beliefs of the livers at $t = 1$ are crucial. If a representative liver believes others will withdraw at $t = 1$, he will too, and a panic run at $t = 1$ is a Nash equilibrium. On the other hand, if a representative liver believes others will wait until $t = 2$, he will too, and this is a Nash equilibrium as well. These beliefs are unrelated to the quality of the bank's assets.

How do you preclude the bad Nash equilibrium? One way is to provide deposit insurance.[17] If the claims of all depositors are insured, then the livers know that they are guaranteed a payoff at $t = 2$ that is independent of the actions of other depositors. Hence, all livers will withdraw only at $t = 2$, and there will be no bank run. The example in the box below makes these ideas concrete.

Example 12.2

Suppose there are 100 risk-averse individuals, each with \$1 to invest in a project at $t = 0$. The project will yield \$1 if liquidated at $t = 1$ and \$2.25 if liquidated at $t = 2$. At $t = 0$, no individual knows what his "type" (denoting his consumption preference) will be at $t = 1$. If the individual turns out to be a "dier" (type D), then his utility function for consumption will be

$$U_D = \sqrt{C_1^D}.$$

If he turns out to be a "liver" (type L), then his utility function for consumption will be

$$U_L = 0.6\sqrt{C_1^L + C_2^L}.$$

These utility functions capture the idea that the dier benefits from consumption at $t = 1$ only, and the liver is indifferent between consuming at $t = 1$ or $t = 2$ (he gets equal utility from each) so that he will prefer the higher of the two consumptions. It is known

---

16. The terms "diers" and "livers" are not meant to be taken literally, but merely represent those with preferences for immediate consumption (diers) and for deferred consumption (livers).

17. Jacklin (1987) offers another solution. If the owners of projects could issue traded equity to finance their projects at $t = 0$ and then paid dividends on the equity at $t = 1$, a scheme can be designed such that livers and diers could trade among themselves and achieve the same risk sharing as the deposit contract, thereby obviating the need for a bank and eliminating runs.

at $t = 0$ that 40% of the individuals will end up being diers and 60% will be livers at $t = 1$. Compute the *ex ante* ($t = 0$) expected utility of each individual if (i) there is no bank and each individual invests in his own projects, and (ii) there is a bank that accepts a $1 deposit from each individual and invests all the proceeds in 100 projects.

Solution

We will solve this problem in six steps. First, we calculate each individual's expected utility absent banks. In this scheme, an individual receives $1 if he consumes at $t = 1$ and $2.25 if he consumes at $t = 2$. Second, we introduce a bank that is a mutual owned by the 100 depositors. It promises $1.1 to each depositor withdrawing at $t = 1$ and $2.1 each to those withdrawing at $t = 2$. Each depositor experiences a higher expected utility at $t = 0$ with this scheme than in the nonbank case. Third, we show that the intermediated outcome leads to a (good) Nash equilibrium in which all type-D depositors withdraw at $t = 1$ and all type-L depositors wait until $t = 2$. Fourth, we show that there is also a bad Nash equilibrium in which all depositors withdraw at $t = 1$. Fifth, we note that the bank run described in Step 4 arises for no particular reason, but that it is possible whenever the existence of the bank makes depositors better off. Finally, in Step 6 we show how deposit insurance can eliminate the Nash equilibrium.

Step 1

Consider first the nonintermediated situation. Let us assume, for simplicity, that the diers/livers fractions (0.4 and 0.6) can be viewed as subjective probability assessments of all individuals at $t = 0$. Then each individual believes that he faces a 0.4 chance of being of type-D at $t = 1$ and a 0.6 chance of being of type-L. In the nonintermediated case, $[C_1^D = 1, C_2^D = 0]$, and $[C_1^L = 0, C_2^L = R = \$2.25]$. Hence, each individual's expected utility will be

$$E(U) = 0.4 \times \sqrt{10} + 0.6 \times 0.6 \times \sqrt{2.25}$$
$$= 0.9400.$$

Step 2

Now consider a bank, owned by its 100 depositors. It provides insurance against depositor preference shocks with a demand deposit offering $C_1^* > \$1$ and $C_2^* < \$R$ (where asterisks denote first- and second-period consumptions in the intermediated case), with the stipulation that C_1^* and C_2^* are mutually exclusive. For example, suppose the bank announces at $t = 0$ that $C_1^* = \$1.1$. Then, with 40 depositors withdrawing at $t = 1$, the bank will need to pay out $44, and this requires premature liquidations of 44 projects. The remaining 56 projects will yield a total payoff of $56 \times \$2.25 = \$126$ at $t = 2$. The bank will be able to promise each of the 60 depositors withdrawing at $t = 2$ an amount $C_2^* = \$126/60 = \$2.1$. The expected utility of a depositor at $t = 0$ will be

$$E^*(U) = 0.4 \times \sqrt{1.1} + 0.6 \times 0.6 \times \sqrt{2.1}$$
$$= 0.9412.$$

Hence, every individual is made better off by the bank that provides *consumption smoothing*.

Step 3

The Step-2 outcome is a Nash equilibrium among depositors. Each type-D depositor's Nash equilibrium strategy is to withdraw at $t = 1$ since that gives him his highest utility (his utility from consumption at $t = 2$ is zero). If each type-L depositor *takes as given* the Nash equilibrium strategy of the *other* type-L depositors (to wait until $t = 2$ to withdraw), then no type-L depositor can do better by withdrawing at $t = 1$. This is because withdrawal at $t = 2$ gives a type-L a utility of

$$0.6 \times \sqrt{2.1} = 0.8695 \text{ whereas}$$

withdrawal at $t = 1$ gives a utility of

$$0.6 \times \sqrt{1.1} = 0.6293.$$

Thus, a Nash equilibrium is needed for all type-D depositors to withdraw at $t = 1$ and all type-L depositors to wait until $t = 2$.

Step 4

The "good" outcome is not the only Nash equilibrium, however. There is also a "bad" Nash equilibrium with a bank run. To see this, suppose that the representative type-L depositor believes that all the other type-L depositors will withdraw at $t = 1$ rather than $t = 2$.[18] What should you, as the "representative" type-L depositor, do?

Suppose you also decide to withdraw at $t = 1$. The bank will then observe that all 100 depositors wish to withdraw. All 100 projects will have to be liquidated to obtain $100. According to the SSC, the bank will pay $1.1 each to the first 90 depositors and the remaining $1 to the 91st depositor; the last nine depositors receive nothing. If you wait until $t = 2$ to withdraw (when all the other depositors withdraw at $t = 1$), you get nothing. If you rush to the bank at $t = 1$, then assuming that your position in the queue is decided randomly (with equal probability of being at any position in the queue), you have a 0.9 probability of receiving $1.1, a 0.01 probability of receiving $1, and a 0.09 probability of receiving nothing. Clearly, your optimal strategy is to withdraw at $t = 1$ too. Thus, it is also a Nash equilibrium for *all* depositors to withdraw $t = 1$. This equilibrium is a *bank run*.

---

18. Do not ask why. This point is to see if this *can* be a Nash equilibrium. That is, conditional on such a belief about the behavior of others, does it pay for the representative type-L depositor to also behave like that?

Step 5

Two points are noteworthy. First, the bank run in Step 4 arises for no particular reason. We are not in a position to say which Nash equilibrium will arise. Hence, while we can say that a bank run is a possibility, we cannot say *why*. Second, a simple way for the bank to eliminate this type of run is to stipulate that withdrawers of demand deposits at $t = 1$ can receive only $1. In this case, the bank does not need to liquidate more projects than there are withdrawers at $t = 1$, so that a depositor who waits until $t = 2$ will surely receive $R, Thus, it is optimal for *every* type-L depositor to wait until $t = 2$, regardless of what the other type-L depositors do. But in this case the bank's demand deposit contract provides no risk sharing and the bank adds no value over the nonintermediated case. Hence, runs are a possibility whenever the bank adds value.[19]

Step 6

Deposit insurance can eliminate the bank run equilibrium *without* trivializing the bank. To see this, imagine that a governmental insurer were to guarantee that any individual withdrawing at $t = 1$ will receive $1.1 and any individual withdrawing at $t = 2$ will receive $2.1. Then, only the good Nash equilibrium survives.[20]

The message of this theory is this: In the absence of deposit insurance, even a perfectly healthy bank faces the threat of a run, given the SSC associated with demand deposits. In other words, runs can result from shifts in the beliefs of individuals, unrelated to the "real" economy or the health of the banking system. Bank runs are simply random manifestations, a *force majeure* triggered even by "sunspots." In French, the term for a bank run is colloquially *sauve qui peut* (every man for himself).

Although some runs reflect sunspot phenomena, it is difficult to verify empirically what precisely triggered a run. Banking panics, on the other hand, have often been triggered by adverse information about banks. We now turn to an informational theory of bank runs.

2. *Adverse Information and Bank Runs:* Suppose that we have three types of individuals.[21] We still have the diers (type-D individuals) who must consume at the end of the first period and represent a fraction, f, of all individuals. But among the livers (type-L individuals), we now have a fraction who receives information about the terminal ($t = 2$) value of the bank's assets. In the previous theory, we assumed that this value, $R, was nonrandom and known to everyone. Assume now that $\tilde{R}$ is a random variable with a commonly known expected value, R. Let $\tilde{R} = H > 0$ with probability p and $\tilde{R} = 0$ with probability $1 - p$. Thus, at $t = 0$, no individual knows either the $t = 2$ value of $\tilde{R}$ or what his type (D or L) will be at $t = 1$. However, at $t = 1$, each individual discovers whether he is a D or L, and some fraction, q, of the Ls also comes to know the value $\tilde{R}$ will take at $t = 2$. Nobody knows how many individuals of each type are there at $t = 1$ (i.e., both the fraction f and the fraction q are random).

The choice problem faced by the Ds and the informed Ls at $t = 1$ is straightforward. All the Ds will line up to withdraw their deposits. If the informed Ls learn that $R = H$, then it is better for them to defer withdrawal until $t = 2$, thereby avoiding premature project liquidation. But if the informed Ls learn that $R = 0$, then it pays for them to withdraw whatever they can at $t = 1$.

Consider now the choice problem of the uninformed Ls. They can withdraw at $t = 1$ or wait until $t = 2$. Their decision will be based on their assessment of the $t = 2$ value of the bank's assets. Although they cannot directly observe this value, they can infer it by observing the length of the withdrawal queue at $t = 1$.[22] In drawing this inference, they realize that some people are in the withdrawal queue at $t = 1$ because they have discovered that they are Ds. But they do not know *how many* such individuals there are. This means that when they observe the length of the withdrawal queue at $t = 1$, they are unsure whether all are Ds or whether some are informed Ls.

It is true, however, that the longer the queue the more likely it is that it contains some informed Ls with adverse information about the bank. If the uninformed Ls knew for sure that the queue contained informed Ls, they would withdraw their money at $t = 1$, and if they knew for sure that it contained only Ds, they would defer withdrawal until $t = 2$. But when they cannot be sure, they use the queue length as a *noisy* signal of the information possessed by the informed Ls. Thus, they withdraw their deposits at $t = 1$ if the queue is sufficiently long, and they defer withdrawal until $t = 2$ if the queue is shorter.

Defining a bank run as a situation in which uninformed Ls withdraw at $t = 1$, we see that a bank run is more likely when some depositors receive adverse information about the bank. The reason is that as the informed Ls line up to withdraw their funds, they increase the queue length. This induces the uninformed Ls also to seek withdrawal of their deposits. Thus, a bank run results from depositors attempting to detect the bank's condition from the length of the

---

19. You will note that the bank exists here for a different reason from that in Chapter 3.

20. Suspension of convertibility will work just as well. The bank could announce at $t = 0$ that only the *first* 40 withdrawers at $t = 1$ will be paid $1.1 each. Remaining withdrawals can occur only at $t = 2$. This will do the trick, but only if the fraction of diers is known deterministically at $t = 0$. If this fraction is random, then the bank will not know *ex ante* when to suspend convertibility. In this case, deposit insurance is necessary to eliminate the bad Nash equilibrium without sacrificing the risk-sharing service banks.

21. This discussion is based on Chari and Jagannathan (1988).

22. This inference will usually be noisy. Formally, the inference may be made using Bayes' rule (see Chapter 1).

withdrawal queue. However, since their learning is "noisy" (they occasionally confuse liquidity-motivated withdrawals with informed withdrawals), they make both type-I and type-II errors.[23] That is, they sometimes do not run the bank when they should (when the queue is relatively short but consists of informed Ls: a type-II error if the null hypothesis is that the bank is healthy); and they sometimes run the bank when they should not (when the queue length is relatively long but consists only of Ds: a type-I error). Because runs can sometimes occur when they should not, deposit insurance may improve welfare by eliminating the possibility that uninformed Ls will erroneously withdraw.

3. *The Empirical Evidence on Panics:* Strictly speaking, neither of the two theories of bank runs discussed just above explains *panics*. According to the sunspots theory, a bank run is a completely random event, so there is no reason for a run to precipitate a panic, although a panic could come about by pure chance. According to the adverse information theory, a run is caused by information *specific* to a bank. Once again, there is no reason for a run to be contagious. These then are theories of bank runs and not banking panics.

The adverse information theory, however, can be adapted to provide an explanation for banking panics. Suppose there is information about some event that is relevant to the fortunes of all banks. That is, there is a systematic risk element that affects all banks. Unlike the standard Capital Asset Pricing Model, however, assume that the systematic risk is *not* commonly known. Individuals may then attempt to infer something about systematic risk from their observations of presumably related events. For example, the failure of a large bank may cause depositors to believe that general economic conditions have deteriorated, and this may lead to a panic. The intuition is similar to that of the adverse information theory. According to that theory, depositors infer something about their bank from the behavior of fellow depositors. Here, depositors at one bank infer something about their bank from the behavior of depositors in *other* banks.[24]

An example of an event that may reveal adverse systematic information is a recession, or a bank run during a recession. During the period from 1873 to 1914, every major business cycle downturn was accompanied by a banking panic.

Empirical evidence supports this version of the adverse information hypothesis. If banking panics are indeed systematic events, then there must be a change in the risk perceptions of individuals prior to a panic, and this, in turn, must cause a change in the deposit/currency ratio. That is, the perceived risk variable must achieve some critical value at the panic date. Also, the movements in the risk predictors and in perceived risk should occur at panic dates and not at other dates. If such movements occurred at other dates, then there should have been panics at those dates.

An empirical examination of panics in the pre-Federal Reserve era provides insight into the relationship between changes in risk perceptions and banking panics.[25] To serve as a proxy for perceived risk, empiricists use unanticipated changes in the liabilities of failed businesses.[26] This is reasonable since the fortunes of nonfinancial firms affect the fortunes of banks. As Table 12.2 shows, panic dates correspond to the timing of the largest values of the liabilities shocks. Panics also follow the business cycle peak by several months.

TABLE 12.2 The Relationship Between the Timing of the Largest Unanticipated Changes in the Liabilities of Failed Businesses and the Timing of Banking Panics in the National Banking Era

NBER Chronology Peak-Trough (Business Cycle)	Timing of Largest Value of Unanticipated Changes in Liabilities of Failed Businesses	Panic Date
Oct. 1873–Mar. 1879	Dec. 1873	Dec. 1873
Mar. 1882–May 1885	June 1884	June 1884
Mar. 1887–Apr. 1888	Nov. 1887	No panic
July 1890–May 1891	Dec. 1890	Dec. 1890
Jan. 1893–June 1894	July 1893	July 1893
Dec. 1895–June 1897	Oct. 1896	Oct. 1896
June 1899–Dec. 1900		No panic
Sep. 1902–Aug. 1904		No panic
May 1907–June 1908	Feb. 1908	Dec. 1907
Jan. 1910–Jan. 1912	Mar. 1910	No panic
Jan. 1913–Dec. 1914	Mar. 1914	Sep. 1914

Source: Gorton, Gary, "Banking Panics and Business Cycles," *Oxford Economic Papers* 40, 1988, 751–781.

23. A type-I error in statistics is when the decision maker rejects the (null) hypothesis although it is true and a type-II error is when he accepts (or more appropriately, fails to reject) the null hypothesis although it is false.

24. For a recent theory that captures this intuition, see Acharya and Thakor (2015).

25. The evidence reported here is from Gorton (1988).

26. In an empirical study by Gorton (1988), this variable was measured by the residuals (error terms) from an estimated time-series model.

TABLE 12.3 The Relationship Between the Timing of the Largest Unanticipated Changes in the Liabilities of Failed Businesses and the Timing of Banking Panics in the Federal Reserve Era

Peak-Trough (Business Cycle)	Timing of Largest Value of Unanticipated Changes in Liabilities of Failed Businesses	Panic Date
Aug. 1918–Mar. 1919	Nov. 1918	No panic
Jan. 1920–July 1921	June 1920	No panic
May 1923–July 1924	Nov. 1923	No panic
Oct. 1926–Nov. 1927	Apr. 1927	No panic
Aug. 1929–Mar. 1933	Dec. 1929	Oct. 1930
		Mar. 1931
		Jan. 1933

Note: The change in perceived risk in June 1920 was large enough to have caused a panic in the pre-Fed Era.
Source: Gorton, Gary, "Banking Panics and Business Cycles," *Oxford Economic Papers* 40, 1988, 751–781.

The study also indicates that the percentage change in the currency/deposit ratio is significantly correlated with the perceived risk measure. Thus, the data for the pre-Fed period support the notion of a threshold value of perceived risk that triggers panics. More recent research indicates that the banking panics during 1890–1909 were triggered by net movements of deposits away from the money-center banks and low levels of excess reserves. Changes in stock market values had little effect.[27]

The formation of the Federal Reserve System in 1914 and the initiation of deposit insurance in 1934 had a significant influence on the timing of panics. In the period from 1914 to 1933, we can see from Table 12.3 that changes in the perceived risk measure were large enough in at least one instance (June 1920) to cause panics during the pre-Fed period, but resulted in no panics in the post-Fed period.

The introduction of deposit insurance again significantly changed depositor behavior. In the period from 1935 to 1972, until after deposit insurance was introduced, there were several instances of large failed business liabilities shocks, none of which resulted in panics. Thus, deposit insurance appears to have served its purpose.

Deposit Insurance Pricing and Moral Hazard

Until the 1980s, the pricing of federal deposit insurance was largely *risk insensitive.* That is, each bank was charged an insurance premium that depended only on its volume of deposits, and not on its riskiness. Many have charged that this heightened incentives for insured depository institutions to take excessive levels of risk. Note that institutions like banks can increase risk in a variety of ways. However, for the purposes of this discussion, we will focus on the bank's incentive to invest in assets with high default risk. Although deposit insurance premiums are now risk sensitive, only a limited number of risk categories are used and at best, the premiums are only crudely related to risk for most banks. In this section, we will show how the imperfectly risk-sensitive structure of deposit insurance pricing also creates incentives for excessive risk-taking by banks.[28]

Deposit Insurance as an Option: Consider an insured bank (both principal and interest on deposits are insured) that has raised deposits requiring the bank to repay B at the end of the period. Let V be the total value of the bank's assets at the end of period. Now, if $V \geq B$, then the depositors receive B from the bank and the bank's shareholders receive $(V - B)$. If $V < B$, then the bank fails. Its shareholders receive nothing, whereas the deposit insurer takes possession of the bank's assets and pays out B to the depositors. The net *loss* to the deposit insurer in this case is $(B - V)$. Thus, the end-of-period payoffs to the different parties can be written as

Shareholders:	$\text{Max}[0, V - B]$
Depositors:	B
Deposit Insurer:	$\text{Min}[0, V - B]$, which is either zero (when $V > B$) or negative (when $V < B$).

---

27. See McDill and Sheehan (2006).
28. The discussion here is based on Merton (1977).

The effect of deposit insurance is to create an additional cash inflow to the firm of $-\text{Min}[0, V - B]$ dollars. But $-\text{Min}[0, V - B]$ can also be written as $\text{Max}[0, B - V]$. Hence, if $G(T)$ is the value to the firm of the deposit insurance guarantee when the length of time remaining to maturity of the deposits is T, then on the date of maturity,

$$G(0) = \text{Max}\,[0, B - V]. \tag{12.1}$$

You will recall now from our discussions of options in Chapters 1 and 10 that the payoff structure in Equation (12.1) is identical to that of a *put option* at expiration. To see this, imagine that V is the (random) value of the underlying security on which the option is written, and B is the exercise (or strike) price. Then, as the owner of the put, you will exercise your option to *sell* the security to the option writer at $\$B$ if the value of the security, V, is less than B. In this case, your gain from exercising the option will be $\$(B - V)$. On the other hand, if $B < V$, then you will let the option expire unexercised, and your gain will be zero.

The Cost of the Option

In other words, when the FDIC insures a bank's deposits, it is writing a put option in favor of the bank. The cost to the FDIC of providing this insurance is simply the value of the put option. We can calculate this value using the option pricing formula developed by Black and Scholes (1973):

$$G(T) = Be^{-rT}\Phi(x_2) - V\Phi(x_1) \tag{12.2}$$

where

$$x_1 \equiv \frac{\log(B/V) - \left[r + \frac{\sigma^2}{2}\right]T}{\sigma\sqrt{T}}$$

$$x_2 \equiv x_1 + \sigma\sqrt{T}.$$

Here r is the instantaneous risk-free interest rate, $\Phi(\bullet)$ is the standard normal cumulative distribution function, V is the current value of the bank's assets, and σ^2 is the variance rate per unit time of the logarithmic changes in the value of the assets. It is assumed that all the Black–Scholes assumptions are satisfied.

The Cost Per Dollar of Deposits

We can also compute the appropriate deposit insurance premium per dollar of deposits. If depositors are promised a repayment of $\$B$ at a time, T, in the future, then the current value of these (riskless) deposits will be

$$D = Be^{-rT}. \tag{12.3}$$

Let $g = G(T)/D$ be the cost (to the FDIC) of the deposit insurance guarantee per dollar of insured deposits. Then, using Equations (12.2) and (12.3) we can write

$$g(d,\tau) = \Phi(h_2) - \frac{1}{d}\Phi(h_1) \tag{12.4}$$

$$\text{where } h_1 \equiv \frac{[\log(d) - \frac{\tau}{2}]}{\sqrt{\tau}} \tag{12.5}$$

$$h_2 \equiv h_1 + \sqrt{\tau}. \tag{12.6}$$

Here $d \equiv D/V$ is the current deposit-to-asset value ratio for the bank, and $\tau \equiv \sigma^2 T$ is the variance of the logarithmic change in the value of the assets during the term of the deposits.

Properties of a Risk-Sensitive Deposit Insurance Pricing Scheme

A few points are worth noting. First, an increase in the deposit-to-asset value ratio causes an increase in the cost per dollar of deposit insurance to the FDIC, that is,

$$\partial g/\partial d = \Phi(h_1)/d^2 > 0.$$

Similarly, as τ increases, so does the cost of deposit insurance, that is,

$$\partial g/\partial t = \Phi'(h_1)/2d\sqrt{T} > 0.$$

Here the prime denotes a derivative; hence, $\Phi'(h_1)$ is the standard normal density function at h_1. This is a well-known property of options; their value increases with the volatility of the underlying security. Hence, the FDIC should charge a higher deposit insurance premium for banks with lower capital-to-total-assets ratios and higher volatility in the value of total assets. Alternatively, in a regime in which the FDIC charges each bank a fixed premium per dollar of insured deposits, rather than g (which is a function of d and τ), banks with higher capital ratios and lower asset risks *subsidize* those with lower capital ratios and higher asset risks, assuming that the FDIC breaks even on average.

The Option Feature and Moral Hazard

These observations also highlight the moral hazard inherent in deposit insurance. Since g is the *value* to the bank of deposit insurance per dollar of insured deposits, a bank can increase this value by reducing its capital and increasing its asset volatility. To the extent that the premium charged is insensitive to these initiatives of the bank, a *shareholder-wealth-maximizing* bank has an incentive to increase financial leverage and asset volatility. Figure 12.1 illustrates this incentive graphically.

In Figure 12.1, the curve AB is the total expected return on the bank's assets, net of bankruptcy costs.[29] This curve peaks at σ^*. The expected return to depositors, as represented by the straight line CD, remains constant because we assume that deposits are completely insured. The total expected return to depositors and the FDIC is equal to the deposit yield plus the deposit insurance premium minus the expected bankruptcy costs. This total *expected* return, represented by the curve BF, is constant for $\sigma < \sigma_f$ (some threshold variability) because the probability of bankruptcy is zero in this range. Then, as the probability of bankruptcy rises, the total expected return to the FDIC and the depositors declines. Since the depositors are completely protected and the deposit insurance premium is insensitive to σ, it is the expected return to the FDIC that falls

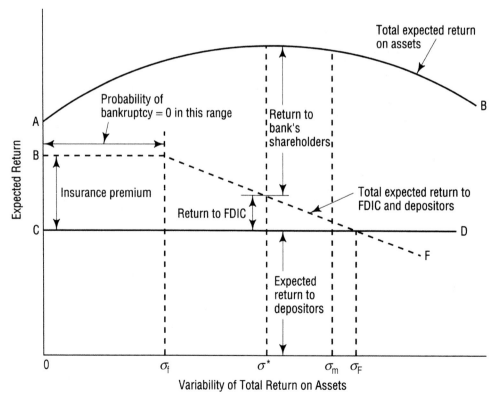

FIGURE 12.1 The Relationship Between Expected Return and Risk.

---

29. Figure 12.1 is based on Keeton (1984), who provides a similar figure (see p. 32 in that paper).

very rapidly as σ arises. Consequently, even though the total expected return on the bank's assets is falling as σ increases beyond σ^*, the expected return to the bank's shareholders is increasing in this range. In fact, the shareholders' expected return peaks at $\sigma_m > \sigma^*$.

The optimal level of risk (as represented by σ) depends on the decision maker's objective. If the objective is to minimize the liability of the deposit insurer, then the optimal risk choice is $\sigma = \sigma_f$. If the objective is to maximize the bank's total expected return on assets, then the optimal risk choice is $\sigma = \sigma^*$. But if decisions are made to maximize the wealth of shareholders, the optimal risk choice is $\sigma = \sigma_m$. Thus, if the "socially desired" risk choice is σ^*, the bank will take more risk than the social optimum by choosing σ_m. This is the moral hazard of deposit insurance.

Why the Concern With Moral Hazard in Banking?

You will recall from Chapters 7 and 8 that a similar moral hazard exists for nonfinancial firms that borrow from banks. However, with nonfinancial firms, the costs of this moral hazard are borne *ex post* by private lenders, who pass along these costs *ex ante* (through the pricing mechanism) to the borrower. Thus, the moral hazard gets priced among the contracting parties in equilibrium. In the case of banks and other federally insured depository institutions, however, these costs are borne *ex post* by the FDIC, and hence, eventually by the taxpayers. Of course, if the FDIC breaks even in aggregate, then these costs are passed along *ex ante* to the banking industry as a whole, and there is simply a redistribution of wealth across banks. That is, less risky banks end up subsidizing their riskier counterparts, with no direct wealth consequences for the taxpayers.

This analysis, as well as our earlier discussion of the similarity between a deposit insurance guarantee and a put option, indicates a role for safety regulation in banking. Given deposit insurance, banks have a propensity to lower capital and increase risk. Capital requirements and asset portfolio restrictions seek to address these distorted incentives arising from deposit insurance. However, the implementation of these regulatory devices has not always been effective.

In the box below, we provide an illustration of the effect of moral hazard in the context of the put option pricing formula.

Example 12.3
Consider a bank with federally insured deposits maturing in one year. Imagine that the bank's asset value changes monthly and you have been provided the following data on asset values for the past seven months (you may assume that the probability distribution of asset value changes remains stationary through time).

Month	Bank Asset Value (in millions of dollars)
1	100
2	101
3	99
4	102
5	100
6	98
7	97.605074

Suppose the bank's current deposit-to-asset value ratio is 0.95. Compute the value to the bank of the deposit insurance guarantee per dollar of insured deposits. Also compute the value of this guarantee for a higher deposit-to-total-asset-value ratio (of your choice), holding fixed the variance of asset value changes, and the value of this guarantee for a higher variance, holding fixed the deposit-to-total-asset-value ratio.

Solution
We solve this problem in three steps. First, we will compute τ, the variance of bank asset values. Second, we compute h_1 and h_2 using the value of τ obtained in the previous step. Finally, in Step 3 we calculate the cost of deposit insurance per dollar of insured deposits.

Step 1
To compute τ, we define V_t as the asset value in month t and V_{t-1} as the asset value in month $t-1$. Thus, when we write the asset value in month 2, for example, we will write V_2, and when we write the ratio V_t/V_{t-1} in month 2, we will write V_2/V_1. We can construct Table 12.4.

TABLE 12.4 Calculation of Asset Value Variance

A Month	B Asset Value V_t	C V_t/V_{t-1}	D $\log(V_t/V_{t-1})$	E D-Sample Mean	F $(E)^2$
1	100	–	–	–	–
2	101	1.01	0.00995	0.013988	0.0001957
3	99	0.9802	–0.02000	–0.015962	0.0002548
4	102	1.0303	0.02985	0.033888	0.0011484
5	100	0.9804	–0.01979	–0.015752	0.0002481
6	98	0.9800	–0.0202	–0.016162	0.0002612
7	97.605074	0.9959701	–0.004038	0	0

In this table, we compute the "sample mean" by adding up the entries in column D and dividing by 6 to obtain –0.004038. Column E is then obtained by subtracting the sample mean from each entry in column D. Column F is merely each entry in column E squared. Now,

$$\sigma^2 = \frac{\text{sum of all entries in column F}}{5}$$
$$= \frac{0.0021082}{5} = 0.0004216.$$

Note that we divide by 5 because we lose one degree of freedom in computing the variance. Now, $\tau = \sigma^2 T = 0.0004216 \times 12 = 0.005$ approximately. Note that $T = 12$ since the deposit maturity is 1 year and asset values change monthly.

Step 2
Next, we compute h_1 using Equation (12.5) as

$$h_1 = \frac{\log(0.95) - (0.005/2)}{\sqrt{0.005}}$$
$$= -0.76076$$

and h_2 using Equation (12.6) is

$$h_2 = -0.76076 + \sqrt{0.005} = -0.69005.$$

Step 3
Using Equation (12.4), we can now compute g as

$$g = \Phi(-0.69005) - \frac{1}{0.95}\Phi(-0.76076) \cong 0.0099.$$

Thus, the value to the bank of having the deposit insurance guarantee is roughly 99 cents per $100 of insured deposits. This is much higher than the premia often charged in the past (e.g. 25 cents per $100 of insured deposits). In Table 12.5, we present calculations for a variety of deposit-to-asset value ratios and values of τ. Note that if we increase d to 1 and hold τ fixed at 0.005, the value of g rises to $2.82 per $100 of insured deposits. This illustrates the bank's incentive for leverage emanating from deposit insurance. Similarly, if we hold d fixed at 0.95 and increase τ to 0.006, the value of g rises to $1.209 per $100 of insured deposits. This illustrates the bank's incentive to take on more risky assets.

The option pricing approach indicates factors that must be considered in setting the deposit insurance premium. The premium per dollar of insured deposits must be sensitive to the volatility of the bank's assets and to its deposit-to-total-asset ratio. If not, the bank will have an incentive to reduce its capital and increase its asset risk in the interests of its shareholders. The option pricing approach is not meant to be taken literally as a precise way to set the deposit insurance premium, since many of the standard Black–Scholes assumptions are not satisfied.[30] For example, the asset values of banks often exhibit jumps rather than following a continuous path through time as assumed by Black–Scholes. In any case, the numerical values in Table 12.5 suggest the magnitude of the gains to banks from exploiting risk-insensitive deposit insurance pricing.

---

30. In addition, it may be difficult to ensure that the deposit insurer measures bank risk without error. See Flannery (1991) for a discussion of the implications.

TABLE 12.5 Cost of Deposit Insurance Per Dollar of Insured Deposits

Cost of Deposit of Insurance (g)	Deposit-to-Asset Value Ratio	Variance (τ)
0.00055	0.85	0.00600
0.00040	0.85	0.00550
0.00028	0.85	0.00500
0.00018	0.85	0.00450
0.00011	0.85	0.00400
0.00326	0.90	0.00600
0.00274	0.90	0.00550
0.00223	0.90	0.00500
0.00176	0.90	0.00450
0.00132	0.90	0.00400
0.00093	0.90	0.00350
0.00060	0.90	0.00300
0.00015	0.90	0.00200
0.01209	0.95	0.00600
0.01102	0.95	0.00550
0.00992	0.95	0.00500
0.00880	0.95	0.00450
0.00765	0.95	0.00400
0.00647	0.95	0.00350
0.00528	0.95	0.00300
0.00287	0.95	0.00200
0.00172	0.95	0.00150
0.00072	0.95	0.00100
0.00033	0.95	0.00075
0.03089	1.00	0.00600
0.02958	1.00	0.00550
0.02820	1.00	0.00500
0.02676	1.00	0.00450
0.02523	1.00	0.00400
0.02360	1.00	0.00350
0.02185	1.00	0.00300
0.01784	1.00	0.00200
0.01545	1.00	0.00150
0.01262	1.00	0.00100
0.01093	1.00	0.00075
0.00892	1.00	0.00050
0.00631	1.00	0.00025
0.00564	1.00	0.00020
0.00489	1.00	0.00015
0.00399	1.00	0.00010
0.00282	1.00	0.00005
0.00126	1.00	0.00001

Source: Merton, Robert C., "The Cost of Deposit Insurance and Loan Guarantees," *Journal of Banking and Finance* 1, June 1977, 10.

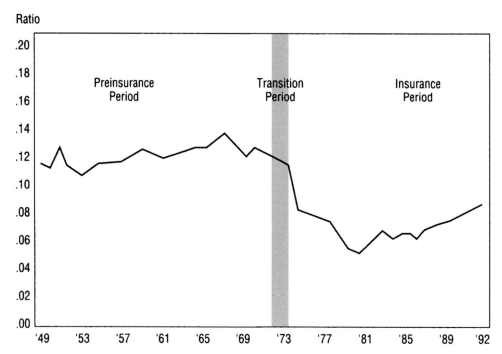

FIGURE 12.2   Capital Ratio for Federal Credit Unions. *(Source: National Credit Union Administration).*

Empirical Evidence on Moral Hazard

Apart from the anecdotal evidence on moral hazard, there is now substantial scientific evidence to support the theories we have reviewed. Federal deposit insurance has been in existence for banks since 1934, but the more visible problems were encountered only during 1970–1990. This suggests that there must have been *countervailing forces* in the past that diminished the risk-taking propensity created by deposit insurance. The empirical evidence we discuss here sheds some light on these forces.

1. *Some Evidence on the Effect of Federal Deposit Insurance on Risk-Taking: The Case of Credit Unions*: Federal deposit insurance was extended to credit unions in 1971 when the National Credit Union Administration (NCUA) was formed, and the coverage limits are currently the same as for banks and thrifts.

    Credit unions: (i) make loans to their own members, (ii) make loans to other credit unions, and (iii) engage in loan participations with other credit unions. A credit union's asset portfolio consists primarily of: (i) secured loans for the purchase of consumer durables, and (ii) investments in low-risk assets such as government bonds, loans to other credit unions, and deposits with commercial banks.

    A credit union can increase its risk by decreasing its capital cushion and by increasing the fraction of its total assets invested in high-risk assets. An empirical examination provided support for this hypothesis.[31] Figure 12.2 is a graph illustrating the behavior of capital ratios (defined as capital divided by total assets) for federal credit unions over the 1949–1992 period. In 1970, just prior to the adoption of federal deposit insurance, the capital ratio was about the same as in 1949. There was a slight decline during the transition period from the preinsurance regime to the insurance regime. The sharpest decline occurred during the insurance period. This is consistent with the prediction of a moral hazard associated with deposit insurance.

    A similar pattern can be seen by examining the behavior of bank capital ratios over time, as shown in Figure 12.3. As is apparent, banks kept much higher levels of capital before the advent of deposit insurance.[32]

2. *The Relationship Between Market Power in Banking and Moral Hazard:* As mentioned earlier, a major puzzle is why the deposit insurance system in the United States worked so well for so many years despite the risk-taking incentives provided by federal deposit insurance and why problems surfaced only recently. One explanation is that a bank's risk-taking propensity depends on the value of its charter. The higher the charter value – the capitalized value of its future cash flows – the weaker is the bank's incentive to take risk. This is because higher risk implies a higher likelihood of insolvency, in which case the insurer takes possession of the bank, and the charter is lost. Thus, the higher the value of this charter, the greater is the bankruptcy cost for the bank. In the past, various anticompetitive restrictions gave banks market power that enhanced

---

31. See Clair (1984).

32. In Chapter 2, we discuss the divergent developments in the capitalization of key financial institutions in the period leading up to the 2007-09 financial crisis.

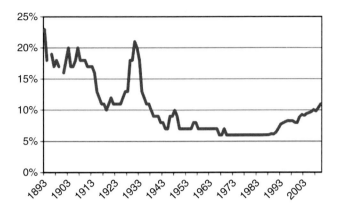

FIGURE 12.3   Book Equity Ratios for U.S. Banks. *(Source: Flannery and Rangan (2008), Y-9C Reports, and Acharya, Mehran, Schuerman and Thakor 2012).*

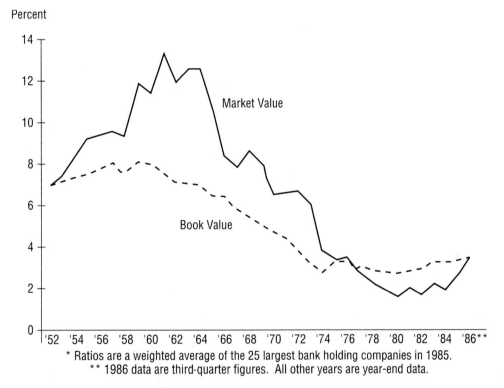

* Ratios are a weighted average of the 25 largest bank holding companies in 1985.
** 1986 data are third-quarter figures. All other years are year-end data.

FIGURE 12.4   Capital-to-Asset Ratios, Market and Book Values. *(Source: Keeley, Michael C., "Deposit Insurance, Risk, and Market Power in Banking," American Economic Review 80, December 1990, 1183–1200).*

the value of charters. The loss to the bank from losing its charter in the event of bankruptcy provided a counterbalance to the incentive for excessive risk-taking due to fixed-rate deposit insurance.[33] The deregulation that took place in the 1980s increased banking competition but lowered the value of bank charters. Greater risk-taking was predictable.

Evidence supports this theoretical prediction. Figure 12.4 is a graph of the time series behavior of the average capital/total assets ratio of the 25 largest bank holding companies in the United States from 1952 to 1986. The decline in this ratio is significant.

A *direct* test of the relationship between risk-taking and charter value would need to have some measure of the capitalized value of future rents, or market power. One such measure is "Tobin's q," which is approximated as the ratio of the market value of assets (market value of common equity plus the book value of liabilities) to the book value of assets. The higher the q ratio, the larger is the charter value, relative to the book value of its assets. Since bank risk-taking is also not directly observable, a proxy is needed. A reasonable proxy is the interest cost on large uninsured CDs. The holders of such CDs should be sensitive to the bank's riskiness and demand higher interest rates from riskier banks. The evidence

---

33. For the theory, see Chan et al. (1992). The empirical evidence discussed below is from Keeley (1990).

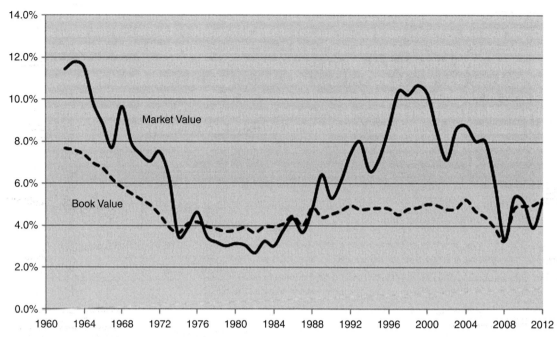

FIGURE 12.5 Capitalization of the 25 Largest Bank Holding Companies During 1962–2012. This figure shows the weighted average capitalization of the 25 largest bank holding companies from 1962 to 2012. Capital ratios are expressed in book values (shareholder equity/total assets) and market values (market value of equity/market value of assets). *(Source: Compustat and own calculations).*

is quite compelling. Each 1% increase in the *q* ratio results in a 16–18 basis point reduction in the average CD cost. Moreover, this relationship is statistically significant. Thus, bank risk-taking appears to have increased substantially in the 1980s owing to deregulation that diminished bank charter values.

To provide a comparison with more recent data, we have provided in Figure 12.5 the capital ratios in book and market value terms for the 25 largest bank holding companies from 1959 to 2012. The effect of the capital regulation that began with the Basel I Accord is evident, as capital ratios exhibit an upward drift beginning in the late 1980s, but note the divergent experience that we documented in Chapter 2.[34]

In Figure 12.6, we show the number of bank failures during 1992–2011. As is evident, the number of failures decreased dramatically during the early 1990s and has stayed relatively low as banks have operated with healthy capital ratios. Then there was an increase in bank failures during the financial crisis.

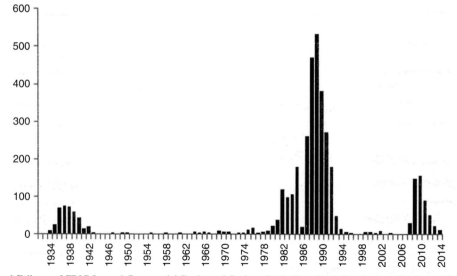

FIGURE 12.6 Annual Failures of FDIC Insured Commercial Banks and Savings Institutions (including Savings Banks and Savings Associations). *(Source: FDIC Historical Statistics on Banking).*

---

34. Recall that we documented in Chapter 2 that many banks that were involved in investment banking increased leverage prior to the 2007–2009 financial crisis.

THE GREAT DEPOSIT INSURANCE DEBACLE

General Background

We have now reviewed both the theory and some empirical evidence about the effects of deposit insurance on depository institutions' risk-taking behavior. In trying to understand the great deposit insurance debacle of the 1980s, it is important to remember that until the mid-1970s deposit insurance worked remarkably well. But, two developments undermined federal deposit insurance. One is the lowering of bank charter values, which increased managers' incentives to take more asset risk and to also engage in fraud. The other is the decline in regulatory vigilance over the same period; this simply exacerbated the moral hazard problem of federally insured depository institutions.

The waste that resulted from the collapse of the thrift industry and the many banking failures in the 1980s can be classified into three categories: excessive risk-taking, excessive consumption of perquisites by top executives, and outright fraud. Moreover, these diversions/destructions of wealth were possible due to three factors working in concert: deposit insurance with risk-insensitive pricing, low charter values due to deregulation, and lax monitoring by regulators. This laxity in monitoring, caused by a lowered commitment of resources to supervision, was also compounded by cozy relationships between some regulators and the institutions they were supposed to be watching over. In Figure 12.7, we have provided a simple schematic to summarize these effects.

It is not as if S&L and bank managers woke up one morning in the 1980s and decided to change the way they made decisions in order to "rip off" the taxpayers.

The point is that their *incentives* were altered. Their *decision rule* was still the same, but the altered incentives changed their behavior. The reasons for the deposit insurance crisis can therefore be traced not just to the managers of depository institutions, but also to the politicians and regulators who pursued myopic and hasty policies. In what follows, we briefly discuss the causes and effects depicted in Figure 12.7.

Regulatory and Political Culpability

For some years, S&L regulators tried to ignore problems in the thrift industry. Hoping that problems would improve, regulators permitted insolvent institutions to continue to operate. Our analysis of credit risk in Chapters 7 and 8 highlighted the important incentive effects of capital on a borrower's risk-taking propensity. The same is true of depository institutions; their propensity to take risk is greater when capital is lower. When capital is negative, excessive risk-taking is easy to predict. Indeed, the Federal Home Loan Bank Board (FHLBB) was quite aware that the thrift industry was in deep trouble in 1981, but chose not to close all the insolvent institutions.[35]

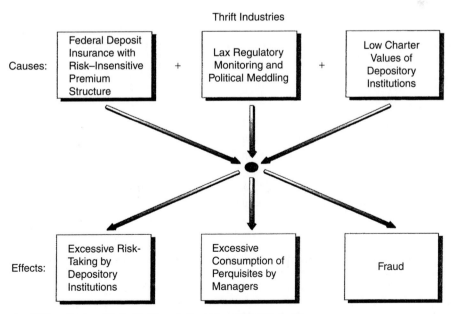

FIGURE 12.7   Schematic of Effects Responsible for Problems in Banking and Thrift Industries.

---

35. A 1990 issue of *The American Banker* quoted Mr. Richard T. Pratt, then chairman of the FHLBB, "Had we liquidated the S&L industry in 1981, it would have cost $178 billion–$380 billion in today's dollars. It would have been the most foolish public policy that could have possibly been undertaken."

This inaction was part of a broader regulatory malaise. The main findings of a 2-month *USA Today-Gannett* News Service investigation are listed below.[36]

- Some regulators had close ties to the industry.[37]
- In some cases, *regulators* suggested that S&Ls try to grow rapidly and to invest in risky ventures as a way of quickly boosting profits.
- Regulatory agencies lacked the powers and the human resources to monitor rapidly growing S&Ls.
- Congress repeatedly refused requests to add S&L examiners, and told the FHLBB to go easy on problem S&Ls.[38]

Excessive Risk-Taking

As previously discussed, the three prominent ways to detect excessive risk-taking involve examining capital-to-total-asset ratios, interest rates on large (uninsured) CDs, and the assets in the institution's portfolio. The last two are briefly discussed below.

Higher Interest Rates on CDs

Riskier institutions must pay higher interest rates on large CDs, or conversely, those institutions that offer to pay higher interest rates on their deposits anticipate investing in high-risk, high-yield assets to cover their deposit funding costs. Since risk-taking incentives are the strongest in insolvent and nearly insolvent institutions, one would expect such institutions to be paying the highest rates. This is precisely what happened in the southwestern United States, where the S&L industry was devastated. Higher interest rates offered by insolvent institutions led to a self-fulfilling prophecy. When a depository institution has low net worth, it is expected to invest in riskier assets, so that depositors demand relatively high interest rates. These high interest rates, in turn, increase the attractiveness of high-yield, high-risk assets to the institution, thus completing the cycle. Moreover, in order to compete with insolvent institutions, solvent institutions may be compelled to offer higher interest rates on their deposits, leading to stronger incentives to invest in riskier assets.

Investments in High-Risk Assets

There is ample evidence of excessively risky investments by S&Ls. These investments included loans to developers to build ski resorts, speculative positions in government securities, junk bond portfolios, and so on.

Excessive Consumption of Perquisites by Managers

Although it is empirically difficult to determine whether a given level of perquisites consumption by a manager is "appropriate," some of the examples are striking and suggestive of abuse. These include institutional purchases of planes to transport top managers from their places of residence to their offices, payments for escort services, offices lined with expensive antiques and paintings, and gold-painted toilets. Many of the institutions where such apparent abuse occurred were investigated by the FSLIC.

Fraud

Estimates of *direct* losses to the government due to fraud by S&L managers range from $8 billion to $15 billion, and fraud is suspected in 80% of failed S&Ls. Parties, mansions, airplanes, women, Rolls-Royces, and Cayman Island bank accounts are some of the perks that S&L executives showered upon themselves as they looted federally insured deposits.

The S&L crooks also caused failures of S&Ls run by honest managers, by selling them stakes in their bad loans. For example, the now-insolvent First Federal Savings and Loan of Malvern, Arkansas, bought an interest in a doomed $44 million loan to a high-rise condo in Honolulu, which subsequently defaulted.

---

36. See *USA TODAY,* February 14, 1989.

37. Mr. Tom Huston, former Iowa state banking superintendent, claims that regulators traveled too much at industry expense. He said, "They were so loved and so well-treated . . . that no wonder they couldn't make a rational decision."

38. Mr. Edwin Gray, FHLBB chairman from May 1983 to June 1987, blames Congress and the Reagan administration for failing to give regulators more power, and he blames the powerful S&L lobby for influencing them. In *USA TODAY* (2/14/1989), Mr. Gray was quoted as saying the following: "We were asking Congress and the Reagan administration for help and getting nothing. We had a rag-tag bank of 700 examiners, who were expected to monitor $1 trillion in assets and 3300 S&Ls. Sometimes our examiners were hired away by the S&Ls they were examining." It turns out that entry-level examiners were paid $14,000 per year during this time, and the turnover rate was 25%.

Many of the fraud cases are very complex. Shady S&Ls and equally shady borrowers combined dozens of loans, companies, and properties into convoluted deals to cover personal use of S&L deposits. Some S&Ls made borrowers pay big one-time fees – 4–10% of the loan – in order to obtain loans. The S&Ls would report these fees as income, which boosted profits. Many loans were never repaid, leaving the property in the S&L's hands. An S&L executive might get a kickback for participating in the scheme. In Texas, this strategy was described as: "Heads, I win. Tails, FSLIC loses."

Following the S&L debacle, the government has filed approximately 100,000 civil suits against S&L executives, directors, owners, borrowers, and others believed responsible for contributing to the insolvency of S&Ls. The success of these prosecution efforts, and of attempts to recover some of the losses due to fraud, negligence, and simple mismanagement, remains uncertain.

To summarize, the greatest banking debacle since the Great Depression was *not* just an "unfortunate break" or an outcome of exogenous changes in the banking environment. Increasing competition increased interest-rate volatility and deregulation reduced the profitability of depository institutions, substantially diminishing charter values. Models of bank behavior predict increased risk-taking by federally insured institutions in such a setting, suggesting a need for improved regulatory monitoring. Unfortunately, safety was sacrificed at the same time that the industry was deregulated, as resources devoted to regulatory supervision were decreased. Regulatory ineptness and political meddling compounded the effects of poorly-thought-out initiatives.[39]

In later years, the subprime crisis of 2007–2009 eclipsed the S&L crisis in terms of its magnitude and global impact. Although it affected the shadow-banking system more than depository institutions in the United States, it also affected depository institutions in other countries. We will say more about this in Chapter 14.

Banking Fragility, Deposit Insurance, and Developments Since the Great Deposit Insurance Debacle

We have seen in this chapter that deposit insurance induces moral hazard and invites banks to engage in reckless risk-taking. That is, there is an inherent paradox in the use of deposit insurance as a way to diminish the likelihood of bank runs and banking fragility. The safer banks feel due to deposit insurance, the greater is their risk-taking propensity! It is for this reason that it may be socially efficient to impose a limit on the level of deposit insurance, thereby leaving room for market discipline, which then opens up the possibility of bank runs and banking fragility. In other words, there may be an "optimal" amount of banking fragility that strikes the right balance between the market discipline associated with the possibility of bank runs to temper banks' risk-taking incentives and the need to ensure that the likelihood of runs is not so high as to make banking excessively fragile.[40] Of course, the subprime crisis of 2007–2009 has taught us that even though such thought out experiments may make sense on paper, in reality regulators often have a hard time saying no to bailouts *ex post*, especially when confronted with the possibility of large and interconnected institutions failing. Thus, market discipline may be substantially weakened by the *ex ante* expectation by creditors of banks that there will be regulatory forbearance *ex post*, regardless of whether there is deposit insurance.

One could argue that one way to cope with the moral hazard related to regulatory forbearance and deposit insurance is to use capital requirements as an instrument to reduce banks' proclivity to take excessive risk. Regulatory reforms associated with the Basel I accord and FDICIA of 1991 (see subsequent chapters) lend strong support to the hypothesis that sufficiently high capital requirements can be effective in controlling risk.[41]

The real question, however, is whether we need deposit insurance in the first place, for a lot of the regulatory apparatus we observe would be unnecessary were it not for deposit insurance.[42] But would we not have excessive bank runs without deposit insurance? This is actually an open question. Mutual funds have no deposit insurance and we had not observed any runs until the 2007–2009 subprime crisis, and even those runs were induced by concerns about the risks of the investments made by these mutual funds. At the end of the day, a fundamentally sound banking system, backed up by a credible lender of last resort, may not be as fragile without deposit insurance today as it may have been in the past, especially when one

39. We recommend reading Adams (1990), Mayer (1990), and White (1991) for accounts of the many factors that contributed to the implosion of the thrift industry in the United States.

40. This implication can be drawn from Calomiris and Kahn (1991) and is discussed in Diamond and Rajan (2001). For other analyses of banking fragility, see Allen and Gale (2001) and Yorulmazer (2014).

41. Basel II had more mixed effects (see Chapter 15).

42. See Miller (1995) for a forceful argument in favor of dismantling federal deposit insurance.

considers that selective bailouts of uninsured institutions may be used to promote the safety of the financial system, as in the subprime crisis.[43] If this is true, the entire system of deposit insurance and regulations may have to be reconsidered.

FUNDING IN THE SHADOW-BANKING SECTOR

With depository financial intermediaries – the traditional banking sector – savers deposit money in banks which is then channeled to investors through bank loans. By contrast, the shadow-banking system is a web of specialized nondepository financial institutions that channel funding from savers to investors through a range of securitization and secured funding techniques.[44] Shadow banks engage in credit and maturity transformation, just like traditional banks do, but without formal access to public sources of liquidity (e.g., discount window) and deposit insurance.

Growth of Shadow Banking

Funding in the shadow-banking sector has actually grown much faster than bank deposit funding, as shown in Figure 12.8[45]. Included in shadow banks are various nondepository financial institutions like investment banks, insurance companies, mutual funds, hedge funds, and finance companies; securitization structures such as ABCP and ABS; and key investors in securitized structures, such as money market mutual funds.

Shadow banks raise their financing by using tradable instruments like commercial paper and "repos." A "repo" is a repurchase agreement whereby an institution borrows short-term using traded securities as collateral, having the collateral returned to it when the loan is repaid. The collateral used in these transactions comes from the creation of asset-backed securities created by the securitization of loans, leases, and mortgages. Savers hold money-market mutual fund (MMF) balances, instead of deposits with banks.

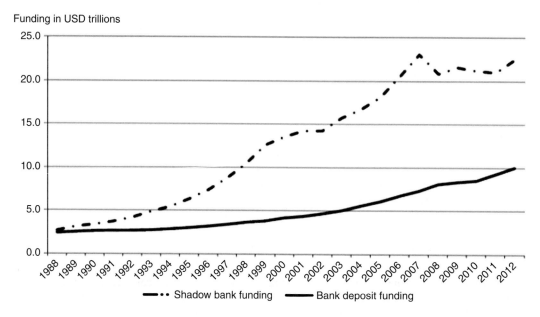

FIGURE 12.8 Shadow-Bank Funding and Traditional Bank Deposit Funding from 1988 to 2012. *(Source: FDIC's Historical Statistics on Banking, and Bouwman (2014)).*

---

43. Acharya et al. (2013) develop a theory in which regulators engage in selective, state-contingent bailouts, based on inferences about whether the observed failures represent a systemic risk.
44. This discussion is based in part on Adrian and Ashcraft (2012).
45. Taken from Bouwman (2014). See also Yorulmazer (2014).

The Funding Process: How it Works

In the shadow-banking system, there is a chain of wholesale-funded, securitization-based lending that transforms risky, long-maturity loans (e.g., subprime mortgages) into lower-risk, short-term money-like instruments. The process by which this transformation occurs is described below:[46]

Loan Origination: Finance companies originate auto loans, leases, nonconforming mortgages, whereas banks originate many different types of mortgages.

Loan Warehousing: This is conducted by conduits and is funded through asset-backed commercial paper (ABCP). That is, the conduits provide an institution where loans can be warehoused for securitization.

Securitization: involving the pooling and structuring of loans into term asset-backed securities (ABS), is conducted by broker-dealers' ABS syndicate desks.

ABS Warehousing: is funded through repos and swaps and facilitated by trading books.

The Creation of Collateralized Debt Obligations (CCDOs): occurs through the pooling and structuring of ABS, and is also conducted by broker-dealers' ABS.

ABS Intermediation: is performed by limited-purpose finance companies, structured investment vehicles (SIVs) and credit hedge funds, which are funded by repos, ABCP, bonds, and capital notes.

Funding: of all of these activities is conducted in wholesale funding markets by a mix of regulated unregulated intermediaries like MMFs and securities lenders. These cash investors fund shadow banks through short-term repos, commercial paper ABCP, bonds, etc.

Figure 12.9 summarizes the credit intermediation process in the shadow-banking system.

The Role of Commercial Banks in Shadow Banking

Commercial banks get involved in shadow banking in various ways. The most obvious is that commercial banks are owned by bank holding companies (BHCs). A BHC might own a wealth management unit with a money market mutual fund, that is, a shadow bank within the BHC. Another example is triparty repo funding by the broker–dealer subsidiary of a BHC. Similarly, a BHC might have an ABCP conduit, which would be off-balance-sheet to the BHC, but may be supported by a commercial bank subsidiary of the BHC through loan commitments.[47] Another connection is that commercial banks originate the loans whose securitization creates the securities that shadow banks hold and then borrow against these securities which are used as collateral in repo transactions.

In the future, as BHCs are subjected to more stringent and liquidity requirements, some shadow-banking activities may migrate out of BHCs into the shadow-banking system.

CONCLUSION

We have devoted this chapter to an extensive discussion of the deposit contract, liability management, and deposit insurance. The nature of the deposit contract is such that it leaves the bank vulnerable to runs, and the banking system vulnerable to panics. It appears that deposit insurance served its purpose of minimizing bank runs and panics. Indeed, for almost 50 years since the inception of federal deposit insurance in 1933, failure rates in the banking and thrift industries have been abnormally low compared to other industries. Moreover, this stable environment meant that liability management was not a pressing issue for banks.

But all that changed in the 1970s and 1980s. As interest-rate volatility increased and interest-rate restrictions were relaxed and then eliminated, liability management became a significant concern for banks. Moreover, a combination of deregulation, heightened volatility in market prices, lax regulatory monitoring, political interference, and corrupt executives in federally insured institutions significantly undermined the safety of the industry, and imposed monstrous losses on the deposit insurance funds. It is somewhat ironic that these events were quite predictable, in light of what was known *prior* to these events.

The 2007–2009 financial crisis offered new challenges, particularly the fragility of funding structures in the shadow-banking sector. Chapter 14 covers this in depth.

---

46. See Adrian and Ashcraft (2012).

47. Avraham et al. (2012) document that each of the five largest BHCs in the U.S. had over 1500 subsidiaries in 2012. See Cetorelli (2014) for a characterization of BHCs as a "web" in the shadow system.

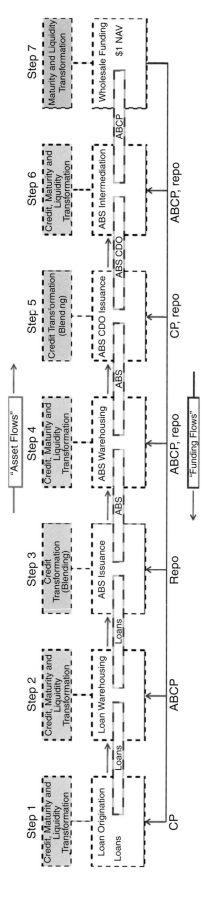

FIGURE 12.9 The Shadow Credit Intermediation Process. *(Source: Pozsar et al. (2010)).*

REVIEW QUESTIONS

1. What are the main economic features of the demand deposit contract and how do these features discipline management when deposits are uninsured?
2. What measures were used to cope with bank runs and panics prior to federal deposit insurance? Why were these not entirely satisfactory?
3. What is a bank run and how can you explain a run on *economic* grounds?
4. How does deposit insurance prevent runs and panics?
5. Explain the similarity between deposit insurance and a common stock put option and how this leads to moral hazard.
6. Why did deposit insurance work so well in the United States until 1980 despite the obvious moral hazard, and why did it fail after that?
7. Discuss the roles of bank managers, accountants, regulators, and politicians in the "great banking/S&L debacle."
8. What is liability management and what are its main objectives?
9. What is the agency problem between the shareholders and managers of a bank in liability management?
10. Is moral hazard unethical, illegal, or neither? Can you outline a conceptual framework for defining unethical behavior by a depository institution?
11. What aspects of S&L/bank behavior would you consider unethical? For example, were junk bond investments unethical? Be sure to take an *ex ante* perspective and not use "20-20 hindsight."
12. Why do you think unethical behavior became so rampant in the last decade and not prior to that? Did people change? Did morals decline in general? Did the environment change? Can you relate unethical behavior during this period to similar behavior during other periods in history?
13. Consider a bank that receives a $1 deposit from each of 200 different depositors at $t = 0$. It invests $25 of shareholders' equity in the bank and lends $200, keeping $25 as cash reserves. Out of the 200 depositors, there are 75 depositors (called type-D_1 depositors) who are capable of monitoring the bank's management; the remaining depositors (called type-D2 depositors) have kept their money in the bank simply for transactions and safekeeping. The cost of monitoring the bank for an individual type-D_1 depositor is $0.03 per period.

    The bank has two mutually exclusive investment opportunities. Project (or loan) A pays $300 with probability 0.6 and zero with probability 0.4 at $t = 1$. Project B pays $250 with probability 0.8 and $220 with probability 0.2 at $t = 1$. If the bank chooses one of these two projects, the probability that the bank will actually end up with that project is 0.7. With probability 0.3, the bank will have inadvertently chosen the other project. Thus, we assume that the bank may make errors in project choice. By monitoring the bank, a type-D_1 depositor can discover the bank's true project choice at some point in time intermediate between $t = 0$ and $t = 1$, say at $t = 1/2$. These depositors can, if they desire, force liquidation of the bank by withdrawing their deposits at $t = 1/2$. Note that the bank's loans/projects mature at $t = 1$. If they are liquidated at $t = 1/2$, they are worth only $70 to the bank. Under the terms of the deposit contract, the bank promises to pay 15% interest (conditional on the bank having the financial capacity to do so) if deposit withdrawal occurs at $t = 1$, and no interest if withdrawal occurs before that. Thus, a depositor is entitled to $1.15 if she withdraws at $t = 1$, and $1 if she withdraws at $t = 1/2$. The risk-free discount rate is zero and all agents are risk neutral.

    All the type-D_2 depositors plan to withdraw at $t = 1$, but each is subject to a random liquidity-motivated desire to withdraw at $t = 1/2$. To simplify, we will assume that even though no one knows in advance which (type-D_2) depositors will wish to withdraw at $t = 1/2$, the fraction of those who will wish to withdraw is known to be 25/125. That is, 25 type-D_2 depositors will wish to withdraw at $t = 1/2$. Assume that the bank's managers make decisions in the best interests of their shareholders. Compute the equilibrium strategies for the bank and its depositors.
14. Why do you think shadow banking grew so much in the last two decades? What does it imply about systemic financial risks?

REFERENCES

Acharya, V., Mehran, H., Schuermann, T., Thakor, A.V., 2012. Robust capital regulation. Federal Reserve Bank NY Capital Issues Economics Finance 18 (3).

Acharya, V., Mehran, H., Thakor, A.V., 2013. Caught between Scylla and Charybdis? Regulating bank leverage when there is no rent-seeking and risk shifting, Working Paper.

Acharya, V., Thakor, A.V., 2015. The dark side of liquidity creation: leverage-induced systemic risk and implications for the lender of the last resort. Paper Presented at the JFI-Hoover Institute Conference on the Lender of Last Resort. April, Washington DC.

Adams, J.R., 1990. The Big Fix: Inside the S&L Scandal. Wiley, New York.

Adrian, T., Ashcraft, A.B., 2012. Shadow Banking: A Review of the Literature. Federal Reserve Bank of New York, Staff Report No. 580.

Allen, F., Gale, D., 2001. Comparing Financial Systems. MIT Press, Cambridge, MA.

Avraham, D., Selvaggi, P., Vickrey, J., 2012. A structural view of bank holding companies. Federal Reserve Bank of New York Economic Policy Review 18, 65–82.

Black, F., Scholes, M., 1973. The pricing of options and corporate liabilities. J. Polit. Econ. 81, 637–659.

Bouwman, C.H.S., 2014. Liquidity: how banks create it and how it should be regulated. In: Berger, A.N., Molyneaux, P., Wilson, J. (Eds.), The Oxford Handbook in Banking, second ed., Oxford University Press, New York, forthcoming.

Bryant, J., 1980. A model of reserves, bank runs, and deposit insurance. J. Bank. Financ. 4, 335–344.

Calomiris, C.W., Kahn, C.M., 1991. The role of demandable debt in structuring optimal banking arrangements. Am. Econ. Rev. 81, 497–513.

Cetorelli, N., 2014. Hybrid intermediaries, Federal Reserve Bank of New York Staff Report 705.

Chan, Y.-S., Greenbaum, S.I., Thakor, A.V., 1992. Is fairly priced deposit insurance possible? J. Financ. 47, 227–246.

Chari, V.V., Jagannathan S R., 1988. Banking panics, information, and rational expectations equilibrium. J. Financ. 43, 749–761.

Clair, R.T., 1984. Deposit insurance, moral hazard, and credit unions. Econ. Rev. (Federal Reserve Bank Dallas), 1–8.

Diamond, D., Rajan, R., 2001. Liquidity risk, liquidity creation and financial fragility: a theory of banking. J. Polit. Econ. 109, 287–327.

Diamond, D.W., Dybvig, P., 1983. Bank runs, deposit insurance, and liquidity. J. Polit. Econ. 91, 401–419.

Flannery, M., 1991. Pricing deposit insurance when the insurer measures bank risk with error. J. Bank. Financ. 15, 975–998.

Flannery, M., Rangan, K., 2008. What caused the bank capital build-up of the 1990s? Rev. Financ. 12, 391–430.

Gibbons, J.S., 1968. The Banks of New York, Their Dealers, the Clearing House, and the Panic of 1857. Greenwood Press, New York, reprint of 1859 original.

Gorton, G., 1988. Banking Panics and Business Cycles. Oxford Econ. Papers 40, 751–781.

Jacklin, C., 1987. Demand deposits, trading restrictions and risk sharing. In: Prescott, E.C., Wallace, N. (Eds.), Intertemporal Trade. University of Minnesota Press, Minneapolis, MN, pp. 26–47.

Jacklin, C., Bhattacharya, S., 1988. Distinguishing panics and information-based bank runs: welfare and policy implications. J. Polit. Econ. 96, 568–592.

Keeley, M.C., 1990. Deposit insurance, risk, and market power in banking. Am. Econ. Rev. 80, 1183–1200.

Keeton, W.R., 1984. Deposit insurance and the deregulation of deposit rates. Econ. Rev. (Federal Reserve Bank Kansas City), 28–46.

Mayer, M., 1990. The Greatest-Ever Bank Robbery. Charles Scribner's Sons, New York.

McDill, K.M., Sheehan, K.P., 2006. Sources of historical banking panics: a Markov switching approach, FDIC Working Paper.

Merton, R.C., 1977. An analytic derivation of the cost of deposit insurance loan guarantees. J. Bank. Financ. 1, 3–11.

Merton, R.C., 1989. On the application of the continuous-time theory of finance to financial intermediation and insurance. The Geneva Papers on Risk and Insurance 14, 225–262.

Merton, R.C., 1993. Operation and regulation in financial intermediation: a functional perspective. In: Englund, P. (Ed.), Operation and Regulation of Financial Markets. Economic Council, Stockholm, pp. 17–68.

Merton, R.C., Thakor, R.T., 2015. Customers and investors: A framework for understanding financial institutions. NBER Working Paper No. 21258.

Miller, M., 1995. Do the M&M propositions apply to banks? J. Bank. Financ. 19, 483–489.

Noyes, A.D., 1909. Forty Years of American Finance. G.P. Putnam's and Sons, New York.

Pozsar, Z., Adrian, T., Ashcraft, A., Boesky, H., 2010. Shadow banking. Federal Reserve Bank of New York Staff Report 458.

Song, F., Thakor, A.V., 2007. Relationship banking, fragility and the asset-liability matching problem. Rev. Finan. Stud. 20, 2129–2177.

Yorulmazer, T., 2014. Literature review of the stability of funding models. Federal Reserve Bank N.Y. Econ. Policy Rev. 20, 3–16.

White, L., 1991. The S&L Debacle. Oxford University Press, New York.

Chapter 13

Bank Capital Structure

"An essential message of the M&M Propositions as applied to banking, in sum, is that you cannot hope to lever up a sow's ear into a silk purse. You may think you can during good times; but you'll give it all back and more when the bad times roll around."

Merton Miller (1995)

GLOSSARY OF TERMS

Bank Capital Typically thought of as common equity. The Basel III definition of "Tier One" capital includes primarily common stock as well as some qualifying preferred stock.

BIS Bank for International Settlements, which is the coordinating body for international capital regulation.

Leverage Ratio In corporate finance, this is typically defined as the firm's debt/total assets. In bank regulation, it is the opposite: equity/total assets.

Capital Requirements Bank regulators require banks to hold at least some fraction of their assets as equity capital. Regulatory capital requirements additionally allow some types of nonequity claims to be counted as capital. Moreover, the measure of assets in the calculation of capital ratios is adjusted for asset risk (based on risk-weights) in the calculation of risk-based capital ratios.

Subordinated Debt This is uninsured debt that the bank holds, that is, bonds. This debt is senior to equity (of course) but junior to deposits.

INTRODUCTION

Bank capital structure basically represents the bank's choice of how to finance its balance sheet, that is, what mix of equity, subordinated debt, and deposits to use. It is an issue of central importance in any discussion of bank stability, and thus of great interest to regulators. The reason is that the bank's capital structure affects its fragility and its ability to withstand economic shocks. Banks are especially vulnerable to such shocks because they provide a variety of qualitative asset transformation (QAT) services that expose them to risks of various sorts. These QAT services were discussed in detail in previous chapters. The risks that banks face can generate unexpected shocks that jeopardize the bank's continued access to funding and cause failure. The higher the amount of capital in the bank's capital structure, the greater its ability to withstand these shocks. Bank capital is like "breaking distance" – the higher the bank's capital, the longer the distance between it and economic failure, and thus the greater the time that its managers have to react to warning signs, and make decisions that enhance the odds of survival.

If banks were uninsured entities or if their failures were not viewed as creating costly economic externalities, the bank's capital structure decision would be a "private matter," something left to the bank's shareholders and managers. But this is not the case. First, banks' deposits are insured, and this means that the banks' shareholders have been given a put option on the bank's assets by the deposit insurer.[1] This incents the bank to keep too low a level of capital (relative to what may be socially efficient) in order to increase the value of that put option. Second, bank failures are often contagious. In part because banks hold highly correlated asset portfolios, the failure of one bank can cause depositors and uninsured creditors to withdraw their funds from other banks, resulting in a financial crisis, as we discussed in the previous chapter. Thus, regulators would like to see banks keep enough capital so that individual bank failures are avoided in the first place. And if some banks do fail, regulators would like adequate capital in other banks to mitigate domino risks. For these reasons, regulators restrict the bank's capital structure to have some minimum amount of equity.

To understand why banks choose the capital structures they do and why regulators impose capital requirements, it is important to first start asking: is there a privately optimal capital structure for a bank, that is, a mix of debt and equity that maximizes the total value of the bank? This is, of course, the classic capital-structure question that corporate finance students are familiar with. It is therefore appropriate to begin with a discussion of the applicability of the Modigliani and Miller (1958) leverage indifference theorem to banking. This will be done in the next section. In that section we will also discuss some common fallacies when it comes to the applicability of the M&M theorem, that is, wrong reasons that are sometimes used to say that M&M does not apply to banks. We will then move to capital structure theories that violate the

---

1. See Merton (1977).

key assumptions of M&M to establish an optimal capital structure for a bank. We will also discuss why the private optimum may involve less capital than what is socially optimal. We will then discuss some of the empirical evidence on the relation between bank capital, bank lending, and bank value.

The chapter concludes with different ways in which capital is defined in banking and measured in banking supervision and regulation. There are many instances in which the issue of capital structure in banking differs from its treatment in corporate finance theory.

DOES THE M&M THEOREM APPLY TO BANKS? DISPELLING SOME FALLACIES

In his 1995 paper titled, "Do the M&M propositions apply to banks?" Merton Miller provided a two-word Abstract: "Yes and no." He begins that paper by expressing the popular view of bankers that equity capital in banking is so expensive that asking banks to raise capital to meet higher capital requirements would reduce shareholder value in banking and reduce bank lending. His view of this issue is succinctly summarized in the opening paragraph of his paper[2]:

> "*The banker sitting next to me was lamenting the profitable lending opportunities being passed up by capital constrained banks, when I broke in to ask: "Then, why don't they raise more capital?" "They can't," he said, "It's too expensive. Their stock is selling for only 50% of book value." "Book values have nothing to do with the cost of equity capital," I replied. "That's just the market's way of saying: We gave those guys a dollar and they managed to turn it into 50 cents."*

Miller's overall conclusion is that there would be no harm to banks from operating with higher amounts of capital, because the (equity) cost of capital would decline in response to the additional safety provided by the higher capital. In other words, Miller's view is that the cost of equity capital in banking is too high because equity capital is too low. Miller says[3]:

> "*And indeed, people often tell me they can easily imagine a viable bank with 95% deposits and 5% equity, but they cannot imagine a viable bank with 5% deposits and 95% equity. Well, I can certainly imagine one. That seems hard only to those who think of the cost of equity capital as a single fixed number. But the cost of equity is* not *a fixed number; it's a* function *that depends both on the* risk of the firm's earning assets *and the degree of leverage in the firm's capital structure.*"

Miller also goes on to say that regulatory deposit insurance and too-big-to-fail safety nets create incentives for banks to keep inadequate capital levels, and capital requirements are necessary for regulators to protect their interests, just the way banks require their own borrowers to maintain adequate net worth.[4]

There are many who disagree with Miller's views on the subject, and it is often argued that the M&M propositions clearly do not apply to banks because they depart in so many ways from the set of assumptions that are needed for the M&M theorem to hold. While this may be true, it is nonetheless important to *start* with one of the foundational pillars of modern finance – the M&M capital structure theorem – and then ask whether the reasons given for this theorem do not apply to banks can stand up to rigorous scrutiny. In doing so, it is important to first dispel some myths or fallacies about why capital is very expensive in banking and why the M&M theorem does not apply.[5]

Myth 1: Capital is money that banks have to set aside and is therefore unavailable for lending, so an increase in bank capital requirements will reduce bank lending.

Banks have been subject to two kinds of regulatory requirements: reserve requirements and capital requirements. A reserve requirement is essentially a liquidity requirement. It requires the bank to keep as cash (or as a deposit with the central bank) a certain fraction of its funding.[6] The reserve requirement may also include an additional buffer of cash reserves that the bank voluntarily holds in order to cope with its deposit-withdrawal and refinancing (rollover) risk. Thus, the direct impact of a reserve requirement will be seen in terms of the cash the bank holds on the *asset* side of its balance sheet, and this cash is indeed tied up and cannot be loaned out.

A capital requirement is entirely different. It has to do with equity as a fraction of total assets in the bank's funding mix. Thus, the direct impact of a (binding) capital requirement will be seen on the *liability* side of the bank's balance sheet in terms of how much equity capital the bank holds, and unlike cash reserves, equity capital can be directly invested in risky loans, just like any other form of financing the bank uses. That is, equity does not directly constrain the bank's investment.

2. See Miller (1995).

3. See Miller (1995).

4. Miller (1995) notes: "So close is the mimicry in fact, that I can't help smiling at complaints from bankers about their capital requirements, knowing that they have always imposed even stronger requirements on people in debt to them."

5. The discussion below follows Thakor (2014). In their book, Admati and Hellwig (2013) also have an extensive discussion of the common myths and fallacies about banking capital. See also the review by Berlin (2011).

6. Reserve requirements exist typically against deposits.

In fact, one cannot draw arrows on the balance sheet and suggest that a particular asset was funded by a particular liability – the entire funding mix of the bank, which includes all of its equity and liabilities, is used to support its entire asset portfolio. In this sense, there is *no* difference between a bank's equity and its debt or deposits in that all of the money gathered from these sources is used to finance the asset side of the bank's balance sheet. Thus, equity does *not* reduce lending by somehow freezing up potentially loanable funds into immobility.

Myth 2: Banks must necessarily have high leverage because deposits are a factor of production in banking.

Banks are different from nonfinancial corporations in the sense that a large fraction of their liabilities is in the form of deposits that are an essential part of the financial intermediation services that banks provide. For example, deposits are an integral part of the bank's liquidity creation services. Banks also provide various transactions and related services on deposits.[7] So, just as milk is a factor of production in the making of cheese, deposits are a factor of production in what a bank produces. That is, deposits are both a liability and a factor input for the bank. Thus, high leverage in banking is hard-wired by its production process, the argument goes, and an institution that is not highly levered is not really a bank.

While superficially plausible, this reasoning is largely incorrect. Banks do provide valuable liquidity and transaction service to their depositors, and this generates profits. This is why banks are willing to invest resources in building branch networks to gather deposits, and are willing to pay premia for purchasing core deposits or branches from other banks. But these deposits and the profits they generate are not unlimited. So imagine a bank that has raised all of the core deposits as is cost-effective for the bank to do, and it now has a particular level of leverage. If one wants the bank to have more capital, all that one needs to ask the bank to do is to put as much equity on its balance sheet as is necessary to achieve the desired leverage ratio. Of course, the bank's investment opportunities may not be large enough to fully utilize all of the capital and deposits this will cause the bank to accumulate. But in this case the bank can invest its surplus funds – those left over after its lending opportunities are exhausted – in marketable securities that have zero net present value (NPV).[8] Thus, requiring more equity does not constrain deposit services, and a bank can be required to finance itself with as much equity as is deemed efficient for prudential regulation.[9]

Myth 3: Deposits cost less than equity, so higher capital will decrease the value of the bank by forcing it to rely on more expensive funding.

Ask any banker and you will be told that the interest rate the bank pays on deposits is far lower than the rate of return demanded by the bank's shareholders. So, the argument goes, if we hold the size of the bank fixed and increase capital in the bank, the bank will be forced to replace deposits with more costly equity, thereby causing the bank's value to decline.

While it is true that a bank's cost of deposits is less than its cost of equity, this reasoning is incorrect to make the point that higher equity capital will lead to lower bank value. Consider the following example.[10] Consider two banks, A and B, each with $100 loan portfolios, an unlevered equity cost of capital of 10%, and a cost of deposits of 5%. There are no taxes. Let bank A be financed with $10 in equity and $90 in deposits, and bank B be financed with $20 in equity and $80 in deposits. Assume that each bank earns 10% per year on its loans, and that this is also the appropriate risk-adjusted discount rate for valuing the loan cash flows. All cash flows are perpetual. Using the corporate finance formula that relates the bank's unlevered and levered costs of capital, it follows that the levered equity costs of capital for banks A and B are 55% and 30%, respectively.[11] The market values of equity for banks A and B are $10 and $20, respectively. Thus, the NPV to the bank's

---

7. Complementarities may exist. For example, transaction services on deposit accounts could offer informational benefits in lending (Mester et al., 2007).

8. The assumption that unlimited zero-NPV investment opportunities are available is common in finance theory and lies at the heart of basic valuation — the NPV rule in capital budgeting. No-arbitrage equilibrium pricing of marketable securities would also imply that what the bank would pay for such securities should equal the present value of the future cash flows of the security — a zero-NPV investment. In the banking context, one way in which this argument can fail is if the bank's capital structure directly affects the bank's cash flows or asset values, as in Calomiris and Kahn (1991) or Diamond and Rajan (2000).

9. In other words, the result that banks should be highly levered due to presence of profitable deposits should not arise simply because one assumes that the bank has an arbitrary fixed size, thereby ruling out the possibility of having more equity in the bank mainly by assumption. A more nuanced argument is needed. See DeAngelo and Stulz (2015) for a different perspective on why banks are highly levered and why asking banks to keep equity on their balance sheets may be socially costly, a perspective based on liquidity creation. That is, this is one of the papers that relaxes the Modigliani and Miller (1958) assumptions to show why high bank leverage may be optimal.

10. This example is taken from Mehran and Thakor (2011).

11. The formula is from M&M and is:

$$r_e = r_u + [r_u - r_d][1-T][D/V_S]$$

where r_e is the levered equity cost of capital, r_u is the unlevered equity cost of capital, r_d is the (pre-tax) cost of debt, T is the tax rate, and D/V_S is the debt-equity ratio in market value terms, that is, V_S the market value of the bank's equity (e.g., stock price $\times$ # of shares). Thus, for bank A, we have:

$$r_e = 0.10 + [0.10 - 0.05][D/V_S]$$

and since $V_S = [r_L L - r_D D]/r_e$, where r_L = loan rate, we have $V_S = \{[0.10 \times 100] - [0.05 \times 90]\}/r_e = 5.5/r_e$, and substituting this in the expression for r_e yields: $r_e = 0.10 + [0.05][90 r_e / 5.5]$. This yields $r_e = 55\%$. The r_e for bank B can be derived similarly.

shareholders, measured as the market value of equity minus the book value of equity (invested capital), is $10 − $10 = 0 for bank A and $20 − $20 = 0 for bank B. Moreover, the total value of the bank in each case is $100. Shareholders like the capital structure in bank A no more or no less than that in bank B.

It also does not make any difference if the unlevered cost of equity in this example is the same as the loan interest rate; the same conclusion is reached if the loan yield is assumed to be higher, for example.

The key error made by those who assert this myth to be true is that they fail to recognize that the infusion of equity into the bank lowers the costs of all uninsured sources of financing, leaving total bank value (and the NPV to the bank's shareholders) unchanged. That is, as we pointed out in an earlier quote by Merton, infusing equity in the bank lowers its equity cost of capital. Of course, while we have held bank size fixed as capital structure has been varied, it has also been assumed that there are no profits associated with deposits. If one were to introduce such profits (e.g., a debt tax-shield subsidy), then one would go immediately to an all-debt corner solution for optimal capital structure, as in Modigliani and Miller (1963). This is an old insight from corporate finance, and it applies to all firms, not just banks. But, as indicated previously, if acquiring deposits is profitable, then one should assume that these profits are captured to the fullest and then as much equity as is desirable is added on top of it, without worrying about the thought-experiment condition of a fixed bank size.

Myth 4: Increasing equity capital in banking will reduce the return on equity for banks, and therefore diminish share-holder value in banking and reduce bank lending.

There are multiple claims here, so we will address each in turn. First, it is a mathematical fact that increasing the bank's capital ratio (or reducing its leverage ratio) will reduce its return on equity (ROE) *ceteris paribus*. However, in a world without taxes, a reduction in ROE due to a reduction in leverage does not affect the bank's shareholder value. The reason is that the reduction in ROE is accompanied by a reduction in the shareholders' required rate of ROE, as the shareholders' risk decreases as more equity is infused into the bank. The only way that an increase in capital can reduce the bank's shareholder value is if there are taxes and, holding the size of the bank fixed, equity replaces debt. But this is the familiar debt-tax-shield argument of Modigliani and Miller (1963), and there is nothing special about banks as far as this argument goes. The various arguments for why all-debt leverage is not optimal when various frictions – such as the agency costs identified by Jensen and Meckling (1976) – are introduced are also well known, and apply to all firms.

The final point is that banks will reduce lending if required to hold more capital, due to the reduction of ROE due to higher capital. Suppose the bank views 20% as the ROE target it must set in order to deliver to its shareholders the rate of return they demand. With say, 4% equity capital, the bank's loan portfolio allows it to deliver this return. But if the bank is now required to hold 8% capital, it will earn a lower ROE if its loan pricing, deposit funding cost and all other variables remain unchanged. In order to regain its original ROE of 20% or more, the bank will need a loan portfolio with a higher average loan interest rate. Given the same investment opportunity set as before, the only way that a bank faced with more equity in its capital structure can earn the same ROE as before is to get rid of the lower-yielding part of its loan portfolio. This, in turn, reduces bank lending.

The reasoning above is wrong.[12] To see why, it is useful to return to the observation that the bank's ROE target cannot be viewed as fixed. If its capital ratio increases from 4% to 8%, the rate of return that the bank's shareholders demand will also fall below 20%. In the absence of the effect of taxes, there is no reason why the bank would need to reduce lending in response to higher capital requirements. If there is any change in the bank's lending policy, it is likely to be an *increase* in lending as a bank with higher capital will view itself as less vulnerable to risk and is likely to shift some of its cash into lending. Specifically, a bank with higher capital is likely to have better access to liquidity in the interbank market, which enables it to operate with lower cash reserves.

THE THEORIES OF BANK CAPITAL STRUCTURE

There are two sets of theories about bank capital structure and they produce very different predictions.

Theory 1: High Leverage in Banking is Essential

This theory is the one that we discussed in the last chapter at length. It asserts that the sequential service constraint (or more generally, having deposit liabilities of shorter maturity than assets) associated with bank deposits leads to disciplining of the bank. This theory argues that such discipline is unavailable with equity. Hence, banks must be highly leveraged in order to have the proper market discipline and produce the liquidity that the economy requires. Since this theory acknowledges

---

12. Admati et al. (2013) provide an extensive discussion of many fallacies in discussions of the cost of bank capital.

that high leverage also makes banks fragile and vulnerable to runs, a tradeoff is suggested between bank stability on the one hand and bank liquidity creation and lending on the other.

Theory 2: Banks Need to Have More Capital

This set of theories highlights the positive aspects of bank capital. These theories fall into two groups. In the first group, are older theories that have recognized and have built on the insight of Jensen and Meckling (1976) that there is an asset-substitution moral hazard problem in banking in that equity represents a call option on the bank's total assets, and the value of this call option can be increased by investing in riskier assets. With sufficiently high leverage, the bank might even choose risky negative-NPV investments. To deal with this moral hazard, a sufficiently high amount of capital may be needed in the bank. Numerous models have used this argument as their centerpiece.[13]

The view that more tangible equity capital is needed in banking to limit excessive risk-taking by thinly capitalized banks is an idea that came into vogue in the 1980s, especially in the aftermath of the S&L crisis in the United States. This idea was at the heart of many landmark regulatory reforms, such as the Basel I Capital Accord in 1987, FIRREA in 1989, and the FDICIA in 1991.

A second, more recent, set of theories uses a different argument to highlight the value of capital in banking. This argument is that higher capital provides stronger incentives for banks to monitor their borrowers.[14] This not only improves the terms of financing and access to bank credit for borrowers, but also improves their access to nonbank sources of finance because those financiers benefit as well from the improvement in borrower credit quality due to the bank's monitoring. Moreover, bank equity capital serves not only to strengthen the bank's monitoring incentives, but it also enhances its survival probability, and this increases the value of its relationship loans, creating a positive feedback effect that further strengthens the bank's incentive to monitor.[15]

These monitoring-based theories of bank capital structure reinforce the idea of bank capital promoting financial system stability that the earlier asset-substitution-moral-hazard theories had highlighted. Unless there is a reason for bank equity capital to be more expensive than bank debt, banks should have as much bank equity capital as possible.

Of course, debt financing provides a tax advantage to banks due to the deductibility of interest payments on debt for tax purposes, just like it does for other firms. This can create a tradeoff between the monitoring benefit of equity and the tax benefit of debt, and generate an optimal capital structure for the bank. This is illustrated in the example below.

Example 13.1

Suppose there is a bank that can make a loan of $100 at $t = 0$. The loan will repay at $t = 1$. The loan finances a project that a borrower can invest in. The borrower can choose one out of three mutually exclusive projects: G, N, and n, each of which requires a $100 investment at $t = 0$ and produces a random payoff of $t = 1$. Project G yields a payoff of $150 with probability (w.p.) 0.9 and zero w.p. 0.1. Projects N and n both yield $150 w.p. 0.6 and zero w.p. 0.4. Project N produces a (noncontractible) private benefit of $10 for the borrower. These private benefits can be viewed as prerequisites the borrower can consume which are associated with a given project or cash flow diversions from the project that cannot be controlled/prevented by the bank.

The bank can monitor the borrower's project choice at a cost of $6. This is the monetary equivalent of what may be a nonpecuniary cost of the effort involved in monitoring what project the borrower is choosing. Bank monitoring can prevent the borrower from choosing Project N, but not project n. That is, despite bank monitoring, the borrower can choose either project G or project n, and the bank would not be able to observe which project was chosen,

The bank can raise financing for the loan with a mix of deposits and equity. Assume for simplicity, that all of the bank's equity is "inside equity," that is, it is provided by the bank manager who incurs the cost of monitoring the loan. Depositors cannot observe whether the bank monitored the loan.

The riskless interest rate is 1%. Everybody is risk neutral, so both shareholders and depositors require an expected return of 1%. Banks are relatively scarce, so that they can charge the borrower whatever interest rate they want. The bank faces a tax rate of 30% on its net income of $t = 1$. For simplicity, assume that the depositors and the borrower pay no taxes.[16] Deposits are available to the bank in whatever quantity it desires as long as depositors are promised an expected return of 1%. Similarly, the bank can put up as much inside equity as needed, as long as shareholders are promised an expected return of at least 1%.

What should be the bank's capital structure?

---

13. See, for example, the debt overhang arguments in Admati and Hellwig (2013). See also Furlong and Keely (1989) and Merton (1977), as well as the review by Bhattacharya et al. (1998).
14. See Holmstrom and Tirole (1997).
15. See Mehran and Thakor (2011).
16. This example is an illustration of a theoretical model developed by Holmstrom and Tirole (1997).

Solution
We will solve this problem in four steps.

Step1
We begin by noting that only project G can be financed by a borrower seeking a $100 bank loan. The reason is that project G has an expected present value of 0.9[150]/[1.01], which exceeds the initial investment of $100. That is, there is enough value in the project for it to be viably financed. As for either project N or n, from the bank's standpoint, the maximum repayment it can extract is $150, so the maximum expected present value of the loan would be

$$0.6[150]/[1.01] < 100, \tag{13.1}$$

which means the present value of what the bank can receive by making the loan falls short of the initial loan.

Step 2
We now solve for the borrower's "pledgeable income". By this we mean the maximum repayment the borrower can pledge to the bank as repayment on the loan. Let us refer to this as L. Then L solves the following:

$$0.9[150 - L] = 0.6[150 - L] + 6 \tag{13.2}$$

To understand Equation (13.2), note that the left-hand side (LHS) is the borrower's expected payoff if it chooses the G project, and the right-hand side (RHS) is the borrower's expected payoff if it chooses the n project (which the bank cannot prevent it from choosing even if it monitors). Note that the RHS includes 6, which is the borrower's private benefit from choosing n. Any repayment obligation *exceeding* L will make the RHS of Equation (13.2) greater than the LHS of Equation (13.2), therefore tilting the borrower's preference to project n over project G. We know this is not a viable financing situation since in this case there will be no bank loan forthcoming. Thus L is the maximum loan repayment or pledgeable income of the borrower. Solving Equation (13.2) yields $L = \$130$.

Step 3
We check and verify that the borrower will prefer project N to G if it is not monitored by the bank. That is, if the borrower I given a loan with a repayment of $130, then its expected profit from investing in project G is:

$$0.9[150 - 130] = \$18,$$

and its expected profit from investing in Project N is:

$$0.6[150 - 130] + 10 = \$22.$$

So the borrower prefers project N. But we know that the bank would never finance such a project. Hence, if a bank loan is made, the bank must find it profitable to monitor the borrower.

Step 4
We begin by noting that, due to the tax deductibility of payments on debt, the bank will wish to choose the maximum leverage that is consistent with satisfying the incentive compatibility and participation constraints of the problem. So, what is the maximum amount of deposits the bank can finance with, while still making it profitable for the bank to monitor the borrower? Let D be this deposit level. Then to raise D at $t = 0$, the bank must promise the (uninsured) depositors an amount D[1.01]/0.9 at $t = 1$ since the expected present value of this is

$$\frac{0.9}{1.01}\left[\frac{D[1.01]}{0.9}\right] = D \tag{13.3}$$

In writing Equation (13.3), we are taking the expected value of D[1.01]/0.9 by multiplying it with the repayment probability of 0.9, and then discounting it back at the riskless rate of 1% for one period.

Thus, D can be obtained by solving:

$$0.9\left[130 - \frac{D[1.01]}{0.9}\right][1 - 0.3] - 6 \geq 0.6\left[130 - D\frac{[1.01]}{0.9}\right][1 - 0.3] \tag{13.4}$$

The LHS of Equation (13.4) has the expected value of the bank's pretax income, which is

$$0.9\left[130 - \frac{D[1.01]}{0.9}\right],$$

since the borrowers repays the bank w.p. 0.9 an amount $130, and in this case the bank repays depositors D[1.01]/0.9. If the borrower defaults, then by limited liability, the bank does not repay its depositors anything either. This pretax income in the state in which the borrower repays the bank is then multiplied by [1 – 0.3], where 0.3 is the tax rate, in order to arrive at the bank's net income. From this, the monitoring cost of $6 (to ensure choice of project G by the borrower) is subtracted.

The RHS of Equation (13.4) has the bank's net income if it does not monitor and hence project N is selected by the borrower. Solving Equation (13.4) as an equality yields the maximum value of D as:

$$D = \$90.38$$

If $D > \$90.38$ the RHS of Equation (13.4) will exceed the LHS of Equation (13.4), and the bank will not monitor.

This means that the bank's optimal capital structure will be \$9.62 in equity (for a capital ratio in book value terms of 9.63%) and \$90.38 in deposits. The depositors receive an expected return of exactly 1%. The borrower's NPV is:

$$\frac{0.9[150-130]}{1.01} = \$17.82$$

and the bank's shareholders enjoy an NPV of:

$$0.9\left[130 - \frac{90.38[1.01]}{0.9}\right][1-0.3]-6 = \$12$$

This example shows how we can arrive at an optimal structure for the bank by ensuring that there is enough capital in the bank to make it in the best interest of the bank to monitor the borrower. A key aspect of the example is that deposits are uninsured and there is *no* possibility of a bailout of the bank by the government, so deposit pricing accurately reflects risk. If either of these conditions is violated, the pricing of deposits will become insensitive to the bank's risk, and the bank's privately optimal capital structure will involve more leverage. In fact, these government safety nets may provide the best explanation for why banks are so much more highly levered than nonfinancial firms.

While the monitoring-based theories explain how higher capital reduces the bank's insolvency risk, research suggests that higher banking capital may also reduce funding/liquidity risk in banking. This is because better-capitalized banks face less pressure to dump assets in fire sales in order to cope with unexpectedly low profits or other shocks that deplete their net worth.[17] The reason is that they have more of a capital cushion to deal with such shocks. A reduced incidence of fire sales means that there is less liquidity risk in the market because it is the incidence of fire sales that causes the values of assets for banks to decline and consequently diminishes their borrowing capacity or access to liquidity. Yet another advantage of higher capital in banking that has been identified by recent theories is a reduced risk of contagion arising from individual bank failures.[18]

EMPIRICAL EVIDENCE ON BANK CAPITAL, BANK LENDING, AND BANK VALUE

On the issue of the impact of bank capital on lending, the debt-discipline theories predict that higher bank capital will reduce bank lending, whereas the monitoring-based theories predict that higher capital should result in more lending. The empirical evidence seems to support the prediction of the monitoring-based theories, although calibrating these (potential) effects is challenging.

Let us begin by briefly discussing some of the empirical evidence on how the level of capital in banking affects bank lending. In general, establishing a causal link is a daunting task due to the difficulty in achieving a meaningful segregation of demand and supply effects. However, there are a few papers that have employed clever identification strategies to establish causal linkage. For example, one paper examines how the depleted capital levels of Japanese banks due to the sharp decline in the Japanese stock market during 1989–1992 affected lending by the U.S. branches of these banks.[19] It documents that these U.S. branches displayed significantly lower lending. Based on this and other studies, it appears that when banks experience negative exogenous shocks to their capital, they reduce their lending. This reduction in lending can jeopardize relationships banks have with their borrowers, since these relationships rely on borrowers' continued access to bank credit. Research has shown that banks that enter a financial crisis with more capital are able to perform their relationship lending role more effectively.[20]

What about the effect of bank capital on liquidity creation by banks? A study that used a comprehensive measure of bank liquidity creation that includes both on-balance-sheet and off-balance-sheet items has documented that, for most of the dollar volume of liquidity creation in the United States, higher capital leads to greater liquidity creation.[21] That is, the relationship between capital and liquidity creation is positive for large banks, which create most of the liquidity (81%) in the U.S. economy.

17. A fire sale occurs when firms in an industry simultaneously sell assets, causing the asset price to spiral downward. See Chapter 14 for more on this. A review of the role of fire sales appears in Shleifer and Vishny (2011).
18. See Acharya and Thakor (2015). They develop a model in which the failure of one bank causes the creditors of other banks to infer deterioration in the asset values of their banks, causing those banks to fail. They show that as banks increase their equity capital, the probability of such contagion decreases.
19. See Peek and Rosengren (1997).
20. See Bolton et al. (2014).
21. See Berger and Bouwman (2011).

There is also empirical evidence that having higher capital strengthens the bank's competitive position, and allows it to grow faster by gaining an edge over its lower-capital counterparts in both its deposit and loan markets. Moreover, higher capital also allows banks to gain market share during financial crises.[22] Let us now turn to the relationship between bank capital and bank value. There has been surprisingly little work done on this issue. An exception is a recent study that develops a theoretical model and tests it.[23] The theoretical predictions of the model are as follows: (i) total bank value and the bank's equity capital are positively correlated in the cross-section, and (ii) the various components of bank value in an acquisitions context are also positively related to bank capital. The empirical tests of the study provide strong support for these predictions. The empirical results are consistent with the monitoring-based view of the role of bank capital that features prominently in the theory, and the results are robust to a variety of alternative explanations – growth prospects, desire to acquire toe-hold positions, the desire of capital-starved acquirers to buy capital-rich targets, market timing, pecking order, and the effect of banks with binding capital requirements.

Thus, it appears that higher bank capital is associated with higher lending, higher liquidity, and higher bank values. Nonetheless, it does appear that financial institutions seem resistant to keeping higher levels of capital, and engage in "regulatory arbitrage" that involves for example, engaging in activities with lower capital requirements.[24] Why they may do so will be taken up in the next section.

WHY THEN DO BANKS DISPLAY A PREFERENCE FOR HIGH LEVERAGE?

Our discussion in the preceding section seems to suggest that banks should voluntarily keep high levels of capital, thereby obviating the need for regulatory capital requirements. But this is not the case. As indicated earlier, not only are banks highly levered, but they seem to take advantage of every opportunity to lower the amount of equity they keep on their balance sheets. This section discusses possible reasons for this behavior.

1. Tax Benefits: All firms benefit from using debt because interest on debt is tax deductible at the firm level, whereas dividends paid to shareholders are not. Even Modigliani and Miller noted that this leads firms to the corner solution of an all-debt (and one share of stock) capital structure. But in the case of banks, the tax advantage of debt is even more alluring because banks have competitors (e.g., credit unions) that pay no taxes. Hence, to compete more effectively with these tax-exempt competitors, banks adopt high leverage to minimize taxes.

2. Debt Overhang: When a firm has a high level of debt, it may pass up positive-NPV projects rather than issue equity to finance them because doing so would reduce the value of equity, as most of the benefits go to the bondholders and decrease the value of equity.[25] Consider the following example:

Example 13.2

Suppose a firm has to repay its bondholders $70 based on its past borrowing. Its current end-of-period payoff distribution is $100 with probability (w.p.) 0.5 and $0 w.p. 0.5. Now suppose the firm could invest $20 to make its payoff $75 for sure. This is a positive-NPV investment. However, the value of equity before the investment was 0.5[$100 − $70] = $15. If the shareholders put in $20 in equity, the value of equity will be $75 − $70 = $5, which is lower than $15, so the shareholders will be unwilling to do it.

If bondholders agree to reduce their repayment to $50 and additionally provide the $20 investment needed to achieve the $75 payoff, the shareholders would be willing to make the investment of $20 to achieve the sure payoff. This is because the value of equity is equal under both scenarios:

$$0.5[\$100 - \$50] = \$75 - \$50 = \$25$$

But the bondholders' expected payoff now declines from

$$0.5[\$70] = \$35$$

to

$$\$50 - \$20 = \$30$$

---

22. Calomiris and Powell (2001) find that capital enhanced banks' ability to acquire deposits in Argentina in the 1990s. Calomiris and Mason (2003) encountered a similar result for U.S. banks during the Great Depression. And in a study of New York banks in the 1920s and 1930s, Calomiris and Wilson (2004) found that higher-capital banks had a competitive advantage in the market for risky loans. See also Berger and Bouwman (2013).

23. See Mehran and Thakor (2011).

24. Becker and Opp (2013) examine the effect of a recent change in the manner in which capital requirements are computed for the insurance holdings of mortgage-backed securities. The change replaced credit ratings with regulator-paid risk assessments by Pimco and Blackrock. They document that replacing ratings has led to significant reductions in aggregate capital requirements, and conclude that insurance industry interests, rather than financial stability concerns, drove this regulatory change.

25. See Myers (1977).

3. Preference for Return on Equity (ROE) due to Executive Compensation: Many bank executives are compensated based on ROE and on how their bank's ROE compares with that of peer banks. In practice, the ROE target is not typically adjusted for how the bank's capital changes over time, as long as it satisfies regulatory capital requirements and the bank's own target ratio. This encourages high leverage.[26]

4. Government Safety Nets: As we saw earlier, the value of the deposit insurance put option is decreasing in the bank's capital. So, if the deposit insurance premium does not charge the bank for the additional risk, then banks will have an incentive to increase their leverage to increase the value of their option. Other government safety nets like bailouts produce similar incentives.

BANK CAPITAL AND REGULATION

So far we have made no distinction between bank capital and bank equity. The word "capital" points to the liability side of the bank, just like equity; it is part of the funding of the bank. At a general level, although capital is broader than equity, one similarity between them is that they both represent a cushion that creates a "breaking distance", and hence preserves the viability and solvency of the institution for depositors. That is, capital in general provides a safety cushion for deposits.

Nonetheless, bank capital is not equivalent to bank equity. While equity is a part of capital, some types of hybrid and subordinated debt-like funding sources are also included in some definitions of regulatory capital. The Bank for International Settlements (BIS) – the institution that coordinates the determination of capital standards for all countries that are signatories to the Basel accord – distinguishes between Core Tier 1, Tier 1, Tier 2, and Tier 3 sources of capital. Core Tier 1 capital represents the most stringent definition of capital – it is book common equity (paid-in capital and retained earnings), that is, what any nonfinancial corporation would consider its capital (equity). It is supposed to "support losses on an on-going basis without triggering liquidation,"[27] and should be unconditionally risk absorbing and permanently available to the business. Tier 1 is broader than Core Tier 1 in that certain other instruments can be included.

All the other definitions of regulatory capital are broader in the sense that they allow more sources of the bank's financing to count as capital and therefore compromise on the straightforward interpretation and loss-absorbing features of Core Tier 1. For example, Tier 1 also includes noncumulative, nonredeemable preferred stock, in addition to common equity. Successively higher tiers allow more and more financing sources to be included. In addition to common stock and preferred stock, Tier 2 allows for some types of hybrid (of debt and equity) capital instruments, and term (i.e., of sufficiently long maturity) subordinated debt, while acknowledging that "Subordinated term debt instruments have significant deficiencies as constituents of capital in view of their fixed maturity and inability to absorb losses except in a liquidation. These deficiencies justify an additional restriction on the amount of such debt capital which is eligible for inclusion within the capital base." Tier 3 – introduced as part of the Basel II Accord – is meant to help absorb the bank's exposure to foreign currency risk and commodities risk. In addition to what is included in Tier 2 capital, Tier 3 also includes some short-term subordinated debt.

One of the justifications for these different categories is that bank regulators look at capital in two different ways. One is as a source of financing that boosts the bank's probability of solvency. This would require more capital that is a residual claim, that is, it comes from financiers who cannot force the bank into bankruptcy. This, of course, is "real" capital, which is common equity. It is available to absorb losses without jeopardizing solvency. The other way regulators look at capital is that it should help protect the deposit insurance fund. From this vantage point, all that is needed is that capital is subordinated to deposits, which justifies the inclusion of many instruments that are junior to deposits.

Following the 2007–2009 financial crisis, capital rules have been tightened. The crisis exposed the inadequacy of capital that was not equity in the sense that debt financing could flee the bank when solvency concerns were sufficiently elevated. In the peculiar language of rule makers, it was concluded that the "quality of capital" had to be improved, meaning that there should be more "real" capital.[28]

A second aspect of bank regulatory capital that distinguishes it from the way one thinks about capital for nonfinancial firms is the "flexibility" that is used in the definition of assets in the denominator of the capital ratio. Unlike nonfinancial

---

26. Observe that it follows from standard corporate finance theory that an increase in leverage increases the (expected) ROE of the bank. This, however, should not be interpreted as value creation for shareholders because the minimum expected return demanded by shareholders also goes up to reflect the higher financial risk to the shareholders due to the higher leverage. Bank shareholders, however, often seem to applaud such ROE-increasing strategies. One explanation, apart from the debt overhang argument given earlier, could be that in good times risks are not fully priced and/or are underestimated (see Boot (2014) and Thakor (2015)).

27. See BIS, 2006.

28. This was the so called Basel III amendment (BIS, 2011) of the 2006 rules (BIS, 2006); the 2006 rules are known as Basel II. The major changes are that Tier 1 has become more stringent; after a transition period it will essentially become "real" fully loss absorbing capital, and Tier 3 capital (relatively short-term subordinated debt) is abolished.

firms, for which one would simply use the book value of total net assets in the denominator to compute a capital ratio, bank capital ratios are often computed using "risk-weighted" assets. That is, "risk weights" are used to adjust the value of the assets to reflect differences in the risks of the assets. This way, a bank consumer (nonmortgage) loan may be given a 100% risk weight, so $1 of the asset would count as $1 in the denominator, whereas some other asset, say a sovereign government bond, might be given a zero risk weight, so this asset would simply vanish from the asset base for purposes of calculating the capital ratio. While there are some highly risky assets that are given more than a 100% risk weight, most assets have risk weights that fall between 0% and 100%, so the overall effect of risk-weighting the assets is to reduce the denominator (assets), and thereby boost the calculated capital ratio of the bank. In other words, the practical effect of computing risk-based capital is that capital ratios look better than they otherwise would. The 2007–09 financial crisis has led to a reassessment of this practice in the sense that regulators have determined that risk-based capital ratios cannot be the only ratios that are tracked for prudential regulation. So regulators now also focus on a (complementary) capital ratio that is not based on risk-weighted assets, the so-called "leverage ratio." This ratio is familiar from the way we think of capital for nonfinancial firms: it is book equity capital as a fraction of total assets.

CONCLUSION

This chapter has considered the issue of how banks arrive at an optimal capital structure. Our starting point was whether the Modigliani and Miller (M&M) capital structure irrelevance theorem applied to banks, and if not, what assumptions of the theorem were violated. In this discussion we dispelled some common fallacies that have been commonly used (incorrectly) to argue that the M&M theorem does not apply to banks.

Having done this, we presented two theories of bank capital structure that produce opposite predictions – the debt-discipline theory, which says that having more leverage (and hence less capital) in banking is good for promoting bank lending and liquidity creation, and the monitoring theory which says that having more capital (and hence less leverage) in banking is good for promoting bank lending and liquidity creation. The empirical evidence seems to support the monitoring theory. For the most part, banks with more capital lend more, create more liquidity, are more competitive, face lower insolvency and liquidity risks, exhibit higher probabilities of surviving financial crises, and are worth more. This is good news for public policy, since more highly capitalized banks also lead to greater bank stability.

Private incentives, however, run in the direction of maintaining low levels of capital. Even apart from deposit insurance and bailout safety-net considerations, there are tax advantages to high leverage, so as in the M&M theory with taxes, banks would wish to maximize deposit funding because this minimizes their weighted average cost of capital.[29] What keeps them from going to this extreme, however, is that capital is essential to induce banks to monitor their (relationship) borrowers, so enough capital must reside in the bank's capital structure to support good lending decisions and good postlending behavior by the bank.[30] That is, capital affects both the numerator (cash flows) and the denominator (cost of capital) in the value of the bank. Moreover, it is often the case that the private incentives of banks do not account for the social externalities created by the systemic fragility that results from having banks with too little capital. As we have discussed, regulators have responded to the propensity of banks to keep low capital by formulating a variety of regulatory capital ratios, some of which differ markedly from how capital ratios are thought of for non-financial firms in corporate finance. We return to these issues in the Chapters 15 and 16.

REVIEW QUESTIONS

1. What are the common myths related to the role of capital in banking? Why are these myths wrong?
2. Is the M&M capital structure irrelevance theorem applicable in banking? Why or why not?
3. What are the two main theories of bank capital structure? Provide an assessment of each based on empirical evidence.
4. Why do you think banks have so much more leverage than non-financial firms?
5. Suppose a bank can make a loan of $120 at $t = 0$. The loan will repay at $t = 1$ and it finances a project that a borrower can invest in. The borrower can choose from one of the three mutually exclusive projects: G, N, and n, each of which requires an initial investment of $120 at $t = 0$ and produces a random payoff at $t = 1$. Project G pays off $200 w.p. 0.8 and zero w.p. 0.2. Projects N and n both yield $200 w.p. 0.5 and zero w.p. 0.5. Project N produces a noncontractible private

---

29. From a public policy standpoint, this suggests that if the goal is to encourage banks to keep more equity capital, the tax code ought to be revised to reduce the tax disadvantage of equity relative to debt. Schepens (2014) documents that when this was done in Belgium in 2006, banks responded by increasing their capital ratios.

30. What then counteracts this and pushes banks to be more highly levered is the effect of deposit insurance (as shown by Merton, 1977) and government bailouts.

benefit of $15 for the borrower. The bank has an option to monitor the borrower's project choice at a cost of $12. Bank monitoring, however, can only prevent the borrower from choosing Project N, and not project n.

The bank can raise financing for the loan with a mix of deposits and equity. For simplicity, as in Example 13.1, assume that all of the bank's equity is "inside equity." Depositors cannot observe whether the bank monitored the loan.

Assume the riskless interest rate is 2% and that everybody in the economy is risk neutral. Banks are relatively scarce and as such they can charge the borrower whatever interest rate they want. For simplicity, assume that only the net income of banks at $t = 1$ is taxed at a rate of 30%. Deposits are available to the bank in whatever quantity it desires as long as depositors are promised an expected return of 2%. Similarly, the bank can put up as much inside equity as needed, as long as shareholders are promised an expected return of at least 2%. *What should be the capital structure of the bank?*

REFERENCES

Acharya, V., Thakor, A.V., 2015. The dark side of liquidity creation: leverage-induced systemic risk and implications for the lender of the last resort. Paper Presented at the JFI-Hoover Institute Conference on the Lender of Last Resort. April, Washington DC.

Admati, A., Hellwig, M., 2013. The Bankers' New Clothes: What's Wrong with Banking and What to do About it. Princeton University Press, Princeton, NJ.

Admati, Anat, DeMarzo, P.M., Hellwig, M.F., Pfleiderer, P., 2013. Fallacies, irrelevant facts, and myths in the discussion of capital regulation: why bank equity is not socially expensive. Working Paper, Stanford University.

Becker, B., Opp, M., 2013. Replacing Ratings, Harvard Business School and UC-Berkeley.

Berger, A.N., Bouwman, C.H.S., 2013. How does capital affect bank performance during financial crises? J. Financ. Econ. 109, 146–176.

Berger, A.N., Bouwman, C.H.S., 2011. Bank liquidity creation. Rev. Financ. Stud. 22, 3779–3837.

Berlin, M., 2011. Can we explain banks' capital structures. FED Philadel. Bus. Rev. Q2, 1–11.

Bhattacharya, S., Boot, A., Thakor, A.V., 1998. The economics of bank regulation. J. Money Credit Bank. 30, 745–770.

BIS, 2006. Basel II: International Convergence of Capital Measurement and Capital Standards: A Revised Framework – Comprehensive Version, Basel Committee on Banking Supervision, Bank for International Settlements (BIS).

BIS, 2011. Basel III: A Global Regulatory Framework for More Resilient Banks and Banking Systems, Basel Committee on Banking Supervision, Bank for International Settlements (BIS) (revised).

Bolton, P., Freixas, X., Gambacorta, L., Mistrulli, P., 2014. Relationship and Transaction Lending in a Crisis. Working Paper, Columbia University.

Boot, A., 2014. Financial sector in flux. J. Money Bank. 46, 129–135.

Calomiris, C.W., Kahn, C., 1991. The role of demandable debt in structuring optimal banking arrangements. Am. Econ. Rev. 81, 497–513.

Calomiris, C.W., Wilson, B., 2004. Bank capital and portfolio management: the 1930s "capital crunch" and the scramble to shed risk. J. Bus. 77, 421–455.

Calomiris, C.W., Mason, J.R., 2003. Consequences of bank distress during the great depression. Am. Econ. Rev. 93, 937–947.

Calomiris, C.W., Powell, A. 2001. Can emerging market bank regulators establish creditor discipline? The case of Argentina 1992–1999. In: Mishkin, F.S. (Ed.), Prudential Supervision: What Works and What Doesn't, NBER, University of Chicago Press, Chicago, pp. 147–191.

DeAngelo, H., Stulz, R., 2015. Why high leverage is optimal for banks. J. Financ. Econ. (forthcoming).

Diamond, D., Rajan, R., 2000. A theory of bank capital. J. Financ. 55, 2431–2465.

Furlong, F.T., Keeley, M.C., 1989. Capital regulation and bank risk taking: a note. J. Bank. Financ. 13, 883–891.

Holmstrom, B., Tirole, J., 1997. Financial intermediation, loanable funds, and the real sector. Q.J. Econ. 112, 663–691.

Jensen, M.C., Meckling, W.H., 1976. A theory of the firm: managerial behavior, agency costs and ownership structure. J. Financ. Econ. 3.

Mehran, H., Thakor, A.V., 2011. Bank capital and value in the cross-section. Rev. Financ. Stud. 24, 1019–1067.

Merton, R.C., 1977. An analytic derivation of the cost of deposit insurance and loan guarantees: an application of modern option pricing theory. J. Bank. Financ. 1, 3–11.

Mester, L., Nakamura, L., Renault, M., 2007. Transactions accounts and loan monitoring. Rev. Financ. Stud. 20, 529–556.

Miller, M., 1995. Do the M&M propositions apply to banks? J. Bank. Financ. 19, 483–489.

Modigliani, F., Miller, M., 1958. The cost of capital, corporation finance and the theory of investment. Am. Econ. Rev. 48, 261–297.

Modigliani, F., Miller, M., 1963. Corporate income taxes and the cost of capital: a correction. Am. Econ. Rev. 53, 433–443.

Myers, S.C., 1977. Determinants of corporate borrowing. J. Financ. Econ. 5, 147–175.

Peek S J., Rosengren, E.S., 1997. The international transmission of financial shocks: the case of Japan. Am. Econ. Rev. 87, 496–505.

Schepens, G., 2014. Taxes and Bank Capital Structure. Working Paper, Department of Financial Economics, Ghent University.

Shleifer, A., Vishny, R., 2011. Fire sales in finance and macroeconomics. J. Econ. Perspect. 25, 29–48.

Thakor, A.V., 2014. Bank capital and financial stability: an economic tradeoff or a faustian bargain? Annu. Rev. Financ. Econ. 6, 185–223.

Thakor, A.V., 2015. Lending booms, smart bankers and financial crises. Am. Econ. Rev. 105, 305–309.

Part VII

Financial Crises

Chapter 14

The 2007–2009 Financial Crisis and Other Financial Crises

"In its analysis of the crisis, my testimony before the Financial Crisis Inquiry Commission drew the distinction between triggers and vulnerabilities. The triggers *of the crisis were the particular events or factors that touched off the events of 2007–2009 – the proximate causes, if you will. Developments in the market for subprime mortgages were a prominent example of a trigger of the crisis. In contrast, the* vulnerabilities *were the structural, and more fundamental, weaknesses in the financial system and in regulation and supervision that served to propagate and amplify the initial shocks."*

Chairman Ben Bernanke (April 13, 2012).[1]

GLOSSARY OF TERMS

Breaking the Buck Money market funds invest in relatively safe securities and seek to maintain a stable net asset value (NAV) of $1 per share. When the NAV drops below $1, it is said that the fund "broke the buck."

EBRD European Bank for Reconstruction and Development. This is an institution – funded by many western countries – that provides help to countries in central and Eastern Europe, Central Asia, and the Southern and Eastern Mediterranean to make transitions to market economies.

ECB European Central Bank

FDIC Federal Deposit Insurance Corporation

Fannie Mae Federal National Mortgage Association (FNMA)

Fire Sales The simultaneous sale of similar assets by many firms in an industry, which results in a downward price spiral.

Freddie Mac Federal Home Loan Mortgage Corporation (a government-sponsored enterprise for securitizing home mortgages in the United States)

IMF International Money Fund

LIBOR London Interbank Offer Rate, which is the average interest rate estimated by leading banks in London that they would be charged if borrowing from other banks.

MBS Mortgage-backed securities

OTD Originate-to-distribute model in securitization, wherein a bank originates a loan to securitize it (distribute securities to others) rather than hold it on its books.

Tail Risks Extreme risks involving large losses but very low probabilities of occurrence.

INTRODUCTION

The financial crisis of 2007–2009 is widely regarded as the worst financial crisis since the Great Depression of the 1930s.[2] The crisis threatened the global financial system with total collapse, led to the bailouts of many large financial institutions by their national governments, caused big declines in stock prices, followed by smaller and more expensive loans for corporate borrowers as banks pulled back from lending, and decline in consumer lending, as well as lower investments in the real sector.[3] The decline in lending to consumers and corporations also caused unemployment to rise.[4] In the United States, Lehman Brothers, a global 158-year old investment bank, filed for bankruptcy, whereas Fannie Mae and Freddie Mac, two huge government-sponsored enterprises that have been key players in the securitization market in the United States, as well as the insurance giant AIG, were bailed out by the government, and Wachovia (the fourth largest bank in the United States) was bought out by Citigroup. In response to these events, financial markets became highly volatile, and the Dow Jones

---

1. See Bernanke, Ben, S., "Some Reflections on the Crisis and the Policy Response", speech at the Russell Sage Foundation and the Century Foundation Conference on "Rethinking Finance," New York, April 13, 2012. See also Bernanke (2010).

2. The material in this chapter relies on the review of the 2007–2009 financial crisis in Thakor (forthcoming).

3. See Campello et al. (2011), Gorton and Metrick (2012), and Santos (2011).

4. Halfenhof et al. (2014) document that the reduction in consumer lending was the major driver of the rise in unemployment as it resulted in a decline in consumer purchasing power and hence a drop in the demand for products and services.

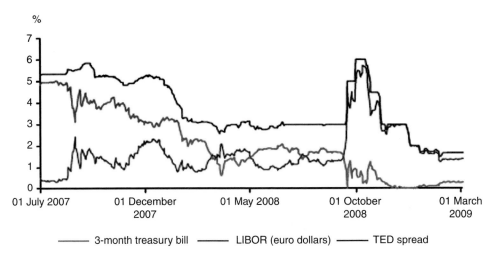

FIGURE 14.1   TED Spread. *(Source: Federal Reserve and Marshall (2009)).*

TABLE 14.1 Different Dimensions of the Costs of the Crisis

	Cost of Lost Income		Cost of National Trauma and Lost Opportunity	Extraordinary Government Support
	According to the path of output	According to total wealth, implied by the path of consumption		
Trillions of 2012 dollars	6–14	15–30	Up to 14	12–13
Percent of 2007 output	40–90	100–190	Up to 90	80–85
Source: Atkinson et al. (2013).				

Industrial Average experienced its largest single-day point drop in value on September 29, 2008. Investor confidence fell dramatically and credit channels tightened considerably as the difference between the 3-month London Interbank Offer Rate (LIBOR) and the 3-month Treasury bill rate – known as the TED spread – shot up, as shown in Figure 14.1, a reflection of growing fears about counterparty risk.[5]

The Federal Reserve Bank of Dallas estimates that the financial crisis cost the United States an estimated 40–90% of 1 year's output, an estimated $6–$14 trillion, the equivalent of $50,000–$120,000 for every U.S. household.[6] Even these staggering estimates may be conservative. The loss of *total* U.S. wealth from the crisis – including human capital and the present value of future wage income – may be as high as $15–$30 trillion, or 100–190% of the 2007 U.S. output.[7] Table 14.1 provides estimates of different dimensions of the costs of the crisis, and Figure 14.2 shows that the rebound in output has been much weaker than in previous business cycles.

In the aftermath of the crisis, the U.S. Congress passed the Dodd–Frank Act, an enormous piece of legislation that introduced sweeping changes in the regulation of the U.S. financial system and numerous regulatory changes were contemplated and implemented in Europe as well. In this chapter, we describe and analyze this financial crisis. We begin in the next section with an overview of what happened and the time-line of events. In the section after that, we develop a causal link of events to shed light on what caused the crisis, explaining where there seems to be consensus and where we still have differing opinions, and then discuss the real effects of the crisis. This is followed by a section that provides a brief description of the regulatory responses to the crisis, and assesses these responses. The penultimate section discusses crises in some other countries and compares these with the U.S.. The final section concludes.

---

5. See Marshall (2009). For a detailed account of these events, see Brunnermeier (2009).
6. See Atkinson et al. (2013).
7. These estimates are provided by Atkinson et al. (2013).

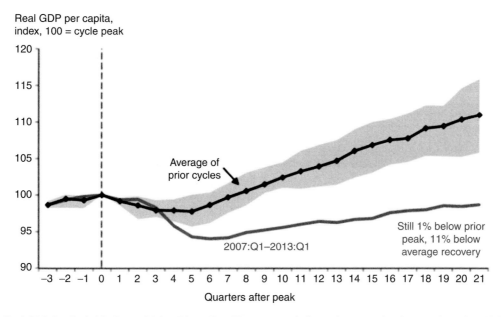

FIGURE 14.2   Real GDP Per Capital Before and After Crises. *Note:* The gray area indicates the range of major recessions since 1960, excluding the short 1980 recession. *(Source: Bureau of Economic Analysis, Census Bureau, and Atkinson et al. (2013)).*

WHAT HAPPENED

The financial crisis of 2007–2009 came on the heels of a credit crunch that began in the summer of 2006 and continued into 2007. Most agree that the crisis was rooted in the U.S. housing market. The factors that contributed to the housing price bubble that burst during the crisis will be discussed later in this chapter. The first signs of problems surfaced in early 2007 when Freddie Mac announced that it would no longer purchase high-risk mortgages, and New Century Financial Corporation, a leading mortgage lender to risky borrowers, filed for bankruptcy. These developments elevated concerns about the credit risks in mortgages and the solvency of institutions that held them. A timeline of these events and those that followed is discussed below and summarized in Table 14.2.

These elevated insolvency concerns caused investors to withdraw their funds from various institutions. The crisis, according to most people, began in August 2007, with large-scale withdrawals of short-term funds from various markets previously considered safe, as reflected in sharp increases in the "haircuts" on repos and difficulties experienced by ABCP (asset-backed commercial paper) issuers experiencing difficulty in rolling over their outstanding paper.[8]

It was the sharp decline in U.S. house prices that caused this stress in the short-term funding markets in the shadow-banking system during 2007. This caused credit rating agencies (CRAs) to downgrade their assessments of the creditworthiness of asset-backed financial instruments in mid-2007. Between the third quarter of 2007 and the second quarter of 2008, $1.9 trillion of mortgage-backed securities (MBS) received downgrades that reflected a higher assessment of risk. This came as a shock to investors.[9] This caused credit markets to continue to tighten, and led the Federal Reserve to provide relief by opening up short-term lending facilities (Term Securities Lending Facility, TSLF) and auctions for the sale of mortgage-related financial products. But this failed to prevent the hemorrhaging, as asset prices continued to decline.

In early 2008, these stresses began to show up in institutional failures. Mortgage lender Countrywide Financial was bought by Bank of America in January 2008, and then in March 2008, Bear Stearns, the sixth largest U.S. investment bank, was unable to roll over its short-term funding due to losses on MBS whose prices were plunging. Bear Stearns' stock price had a precrisis 52-week high of $133.20 per share, but dropped like a rock as revelations of losses in its hedge funds and other businesses came to light. JP Morgan Chase made an initial offer of $2 per share for all the outstanding shares of Bear Stearns, and the deal was consummated at $10 per share when the Federal Reserve intervened with a financial assistance package. The problems continued with the failure of IndyMac, the largest mortgage lender in the United States, which was

---

8. See Gorton and Metrick (2012). A "haircut" on a repo is the discount relative to the market value of the security offered as collateral in a repurchase transaction that the borrower must accept in terms of how much it can borrow against that collateral.
9. "The odds are only about 1 in 10,000 that a bond will go from highest grade, AAA, to the low-quality CCC level during a calendar year," as reported in "Anatomy of a Ratings Downgrade," *BusinessWeek*, October 1, 2007. Benmelech and Dlugosz (2009) document that the average downgrade of mortgage-backed securities was 5–6 notches, significantly higher than the average downgrade of corporate bonds. See also Marshall (2009).

TABLE 14.2 Financial Crisis Major Events Timeline

2007	
Jan.–July	Subprime mortgage underwriters Ownit Mortgage Solutions and New Century Financial Corporation file for bankruptcy. Massive downgrades of mortgage-backed securities by rating agencies. Kreditanstalt für Wiederaufbau (KfW), a German government-owned development bank, supports German bank IKB
August	Problems in mortgage and credit markets spill over into interbank markets; haircuts on repo collateral rise; asset-backed commercial paper issuers have trouble rolling over their outstanding paper; large investment funds in France freeze redemptions
August 17	Run on U.S. subprime originator Countrywide
September 9	Run on U.K. bank Northern Rock
December 15	Citibank announces it will take its seven structured investment vehicles onto its balance sheet. $49 billion
December	National Bureau of Economic Research subsequently declares December to be the business cycle peak
2008	
March 11	Federal Reserve announces creation of the Term Securities Lending Facility to promote liquidity
March 16	JPMorgan Chase agrees to buy bear Stearns, with Federal Reserve assistance, and Federal Reserve announces creation of the Primary Dealer Credit Facility
June 4	Monoline insurers MBIA and AMBAC are downgraded by Moody's and S&P
July 11	IndyMac collapses and is taken over by the government
July 15	U.S. Securities and Exchange Commission issues an order banning naked short-selling of financial stocks
September 7	Federal government takes over Fannie Mae and Freddie Mac
September 15	Lehman Brothers files for bankruptcy
September 16	The Reserve Primary Fund, a money market fund, "breaks the buck," causing a run on MMFs. Federal Reserve lends $85 billion to AIG to avoid bankruptcy
September 19	U.S. Treasury announces temporary guarantee of MMFs, and Federal Reserve announces the Asset-Backed Commercial Paper Money Market Mutual Fund Liquidity Facility
September 25	Washington Mutual, the largest savings and loan in the United States with $300 billion in assets, is seized by the authorities
October	Financial crisis spreads to Europe.
October 3	U.S. Congress approves the Troubled Asset Relief Program, authorizing expenditures of $700 billion
October 8	Central banks in the United States, England, China, Canada, Sweden, Switzerland, and the European Central Bank cut interest rates in a coordinated effort to aid world economy
October 13	Major central banks announced unlimited provision of liquidity to U.S. dollar funds; European governments announce system-wide bank recapitalization plans
October 14	U.S. Treasury invests $250 billion in nine major banks
2009	
May	Results of the Supervisory Capital Assessment Program ("stress tests") announced
June	National Bureau of Economic Research subsequently declares June to be the business cycle trough
October	Unemployment rate peaks at 10.0%

Source: Adapted (with changes) from Gorton and Metrick (2012).

taken over by the U.S. government. Then, Fannie Mae and Freddie Mac (with ownership of $5.1 trillion of US mortgages) became sufficiently financially distressed and were also taken over by the government in September 2008.

The next major tremor occurred when Lehman Brothers filed for Chapter 11 bankruptcy on September 15, 2008. It was unable to raise the capital it needed to underwrite its downgraded securities. On the same day, AIG, a leading insurer of credit defaults, received $85 billion in government assistance, as it faced a severe liquidity crisis. The dominos continued to topple as on the next day, the Reserve Primary Fund, a money market fund, "broke the buck," with its per-share value falling below $1. This caused a run on these funds. Interbank lending rates rose significantly.

The news kept getting worse. On September 25, 2008, a very large savings and loan institution, Washington Mutual, was taken over by the FDIC, and most of its assets were transferred to JP Morgan Chase. By October, the crisis had spread to Europe, forcing central banks around the globe to cooperate and announce coordinated interest rate cuts and a commitment to unlimited liquidity provision. But there was also growing recognition that this was perhaps an insolvency crisis, and banks needed higher levels of equity capital to deal with it. The U.S. government provided some of this capital. By mid-October, the US Treasury had invested $250 billion in nine major banks.

The crisis continued into 2009. By October, the unemployment rate in the United States had hit 10%. In Table 14.2, a summary of these events is provided.

CAUSE AND EFFECT: THE CAUSES OF THE CRISIS AND ITS REAL EFFECTS

Although there is some agreement on the causes of the crisis, there are disagreements among experts on many of the links in the causal chain of events. We begin by providing a pictorial depiction of the chain of events that led to the crisis, and then discuss each link in the chain (Figure 14.3).

External Factors

In the vast number of books and articles written on the financial crisis, various authors have put forth a variety of precrisis factors that created a powder keg just waiting to be lit.[10] There is no consensus on which of these factors were the most significant, but we will discuss each in turn.

Political Factors

Some have pointed to politics playing a major role in planting the seeds of the crisis. One viewpoint is that economic inequities had widened in the United States due to structural deficiencies in the educational system that created unequal access for various segments of society.[11] Politicians from both parties viewed the broadening of home ownership as a way to deal with

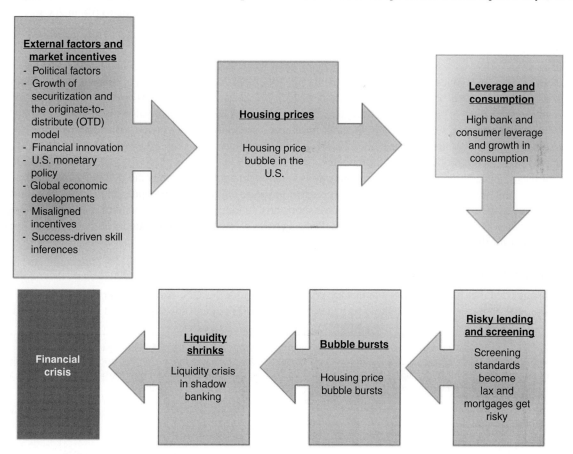

FIGURE 14.3 The Chain of Events Leading Up to the Crisis.

10. Lo (2012) provides an excellent and succinct summary and critique of 21 books on the crisis, written by academics and journalists.
11. See Rajan (2010) for this line of reasoning.

this growing wealth inequality, and therefore undertook legislative initiatives and other inducements to make banks extend mortgage loans to a broader borrower base by relaxing underwriting standards, and this led to riskier mortgage lending.[12] The elevated demand for houses pushed up house prices, and led to the housing price bubble.

A somewhat different view of political influence lays the blame on deregulation motivated by political ideology. Deregulation in the 1980s created large and powerful financial institutions with significant political clout to block future regulation, goes the argument.[13] This "regulatory capture" created a crisis-prone financial system with inadequate regulatory oversight and a cozy relationship between government and big banks.

Growth of Securitization and the OTD Model

It has been suggested that the desire of the U.S. government to broaden ownership was also accompanied by an "easy money" monetary policy that encouraged softer lending standards by banks. In particular, an empirical study of Euro-area and U.S. Bank lending standards finds that low short-term interest rates (generated by an "easy money" monetary policy) lead to softer standards for household and business loans. Moreover, this softening is magnified by securitization, weak regulatory supervision over bank capital, and a lax monetary policy for an extended period.[14] These conditions thus made it profitable for banks to expand mortgage lending in the period prior to the crisis. Empirical evidence has also been provided showing that the OTD model encouraged banks to originate increasing volumes of risky loans, and caused banks to be less diligent in screening loans than if these were held on the books.[15] A one-standard deviation in a bank's propensity to sell off its loans has been documented to increase the default rate by about 0.45%; given the low levels of default rates in general, this represents an overall increase of 32%.[16]

These developments led to a substantial increase in the credit that flowed into the housing market to enable consumers to buy homes. Loan originations (new loans issued) rose from $500 billion in 1990 to $2.4 trillion in 2007, before declining to $900 billion in the first half of 2008, and mortgage loans outstanding increased from $2.6 trillion to $11.3 trillion over the same period. The subprime share of home mortgages grew from 8.7% in 1995 to a peak of 13.5% in 2005.[17]

Financial Innovation

Numerous financial crises have been preceded by financial innovations that worked hand-in-hand with high bank leverage and produced asset price bubbles. This crisis was no different.[18] We witnessed an explosion of financial innovation for over two decades prior to the crisis. Part of the reason is that financial markets are very competitive, so with standard financial products – those whose payoff distributions everybody agrees on – it is hard for financial institutions to have high profit margins. This encourages the search for new financial products, especially those whose creditworthiness not everybody agrees on. This limits how competitive the market for those products will be, and allows the institutions involved in offering those products to earn high profits, at least for a while.

Many of these financial innovations produce enormous benefits for society. But they are also innately more risky. The reason is that it is not only competitors who may disagree that these are creditworthy products, but also the financiers of the institutions offering these products. When this happens, short-term funding to the innovators will not be rolled over, and a funding crisis ensues. The explosion of new asset-backed securities created by securitization prior to the crisis created an ideal environment for this to occur.[19]

U.S. Monetary Policy

It has been suggested that the easy-money monetary policy followed by the U.S. Federal Reserve, especially in the 6 or 7 years prior to the crisis, was a major contributing factor to the price boom and subsequent bust that led to the crisis. The

12. One of these initiatives involves the strengthening of the Community Reinvestment Act (CRA) in the mid-1990s. Agarwal, Benmelech, Bergman and Seru (2012) provide evidence that they interpret as suggesting that the CRA led to riskier lending by banks. They find that in the six quarters surrounding the CRA exams, lending increases on average by 5% every quarter, and loans in those quarters default about 15% more often.
13. See Johnson and Kwak (2010) for this viewpoint.
14. See Maddaloni and Peydró (2011). As we saw in the chapter on securitization, the OTD model makes it less costly for banks to relax credit standards, invest less in screening, and make riskier loans.
15. See Keys et al. (2010).
16. See Purnanandam (2011) for this evidence.
17. As of early 2009, the U.S. housing market was valued at about $19.3 trillion. See Barth, Li, Lu, Phumiwasana, and Yago (2009).
18. See Reinhart and Rogoff (2008, 2009).
19. See Thakor (2012) for this viewpoint. An alternative but related explanation is that financial innovations involved "tail risks" that were ignored by investors, leading to excess demand for these risky securities. When these risks were recognized by investors, they dumped these securities, leaving financial institutions to hold them and eventually precipitating a crisis. See Gennaioli et al. (2012) for this view.

argument is that monetary policy was too "loose fitting" during 2001–2007 in the sense that actual interest rate decisions fell well below what historical experience would suggest policy should be. See Figure 14.4.

These unusually low interest rates, a part of a monetary policy choice by the Federal Reserve, were viewed as responsible for accelerating the housing boom and thereby ultimately leading to the housing bust. There is research to support this view. A regression to estimate the empirical relationship between the interest rate and housing market shows that there was a high positive correlation between the decline in interest rates during 2001–2007 and the boom in the housing market. Moreover, a simulation to see what would have happened in the counterfactual event that the Taylor rule[20] interest rate policy in Figure 14.5 had been followed indicates that we would not have witnessed the same housing boom that occurred.[21] Of course, in the absence of the housing boom, there would be no bubble to burst and no crisis.

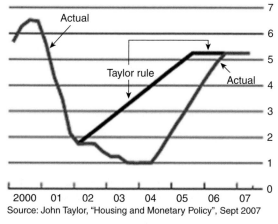

Loose fitting

Federal funds rate, actual and counterfactual, %

Source: John Taylor, "Housing and Monetary Policy", Sept 2007

FIGURE 14.4   Actual Interest Rates versus Rates Implied by the Taylor Rule. *(Source: Chart from The Economist, October 18, 2007).*

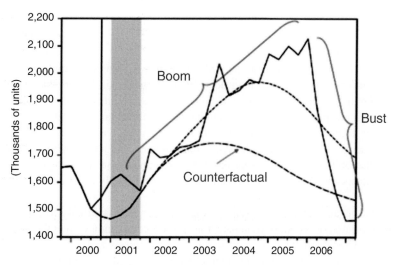

FIGURE 14.5   Housing Construction During the Precrisis Boom and Under Taylor Rule Counterfactual. *(Source: Taylor (2009)).*

---

20. The "Taylor rule" is a monetary policy rule that stipulates how much the central bank should change the nominal interest rate in response to changes in inflation, output, or other economic conditions. Specifically, the rule, attributed to Stanford University economist John B. Taylor, stipulates each 1% increase in inflation should be met with a more than 1% increase in the nominal interest rate by the central bank.
21. See Taylor (2009) for this research.

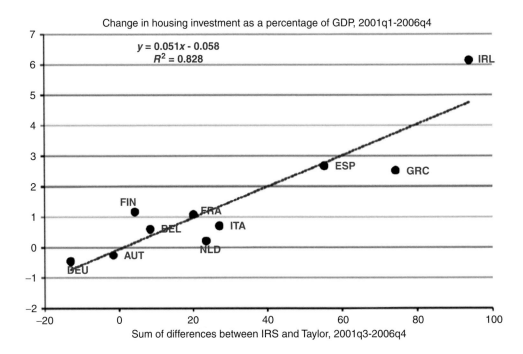

FIGURE 14.6 Housing Investment versus Deviations from the Taylor Rule in Europe. *(Source: Taylor (2009)).*

Similar developments occurred in Europe where deviations from the Taylor rule varied in size across countries due to differences in inflation and GDP (Figure 14.6). The country with the largest deviation from the rule was Spain, and it had the biggest boom in housing, as measured by the change in housing investment as a share of GDP. Austria had the smallest deviation from the rule, and also experienced the smallest change in housing investment as a share of GDP.

It appears that there was coordination among central banks to follow this easy-money policy. Apparently, a significant fraction of the European Central Bank (ECB) interest rate decisions can be explained by the influence of the Federal Reserve's interest rate decisions.[22]

Global Economic Developments

There are some who have pointed to developments in the global economy as a contributing factor.[23] In the past two decades, emerging-market countries – most notably China – have accounted for an increasing percentage of global GDP. This growing wealth has led to the accumulation of large amounts of savings in these countries, and the lack of extensive social safety nets means that there have been incentives for individuals to hang on to these savings and not reduce them by indulging in higher domestic consumption. Rather, the savers have sought to invest in safe assets, resulting in huge inflows of investments in the United States in assets like bank debt, AAA-rated mortgages, and so on. When coupled with the easy-money monetary policy pursued in the United States over approximately the same time period, the result was a very large infusion of liquidity into the United States and Western Europe. This led to exceptionally low mortgage interest rates, as shown in Figure 14.7.

This would normally lead to an increase in inflation as more money is available to purchase goods and services. However, the rise of emerging-market economies meant that global companies in the West could move procurement, manufacturing, and a variety of back-office support services to these countries with lower labor costs. Consequently, core inflation stayed low in the West, and provided no signals to central banks to discontinue their easy-money monetary policies. Moreover, the flood of this "hot money" found its way into real estate, increasing demand for housing, and pushing up house prices.

---

22. See Taylor (2009) for details.
23. The discussion here is based in part on Jagannathan et al. (2013).

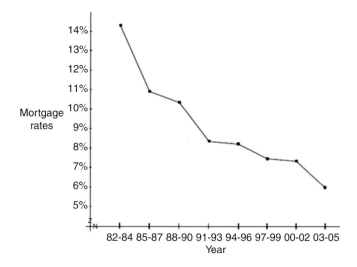

FIGURE 14.7   Average Mortgage Interest Rates from 1982 to 2005. *(Source: Holt (2009)).*

Misaligned Incentives

There are many who have suggested that misaligned incentives also played a role. The argument goes as follows. Financial institutions, especially those that viewed themselves as too big to fail (TBTF), took excessive risks because *de-jure* safety-net protection via deposit insurance and *de-facto* safety-net protection due to regulatory reluctance to allow such institutions to fail.[24] Such risk-taking was permitted due to lax oversight by regulators whose incentives were not aligned with those of taxpayers.[25] Moreover, "misguided" politicians facilitated this with their overzealous embrace of unregulated markets. This is also the essence of the report of the U.S. government's *Financial Crisis Inquiry Commission* (FCIC).[26]

The risk-taking was a part of the aggressive growth strategies pursued by banks. This meant that banks were willing to substantially increase their mortgage lending. This increase in financing meant another facilitating factor in pushing up home prices.

Success-Driven Skill Inferences

While misaligned incentives clearly played a role in this crisis, as they have in previous financial crises, they do not tell the whole story. There was more to the 2007–2009 crisis. In particular, the recent crisis followed a long period of high profitability and growth for the financial sector, and during those good times, there was little warning of the onset and severity of the crisis from any of the so-called "watch dogs" of the financial system – rating agencies, regulators, and creditors of the financial system.[27] This suggests that other, possibly complementary, forces were at work besides misaligned incentives.

A major driver of the conditions that made the crisis likely was that the long period of success that preceded the crisis caused everyone to develop a very high regard for the skills of bankers in managing risks.[28] To see how this can lead to a high probability of a financial crisis, imagine there is a high probability that loan defaults are affected by the skills of bankers in managing credit risk, and a small probability that these outcomes are driven solely by luck or factors beyond the control of bankers. Banks start out initially making fairly safe loans because riskier (and more profitable) loans are viewed by the financiers of banks as being too risky. Now, if these loans successfully pay off over time, everybody raises their assessment of their beliefs about the abilities of banks to manage (credit) risk, even though the performance of the loan portfolio may have been just due to luck. As this happens, it becomes possible for banks to finance riskier loans as investors view these loans

---

24. See Bebchuk and Fried (2010), Litan and Bailey (2009), for example.

25. See, for example, Boot and Thakor (1993), Kane (1990), and Barth et al. (2012).

26. The report claims that industry players and government regulators saw warning signs of the impending crisis, but chose to ignore them. It blames the Federal Reserve for being too supportive of industry growth objectives, citing, for example, Federal Reserve Governor Edward Gramlich in 2004, "We want to encourage growth in the subprime lending market." See also Johnson and Kwak (2010) and Stiglitz (2010).

27. In fact, there was a report by the Independent Evaluation Office (IEO) of the IMF which stated: "The banner message was one of continued optimism after more than a decade of benign economic conditions and low macroeconomic volatility ... the belief that financial markets were sound and that large financial institutions could weather any likely problem lessened the sense of urgency to address risks or to worry about the possible severe adverse outcomes." During 2004–2007, the period leading right up to the crisis, the IMF reported that individual financial institutions were sound. The *Independent Evaluation Office* (IEO) of the IMF (2011) went on to criticize the IMF for failing to warn about shocks and vulnerabilities in the financial system.

28. This reasoning is based on Thakor (2015).

as being less risky due to their elevated regard for bankers' skills. And if these successfully pay off, then even more risky loans are financed. This way, risk taking in banking continues to rise, and no one issues warnings about an impending crisis.

Of course, even low-probability events (the so-called "black swans") sometimes occur. Thus, it is possible that investors eventually find themselves in a state in which they believe outcomes are purely luck-dependent. When this happens, beliefs revert sharply to *prior* beliefs. And since only relatively safe loans could be financed with these prior beliefs, the sudden drop in beliefs about the risk-management abilities of banks causes investors to withdraw funding for the loans that are suddenly viewed as being "excessively risky." This theory predicts that it is precisely when there is a sufficiently long period of high profitability and low loan defaults that bank risk-taking increases, and that a financial crisis occurs only when its *ex ante* probability is being viewed as being sufficiently low.

Housing Prices

As a consequence of the factors just discussed, house prices in the United States experienced significant appreciation prior to the crisis, especially during the period 1998–2005. The Case-Shiller U.S. national house price index more than doubled between 1987 and 2005, with a significant portion of the appreciation occurring after 1998. See Figure 14.8.

Further supporting empirical evidence that there was a housing price bubble, came from the observation that the ratio of house prices to renting costs appreciated significantly around 1999.[29] See Figure 14.9.

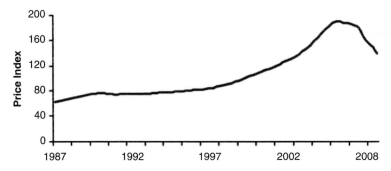

FIGURE 14.8 S&P/Case-Shiller US National Home Price Index, 1978–2008. *(Source: S&P/Case-Shiller Home Price Index, Standard and Poor's, and Marshall (2009)).*

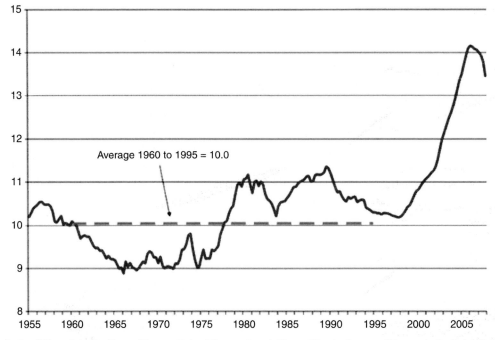

FIGURE 14.9 Ratio of Home Prices to Rents. *(Source: Federal Reserve Board: Flow of Funds, Bureau of Economic Analysis: National Income and Product Accounts, and Cecchetti (2008)).*

---

29. See Cecchetti (2008).

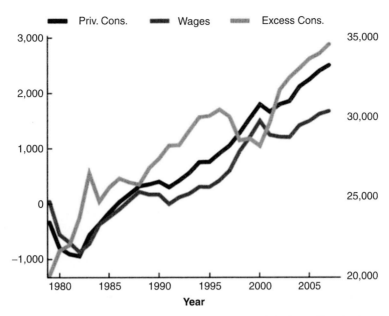

FIGURE 14.10   Per Capital Consumption from 1978 to 2008. *Note:* All Numbers are in 1980 Dollar per Household. *(Source: Jagannathan et al., 2013).*

Leverage and Consumption

The housing price bubble facilitated a substantial increase in individual consumption. U.S. households, feeling rich in an environment of low taxes, low interest rates, easy credit, expanded government services, cheap consumption goods, and rising home prices, went on a consumption binge, letting their personal savings rate drop below 2% for the first time since the Great Depression. The increase in U.S. household consumption during this period was striking. Per capita consumption grew steadily at the rate of $1994 per year during 1980–1999, but then experienced a big jump to approximately $2849 per year from 2001 to 2007.[30] See Figure 14.10.

Some of this higher consumption was financed with higher borrowing, which was supported by rising home prices. Indeed, the simplest way to convert housing wealth into consumption is to borrow against the equity built up in one's house. As the value of residential real estate rose, mortgage borrowing increased even faster. Figure 14.11 shows this phenomenon – home equity fell from 58% of home value in 1995 to 52% of home value by 2007.[31]

This increase in consumer leverage, made possible by the housing price bubble, had a significant role in the crisis that was to come. An empirical study, conducted using detailed zip-code level data, shows that the sharp increase in mortgage defaults during the crisis was significantly amplified in subprime zip codes, or zip codes with a disproportionately large share of subprime borrowers as of 1996.[32] The study shows that, during 2002–2005, the subprime zip codes experienced an unprecedented relative growth in mortgage credit, despite significantly declining relative income growth – and in some cases declining absolute income growth – in these neighborhoods. The study also notes that this was highly unusual in that 2002–2005 is the only period in the past 18 years during which personal income and mortgage credit growth were negatively correlated.[33] That is, it is the only period during which people were borrowing more while their incomes were falling.

What exacerbated the situation is that this increase in consumer leverage was by those who were perhaps least equipped to handle it and was also accompanied by an increase in the leverage of financial institutions, especially those in the shadow-banking system, which turned out to be the epicenter of the crisis. This made these institutions fragile and less capable of handling defaults on consumer mortgages and sharp declines in the prices of MBS than they would have been had they been not as thinly capitalized.

Risky Lending and Screening

In the chapter on securitization, we discussed the empirical evidence which indicates that securitization may have weakened the incentives of banks to screen their borrowers. There is also additional evidence that during the dramatic growth of

---

30. See Jagannathan et al. (2013).

31. See Cecchetti (2008).

32. See Mian and Sufi (2009).

33. The study attributes this disassociation during 2002–2005 to the increase in the securitization of subprime mortgages. The *correlated* increase of consumer leverage with that of financial institutions made the system especially fragile (see Goel et al., 2014).

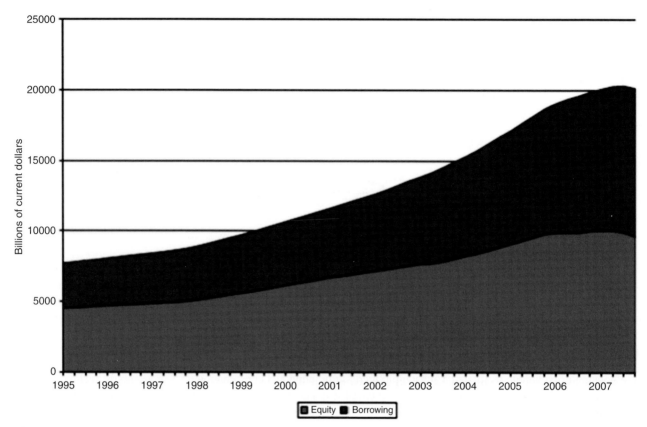

FIGURE 14.11   Evolution of Equity and Borrowing in Residential Real Estate. *(Source: Federal Reserve Flow of Funds, and Cecchetti (2008)).*

the subprime (securitized) mortgage market, the quality of the market declined dramatically and that lenders seemed to be aware of this.[34] In particular, the quality of loans, measured as the performance of loans, deteriorated for six consecutive years prior to the crisis, and this deterioration is statistically significant even after loan performance is adjusted for differences in borrower characteristics like the credit score, level of indebtedness, loan amount, and ability to provide documentation; differences in loan characteristics like product type, amortization term, loan amount, and mortgage interest rate; and macroeconomic conditions like house price appreciation, level of neighborhood income, and change in unemployment. The fact that lenders seemed aware of the growing default risk of these loans is suggested by the higher rates lenders charged borrowers as the decade prior to the crisis progressed. For a similar decrease in the quality of the loan (e.g., a higher loan-to-value ratio), a loan made early in the decade was associated with a smaller interest rate increase than a loan made late in the decade. Thus, even though it is possible that lenders underestimated the credit risks in the loans they were making, they do seem to have been aware that they were making riskier loans.

These lenders also seem to have taken steps to reduce some of these risks from their balance sheets. Research shows that from the end of 2006 until the beginning of 2008, originators of loans tended to sell their loans, collect the proceeds, and then use them to originate new loans and repeat the process.[35] The research also shows that banks with high involvement in the OTD market during the precrisis period originated excessively poor-quality mortgages, and this result cannot be explained by differences in observable borrower quality, geographical location of the property, or the cost of capital for high-OTD and low-OTD banks. This evidence indicates that the OTD model induced originating banks to have weaker incentives to screen borrowers before extending loans. However, this effect is stronger for banks with lower capital, suggesting that capital strengthens banks' incentives to screen their borrowers and operate with lower levels of credit risk.

---

34. This evidence is provided by Demyanyk and Van Hemert (2011).
35. See Purnanandam (2011).

The Bubble Bursts

The start of the crisis, according to most accounts of the financial crisis, can be traced to the bursting of the housing price bubble, and the fact that the failure of Lehman Brothers in September, 2008 was a sign that the crisis was deepening. But exactly what caused the housing price bubble to burst?

Some studies cite evidence that run-ups in house prices are a common place occurrence prior to the start of a crisis.[36] But they do not explain what caused the bubble to burst. However, we can get some insights into what happened by examining the dynamics of loan defaults in relation to initial home price declines, and how this fueled larger subsequent price declines, causing the bubble to burst. Home prices reached their peak in the second quarter of 2006. The initial decline in home prices from that peak was a rather modest 2% from the second quarter of 2006 to the fourth quarter of 2006.[37]

With prime mortgages held by creditworthy borrowers, such a small decline is unlikely to lead to a large number of defaults, and especially not defaults that are highly correlated across geographic regions of the United States. The reason is that these borrowers have 20% of equity in the home when they buy the home, so a small price drop does not put the mortgage "under water" and threaten to trigger default.

Not so with subprime mortgages. Even the small decline in home prices pushed these highly risky borrowers over the edge. Foreclosure rates increased by 43% over the last two quarters of 2006, and increased by a staggering 75% in 2007 compared to 2006.[38] Homeowners with adjustable rate mortgages that had low teaser rates to attract them to buy homes were hit the hardest. The drop in home prices meant that they had negative equity in their homes (given how little of their own money many of them had put down in the first place). So, when their rates adjusted upward, they found themselves hard pressed to make the higher monthly mortgage payments. As these borrowers defaulted on their mortgages, CRAs began to downgrade MBS, and many of the adverse events described in Table 14.1 began to kick in. This caused credit availability to decline, pushed up interest rates, and accelerated the downward house price spiral, eventually threatening the repayment ability of even prime borrowers. From the second quarter of 2006 to the end of 2007, foreclosure rates for fixed-rate mortgages increased by about 55% for prime borrowers and by about 80% for subprime borrowers. Things were much worse for those with adjustable-rate mortgages – their foreclosure rates increased by about 400% for prime borrowers and by about 200% for subprime borrowers.

Liquidity Shrinks in Response to Insolvency Concerns

Before the financial crisis, the shadow banking sector of the U.S. economy had grown dramatically. One notable aspect of the shadow banking system is its heavy reliance on short-term debt, mostly repurchase agreements (repos) and commercial paper. Repo liabilities of U.S. broker dealers increased 2 ½ times in the 4 years before the crisis.[39] The IMF (2010) estimates that total outstanding repo in U.S. markets at between 20% and 30% of U.S. GDP in each year from 2002 to 2007. The IMF estimates for the European Union are even higher – a range of 30% to 50% E.U. GDP per year during 2002–2007.

A repo transaction is basically a "collateralized" deposit.[40] The depositor (or lender) deposits money in a financial institution for a short period of time, typically overnight. The amount deposited is usually large and exceeds deposit insurance coverage limits. The interest rate paid on this deposit is the overnight repo rate. To reduce the depositor's risk, given the absence of deposit insurance, the institution that accepts the deposit gives the depositor a marketable security as collateral. If the institution that has the deposit fails, then the depositor can sell the collateral to recover the deposited amount. Such transactions often involve "haircuts." If the deposit is $80 and the security given by the institution to the depositor as collateral is also worth $80, there is no "haircut." But if the deposit is $80 and the security provided as collateral is worth $100, then the haircut is 20%.

The repo transactions used Treasury bonds, MBS, commercial paper, and so on as collateral. As news about defaults on mortgages began to spread, concerns about the credit qualities of MBS began to rise. The bankruptcy filings of subprime mortgage underwriters and the massive downgrades of MBS by the rating agencies in mid-2007 created significant concerns about the credit qualities of many types of collateral being used in repo transactions, as well as possibly the quality of the credit screening conducted by the originators of the underlying mortgages. This caused repo haircuts to spike up significantly, causing the short-term borrowing capacity in the shadow banking sector to decline substantially, creating what appeared to be a liquidity crunch.

---

36. See Reinhart and Rogoff (2008, 2009) for evidence on this.
37. See Holt (2009).
38. See Liebowitz (2008).
39. See Bernanke (2010).
40. See Gorton and Metrick (2012).

An important question is whether this was a market-wide liquidity crunch or a bank-specific increase in concerns about solvency risk that caused the availability of funding to shrink for some banks but not for others. That is, one viewpoint is that when people realized that MBS were a lot riskier than they thought, liquidity dried up across the board because the high level of asymmetric information and opaqueness in MBS arising from the multitude of steps in the creation of a MBS – from the originations of multiple mortgages to their pooling and then to the specifics of the tranching of this pool – meant that it was hard for an investor to determine which MBS was of high quality and which was not.[41] So when bad news arrived about mortgage defaults, there was a (nondiscriminating) market-wide effect. According to this view of the events, this was a liquidity crunch.

Another viewpoint is that this was, at its core, a bank-specific solvency issue, and not a liquidity crisis. A recent study examines funding sources and asset sales at commercial banks, investment banks, and hedge funds.[42] It hypothesizes that if liquidity dries up in the financial market, institutions that rely on short-term debt will be forced to sell assets at fire-sale prices.[43] The empirical findings are, however, that the majority of commercial and investment banks did not experience funding declines during the crisis, and did not engage in the fire sales predicted to accompany liquidity shortages. The problems at financial institutions that did experience liquidity shortages during the crisis originated on the asset side of their balance sheets in the form of bad news about the credit risks embedded in the assets they held. Commercial banks' equity and asset values were strongly negatively affected by the levels of net charge-offs, whereas investment banks' asset changes seemed to reflect changes in market valuation.[44] Thus, this was an insolvency crisis, according to this viewpoint.

Nonetheless, there were events that seemed to have market-wide implications. The failure of Lehman Brothers was followed by larger withdrawals from money market-mutual funds after one large fund "broke the buck." The ABCP market also experienced considerable stress. By July 2007, there was $1.2 trillion of ABCP outstanding, with the majority of the paper held by MMFs. Issuers of commercial paper were unable in many cases to renew funding when a portion of the commercial paper matured, and some have referred to this as a "run."[45] As Figure 14.12 shows, things deteriorated quite dramatically in this market beginning August 2007.

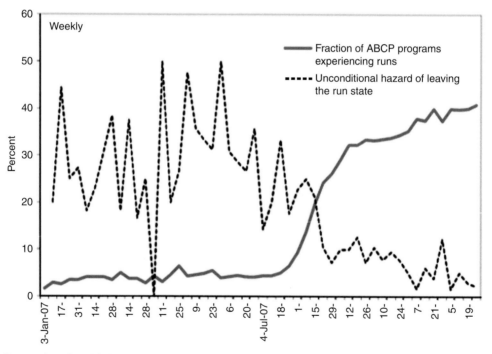

FIGURE 14.12 Runs on Asset-Based Commercial Paper Programs. *(Source: Covitz et al., (2013)).*

41. See Gorton (2010) for this viewpoint.

42. See Boyson et al. (2013).

43. "Fire sales" occur when many institutions, faced with similar constraints, become excessively highly leveraged and have to sell assets simultaneously, resulting in a downward price spiral for the assets being dumped in the market. This can happen, for example, if institutions find that their funding has dried up. See Shleifer and Vishny (2011) for an explanation of this phenomenon.

44. Supporting the idea that problems faced by institutions in this crisis were specific to these institutions and not market-wide phenomena, is a study by Fahlenbrach et al. (2012). It shows that a bank's stock return performance during the 1998 crisis predicts its stock return performance and failure likelihood during the 2007-09 crisis, which highlights the importance of bank-specific attributes like business models and credit culture.

45. See Gorton and Metrick (2012), and Covitz et al. (2013).

The ABCP market fell by $350 billion in the second half of 2007. Many of these programs required backup support from their sponsors to cover this shortfall. As the major holders of ABCPs, MMFs were adversely affected. This culminated in the Reserve Primary Fund, a large MMF, "breaking the buck." Consequently, ABCP yields rose for outstanding paper. Many shrinking ABCP programs sold their underlying assets, putting further downward pressure on prices. All of these events led to numerous MMFs requiring assistance from their sponsors to avoid breaking the buck. But even in this case, the empirical evidence indicates that the runs suffered by MMFs were mainly due to asset risk and solvency concerns rather than a liquidity crisis *per se*.[46]

On balance, it appears that the evidence suggests that this was, in the end, an insolvency crisis in which rising perceptions of the default risks of mortgages caused investors to withdraw funding from the institutions that held MBS and especially those that used them as collateral for short-term funding. The massive withdrawal of funding created the appearance of a liquidity crisis.

The Real Effects of the Crisis

This financial crisis had significant real effects. These effects can be pictorially depicted as shown in Figure 14.13.

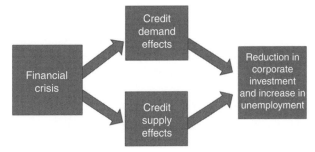

FIGURE 14.13   The Real Effects of the Crisis.

Credit Demand Effects

The argument for why the crisis adversely affected household demand for credit goes as follows.[47] First, due to a variety of reasons discussed in this chapter (including easy credit with relaxed underwriting standards, booming house prices, low interest rates, etc.), household debt went up significantly. Then, the bursting of the house price bubble significantly depleted household net worth. In response, the highly levered households cut back on consumption. However, the relatively unlevered households did not increase consumption to offset the decline in consumption by the levered households. This is not surprising. Many of the unlevered households were probably consuming what they wanted to consume, so they may have had little reason to consume more.

Empirical evidence shows that this interaction between precrisis household leverage and decline in consumption made a major contribution to the events witnessed during the crisis. In particular, the research indicates that the large accumulation of household debt prior to the recession, in combination with the decline in house prices, explains the onset, severity, and length of the subsequent consumption collapse. Consumption declined much more in high-leverage countries with larger house price declines and in areas with greater reliance on housing as a source of wealth. Thus, as house prices dropped, so did consumption and the demand for credit to finance that consumption.

Credit Supply Effects

There is overwhelming empirical evidence that the crisis also caused a significant decline in the supply of credit by banks. One piece of evidence is that syndicated loans declined during the crisis, which is important since syndicated lending is a major source for credit for the corporate sector.[48] The syndicated loan market includes not only banks, but also investment banks, institutional investors, hedge funds, mutual funds, insurance companies, and pension funds (see Chapter 9 for more on syndicated lending). The evidence is that syndicated lending began to fall in mid-2007, and this decline accelerated starting in September 2008. Syndicated lending volume in the last quarter of 2008 was 47% lower than in the prior quarter

---

46. See Kacperczyk and Schnabl (2010).
47. See Mian et al. (2013).
48. The decline in syndicated lending is documented by Ivashina and Scharfstein (2010).

and 79% lower than in the second quarter of 2007, which was the height of the credit boom. Lending declined across all types of corporate loans.

Not only did the volume of lending fall, but the price of credit rose significantly as well. Firms paid higher loan spreads during the crisis.[49] This increase in loan spreads was higher for firms that borrowed from banks that incurred larger losses. This result holds even when firm-specific, bank-specific, and loan-specific factors are controlled for, and the endogeneity of bank losses is taken into account.

It is quite challenging to separate supply and demand effects. One study examines whether there are discernible reductions in credit supply, even when overall demand for credit is going down.[50] This study examined German Savings banks, which operate in well-defined geographies and are required by law to serve only local customers. In each geography there is a *Landesbank*, owned by the savings bank in that area. These Landesbanken (the regional banks) had varying degrees of exposure to U.S. subprime mortgages. These exposures created varying amounts of losses for these Landesbanken, and therefore required different amounts of equity injections from their respective savings banks. In other words, different savings banks were affected differently, depending on the losses suffered by their Landesbanken due to their subprime mortgage exposures. What the research uncovers is that the savings banks that were hit harder cut back more on credit. The average rate at which loan applicants were rejected by the harder-hit banks was significantly higher than the rate at which rejections occurred at unaffected banks.

There is also survey evidence that shows that credit supply fell as a result of the crisis.[51] A survey of 1050 Chief Financial Officers (CFOs) in 39 countries in North America, Europe, and Asia was completed in December 2008. About 20% of the surveyed firms in the United States (about 14% in Europe and 8.5% in Asia) indicated that they were very affected in the sense that they faced reduced availability of credit. Consequently, they reduced capital expenditures, dividends, and employment.

Reduction in Corporate Investment and Increase in Unemployment

With both household consumption going down and credit becoming more scarce and more expensive, it is not surprising that corporate investment fell and unemployment rose. The United States entered a deep recession, with almost 9 million jobs lost during 2008 and 2009, which represented about 6% of the workforce. It also discouraged many from trying to re-enter the workforce after the crisis abated, leading the labor participation rate to decline to historically low levels. This meant that subsequent measurements of the unemployment rate tended to understate the true unemployment rate. Even measured unemployment rose every month from 6.2% in September 2008 to 7.6% in January 2009. U.S. housing prices declined about 30% on average and the U.S. stock market fell approximately 50% by mid-2009.

The U.S. automobile industry was particularly hard hit. Car sales fell 31.9% in October 2008 compared to September 2008. Retail sales in the U.S. declined by 2.8% between September and October 2008, and by 4.1% compared to September 2007.

THE POLICY RESPONSES TO THE CRISIS

Beginning in August 2007, the governments of all developed countries undertook a variety of measures to deal with the financial crisis. The IMF (2009) identifies as many as 153 separate policy actions taken by 13 countries, including 49 in the United States alone. That represents too large a set of policy interventions to discuss here. So we will briefly describe the major categories of interventions here (Figure 14.14).[52]

Expansion of Traditional Role of Central Bank as Lender of Last Resort

This set of interventions included the discount window, Term Auction Facility (TAF), Primary Dealer Credit Facility (PDCF), and Term Securities Lending Facility (TSLF). The Federal Reserve also approved bilateral currency swap agreements with 14 foreign central banks to assist these central banks in the provision of dollar liquidity to banks in their jurisdictions, with the largest of these arrangements being with the ECB.

The discount window has long been a primary liquidity-provision tool used by the Fed. In December 2007, the TAF was introduced to supplement the discount window. The TAF provided credit to depository institutions through an auction

---

49. See Santos (2011).

50. See Puri et al. (2011).

51. The evidence discussed here is provided by Campello et al. (2010).

52. This discussion is based on *Board of Governors of the Federal Reserve* www.federalreserve.gov/monetarypolicy/bst_crisisresponse.html

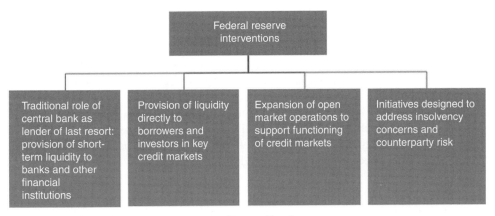

FIGURE 14.14   The Major Categories of Interventions by the Federal Reserve Board.

mechanism. Like discount window loans, TAF loans had to be fully collateralized to the satisfaction of the lending Federal Reserve bank. The final TAF auction was held on March 8, 2010.

The PDCF was established in March 2008 in response to strains in the *tri-party repo* market and the resulting liquidity pressures faced by primary securities dealers. Primary dealers are broker-dealers who serve as the trading counterparties for the Federal Reserve's open-market operations, and thus play a pivotal role in providing liquidity in the market for U.S. treasuries. The PDCF serves as an overnight loan facility for primary dealers, similar to the discount window for depository institutions. Credit extension required full collateralization. This facility was closed on February 1, 2010.

The TSLF was a weekly loan facility designed to promote liquidity in Treasury and other collateral markets. The program offered Treasury securities for a loan for 1 month against other program-eligible collateral. The borrowers were primary dealers who participated in single-price auctions to obtain these loans. The TSLF was closed on February 1, 2010.

Provision of Liquidity Directly to Borrowers and Investors in Key Credit Markets

These interventions included the Commercial Paper Funding Facility (CPFF), ABCP MMF Liquidity Facility (AMLF), Money Market Investors Funding Facility (MMIFF), and the Term Asset-Backed Securities Loan Facility (TALF). Of these, we earlier discussed the AMLF in the chapter on securitization (see Chapter 11).

The CPFF was established in October 2008 to provide liquidity to U.S. issuers of commercial paper. Under the program, the Federal Reserve Bank of New York provided 3-month loans to a specially created limited liability company that then used the money to purchase commercial paper directly from issuers. The CPFF was dissolved on August 30, 2010.

The MMIFF was designed to provide liquidity to U.S. money market investors. Under this facility, the Federal Reserve Bank of New York could provide senior secured loans to a series of special purpose vehicles to finance the purchase of eligible assets from eligible investors. The MMIFF was announced on October 21, 2008 and dissolved on October 30, 2009.

TALF was created to help market participants meet the credit needs of households and small businesses by supporting the issuance of asset-backed securities collateralized by consumer and small-business loans: auto loans, student loans, credit card loans, equipment loans, floor plan loans, etc. The goal was to revive the consumer-credit securitization market. The facility was launched in March 2009 and dissolved by June 2010.

Expansion of Open Market Operations

The goal of these initiatives was to support the functioning of credit markets and put downward pressure on long-term interest rates. These initiatives involved the purchase of longer-term securities for the Federal Reserve's portfolio. For example, starting in September 2012, the Federal Open Market Committee (FOMC) decided to purchase agency-guaranteed MBS at the rate of $40 billion per month. In addition, starting January 2013, the Fed began purchasing longer-term Treasury securities at the rate of $45 billion per month.

Initiatives Designed to Address Insolvency Concerns and Counterparty Risk

As the crisis progressed and the vast amounts of liquidity-injection seemed incapable of ending the crisis, the Fed began to realize that insolvency risk concerns had to be dealt with. One measure to deal with insolvency risk was the Troubled Asset

Repurchase Program (TARP), which was initially authorized in October 2008 and ended on October 3, 2010. The original intent was for the government to buy risky "toxic" assets from financial institutions in order to "clean up" their balance sheets, reduce market perceptions of the credit risks in the assets on the balance sheets of financial institutions, and unfreeze credit markets.[53] However, in practice the program evolved into one in which the government bought equity securities (the Capital Purchase Program) and took ownership positions in various financial and nonfinancial firms.

This was accompanied by regulatory pressure on U.S. banks to recapitalize themselves through other means. To not comply may have meant more equity injections by the government and even greater government ownership – a prospect most banks wished to avoid. As a result, U.S. banks recapitalized quickly and counterparty risk concerns dissipated. This may have been the most effective policy response to the crisis. In contrast, European banks were not compelled to recapitalize to the same extent, so the after-effects of the crisis lingered on much longer there.

Assessment of Policy Initiatives

Many believe that the liquidity support provided by central banks was effective in calming markets in the initial phases of the crisis. However, there is no consensus on whether these were the right measures for the long run, or whether the problem was even correctly diagnosed. At the very least, markets exhibited considerable volatility after the collapse of Lehman Brothers, which indicates that central banks were learning as they went along – building the bridge as they walked on it, so to speak – and not all the initiatives had the intended effects.

A key issue for central banks was to determine whether the events they were observing were due to liquidity or counterparty risk arising from asymmetric information about the quality of assets on the balance sheets of institutions and the opaqueness of those balance sheets. The Federal Reserve and the ECB clearly believed it was a liquidity problem, which is reflected in the first three categories of measures we discussed earlier. But if the issue was counterparty risk, then the proper approach would be to require banks to make their balance sheets more transparent, deal directly with the rising mortgage defaults, and undertake measures to infuse more capital into financial institutions,[54] something that only occurred when the U.S. government began the process of recapitalizing banks.

How do we know what was really going on? One study tackled this question.[55] It began by examining the *LIBOR–OIS Spread*. This spread is equal to the three-month LIBOR minus the three-month Overnight Index Swap (OIS). The OIS is a measure of what the market expects the federal funds rate to be over the three-month period comparable to the three-month LIBOR. Subtracting OIS from LIBOR controls for interest rate expectations, thereby isolating risk and liquidity effects. Figure 14.15 shows the behavior of this spread just before and during the crisis.

The figure indicates that the spread rose in early August 2007, and stayed high. This was a problem because the spread not only is a measure of financial stress, but it affects how monetary policy is transmitted due to the fact that rates on loans and securities are indexed to LIBOR. An increase in the spread, holding fixed the OIS, increases the cost of loans for borrowers and contracts the economy. Policymakers thus have an interest in bringing the spread down. But just like a doctor

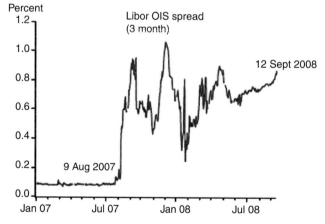

FIGURE 14.15 The LIBOR–OIS Spread During the First Year of the Crisis. *(Source: Taylor, 2009).*

---

53. See Tirole (2012) for a theory in which such intervention by the government reduces adverse selection and unfreezes the credit market.
54. Berger and Bouwman (2013) document empirically that higher-capital banks have a higher probability of surviving crises.
55. See Taylor and Williams (2009).

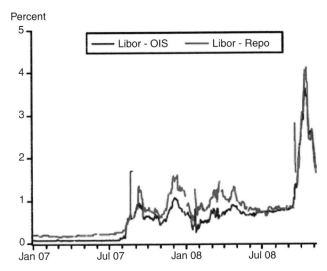

FIGURE 14.16   The LIBOR–OIS Spread. *(Source: Taylor, 2009)*

who cannot effectively treat a patient if he misdiagnoses the disease, so can a central bank not bring the spread down if it does not correctly diagnose the reason for its rise in the first place.

To see whether the spread increased due to elevated risk concerns or liquidity problems the study measured the difference between interest rates on unsecured and secured interbank loans of the same maturity.[56] The study referred to this as the unsecured–secured spread.[57] This spread is essentially a measure of risk. The study then regressed the LIBOR–OIS spread against the secured–unsecured spread, and found a very high positive correlation. It concluded that the LIBOR–OIS spread was driven mainly by risk concerns, and there was little role for liquidity.

As further support for this conclusion, the study shows that the TAF had little effect on the LIBOR–OIS spread. Moreover, the sharp reduction in the federal funds rate during the crisis – the fed funds target rate went from 5 ¼% in August 2007 to 2% in April 2008 – also did not succeed in reducing the LIBOR–OIS spread (see Figure 14.15). However, it also caused a depreciation of the dollar and caused oil prices to jump, causing a sharp decline in world economic growth.

The study goes on to show that in October 2008, the crisis worsened as the LIBOR–OIS spread spiked up even further, as shown in Figure 14.16. That is, more than a year after it started, the crisis got worse. Some suggest that the failure of Lehman Brothers in September 2008 was a proximate cause. The study suggests, however, that that may have been more a symptom than a cause, and that the real culprit was that the market participants were concerned that default risks had increased substantially, fueled by sinking house prices and rising oil prices. That is, this paper provides strong evidence that this was a crisis caused by insolvency risk.

It also appears that central banks – especially the U.S. Federal Reserve – eventually came to recognize that this was an insolvency crisis at its very root, and that measures like recapitalizing banks were needed to reduce concerns about counterparty risk. These measures eventually helped to end the crisis.

FINANCIAL CRISES IN OTHER COUNTRIES AND REGULATORY INTERVENTIONS

Financial crises have occurred in many different countries, and many have involved various forms of central bank intervention. The IMF found that governments intervened with some form of recapitalization or capital injection in 32 of the 42 banking crises around the world. So in this sense, the recapitalization initiatives of the U.S. Federal Reserve in the 2007–2009 crisis were not exceptions. Below we discuss a handful of other crises to provide a contrast in regulatory responses.[58]

Sweden

As has been the case with so many other financial crises, Sweden too experienced a financial crisis that was preceded by very high real estate prices. In the 1970s and 1980s, there was a substantial credit expansion in Sweden and a real-estate boom, with house prices doubling between 1981 and 1991. Sweden's exchange rate was tied with Germany, so when interest rates

---

56. This is the earlier-mentioned study by Taylor and Williams (2009).
57. Unsecured-secured spread = LIBOR minus Repo rate on government-backed collateral.
58. The discussion below is based on Contessi and El-Ghazaly (2011).

increased in 1990 in Germany due to the unification of East and West Germany, Sweden's interest rates also increased substantially, causing a recession in Sweden and a precipitous drop in prices. As a result, nonperforming loans at banks increased to 11% of GDP in 1993.

This significantly impaired the capital ratios of Sweden's largest banks, and these banks were unable to satisfy regulatory capital requirements. Instead of injecting capital into banks – as was done by the Fed during the subprime crisis – the Swedish government nationalized two of Sweden's largest banks and provided a loan guarantee to the third. The ownership of these banks by the government permitted expeditious liquidation of bad assets and restructuring of insolvent firms. The process took less than six years and cost Sweden less than 2% of GDP.

Latvia

Latvia's transition from a centrally planned economy (as part of the Soviet Union) to a free-market economy resulted in the creation of more than 60 licensed banks within 4 years. However, the rapid growth in private banking also occurred with little or no supervision from the central bank. As a result, poor lending practices went unchecked.

A crisis occurred when the central bank requested all banks to present audited financial statements in 1995. The largest bank failed to present its statements, was discovered to be insolvent, and was liquidated in 1996. Several other banks were also discovered to be insolvent. During the crisis, non-performing loans increased all across the banking sector. It was difficult for banks to collect on loans in the absence of laws governing loan collateral.

A series of interventions helped stabilize the banking system. Some banks were liquidated, new banking laws were established which strengthened the regulatory powers of the central bank, deposit insurance was established, and some assistance was received from the EBRD.

Argentina

This country has experienced four banking crises since the 1980s, with a "triple crisis" in 2001. The banking sector was transformed during the 1990s through privatization and consolidation. This allowed foreign bank entry. However, bank profitability was low and a large fraction of bank assets were Argentinian government debt.

In 2001, as the economy deteriorated, concerns about bank solvency and the health of the national currency, the Peso, caused large-scale deposit withdrawals, conversions into U.S. dollars and deposits abroad. This was a classic banking crisis, the first of the "triple" crisis.

Then, the government defaulted on its debt in December 2001, devastating the asset portfolios of the already-weakened banks. This was the second part of the "triple crisis."

The third part of the triple crisis was when the financial distress forced the country to exit its currency board regime, which was a convertibility program that tied the Argentinian peso to the dollar. Since there were bank runs still going on, the government restricted deposit withdrawals and froze all deposit accounts. This fueled further declines in deposit inflows to banks and diminished bank lending.

Government intervention also involved additional steps, including the conversion of dollar-denominated loans and deposits from dollar to peso at different rates, the authorization of regulatory forbearance, the nationalization of three banks, and the closure of another.

CONCLUSION

This chapter has reviewed a very large body of research on the causes and effects of the most devastating financial crisis since the Great Depression, and the policy responses undertaken by central banks to deal with the crisis. It appears that the crisis resulted from a toxic brew of many factors that interacted with each other: politics, monetary policy, global economic developments, misaligned incentives, the growth of securitization, and a complacency born of success-driven skill inferences.

Whatever the cause, the crisis lasted longer than expected and had a huge impact on the United States and global real economies. Central banks took unprecedented measures to deal with the crisis. Whether these were the right measures is an issue on which there is no consensus, and this will be the subject of research for many years to come.

It does appear, however, that having significantly higher levels of capital in banking (including shadow banking) would have gone a long way in reducing the likelihood of this crisis. Research indicates that higher levels of bank capital reduce both insolvency risk, and funding or liquidity risk.[59] Thus, better capital regulation should be a central focus in discussions of how to reduce the likelihood of future crises.

---

59. See Chapter 13 on bank capital and Brunnermeier (2009).

REFERENCES

Agarwal, S., Benmelech, E., Bergman, N., Seru, A., 2012. Did the Community Reinvestment Act (CRA) Lead to Risky Lending? NBER Working Paper No. 18609, December.

Atkinson, T., Luttrell, D., Rosenblum, H., 2013. How bad was it? The costs and consequences of the 2007–2009 Financial Crisis. Staff Paper No. 20, Federal Reserve Bank of Dallas.

Barth, J.R., Caprio, G., Levine, R., 2012. The Guardians of Finance: Making Them Work for Us. MIT Press, Cambridge, MA.

Barth, J.R., Li, T., Lu, W., Phumiwasana, T., Yago, G., 2009. The Rise and Fall of the U.S. Mortgage and Credit Markets: A Comprehensive Analysis of the Meltdown. Wiley, Hoboken, NJ.

Bebchuk, L., Fried, J.M., 2010. Paying for long-term performance. Univ. Pennsylvania Law Rev. 158, 1915–1960.

Benmelech, E., Dlugosz, J., 2009. The credit rating crisis. NBER Macroecon. Annu. 24, 161–207.

Berger, A., Bouwman, C.H.S., 2013. How does capital affect bank performance during financial crises? J. Financ. Econ. 109, 146–176.

Bernanke, B.S., 2010. Causes of the Recent Financial and Economic Crisis. Statement before the Financial Crisis Inquiry Commission, Washington D.C., September 2.

Bernanke, B.S., 2012. Some Reflections on the Crisis and the Policy Response. Speech at the Russell Sage Foundation and the Century Foundation Conference on "Rethinking Finance," New York.

Boot, A., Thakor, AV., 1993. Self-interested bank regulation. Am. Econ. Rev. 83, 206–212.

Boyson, N., Helwege, J., Jindra, J., 2013. Crises, liquidity shocks, and fire sales at financial institutions.' Working Paper, University of South Carolina.

Brunnermeier, M.K., 2009. Deciphering the liquidity and credit crunch 2007–2008. J. Econ. Perspect. 23, 77–100.

Campello, M., Giambona, E., Graham, J.R., Harvey, C.R., 2011. Access to liquidity and corporate investment in Europe during the financial crisis. Rev. Financ. 16, 323–346.

Campello, M., Graham, J.R., Harvey, C.R., 2010. The real effects of financial constraints: evidence from a financial crisis. J. Financ. Econ. 97, 470–487.

Cecchetti, S.G., 2008. Monetary Policy and the Financial Crisis of 2007-08. Working Paper.

Contessi, S., El-Ghazaly, H., 2011. Banking crises around the world: different governments, different responses. The Regional Economist 19, 11–16 Federal Reserve Bank of St. Louis.

Covitz, D., Liang, N., Suarez, G., 2013. The evolution of a financial crisis: collapse of the asset-backed commercial paper market. J. Financ. 68, 815–848.

Demyanyk, Y., Van Hemert, O., 2011. Understanding the subprime mortgage crisis. Rev. Financ. Stud. 24, 1848–1880.

Gennaioli, N., Shleifer, A., Vishny, R.W., 2012. Neglected risks, financial innovation, and financial fragility. J. Financ. Econ. 104, 452–468.

Goel, A., Song, F., Thakor, A.V., 2014. Correlated leverage and its ramifications. J. Financ. Intermed. 23, 2777–2817.

Gorton, G., Metrick, A., 2012. Getting up to speed on the financial crisis: a one-weekend reader's guide. J. Econ. Lit. L, 128–150.

Gorton, G.B., 2010. Slapped by the Invisible Hand: the Panic of 2007. Oxford University Press, Oxford and New York.

Fahlenbrach, R., Prilmeier, R., Stulz, R., 2012. This time is the same: using bank performance in 1998 to explain bank performance during the recent financial crisis. J. Financ. LXVII, 2139–2185.

Halfenhof, S., Lee, Seung J., Stebunovs, V., 2014. "The Credit Crunch and Fall in Employment During the Great Recession," FEDS Working Paper 201406, Finance and Economics Discussion Series, Federal Reserve Board, Washington, D.C., March 31.

Holt, J., 2009. A summary of the primary causes of the housing bubble and the resulting credit crisis. A non-technical paper. J. Bus. Enquiry 8, 120–129.

Independent Evaluation Office of the International Monetary Fund, 2011. IMF Performance in the Run-Up to the Financial and Economic Crisis: IMF Surveillance in 2004-07. International Monetary Fund.

International Monetary Fund, 2009. Global Financial Stability Report, October 2009: Navigating the Financial Challenges Ahead. International Monetary Fund, Washington, D.C.

International Monetary Fund, 2010. Global Financial Stability Report: Sovereigns, Funding, and Systemic Liquidity. International Monetary Fund, Washington, D.C.

Ivashina, V., Scharfstein, D., 2010. Bank lending during the financial crisis of 2008. J. Financ. Econ. 97, 319–338.

Jagannathan, R., Kapoor, M., Schaumburg, E., 2013. Causes of the great recession of 2007–09: the financial crisis was the symptom not the disease! J. Financ. Intermed. 22, 4–29.

Johnson, S., Kwak, J., 2010. 13 Bankers: The Wall Street Takeover and the Next Financial Meltdown. Random House, Pantheon Books, New York.

Kacperczyk, M., Schnabl, P., 2010. When safe proved risky: commercial paper during the financial crisis of 2007–2009. J. Econ. Perspect. 24, 29–50.

Kane, E., 1990. Principal-agent problems in S&L salvage. J. Financ. 45, 755–764.

Keys, B.J., Mukherjee, T., Seru, A., Vig, V., 2010. Did securitization lead to liax screening? Evidence from subprime loans. Q. J. Econ. 125, 307–362.

Liebowitz, S.J., 2008. Anatomy of a Train Wreck, Causes of the Mortgage Meltdown. Independent Policy Report, http://www.independent.org/pdf/policy_reports/2008-10-03-trainwreck.pdf.

Litan, R.E., Bailey, M.N., 2009. Fixing Finance: A Roadmap for Reform. Initiative on Business and Public Policy at Brookings, February.

Lo, A., 2012. Reading about the financial crisis: a twenty-one book review. J. Econ. Lit. L, 151–178.

Maddaloni, A., Peydró, J., 2011. Bank risk-taking, securitization, supervision, and low interest rates: evidence form the euro-area and the U.S. lending standards. Rev. Financ. Stud. 24, 2121–2165.

Marshall, J., 2009. The Financial Crisis in the U.S.: Key Events, Causes and Responses, Research Paper 09/34. House of Commons Library, April 22.

Mian, A., Rao, K., Sufi, A., 2013. Household balance sheets, consumption, and the economic slump. Q. J. Econ. 128, 1687–1726.

Mian, A., Sufi, A., 2009. The Consequences of Mortgage Credit Expansion: evidence from the U.S. mortgage default crisis. Q. J. Econ. 124, 1449–1496.

Puri, M., Rocholl, J., Steffen, S., 2011. Global retail lending in the aftermath of the U.S. financial crisis, distinguishing between supply and demand effects. J. Financ. Econ. 100, 556–578.

Purnanandam, A., 2011. Originate-to-distribute model and the subprime mortgage crisis. Rev. Financ. Stud. 24, 1881–1915.

Rajan, R.G., 2010. Fault Lines: How Hidden Fractures Still Threaten the World Economy. Princeton University Press, Princeton and Oxford.

Reinhart, C.M., Rogoff, K.S., 2009. This Time is Different: Eight Centuries of Financial Folly. Princeton University Press, Princeton, NJ.

Reinhart, C.M., Rogoff, K.S., 2008. Is the 2007 U.S. sub-prime financial crisis so different? An international historical comparison. Am. Econ. Rev. 98, 339–344.

Santos, J.A., 2011. Bank corporate loan pricing following the subprime crisis. Rev. Financ. Stud. 24, 1916–1943.

Shleifer, A., Vishny, R.W., 2011. Fire sales in finance and macroeconomics. J. Econ. Perspect. 25, 29–48.

Stiglitz, J.E., 2010. Free Fall. W.W. Norton and Company, New York.

Taylor, J.B., 2009. The Financial Crisis and the Policy Responses: An Empirical Analysis of What Went Wrong. Working Paper #14631, National Bureau of Economic Research.

Taylor, J.B., Williams, J.C., January 2009. A black swan in the money market. Am. Econ. J. Macroecon. 1, 58–83.

Thakor, A.V., 2012. Incentives to innovate and financial crises. J. Financ. Econ. 103, 130–148.

Thakor, A.V., 2015. Lending booms, smart bankers and financial crises. Am. Econ. Rev. 105, 305–309..

Thakor, A.V., forthcoming. The financial crisis of 2007–09: why did it happen and what did we learn?, Rev. Corp. Finan. Stud.

Tirole, J., 2012. Overcoming adverse selection: how public intervention can restore market functioning. Am. Econ. Rev. 102, 29–59.

Part VIII

Bank Regulation

Chapter 15

Objectives of Bank Regulation

"There have been three great inventions since the beginning of time: fire, the wheel, and central banking."

Will Rogers

GLOSSARY OF TERMS

Basis Point One hundredth of a percent.
BHC Bank Holding Company.
ECB European Central Bank, which is the central bank of Europe's single currency: the Euro. Its main task is to maintain the Euro's purchasing power, and hence price stability in the euro area.
FDIC Federal Deposit Insurance Corporation.
Federal Funds Market A market in which banks borrow and lend their cash-asset reserves for short durations.
FHLMC Federal Home Loan Mortgage Corporation.
FNMA Federal National Mortgage Association.
GAAP Generally Accepted Accounting Principles.
GNMA Government National Mortgage Association.
IMF International Monetary Fund.
LBO Leveraged Buyout, the highly leveraged purchase of a firm.
LDC Loans to Developing Countries.
LLR Lender of Last Resort.
NOW Negotiated Orders of Withdrawal, a deposit account.
OECD Organization for Economic Cooperation and Development.
OCC Office of the Comptroller of the Currency, an agency within the U.S. Treasury Department that charters and regulates national banks.
Regulatory Arbitrage Banks taking actions to avoid regulatory requirements.
SEC Securities and Exchange Commission, a regulatory body for capital markets in the United States.

INTRODUCTION

In the previous chapter, we discussed one aspect of bank regulation, namely, deposit insurance. In this chapter, we discuss bank regulation in a more general context, with attention to the objectives and incentive effects of regulation.

Public regulation of banking has a long and checkered history, with roots extending back to sovereigns who reserved to themselves the rights of coinage. By impressing their imprimatur on a flat piece of metal, a coin would be struck that would trade at a premium to the metal's intrinsic value. The premium derived from the monetary services provided by the coin, which in turn was enabled by the coin's managed scarcity and the authenticity of the coin's ingredients signaled by the imprimatur. The premium or monopoly profit earned from the coin, called seigniorage, was appropriated by the sovereign, owner of the imprimatur. Seigniorage was one of the more efficient modes of taxation.

Like coins, bank deposits provide monetary services, and they too are artificially scarce, even if their ingredients are altogether ephemeral. They also generate seigniorage, and this makes banks an obvious target of government regulation. But public regulation has encouraged circumventing adaptations on the part of the banks, which in turn has led to ever more intrusive forms of regulation. This dynamic, sometimes referred to as the regulatory dialectic, has led to more encompassing regulation.

Numerous rationales for regulation have been advanced including:

- protecting safety and soundness of an individual institution,
- protecting the stability of the financial system,
- fostering competition,
- consumer protection,
- credit allocation, and
- monetary control.

S. I. Greenbaum, A. V. Thakor & A. W. A. Boot: Contemporary Financial Intermediation, Third edition. http://dx.doi.org/10.1016/B978-0-12-405196-6.00015-X

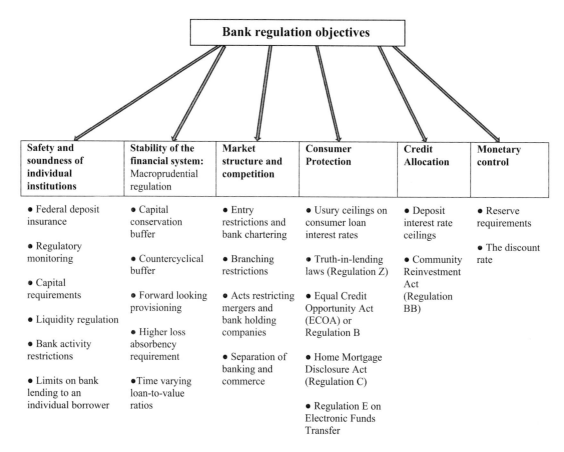

FIGURE 15.1 Objectives of Regulation.

The manifestations of government regulation include disclosure requirements, antidiscrimination restrictions, community reinvestment standards, cash-asset reserve requirements, minimum capital requirements, branching and bank holding company (BHC) restrictions, asset proscriptions, loans-to-one-borrower limitations, and deposit interest-rate ceilings, among others. Figure 15.1 summarizes the major objectives of regulation.

In the next section, we explain the most basic reason for bank regulation that arises from the governmental safety net (including deposit insurance). This is followed by a description of the agencies responsible for bank regulation, including those in the United States, Japan, the United Kingdom, and the European Union (EU). Subsequently, the various "categories" of regulation will be discussed: safety and soundness, macroprudential regulation, governmental regulation of bank market structure and competition, consumer protection, credit allocation, and monetary control. The history of regulation and regulatory reform are covered in Chapter 16.

THE ESSENCE OF BANK REGULATION

The stability of a financial system is of crucial importance for the smooth operations of the real economy. Several examples of financial crises, including the global financial crisis of 2007–2009, demonstrate how costly bank failures are for the real economy (see Chapter 14). The safety and soundness of individual institutions is thus important, but thinking beyond individual institutions – focusing on the stability of the financial system at large – is paramount. Financial crises typically involve stress in several institutions all at once. This explains why we highlight both the safety and soundness of individual institutions and the stability of the financial system. One view is more micro, focusing on an individual institution, and the other is more macro, looking at the system.

Chapter 14 on financial crises discusses ways in which these two views are often related – an individual bank failure may trigger problems in other banks and thus in the "system" through contagion. In any case, both safeguarding the safety and soundness of individual institutions and the stability of the system are foremost objectives of bank regulation.

To illustrate the essence of bank regulation and safety concerns, consider the provisioning of a governmental "safety net" for banks in the form of a lender-of-last-resort (LLR) facility, deposit insurance, or other guarantees. These create the possibility of exploitation of the government by the banks.[1] This moral hazard necessitates a response if the safety net is to remain viable, and the response is normally some form of public regulation.

The Primitive Banker without a Governmental Safety Net

Recall the goldsmith of Chapter 3 who evolved into a fractional reserve banker by printing warehouse receipts in excess of his or her gold holdings. The earnings on loans in that setting were seigniorage, a monopoly profit on the production of money in the form of receipts.[2] Now consider this same monopolist goldsmith confronted by a nascent central bank. Suppose the goldsmith's stock of gold has been purchased by the central bank in exchange for noninterest-bearing demand deposits at the central bank, and the central bank has in turn sold the gold in order to purchase interest-bearing government securities.[3] Balance sheets might appear as follows:

Central Bank		Goldsmith	
Government Securities	Deposits (Goldsmith's)	Deposits at Central Bank	Receipts
150	150	150	1,000
		Loans	
		850	

First, notice that the 150 in deposits at the central bank are the voluntary cash asset reserves of the goldsmith. These are optimal in light of the goldsmith's decision to circulate receipts of 850 in excess of liquid asset holdings. Second, notice that supporting the 1000 in goldsmith receipt liabilities is 1000 in collateral, 850 in the form of earning assets, and 150 in deposits at the central bank.

Thus, the seigniorage on the receipts money is shared between the goldsmith in the form of lower earnings and the central bank in the form of government securities earnings. The sharing is determined, to a first approximation, by the goldsmith's decision about how many excess receipts to circulate by making loans. This decision presumably reflects the goldsmith's own risk-taking preferences. Notably, the central bank does *not* dictate a minimum fraction of deposits to be held at the central bank to back the goldsmith's receipt liabilities. Hence, there is no legal cash-asset reserve requirement.

The Governmental Safety Net and Moral Hazard

Now, in recognition of the goldsmith's vulnerability to bank runs (see Chapter 2), let the central bank institute have an LLR facility. For concreteness, assume that the central bank stands ready to lend without limit to the goldsmith against performing (but illiquid) loan collateral at an interest rate of say 1 or 2% above the risk-free rate. Let us further assume that the volume of goldsmith receipts remains fixed. We can think of the volume of receipts as the monetary policy indicator, and

1. See, for example, Freixas (2010) and Kane (2014). The literature dealing with the economics of bank regulation is reviewed by Bhattacharya et al. (1998).
2. Others could enter the business, of course, and drive down the profit, but even the first entrant could expand until the fear of withdrawals called a halt. In any case, owing to consideration of withdrawal risk, proliferation of receipts can be expected to terminate before the pressure on spreads has eliminated all seigniorage.
3. This would require that the goldsmith's customers accept deposits at other institutions or currency in lieu of the gold originally deposited. But this is not quite as bizarre as it might at first appear. U.S. bank deposits were (not easily) redeemable in gold until 1972 when President Nixon severed the last official link between gold and dollars. Few today seem to be aware or concerned. When President Reagan was elected in 1980, he appointed a commission to study the possibility of a return to the gold standard, but the idea soon died.

the central bank can do *open market operations* (purchases and sales of government securities) to offset the bank's possible inclination to expand receipts as a result of the introduction of the LLR facility.[4]

Now the question is: How does the introduction of the LLR facility affect the bank's choice of reserve ratio, or to put it differently, how does the introduction of the LLR affect the bank's decision as to how many loans to make? Clearly, since the LLR represents an additional source of liquidity for the goldsmith, there is a diminished need to hold nonearning central bank deposits.

The goldsmith/bank will therefore increase its lending, which will temporarily increase the volume of receipts outstanding. The central bank will feel compelled to sell government securities in order to restore the amount of receipts to 1000.[5]

If we look at the new balance sheets, after the introduction of the LLR, we might find the following:

Central Bank		Goldsmith	
Government Securities	Deposits (Goldsmith's)	Deposits at Central Bank	Receipts
100	100	100	1000
		Loans	
		900	

Thus, the introduction of the LLR facility resulted in 50 of earning assets being shifted from the central bank to the goldsmith. This redistribution of earning assets is tantamount to a transfer of seigniorage from the government to the privately owned fractional-reserve goldsmith/bank, and is symptomatic of the moral hazard inherent in the LLR facility. The central bank provides the privately owned banks with a new layer of protection, the LLR facility, and because of its more secure position the goldsmith/bank sheds some of its own protection (cash assets) in order to expand earnings. But the expanded earnings of the goldsmith come, at least partly, at the expense of the central bank. From the central bank's viewpoint, this is clearly an unintended and exploitative side-effect of the LLR facility. And if carried far enough, all of the goldsmith's withdrawal or liquidity risk (see Chapter 6) will be transferred to the central bank. A private-sector risk of banking will have been nationalized, and all seigniorage will be transferred to the goldsmiths/banks. From an immediate safety and soundness perspective (or stability perspective) the LLR facility helps in reducing the goldsmith's vulnerability to bank runs but it comes at a cost: the goldsmith may exploit the LLR facility.

Regulatory Response to Moral Hazard

This moral hazard threatens the viability of the LLR, and it therefore evokes an adaptive response by the central bank in the form of restrictions on bank behavior, such as legal cash-asset reserve requirements. These, together with sanctions for their violation, have clear analogs in private contracting. A fire insurance policy typically reduces the vigilance of the insured and thereby shifts additional risk to the insurer. The insurer reacts by requiring that the insured maintain minimum safety standards, and violations void the insurance coverage. In the case of deposit-taking banks, a large part of public regulation can be explained as protective responses to the moral hazards arising from safety-net provisions provided by the government. The most important among these are the LLR facility, deposit insurance, protection of the payments system, and the too-big-to-fail policy.[6] All of these create moral hazards that shift costs and risks from the private banks to the public (central bank) and, therefore, elicit restrictions on bank behavior designed to limit such exploitation.

The key of this theory of bank regulation is that the potential for deregulation is intricately tied to the span of the safety net. Deregulation, beyond the elimination of redundancies, requires *pari passu* shrinkage of the safety net that prompted the regulation. This nexus is inescapable, and deregulation rhetoric that ignores the trade-off is just that. The problem is that the (perceived) immense costs of bank failure and instability give rise to government bailout guarantees which for that very same reason cannot be shrunk. Recent regulatory initiatives try to counter this inevitability by attempting to contain the public cost of bank failures. The Dodd–Frank Act and Volcker Rule discussed in the next chapter are attempts in that direction.

---

4. The assumption of a fixed volume of receipts is for simplicity only and does not compromise the basic argument.

5. The central bank's sale of its U.S. government securities extinguishes its deposit liabilities and thereby reduces the goldsmith's liquid assets. This prompts the goldsmith to reduce loans until the original 1000 in receipts is re-established.

6. A concept closely related to "too-big-to-fail" is "too-many-to-fail." When too many banks are likely to fail, the regulator is inclined to bail out a lot of them. See Acharya and Yorulmazer (2007).

THE AGENCIES OF BANK REGULATION

Paralleling the fragmented structure of the financial services industry is a similarly fragmented collection of public regulatory agencies. Responsibilities are organized primarily along national lines with substantial differences with respect to their regulatory frameworks. In a large majority of countries (63%), central banks maintain supervisory powers over banks. In 27% of countries, bank supervision is delegated to special supervisory agencies outside the central bank. In 4% of countries, multiple bank supervisory agencies exist but other arrangements are also possible (World Bank, 2013).[7]

Typically, the bank supervisory agency has multiple mandates (see Figure 15.2). It may include not just supervision and maintaining systemic stability, but also prevention of financial crime such as anti-money laundering and combating financing of terrorism, bank restructuring and resolution, market conduct, consumer protection, and competition and antitrust policy. But a great diversity is observed: multiple intuitions may exist and also bank supervisory powers might be distributed over different agencies. A separate deposit insurance agency may exist, but it can also be a part of the central bank (in 18% countries with explicit deposit insurance) but it is rarely a part of a bank supervisory agency (2% of countries) or even a part of the Ministry of Finance (1% of countries).

Via several multilateral organizations, attempts are made to create a more international overlay. Institutions like the Financial Stability Board (FSB), IMF, and the BIS seek to stimulate harmonization and go beyond local arrangements. In the EU, the common currency (the Euro) – and particularly the crisis surrounding it – has led to attempts to move to a pan-European supervision for key financial institutions.

The Regulatory Landscape in the United States

In the United States each major fragment of the industry has its own dedicated regulatory agency, often duplicated at state and federal levels. For example, commercial banks, thrifts, and credit unions can be chartered (licensed) at either the state or the federal level. Therefore, each state will have a governmental agency charged with licensing, examining, supervising, and regulating thrifts, credit unions, and commercial banks. Likewise, the federal government licenses, regulates, supervises, and insures institutions. And deposit insurance is managed by a federal agency, the Federal Deposit Insurance Corporation (FDIC). The financial crisis has led to some attempts to strengthen the role of the federal government in supervising banks with a more explicit mandate for the Federal Reserve. Life and casualty insurance companies are regulated principally at the state level, but recent failures, with effects that spilled across state borders, have evoked calls for more coordination of insurance regulation at the federal level. Even in the securities business, where the Securities and Exchange Commission (SEC) dominates, corporations must seek approval of the states in which they are incorporated when issuing equity or debt securities.[8]

In this section, we discuss the agencies that regulate commercial banks. The complexity and fragmentation should be clear, even though we address only a smallish slice of the financial services industry.

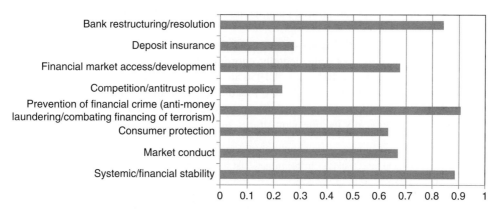

FIGURE 15.2   Mandates of the Bank Supervisory Agency. *(Source: World Bank (2013), bars present a proportion of countries where a bank supervisory agency has a specified mandate).*

---

7. See Čihák et al. (2013), and Barth et al. (2001, 2003, 2008, 2013).
8. Futures have their own dedicated federal regulatory agency, the Commodities Futures Trading Commission (CFTC).

Dual banking in the United States means that a bank can be licensed by either the federal government (the OCC), or by the state in which it is domiciled.[9] Even state-chartered commercial banks are likely to be regulated by at least two federal bank regulatory agencies since they are required to satisfy the Federal Reserve's cash-asset reserve requirements, and they are almost universally insured by the FDIC. National banks are subject to regulation by three or more federal agencies. A distinction is typically drawn between regulation, the setting of rules, and supervision, which is monitoring compliance. The latter subsumes examinations and related activities. All of the federal bank regulatory agencies – the OCC, the Federal Reserve, and the FDIC, as well as the state banking agencies – have both regulatory and supervisory responsibilities.[10]

Office of the Comptroller of the Currency (OCC)

Lodged within the U.S. Treasury Department, the OCC historically played an important role as a federal bank regulatory agency. It was created pursuant to the National Bank Act of 1864 for the purpose of chartering and regulating "national banks." At the time, virtually all banks in the United States were state chartered and state regulated. Indeed, the federal government had been out of the business of regulating banks since the early 1830s when President Andrew Jackson stifled the rechartering of the Second Bank of the United States.[11]

Recall that 1864 was the time of the Civil War, and a national banking system was seen as an opportunity to provide a marker for Union bonds that were being sold in record amounts to finance the hostilities. So the National Bank Act imposed a 5% tax on the liabilities of state-chartered banks and commenced the chartering of national banks, which were required to hold U.S. government securities to satisfy reserve requirements. Deposits were far less important than bank notes at the time both as a means of payment and as a financing instrument of banks. The OCC's primary responsibility was the chartering and supervision of national banks which are a minority among commercial banks, but they tend to be the larger banks.

Following the global financial crisis of 2007–2009 (the Great Recession), some changes have been made to the OCC. The Dodd–Frank Act has dissolved the Office of Thrift Supervision and shifted its responsibilities to the OCC as the charterer of savings and loans, and the Fed as the overseer of thrift holding companies. Simultaneously, the Federal Reserve got additional powers over systemically significant financial institutions (SIFIs), which might effectively reduce the importance of the OCC.

The Federal System

The Federal Reserve System was established in 1913 following a searching investigation prompted by a particularly disruptive financial panic in 1907. The principal purpose of the Federal Reserve was to provide LLR services to a banking system vulnerable to liquidity crises.[12] As LLR, the Federal Reserve stands ready to lend for short periods to liquidity-strapped banks against eligible collateral. So from the very outset, the Federal Reserve used cash-asset reserve requirements to deter banks from substituting the liquidity of the LLR facility for previously held cash assets.

All national banks were required to be members of the Federal Reserve System, whereas membership was voluntary for state-chartered banks. Only in 1980 were all insured commercial banks compelled to meet the cash-asset reserve requirements of the Federal Reserve.

The Federal Reserve has been a remarkably successful regulatory agency in at least two senses. It has managed to remain relatively free of scandal and it has, not coincidentally, enormously expanded the scope of its regulatory turf. Perhaps most important in the latter regard were the BHC Act of 1956 and the Douglas Amendments thereto of 1970. These laws gave the Federal Reserve regulatory control over all BHCs. Practically every important bank in the United States is owned by a BHC, and the Federal Reserve has immense discretionary power over virtually every initiative taken by banks via their holding companies.[13] These typically include acquisitions and mergers both within and outside of banking. Explicit

---

9. Federally chartered banks are required to have "national" in their names, and state-chartered banks are prohibited from including "national" or N.A. (national association) in their names. Likewise, federally chartered thrifts are required to have "federal" in their names whereas their state-chartered counter parts are prohibited from using "federal" in their name.

10. For some regulations, however, a regulator may not be a supervisor. For example, the Federal Reserve sets truth-in-savings regulations for all deposit-taking institutions, but supervises mainly banks (and thrift holding companies).

11. For further reading on the early history of U.S. banking, see Lash (1987).

12. The Federal Reserve was also charged with providing a flexible currency, and this led to the Federal Reserve note in use.

13. The regulatory discretion derives from the vagueness of the legislative mandate. For example, in evaluating nonbank acquisitions by bank holding companies, the Federal Reserve is instructed to judge whether the contemplated acquisition is so closely related to banking as to be a "proper incident thereto." Some decry such vagueness as the hallmark of bad legislation. Others laud the ambiguity as a possible benefit in mitigating moral hazard problems.

permission is required from the Federal Reserve for each and every subsidiary formed or purchased by a BHC, and the criteria for approval leave broad scope for discretion by the Federal Reserve. No wonder the chairman of the Federal Reserve is sometimes described as the second most powerful person in the United States.

The financial crisis of 2007–2009 led to a further expansion in the role of the Federal Reserve, as it became involved in providing liquidity and capital to a vast array of nondepository, uninsured institutions in the shadow-banking system like mutual funds, investment banks, and insurance companies (see Chapter 12 for a discussion of shadow banking). The Federal Reserve's vast regulatory discretion together with its power to influence capital markets places it first among the many public regulators of financial institutions. The major weaknesses in the U.S. supervisory structure of the financial system that were revealed by the 2007–2009 financial crisis – specifically the inefficiency of supervising interconnected depository institutions and shadow banks in different regulatory silos – have led to a further clarification (and strengthening) of the mandate of the Federal Reserve. In particular, the Federal Reserve got additional oversight responsibilities for SIFIs, regardless of whether these SIFIs are commercial banks or not.

The Consumer Financial Protection Bureau (CFPB)

The global financial crisis involved banks making loans (mostly home mortgage loans) to borrowers who were ill-equipped to repay them. This was part of a general trend of increasingly lax lending standards that were discussed in the Introduction to this book. This practice came to be called "predatory lending", which is meant to imply that uninformed (and financially unsophisticated) borrowers were lured into taking unaffordable mortgages through the aggressive and misleading sales tactics of banks.[14] As a response, the CFPB was established as an independent agency by the Dodd–Frank Act with a task of consumer protection in the field of mortgages, credit cards, and financial products and services at large. The CFPB is located inside the Federal Reserve but is independent of it.

The Federal Deposit Insurance Corporation (FDIC)

The FDIC was established during the Great Depression in 1933. As with its predecessors, there was profound political ambivalence about government deposit insurance. Despite a collapsing banking industry and a similarly compelling need to restore public trust, President Roosevelt spoke out strongly against federal deposit insurance for the very reasons we now use to explain recent S&L and bank losses. The patrician Roosevelt was a half century ahead of his time. Nevertheless, he ultimately signed the Banking Act of 1933 that provided federal insurance of bank deposits for the first time in U.S. history, and with it came the FDIC.[15] The original plan called for protections of the first $2500 in each bank account, but over the years coverage has expanded to $250,000.[16]

In addition to the explicit insurance, the FDIC has often remunerated depositors with balances in excess of the stated limit so that very few "uninsured" depositors since 1933 have lost money owing to bank or S&L failures. This second layer of implicit insurance coverage is provided at the discretion of the FDIC and is typically rationalized in one of two ways. It is either less costly to compensate all rather than some, or imposing losses on some is too destabilizing to the financial system and the failed bank. This is of value since liquidation adds costs to compensate uninsured depositors and preserve the bank as an ongoing entity, possibly as a part of another bank.

These arguments can be self-serving, and specious too. Nevertheless, for many years the *modus operandi* worked acceptably. Deposit insurance premiums were low (6–12 basis points) per annum, levied against insured as well as uninsured domestic deposits. Bank failures were few (averaging less than 10 per year before 1975, and almost all of these were small banks), and the deposit insurance funds (the FDIC's and the FSLIC's) grew steadily, until the 1980s. The FDIC was a regulatory backwater during most of this time, rarely seen or heard from. Its anonymity was testimony to its success.

This changed when bank failures ran at 200 per year in the late 1980s, with very large banks represented among the failed. These traumas led to insurance premia rising to about 25 basis points in 1993. The FDIC Combined deposit

---

14. Aggressive lending practices due to lax mortgage standards are perceived as one of the causes for the subprime crisis (Keys et al., 2010). However, Agarwal et al. (2014) find limited support for the theory that predatory lending triggered the subprime mortgage crisis. Thus, there is no consensus on this issue.

15. Some (see Golembe (1960)) prefer to describe the program as a government guarantee rather than insurance since the program is ultimately backed by the government's power to tax rather than by a finite pool of resources contributed by the insured.

16. Coverage of collectively owned accounts (e.g., the deposit of a pension fund) can be far greater than $250,000. These accounts are protected for $250,000 multiplied by the number of participants in the collective.

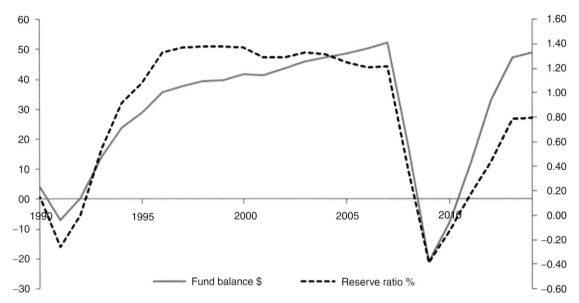

FIGURE 15.3 FDIC Combined Deposit Insurance Fund (Fund Balance in Billions of Dollars: Left Axis; Reserve Ratio in % on the Right Axis). *(Source: FDIC).*

insurance funds was in deficit in 1991, but recovered in 1992, and since then grew steadily until the global financial crisis. The FDIC's measure of "well being" is its fund balance as a percentage of the total deposits insured. It is called the *reserve ratio,* defined as:

$$\text{Reserve Ratio for a year} = \frac{\text{Fourth-Quarter Fund Balance}}{\text{Fourth-Quarter Estimated Insured Deposits}}$$

Figure 15.3 shows the behavior of the reserve ratio through time. Regulation requires that the designated (minimum) reserve ratio is 1.25%. The deposit insurance assessment rate during 2006 ranged between 0% and 0.27%, with most banks paying no deposit insurance premiums and the average annual assessment at roughly 0.11%. The reserve ratio became negative during the global (or subprime) financial crisis in 2009 and 2010.

The Dodd–Frank Act has established a separate fund, the so-called *Orderly Liquidation Fund*, funds from which can be used in the case of liquidation of a large, complex financial company whose failure poses a systemic threat to financial stability in the United States.

The Financial Stability Oversight Council (FSOC)

The Dodd–Frank Act created the FSOC with the objective to have a more integral (macro) picture of the stability of the U.S. financial system. It seeks to identify risks to the financial stability of the United States, promote market discipline, and respond timely to the threats to the stability of the U.S. financial system. Council members include senior representatives of the major regulatory agencies. The FSOC is chaired by the Secretary of the Treasury and has a broad authority to monitor, analyze, and estimate risks in the U.S. financial system. It suggests to Congress and the Federal Reserve changes in the regulation of financial institutions or markets in order to mitigate systemic risk in the financial system. Its mandate is broad. For example, the FSOC (with a two-thirds super majority among its voting members) can place a nonbanking financial institution under the supervision of the Federal Reserve if it poses a serious threat to the stability of the U.S. financial system.

The Office of Financial Research (OFR)

The OFR was established by the Dodd–Frank Act within the Treasury Department to provide support to the Council and other bank regulatory agencies. The salaries within the OFR are exempted from the General Schedule pay rates that apply to the majority of the Federal employees in order to attract the most qualified personnel. Its director is appointed for a 6-year term and can issue subpoenas; that is, the director can issue orders to collect all data necessary to achieve the OFR's objectives.

Other Federal Agencies that Regulate Banks

Nonbank government agencies involved in banking include the Environmental Protection Agency, the Department of Labor, the Internal Revenue Service, and the Federal Bureau of Investigation (every cash transaction of $10,000 or more, with certain exceptions, must be reported to the FBI). Banks also face financial market regulators (like the FTCC) and the Department of Justice that can impose substantial fines for misbehavior. However, these agencies are less involved in the day-to-day operations of banks than the banking agencies.[17]

Noteworthy are also the SEC and the Antitrust Division of the Department of Justice. The former regulates the sale of debt and equity securities in public markets. The latter has the responsibility for administering antitrust laws in cases of bank mergers and acquisitions, and in cases of collusion and other anticompetitive behaviors.

The SEC has asserted itself also in the debate over bank accounting, e.g. the choice of GAAP accounting versus market value accounting. This is an SEC issue because it relates to financial reporting and disclosure to the financial market. We shall return to this issue later.

The Regulatory Landscape in Japan

Bank regulation in Japan falls under the scope of the Financial Services Agency. The Financial Services Agency is an external body of the Cabinet Office of Japan. Its goal is to safeguard the stability of Japan's financial system and protect depositors. In addition, it is also responsible for protection of insurance policyholders and securities investors, and the establishment of fair and transparent financial markets. Its tasks include financial system planning, policymaking, and supervision of financial institutions (i.e., banks, insurance companies, and financial markets participants). Its affairs also cover the review of accounting standards and the supervision of certified auditing firms and public accountants (see http://www.fsa.go.jp/en/index.html).

Deposit insurance in Japan is the responsibility of the Deposit Insurance Corporation of Japan (DICJ). The DICJ's main operations include deposit insurance operation (e.g., collection of insurance premium from insured financial institutions), failure resolution, capital injection, purchase of nonperforming loans, and pursuit of civil and criminal liability of managers of failed banks. Deposits for settlement and payment purposes are entirely covered by deposit insurance. Time deposits are covered up to the maximum amount of ¥ 10 million in principal plus accrued interests (www.dic.go.jp/english/index.html).

Although equipped primarily with the responsibility of monetary policy, the central bank of Japan – the Bank of Japan – also provides settlement services and is responsible for the stability of the financial system. It also acts as a LLR.[18]

The Regulatory Landscape in the United Kingdom

Before 2013, bank regulation in the United Kingdom was based on the tripartite system that involved three regulatory agencies: the Financial Services Authority (FSA), the Bank of England (the central bank of the UK), and the Treasury. The FSA was the main UK bank regulatory agency and was responsible for maintaining confidence and stability in the UK financial system. Its role also included consumer protection and the reduction of financial crime.

The inability to foresee the beginning of the global financial crisis in 2007 led to major regulatory changes in the United Kingdom. Following the enactment of the Financial Services Act (2012), the FSA was abolished and two new regulatory authorities, the Prudential Regulation Authority (PRA) and the Financial Conduct Authority (FCA), were created.

The FCA is responsible for financial markets and proper conduct of financial markets participants with an aim to protect consumers from abusive practices of financial firms. The FCA is an independent regulatory agency and is funded by charging fees to the members of the financial services industry that it regulates.

Substantial regulatory and supervisory powers were placed under the umbrella of the Bank of England. The PRA is, as a part of the Bank of England, responsible for the stability of the UK financial system. It regulates and supervises deposit taking institutions, insurance companies, and large investment firms. It is also responsible for appropriate protection of insurance policyholders.

In addition to the PRA, an independent Financial Policy Committee (FPC) was created as a subsidiary of the Bank of England. The primary objective of the FPC is to identify, monitor, and reduce systemic risk and safeguard the stability

---

17. In the Libor scandal and the misbehavior surrounding subprime mortgages (for some a primary cause of the global financial crisis) substantial fines were imposed. For example, Barclays was fined for its alleged role in the Libor scandal by the CFTC ($200 million), by the US Department of Justice ($160 million) and by the UK Financial Services Authority (£59.5 million). UBS was fined $1.5 billion in total for its involvement in the Libor scandal. Several major U.S. banks have been fined in the billions for their involvement in issues related to misrepresentation in subprime mortgages.
18. See Tamaki (2008).

of the UK financial system. It is responsible for the supervision of providers of financial market infrastructure and also helps the Government in its economic policy.

Earlier, the Banking Act of 2009 had already given the Bank of England substantial powers in dealing with bank failures. In particular, the Resolution Directorate within the Bank of England plays a key role within the Special Resolution Regime with tools to successfully restructure failing banks.

Deposit insurance in the United Kingdom was formally introduced by the 2000 Financial Services and Markets Act. It allocated responsibility to the Financial Services Compensation Scheme, an independent agency accountable to the regulators and to the Treasury with its directors appointed by the FCA and PRA. It covers £85,000 of deposits per person per bank but also £50,000 of investments and £50,000 of home finance instruments per person per bank. It also protects 90% of insurance claims with no upper limit.[19]

The Regulatory Landscape in the EU

Bank regulation and supervision in the EU was historically under the authority of domestic regulators. The global financial crisis showed that national regulation and supervision of banks was inadequate in the highly interconnected European banking market, especially in the euro area where the single currency (the Euro) led to a fast integration of the financial system. The regulatory overhaul in the EU has led to the establishment of a (proposed) common regulatory and supervisory framework in the EU, the so-called *Banking Union*. The Banking union is built on a single rulebook for financial institutions in the EU and comprises the *Single Supervisory Mechanism* (SSM) and *the Single Resolution Mechanism* (SRM).

The single rulebook contains the legal framework of regulatory rules that all EU financial institutions must comply with. It legislates capital regulation, synchronizes rules for deposit insurance, and sets up the rules for bank regulation and prevention of bank failures.

The SSM gives the ECB the authority to supervise the largest banks in the Euro area. The national supervisors maintain supervision over the remaining – smaller – national banks, but they are subject to control from the ECB. The ECB monitors whether banks comply with the single rulebook (in particular, whether they are adequately capitalized) and is responsible to trigger early intervention into failing banks. The SSM became operational in 2014.

The SRM establishes a new, independent EU Agency called the *Single Resolution Board* to deal with failing banks within the EU. It also establishes the *Single Bank Resolution Fund* built up by contributions from banks in the EU. The Single Resolution Board will use resolution tools granted by the SRM and the funds from the Single Bank Resolution Fund to effectively deal with failures of national banks and of cross-border banks. The SRM will become fully operational starting January 1, 2016.

The proposed Banking Union is a product of the massive crisis surrounding the Euro. Several governments were not able to contain deficits and be sufficiently competitive to comply with rules set for the single currency. Domestic banks with substantial exposure on the sovereign bonds of their countries were part of the general confidence crisis. The Banking Union seeks to strengthen banks in Europe and in doing so also strengthen the foundation for the single currency. How this will evolve will be a big unknown as the Euro area consists of 19 countries with strong domestic mandates that may conflict with the coordination that a currency union demands.

The Banking Union follows an earlier attempt to integrate the European financial sector. In 2008, the EU established the *European System of Financial Supervision* (ESFS) consisting of three new *European Supervisory Authorities* (ESAs) – for banking, insurance and financial markets – and the *European Systemic Risk Board* (ESRB).[20] The ESRB is responsible for macroprudential surveillance of the financial system in the EU, somewhat like the Financial Stability Oversight Council in the United States. Its tasks include prevention of systemic risk, safeguarding financial stability, and the smooth operation of the financial sector in support of the real economy.

The three European supervisory authorities – the *European Banking Authority* (EBA), the *European Insurance and Occupational Pensions Authority* (EIOPA), the *European Securities and Markets Authority* (ESMA) – are three independent regulatory agencies, each responsible for supervision in a particular industry. But contrary to the ECB-linked Banking Union, each ESA primarily has "soft" powers, meaning that its role is mainly to provide coordination. The EBA is responsible for determining the uniform regulatory and supervisory technical standards, guidelines and best practices and their

---

19. The regulatory overhaul after the crisis in the UK also included the abolishment of the competition agencies Office of Fair Trading and the Competition Commission. Their tasks were largely merged into a single newly established agency, the Competition and Markets Authority.

20. The ESAs were established by Regulations (EU) No 1093/2010, 1094/2010, and 1095/2010 of the European Parliament and of the Council of 24 November 2010; OJ of 15 December 2010, L 331, 12–119.

applications across the EU.[21] The EBA can provide opinions to the European Parliament, the Council, and the European Commission. The EBA also acts as a mediator to resolve potential conflicts between national supervisors and acts as a coordinator in emergency situations.[22] How the ESAs and ESRB fit within the Banking Union is still open to debate. Several issues may come up, including the different geographic reach (the ESAs and ESRB are linked to the 28 EU member states; the Banking Union primarily addresses the 18 Euro members), and also turf battles between the EU and the ECB are possible (the Banking Union is linked to the ECB while ESAs and ESRB "belong" to the EU). In any case, the "European project" is work in progress.

International coordination

Following the 2007–2009 financial crisis, international coordination has gained additional momentum. Agencies such as the Basel Committee, the FSB and the G-20 – comprising government leaders of the largest 20 economies in the world – have urged the adoption of initiatives to promote global financial stability. In the following sections, we will discuss the Basel Committee that plays a key role in setting capital requirements around the globe. The FSB consists of senior policymakers from Ministries of Finance, Central Banks, and supervisory and regulatory bodies and promotes international financial stability "by coordinating national financial authorities and international standard-setting bodies as they work toward developing strong regulatory, supervisory and other financial sector policies. It fosters a level playing field by encouraging coherent implementation of these policies across sectors and jurisdictions."[23] The FSB is closely linked to the G-20.

Apart from these bodies, the *International Monetary Fund* (IMF) plays an important role in safeguarding financial and economic stability across the world.

SAFETY AND SOUNDNESS REGULATION

Bank regulation seeks to promote the "safe and sound" operation of banks, and in tandem preserve the stability of the financial system. The latter has a macro-prudential focus that is the subject of the next section. We focus first on the safety and soundness of individual financial institutions. In Chapter 12, we explained how deposit insurance creates a risk-inducing moral hazard. Thus, restrictive regulations are deployed to mitigate these endogenous risks that arise due to the government safety net. Government safety net includes the explicit deposit insurance scheme (see the discussion of the FDIC in the United States and deposit insurance arrangements in the previous section) but also consists of implicit government guarantees to financial institutions that are deemed too big (or important) to fail. Figure 15.4 summarizes the types of safety regulation. Redundancy in these regulations recognizes the difficulty of achieving safety objectives, especially when the regulated institutions can circumvent these regulations.

Regulatory Monitoring

The periodic examination of banks by public regulatory agencies is a central part of regulation in the United States. Indeed, each of the three federal bank regulatory agencies employs bank examiners and each of the state banking agencies has theirs as well.

Although bank examiners have overlapping jurisdictions, there is a formal division of labor. The OCC examines all national banks, the Federal Reserve all state-chartered Federal Reserve member banks (and BHCs), and all remaining FDIC insured banks.[24] Of course, the states are responsible for examining all state-chartered banks, too. Often state and federal agencies accept each other's exams. Sometimes they examine jointly. There is some coordination, along with considerable redundancy. Examination details in the U.S. Regulatory Rating System are discussed below.

A uniform interagency bank rating system known as CAMEL (capital adequacy (C), asset quality (A), management ability (M), earning quality (E), liquidity level (L)) was adopted in 1978. In 1997, a sixth factor, "Sensitivity to Market

21. Bank regulation in the EU was often first introduced as EU Directive, which member states are then obligated to introduce in their national legislation but are given some discretion in its implementation. To achieve a harmonized regulatory framework, the EBA's task is to draft legal acts, Binding Technical Standards, that are legally binding and directly applicable in EU countries (after being adopted by the European Commission in the form of Regulation or Decision).
22. The predecessors of the ESA's were EU committees in charge of harmonizing financial sector rule making and oversight practices. The ESA's and ESRB came into existence as recommendations of the so-called de Larosière Committee that had been installed by the EU immediately at the onset of the global financial crisis in 2008 (see European Commission (2014)).
23. See http://www.financialstabilityboard.org/about/.
24. The new responsibilities of the Federal Reserve for SIFIs (systemically important financial institutions) following the 2007–2009 financial crisis has created more overlap in the regulatory system.

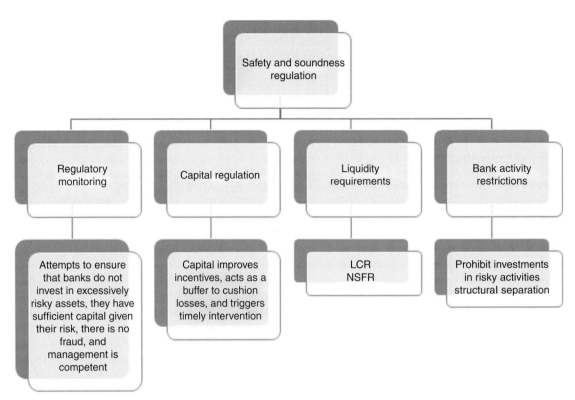

FIGURE 15.4 Types of Safety and Soundness Regulation. *(Source: FDIC Historical Statistics on Banking).*

Risk" (S), was added, to make it CAMELS. None of these factors is judged in isolation. For example, what is considered acceptable asset quality will depend on how much capital the bank has.

- *Capital Adequacy*: The bank's capital is evaluated on the basis of both the bank's sizes as well as the composition of its assets and liabilities, both on- and off-balance sheet. We will have more to say about capital shortly.
- *Asset Quality*: Examiners assess the credit risks in the various loans in the bank's portfolio and classify these loans as: good, substandard, doubtful, or loss.
- *Management Ability*: Examiners attempt to gauge not only the bank's management but also its board of directors. Competence, management acumen, integrity, and willingness to comply with banking regulations are some of the factors assessed.[25]
- *Earnings*: There is an evaluation of the earnings as well as their level relative to peers. One objective is to assess the impact of internally generated funds on the bank's capital.
- *Liquidity*: Regulators assess liquidity by examining credit conditions, deposit volatility, loan commitments, and other contingent claims against the bank, capital, current stock of liquid assets, and the bank's perceived ability to raise funds on short notice.
- *Sensitivity to Market Risk*: Regulators assess how sensitive the bank's asset, liability, and net worth values are to changes in market condition like interest rates.

Until recently, regulatory examinations served in lieu of external audits for most banks. However, bank examinations are not the equivalent of an external audit. External audits focus on financial reporting and consistency with GAAP and are put to external as well as internal use. Bank examinations focus on asset quality and the effectiveness of monitoring and are for internal use exclusively. Indeed, it is illegal to disclose bank examinations (e.g., CAMELS ratings) outside the bank. Both regulatory exams and external audits also seek to uncover fraud, but some would say with mixed success.[26]

---

25. Gaul and Palvia (2013) find that a weak CAMELS rating M for management ability is strongly associated with poor accounting returns. Their study suggests that regulatory management assessment is informative (see also DeYoung et al. (2001)).

26. Banks and bank holding companies have been required to have audits if the number of shareholders exceed 500, but these are SEC requirements. Only with the 1991 Federal Deposit Insurance Corporation Improvement Act (FDICIA) were banks (holding companies) with assets exceeding $500 million required to have external audits (74 Fed. Reg. 35745, July 20, 2009).

The Federal Deposit Insurance Corporation Improvement Act (FDICIA) of 1991 mandates annual, full-scope examinations of banks by regulators. These regulatory examinations and audits are predicated on the assumed informativeness of ratings-based classifications resulting from the examinations in terms of their ability to reveal the bank's true financial health.

The result of the bank's regulatory examination are reported to the bank's board of directors, with subsequent dialog between the examiners and directors to clarify issues and to discuss steps for dealing with the problems uncovered by the examination. The examination report is then submitted to the supervisory authorities whose relationship with the bank is guided by the findings of the report.

Supervisors can impose wide-ranging sanctions for improper actions by the management or the board. Advice is followed by warnings, then cease and desist orders, in which a supervisor requests that the management halts an activity or does not repeat it in the future, or else faces legal action. Management can be discharged. Directors can be fined, discharged, and barred from banking. The bank can be put into conservatorship or into receivership. Directors and officers can be sued civilly and/or criminally for failure to discharge fiduciary responsibilities, for negligence, gross negligence, or criminal negligence. The regulators' power to impose sanctions is expansive.

How informative CAMELS ratings are in assessing a bank's financial condition is an open question. It seems plausible that during stable periods in the banking industry, these ratings are more informative about banks' financial conditions than during times of crises when some of the factors in CAMELS may be less relevant.[27]

The Federal Reserve uses a wider rating system for the BHCs, named RFI/C(D), an acronyms derived from the main components of the rating systems: risk management (R), financial condition (F), potential impact (I) of the parent company and non-depository subsidiaries, and the depository institutions (D) component (see Section 4070 of the BHC Supervision Manual, Federal Reserve Board, 2014a). Risk management (R) measures the effectiveness of BHC's risk management and controls and is constructed based on four subcomponents: board and senior management oversight, risk monitoring and management information systems, internal controls, and policies, procedures, and limits. Financial condition (F) measures the stability of a BHC through the assessment of earnings, capital, liquidity, and asset quality. Impact (I) assesses the downside risk of nondepository entities within a BHC on the subsidiary depository institution. The depository institution (D) component is computed based on the CAMEL rating of the subsidiary depository institution. All the ratings are then combined in the composite rating (C).

The largest and systemically important BHCs are also subject to the additional comprehensive capital analysis and review (CCAR) in which the Federal Reserve assesses (based in part on stress tests) whether they have sufficient capital and sufficiently robust risk-management practices to sustain prolonged periods of financial distress (see Federal Reserve Board, 2014b).

Supervisory processes differ substantially across countries. To improve supervision across the international banking system, The Basel Committee on Banking Supervision (BCBS, 2012) provides key principles for effective banking supervision. Key principles address supervisory powers, responsibilities, and functions and include supervisory expectations of bank behavior focusing on good corporate governance, risk management, capital adequacy, and compliance with supervisory standards. For example, an important supervisory principle is to monitor concentration risk and large exposure limits. That is, a bank may become exposed excessively to a single large borrower or to a group of connected borrowers. The supervisor needs to carefully monitor whether banks adequately identify, measure, and control concentration risks.

The effectiveness of safety and soundness regulation cannot be taken for granted. Institutions can take actions to undermine it. Such actions are referred to as regulatory arbitrage. An example of regulatory arbitrage is how the once imposed deposit interest-rate ceilings were bypassed by disintermediation (see the box below).

Deposit Interest-Rate Ceilings

Deposit interest-rate ceilings, enforced via Regulation Q, came into existence with the Banking Act of 1933. Payment of interest on demand deposits was prohibited and the Federal Reserve was authorized to impose ceilings on the interest rates paid on time and savings deposits by member banks. *Regulation Q* ("Reg Q" for short) was subsequently extended to all FDIC-insured banks.

The Reg Q ceilings lowered deposit costs and thereby offset unpopular deposit insurance premiums. Deposit interest-rate ceilings were defended on two grounds. First, it was thought that the incentives of banks to invest in risky assets would be weakened, and bank's profits would be both higher and less volatile. Second, it was believed that if interest rates were not restricted, larger banks in the money centers would attract deposits away from rural areas.

---

27. This is precisely what Gasbarro et al. (2002) found for Indonesian banks during the Southeast Asian financial crisis. While most of the CAMELS variables were informative during Indonesia's stable economic periods, the informativeness of the CAMELS variables declined during crisis periods.

Whether deposit interest-rate ceilings can achieve either of these objectives depends on the effectiveness of *nonprice* competition. When a bank wishes to attract more deposits and finds the Reg Q ceilings binding, it will compete on other dimensions. During periods in which Reg Q ceilings were binding (such as 1969–1970, 1973–1974, and 1978–1980), banks engaged in nonprice competition, ranging from merchandise giveaways to subsidized cash-management services.[28]

Of course, the fact that banks and other depository institutions could circumvent deposit interest-rate ceilings does not mean that the ceilings were without effect. The nonprice competition induced by the ceilings distorted the allocation of resources. To see this, note that banks could have offered nonprice inducements to depositors even in the absence of ceilings, and it is possible that the *unconstrained* optimal allocation involves both the payment of explicit interest and the provision of other services to depositors. But when the Reg Q ceiling is binding, *more* resources will be allocated to the provision of these ancillary services, and this additional allocation represents an almost certainly inefficient distortion. Moreover, like reserve requirements, Reg Q ceilings induced innovation of new liability instruments. Eurodollar deposit growth was stimulated by both reserve requirements and Reg Q.

By 1986, virtually all deposit interest ceilings were phased out.[29] Massive deposit outflows (disintermediation) due to the increasing disparity between market interest rates and the Reg Q ceilings were one justification for the phaseout (Mertens (2008)).

Capital Requirements

In book-value terms, capital is the sum of retained earnings and the purchase price of outstanding common stock, whereas in market value terms it is the current market price per share multiplied by the total number of shares outstanding. For regulatory purposes, however, capital is defined also to include general, but not specific, *loan loss reserves,* permanent preferred stock, and certain *long-term debt.*[30] Loan loss reserves are capital that has been earmarked to absorb future loan losses; when these losses occur, they are charged against the loan loss reserve account rather than against current earnings. This practice of reserving for losses smooths the time pattern of income. As a form of capital, loan loss reserves improve the value of the bank's creditors' claims. Similarly, long-term debt (which includes mainly subordinated notes and debentures) is junior to deposits, so that a greater amount of long-term debt on the bank's balance sheet implies greater protection for depositors. Hence, the regulatory rationale for including loan loss reserves and long-term debt in bank capital is that both are junior to deposits, and therefore serve to protect the depositors as well as the deposit insurer. As we will see, more recently, following the global financial crisis, the definition of capital is narrowing and tends to exclude debt claims. The rationale is that debt, in whatever form, may cause financial distress, and ultimately threaten stability. Federal bank regulators make a distinction between Tier-1 and Tier-2 capital. Capital requirements apply to total (Tier-1 plus Tier-2) capital, with an upper limit on the amount of Tier-2 capital contributing to the total. In the box below, these two types of capital are defined.

Tier-1 and Tier-2 Capital

Tier-1 (Core) Capital:
- Common Stock
- Retained Earnings
- Capital Surplus (amount received from sale of common stock or preferred stock in excess of par)
- Disclosed Capital Reserves (reserves set aside for cash dividends not declared plus amounts for unforeseen contingencies)

Tier-2 (Supplementary) Capital:
- Loan and Lease Loss Allowances
- Preferred Stock with Maturity of at Least 20 Years
- Subordinated Obligations (Both Stock and Debt) With an Original Average Maturity of at Least 7 Years
- Undisclosed Capital Reserves
- Hybrid Capital Instruments (instruments that have debt and equity characteristics, but might be included in regulatory capital, e.g., preference shares, and convertible debt).

Total Capital:
Tier-1 Capital + Tier-2 Capital

---

28. Other manifestations of nonprice competition included oversupply of branches, automated teller machines (ATMs), and additional hours during which banks were kept open.

29. Banking institutions were prohibited from paying any interest on demand deposits until recently. However, the prohibition was of little consequence because consumer transaction accounts were classified as NOW or share draft accounts. Since NOW accounts were available to individuals, nonprofit entities, and public agencies, the prohibition on demand deposit interest payments applied only to business deposits. Banks might, however, provide their business customers with cash management, lockbox, payroll, and similar services without violating the interest payment prohibition. See Huber (1989).

30. Specific reserves are dedicated to a particular impaired asset, whereas general reserves are not assigned to identifiably impaired assets, and are therefore generally available.

Until the 1980s, legal cash-asset reserve requirements were a more important constraint on bank's balance sheets than capital requirements. To be sure, newly chartered banks had reasonably well-defined initial capital requirements, and the Federal Reserve Bank of New York had a capital standard that was similar to the present risk-related capital rules. Nevertheless, bank capital regulation was in striking contrast to thrift regulation where capital requirements had primacy over liquidity requirements as a regulatory desideratum.

This contrast reflected the traditional view that the principal risk in banking was withdrawal risk rather than credit risk, and the reverse was the presumption regarding thrifts. Commercial banks were designed to make short-term, self-liquidating business loans, financing trade, inventories, and receivables with highly predictable patterns of repayment. But LBO, LDC, commercial real estate, term lending, off-balance sheet activities, and BHC extensions into nonbank activities expanded the credit risk asset transformation of commercial banks.

The banks' expanded credit risk implied greater exposure of the governmental safety net, and the regulatory response was more stringent bank capital requirements. Bank shareholders were required to put up greater stakes in order to control banking assets.

The first effective nationwide capital requirement for commercial banks was mandated by the International Banking Act (IBA) of 1978. Previously, the only federal capital standards were for newly chartered banks. Otherwise, capital standards were *ad hoc,* usually implemented as an incident to a BHC application. For example, if a BHC sought permission to acquire a mortgage banking affiliate, the Federal Reserve would require additional capital in order to enter this new line of business.

The 1978 legislation required bank capital of at least 5.5% of total assets, and capital was defined to include paid-in equity, retained earnings, general (but not specific) loan-loss reserves, limited amounts of permanent stock, and certain classes of convertible long-term debt.

The Basel I Capital Accord

Since 1978, bank capital has become a focal point of bank regulation. With increasing international competition among banks in a global market, public regulators have come to recognize the need to coordinate capital requirements for banks across countries. Hence, meetings were held among the United States, Japan, and the major Western European countries under the auspices of the *Bank for International Settlements* in Basel, Switzerland, in 1987. After long and arduous negotiations, the Basel (BIS) Accord provided a more-or-less uniform capital standard for all banks in the 12 participant countries. The new BIS (or Cooke, after the name of the British organizer) ratios were to be fully implemented by 1993 and to cover all insured banks. By 1993, all of the world's major banks had satisfied the Basel capital requirements.[31] The accord, now referred to as the Basel I Accord, was lauded as a great victory in international banking cooperation and as the harbinger of the "level playing field." Its main elements are summarized in Table 15.1. The definitions of Tier-1 capital are those given in the box earlier. The guidelines specifically exclude the following items (included in earlier capital ratio calculations) from the capital base for computing capital ratios: (i) goodwill, (ii) other intangibles, (iii) capital investments in most unconsolidated subsidiaries, (iv) reciprocal holdings of capital instruments in banking organizations, and (v) revaluation reserves.

The Basel I Accord relates required capital to the composition of the bank's assets. Hence, capital requirements are stated as a percentage of *risk-weighted assets* rather than total assets. A bank's risk-weighted assets are an average of the bank's booked assets and *credit equivalent amounts* of its off-balance sheet exposure. There are five asset categories for risk-weighting purposes, numbered 1 through 5 in Table 15.1. The Basel I Accord called for a minimum overall risk-weighted capital ratio of 8%, with at least 50% in the form of Tier-1 capital. To compute how much capital it needs, a bank must first determine the dollar volume of assets in each of the five risk categories. Say A_i represents the dollar volume in risk category i, with $i = 1, 2, 3, 4,$ or 5. Let C_i represent the conversion factor for category i, that is, $C_1 = 0, C_2 = 0.10,$ $C_3 = 0.2, C_4 = 0.5,$ and $C_5 = 1.0$. Then the total capital a bank is required to have is 8% of $C_1A_1 + C_2A_2 + C_3A_3 + C_4A_4 + C_5A_5$ or $0.08 \times (C_2A_2 + C_3A_3 + C_4A_4 + C_5A_5)$ since $C_1 = 0$. Moreover, the bank must have at least $0.04 \times (C_2A_2 + C_3A_3 + C_4A_4 + C_5A_5)$ as Tier-1 capital. U.S. banking regulators have additionally imposed a Prompt Corrective Action (PCA) requirement in terms of a leverage ratio constraint mandating that Tier-1 capital can be no lower than 3% of *total assets* for banks earning the highest CAMEL rating. Other banks are required to keep a 4% ratio. Weaker-rated banks may have to keep higher capital, as much as 6%. Table 15.2 summarizes the three capital constraints U.S. banks face.

Signatories to the Basel I Accord were free to impose higher capital requirements on banks in their own countries. As indicated previously, the capital requirements are risk sensitive for various classes of assets, both on- and off-balance sheet items. Although the focus of the Basel I capital requirement is credit risk, limited recognition is also made of interest-rate risk. For example, the capital requirement on federal government debt with initial maturity exceeding 91 days is 0.8%, whereas the requirement on shorter-maturity government debts is 0. The imposition of capital requirements on

---

31. See Reuters (1993).

TABLE 15.1 The Basel I (BIS) Capital Requirements

Minimum Overall Capital Ratio: 8%

Mix in Capital Ratio: Not More Than 50% Tier-2 Capital

Requirements Against Specific Assets

Asset Risk Category	Conversion Factor in Percentage	Qualifying Assets
1	0	Cash (including foreign currency), claims on Federal Reserve Banks, direct obligations of the United States with a maturity of up to 91 days, claims on OECD central government and banks, and loan commitments with maturities less than 1 year
2	10	Longer-term federal government debt, loans secured by government paper or deposits at the official lending institution, and Federal Reserve System bank stock (at book value)
3	20	Claims on domestic depository institutions, short-term claims on foreign banks in OECD countries, cash items in the collection process, obligations of or claims guaranteed by federal entities, claims backed by the full faith and credit of state and local governments, and the lowest-risk standby letters of credit
4	50	Government obligations whose repayment is not backed by the full faith and credit of the issuing entity (revenue bonds and similar paper), residential mortgages, unused loan commitments with maturities exceeding 1 year, note issuance facilities, and medium-risk standby letters of credit
5	100	Claims on corporations (including loans and bonds), guaranty-type instruments, sales subject to repurchase agreements and other credit substitutes, and certain standby letters of credit.

TABLE 15.2 Summary of Capital Constraints on U.S. Banks

1. Total capital $\geq 0.008 \times \sum_{i=2}^{5} C_i A_i$

2. Tier-1 capital $\geq 0.08 \times \sum_{i=2}^{5} C_i A_i$

3. Tier-1 capital $\geq \left[0.03 \times \sum_{i=2}^{5} A_i \right] + d$

where A_i = dollar volume of assets in category i, and i varies from 1 to 5 as in Table 15.1.

$\quad$ C_i = Basel risk weight or conversion factor attached to category i.

$\quad$ d = an add-on usually between $0.02\Sigma A_i$ and $0.03\Sigma A_i$ for banks with CAMEL ratings below the best

Note that Equations (2) and (3) can be combined as:

4. Tier-1 capital $\geq \text{Max} \left\{ 0.04 \times \sum_{i=2}^{5} C_i A_i, \left[\left(0.03 \times \sum_{i=2}^{5} A_i \right) + d \right] \right\}$

where "Max" means the greater of the two enclosed quantities in the parenthesis. The bank's capital must then satisfy both (1) and (4), above.

shorter-maturity government debts is 0. The imposition of capital requirements against off-balance sheet items (e.g., loan commitments, standby L/Cs, and interest-rate and currency swaps) is another innovation of the Basel I requirements.

From one perspective, capital requirements look like a naïve first step in international banking cooperation. There are numerous criticisms. First, the risk classes are crude to the point of inviting exploitation. Mortgages require half the capital of business loans, yet it is easy to find mortgages with greater credit risk than business loans. Indeed, at the margin, business loans can be repackaged in the form of mortgages. Regulators always seem to underestimate the adroitness and plasticity of the capital markets. Loans are merely written contracts that can be adapted to meet the imperatives of the moment.

Second, the risk classes can be manipulated.[32] For instance, suppose a bank invests in U.S. Treasury bonds that require zero capital and then enters into an amortizing swap (recall Chapter 8) in which it *pays* the total return on those bonds and *receives* the total payments on mortgages. Even though this bank effectively holds mortgages, the bank faces a BIS capital requirement that is lower than the 4% attached to mortgages.

Third, interest-rate risk failed to receive its due under Basel I, although the 1991 legislation mandates that regulators develop new capital guidelines that reflect interest-rate risk as well as credit risk.

Fourth, many concessions were made to accommodate special interests. For example, 45% of unrecorded capital gains on equity holdings can be counted as Tier-2 capital. This concession was especially important to Japanese banks with large equity holdings valued at purchase prices. U.S. banks are prohibited from treating unrealized capital gains as capital.

Fifth, the Basel I capital requirements assume that banking risk is substantially the same in different countries. However, there are striking differences in the variability of bank rates of return across countries. This suggests that the basic asset-risk categories may be too crude and that minimum capital ratios should vary across countries.

Finally, since the capital ratios are prescribed on a book-value basis, they fail to adjust for changing return volatilities and the relationship between book and market values of bank equity. Moreover, the capital requirements do not recognize the portfolio aspects of bank balance sheets. Since requirements are linear in individual asset categories, there is no recognition of the covariability of returns that affects diversification and portfolio risk.

Despite these shortcomings, the accord is noteworthy as a historic first step in the international harmonization of capital standards, linking capital to risk, and in recognizing the significance of off-balance sheet items. As it turned out, it was basically only a first step, as a revised accord, the Basel II Accord, was adopted in 2004; this will be discussed next. Note also that the PCA requirements of FDICIA increase the importance of capital since regulators are required to close banks with sufficiently deficient capital.

The Basel II Capital Accord

In June 2004, central bank governors and heads of bank supervisory authorities in the Group of Ten (G10) countries issued a press release and endorsed the publication of International Convergence of Capital Management and Capital Standards: A Revised Framework, a new capital adequacy framework, commonly known as Basel II. The planned implementation of the basic approach was to be completed by the end of 2006, with the more advanced approaches to be adopted by end of 2007.[33] Basel II is viewed by many as the outcome of a process of evolution started by Basel I.

Objectives of Basel II: Basel II has numerous objectives. The main ones are listed below:

- Ensure that capital adequacy regulation is not a source of competitive disadvantage.
- Adopt more risk-sensitive capital requirements.
- Make greater use of banks' own internal risk assessments.
- Bring market discipline and regulatory monitoring to bear as part of regulation to ensure prudent risk-taking rather than relying solely on capital requirements.
- Cover a more comprehensive set of risks, including credit risk, interest rate risk, and operational risk.
- Account for the risk-mitigation efforts of banks.
- Adopt a more forward-looking approach that can evolve with time.

The Three Pillars of Basel II: Basel I focused exclusively on bank capital requirements. In contrast, Basel II takes a more comprehensive approach, relying on three "pillars" to ensure appropriate risk-taking by banks. These three pillars are:

- First pillar: Minimum Capital Requirements;
- Second pillar: Supervisory Review Process; and
- Third pillar: Disclosure (or Market Discipline).

The idea is that regulators are supposed to rely on three mechanisms for controlling bank risk: capital requirements (as in Basel I, but with modifications to link capital requirements to a broader array of risks than just credit risk), regulatory monitoring, and market discipline. We discuss each pillar briefly in what follows. The interested reader should visit the Bank for International Settlements Web site for a more detailed discussion.

The First Pillar: Minimum Capital Requirements: Total minimum capital requirements have to be calculated for credit, market, and operational risks. The capital ratio is calculated using the definitions of regulatory capital and risk-weighted assets. The total capital ratio must be no lower than 8%. Tier-2 capital is limited to 100% of Tier-1 capital.

---

32. This was pointed out by Merton (1994) and more recently by Goodhart (2013).
33. The U.S. was very reluctant to adopt Basel II, and decided to do so only for the largest 25 banks.

With a few modifications, the definition of eligible regulatory capital is essentially the same as in the 1988 Basel I Accord.[34]

Basel II defines Risk-Weighted Assets as

Total Risk-Weighted Assets = [Risk-weighted assets determined by credit risk] + [12.5 × Capital requirement for market and operational risks].

Note that the number 12.5 above is the reciprocal of the minimum capital requirement of 8%.

Determination of risk-weighted assets for credit risk is as follows. Banks are allowed a choice between two broad methodologies for calculating their capital requirements for credit risk: the standardized approach and the internal ratings-based (IRB) approach. We consider the standardized approach first. In Table 15.3, we provide the weights to be assigned for different kinds of credits under this approach.

TABLE 15.3 Risk weights for different credits under the standardized approach

Types of Claims	Risk Weights Assigned
1. Claims on sovereign governments and their central banks	Depends on credit ratings: 0% for AAA to AA–; 20% for A+ to A–; 50% for BBB+ to BBB–; 100% for BB + to B–; 150% below B–; and 100% if unrated.
2. Claims on noncentral government public sector entities (PSEs)	Risk-weighted at national discretion, with claims on certain domestic PSEs being treated as claims on the sovereigns in whose jurisdictions the PSEs are established.
3. Claims on multilateral development banks (MDBs)	Risk weights are based on external risk assessments, with a 0% risk weight applied to claims on highly rated MDBs (e.g., those with external assessments of AAA).
4. Claims on banks	National supervisors can choose from one of two options: (i) assign all banks incorporated in a given country a risk weight one category less favorable than that assigned to claims on the sovereign of that country, with a cap of 100% on the risk weight; or (ii) base the risk weighting on the external credit assessment of the bank itself, subject to a floor of 20% and claims on unrated banks being risk weighted at 50%.
5. Claims on securities firms	To be treated as claims on banks if securities firms are subject to supervisory and regulatory arrangements similar to banks, including risk-based capital requirements; otherwise, the rules for claims on corporates apply.
6. Claims on corporates	Depends on credit ratings: 20% for AAA to AA–; 50% for A+ to A–; 100% for BBB+ to BB–; 150% below BB–; and 100% for unrated. At national discretion, supervisory authorities may permit banks to risk weight all corporate claims at 100% without regard to external ratings.
7. Claims included in regulatory retail portfolios, such as revolving credit and lines of credit (such as credit cards and overdrafts), personal term loans and leases, and small-business facilities and commitments.	Risk-weighted at 75%
8. Residential mortgages and claims secured by residential property.	Risk-weighted at 35%
9. Claims secured by commercial real estate.	Risk-weighted at 100%
10. Past due loans (past due for more than 90 days).	Risk-weighted at 100–150% depending on specific provisions.
11. High-risk categories such as claims on sovereigns, PSEs, banks, and securities firms rated below B–, claims on corporates related below BB–, securitization tranches rated between BB+ and BB–.	Risk-weighted at 150% or higher, with securitization tranches rated between BB+ and BB– risk-weighted at 350%
12. Other assets such as investments in equity or regulatory capital instruments issued by banks or securities firms.	Risk-weighted at 100%
13. Off-balance sheet items	• Credit conversion factors (CCFs) will be used. Commitments with an original maturity of up to 1 year will receive a CCF of 20%, commitments of original maturity over 1 year will receive a CCF of 50%, whereas commitments with a material adverse change (MAC) clause receiving a 0% CCF. • Short-term self-liquidating trade letters of credit will receive a 20% CCF.

---

34. An example of a deviation is that under one of the permissible approaches (the internal ratings-based approach, IRB), general loan-loss reserves cannot be included in Tier-2 capital.

In addition to stipulating risk weights to reflect credit risks embedded in a variety of different assets, Basel II also recognizes that the risk mitigation efforts of banks can affect their risk exposure, and seeks to account for this in the computation of minimum capital requirements. For example, the bank may be able to lower the capital it posts against a transaction if it is collateralized, that is, the bank's credit exposure is limited by collateral. If, however, the claim in question has an issue-specific rating that reflects the bank's risk mitigation efforts, then no additional capital reduction is granted beyond what is already made possible by the effect of the risk mitigation on the credit rating.

Next, we turn to the IRB approach to credit risk. This approach permits some banks to rely on their own estimates of risk components in determining the capital requirement for a given exposure, as long as the banks using this approach meet certain conditions and disclosure requirements. The risk components in the IRB approach include measures of the probability of default (PD), loss given default (LGD), the exposure at default (EAD), and effective maturity (M). In some cases, banks may be required to use a supervisory value as opposed to an internal estimate for one or more of the risk components.

The first step in the IRB approach is to categorize banking-book exposures into broad classes of assets with different underlying risk characteristics: corporate, sovereign, bank, retail, and equity. Within those broad classes, there are subcategories. For each of these asset classes, there are three key elements:

- Risk Components: estimates of risk parameters provided by banks, some of which are supervisory estimates;
- Risk-Weighted Functions: the means by which risk components are transformed into risk-weighted assets and therefore capital requirements;
- Minimum Requirements: the minimum standards that must be met in order for a bank to use the IRB approach.

For many of the asset classes, there are two broad approaches within the IRB approach: a foundation approach and an advanced approach. Under the foundation approach, as a general rule, banks provide their own estimates of PD and rely on supervisory estimates for other risk components. Under the advanced approach, banks provide more of their own estimates of PG, LGD, and EAD, and their own calculation of maturity M.

Securitization receives special treatment under Basel II. Banks are required to determine regulatory capital requirements on exposures arising from traditional and synthetic securitizations, keeping in mind the economic substance of the securitization rather than its legal form. The securitization structures subject to capital requirements include exposures arising from the provision of credit-risk mitigants to a securitization transaction, investments in asset-backed securities (ABS), retention of a subordinated tranche, and extension of a liquidity facility or credit enhancement. The actual capital requirements against these exposures depend on the credit ratings of the exposures.

Operational risk is defined as the risk of loss resulting from inadequate or failed internal processes, people or systems, or from external events. It includes legal risk, but excludes strategic and reputational risk. Several approaches for determining the capital requirements against operational risk are included in Basel II (see the box below for details).

Box: Capital requirements for operational risk

Basel II dictates three methods for calculating operational risk capital charges: (i) the Basic Indicator Approach; (ii) the Standardized Approach; and (iii) Advanced Measurement Approaches (AMA). Banks are encouraged to move along the continuum of available approaches as they develop more sophisticated operational risk measurement systems and practices, with specific qualifying criteria specified for the Standardized Approach and the AMA.

Under the Basic Indicator Approach, the bank must hold capital for operational risk equal to 15% of the positive average annual gross income for the previous three years. Figures for any year in which annual gross income is negative are excluded.

Under the Standardized Approach, banks' activities are divided into eight business lines: corporate finance, trading and sales, retail banking, commercial banking, payment and settlement, agency services, asset management, and retail brokerage. The total capital charge is calculated as the 3-year average of the simple sum of the regulatory capital charges across each of the business lines in each year. In any given year, negative capital charges (resulting from negative gross income) in any business line may offset positive capital charges in other business lines without limit. However, when the aggregate capital charge across all business lines within a given year is negative, then that year is excluded from the calculations. The percentages of gross income to be kept as capital vary across business lines.[35]

Under the AMA, the regulatory capital requirement equals the risk measure generated by the bank's internal operational risk measurement system. Use of the AMA is subject to supervisory approval.

---

35. It is 18% for Corporate Finance, Sales and Trading, and Payment and Settlement; 15% for Commercial Banking, and Agency Services; and 12% for Retail Banking, Asset Management, and Retail Brokerage.

Basel II also includes capital requirements against market risk. Under Basel II, banks are required to have procedures that enable them to assess and actively manage all material market risks. The assessment of internal capital adequacy for market risk should be based on both Value-at-Risk (VAR) modeling and stress testing, including an assessment of concentration risk and assessment of illiquidity under stressful market scenarios. The bank's internal capital assessment is required to demonstrate that it has enough capital to not only meet the minimum capital requirements but also to withstand a range of severe but plausible market shocks.[36]

The Second Pillar: Supervisory Review Process: The supervisory review process of Basel II is intended to ensure that banks have adequate capital to support all the risks in their business, but also to encourage banks to develop and use better risk-management techniques in monitoring and managing their risks. This review process recognizes the responsibility of bank management in developing an internal capital assessment process and setting appropriate capital targets.

Supervisors are expected to evaluate how well banks are assessing their capital needs relative to their risks and to intervene when appropriate. This interaction is intended to foster an active dialog between banks and supervisors such that when deficiencies are identified, PCA can be taken to either reduce risk or restore capital.

There are three main areas that might be particularly suited to treatment under Pillar 2: risks considered under Pillar 1 that are not fully captured by the Pillar 1 process (e.g., credit concentration risk), factors not accounted for by Pillar 1 (e.g., interest-rate risk in the banking book, business and strategic risk), and factors external to the bank (e.g., business cycle effects). Moreover, Pillar 2 also involves an assessment by regulators of compliance with the minimum standards and disclosure requirements of the more advanced methods in Pillar 1, such as the IRB framework for credit risk and the treatment of operational risk.

Basel II also cautions bank supervisors to carry out their obligations in a transparent and accountable manner. Moreover, it encourages enhanced cooperation between national supervisors, especially for the cross-border supervision of complex international banking organizations.

The Third Pillar: Disclosure (or Market Discipline): Given the increasing complexity of banking activities, it is extremely difficult, if not impossible, for banking supervisors to monitor these activities in detail. Basel II therefore seeks to encourage market discipline by asking for more transparency and disclosure. In doing so, it hopes to encourage monitoring of banks by professional investors and financial analysts as a complement to banking supervision. However, this is where Basel II provides the least detail and precision. Other than emphasizing the need for increased transparency and disclosure, it says little about how to make it effective.[37]

The Basel III Capital Accord

The global financial crisis highlighted substantial shortcomings in the regulation of banks and the financial system. Basel II, introduced on the verge of the 2007–2009 financial crisis, did not escape criticism. It is criticized for amounting to little more than lightweight procyclical bank capital regulation with ample possibilities for regulatory arbitrage,[38] and as such has contributed to banks being undercapitalized and unable to weather a serious economic storm. In particular, the "model-based" approaches were criticized as being easily manipulated and producing excessively optimistic assessments of risk in good times (and hence low capital requirements). The latter created substantial procyclicality in the operations of banks. Also the "quality" of capital was criticized – debt-like sources of financing were still allowed to be counted in meeting capital requirements. Criticism was that the focus on models that needed to be certified by regulators led to a standardization of these models possibly forcing greater similarity in bank strategies. This could make bank asset portfolio choice become more highly correlated and elevate systemic risk. Finally, counterparty risk was inadequately addressed, which threatened not just the safety and soundness of individual financial institutions but also the stability of the system at large. As a response, the Basel Committee proposed the new Basel III Capital Accord on 1 June, 2011 (see BCBS (2011, 2012)).

The Basel III Capital Accord works to strengthen the global capital framework by raising the quality of bank capital, enhancing risk coverage, and adding a leverage ratio that is not model-based.

Raising the quality of bank capital: The total regulatory capital comprises Tier 1 capital and Tier 2 capital. Tier 1 capital is seen as high-quality bank capital; that is, bank capital that is able to absorb losses on a going concern basis (i.e., under

---

36. Basel II also includes other refinements. Wherever appropriate, banks are required to factor in: illiquidity/"gapping" of prices, position concentration (relative to market turnover), nonlinear products/deep out-of-the-money positions; events and jumps-to-defaults; significant shifts in correlations, and other risks that may not be appropriately captured by VAR, such as recovery rate uncertainty and skewness risk.

37. Various proposals have been put forward to incentivize private sector investors to monitor banks, among them forcing banks to finance themselves in part with subordinated debt. The pricing of such debt would give potential signals by investors about the well being of banks and could provide useful complementary information for supervisors; see Bliss (2001), Calomiris (1998), and Evanoff and Wall (2000).

38. See OECD (2012).

normal operations of the bank). In contrast, Tier 2 capital is lower-quality bank capital; that is, bank capital that is able to absorb bank losses on a gone-concern basis (i.e., if the bank enters the insolvency procedures) and thus does not prevent financial distress but provides some protection to depositors.

Definitions of bank capital (and its decomposition into high-quality-Tier-1 and low-quality-Tier-2 capital) were imprecise and varied substantially across countries before the 2007–2009 crisis. This created two problems. First, it was difficult to compare the levels of bank capital across banks and banking systems as indicators of comparative or relative bank stability. Second, banks could engage in capital arbitrage by letting various nonequity sources of funding qualify as bank capital. To deal with these problems, the Basel III Capital Accord more clearly defines which funding sources can count as bank capital and focuses more on the highest quality tier of bank capital (i.e., Tier-1 bank capital). In particular, Tier-1 capital is supplanted by Common Equity Tier-1 capital which comprises common shares, retained earnings, and stock surplus, accumulated other comprehensive income and other disclosed reserves, and regulatory adjustments.

Additional Tier 1 bank capital, which comprises hybrid instruments that need to be among others: (1) subordinated to depositors, general creditors, and subordinated debtholders of the bank, (2) perpetual without incentives to redeem, and (3) the bank needs to contain full discretion with respect to dividend/coupon payments. The latter requires that dividends/coupons must be paid out of distributable income available for payment to common shareholders, and nonpayment of dividends cannot impose any restriction on the bank (except for triggering nonpayment of dividend to common shareholders).

A major change compared to the Basel II Capital Accord pertains to the phase out of Tier-1 bank capital hybrid capital instruments that have redemption incentives (due to step-up clauses). Basel II also permitted "Tier-3 bank capital" to cover market risks (Tier-3 bank capital included general loss reserves, undisclosed reserves, and a greater variety of subordinated debt). Tier-3 bank capital is now abolished under Basel III. In addition, Tier-2 bank capital is to be better synchronized across jurisdictions.

The main task of Tier-2 capital is to cover the losses of depositors or general creditors of the bank in the case of default. Therefore, the Basel III Capital Accord stipulates that Tier-2 bank capital needs to be subordinate to depositors and general creditors of the bank. It should not be securitized to enhance its seniority. It should have a minimum maturity of at least 5 years and can be callable only after 5 years. The buyer of Tier-2 capital should not be the issuing bank or a related party neither should the issuing bank provide funds for its purchase.[39]

Raising the quantity of bank capital: The Basel III Capital Accord demands from banks to have Common equity Tier-1 capital of at least 4.5% of risk-weighted assets. Tier-1 capital to risk weighted assets must be at least 6% and Total capital to risk-weighted assets must be at least 8%.

Enhancing Risk Coverage: In addition to raising the quantity and quality of bank capital, it is crucial that capital regulation covers the main risk exposures of banks. The global financial crisis has shown that several on-balance sheet and off-balance sheet risks were largely unaccounted for. Therefore, the Basel III Capital Accord aims at raising capital to improve its risk coverage function, especially with respect to complex financial derivatives holdings and for the trading book.

Banks need to compute their minimum capital requirements for counterparty credit risk using stressed value-at-risk capital requirements. Stressed VAR capital requirements are computed on a continuous 12-month period of significant financial stress. The idea behind the stressed VAR capital requirements is to build up sufficient capital to weather a prolonged period of financial distress.

Whereas the Basel II Capital Accord obliged banks to provide a capital cushion to cover potential *default risk* of a counterparty, the global financial crisis of 2007–2009 has shown that the deterioration of the credit standing of a counterparty (and not necessarily its default) can already put a bank under substantial stress. Therefore, the Basel III Capital Accord stipulates from banks to build sufficient capital to cover mark-to-market losses (so-called credit valuation adjustment CVA risk) due to a decrease in the credit worthiness of a counterparty. The Basel III Capital Accord also prescribes a methodology to deal with the so-called wrong-way risks. Wrong-way risks are defined as situations in which exposure increases with the deterioration of the credit standing of the counterparty. Standards for collateral risk-management practices are also being improved.

The Basel III Capital Accord also addresses *systemic risk* within the banking system. It raises the capital requirements for bilateral OTC derivatives exposures, giving strong incentives to banks to move derivative exposures to central counterparties (such as clearing houses). The central counterparties will also need to comply with rigorous standards (such as capital requirements) in order to ensure a robust financial market infrastructure.

---

39. The Basel III Capital Accord also provides rules for the inclusion of capital for the Bank holding company and for the nonjoint stock companies such as mutual and cooperative or savings institutions.

Available unencumbered assets identify the amount of assets that are available to be pledged as a collateral if there is a need to raise additional funding
LCR by significant currency to monitor liquidity risk within certain currencies
Market-related monitoring tools to use market data as an early indication of liquidity risk within a bank.

Bank Activity Restrictions

The legal separation of commercial and investment banking in the United States was memorialized with the Glass–Steagall Act of 1933. Federal Reserve member banks were prohibited from underwriting, distributing, or dealing in stocks, bonds, or other securities, the exceptions being U.S. government bonds, general obligation municipal securities, and the obligations of specified government agencies. The act also prohibited banks from affiliating with investment banking firms or otherwise engaging in investment banking. The separation of commercial and investment banking was based on the controversial notion that the massive banking disruption of the period was due to the securities activities of banks.

The Glass–Steagall Act also affirmed the authority of the states regarding geographic expansion, originally spelled out by the McFadden Act in 1927. Thus, branching and holding company issues were deferred to the states, effectively blocking the development of interstate banking and ensuring a fragmented industry. The assets that banks could intermediate as well as their geographic origin were severely restricted. This meant that banks were closely tied to the fortunes of their local communities, and the opportunities for diversification were limited, as were opportunities to exploit economies of scale and scope.[46] Notably, the restrictions were based on an increasingly tenuous distinction between loans and securities. Private placements of debt securities are, for all practical purposes, loans, and securitized loans are, for all practical purposes, securities. The all-but-vacuous distinction between loans and debt securities was not lost on bankers seeking to expand their activities.

A relentless testing of limits by bankers prompted regulatory reinterpretations through time, leading to bank entry into a variety of previously prohibited areas. For example, through holding company affiliates, banks were able to underwrite municipal debt, commercial paper, and even corporate bonds and equity, within strict limit as to the volume of this business. Without the benefit of legislation, the rules governing asset proscriptions were substantially relaxed by regulators. To be sure, these initiatives were tested in the courts, but the regulatory liberalizations were judicially sustained for the most part. This is actually quite remarkable because the reinterpretations of the 1930s legislation were fundamental. Underwriting corporate debt and equity securities by commercial banks and their holding companies was for decades simply illegal under Glass–Steagall. When the banks and their regulators sought to have the law liberalized, their efforts were wasted time and again by a variety of other interest groups. Then, however, the bank regulators simply reinterpreted Glass–Steagall, and the courts upheld their prerogative to do so.

The once impregnable wall separating commercial and investment banking was dismantled piecemeal, without legislation. Likewise, banks found their way into the asset-management business via mutual funds. Banks could sell and manage mutual funds. This too was thought to be foreclosed by Glass–Steagall. The separation of banking and insurance proved to be more stubborn. Lobbying by insurance interests kept banks out of this business for the most part. However, banks competed vigorously in the business of financial guarantees. Moreover, some insurance companies offered depository financial intermediation services.[47] Standby letters of credit sold by banks and financial guarantees sold by insurance companies are close substitutes, especially as credit enhancements for securitization.[48] Likewise, banks and insurance companies competed directly in the market for annuities.

Prior to the dismantling of the Glass–Steagall Act, the expanding securities activities of banks were being forced into holding company affiliates in order to achieve a measure of separation (see the box on Holding Companies and Separability) between the deposit-taking bank and its nontraditional activities.

Bank holding companies and separability

BHC legislation of 1956 and 1970 clearly established the Federal Reserve as the primary federal bank regulatory agency. The BHC Act of 1956 brought the multi-BHC under the supervision of the Federal Reserve. All holding company formations and their bank acquisitions thereafter required the explicit permission of the Federal Reserve. What the 1956 legislation did

---

46. As an offset to excessive concentration, banks are allowed to lend to any one person (legal or biological) no more than 25% of their capital (15% of capital, plus an additional 10 percent of capital upon having high-quality collateral as a backup; see 12 U.S.C. § 84; 12 C.F.R. Part 32.), but there are exceptions (e.g., large systemically important financial institutions (SIFIs) must limit their exposures to other large SIFIs to at most 10% of capital).
47. For example, some insurance companies own thrift institutions.
48. These comments apply to nationally chartered banks. Some states allow banks to engage in agency, brokerage, underwriting, and a broad range of insurance activities.

not anticipate was the use of the BHC for purposes other than the purchase of banks. In the 1960s, there emerged a new kind of BHC, referred to as the one-BHC. It was used for a variety of circumventing purposes. For example, one-BHCs issued commercial paper, which banks were not permitted to do. They downstreamed the proceeds to their affiliate bank, which issued nondeposit liabilities for the proceeds of the commercial paper. The banks thereby avoided cash-asset reserve requirements against these liabilities.

The one-BHC also was a vehicle for increasing financial leverage. By purchasing the banks' equity with a mix of holding company debt and equity, the banks' owners increased their leverage. The holding company also was used as a tax shield in that dividends from the bank to the holding company could be used to retire holding company debt without being taxed as income to the holding company owners.

Finally, the one-BHC was used to expand the powers of banks. BHCs purchased travel agencies, consulting companies, securities affiliates, and other businesses that banks would not have been permitted to purchase directly. Not surprisingly, one-BHCs experienced rapid growth after the 1956 legislation.[49] The 1970 Douglas Amendments to the BHC Act brought one-BHCs under the supervision of the Federal Reserve. Thereafter, all holding company formations and all acquisitions, bank or nonbank entities, would require the explicit permission of the Federal Reserve. As indicated earlier, the vagueness of BHC legislation gave the Federal Reserve expansive discretionary powers. Prior to the bank capital requirements legislated in 1978, BHC applications became the Federal Reserve's foremost lever for coercing additional capital into the banks.

Both public regulators and the banks themselves often prefer to lodge less traditional activities in a separately incorporated holding company subsidiary instead of having the bank itself engage in new businesses. The rationale is based on two considerations. First, the holding company is viewed as a "source of strength."[1] According to Regulation Y of the Federal Reserve, "A BHC shall serve as a source of financial and managerial strength to its subsidiary." Second, prohibiting the bank from engaging directly in an activity achieves a measure of separation so that if something goes wrong at the new business, the bank, where most of the assets and net worth usually reside, will be insulated from the adversity.

But is it possible to insulate the bank in this fashion? This will depend on a variety of considerations. First, is the question of whether creditors of the subsidiary have legal remedy against the bank and/or the holding company. This is an issue the lawyers call "piercing the corporate veil." The courts usually respect the legal partitioning of related companies, but this depends on how the courts may act on such representations. The company's advertising may well influence the courts in deciding whether to respect the format separation. Thus, if a bank gives the public to understand that it stands behind the commitments of a subsidiary, the courts might feel justified in permitting creditors of the subsidiary to seek satisfaction from the bank or the holding company. The standards in this area are of necessity judgmental and less than clearly defined.

Perhaps even more important than legal considerations are the reputational issues. For example, will adversity at some nonbank subsidiary result in higher costs or lost business to other holding company affiliates? The failure of a subsidiary might lead to downgrading in the credit rating of the parent or the bank affiliate. In order to forestall such a possibility, the management of the parent might voluntarily divert resources to support the floundering subsidiary. Either one of these possibilities, the customer's reaction or the voluntary diversion of resources to support the floundering subsidiary, would subvert the separation achieved by the holding company structure.

Hence, the holding company's ability to insulate members can easily be overstated, and often is. Those who argue that banks can be permitted to do any legal businesses with impunity so long as the nonbank activities are isolated in holding company subsidiaries fail to appreciate the fragility of the separation provided by the holding company structure.

Ultimately, the Glass–Steagall Act was dismantled in 1999, with the passage of the Financial Services Modernization Act of 1999. This act is also known as the Gramm–Leach–Bliley Act of 1999, to reflect the names of the senators who sponsored the bill. This legislation repealed Sections 20 and 32 of the Glass–Steagall Act. It further authorizes a wide range of activities for BHCs and foreign banks that meet eligibility criteria.

In the case of such organizations, it allows United States financial service providers, including banks, securities firms, and insurance companies to affiliate with each other and enter into each other's markets. The affiliation of financial services providers allows open and free competition in the financial services industry.

The 2007–2009 global financial crisis has revived the idea of structural separation of activities in banking. Several trading and more transaction-oriented activities, such as investments in financial derivatives, engagement in structured finance products and activities, and risky trading on financial markets, imposed substantial risk and losses on banks and it is perceived that they contributed to an increased fragility of the financial systems during and leading up to the crisis. Regulators in different countries all recognized the importance of these root causes but approached the problem of dealing with these root causes differently. We focus here on three major initiatives: the Volcker rule in the U.S. (part of the Dodd–Frank Act that was a legislative response to the crisis), recommendations by the Vickers Commission in the United Kingdom, and the Liikanen proposals in the EU.

---

49. See Fischer (1986) and Mester (1992).

The Volcker Rule: In the United States, Section 619 of the Dodd–Frank Act, the so-called Volcker Rule, prohibits the involvement of any bank in proprietary trading, which is trading for profit on financial markets for its own account. In addition, the Volker Rule prohibits an ownership in hedge funds or private equity funds.

The main idea behind the Volker Rule is to protect the stability of the financial sector and the government safety net ("the tax payer") against risks stemming from (opportunistic) speculative activities. It recognizes that banks can use their core banking activities, including the supporting government safety net, to support highly risky trading activities. The Volcker Rule seeks to address the issue by separating trading from banking activities. Whether this can be done effectively is still open for debate. Actually, the implementation of the Dodd–Frank Act will take some time.

Several exemptions exist to the Volcker Rule to deal with grey areas. An important one is "market making," which involves the bank participating in trades to provide continuity and liquidity to the market in a security. For example, the bank can keep some securities in inventory to satisfy customers' purchase orders in the future or absorb the supply of securities from a customer who wishes to sell even when there is no buyer on the other side of the transaction. Another exemption is when trading is used for hedging purposes rather than for speculation. The idea behind the hedging exemption is clear: banks should be allowed to manage and lower their risk exposures. Thus, permitted activities include investments for market making and underwriting activities, trading in the name of bank clients, and trading in the U.S. government debt instruments (Financial Stability Board (2012)).

In practice, the distinction between permitted and prohibited activities by the Volcker Rule is difficult to make, which led to substantial complexity in the operational formulation of rule and ongoing challenges with respect to its implementation. The rule came into effect as of April 1, 2014.[50] For example, how do you determine whether the bank was hedging or speculating? How do you distinguish between market making and speculating? Some of the proposed metrics for making these fine *ex-post* distinctions may end up discouraging market making.

The UK Vickers Report: The UK took a slightly different approach on structural reforms in banking; that is, on the separation of risky activities from standard banking activities. The so-called Vickers Report (Independent Commission on Banking, 2011) aims at separating retail banking services that are crucial for the smooth operation of the real economy from global wholesale and investment banking operations. Banks are required to *ring-fence* their retail banking operations. More specifically, banks are required to move retail banking operations under a special subsidiary that is separated from the rest of the bank in a legal, economic, and operational sense. The retail subsidiary should comply with all minimum regulatory requirements (including requirements on capital, liquidity, funding, and large exposures). Its ties with the rest of the banking group should be limited. It should have an independent corporate governance structure with a majority of independent directors and report in the same way as an independent listed company.

The activities that need to be ring-fenced include deposit taking and provision of overdrafts to individuals and to small and medium enterprises. The prohibited activities in the ring-fence include trading related activities, underwriting of security issues, market making, activities on a secondary markets, derivatives trading (for the purpose other than hedging), and the provisioning of nonpayment-related services to clients outside the European Economic Area or to financial customers.

The permitted activities, subject to certain limits on wholesale funding, include secured and unsecured lending to individuals and corporations (e.g., mortgages, credit cards), deposit taking and lending to large nonfinancial corporations, trade finance, and selling products from the nonring-fenced parts of a bank that bring no exposure to the ring-fenced part.

The EU Liikanen Report: Following the regulatory overhaul in the United States and the United Kingdom through the enactment of the Dodd–Frank Act and the work of the Independent Commission on Banking, the European Commission installed a commission to evaluate the regulatory framework in banking and suggest improvements, with a particular focus on structural measures.

The report, called the Liikanen Report (Liikanen et al. (2012)), proposes that a bank that has substantial trading activities should move these activities to a separate legal entity (a so-called "trading entity"), walled off from deposit-taking and retail-payment operations. Separation is intended to ensure that trading activities are no longer either the explicit or implicit recipients of government safety nets that protect standard banking operations. The activities required to be moved into the trading entity are proprietary trading, assets, or derivative positions that arise due to market-making activities, lending to hedge funds and SIVs, and private equity investments.

Compared to Vickers, the approach employed in the Liikanen Report is to build a wall around the trading activities and not around the retail operations. The basic idea, however, is the same: trading should not benefit from government safety

---

50. See 78 F.R. 5536 (January 31, 2014); http://www.gpo.gov/fdsys/pkg/FR-2014-01-31/pdf/2013-31511.pdf

nets nor should it put the bank's retail operation at risk. Also, in both cases, all activities (albeit separated) can be continued under one roof, consistent with the universal banking model, common in Europe.

How to evaluate? The big question is whether the structural remedies as proposed by either the Volcker Rule, Vickers Report, and the Liikanen Report are effective. This is not obvious. Recall that market forces effectively undermined the Glass–Steagall Act. Why will the new structural approaches not suffer the same fate? This is one unanswered question. Another is whether driving out (Volckers) or separating financial market activities (Vickers, Liikanen) will make the financial system more stable. Can we afford widespread failures of those activities across the financial system?[51] For example, if a bank's trading unit fails, what is the consequence of the reputational spillovers on the rest of the bank? What would be the implications for the real economy? Recall that Lehman Brothers was an investment bank, and yet its failure is considered by some as one of the events of the 2007–2009 crisis that deepened the crisis. Note also that retail operations can be risky (Northern Rock). So the effectiveness of the proposed measures remains an untested hypothesis. Moreover, we do not have a good sense of the costs of the measures.

STABILITY: MACROPRUDENTIAL REGULATION

Before the 2007–2009 global financial crisis, the focus of bank regulation was on microprudential regulation, in which, the main goal of a bank regulator is to prevent the failure of an individual bank. Now macroprudential regulation occupies much greater regulatory focus. In macroprudential regulation, the main goal is to guarantee stability of the financial system at large. The regulator focuses on the risk that the system fails, meaning typically that many financial institutions fail simultaneously, or are simultaneously in distress. This is called systemic risk. As pointed out in Chapter 14, a financial crisis, in which the whole financial system is distressed, typically follows euphoric periods of asset price booms fueled by excessive lending by highly levered financial institutions. Macroprudential regulation would seek to dampen these boom–burst cycles. As Federal Reserve Chair Janet L. Yellen (2014) noted:

"I believe a macroprudential approach to supervision and regulation needs to play the primary role. Such an approach should focus on "through the cycle" standards that increase the resilience of the financial system to adverse shocks and on efforts to ensure that the regulatory umbrella will cover previously uncovered systemically important institutions and activities. These efforts should be complemented by the use of countercyclical macroprudential tools…"

Macroprudential regulation seeks to minimize episodes of fire-sale prices in asset markets due to selling of assets by distressed financial institutions, the consequently adverse effects of these fire-sale prices on the capital positions of these institutions, and then the reduced lending by these institutions that causes a credit crunch. Whatever the initial adverse economic shock that caused asset price declines and led to fire sales of assets by financial institutions, a credit crunch exacerbates the initial economic shock by causing a shrinkage in the economic activity of firms that are left without financing. This drags the real economy further down, accentuating the economic doldrums and resulting in greater procyclicality. The goal of macroprudential policies is to strengthen resilience of the banking system during times of economic growth so that banks are better prepared for times of economic downturn.[52]

One of the criticisms of the Basel II Capital Accord is that risk-based minimum capital requirements would increase procyclicality in banking. In particular, banks that estimate risks to be low during periods of economic growth are easily able to satisfy minimum capital requirements with relatively low capital levels, and may even have "excess" capital. This encourages additional lending and further fuels economic growth. In recessions, banks perceiving higher risks need to build up higher capital cushions to meet risk-based capital requirements. Since it is difficult to raise additional capital during a recession, banks cut back on lending, which then exacerbates the recession.

Within the context of the Basel II Capital Accord, there is some scope to limit procyclicality: that is, if the metrics to estimate risks include sufficiently long time periods that cover recessions. If so, the estimated risks would not vary substantially across economic cycles and consequently would not add cyclicality to the minimum capital requirements. In addition, bank supervisors can work to lower procyclicality through the Pillar II supervisory process. For example, the supervisors can demand higher risk estimates and capital levels during economic booms.

The Basel III Capital Accord proposes several additional measures to reduce procyclicality in banking (BCBS, 2011). *A capital conservation buffer* is additional capital formed in the period of normal operations of a bank that can be drawn

---

51. See Goodhart and Lastra (2012).
52. See also BIS (2008) and IMF (2011). IMF (2013) and Galati and Moessner (2013) discuss the interaction between macroprudential regulation and other policies such as monetary policy.

down in times of stress. The Basel III Capital Accord prescribes a capital conservation buffer of 2.5% of Common equity Tier-1 capital over risk-weighted assets. Common equity Tier-1 capital can only be used as a capital conservation buffer if minimum capital requirements are already satisfied (including the minimum 4.5% Common equity Tier-1 capital, 6% Tier 1, and 8% Total capital requirements).

If the capital conservation buffer is depleted, the bank needs to restore it by limiting the redistribution of profits to its shareholders, other capital providers, and employees (e.g., by limiting dividend payments, share buybacks, and discretionary bonus payments to employees). The constraints on redistribution increase with the extent to which the capital conservation buffer is depleted.

The Basel III Capital Accord also prescribes the formation of *a countercyclical buffer*. A countercyclical buffer will be implemented on a national basis if excess credit growth in a country indicates that systemic risk is piling up in the banking system. More specifically, a national bank supervisor could impose a countercyclical buffer requirement between 0% and 2.5% of risk weighted assets.

Forward-looking provisioning is another tool to lower procyclicality in banking. Forward-looking provisioning refers to the accounting practices for loan-loss provisioning that are based on the "expected loss" approach rather than on the current "incurred-loss" approach. The incurred-loss model requires for banks to make provisions (for loan losses) only after a loss event occurs. However, this has granted banks substantial leeway in delaying the recognition of losses during the 2007–2009 global financial crisis, something that the expected-loss approach seeks to avoid.[53]

In response, the International Accounting Standards Board (IASB) published a new Standard IFRS 9, which prescribes the application of an expected-credit-loss model that encompasses all financial instruments subject to impairment accounting. Under IFRS 9, provisions need to be based on expected credit losses. In addition, full lifetime expected credit losses need to be recognized when the credit quality of a financial instrument falls substantially (IASB (2014)). IFRS becomes effective on January 1, 2018. The IASB, however, has not reached a unified view with the US Financial Accounting Standards Board (FASB); the FASB is working on its own standards for financial instruments.

Higher loss absorbency requirement: Rather than focus on the time dimension of systemic risk that is reflected in procyclicality, the regulators could also aim to contain the cross-sectional dimension of systemic risk. In particular, risks can be concentrated in the financial system in the way that they threaten the stability of the whole financial system. For example, the risks concentrated in a bank that is too-big-to-fail may lead to a systemic banking crisis. In this light, the Basel Committee on Banking Supervision[54] proposes additional capital requirements for globally systemically important banks (GSIBs). The so-called higher loss absorbency requirement needs to be in a form of Common Equity Tier 1 capital and ranges from 1% to 3.5% of risk-weighted assets, depending on the global systemic importance of a bank. The global systemic importance of a bank reflects the loss that a bank's failure imposes on the global financial system. It is measured by several indicators, including the size, interconnectedness and complexity of a bank, how globally the bank operates and how substitutable its services are.

Leverage ratio: Capital regulation based on a simple, nonrisk-based leverage ratio could also work to lower procyclicality. A minimum leverage ratio provides a minimum fraction of capital that does not change through the economic cycle. It constraints banks that would want to expand excessively in good times when risks are considered to be low and, therefore, could compensate for risk-based minimum capital requirements that might be too low.

Liquidity regulation: Liquidity regulation works to reduce liquidity risk in banking, by requiring banks to keep sufficient liquid assets on their balance sheets.[55]

Other measures: Various other instruments may help limit systemic risk. An important one that is being proposed in the EU are time-varying loan-to-value ratio requirements. Central banks could be given the right to impose higher loan-to-value requirements on banks when they suspect high asset prices could be forming bubbles that could burst suddenly. This can force borrowers to rely more on internal funds and arrest ruinous asset price increases in markets like real estate, where subsequent price drops bring with them financial crises. Another item that is much on the agenda of particularly EU policymakers is executive compensation. Measures have been introduced to limit variable pay and facilitate "clawbacks," whereby a bonus given to a bank executive for high earnings during good times can be "clawed back" during bad times. The idea is to limit the compensation benefits executives can get from risk taking and the high profit variability that comes with it.

---

53. G20 (2009) has encouraged the accounting standard setters to improve accounting standards, i.e., to lower complexity of accounting standards, improve loan-loss provisioning to better reflect the credit quality of financial instruments, and unify accounting standards internationally.
54. See BCBS (2013b).
55. See Brunnermeier and Oehmke (2013) for an analysis of liquidity regulation.

Empirical Evidence on capital structure and liability structure through time

Ultimately, the effectiveness of capital requirements in elevating capital levels should be assessed empirically. In this respect, the Basel I and Basel II Capital Accords, along with the FDICIA of 1991, cannot be considered an unqualified success, whereas it is too early to judge the Basel III Capital Accord. While on smaller financial institutions the picture is mixed, the average capital ratios among the largest U.S. financial institutions (i.e., BHCs) *declined* significantly before the 2007–2009 financial crisis. The decline was the most pronounced for large BHCs, see Figures 15.5, 15.6, and also the evidence reported in Chapter 2.

In addition to declining capital ratios, it is also apparent that banks have exploited the rather broad regulatory definitions of capital and assets to reduce the level of equity capital even below what their regulatory capital ratios might suggest. That is, the flexibility afforded by *risk-based* capital requirements in the Basel framework has been used to reduce the amount of equity. See Figure 15.7 to see how much lower European banks' common equity/total assets ratios have been than their (regulatory) ratios of tier-1 capital to risk-weighted assets.

Moreover, insufficient bank capital led to a substantial number of banks failing in the United States during the 2007–2009 financial crisis (see Figure 15.8). The magnitude of the losses due to failures during the 2007–2009 financial crisis eclipsed the magnitudes of losses during the previous episodes of banking crises as Figure 15.9 shows.

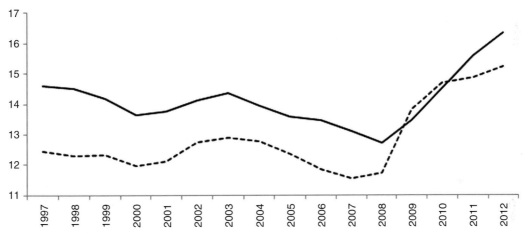

FIGURE 15.5   Average Risk-Weighted Capital Ratios for U. S. Bank Holding Companies (in Percentage Points). *(Source: Quarterly data from FR Y-9C, sample period: 1997:Q1–2012:Q4. Full line represents all BHCs, dashed line represents the largest BHCs with total assets bigger than $50 billion).*

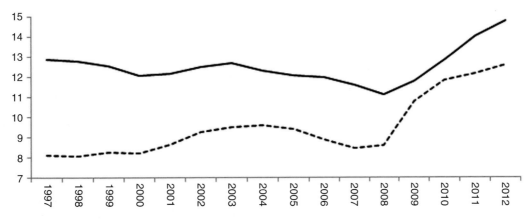

FIGURE 15.6   Average Risk-Weighted Tier 1 Capital Ratios for U.S. Bank Holding Companies (in Percentage Points). *(Source: Quarterly data from FR Y-9C, sample period: 1997:Q1–2012:Q4. Full line represent all BHCs, dashed line represents the largest bank holding companies with total assets bigger than $50 billion).*

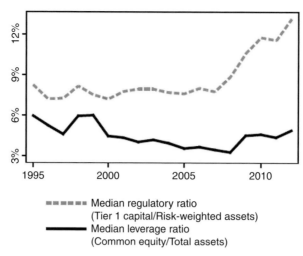

FIGURE 15.7 Book Leverage Ratio versus Regulatory Capital Ratio for European banks (median of top 20 Banks). *(Source: Bloomberg and "Is Europe Overbanked?", Advisory Scientific Committee of the ESRB(2014)).*

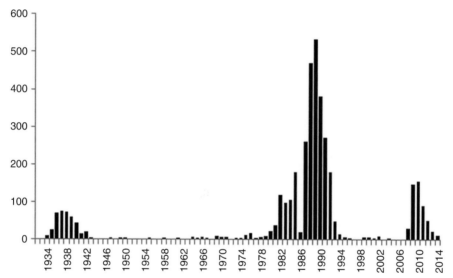

FIGURE 15.8 Annual Failures of FDIC Insured Commercial Banks and Savings Institutions (including Savings Banks and Savings Associations). *(Source: FDIC Historical Statistics on Banking).*

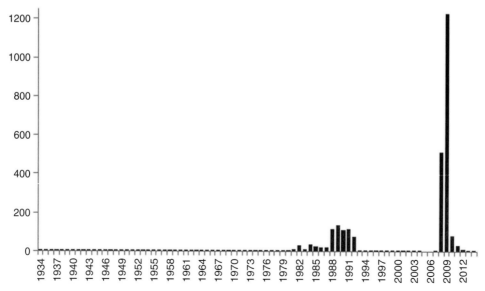

FIGURE 15.9 Annual Failures of FDIC Insured Commercial Banks and Savings Institutions (including Savings Banks and Savings Associations) in Billion $ of Failed Institutions' Deposits. *(Source: FDIC Historical Statistics on Banking.)*

MARKET STRUCTURE, CONSUMER PROTECTION, CREDIT ALLOCATION, AND MONETARY CONTROL REGULATION

Market Structure and Competition

As in other markets, competition among banks can be good for its customers – borrowers who might obtain cheaper financing and depositors who are paid higher interest rates. But excessive competition among banks can encourage excessive risk taking by banks, as we discuss below.

On the one hand, competition facilitates the efficient allocation of resources in the financial system. Competitive pressures force banks to improve efficiency, and these efficiency gains are shared with the bank's customers.

On the other hand, competition may also lead to instability in the banking system as banks take excessive risks by pursuing riskier borrowers and investments because profit margins in traditional businesses are squeezed by competition. Bank regulation may thus seek to limit competition by elevating barriers to entry, branching restrictions, BHC limitations, and merger controls. You will recall from Chapter 12 that safety might be enhanced by improving the charter values of existing banks and thrifts. Charter values of existing banks can be enhanced by limiting entry of new banks, so as to increase the economic rents earned by incumbents. Technological advances may have lowered entry barriers in recent years. Also, prior to the 2007–2009 global financial crisis public policy might also have favored increasing competition. Recent regulatory initiatives point at a renewed emphasis on increasing entry barriers. We now turn to the ways in which market structure and competition regulation can affect industry structure.

Bank Chartering in the United States: Chartering policy is designed to influence industry structure and also to foster adequate capitalization as well as ethical and competent management. Prior to the FDIC, entry controls were shared by the OCC and the state banking agencies and consequently varied widely. The advent of the FDIC added a measure of uniformity to the standards for chartering banks and thrifts. The FDIC, the Fed, and the OCC collaborated to implement a restrictive chartering policy until the mid-1960s. For example, only 70 new banks were chartered between 1936 and 1955. Subsequently, chartering requirements have become more transparent: to obtain a bank charter, one must submit a well-designed operating plan along with adequate capital and credible management.

Branching and BHC Restrictions in the United States: The United States had over 11,000 banks in 1993, more than any other nation. The main reason for this proliferation of banks was a highly restrictive branching policy that existed until the Riegel–Neal Interstate Banking and Branching Efficiency Act of 1994 permitted interstate banking. Both national- and state-chartered banks were limited in their geographic expansion by laws of their domicile states. This is the heritage of the McFadden Act of 1927. Pursuant to the U.S. Treasury's proposal of February 1991, legislation was drafted to permit adequately capitalized banks to branch without regard to state boundaries, but the bill failed. To be sure, along with multistate pacts, many failed institutions provided opportunities for interstate expansion.[56] Thus, even prior to the Riegel–Neal Act, Citicorp claimed to do business in 30 states and Norwest (now Wells Fargo) in all 50 states through a patchwork of failed thrifts and banks they had purchased, along with mortgage banking and consumer finance companies. Others like Bank of America also built formidable interstate organization, but the pattern was checkered.

Before the BHC Act of 1956, holding companies were permitted in a number of upper Midwest, West Coast, and Southern states and became an instrument for circumventing restrictions on branch banking. Thus, if a bank desired to expand in a state that severely restricted branching, it could establish a holding company that could, in turn, purchase separately incorporated banks within the state. Such a structure permitted the exploitation of economies of scale in marketing, finance, and processing, but each bank also needed to sustain the cost of being a separate corporate entity. Reserve requirements and capital requirements needed to be maintained separately, and each bank needed a separate board of directors. Clearly, the multiBHC could not achieve all the potential savings of a branch structure.

The passage of the Reigel–Neal Act in 1994 finally permitted banks to branch across state lines. However, given the overcapacity in bank branches at that time, the way that banks expanded subsequently across state lines was by acquiring banks in various states rather than opening new branches. An important consequence of this consolidation was a dramatic decline in the number of U.S. banks, which was further fueled by the global financial crisis and stood at 5876 by the end of 2013. Note that the number of branches quickly increased until 2008 and then stayed at similar levels until 2013. (See Figure 15.10.)

Merging with another bank is an alternative method of branching, but the BHC Act of 1956, its 1970 amendment, and the Bank Merger Act of 1960 require banking authorities to review all proposed mergers, after obtaining the opinion of the

---

56. Falling institutions provide an opportunity to circumvent state laws because the federal government can arrange sales of impaired institutions without regard to state restrictions.

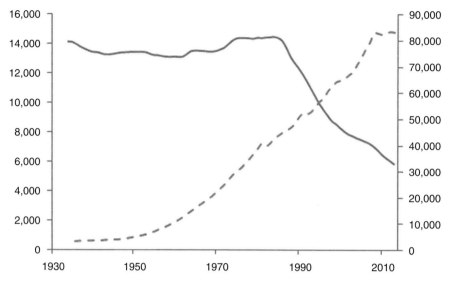

FIGURE 15.10 Number of Commercial Banks in the United States (Full Line and Left Axis) and the Number of Branches (Dashed Line and Right Axis). *(Source: FDIC Historical statistics on banking).*

Department of Justice regarding the anticompetitive effects. A 1966 amendment to the Bank Merger Act shifted more of the responsibility to the Department of Justice where anticompetitive considerations were elevated. Although guidelines were revised again in 1982, the basic idea is to determine whether a bank merger would significantly reduce competition.[57]

Competition policy in the EU during the global financial crisis: Competition policy is generally based on three pillars: anti-cartel policy, merger policy, and state-aid control. Anti-cartel policy in the EU resides mainly on Article 101(1) of the Treaty of the Functioning of the European Union (TFEU) that prohibits "all agreements between undertakings, decisions by associations of undertakings and concerted practices which may affect trade between Member States and which have as their object or effect the prevention, restriction or distortion of competition within the internal market…" It is explicitly prohibited to fix prices or other trading conditions, to restrict production, markets, technical development or investment, to share markets or sources of supply, to put other trading parties at a disadvantage and to demand that contracts are subjected to other nonrelated obligations.[58]

The European Commission as a competition authority fiercely combats cartels in banking. For example, the European Commission imposed fines in total of €1.7 billion to eight international banks for their collusion in the financial derivatives market. The banks manipulated LIBOR and EURIBOR interest rates to earn trading profits on financial derivatives that are priced based on these interest rates.[59]

Merger control in the EU is mainly defined by the EC merger regulation (ECMR) and the implementing regulation (IR). Article 2(2) of the ECMR states that "[a] concentration which would not significantly impede effective competition, in the common market or in a substantial part of it, in particular as a result of the creation or strengthening of a dominant position, shall be declared compatible with the common market." The European Commission evaluates mergers with a community dimension (i.e., mergers that have an impact on a substantial number of EU countries). National competition authorities evaluate other mergers within EU member states.[60]

Financial support for their banks by national governments in the EU is also prohibited because it may hinder cross-border competition and the operation of the common internal market. Another reason for prohibition is that such support creates unfair competition (through e.g., too-big-to-fail guarantees) in which inefficient banks may unduly benefit at the expense of more efficient competitors, resulting in a loss of welfare for consumers. Moreover, government protection may also increase risk-taking by banks.

---

57. In measuring competition, the Department of Justice includes thrifts if they are engaged primarily in retail banking. The courts viewed the Bank Merger Act and amendments as applying the Clayton and Sherman acts standards to banks (see Pekarek and Huth, 2008). During the recent financial crisis, questions were raised about the potential lax way that antitrust policy was implemented particularly concerning the high levels of aggregate concentration of large financial conglomerates (Foer and Resnikoff, 2014).
58. See European Commission (2013).
59. See http://europa.eu/rapid/press-release_IP-13-1208_en.htm
60. See European Commission (2013).

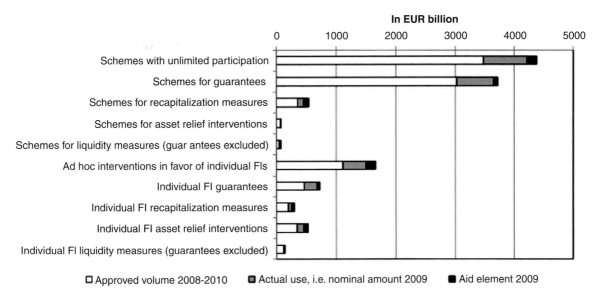

In EUR billion

- Schemes with unlimited participation
- Schemes for guarantees
- Schemes for recapitalization measures
- Schemes for asset relief interventions
- Schemes for liquidity measures (guar antees excluded)
- Ad hoc interventions in favor of individual FIs
- Individual FI guarantees
- Individual FI recapitalization measures
- Individual FI asset relief interventions
- Individual FI liquidity measures (guarantees excluded)

☐ Approved volume 2008-2010   ▨ Actual use, i.e. nominal amount 2009   ■ Aid element 2009

FIGURE 15.11   The Maximum Approved Volumes, Actual Use, and Aid Element of Aid Measures. *(Source: Hasan and Marinč (2013) and EC (2010b); schemes for organizations with unlimited participation include guarantees, recapitalization measures, asset-relief interventions, and liquidity measures. Ad hoc interventions in favor of individual financial institutions (FIs) consist of the sum of individual FI guarantees, recapitalization measures, asset-relief interventions, and liquidity measures).*

During the 2007–2009 global financial crisis, government intervention was viewed as unavoidable in order to prevent a complete meltdown. Governments largely supported banks and provided guarantees, additional liquidity, capital and transferred assets of failing banks in order to safeguard stability. They supported banks collectively and individually (see Figure 15.11), as restoring stability was the overarching objective.

The European Commission permitted government assistance during the 2007–2009 crisis by invoking an exception in the state-aid control procedures arguing that state aid was needed to "remedy serious disturbances in the economy of a Member State." The European Commission issued several communications to provide legal certainty and to give guidance regarding the rules of state aid. However, the stipulation was that state aid needed to be accompanied by additional remedies and restrictions for the recipient. The additional remedies and restrictions would be particularly high if the state aid was directed to an individual bank rather than all banks in the system or if state aid was given to insolvent banks rather than to illiquid banks.

Consumer Protection Regulation

Consumer protection regulation in the United States takes many forms. For example, *usury laws* restrict interest rates that lenders can charge on consumer loans. The idea of protecting borrowers from exploitative loan interest rates has biblical origins. In the United States, legislation goes back to 1641 when Massachusetts passed a usury law. From an economic standpoint, usury ceilings do not make much sense unless the lender is a monopolist. When a bank encounters a borrower whose assessed risk warrants a loan interest rate higher than the usury ceiling, the bank will withhold credit.[61]

Another form of fairness regulation mandates the disclosure of information by lenders. The *Truth-in-Lending Act* (Federal Reserve Regulation Z) requires that lenders provide their customers with standardized credit information regarding finance charges and annual percentage rates in order to permit more informed borrower decisions. Similarly, the *Real Estate Settlement Procedures Act* (RESPA) requires that mortgage borrowers be provided all relevant information about the real estate settlement process, and a uniform settlement statement that discloses all fees and charges at closing.

The 2007-09 global financial crisis has caused regulators to focus on questionable business practices of banks in their quest for higher profits, particularly those related to mortgages. Consequently, new legislation within the Dodd–Frank Act – Title XIV: Mortgage Reform and Anti-Predatory Lending Act – was adopted, amending the Truth-in-Lending Act. The

---

61. Robins (1974) conducted a study of real estate lending and found that when usury ceilings were lower than market mortgage rates, the level of residential construction declined by approximately 25 percent.

Mortage Reform and Anti-Predatory Lending Act aims at limiting lending practices that: (1) granted loans to borrowers who were not creditworthy and (2) targeted lending to financially unsophisticated borrowers who did not understand the terms of the credit they were getting. As indicated earlier, the Dodd–Frank Act (under Title X) also establishes the CFPB.

In addition to protecting borrowers, legislation seeks to protect depositors. The *Truth in Savings Act* (TIS) was enacted in 1991 as part of the *Comprehensive Deposit Insurance Reform and Taxpayer Protection Act or* for short. The purpose of TIS, which went into effect June 1993, is to promote competition among depository decisions. TIS requires uniform disclosure of the terms and conditions for the payment of interest and the charging of deposit fees. It applies to all banks and thrifts, insured and uninsured. Credit unions are not directly subject to TIS, but the *National Credit Union Association* (NCUA) – the regulatory agency governing credit unions – adopted similar rules.

Given the rapid growth in electronic funds transfer (EFT), it is not surprising that regulation governs this activity as well. The *Electronic Funds Transfer Act* (EFTA) of 1978 is designed to protect consumers by establishing the rights, liabilities, and responsibilities of EFT participants. The EFTA focuses on the types of transactions rather than the type of institution providing the service. It applies to most fund transfers initiated through an electronic terminal, telephone, computer or magnetic tape to authorize the debiting or crediting of an account by a financial institution (e.g., automate teller machine transfers, telephone payment, point-of-sale terminal transfers). Thus, payment by check, for example, would not be covered by the EFTA.

The EFTA is a complex web of requirements, one of which is that the consumer be provided "means of access" (e.g., a card and a personal identification number) that can be used to initiate an EFT transaction. Other requirements have to do with disclosure and documentation. Prior to a consumer's first EFT transaction, the financial institution must provide a written disclosure statement that clearly explains the terms and conditions under which the EFT service is provided. Moreover, for each transaction initiated at an electronic terminal, the financial institution must provide a written receipt that clearly states the relevant information about the transaction.

Credit Allocation Regulation

Because bank credit availability affects the pattern of economic activity, governments are often tempted to influence the allocation of this credit to achieve social and political objectives. Some form of governmental credit allocation is found in almost every country. Atypically, *overt* governmental credit allocation has been used only sparingly in the United States, except during times of war or national emergencies. However, numerous indirect credit allocation mechanisms have been extensively employed in the United States. We discuss some of these below.

- *Credit for the Purchase of Securities:* Credit to finance securities has been regulated by the Federal Reserve since 1934. Initial credit is limited to a percentage of the value of the security. If the value of the security drops after credit is extended, a borrower is subject to a margin call. The borrower must then provide additional collateral or sell stock. Moreover, the Federal Reserve may limit a member bank's total lending in support of securities transactions. The obvious effect of this restriction and the margin requirements is to limit credit for the purchase of securities.
- *Tax Policy and Guarantee Programs:* Tax credits and tax deductions have been used to influence a variety of economic activities, including credit allocation. For example, tax credits are used to encourage capital investment and greater energy efficiency in homes. Tax deductibility of charitable contributions has increased the flow of capital to eligible organizations.
- *Credit Programs for Specific Sectors of the Economy:* The government has a long history of credit programs to promote specific sectors of economy. Examples are housing, education, and agriculture.

  For example, the thrift industry was nurtured by the government primarily to encourage home ownership. The investment portfolios of these institutions were restricted and tax incentives were provided to encourage investments in residential mortgages. A major objective of Regulation Q was to keep funding costs low so that home buyers could obtain low-cost credit. Fannie Mae (FNMA), Ginnie Mae (GNMA), and Freddie Mac (FHLMC) were created and subsidized to provide a secondary market for mortgage loans in order to further encourage the flow of credit into housing. The government's role in directing credit to housing has been massive.

  In 1970, the federal government began directing credit to education with the adoption of the Guaranteed Student Loan Program. Loans were made available to students at favorable interest rates and liberal repayment terms. Sallie Mae (Student Loan Marketing association) was created to provide a secondary market for student loans.

  The federal government also subsidizes *agriculture*. The Farm Credit System (FCS) gives farmers subsidized loans, and the Rural Electrification Administration (REA) makes low-interest loans to rural cooperatives, and guarantees loans for rural telephone and cable television. In 1988, Congress created Farmer Mac (Federal Agricultural Mortgage Corporation) to provide a secondary market for farm mortgages and rural housing loans.[62]

Following the global financial crisis strong pressure came into existence to reform the various federal agencies, including Fannie Mae and Fredie Mac. They were seen as culprits in facilitating the massive overselling of mortgages. So far reform has been limited, but is subject of discussion.[63]

• *Influencing Credit Allocation Through Consumer Protection Regulation:* Regulation also seeks to ensure that there is no pernicious discrimination by lenders in the allocation of credit. One such regulation is the *Equal Credit Opportunity Act* (ECOA), which is implemented by Regulation B of the Federal Reserve. The ECOA prohibits discrimination on the basis of race, religion, national origin, marital status, age, and gender.[64] The *Home Mortgage Disclosure Act* (HMDA) of 1975 (Regulation C) and the *Community Reinvestment Act* of 1977 (Regulation BB) seek similar ends; see the box below. Regulation C prohibits "redlining", the practice of withholding credit from particular neighborhoods. Regulation BB encourages financial institutions to serve all legitimate credit needs of their communities.

Community Reinvestment Act, 1977

The Community Reinvestment Act (CRA) requires banks to make loans in their own community, even if business judgment calls for deploying the bank's resources elsewhere. Moreover, well before the adoption of the CRA, mechanisms – such as the federal funds market and the Treasury bills market – were already in place to channel funds from deficit to surplus areas. The logic of the CRA is that banks are chartered by the government with privileges and subsidies, and there is a reciprocal obligation to serve the local community where the bank obtains its financial resources (deposits). But as brokers, banks exist to redeploy funds from surplus to deficit users (locales), motivated by spatial differences in interest rates. For example, for decades funds raised via bank deposits on the East Coast found their way to the West Coast because of differences in rates of economic growth and investment opportunities. This welfare-improving transportation of financial resources could violate CRA, depending on how it is applied. The CRA can counterproductively distort credit flows, and this is the source of much of the controversy surrounding this legislation.

Previously, banks with under $250 million in assets (considered "small banks") were mostly tested on whether they were making loans to the entire community. Banks with assets exceeding $250 million (considered "large banks") were tested for lending practices, but were also required to earn 25% of their grade in service and 25% in community reinvestment. Changes in the CRA rules in 2004 released almost 1800 banks with assets between $250 million and $1 billion from CRA's data collection requirement as well as community investment and service tests. The new community development test covers four areas of activity: affordable housing, community services, economic development, and revitalization of stabilization activities.

"Redlining" or rejecting credit applicants because of their gender, race, religion, and other attributes is divisive.[65] Moreover, it is wrong to state the cost of a loan or other financial service in terms that intentionally confuse or mislead the client. But it should also be understood that banking is about making the most efficient credit decisions possible on the basis of incomplete information, and gender, race, age, handicap, and neighborhood of origin are correlates of creditworthiness, but these attributes are more costly to observe. Thus, the banker need not be a bigot to discriminate. Nor should he or she necessarily be expected to internalize the social costs of using freely available information. But this is the rationale for equal opportunity credit legislation, proponents of which argue that the banker has been privileged to operate with a valuable license, and an obligation attaches to the privilege.

Title XII of the Dodd-Frank Act, entitled Improving Access to Mainstream Financial Institutions, aims at providing low-income and medium-income individuals access to financial institutions for mainstream financial products and services. Title XII supports opening an account at a federal insured bank, provision of microloans, financial education and

---

62. Farmer Mac is an agency created by the U.S. government and operated by a board of directors, five of whom are appointed by the president of the United States. Like Fannie Mae, Freddie Mac, and Sallie Mae, Farmer Mac is a member of a genre referred to as government-sponsored enterprises, or GSEs. They are hybrid institutions with both private and public aspects. Some have privately owned stock outstanding, but all have some government-appointed board members. Their debts are not explicitly guaranteed by the government, but trade as if there exists some government protection; typically, this "agency" debt trades at a spread of less than 50 basis points above Treasury issues of similar duration. The agencies buy, sell, repackage, and guarantee private debts of their constituents, and are exempt from SEC registration requirements.
63. See CBO (2014).
64. Such lending discrimination is called "red lining". Banks must walk a fine line in order to avoid being accused of predatory lending as well as red lining. Denying credit to borrowers from minority groups because they are viewed as not being creditworthy could be misinterpreted as red lining, whereas lending to some borrowers in these groups – that re *ex-post* judged to not have been creditworthy – could be viewed as predatory lending.
65. Studies, based on HMDA data, have found evidence of discrimination in lending. See, for example, Cummins (1993) and Munnell et al. (1996). See also Duca and Rosenthal (1993).

counseling. The aim of Title XII is that low- and medium-income individuals rely on common financial products rather than predatory lending products such as pay-day loans and cash advances.

Monetary Control Regulation

The two major forms of bank regulation relating to monetary control objectives are: reserve requirements and the discount window. Moreover, "moral suasion" by the central bank also plays a role. In addition, several unconventional monetary policy tools were used to tackle disturbances on financial markets due to the global financial crisis. We discuss each in turn.

(1) Legal Reserve Requirements: Cash-asset reserve requirements mandate that the bank retain a certain fraction of its deposits liabilities in a noninterest bearing, liquid form – vault cash or deposits, at the Federal Reserve in the case of Fed member banks, or deposits at member banks in the case of nonmember banks. All depository institutions in the United Stats are subject to reserve requirements on customer deposits.

Reserve requirements also vary depending on the type of the deposit. For instance, reserve requirements against time deposits (CDs) are zero, whereas deposits subject to withdrawal on demand, or net transactions accounts, are subject to a reserve requirement that depends on the level of deposits. No reserves are required for the first $14.5 million in deposits. Between $14.5 million and $103.64 million, there is a 3% reserve requirement, and above $103.64 million there is a 10% reserve requirement.[66] Reserves are computed as the average held over a 14-day period.

The earliest justification for reserve requirements was as a source of liquidity.[67] This notion was derived from the role that specie reserves played as a source of liquidity to redeem notes. However, required reserves are unavailable to meet deposit withdrawals. The reason is that any deposit withdrawal reduces available reserves, and the deficit must be made up. For example, consider a bank with $100 in deposits and a 5% reserve requirement against these deposits. Imagine that the bank has $10 in capital, so that the total asset base is $110. This bank is required to keep $5 in cash reserves. Imagine that it does so and invests the remaining $105 in other assets. Now, suppose there is a $5 deposit withdrawal that the bank meets with its reserves. Since it now has $95 in deposits, it needs to keep $4.75 in reserves. This will require taking in new deposits (note, however, that more than $4.75 in new deposits will be needed since the reserve requirement applies also to the new deposits)[68] or by liquidating other assets.[69]

This is the paradox of fractional reserve requirements. Rather than augmenting liquidity, reserve requirements freeze assets into immobility.[70] The safety of any fractional reserve banking system rests squarely on the availability of a secure and reliable lender of last resort. Fractional reserve requirements cannot help much in this regard.

More recently, reserve requirements have been rationalized as a tool of monetary policy.[71] In its 1931 report, the Fed Committee on Bank Reserves stated: "The most important function served by reserve requirements is the control of credit." Since increasing reserve requirements means that a smaller fraction of deposits can be loaned out by the bank, the Federal Reserve can, in principle, affect the availability of credit by altering reserve requirements.

As a practical matter, however, reserve requirements have played only a minor role in the Fed's monetary policy. From the early years of the Federal Reserve System through the 1920s, the primary instrument of credit policy was the discount window,[72] and from 1942 until the Treasury-Fed Accord in 1951, reserve requirements remained virtually unchanged because the Fed committed itself to a policy of supporting government bond prices.

The current officially stated rationale for reserve requirements is that they are a tool of monetary policy. This position was first articulated in the 1950s, when the Fed came to view reserve requirements as a mechanism for limiting the growth of the money stock as well as credit. It is now believed, however, that this is a specious argument. Without reserve requirements, banks can be expected to voluntarily hold some cash assets, the amount depending on how the LLR facility is priced and administered, and deposit expansion and contraction would ensue more or less as it would with legal reserve requirements. Moreover, reserve requirements have numerous drawbacks: They foster spurious innovation as depository

---

66. See http://www.federalreserve.gov/monetarypolicy/reservereq.htm.

67. See Edgeworth (1888).

68. In fact, at least $5 of new deposits will have to be raised and all of the money invested in cash. If more new deposits are raised, say $10, a greater amount, $5.50 in this case, will need to be invested in eligible reserves.

69. For example, the bank may sell some of its marketable securities or loans.

70. Of course, as reserve requirements approach 100%, these problems vanish since all of the bank's assets are invested in eligible reserves. This limiting argument is the basis for the once popular 100 percent reserve requirement proposal of Henry Simons (1934), Simons (1935).

71. For a detailed discussion of the early history of reserve requirements, see Federal Reserve Staff (1938). For a more recent treatment, see Goodfriend and Hargraves (1983).

72. Friedman and Schwartz (1963) argue that the reserve requirement increases of 1936–1937 precipitated the economic collapse of 1937–1938.

institutions create deposit substitutes to avoid reserve requirements (since there is invariably a lag before regulators respond by imposing reserve requirements on the new liabilities).[73]

The critical feature of reserve requirements is that they determine the sharing of seigniorage on bank deposits between the central bank and the privately owned banks. The higher the reserve requirement, the greater the share of seigniorage that flows to the Federal Reserve, and ultimately back to the U.S. Treasury. Lower reserve requirements direct these monopoly profits to the privately owned banks. This is why reserve requirements are sometimes referred to as a tax on the banks, but they could be defensibly described as a subsidy, depending on who owns the rightful claim to the deposit seigniorage.

Some have argued that the Federal Reserve continues to support reserve requirements because they produce three bureaucratic benefits.[74] First, reserve requirements permit the remission of substantial sums to the Treasury, thereby fostering the Fed's continued budgetary independence; currently, the Federal Reserve's earnings, after expenses and a small contingency reserve charge, are paid to the Treasury as a special franchise tax.[75] Second, reserve requirements provide the Federal Reserve with a natural constituency since financial institutions subject to reserve requirements can be influenced by the Fed.[76] Finally, in the past, when reserve requirements applied only to Federal Reserve member banks, they enabled the Federal Reserve to expand its operations because a variety of subsidized services had to be provided to induce members not to leave the system.[77]

The thing to remember about reserve requirements is that their most basic rationale is to address the moral hazard associated with the LLR facility, and the real issue is the sharing of deposit seigniorage between the government and the privately owned banks.

(2) The Discount Window: The discount window is a mechanism by which the Federal Reserve performs its LLR responsibilities. Banks are allowed to borrow through the discount window to meet short-term liquidity needs. Prior to the passage of the Depository Institutions Deregulation and Monetary Control Act of 1980 (DIDMCA), the discount window was available only to member banks. DIDMCA expanded access to the discount window for nonmember banks and S&Ls, mutual savings banks, and credit unions as well. This was "fair" since DIDMCA also extended federal cash-asset reserve requirements to all institutions.

When a depository institution borrows through the discount window, it ordinarily uses government securities as collateral. This borrowing is used to make up reserves lost due to (unanticipated) deposit withdrawals. Thus, the discount window is closely linked to reserve requirements.

Establishment of the discount window was one of the primary reasons for the creation of the Fed. In addition to providing liquidity, the discount window also facilitates the conduct of monetary policy in that contractionary open market operations can drain the liquidity of individual institutions. The box below provides further details on the discount window.

Discount window details

- *Brief History:* The Fed has three major instruments of monetary policy: open market operations, changes in reserve requirements, and changes in the terms of borrowing from the discount window. Reserve requirement changes have never been used on a consistent basis as a monetary policy tool. One argument is that they represent a very cumbersome policy instrument, although this is largely a calibration issue. That is, reserve requirements can be changed from 10% to 10.0001% rather than to 10.5%, and then they would not be so cumbersome. Nonetheless, the "cumbersome" argument has often been cited as an impediment to using reserve requirements. And, at least in the early years of the Fed, open market operations were not used much either. Administration of the discount window was the key tool for regulating bank reserves.

  Since one of the stated purposes of the discount window was to encourage bank safety, access to the discount window was considered a privilege rather than an entitlement. At the time that the Fed was created, safety and liquidity were to be promoted by encouraging banks to make short-term, self-liquidating loans backed by real goods ("real bills"). In the early years of the Fed, banks could borrow from the discount window only by discounting eligible commercial paper ("real bills"). Banks engaged in risky investments could be denied discount window access by the Fed.

  The banking reforms following the Great Depression resulted in the adoption of the principle that banks should be allowed greater access to the discount window. The "real bills doctrine" was discarded, and banks were allowed to borrow at the discount window using any collateral acceptable to the district Reserve Bank. Thus, in the period immediately following the Great Depression, the discount window was used primarily as a means for the Fed to stand ready to act as a lender of last

---

73. See Greenbaum and Higgins (1983), Porter et al. (1979), and Federal Reserve Staff (1979).
74. See Greenbaum and Thakor (1985).
75. As of July 2006, required reserves were $45 billion. If the Federal Reserve paid interest at say 1% under the discount rate of 6.5% at that time, the annual payment to the banks would approximate $2.475 billion.
76. See Kane (1974).
77. See Gilbert and Peterson (1974).

resort and ensure the overall liquidity of the banking system rather than as an instrument of monetary policy or as a way to influence banks to specialize in real bills.[78] In more recent times, the discount window, in conjunction with federal open market operations, has become an important monetary policy tool. For example, when the Federal Reserve wants to stimulate the economy with a monetary expansion, it may lower the borrowing rate at the discount window. This usually has a ripple effect in the economy, lowering a host of other interest rates and facilitating increased borrowing for investment and consumption.

- *The Discount Rate:* The rate at which a depository institution can borrow at the discount window is known as the *discount rate*. This rate is set at each district Federal Reserve Bank by the board of directors and is subject to approval by the Board of Governors of the Federal Reserve System.

   The costs of borrowing at the discount window are twofold for a depository institution. One is the *discount rate,* and the other is the cost of the accompanying *increased regulatory surveillance.*

- *Forms of Borrowing From the Discount Window:* There are three forms of discount credit: primary credit, secondary credit, and seasonal credit.

- *Primary and Secondary Credit:* Primary credit is typically overnight and available to depository institutions in sound financial condition, usually with minimal administrative conditions. Depository institutions not eligible for primary credit can avail of secondary credit with higher administrative requirements and further oversight.

- *Seasonal Credit:* Because some banks, like rural agricultural banks, are subject to predictably large seasonal credit needs and lack ready access to credit markets, the Federal Reserve amended Regulation A in 1973 to provide seasonal credit to banks. This credit is limited to institutions with deposits less than a stipulated maximum, the rationale being that larger institutions have access to credit markets. The credit extension period lasts from four weeks to nine months.

- *Emergency Credit for Others:* Emergency credit is available to individuals and businesses. Such credit is extended only under very rare circumstances by the district Federal Reserve Bank, and only after consultation with the Board of Governors. Such credit is ostensibly made available only if the borrower is unable to secure credit elsewhere, and failure to obtain credit could have a harmful effect on the economy.

- *Interest on Required Balances and Excess Balances:* The Financial Services Regulatory Relief Act of 2006 allowed the Federal Reserve Banks to pay interest rates on funds at Federal Reserve Banks that are maintained to satisfy reserve balance requirements and on excess balances. The interest rate was set to 0.25% in the period from 2009 to 2013.

(3) Moral Suasion: Central banks around the world also exercise control over banks they regulate by using "moral suasion" or "jawboning." This is simply exerting pressure on banks by persuading, cajoling, or coercing them to act in a particular way. This mode of policy implementation is less feasible in the United States with its thousands of banks than in Europe or Japan where banking tends to be more concentrated.

(4) Unconventional monetary policy tools during the 2007–2009 global financial crisis: The Federal Reserve implemented several unconventional monetary policy tools to deal with the widespread disturbances on various financial markets. For example, the Term Asset-Backed Securities Loan Facility (TALF) was established as a funding facility by the Federal Reserve to provide support for the market of ABS that are collateralized by the loans to consumers and businesses. Under TALF, the Federal Reserve Bank of New York supports market participants by lending on a nonrecourse basis to financial institutions that hold high quality ABS backed by newly issued consumer or small-business loans. Several other facilities are already wound down because conditions on the respective markets have improved.[79] See Chapter 14 for more discussion of this.

CONCLUSION

Banks have been regulated for over two centuries in the United States and even longer so in some other countries. Although regulation has been shaped largely by historical events, as opposed to being the outcome of a well-thought-out regulatory agenda, there have been some important goals that have guided banking regulation. In this chapter, we have explained these goals and described the major regulations to which banks are subjected. In the next chapter, we discuss important milestones in banking legislation in the 1990s, and the early twenty first century.

---

78. The Fed may still utilize the discount window to modify the behavior of potential users. For instance, in 1966 the Fed discouraged member banks from making certain types of business loans, and those who cooperated were assured easier access to the discount window. It is not clear how quantitatively important the discount rate has been. Changes in borrowed reserves seem to be only marginally influenced by changes in the discount rate. Discount rate changes may, however, have a bigger role to play in changing expectations about the future, that is, as a signaling device.

79. These include the Money Market Investor Funding Facility, ABCP MMMF Liquidity Facility, Commercial Paper Funding Facility, Primary Dealer Credit Facility, Term Securities Lending Facility, Term Auction Facility, and Maturity Extension Program and Reinvestment Policy. See http://www.federalreserve.gov/monetarypolicy/expiredtools.htm

REVIEW QUESTIONS

1. What are the main objectives of bank regulation? Discuss each.
2. How inherent is the need for bank regulation? Relate your answer to the *raison d'être* for banks.
3. What is the main conceptual difference between micro-prudential and macro-prudential regulation?
4. Which are the main agencies of bank regulation in the United States, and what is the function of each?
5. Why do we have reserve requirements? What are their drawbacks?
6. What is the purpose of the discount window?
7. Why do we have capital requirements? What are the components of a good capital standard?
8. Critique the Basel I Accord on internationally harmonized capital standards.
9. What improvements does the Basel III Accord seek to make relative to the Basel II accord?
10. Discuss the key elements of safety regulation in banking. What specific role does each play in ensuring bank safety? To what extent are these regulations complements or substitutes in this regard?
11. Discuss the economics of branching and BHC legislation in the United States.
12. What impact has vagueness in BHC legislation had on the behavior of U.S. banks?
13. Discuss the division of a bank's capital into Tier-1 and Tier-2 capital. Contrast this with the usual definition of capital in a nonfinancial firm. Why do you think banks have this more elaborate definition of capital and a division of capital into Tier-1 and Tier-2 components? And explain why following the global financial crisis Tier-1 capital became more dominant.
14. Provide a comparative analysis of the regulatory structures in the United States, United Kingdom, Japan, and the EU.
15. Why do regulators need to regulate market structure and competition in banking?
16. What are the pros and cons of consumer protection regulation?

REFERENCES

Acharya, V.V., Yorulmazer, T., 2007. Too many to fail: An analysis of time inconsistency in bank closure policies. J. Financ. Intermed. 16, 1–31.

Agarwal, S., Amromin, G., Ben-David, I., Chomsisengphet, S., Evanoff, D.D., 2014. Predatory lending and the subprime crisis. J. Financ. Econ. 113, 29–52.

Barth, J.R., Caprio, Jr., G., Levine, R., 2001. Bank regulation and supervision: what works best? World Bank Policy Research Working Paper 2725.

Barth, J.R., Caprio, Jr., G., Levine, R., 2003. Rethinking bank regulations: Till Angels Govern. World Bank.

Barth, J.R., Caprio, Jr., G., Levine, R., 2008. Bank regulations are changing: for better or worse? Comp. Econ. Stud. 50, 537–563.

Barth, J.R., Caprio, Jr., G., Levine, R., 2013. Bank regulation and supervision in 180 countries from 1999 to 2011. J. Financ. Econ. Policy 5, 111–219.

BCBS, Basel Committee on Banking Supervision, 2011. Basel III: A Global Regulatory Framework of More Resilient Banks and Banking Systems. Bank for International Settlements.

BCBS, Basel Committee on Banking Supervision, 2012. Core Principles for Effective Banking Supervision. Bank for International Settlements.

BCBS, Basel Committee on Banking Supervision, 2013a. Basel III: The Liquidity Coverage Ratio and Liquidity Risk Monitoring Tools. Bank for International Settlements.

BCBS, Basel Committee on Banking Supervision, 2013b. Global Systemically Important Banks: Updated Assessment Methodology and the Higher Loss Absorbency Requirement. Bank for International Settlements.

BCBS, Basel Committee on Banking Supervision, 2014. Basel III leverage ratio framework and disclosure requirements. Bank for International Settlements.

BIS, Bank for International Settlements, 2008. Addressing Financial System Procyclicality: a possible framework. Note for the FSF Working Group on Market and Institutional Resilience.

Berger, A., Bouwman, C., 2013. How does capital affect bank performance during a financial crisis? J. Financ. Econ. 109, 146–176.

Bhattacharya, S., Boot, A., Thakor, A.V., 1998. The economics of bank regulation. J. Money Credit Bank. 30, 745–770.

Bliss, R.R., 2001. Market discipline and subordinated debt: a review of some salient issues. Fed. Reserve Bank Chicago Econ. Perspect. 25, 24–45.

Brunnermeier, M.K., Oehmke, M., 2013. The maturity rat race. J. Financ. 68, 483–521.

Calomiris, Ch.W., 1998. Blueprints for a New Global Financial Architecture. U.S. House of Representatives, Joint Economic Committee.

CBO, Congressional Budget Office, 2014. *Transitioning to Alternative Structures for Housing Finance*, CBO, Congress of the United States.

Cummins, C., 1993. Nader Study Accuses 49 Lenders of Redlining. *American Banker*.

Čihák, M., Demirgüç-Kunt, A., Martinez Peria, M.S., Mohseni-Cheraghlou, A., 2013. Bank regulation and supervision in the context of the global crisis. J. Financ. Stabil, 733–746.

DeYoung, R., Flannery, M.J., Lang, W.W., Sorescu, S.M., 2001. The information content of bank exam ratings and subordinated debt prices. J. Money Credit Bank. 33, 900–925.

Duca, J.V., Rosenthal, S.S., 1993. Borrowing constrains, household debt and racial discrimination in loan markets. J. Financ. Intermed. 3, 77–103.

Edgeworth, F.Y., 1888. The mathematical theory of banking. J. R. Statist. Soc. 51, 113–127.

ESRB, 2014. *Is Europe Overbanked?*, Report of the Advisory Scientific Committee, European Systemic Risk Board, No. 4.

European Commission, 2013. EU Competition Law, Rules Applicable to Antitrust Enforcement, Volume I: General Rules, Situation as at 1st July 2013. Luxemburg.

European Commission, 2014. Report from the Commission to the European Parliament and the Council on the Opearion of the European Supervisory Authorities (ESAa) and the European System of Financial Supervision (ESFS). Brussels, 8.8.2014, COM(2014) 509 final.

Evanoff, D.D., Wall, L.D., 2000. Subordinated debt and bank capital: a proposal for regulatory reform. Federal Reserve Bank of Chicago Working Paper no. 2000-07, 2000.

Federal Reserve Board, 2014a. Bank Holding Company Supervision Manual. Prepared by Division of Banking Supervision and Regulation, 2014a, Washington. www.federalreserve.gov/BoardDocs/SupManual/bhc/bhc.pdf.

Federal Reserve Board, 2014b. Comprehensive Capital Analysis and Review 2014 Assessment Framework and Results. Washington. http://www.federalreserve.gov/newsevents/press/bcreg/ccar_20140326.pdf.

Federal Reserve Staff, 1979. Redefining monetary aggregates. Fed. Reserve Bull. 65, 13–42.

Federal Reserve Staff, 1938. The history of reserve requirements for banks in the United States. Fed. Reserve Bull. 24, 953–972.

Fischer, G.C., 1986. The Modern Bank Holding Company: Development Regulation, and Performance. Temple University, Philadelphia, PA.

Foer, A.A., Resnikoff, D.A., 2014. Competition policy and "too big" banks in the European Union and the United States. Antitrust Bull. 59, 9–30.

Freixas, X., 2010. Post-crisis challenges to bank regulation. Econ. Policy 25, 375–399.

Friedman, M., and Schwartz, A.J., 1963. A monetary history of the United States: 1867–1960. National Bureau of Economic Research.

G20, 2009. Declaration on Strengthening the Financial System. London Summit. http://www.eu-un.europa.eu/articles/fr/article_8622_fr.htm.

Galati, G., Moessner, R., 2013. Macroprudential policy – a literature review. J. Econ. Surveys 27, 846–878.

Gasbarro, D.I., Sadguna, G.M., Zumwalt, K.J., 2002. The changing relationship between CAMEL ratings and bank soundness during the Indonesian banking crisis. Rev. Quant. Financ. Account. 19, 247–260.

Gaul, L., Palvia, A., March–April 2013. Are regulatory management evaluations informative about bank accounting returns and risk? J. Econ. Bus. 66, 1–21.

Gilbert, G.G., Peterson, M.O., 1974. Uniform reserve requirements on demand deposits: some policy issues. J. Bank Res. 5, 38–44, Spring.

Golembe, C.r, 1960. The deposit insurance legislation of 1933: an examination of its antecedents and purposes. Polit. Sci. Q. 75, 181–200.

Goodfriend, M., Hargraves, M., 1983. A historical assessment of the rationales and functions of reserve requirements. Economic Review, 2, Federal Reserve Bank of Richmond.

Goodhart, C., 2013. Ratio controls need reconsideration. J. Financ. Stabil. 9, 445–450.

Goodhart, C.A.E., Lastra, R.M., 2012. The boundary problems in financial regulation. In: Barth, James R., Lin, Chen, Wihlborg, Clas. (Eds.), Research Handbook on International Banking and Governance. Edward Elgar Publishing Ltd, Cheltenham, pp. 321–332.

Greenbaum, S.I., Higgins, B., 1983. Financial Innovation. In: Benston, G.J. (Ed.), Financial Services: The Changing Institutions and Government Policy. Prentice Hall, Inc, Englewood Cliffs, NJ, pp. 213–214, The American Assembly, Columbia University.

Greenbaum, S., Thakor, A., 1985. Legal Reserve Requirements in in Banking: a Review and Assessment. *Bank Administration Institute* (monograph).

Hasan, I., Marinč, M., 2013. Should competition policy in banking be amended during crises? Lessons from the EU. Eur. J. Law Econ., Forthcoming.

Huber, S.K., 1989. Bank Officer's Handbook of Government Regulation. Warren, Gorham & Lamont, Inc, Boston.

IMF, International Monetary Fund, 2011. Macroprudential Policy: an Organizing Framework. Prepared by the Monetary and Capital Markets Department. http://www.imf.org/external/np/pp/eng/2011/031411.pdf.

IMF, International Monetary Fund, 2013. Key Aspects of Macroprudential Policy. www.imf.org/external/np/pp/eng/2013/061013b.pdf.

Independent Commission on Banking, 2011. Final Report: Recommendations, London. http://bankingcommission.independent.gov.uk/.

IASB, International Accounting Standards Board, 2014. International Financial Reporting Standard: IFRS 9 Financial Instruments. London.

Kane, E., 1974. All for the best: the Federal Reserve Board's 60th annual report. Am. Econ. Rev. 64, 842–850.

Kane, E., 2014. Shadowy banking: theft by safety. Yale J. Regul., forthcoming.

Keys, B.J., Mukherjee, T., Seru, A., Vig, V., 2010. Did securitization lead to lax screening? Evidence from subprime loans. Q. J. Econ. 125, 307–362.

Lash, N.A., 1987. Banking Laws and Regulations: an Economic Prospective. Prentice-Hall, Inc, Englewood Cliffs, NJ.

Liikanen, E., Bänziger, H., Campa, J.M., Gallois, L., Goyens, M., Krahnen, J.P., Mazzucchelli, M., Sergeant, C., Tuma, Z., Vanhevel, J., Wijffels, H., 2012. High-level Expert Group on Reforming the Structure of the EU Banking Sector. Final Report, Brussels. http://ec.europa.eu/internal_market/bank/docs/high-level_expert_group/report_en.pdf.

Mertens, K., 2008. Deposit rate ceilings and monetary transmission in the US. J. Monetary Econ. 55, 1290–1302.

Merton, R.C., 1994. Influence of Mathematical Models in Finance on Practice: Past, Present and Future. WP #94-045, Division of Research, Harvard Business School.

Mester, L.J., May/June 1992. Banking and Commerce: a Dangerous Liaison? Federal Reserve Bank of Philadelphia Business Review, 17–29.

Munnell, Alicia, H., Lynn, E., Browne, James McEneaney, Geofferey, M.B., March 1996. Tootell, Mortgage Lending in Boston: Interpreting HDMA Data. American Economic Review 86, 25–53.

OECD, 2012. Systemically Important Banks and Capital Regulation Challenges. Working paper.

Pekarek, E., Huth, M., 2008. Bank merger reform takes an extended Philadelphia National Bank holiday. Fordham J. Corp. Financ. Law 13, 594–703.

Porter, R.D., Simpson, T.D., Mauskopf, E., 1979. Financial Innovation and Monetary Aggregates. Brookings Papers on Economic Activity, 213–229.

Reuters, 1993. All of world's big banks said to meet risk-based rules. *Am. Banker*.

Robins, P.K., 1974. The effect of state usury ceilings on single family homebuilding. J. Financ., 227–231.

Simons, H.C., 1935. Rules versus authorities in monetary policy. J. Polit. Econ. 1–30.

Simons, H.C., 1934. A Positive Program for Laissez Faire, Public Policy Pamphlet No. 15, University of Chicago.

Tamaki, N., 2008. Bank Regulation in Japan. CESifo DICE Report 3/2008, 9–13.

World Bank, World Bank Bank Regulation and Supervision Survey (2013) http://econ.worldbank.org/WBSITE/EXTERNAL/EXTDEC/EXTGLOBALF INREPORT/0,contentMDK:23267421~pagePK:64168182~piPK:64168060~theSitePK:8816097,00.html.

Yellen, J.L., 2014. Speech at the 2014 Camdessus Central Banking Lecture, International Monetry Fund, July 2, Washington, DC. http://www.federalreserve.gov/newsevents/speech/yeller20140702a.htm.

Chapter 16

Milestones in Banking Legislation and Regulatory Reform

"In all that the people can individually do well for themselves, government ought not to interfere."

Abraham Lincoln

GLOSSARY OF TERMS

BIF Bank Insurance Fund.
BHC Bank Holding Company.
BHCA Bank Holding Company Act.
CRA Community Reinvestment Act.
ECB European Central Bank.
FDIC Federal Deposit Insurance Corporation.
GAO General Accounting Office.
Golden Parachute A severance payment made to a manager upon termination of employment.
LLR Lender of Last Resort.
Narrow Bank A bank that is restricted in its assets. The original narrow bank proposal called for all of the deposits to be invested in cash and government securities.
OCC Office of the Comptroller of the Currency.
OTS Office of Thrift Supervision (abolished October 19, 2011: supervision powers effectively transferred to the Federal Reserve, the OC, and the FDIC).
SAIF Savings Association Insurance Fund.
Sarbanes – Oxley Act Legislation that mandated more restrictive corporate governance guidelines for publicly traded companies.
SEC Securities and Exchange Commission.
TBTF Too Big to Fail.
Universal Bank A financial intermediary that performs services usually associated with commercial banks, investment banks, and insurance companies.

INTRODUCTION

In this chapter, we discuss milestones in banking legislation and review bank regulatory reform proposals. This chapter is complementary to Chapter 15, which primarily looked at the objectives of regulation and how these have been translated in various regulatory measures around the world. Here we examine first what has happened from a more historic point of view and include a more complete description of key banking acts (the legislative milestones in banking). Subsequently, we will review major problems of bank regulation, and examine the causes of and possible cures for these problems. In particular, we will discuss extensively the Federal Deposit Insurance Corporation Improvement Act (FDICIA) of 1991 and the Dodd–Frank Act of 2010 in the United States, and the recent European Union (EU) legislative agenda. The Dodd–Frank Act and the recent European legislative agenda are largely responses to the global financial crisis; FDICIA was a response to the massive Savings & Loans crisis in the 1980s. We will contrast these responses that followed crises to the deregulation agenda of the 1999 Financial Services Modernization Act ("the Gramm–Leach–Bliley Act"). The Basel Capital Accords (I, II, and III) have been discussed in Chapter 15.

MILESTONES OF BANKING LEGISLATION

Banking legislation has shaped the relationship between government and privately owned banking institutions from the earliest history of the United States. The first banks were chartered by the states, but the federal government reserved to itself the control of interstate commerce and the production of coin and currency.

S. I. Greenbaum, A. V. Thakor & A. W. A. Boot: Contemporary Financial Intermediation, Third edition. http://dx.doi.org/10.1016/B978-0-12-405196-6.00016-1

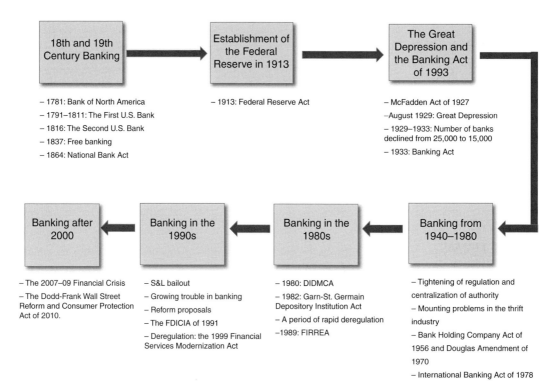

FIGURE 16.1 The Major Eras of U.S. Bank Regulation.

With growing governmental responsibility for stabilizing economic activity came increasing involvement with the banks. Failures and financial panics linked to banks preceded recessions, and many believed that banks were instrumental in producing financial panics and business cycles. Seven major eras of U.S. banking regulation are summarized in Figure 16.1.

Early Bank Regulation

Eighteenth and Nineteenth Century Banking

The creation of the *Bank of North America* in 1781 was driven by the fledgling government's need for a fiscal agent. Soon after the colonies won their independence, the Continental Congress gave a perpetual charter to the Bank of North America. Later, other banks emerged. However, criticism of lending policies and the ability to issue paper currency led to a repeal of the charter given to the Bank of North America.

The First and Second Banks of the United States

With the active support of Alexander Hamilton, then Secretary of the Treasury, the First Bank of the United States was chartered in 1791 for a 20-year period. The bank was an embryonic central bank in that it issued notes, accepted deposits, transferred government funds through its eight branches, made public disbursements, and granted credit to the government as well as the private sector. However, the First Bank did not serve as a depository of bank funds, or as a clearinghouse, or as a creator of bank reserves. Nor did it act as an LLR. The bank was severely criticized for its "anti-South" bias, its inattention to agrarian interests, and its growing English ownership. With Congress not renewing its charter, the bank expired in 1811.

In 1816, Congress chartered the Second Bank of the United States. This bank, initially a fiscal agent for the government, evolved into an embryonic central bank. It would, for example, redeem the bank notes of suspect institutions. The bank was seen, however, as a disciplinary agent representing eastern (lenders) interests at the expense of agrarian (borrowers) interests. When Andrew Jackson, representing the agrarian and frontier interests, was elected president, efforts to recharter the Second Bank of the United States were stifled. Its federal charter expired in 1836.

The period from 1837 to 1864 is commonly referred to as the era of *free banking*. It was a period of minimal federal government involvement in banking. The states had virtual free rein. Colorful stories of "wildcat banking" circulated along with bank notes of heterogeneous value. These banks would open in remote locales in order to frustrate note redemption efforts.

National Bank Act of 1864

The National Bank Act of 1864 marked the return of the federal government to banking. With the 5% tax on state bank notes and licensing of national banks, the era of free banking was brought to a close. The National Bank Act established the *Office of the Comptroller of the Currency* (OCC) to charter and supervise national banks and to regulate the national currency. With the tax on state bank notes, the largest and most reputable banks obtained national bank charters.

The National Bank Act probably had more to do with financing the Civil War than with reforming banks; national banks were required to hold government securities to satisfy liquidity requirements. Moreover, the populist distrust of banks, which sought to avoid undue concentration of power, led to a fragmented banking industry structure.

The period following the Civil War was characterized by periodic financial disruptions as banks' liquidity would be tested by skittish note and deposit holders. Inevitably, some banks would be found wanting and contagious panics would occasionally ensue. Systemic risk arose from provisions that allowed banks to hold their reserves in the form of deposits at other banks. This pyramiding of reserves and attendant panics eventually led to the creation of the Federal Reserve System in 1913. In addition, the pre-Federal Reserve monetary system was inefficient with the notes of thousands of individual banks circulating as imperfect substitutes for one another. This was an era of not only private deposits, but also privately produced currency. There were as many media of exchange as there were banks.

The Federal Reserve Act

Following a particularly disruptive financial panic in 1907, the Congress created the National Monetary Commission to recommend reform of the banking system. Their work led to the Federal Reserve Act in 1913 that established the Federal Reserve System.

The United States was the last major western country to establish a central bank. Unique in its decentralized design, the Federal Reserve reflected the historical ambivalence about creating a powerful quasi-government banking institution. America's deep-rooted populism recoiled at the notion of a centralized hegemony over banking. The genius of the system is that it has been able to function credibly despite its convoluted design. Nominally privately owned, it is a governmental institution. Nominally decentralized with 12 separate corporate entities, virtually all important decisions are made by the presidentially appointed Board of Governors in Washington, DC.

Originally, the Federal Reserve had note-issuing authority, LLR powers, and performed clearing services. But with time, the Federal Reserve took on increasing responsibilities for monetary policy and bank regulation. Perhaps most important among the latter are its responsibilities for oversight of bank holding company (BHC) activities.

Legislation During 1920–1980

The McFadden Act of 1927

The McFadden Act addressed the question of geographic expansion of national banks. Each of the states retained the power to determine the basis on which state-chartered banks could expand their facilities or branches. Thus, states like Illinois limited banks to having only one office (hence the term unit banking). Others, like California, placed no limits on the branching powers of their banks; California banks could establish offices anywhere in the state. Still others like New York permitted limited-area branching. Similarly, some states permitted multibank holding companies whereas others explicitly forbade BHCs.

A question arose about the powers of national banks. Prior to McFadden, some state banks had more expansive branching powers than competing national banks. The McFadden Act gave national banks exactly the same powers as state banks in the states where the national banks are domiciled. Thus, national banks domiciled in California would have the same branching powers as California's state-chartered banks, and national banks located in Illinois would be restricted in the same way as Illinois' state-chartered banks.

This principle of devolution preserved the dual banking system and the fragmentation of banking markets.[1] While it put state and national banks on an equal footing, it also prevented national banks from expanding nationwide, thereby limiting banks' ability to diversify their funding and credit risks and to exploit economies of scale. This diversification problem would come back to plague the industry in the 1980s. The distress and failure of Texas' major banks in the 1990s was in good part due to their undiversified exposure in energy-related industries. And Texas was not alone. The energy industry funk brought down major banks in Oklahoma, Louisiana, and Colorado, too. The subsequent difficulty of New England banks was similarly linked to a regional recession. And still more recently, cutbacks in defense spending and other local problems have stressed California's banks.

The McFadden Act and its litigation of interstate bank expansion was eventually mooted by the Gramm–Leach–Bliley Act, which permitted well-capitalized banks to expand across state lines. Even with the rapid decline in the number of banks and complementary increase in market share of the top-10 banks there is still a paucity of banks in the United States with facilities that are distributed nationwide.

---

1. Later legislation overrode state restrictions on branching for thrifts. For a detailed account of early American banking history, see Hammond (1957).

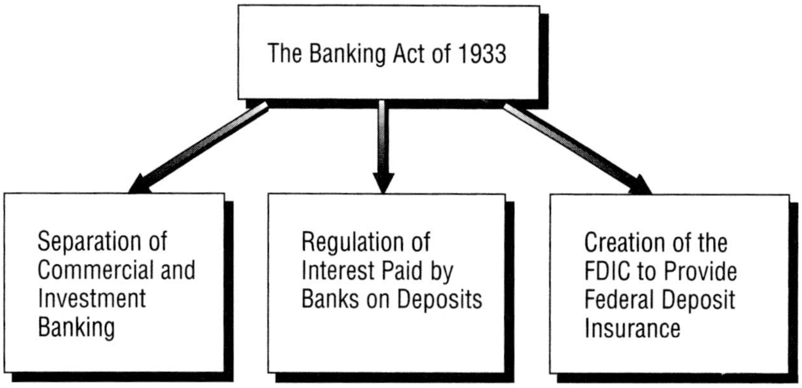

FIGURE 16.2 Significant Provisions of the Banking Act of 1933.

Glass–Steagall Act of 1933

From 1919 to 1929, 6000 banks were suspended or liquidated, and another 4,000 merged with other banks. From 1929 to 1933, another 10,000 banks failed, as the number of banks declined from 25,000 to 15,000. In the depths of the nation's worst economic recession (GNP dropped by 50%, the money supply fell by 33% and the unemployment rate reached 25% in 1932), failing banks were a focal point of discontent. There was no more potent force transforming ordinary folk into revolutionaries than the loss of one's liquid assets in some ostensibly mismanaged bank. (Recall there were no readily available risk-free assets other than currency. Mutual funds came much later and government securities were available only in large denominations.)

This was the ambiance in which newly elected President Franklin D. Roosevelt set out to reform banking. The crisis was memorialized with the Bank Holiday of March 1933 that closed all banks. Congress then shaped legislation that ultimately reconfigured banking more fundamentally than any previous legislation in U.S. history.

The 1933 legislation introduced federal deposit insurance despite President Roosevelt's misgivings. This reform addressed the public's need for a risk-free asset and stemmed the flight from bank deposits to currency. The legislation also capped deposit interest rates, providing banks with a new subsidy. Together with the follow-on Banking Act of 1935, Glass–Steagall took banks out of the securities business and imposed more intrusive supervision than ever before.[2] The most significant provisions of the 1933 legislation are summarized in Figure 16.2.

This legislation was lauded as one of the most successful governmental intrusions into the private sector, ever. President Roosevelt's misgivings about deposit insurance took a full 50 years to be realized. Until the inflation of the 1970s and 1980s, the premium charged for deposit insurance was less than 1/10 of 1% of the deposit base per year. The deposit insurance fund grew steadily, and bank failures were inconsequential. Glass–Steagall, and more particularly the deposit insurance it established, was one of the most admired monuments of the New Deal. As pointed out in Chapters 10 and 11, the remarkable point about deposit insurance is not that it eventually came unraveled, but rather that it lasted as long as it did. President Roosevelt clearly foresaw the moral hazards in the deposit insurance system. What he could not be expected to understand was that these internal contradictions could be held in check for four decades.

Two years after Glass–Steagall, the Banking Act of 1935 became law. It renamed the Federal Reserve Board as the *Board of Governors of the Federal Reserve System* and extended its powers to regulate the discount rates of the district Federal Reserve banks and cash-asset reserve requirements, and impose margin requirements on securities lending. The committee coordinating open-market operations was renamed the *Federal Open Market Committee* (FOMC).

Banking During 1940–1980

The U.S. banking system came out of World War II with immense holdings of U.S. government securities and cash-asset reserves. Banks were well capitalized and credit risk was a minor problem. Indeed banks' loan portfolios had grown very little during the greatest wartime mobilization in U.S. history. Much of the build-up was directly financed by government with the banks serving the secondary role of accumulating government debt. (Recall that the banking industry was still emerging from the trauma of the Great Depression.)

All of this changed when the widely predicted postwar economic funk failed to materialize. Pent-up demand of returning veterans unleashed a sustained prosperity, and bankers sought ways to participate. This required re-examination

2. See Benston (1990) and Lucas (2013).

of their bomb-shelter mentality and the development of methods to prudently process greater risk, principally credit and liquidity risk.

Thus, the postwar period saw banks that had emerged from World War II with over 74% of their assets in government securities replace government securities with business loans. Balance sheets grew, capital ratios fell, and so did cash-asset reserve ratios. It was in this climate that banks expanded their branch systems and began holding company powers more aggressively.

Bank Holding Company Act (BHCA) of 1956 and the Douglas Amendments of 1970

Although group (holding company) banking grew little from 1933 to 1948, activity picked up considerably from 1948 through 1956.[3] Concern about the use of the BHC to expand geographically and functionally prompted the BHC legislation of 1956 and the Douglas Amendments of 1970. Prior to this legislation, the federal government had little power to regulate or supervise BHCs, the corporate parents of the banks. This was viewed as a loophole that needed to be addressed. The BHCA defined a BHC as any entity that owns or controls 25% or more of the voting shares and controls the board of directors of two or more affiliated banks. The 1956 law required BHCs to: (i) divest ownership of businesses other than banking or furnishing services to affiliated banks, (ii) register with the board of Governors of the Federal Reserve, and (iii) seek approval of the board for any bank acquisitions.

Although the Federal Reserve was charged with primary responsibility for regulating BHCs, the focus was on bank acquisitions of holding companies and multibank holding companies. Thus, the 1956 legislation largely ignored questions raised by nonbank acquisitions of one-bank holding companies. This was because nonbank acquisitions were not yet an issue in 1956. But the relentless testing of the limits of banking, symptomatic of the segue away from banking's depression mentality, brought this latter issue to the fore. The 1970 Douglas Amendments required all BHC acquisitions to have explicit Federal Reserve approval. The Federal Reserve developed a laundry list of approvable and prohibited activities, but these lists were merely presumptive, and each individual acquisition required explicit approval. The Douglas Amendment's charge to the Federal Reserve was ambiguous – "[nonbank acquisitions] should be so closely related to banking to be a proper incident thereto" – and the Federal Reserve consequently has virtually boundless discretion in deciding on BHC acquisition applications.

The importance of the BHC regulation, both extant and prospective, is clear in the current debate on reform. First, existing legislation clearly lodges almost boundless power in the Federal Reserve. Second, virtually all proposals to expand banking powers rely on the holding company and its questionable "fire walls" to protect the bank and its insured deposits. Almost certainly, the role of the BHC will expand as banking legislation is liberalized, and the Federal Reserve will be the regulatory focal point.

International Banking Act of 1978

The International Banking Act of 1978 was designed to provide a more "level playing field" between U.S. banks and their foreign-bank competitors operating in the U.S. market. Foreign-bank branches were compelled to select one state as domicile for McFadden purposes. They also were required to satisfy capital and liquidity requirements comparable to those of their U.S. competitors.

Incidental to this complex exercise in defining equivalence came the first explicit continuous capital requirement for banks.[4] This was another testimony to the success of the 1930s legislation. The 5.5% capital requirement of the 1978 legislation was almost an afterthought to defining equivalence between U.S. and foreign banks competing in U.S. markets.

Problems of the Thrift Industry

The 1970s saw a significant increase in interest rate levels and volatility owing to high and volatile inflation rates. In addition, information technology improved dramatically. These two developments profoundly affected banks and thrifts. Interest-rate surprises led to crippling losses for financial institutions with mismatched balance sheets. The thrifts that were legally locked into long-term, fixed-rate mortgages suffered worse than banks that had gradually substituted floating-rate loans for fixed-rate term loans. Advances in information technology weakened barriers to entry and invited competition

---

3. See Fischer (1986). Legislation designed to subject BHCs to stricter regulation had been introduced at every session of Congress between 1933 and 1955, so there was concern among bankers about stricter margin restrictions. This fear of pending legislation prompted a rapid development in multiple-unit banking.

4. Previously banks had to satisfy a minimal capital requirement at their moment of birth, but in the absence of insolvency little was said about capital thereafter.

from a wide variety of nonbank providers of financial services, such as mutual funds, finance companies, and the capital markets. By 1980, the thrift industry was on the brink of insolvency, and banking failures were increasing in size as well as frequency.

Legislation of the 1980s

The legislative developments in the 1980s have a distinct importance because they sought to address the cracks that had started to appear in the rather stable banking environment that had characterized the United States in the years after the Second World War. The more competitive environment of banking and the thrift crisis needed answers.

Depository Institutions Deregulation and Monetary Control Act (DIDMCA) of 1980

DIDMCA addressed two major issues: the disintermediation of deposits that was exacerbated by deposit interest-rate ceilings, and the attrition of Federal Reserve membership as more banks sought to avoid the cost of maintaining cash-asset reserve requirements.

Deposit interest-rate ceilings introduced by the Glass–Steagall legislation had always been a mixed blessing for the banks. When market interest rates for deposit substitutes – government securities, money market mutual funds – were only moderately higher than the ceilings, the banks benefited owing to depositor inertia or convenience. But as the disparity between market and ceiling rates widened, depositors became restless and funds flowed out of the banks. The same deposit interest ceilings that were a major support of banking when interest rates were tranquil became a headache as interest rates became more volatile.

This problem might have been addressed by indexing the deposit interest-rate ceilings to market interest rates, but this was never done. The regulators seemed to prefer unlimited discretion, but their efforts to make timely adjustments in the ceilings could not keep up with the fast-moving capital markets.

DIDMCA addressed this problem by providing for the gradual elimination of all deposit interest-rate ceilings, except those on demand deposits.[5] Banks became free to compete in deposit markets as they saw fit. Even the demand deposit interest-rate restriction was circumvented with consumer NOW accounts. What was not too clearly understood was how important the earlier deposit subsidies had been in discouraging high-risk strategies of banks. DIDMCA also raised the ceiling on federally insured deposits from $40,000 to $100,000 per account. This reduced the incentive of depositors to monitor their banks, further encouraging risk-taking by banks.

The second major initiative of DIDMCA was to subject all insured banks to Federal Reserve cash-asset reserve requirements. This addressed the Federal Reserve's problem of membership attrition. The opportunity cost of satisfying the Federal Reserve's cash-asset reserve requirements increased with the level of market interest rates and declining Federal Reserve membership was yet another piece of the syndrome of the 1970s. Thus, DIDMCA eliminated an opportunity for regulatory arbitrage. Interestingly, since 1980 the Federal Reserve has lowered demand deposit reserve requirements from a maximum of over 16% to 10%. Thus, regulatory hegemony has been accompanied by a transference of the taxpayer's seigniorage to the banks. A summary of the major provisions of DIDMCA appears in the box below.

Major Provisions of DIDMCA
- All depository institutions were permitted to issue interest-bearing checking accounts and required to hold cash-asset reserves as prescribed by the Federal Reserve.
- S&Ls were allowed to have up to 20% of their assets in a combination of consumer loans, commercial paper, and corporate debt instruments.
- Federal S&Ls were allowed to offer credit-card services and engage in trust activities.
- A statutory capital requirement for S&Ls of 5% of deposits was replaced with a range of 3–6% to be set by the Federal Home Loan Bank Board.
- Deposit interest-rate ceilings were phased out over a 6-year period. Interest-rate deregulation was to be administered by the Depository Institutions Deregulation Committee (DIDC) with the Secretary of Treasury as chair and the heads of the Federal Reserve, the FDIC, the Federal Home Loan Bank Board, and the National Credit Union Administration as voting members.
- The deposit insurance limit was raised to $100,000 per account.
- Statewide branching was permitted for federal S&Ls.
- Earlier geographical limits on S&L lending – loans could only be made within a 50-mile radius of an office – were eliminated.
- Authority of federal S&Ls to make acquisition, development, and construction (ADC) loans was expanded.

---

5. One catalyst for DIDMCA was a Supreme Court deadline for addressing the alleged illegality of NOWs, ATMs, and share draft accounts.

Garn-St. Germain Depository Institutions Act of 1982

The Garn-St. Germain Act was directed at thrifts exclusively and sought to enhance their earnings potential by expanding their powers. The initiative was a response to the huge losses suffered by the industry due to the 1980–1981 spike in interest rates.

The prime rate soared to over 21%. The thrift industry was forced to fund its vast portfolio of loans and fixed-rate mortgages with very high cost liabilities. The losses sustained over an 18-month period eroded a significant portion of the industry's capital.[6] Much of the loss was attributable to thrifts having been legally confined to fixed-rate mortgages. In order to earn their way back, it was argued that thrifts needed more liberalized asset empowerments, including the authority to make adjustable-rate mortgages.

Garn-St. Germain provided the expanded asset powers the industry sought. This permitted vastly increased credit risk, and those who had been most devastated by losses were the most eager to pursue high-risk strategies. A summary of the major components of Garn-St. Germain is given in the box below.

Major Provisions of Garn-St. Germain
- Asset powers of federal S&Ls were expanded by permitting:
  - Up to 40% of assets in commercial mortgage loans.
  - Up to 30% of assets in consumer loans.
  - Up to 10% of assets in commercial loans.
  - Up to 10% of assets in commercial leases.
- Elimination of the previous statutory limit on the loan-to-value ratio, allowing S&Ls to lend more relative to the appraised value of a project.
- Authorization of the FDIC and the FSLIC to issue "net worth certificates" that could increase an institution's capital for regulatory purposes without any real infusion of capital.

Financial Institutions and Regulatory Reform Enforcement Act (FIRREA) of 1989

FIRREA was the sequel to Garn-St. Germain. It created the machinery and procedures to dispose of insolvent and near-insolvent thrifts. The regulatory agency for thrifts, the FHLBB, was disenfranchised. A new thrift regulator was created, the Office of Thrift Supervision (OTS), within the Treasury Department. The thrift insurer, the FSLIC, was also reorganized and placed within the FDIC as the Savings Association Insurance Fund (SAIF). The legislation also created the Resolution Trust Corporation (RTC) to dispose of failed thrifts and their assets.

FIRREA laid the groundwork for more aggressive resolutions of impaired thrifts, and subsequently more than 1000 thrifts were restructured via government intervention. FIRREA sought to correct for the passivity and forbearance of earlier regulatory policies.

FIRREA had two important provisions insofar as capital requirements are concerned. First, FIRREA stipulated three types of capital requirements: tangible capital, core capital, and risk-based capital. Tangible capital is common equity and perpetual preferred stock; the OTS required thrifts to keep tangible capital equal to at least 1.5% of total assets. Core Capital was defined as tangible capital plus nonperpetual preferred stock and qualifying subordinated debt; the OTS required thrifts to keep core capital equal to at least 3% of total assets. Intangible assets like goodwill could no longer count as part of core capital by 1994, with a phase-out schedule stipulating the rate at which intangible assets had to be phased out from consideration as regulatory capital. With the passage of FIRREA, the term "supervisory goodwill" was used to denote goodwill created in FSLIC-assisted acquisitions of insolvent thrifts in which there was a specific agreement by regulators to permit the goodwill to count as regulatory capital. It is this goodwill that was subject to a 5-year phaseout. All other goodwill was immediately disqualified as regulatory capital. The risk-based capital ratio had to exceed 8% and was to be computed in the same way as the Tier-1 capital ratio under the Basel Accord.

FIRREA mandated a study by the Treasury that would propose reform of the deposit insurance system. This resulted in a February 1991 proposal by the Treasury. The Treasury proposal was two-fold: limiting the risks in the deposit insurance system in combination with freeing up banking markets. In particular, it advocated limiting deposit insurance coverage in combination with risk-sensitive pricing and higher capital requirements. Simultaneously it advocated full interstate banking and allowing banks to affiliate with other financial institutions. In combination, the Treasury

---

6. Estimates range between $150 billion [Balderstone (1985)] and $165 billion [Kane (1990a)]. See also Kane and Yu (1993). For a perspective, note that thrifts were a trillion-dollar industry with something less than 5% in capital.

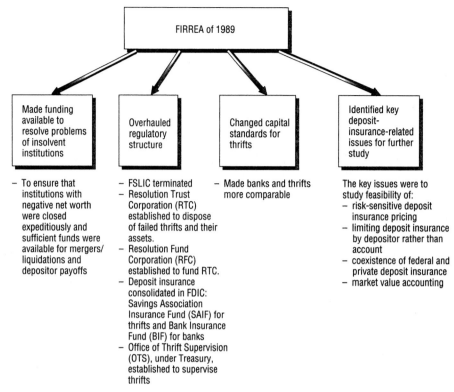

FIGURE 16.3   Major Elements of FIRREA.

proposals were aimed at reducing the taxpayer liability, facilitating a better allocation of credit and strengthening the banking industry.[7] The major elements of FIRREA are summarized in Figure 16.3.

The Treasury's bold reform proposals were rejected in favor of the FDICIA that we discuss later in this chapter.

PROBLEMS OF BANK REGULATION

The Problems

In Table 16.1 we summarize prominent problems among deposit-taking financial institutions, along with possible causes and commonly suggested remedies. Our perspective here is that of a taxpayer desiring a globally competitive banking system in which taxpayer exposure is minimized.

Causes and Possible Cures

In this subsection, we briefly discuss each of the major issues and possible remedies listed in Table 16.1. Our discussion is organized around four issues: deposit insurance, regulatory uncertainty, market value accounting (MVA), and expanded banking powers.

1. ***Deposit Insurance and the Bank's Incentives:*** Our discussion in Chapter 10 highlighted problems associated with deposit insurance. It is commonly believed that these problems arise from: (i) the pricing of deposit insurance, (ii) the incentives of regulators, and (iii) the incentives of bank executives. We discuss each briefly in turn.

   a. *Deposit Insurance Pricing:* Insurance premiums that are risk insensitive or only weakly sensitized to risk shift the burden of restraining risk-taking to the regulators rather than allowing risk to be controlled by the discipline of a pricing mechanism. This problem was recognized in FDICIA as we discuss below. There are, however, numerous difficulties in implementing a risk-sensitive deposit insurance pricing scheme that effectively deters risk-taking. These include risk measurement[8] and asymmetric information.[9] Properly calibrated risk-based deposit insurance

---

7. See, for example, Keeton (1991).

8. See Kareken and Winter (1983) and Flannery (1991). Some risks may even be immeasurable (see Caballero and Krishnamurthy, 2008).

9. See Chan et al. (1992), and Pennacchi (2006).

TABLE 16.1 Symptoms, Causes and Commonly Suggested Cures for the Problems of Depository Institutions in the 1980s

Symptoms	Possible Causes	Commonly Suggested Cures
• Excessive risk-taking • Management fraud	• Distorted incentives arising from the pricing of deposit insurance • Ineffective regulatory monitoring • Low charter values of depository institutions	• Improving capital standards • Risk-sensitive deposit insurance • Restricted entry into banking • "Narrow" banks • Improving monitoring procedures • Providing greater resources for regulatory surveillance
• Excessive delays in closing failed institutions – forbearance.	• Regulatory accounting principles (RAP) • Self-interested bank regulators	• Market value accounting • Improving incentives of regulators
• Unpredictable effects of monetary policy	• Reserve requirements • Financial innovation	• Modify reserve requirements • Reduce regulatory taxes that encourage Financial innovation
• High cost of equity capital for banks	• Regulatory uncertainty	• Make regulation more predictable and eliminate perceived regulatory capriciousness
• Declining competitiveness of U.S. banks	• Improved information processing in economy and reduced value of banking services • Loss of market share to foreign banks	• Less onerous regulation • Expanded powers for banks to permit entry into investment banking and insurance • Dismantling of branching restrictions • International harmonization of capital standards

pricing must depend on many variables, reflecting credit, interest rate, and liquidity risks. How do we measure these risks? Moreover, even if we could measure these risks, how should the deposit insurance premiums be linked to the measured risks? The asymmetric information problem arises from the bank having better information about its own risks than the regulator. Thus, in designing a deposit insurance scheme that accurately reflects risk, the regulator confronts the task of eliciting the bank's private information.

Risk-sensitive deposit insurance premiums were adopted under FDICIA, representing an important step in regulatory reform.

b. *Regulatory Incentives:* Some believe that many banking problems are rooted in defects in political and bureaucratic accountability.[10] Covering up evidence of poor regulatory performance and relaxing restrictions on regulated firms are common governmental responses to industry difficulties. Similarly, aggressive risk-taking by banks is a rational response to regulatory forbearance.

This viewpoint recognizes a principal-agent problem at the level of the public regulator. Regulators and politicians are seen as *agents* of taxpayers, and as agents they possess well-defined objectives that commonly conflict with those of their principals. To understand this viewpoint, imagine a banking or thrift industry that consists of many impaired firms with negative net worths that are attracted to risky portfolio strategies.

Regulators should expeditiously close such firms. But doing so usually upsets incumbent politicians. Moreover, resolute actions by regulators may signal their previous mistakes in allowing conditions to fester to the point where receivership or conservatorship becomes necessary. The larger the troubled firms' hidden economic losses, the more a public acknowledgement of their insolvency threatens the regulators' reputations, and the more inclined regulators will be to forbear. The hope may be that the insolvency can be reversed, or the problem can be passed on to a successor. The idea that the careers of regulators and politicians would be damaged by acknowledging insolvencies is enshrined in the ancient practice of killing messengers bearing bad news. FIRREA and FDICIA dealt with this problem by greatly limiting regulatory forbearance; an institution whose book net worth falls below 2% of assets now has to be closed within a specified period of time.

If we assume that insured institutions constantly develop new and partly unanticipated ways to shift risk to the deposit insurance fund, we can imagine three *regulatory regimes* as shown in Figure 16.4.[11]

---

10. The most forceful proponent of this argument is Kane (1989a, 1989b, 1990a, 1990b, 2014). See also Campbell et al. (1992), Boot and Thakor (1993), and Morrison and White (2013).
11. This is based on Kane (1989a, 1989b).

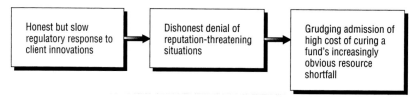

FIGURE 16.4 Sequential Regulatory Regimes.

As shown in Figure 16.4, regulators start out as well-intentioned public servants. However, a "crossover point" is reached when they discover that actions taken by the firms they regulate have gone undetected and now threaten the solvency of the deposit insurance fund. The regulators recognize that the problems are so difficult to resolve that their career interests are better served by procrastination or denial. It appears that, in the case of the thrift industry, this transition to denial occurred in the late 1970s, and the denial continued through 1987. During this period, thrift-industry lobbying generated disinformation about the condition of the industry. Concern seemed limited to the possibility that public acknowledgement of the FSLIC's insolvency could precipitate a crisis. The existence of serious problems and regulatory denial is indicated by the data in Table 16.2.

As this table shows, the industry was insolvent on average for a long time before there was a public awareness. Moreover, closures or resolutions by the FSLIC fell far short of actual insolvencies. Since this was also a period during which the industry was growing rapidly, many firms with negative net worths were not only allowed to stay in business but also to grow their assets.

However, the longer a cover-up goes on, the harder it becomes to sustain the deception. The reasons are twofold. First, not acknowledging losses only defers accounting recognition. Second, allowing economically insolvent institutions to continue may increase losses over time given the bank's increased incentive to assume risk.

The above discussion takes as given the existing structure of federal deposit insurance. Many alternatives to this structure have been proposed, however. One is to *privatize deposit insurance.* This would provide a self-insurance program for the banking industry, in which banks insure and monitor each other. The difficulty is that, with a large number of banks, each member's incentive to monitor is likely to be weak.[12]

A second alternative is to limit deposit insurance to "narrow banks." That is, only those banks that invest in the safest securities like Treasury bills would be able to offer insured deposit accounts. The remaining banks would

TABLE 16.2 Data on Financial Condition and Closures of FSLIC-Insured Thrifts from 1975 to 1984

Year	Ratio of Appraised Market Value of Net Worth to Total Assets in Percent	GAAP-Insolvent Institutions	Insolvencies Resolved by the FSLIC
1975	−7.77	17	11
1976	−7.25	48	12
1977	−6.62	38	10
1978	−6.87	38	4
1979	−9.32	34	4
1980	−12.78	43	32
1981	−15.41	85	82
1982	−10.63	237	247
1983	−6.03	293	70
1984	−2.74	445	336

Source: Edward J. Kane, "The Unending Deposit Insurance Mess," *Science* 246, October 1989b, 451–456.

---

12. These incentives can be further weakened when some of the banks responsible for monitoring are in financial difficulty. The reduced monitoring by financially weak banks can lead to more banks getting into trouble due to the reduction of vigilance. This introduces a systematic risk element and possible contagions. For an analysis of the macroeconomic effects of bank runs, see Loewy (1991) and Gertler and Kiyotaki (2013). See also Donaldson (1992), and Gilchrist et al. (2009).

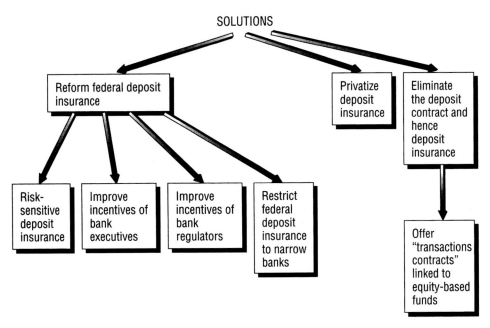

FIGURE 16.5   Possible Solutions to the Deposit Insurance Problem.

invest in assets of their choice, but could finance these assets only with uninsured liabilities. This would limit taxpayers' exposure while preserving federal deposit insurance.

Finally, there are those who would reform deposit insurance by *eliminating the deposit contract itself.* As we saw in Chapter 12, the deposit contract creates the possibility of a bank run because of the *sequential service constraint* that entices each depositor to be the first at the teller window to withdraw his or her deposits as soon as trouble is suspected. While deposit insurance is one response to this potential disruption, another possibility is to do away with the sequential service constraint. This could be achieved if banks issued equity-like claims, such as those of mutual funds. Since any withdrawal from the fund would be commensurate with the fractional ownership of the investor in the fund, there would be no advantage to any investor/depositor in being first to withdraw. Such contracts could be endowed with the full range of transactions services. Individuals would be exposed to "market risk" since the value of the mutual fund would be subject to random fluctuations as market conditions change, but the threat of panic runs would vanish.[13] The issue was also discussed in Chapter 12. Figure 16.5 summarizes possible solutions to the deposit insurance problem.

  c. *Improving the Incentives of Bank Executives:* If the bank's top executives are somehow *rewarded* for failure, then the incentives to take risk are strengthened. One way that executives are rewarded is with *golden parachutes* when they leave troubled firms. The FDIC now has restrictions on such payments by troubled firms. This follows the OCC's decision in 1991 to stop monthly payments of $42,000 to Charles Zwick, former chairman of Southeast Banking Corporation. In February 1991, regulators forced Alan P. Hoblitzell, former chairman and CEO of troubled MNC Financial, Inc., to return $915,865 in severance pay.

The Bank Fraud Act of 1990 authorized the FDIC to set strict golden parachute rules in its role as guardian of the Bank Insurance Fund. The agency must approve any golden parachute offered to departing executives of troubled banks. To gain approval, the institution must demonstrate that the executive committed no fraudulent act, is not substantially responsible for the institution's impaired condition, and has not violated banking and criminal laws. Moreover, all institutions must satisfy similar criteria before they are allowed to pay legal fees for directors and officers.

2. *Regulatory Uncertainty:* Public regulation of banking is aimed in part at dealing with moral hazard problems growing out of the public safety net. This includes not only explicit guarantees, such as deposit insurance and the LLR,

---

13. Elimination of *non par clearance* was one of the motivations for the passage of the Federal Reserve Act of 1913. So to return to it may seem odd, but people are now willing to accept claims on mutual funds in lieu of deposits. Some may argue that it is fanciful to believe that removing the sequential service constraint would remove the threat of bank runs, since we saw runs on money market mutual funds in the United States during the 2007–2009 crisis; see Chapter 14. However, as documented by Kacperczyk and Schnabl (2013) these runs on mutual funds were due to (rational) perceptions of higher risk-taking by these funds and concerns about the possible insolvency of the funds. This is no different from a bank refusing to renew a loan because it believes the borrower is on the verge of insolvency. One could hardly call this a "panic" run.

but also ill-defined governmental guarantees of the payments system and TBTF. Thus, the question transcends that of designing an optimal regulatory monitoring system. Rather, it calls for *jointly* designing the guarantee structure *and* the monitoring system so as to achieve social objectives while controlling moral hazard at minimal *total* social cost.

An appealing approach is to minimize the *need* for regulation, but this means minimizing the span of the safety net. Indeed, this may be the most compelling argument for restricting the government's safety net. However, since even the minimal safety net will entail *some* government exposure, some regulation/supervision is likely to be necessary. We are, therefore, forced to wrestle with the question of optimal regulatory design in the context of a minimally guaranteed system.

In contemplating this issue, it is useful to distinguish between the *discretionary* and *nondiscretionary* aspects of regulation. The latter represent more or less well-defined rules, such as cash-asset reserve requirements, capital requirements, loans-to-one-borrower rules, and deposit insurance premium schedules. On the other hand, discretionary regulations involve greater ambiguity. Examples include the standards for BHC acquisitions contained in the 1970 Douglas Amendments, deposit insurance coverage under current practices, standards for access to the discount window, standards for intervention in cases of distressed institutions, and accounting standards in the banking and thrift industries.

One benefit of ambiguity is that it gives the regulator a weapon against moral hazard.[14] When a bank is not really sure whether the regulator will rescue it in a given set of circumstances, the bank may go to greater lengths to avoid jeopardy. However, ambiguity also has costs. As the probability and nature of regulatory intervention become more difficult to assess, investors begin to demand higher risk premia on the bank's equity. This increases the bank's cost of capital and reduces competitiveness relative to competitors in more predictable environments. To the extent that the regulator does *not* internalize the bank's increased cost of capital, discretion transfers wealth from shareholders to taxpayers or regulators.

3. *MVA:* It is widely believed that Regulatory Accounting Principles (RAP) and Generally Accepted Accounting Principles (GAAP) have contributed to problems in the thrift and banking industries. RAP hid the magnitude of the crisis for some time because it deferred unrealized losses and thereby overstated capital even when economic net worth was negative. Given the risk-taking incentives of economically insolvent institutions, the crisis gathered momentum as thrifts sought ever-increasing risk. GAAP do not help much since they rely substantially on the historical cost (or book value) of transactions.[15]

The alternative, MVA, requires that all assets and liabilities, including all off-balance sheet items (which would be brought on-balance sheet) be carried at current market value. The values of the assets and liabilities would be increased or decreased, as market conditions indicated. MVA can be useful in implementing risk-based capital requirements, risk-based deposit insurance premiums, and improved regulatory supervision. It could, thus, be an important part of the overall reform of the deposit insurance system.

In principle, the case for adopting MVA is impeccable, but there are conceptual, measurement, and incentive problems with implementing MVA.[16] The major problem is assigning market values to nontraded commercial bank loans and guarantees. Many of these instruments are nonmarketable or marketable only at steep discounts. Because of information and monitoring advantages that the bank has relative to potential buyers of these instruments, there is usually a divergence between the value of the asset to the bank and its value if sold, so that measuring value becomes difficult.

Arguing that the system does not need a full-blown accounting system, but only a market-based measure of net worth, simplifies the measurement problem, but raises other issues that need further consideration. For example, it is possible that requiring banks to add capital when the market value of loans (and hence net worth) declines would induce banks to choose loans of shorter maturity, that is, loans that would "liquidate" with fewer possibilities for a market-based revision in value.[17] The reason is that there may be an asymmetry in the effect of revisions on the bank's capital. An increase in loan value would augment the bank's economic net worth and permit it to support deposit and asset expansion, but the bank may be unable to profitably carry out such an expansion

---

14. The constructive role of ambiguity/discretion has been stressed by Allen and Gale (1993), Boot et al. (1993), Corrigan (1990), and DeYoung et al. (2013).

15. See White (1988).

16. See Berger et al. (1991).

17. See O'Hara (1993) for an interesting model that predicts that, under some conditions involving asymmetric information, we could see a shortening of bank asset maturity with MVA, a veritable return to the concept of self-liquidating investments embodied in the "real bills" doctrine.

immediately.[18] Thus, the bank may be unable to fully extract the benefit of an upward revision in loan value. But if the loan value drops, then MVA would force the bank to acquire additional capital or sell off some assets; both initiatives are likely to be costly.[19] Such an asymmetry in the effect of loan value revisions on the bank could create an incentive to minimize potential value revisions, and hence a shortening of loan maturities. Despite these unresolved issues, valuing at market all those assets and liabilities that are actively traded in secondary markets and using best judgment to estimate the values of the remainder seems to be gaining favor among public regulators and the accounting profession.

4. *Expanded Banking Powers:* Prior to the Gramm–Leach–Bliley Act of 1999, both banks and thrifts have lobbied for expanded powers that would increase charter values and reduce failures. The principal objections to *universal banks* were that expanded powers make it more difficult to regulate and limit risk-taking at the expense of the deposit insurance fund, and that expanded powers can give rise to conflicts of interest. The potential conflicts include:[20]

   i. The promotional role of the investment bank in selling securities may conflict with the commercial bank's obligation to provide objective advice to depositors.

   ii. In order to avoid a loss on a loan, the universal bank may encourage the borrower to raise new capital through the bank's securities subsidiary in order to repay the loan.

   iii. A universal bank may use its monopoly power to cross-sell services. Threats of credit rationing, refusal to renew loan commitments, and increasing the cost of loans could all be used to "tie" existing customers to other products of the universal banks.

   iv. A universal bank may avoid losses in underwriting by placing unsold securities in its trust accounts.

   v. Interlocks between the directors of universal banks and their customers may give rise to conflicts.

   vi. Banks may make imprudent loans to bolster a firm taken public through an *initial public offering* (IPO) underwritten by the universal bank.

   vii. The bank may lend imprudently to its securities affiliate, possibly transferring wealth from the deposit insurance fund to the securities affiliate.

The seriousness of these conflicts of interest is widely disputed.[21] Those favoring the separation of commercial and investment banking believe that conflicts are significant,[22] and that the separation is necessary to ensure that the governmental safety net is not significantly expanded in scope. Those favoring expanded bank empowerment believe that market forces will provide the discipline necessary to control abuses.[23] Others believe that moral hazard and other conflicts of interest can be controlled by limiting regulatory forbearance and forcing sufficiently early closure of troubled institutions.[24]

If there are serious conflicts, then there should be evidence that banks in the pre-1933 period deceived investors into investing in securities that imposed losses on investors. A recent study tested this hypothesis by comparing the performance of securities underwritten by affiliates of commercial banks with those sponsored by independent investment banks.[25] It found that securities sold by bank affiliates defaulted less frequently than similar securities sold by stand-alone investment banks. Strikingly, the difference in default rates was the greatest for relatively speculative (private-information-intensive) issues that, because they are the hardest for investors to judge, should have potentially imposed the largest losses on investors. This evidence calls into question the significance of alleged conflicts of interest. Investors with rational expectations will take into account potential conflicts of interest in pricing securities. Consequently, securities sold by bank affiliates with poor reputations for avoiding potential conflicts will sell at steep discounts. Issuers will anticipate this and gravitate to bank affiliates with good reputations, and these institutions will then be observed to underwrite the majority of issues accounted for by bank affiliates. Succinctly put, market discipline apparently worked well in resolving conflicts of interest prior to Glass–Steagall.

---

18. This would be the case, for example, if the marginal cost of deposits is increasing in quantity, and assets yielding more than the deposit funding cost are unavailable without sufficient time to plan for the expansion.

19. Again, this cost may be due to informational frictions. Asymmetric information alone can make equity capital more costly than deposits (see Myers and Majluf, 1984). Moreover, loan sales may involve losses for the bank when it knows more than outsiders about the true value of the loans (see Bhattacharya and Thakor (1993)).

20. See Saunders (1985).

21. See Benston (1990).

22. See Mester (1992).

23. See Huertas (1988) and Saunders (1991). For historical accounts of the separation of investment banking, see Shull (1983).

24. See Eisenbeis and Horvitz (1993).

25. See Kroszner and Rajan (1994).

An additional argument against expanded banking powers is that they may dilute financial innovation incentives. A universal bank that is considering a financial-market innovation will worry about cannibalizing the loan business of its commercial banking arm. A stand-alone investment bank has no such concerns and thus will have stronger financial-innovation incentives.

The effect of expanded powers on banks is ultimately an empirical issue. Empirical research has provided interesting evidence. Using data on 107 countries, one study shows that restricting bank activities has an adverse effect on bank development and stability.[26] This could provide some support for universal banking, which is common in Europe, Latin America, and other parts of the world.[27] Note, however, that this does not provide support for having purely speculative activities become part of banks. The universal banking model works best when it is client-centric, and thus relationship based.

THE 1991 FDICIA AND BEYOND

In 1991, the U.S. Treasury proposed sweeping regulatory reform of banking aimed at promoting the global competitiveness of American banking institutions, reducing taxpayers' exposure deriving from deposit insurance, and promoting the safety and soundness of American financial institutions. The key elements of the proposal were: (i) limiting deposit insurance coverage, (ii) achieving regulatory consolidation, (iii) involving the Treasury as well as the Federal Reserve in TBTF decisions, and (iv) dismantling the Glass–Steagall and McFadden restrictions on banking activities.

This initiative culminated in the Federal Deposit Insurance Corporation Improvement Act (FDICIA) in December 1991. The main focus of FDICIA was on reducing taxpayer exposure deriving from deposit insurance and promoting the safety and soundness of American financial institutions. The key features of FDICIA are discussed below.

Bank Regulation

FDICIA linked *supervision* to *bank capital* (Figure 16.6). Regulators were required to establish five capital compliance categories for banks and thrifts: well-capitalized, adequately capitalized, undercapitalized, significantly undercapitalized, and critically undercapitalized. Regulatory forbearance was restricted by requiring "prompt corrective action" as capital dissipated. In particular, regulators are required to close banks *before* they become insolvent. If capital declines to levels below positive trigger points, regulators must impose caps on growth, enforce reductions or suspension of dividends, instruct bank management to raise capital, and mandate management changes if necessary. Regulators are also permitted to close critically undercapitalized banks, where the ratio of tangible equity capital to total assets is less than 2%. FDICIA also permits bank regulators to place a bank in receivership or conservatorship for other transgressions, including violation of a cease-and-desist order, concealment of records or assets, inability to cover deposit withdrawals, or failure to either develop or implement a required plan to raise capital. Moreover, FDICIA requires bank regulators to take action within 90 days of a bank becoming critically undercapitalized. The key principles of the supervisory review under FDICIA are summarized in Figure 16.6.

Prompt corrective action also requires an *ex-post* review of any bank or thrift failure that imposes material costs on the FDIC. If a material loss occurs, the inspector general of the appropriate banking agency must determine why and must provide recommendations for preventing such a loss in the future. This report must be made available to the Comptroller

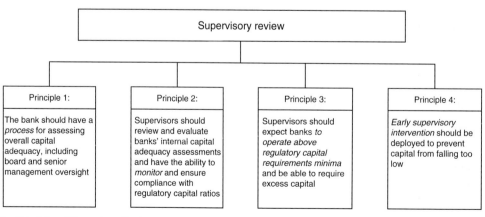

FIGURE 16.6 Key Principles of Supervisory Review.

26. See Barth et al. (2004).
27. See Mester (1992).

General of the United States, to members of Congress upon request, and to the public through the Freedom of Information Act. Further, the GAO must do an annual review of the reports and recommend improvements in supervision.

In addition to supervision, regulators were instructed to come up with a way to link bank capital requirements to interest-rate risk, credit risk of concentrations of credit, and the risk of nontraditional activities, and to draft a new set of noncapital measures of bank safety, such as underwriting standards. Regulators also are required to perform annual on-site bank examinations, place limits on real estate lending by banks and tighten auditing requirements.

Deposit Insurance

FDICIA transferred to the FDIC the responsibility for insuring thrifts as well as commercial banks. (Credit unions continue to have a separate deposit insurance agency, the NCUA.) While the deposit insurance of thrifts and banks was consolidated into the FDIC, the two types of intermediaries retained separate insurance reserve funds – bank deposits are insured by the *Bank Insurance Fund* (BIF) and thrift deposits by the *Savings Association Insurance Fund* (SAIF).

FDICIA also reduced the scope of federal deposit insurance. The most significant change is the restriction on the TBTF initiatives that provide governmental protection of deposits beyond the prescribed $100,000 limit. The FDIC's ability to re-imburse uninsured depositors – those with over $100,000 and those with foreign deposits – was severely limited. FDICIA, however, does permit TBTF initiatives if failure would "have serious adverse effects on economic conditions or financial stability." This exception requires the agreement of a two-thirds majority of the directors of the FDIC, a two-thirds majority of the Board of Governors of the Federal Reserve System, and concurrence of the Secretary of the Treasury. The Secretary of the Treasury is required to document the need to invoke the systemic risk exception. The GAO must review any actions taken, and analyze the potential effect on the behavior of other insured depository institutions as well as uninsured deposi-tors. The rest of the banking industry is required to pay the cost of any bailout through an emergency assessment by the FDIC that is proportional to each bank's average total tangible assets.[28] Only the best-capitalized banks will be able to offer *insured brokered deposits* (large CDs sold through brokerage firms) or accounts established under employee pension plans that offer pass-through insurance.[29] FDICIA also required the FDIC to adopt *risk-sensitive deposit insurance premia.*

FDIC Funding

The shrinking bank deposit insurance fund was bolstered with an additional $70 billion in borrowing authority. The FDIC's authority to borrow from the Treasury was increased from $5 billion to $30 billion. The loans were to be repaid with increased deposit insurance charges on the banks. The FDIC was authorized to borrow additionally for working capital needs. The mon-ey, about $45 billion, and interest would be repaid as the FDIC gradually disposes of the assets of failed banks. The FDIC also was instructed to rebuild the BIF to 1.25% of insured domestic deposits by the year 2006, which was achieved well before that.

The Discount Window

FDICIA limits the Federal Reserve's ability to use the discount window to support a financially troubled bank. Permitting discount window access to a failing bank allows uninsured deposits to be withdrawn prior to FDIC resolution, thereby increasing the exposure of the deposit insurance fund. FDICIA limits the amount of discount window lending to a bank's capital, with restrictions applying to undercapitalized (capital less than 8% of assets) and critically undercapitalized banks. Although the Federal Reserve retains considerable discretion in its discount window policy, it is liable to the FDIC for losses suffered by the deposit insurance fund due to discount window access provided to critically undercapitalized banks.

Another significant change in the discount window is that FDICIA now permits *all* nonbank U.S. firms – brokerage and other financial services firms as well as nonfinancial firms – to borrow at the discount window for emergency purposes under the same collateral terms afforded to banks.

Corporate Governance of Banks

FDICIA contains provisions aimed at strengthening the audit function of the boards of directors of banks and developing guidelines for the compensation of directors and officers. These provisions are designed to protect the deposit insurance fund by enhancing managerial and director accountability.

---

28. FDICIA thereby introduces an incentive for insured banks themselves to question any TBTF initiative.

29. Pass-through insurance refers to a $100,000 coverage for each participant in a collective account. Thus, a $50 million pension fund deposit might be fully insured, provided it had a sufficient number of participants $\left(\frac{\$50\,\text{million}}{\$100.00} = 500\,\text{participants}\right)$.

Specifically, banks are required to have audit committees composed exclusively of "outside" directors who are independent of the management of the institution. Two additional requirements are imposed on large institutions. First, their audit committees cannot include large customers of the institution. Second, audit committee members must have banking or related financial management expertise, and they must have access to independent outside counsel of their own choosing. FDICIA prescribes that the audit committee shall review external audits with management and the independent accountants. These provisions are designed to increase the independence of the audit committee and its ability to monitor management. They in many ways anticipate the requirements of the Sarbanes–Oxley legislation of 2002 which applies to all publicly owned corporations.

FDICIA's impact on board compensation committees is less direct. FDICIA does not specify the composition of the board's compensation committee, but it calls for federal banking agencies to prescribe guidelines for executive and board compensation that preclude employment contracts that could jeopardize the financial health of the institution.

Foreign Banks and Foreign Deposits

FDICIA gives the Federal Reserve new authority to regulate foreign bank operations in the United States. The FDIC is generally prohibited from protecting foreign branch deposits of a failed bank. In cases where the agency determines offshore deposits must be repaid to protect the system, it is required to recover losses through an industry-wide assessment on an expanded base that has the effect of assessing foreign deposits.

Accounting Reforms

The federal banking agencies must issue regulations requiring banks to report *off-balance-sheet items* on financial statements. In addition, the agencies must require disclosure of the fair market value of all assets, to the extent possible.

Restrictions on State Bank Powers

FDICIA prohibits state banks from exercising powers not permissible to federally chartered institutions, including insurance underwriting. The bill "grandfathers" banks already lawfully engaged in underwriting insurance under state law. Another exemption permits state banks to invest up to 10% of their portfolio in stocks listed on national securities exchanges, provided they are already in the business.

Consumer Provisions

The principal consumer protection is the truth-in-savings provision, which requires uniform disclosure of the terms and conditions of savings accounts. A "greenlining" amendment provides incentives for banks to lend money in less affluent neighborhoods. The FDIC is required to start an affordable housing program and to give nonprofit organizations an opportunity to purchase residential properties acquired from failed banks.

Miscellaneous Provisions

FDICIA also relaxes the "qualified thrift lender test" allowing thrifts to invest more of their assets outside of housing-related areas.

An Evaluation of FDICIA[30]

As we have seen in earlier chapters, banks must process risk if they are to serve as qualitative asset transformers. However, because of the regulatory safety net that is needed to foster banking stability, a moral hazard arises stemming from banks' propensities to take *excessive* risks. The goal of bank regulation should be to address this moral hazard without stifling the intermediation function of banks.

FDICIA focused on limiting the deposit insurance exposure of taxpayers.[31] To this end, FDICIA provides banking agencies with a clear goal of minimizing deposit insurance losses and providing incentives to encourage compliance. The

---

30. For additional readings on FDICIA, see Booth (1993), Carnell (1992), Greenspan (1993), and Wall (1993).

31. The focus of FDICIA was not a new concern as the following 1933 rhetorical question by Senator Carter Glass indicates "Is there any reason why the American people should be taxed to guarantee the debts of banks, any more than they should be taxed to guarantee the debts of other institutions, including merchants, the industries, and the mills of the country?"

prompt corrective action requirements limit regulatory forbearance, and risk-sensitive capital requirements and deposit insurance premia may encourage risk abatement.[32]

There are four main criticisms of FDICIA. First, while the principal thrust of FDICIA was to limit the size and scope of the federal financial safety net, the discount window access given to nonbanking firms potentially expands the safety net.[33]

Second, FDICIA may impede desirable risk-taking function of banks as qualitative asset transformers. FDICIA was a reaction to perceived excesses in the industry and to failures of the regulators. However, FDICIA failed to address the question of *optimal* risk-taking by banks.[34] Rather, it focused on recapitalizing the BIF and ensuring that future costs to the deposit insurance fund were better controlled. But this could deter banks from processing the kinds of risks that are also socially optimal.

Third, FDICIA directs each federal banking agency to monitor banks' operations, management, asset quality, earnings, stock values, and the compensation of executives and directors. This mandate could pressure regulators to "micromanage" banks and to discourage desirable risk-taking and innovation.

Fourth, FDICIA failed to address the issue of the competitiveness of U.S. banks *vis à vis* foreign banks and nonbank competitors. The discretionary elements of regulation, including expanded powers to fine and dismiss directors and officers and to review executive compensation, raises potentially nondiversifiable investor risk and, therefore, increases banks' cost of capital. This reduces banks' competitiveness. Also, the increased exposure of directors and officers elevates the cost and difficulty of staffing these positions. While the Act will require greater care on the part of directors and officers, it will discourage those with reputational capital or other forms of wealth from serving as directors and officers of financial institutions.

Another competitive weakness of FDICIA relates to Glass–Steagall and interstate branching prohibitions. When the 1991 Treasury proposal was being discussed, the financial health of banks was thought to be too precarious to permit expanded powers via repeal of Glass–Steagall. When the issue resurfaced in 1993, opponents of repeal argued that bank profits were at historic highs, so that expanded powers were unnecessary to bolster bank profitability. The key impediment to repeal of Glass–Steagall appeared to be the potential for increased taxpayer exposure. Further, the greater number of regulatory requirements (including requirements such as Truth-in-Savings that are unrelated to bank safety) could further damage banks' competitiveness.

While these criticisms might be well founded, in retrospect, one could come up with a very positive assessment of FDICIA that may prevail. Prompt corrective action and the focus on getting banks to keep more capital on the balance sheet – effectively through a leverage ratio – have become a central part of the Basel III Capital Accord, 20 years later.

THE FINANCIAL SERVICES MODERNIZATION ACT OF 1999

After a relentless weakening of its key separation provisions, the Glass–Steagall Act was finally formally dismantled in 1999 with the passage of the Financial Services Modernization Act or the Gramm–Leach–Bliley Act. This act repealed Sections 20 and 32 of the Glass–Steagall Act. It also authorized BHCs and foreign banks that meet eligibility criteria to become financial holding companies, thus allowing them to engage in a broad array of financially related activities. In addition, the Act addressed the functional regulation of financial holding companies, the protection of nonpublic customer information held by financial institutions, the supervision of the Community Reinvestment Act (CRA), and other regulatory practices. A summary of the key elements of the act are provided below.

- *Repeal of Glass–Steagall.* Allows U.S. financial services providers, including banks, securities firms and insurance companies, to affiliate with each other and enter each other's markets.
- *Bank Holding Company Structure.* Generally BHC affiliates will be the vehicles through which to engage in a broad range of financial activities.
- *Qualification to Engage in Financial Activities.* Requires all subsidiary insured depository institutions of the holding company to be well capitalized and well managed in order for the holding company to engage in broader financial activities. Divestiture and/or other restrictions and limitations may be required in the event of noncompliance.

---

32. The crudity of the risk sensitizations may encourage new circumventions with attendant deadweight losses. Some also criticize FDICIA for not going far enough in restricting regulatory forbearance. Many of the important changes are suggestions, so that regulatory discretion remains in the treatment of problem banks. See Carnell (1992). Discretion, however, can be of value to regulators in dealing with banks in a rapidly changing environment. See Boot et al. (1993).

33. Whether this represents a significant risk exposure depends on how easily the Federal Reserve grants access to nonbanks.

34. Greenspan (1993) noted, "The legislative and regulatory process, in my judgment, has never adequately wrestled with the question of just how much risk is optimal."

- *Operating Subsidiary Activities.* Allows national banks with assets of $1 billion or less to conduct financial activities through operating subsidiaries. In order to conduct such activities through a subsidiary, the national bank and all insured depository institution affiliates must be well capitalized and well managed and the national bank must receive the approval of the OCC based on those criteria. A national bank subsidiary engaging in such activities will be subject to affiliate transaction restrictions and to antitying prohibitions. The bank also must deduct from capital the amount of its investment in the subsidiary. National banks with assets exceeding $1 billion must conduct financial activities through holding company affiliates. National banks of any size may engage in financial activities on an agency basis through an operating subsidiary. National banks lawfully conducting activities through operating subsidiaries as of the date of enactment will be permitted to continue such activities.

- *Municipal Revenue Bond Underwriting.* Authorized as a permissible banking activity. Therefore, this activity may be conducted by the bank directly or in an operating subsidiary. Previously, only the general obligations of municipalities could be underwritten by banks.

- *Functional Regulation.* Relies on strong functional regulation of the banking, insurance, and securities components of the holding company, and establishes the Federal Reserve as the umbrella regulator.

- *Reduces Regulatory Burdens.* Streamlines regulatory burdens by requiring the Federal Reserve as umbrella supervisor to rely on reports and examinations conducted by other functional regulators. Also requires sharing of information among affected regulatory agencies as necessary to carry out their official duties.

- *Competition Protection Rules.* Requires the federal banking agencies to issue joint consumer protection regulations governing the sale of insurance products by banks, their employees, or others who engage in such activities on behalf of the banks. The federal banking regulators must consult with the states in the process of formulating their joint rules. Provisions of federal rules deemed more protective will pre-empt state law or rules unless within three years of federal notification the state legislatures enact laws opting out of such coverage.

- *FICO Assessment.* Freezes the BIF-member FICO assessment for 3 years, beginning 1999. This represents a saving of about $18,000 per year for a bank with total assets of $100 million. It is therefore important to smaller community banks. This freeze is important because it will give Congress time to consider other important issues such as the merger of the FDIC insurance funds, merger of banks and thrift charters, and consolidation of regulatory agencies such as the OCC and the OTS. Since 1980, there have been at least 13 congressional hearings on the soundness of the federal deposit insurance system. There have been 11 proposals introduced concerning consolidation of federal regulation of banks and savings and loan institutions; and five proposals to merge bank and thrift charters.

- *Community Reinvestment Act (CRA).* Establishes a rebuttable presumption of CRA compliance with respect to an insured depository institution that has achieved a "satisfactory" or better rating in its most recent CRA exam and in each of its CRA exams during the immediately preceding 36-month period. The presumption of compliance may be rebutted by any person presenting substantial verifiable information to the contrary.

  Banks and savings and loan associations with total assets less than $100 million and located in nonmetropolitan areas are exempted from the provisions of the CRA. This exemption only applies to 38% of all banks and savings and loans, which collectively control only 2.8% of banking assets nationwide.

- *Bank Securities Activities.* While eliminating the broad exemption that banks enjoyed from registration as a broker or dealer under the securities laws, the bill makes clear that banks serving as custodians to self-directed IRAs will not be required to push these activities out of the bank and into a registered broker or dealer. Banks often function as service providers to pension, retirement, profit sharing, bonus, thrift, savings, incentive and other plans. The SEC, with the concurrence of the Federal Reserve Board, may determine by regulation those new products which, if offered or sold by a bank, would subject it to registration with the SEC. A bank may offer or sell "traditional banking products," as defined in this section, without becoming subject to registration with the SEC.

- *Federal Home Loan Bank Reforms.* Includes provisions to modernize the operations of the Federal Home Loan Bank System. As of June 1, 2000, membership in the Federal Home Loan Bank System was made voluntary. Community banks (those banks with total assets less than $500 million) will be able to become members without regard to the percentage of total assets represented by residential mortgage loans. Community banks will be able to use advances for small business, small farm and small agribusiness lending. It also allows community banks to collateralize advances with small business and agricultural loans, and modifies the governance structure of the System to give more authority to the regional banks.

THE DODD–FRANK WALL STREET REFORM AND CONSUMER PROTECTION ACT

In a response to the global financial crisis, the US policymakers enacted The Dodd–Frank Wall Street Reform and Consumer Protection Act (Dodd–Frank Act) in 2010. The Dodd–Frank Act presents a sweeping regulatory overhaul across several aspects of banking regulation and reshapes the banking regulatory and legal environment for years to come.[35]

The Dodd–Frank Act consists of 16 titles. It creates several new regulatory agencies (e.g., the Financial Stability Oversight Council (FSOC), the Office of Financial Research (OFR), and the Bureau of Consumer Financial Protection) and merges or eliminates others (e.g., it abolishes the OTS). The regulatory reform aims at mitigating systemic risk to protect the US economy and consumers, businesses and investors alike. It focuses on the regulation and supervision of financial institutions that are too-big-to-fail with the idea to end the reliance on the tax payer. The Dodd–Frank Act provides mechanisms for orderly wind down of the systemically important institution (SIIs), defines the framework for consumer protection, regulates credit rating agencies, and provides rules on executive compensation and corporate governance.

Title I – Financial Stability

Title I of the Dodd–Frank Act establishes a regulatory structure capable of identifying and mitigating systemic risk. The importance of addressing systemic risk was explained in Chapter 15. A more integral view of the financial system, focusing on the interconnectiveness across financial institutions and the macroprudential regulation needed to address it, has gained importance.

What Made Systemic Risk More Prevalent?

As highlighted in Chapter 3, banks have become increasingly sensitive to financial market developments. This more intertwined nature of banks and financial markets has exposed banks to the boom and bust nature of those markets and possibly augmented instability.[36] Moreover, (opportunistic) decision-making in momentum-driven financial markets may induce herding, and, as a consequence, banks may become more similar in terms of risk exposure. Systemic risk may then become paramount. Meaning, when all institutions make the same bets, risk exposures become more highly correlated and a simultaneous failure of institutions is more likely.[37]

Title I sets the regulatory and supervisory framework for large BHCs and for nonbank financial companies that are deemed important for the U.S. financial stability. Title I also seeks to improve the regulatory standards for U.S. financial institutions and financial markets in general.

Title I creates a new, independent regulatory body entitled the *Financial Stability Oversight Council*. In addition, it establishes the OFR as an independent department within the Treasury department. The FSOC's tasks are to (1) identify risks to the financial stability of the U.S. and of the U.S. financial system, (2) promote market discipline by removing too-big-to-fail guarantees, and (3) respond to the threats to the stability of the U.S. financial system. The FSOC together with the OFR gather data to be able to assess risks to the financial system.

The FSOC's task is also to determine the significant non-bank financial institutions, defined as non-bank financial institutions whose failure may create repercussions for the stability of the U.S. financial system. In addition, the FSOC will make recommendations to the Federal Reserve on the implementation of the improved regulatory and supervisory framework to be applied to significant nonbank financial institutions and to BHCs with consolidated assets of $50 billion or more.

The areas for improved regulation and supervision include: capital requirements, liquidity requirements, resolution plans, credit exposure requirement, concentration limits, contingent capital requirements, improved public disclosure, short-term debt limits, and risk management-requirements. It also stipulates that the Federal Reserve needs to build a framework of early remediation requirements for large BHCs and significant nonbank financial institutions. More specifically, the Federal Reserve needs to define minimum capital and liquidity levels whose breach would trigger remedial actions that include limits

---

35. See ABA (2010) for a review and Acharya et al. (2011b,c), and Krainer (2012) for detailed evaluations.
36. As Shin (Shin, 2009, page 110) puts it, "… in a modern market-based financial system, banking and capital market conditions should not be viewed in isolation."
37. Boot (2014) links the increased exposure to financial markets to developments in information technology. Farhi and Tirole (2012) discuss correlated asset portfolio and leverage choices of banks.

on capital redistribution, mergers, and acquisitions and growth in total assets, but can also include forced recapitalizations, changes in management or asset sales. The Federal Reserve can also take remedial actions under the approval of the FSOC if a BHC or nonbank financial institution is determined to pose a grave threat to the U.S. financial stability. The framework for early remediation requirements reflects the Prompt Corrective Action provision under the FDICIA that applies to insured depository institutions.

The authority over supervision and enforcement actions against large BHCs and systemically important nonbank financial institutions is put squarely in the hands of the Federal Reserve. The stringency of regulation increases with the systemic importance of the regulated BHCs and nonbank financial institutions.

In the case where systemic risk is perceived to be imminently threatening the banking system or financial markets, the FSOC may recommend to any regulatory agency that stricter regulatory requirements are imposed on the relevant entities. In its recommendation, activities or practices that elevate systemic risk may be limited, regulated, or even completely prohibited. The regulatory agency may decide not to follow the recommendation of the FSOC but needs to explain the decision to the FSOC in writing. The FSOC needs to report to the Congress on its recommendations.

The FDIC is granted examination and enforcement authority over BHCs whose subsidiary is an insured depository institution. An examination authority can be used to examine if a BHC is approaching the conditions for orderly liquidation under Title II of the Dodd–Frank Act. An enforcement authority can be used if the actions of a BHC may impose a loss on the Deposit Insurance Fund.

Title I of the Dodd–Frank Act equips the regulator with powers to tackle SIIs, the so-called SIFIs – systemically significant financial institutions (either banks, BHCs, or non-bank financial institutions). Key issues that remain are how to identify SIFIs and whether too much focus on SIFIs would possibly distract from discovering systemic risk building up elsewhere.[38]

Title II – Orderly Liquidation Authority

The global financial crisis showed that regulators had insufficient authority to orderly wind down large, nondepository financial institutions, such as investment banks or BHCs. Title II of the Dodd–Frank Act provides authority for orderly liquidation to the Federal Reserve and to the FDIC, mimicking the resolution process for the depository institution under the FDICIA.

Under Title II, companies eligible for orderly liquidation (so-called covered financial companies) are BHCs, significant nonbank financial institutions, and companies predominantly engaged in financial activities (as determined by the Federal Reserve).

The Federal Reserve or FDIC can make a proposal to the Treasury Secretary to appoint the FDIC as a receiver for the covered financial company (or the SEC for broker/dealers, or the Director of the Federal Insurance Office (FIO) for insurance companies). Such a recommendation must be approved by a two-thirds majority at the Federal Reserve Board and the FDIC Board. The Treasury Secretary needs to determine in consultation with the President whether (1) the covered financial company is in default or is approaching default, (2) its failure will result in serious repercussions for financial stability, (3) there are no other private sector solutions, (4) the repercussions to shareholders, creditors, investors, and counterparties of the company are appropriate in light of the need to safeguard financial stability in the United States, (5) such repercussions should be minimized while considering financial stability, cost to the public funds, and potential future increase in risk taking, (6) convertible debt instruments are converted into equity, (7) the company is a financial company. If all conditions are met, the company is put under receivership (with judicial approval of the Court for the District of Columbia).

The FDIC as a receiver must take actions to safeguard financial stability. In addition, it must assure that the unsecured creditors bear losses according to the priority of their claims, and shareholders are only compensated at the end after all other claimants if there are any proceeds left. The FDIC also must replace the management and the responsible directors of the failed institution.

Under the receivership, the FDIC has far-reaching powers that largely mimic the rights of the FDIC in the case of a failure of a depository institution. The FDIC obtains all rights and powers of the company in receivership and needs to operate

---

38. Systemic risk does not always originate from large institutions. Smaller institutions having similar risk exposures can collectively create a systemic threat (Brunnermeier et al., 2009). Acharya et al. (2011a) argue that the classification of financial institutions based on simple systemic risk indicators (e.g., size, leverage, interconnectedness) needs to be complemented with financial market indicators about systemic risk of individual financial institutions. They argue that systemic risk can often be hidden in the opaque interconnections among financial institutions, for example, through the over-the-counter derivatives markets.

the company or liquidate its business. The FDIC can merge the company with another company and/or transfer assets and liabilities.[39]

Title VI – Improvements to Regulation of Bank and Savings Association Holding Companies and Depository Institutions

Title VI provides for a variety of measures to strengthen the regulation of BHCs, saving and loan holding companies and depository institutions to ensure that these will not threaten the stability of the U.S. financial system. Title VI contains the Volcker Rule, which prohibits banks and BHCs from engaging in proprietary trading, and from investing in private equity funds and hedge funds (see Chapter 15 for a more detailed discussion of the Volcker Rule). It also contains other measures that give the Federal Reserve the power to evaluate mergers and acquisitions based on their impact on stability, and to prescribe countercyclical capital buffers when deemed necessary.

Title VII – Wall Street Transparency and Accountability

Title VII regulates over the counter (OTC) derivatives markets. It requires various OTC to be cleared at the clearinghouses or exchanges. The aim of Title VII is to lower the interconnectedness of financial companies through the OTC market (eliminate counterparty risk) and to increase transparency in the OTC derivatives markets. Under Title VII of the Dodd–Frank Act, over-the-counter derivatives will be subject to robust regulation for the first time. The Commodity Futures Trading Commission (CFTC) will be granted regulatory jurisdiction over interest rate, foreign exchange, and commodity derivatives – swaps and futures primarily. Title VII instructs the CFTC to implement several regulatory mandates, including registration, business conduct standards, central clearing, trading, capital, margin, and reporting requirements.

Title IX – Investor Protections and Improvements to the Regulation of Securities

Title IX devotes significant attention to investor protection and disclosure of relevant information in the securitization process in particular. It also addresses disclosures related to executive compensation.

An important part of Title IX is the regulatory reform of credit rating agencies. Credit rating agencies are companies that evaluate the creditworthiness of debt instruments issued by corporations or (semi) governments by assigning credit ratings; see Table 4.3 in Chapter 4. Credit rating agencies were widely criticized to have contributed to the global financial crisis by being overly generous in assigning ratings.[40]

The criticism of rating agencies is not really new. In the 2002 Sarbanes Oxley Act (SOX) that followed the spectacular demise of companies like Enron and Worldcom, rating agencies were criticized. SOX commissioned the SEC to perform a study to investigate "…the role and function of credit rating agencies in the operation of the securities market" (SOX, 2002, Section 702b). The study was conducted in early 2003 and focused on the privileged position of the three big rating agencies – Moody's Investors Service, Standard & Poors (S&P) and Fitch Ratings – as Nationally Recognized Statistical Rating Organization (NRSRO). This status effectively creates a substantial barrier to newcomers entering the credit rating business to compete with the NRSROs.[41] The Credit Agency Reform Act of 2006 (SEC, 2006) abolished this classification in an attempt to open the rating business for new entrants. While other concerns, including potential conflicts of interest, were also on the table, no actions were taken until the Dodd–Frank Act.

The Dodd–Frank Act seeks to address the conflict of interest within credit rating agencies. Its provisions relate to internal controls that govern the process of determining credit ratings, separation of marketing and production of credit ratings, search for (present and past) conflict of interests of their employees, and to the corporate governance of credit rating agencies.

Title IX also broadens their potential liability and allows the SEC to charge higher penalties. In addition, Title IX asks for higher disclosure standards with respect to the characteristics of a debt instrument that has a credit rating. Greater disclosure of the rating process itself, including the information, procedures, and methodologies used, is also part of Title IX.

---

39. Acharya et al. (2011b) criticize the orderly liquidation process because the government is not allowed to provide funding if needed. See Marinč and Rant (2014) for a cross-country analysis of bank bankruptcy regimes and their implications for severity and frequency of the global financial crisis (see also Cihak et al., 2013).
40. See Altman et al. (2011).
41. See White (2010).

Title X – Bureau of Consumer Financial Protection

Title X establishes the Consumer Financial Protection Bureau (CFPB). The CFPB is equipped with far-reaching powers from several Federal consumer protection laws. It has a broad rule-making authority to shape consumer protection in the United States. Its decisions may in a few instances be overruled by the FSOC.

The CFPB must direct its activities to prohibit abusive, deceptive, or unfair financial practices. Its responsibilities with respect to the mortgage reform are further defined under Title XIV of the Dodd–Frank Act. Title X also sets limits on inter-change fees for debit card transactions.

Title XI – Federal Reserve System Provisions

Title XI sets higher limitations on when the Federal Reserve may use emergency assistance to financial institutions. The Federal Reserve may only provide emergency assistance if needed on a broad-based scale to provide liquidity to the financial system or part of it (under the approval of the Treasury Secretary). Emergency assistance should not be used to support failing institutions. The hope is that such a limitation may enhance its credibility, lower *ex-ante* risk taking of financial institutions and reduce the probability and severity of future crises.

Title XI also provides the FDIC the possibility to guarantee bank debt. In the case of extraordinary financial distress (and upon the approval of two-thirds of the members of the board of the Federal Reserve and FDIC and the Treasury Secretary), the FDIC is to create a program of debt guarantees for solvent insured banks and BHCs. The maximum amount of guarantees is determined by the Treasury in consultation with the President and requires Congressional approval.

Title XII – Improving Access to Mainstream Financial Institutions

Title XII aims to improve access to basic financial services and products for low- and medium-income citizens by offering three voluntary programs that the financial institutions may tap into. First, the Secretary Treasury should establish a program to provide low- and medium-income individuals with the incentives to an open account at a depository institutions. Second, the financial institutions should be supported in their offering of small dollar value loans under attractive interest rates. Such loans are intended to replace payday loans that were often offered by financial institutions under unreasonable and excessive interest rates. Third, additional financial assistance should be provided for community development and financial institutions that provide small dollar loan programs.

Other Titles to the Dodd–Frank Act

Title III – Transfer of Powers to the Comptroller of the Currency, the Corporation, and the Board of Governors, eliminates the OTS and transfers its supervisory responsibilities to the Federal Reserve, the Office of the Comptroller of the Currency, and the FDIC.

Title IV – Regulation of Advisers to Hedge Funds and Others, requires additional obligations (e.g., net worth requirements) to the previously very lightly regulated private funds (e.g., venture capital funds, hedge funds, and equity funds).

Title V – Insurance, provides for a stronger Federal involvement in the insurance industry. The insurance sector is primarily regulated at the state level by individual state agencies. Title V of the Dodd–Frank Act establishes a FIO within the Department of the Treasury to promote national coordination in the insurance sector. It seeks to streamline regulation, but leaves supervision in the hands of the states.

Title VIII – Payment, Clearing, and Settlement Supervision, follows Title I in its focus on systemic risk and sets the regulatory framework to safeguard the stability of the systemically important financial institutions in the payment system and in the clearing and settlement system.

Title XIII – Pay It Back Act, puts constraints on the Troubled Asset Relief Program, which aimed at safeguarding stability in the financial system during the peak of the financial crisis in 2008.

Title XIV – Mortgage Reform and Anti-Predatory Lending Act, focuses on consumer protection on the mortgage markets to prevent abusive mortgage lending. In particular, it aims at prohibiting lending practices involving individuals that do not have the resources to repay loans, and seeks to prevent individuals being pushed into mortgage loans with terms that they cannot understand.

Title XV – Miscellaneous Provisions.

Title XVI – Section 1256 Contracts, preserves pre-Title VII derivative tax law for certain swaps and future contracts.

EU REGULATORY AND SUPERVISORY OVERHAUL AND THE DE LAROSIÈRE REPORT

In 2008, the president of the European Commission José Manuel Barroso established a High-Level Group on financial supervision in the EU, chaired by Jacques de Larosière, to propose regulatory and supervisory overhaul in the EU. The so-called de Larosière Report reviews the causes of the global financial crisis, suggests changes to bank regulation, proposes a better EU supervisory framework, and discusses the regulatory/supervisory developments needed on the global level (de Larosière (2009)).

One of the crucial findings of the de Larosière Report is that the European system of supervision and crisis management was fundamentally flawed and needed repair. The de Larosière Report proposes a number of recommendations. It recommends the establishment of a new regulatory body, tasked with the official mandate to assess macrofinancial risks, issue warnings, and propose recommendations on how to mitigate these risks. The de Larosière Report also proposes recommendations to improve microsupervision in the EU. It recommends further integration and synchronization of bank regulation across the EU and a bolder move toward a European system of financial supervision.

The European policymakers have largely followed the recommendations of the de Larosière Report. They have established the European Systemic Risk Board (ESRB) to be in charge of spotting the systemic risks in the EU financial system. In addition, at the microlevel, existing coordination committees were replaced with three sector bodies: the European Banking Authority (EBA), the European Insurance and Occupational Pensions Authority (EIOPA), and the European Securities and Markets Authority (ESMA), each responsible for primarily pan-European coordination in their particular field. These EU-linked coordinating agencies have little real power. As indicated in Chapter 15, the development of a banking union, with strong supervisory powers in the hands of the ECB, may lessen the significance of these EU agencies.

Other EU Directives

A single rulebook for regulation across the EU has been established by common capital regulation (Capital requirements regulation and directive – CRR[42]/CRD IV[43]), common rules on deposit insurance (Directive on deposit guarantee schemes[44]) and on bank recovery and resolution (Single Resolution Mechanism Regulation[45] and the Bank Recovery and Resolution Directive[46]). Moreover, in November 2013, the Single Supervisory Mechanism (SSM) – conferring bank-supervisory powers on the ECB – came into effect. The SSM creates a new system of financial supervision comprising the ECB and the national supervisory authorities of participating EU countries. In tandem, the Single Resolution Mechanism and the SSM are referred to as the "Banking Union."

The Capital Requirements Regulation (CRR) and *Capital Requirements Directive (CRD IV)* closely implement Basel III regulatory standards on capital, liquidity, and leverage ratio across the EU. Even though the capital requirements under the CRR remain unchanged at 8% of risk-weighted assets, what qualifies as of bank capital has changed. In particular, banks need to hold at least 4.5% of risk-weighted assets in the form of *common equity*, so "lower quality" forms of capital (e.g., intangibles) are now disallowed. The CRD IV defines additional capital buffers for SIIs, a countercyclical capital buffer (i.e., macroprudential buffer), and a capital conservation buffer (see Table 16.3). Bank supervisors can also increase

TABLE 16.3 The Components of Capital Regulation

Share of Risk-Weighted Assets (%)	The Type of Bank Capital	The Groups of Bank Capital
1–2	Bank's own buffer	
0–2	Pillar 2	
0–5	Higher of systemic risk, G-SII and O-SII buffers	Combined buffer (all in the form of Common equity tier 1 capital)
0–2.5	Countercyclical capital buffer	
2.5	Capital conservation buffer	
2	Tier 2	Basic requirement (8%)
1.5	Additional Tier 1	
4.5	Common Equity Tier 1	

Note: See European Commission (2013).

42. Regulation (EU) No 575/2013 of the European Parliament and of the Council of 26 June, 2013 on prudential requirements for credit institutions and investment firms and amending Regulation (EU) No 648/2012, OJ L 176/1 27.6.2013.
43. Directive 2013/36/EU of the European Parliament and of the Council of 26 June, 2013 on access to the activity of credit institutions and the prudential supervision of credit institutions and investment firms, amending Directive 2002/87/EC and repealing Directives 2006/48/EC and 2006/49/EC, OJ L 176/338 27.6.2013.
44. Directive 2014/49/EU of the European Parliament and of the Council of 16 April, 2014 on deposit guarantee schemes, OJ L173/149 12.6.2014.
45. Regulation (EU) No 806/2014 of the European Parliament and of the Council of 15 July, 2014 establishing uniform rules and a uniform procedure for the resolution of credit institutions and certain investment firms in the framework of a Single Resolution Mechanism and a Single Resolution Fund and amending Regulation (EU) No 1093/2010, OJ L225/1 30.7.2014.
46. Directive 2014/59/EU of the European Parliament and of the Council of 15 May, 2014 establishing a framework for the recovery and resolution of credit institutions and investment firms and amending Council Directive 82/891/EEC, and Directives 2001/24/EC, 2002/47/EC, 2004/25/EC, 2005/56/EC, 2007/36/EC, 2011/35/EU, 2012/30/EU and 2013/36/EU, and Regulations (EU) No 1093/2010 and (EU) No 648/2012, of the European Parliament and of the Council, OJ L 173/190 12.6.2014.

a bank's capital requirement to compensate for deficiencies in the bank's risk-management practices that are uncovered by the supervisory process under the Pillar II of Basel III. The CRR also puts a floor on a bank's capital (being effective as of 2017): bank capital cannot fall below 80% of capital requirements under Basel I.

The CRR also implements liquidity regulation following Basel III liquidity standards: the Liquidity Coverage Requirement (LCR) and the Net Stable Funding Requirement (NSFR). The requirement that the LCR is at least 100% is to be phased in gradually and fully implemented in 2018 – one year earlier than Basel III. Early implementation of the LCR standard stresses the importance that the European Commission puts on liquidity regulation.

The exact implementation of the NSFR is still pending on further studies of the Basel Commission on Banking Supervision, the EBA and the European Commission. However, the CDR already sets a general rule that banks should cover long-term obligations with diversified stable funding sources from 2016 onwards.

The leverage ratio (i.e., the ratio of tier 1 capital over nonrisk weighted on- and off-balance sheet items) is currently not being implemented under the Pillar I and is therefore not included as a binding capital requirement. Rather, it is a part of Pillar II. However, banks are required to publically disclose their leverage ratios from 2015 onwards, and will be subject to ongoing evaluations. The implementation of the binding minimum leverage ratio is scheduled to begin in 2018.

Directive on deposit guarantee schemes harmonizes deposit insurance across the EU. The coverage limit of deposit insurance is set at €100,000 per depositor per bank but can be temporarily raised. Individual deposits and deposits of nonfinancial companies are covered (regardless of their currencies). The payment schedule is to be reduced from the current 20 to 7 working days. The deposit insurance fund should be funded *ex-ante* and should reach at least 0.8% of covered deposits in the national banking system. Deposit insurance premia are to be risk adjusted according to the criteria set by the EBA.

The recent developments are an important step forward, especially the funding requirements and further harmonization of deposit insurance across the EU. However, deposit insurance would still be national and backed only by the domestic treasury. Further moves toward a pan-European Deposit Guarantee Scheme might be necessary to reduce fragmentation along national lines in the European banking system. In particular, systemic bank failures in one of the European countries, may leave the national deposit insurance fund incapable of covering all the mandated payments. Even the anticipation of such an event may cause panic withdrawals and flight of deposits to neighboring countries with stronger deposit insurance funds. This might elevate the competitive advantage of banks in stronger countries over those in weaker countries and leads to distortions in competition.

Bank recovery and resolution in the EU is governed by the Single Resolution Mechanism Regulation (SRM) and the Bank Recovery and Resolution Directive. The Bank Recovery and Resolution Directive (BRRD) requires banks to build "living wills," which are resolution plans – to be used in the case of a failure. In addition, it sets a coherent framework for early intervention, giving bank supervisory powers to impose corrective actions on failing banks before insolvency. The BRRD also seeks to provide necessary tools to resolution authorities to be able to wind down failing banks effectively, without repercussions for financial stability, and without the need for public funds. Resolution tools include forced sell-off of (parts of) failing banks, transfer of business to a bridge bank, establishment of a good bank/bad bank structure, and a haircuts for bank creditors (i.e., bail in of bank creditors).

The SRM creates a new, independent EU agency – the Single Resolution Mechanism – responsible for an orderly wind down of failing banks in the EU. It also creates a supporting Single Bank Resolution Fund that provides funds necessary for a smooth resolution of failing banks. The Single Resolution Mechanism's resolution powers encompass the largest (most significant) banks in the EU (these number 120 out of a total of around 6000 banks in the Euro Area[47]) – the same ones that are covered by the SSM.

The *SSM* tasks the ECB with the supervisory authority over significant banks in the EU. The supervisory powers of the ECB include providing and withdrawing licenses to credit institutions, approving mergers and acquisitions and asset disposals of BHCs, supervision of compliance with bank regulation, and increasing regulatory standards if needed to safeguard financial stability. For example, the ECB could demand that a bank strengthen its corporate governance or raise its capital levels. National supervisors retain their supervisory responsibilities toward other, less significant, banks. In addition, they provide support and local knowledge in the supervision of significant banks' operations in their countries.

The European Union also seeks to strengthen the functioning of capital markets, and particularly reduce the fragmentation along national lines. Proposals have been made to create a so-called Capital Market Union. It is hoped that this initiative will make Europe less bank-dependent by easing access to nonbank funding sources.

---

47. EU countries outside Euro Area may choose to join SSM and SRM at their own will.

Structural reform proposals

UK Vickers Report

As discussed in Chapter 15, in the wake of the global financial crisis, the UK government established a commission with a task to analyze how to enhance financial stability and competition in financial services (Independent Commission on Banking (2011)). The objectives of the Independent Commission on Banking were: (i) to reduce the severity and frequency of the future systemic financial crises; (ii) to enhance the ability of the financial system to support the real economy (e.g., by providing credit, risk management, and other financial products to households and businesses), and; (iii) to secure the stability of the payment system and assure capital and liquidity certainty of individuals and small and medium enterprises.

The Independent Commission on Banking explicitly took into account not just financial stability issues but also the competitive environment. It stated as its principles that it seek to curb incentives for excessive risk taking, reduce the costs of the future systemic financial crises, *and* increase the level of competition in the banking system. It considered the costs that more stringent regulatory standards might impose on GDP due to a lower level of banking activity (e.g., lending) and the impact on competitiveness of the UK financial sector and economy.[48] It also evaluated the impact of regulatory reform on the nonbank financial institutions in the UK.

In the final report, called Vickers Report, the Independent Commission on Banking suggests several structural measures as well as improvements in capital regulation and competition in retail banking (Independent Commission on Banking (2011)). The crucial feature of the Vickers report are the proposed structural measures to separate ("ring fencing") retail banking, which is crucial for the smooth operation of the UK real economy, from other, less systemically important banking services (e.g., wholesale and investment banking services).

Ring fencing still allows banks to exploit some economies of scale among retail and wholesale/investment banking activities. Subsidiaries can share information, expertise, and brand name. They can provide a one-stop-shopping access to all banking services. In addition, the banking group can provide "back-stop" capital to the ring-fenced subsidiaries in case of financial difficulty.[49]

The idea is that ring fencing enables an efficient resolution of a failing bank by preserving the ring-fenced part (e.g., moving it to a bridge bank or to a private acquirer) and liquidating the rest. Also, burden-sharing arrangements that include bank shareholders and creditors should minimize the reliance on public funds to rescue the bank. It is also envisioned that ring fencing shields the retail banking part from external financial shocks that affect wholesale and investment banking operations. Finally, ring fencing may allow regulators to focus exclusively on the retail banking operations, and thus keep wholesale and investment banking more competitive by having reduced regulatory scrutiny and lighter regulation.

Besides structural measures, the Vickers Report recommends that loss-absorbing capacity in the UK banking system needs to be increased. The first recommendation is to increase the minimum capital requirements for large UK retail banks to an equity capital level that is at least 10% of risk-weighted assets. This is far above the Basel III minimum, even for globally systemically important banks. The minimum leverage ratio should be increased accordingly.

In addition, the primary loss-absorbing capacity of large UK banking groups should be at least 17–20%. Primary loss-absorbing capacity includes equity and other capital, but also long-term unsecured debt with so-called "bail-in" provisions. The holders of bail-in debt can take losses in the resolution process if the equity of banks is wiped out. Contingent capital ("cocos") that can take losses before the resolution can also be included in the primary loss-absorbing capacity if deemed appropriate by the regulators. The regulator keeps discretion on the level of loss-absorbing capacity within the range of 17–20% and on the type of loss-absorbing capacity. That is, the regulator needs to estimate the risk of a bank dipping into the till of public finances for help, the bank's strength in credit recovery and the viability of its resolution plans, and accordingly adjust the minimum loss-absorbing capacity somewhere in the range from 17 to 20%.

The Vickers Report also suggests that insured deposits have higher priority in potential resolution compared to other uninsured debt. This reinforces the credibility of a stance that losses are imposed on unsecured debt in the case of a bank failure. Creditors anticipate losses in resolution and, therefore, have higher incentives to monitor risks of banks.

The Vickers Report also unveils substantial shortcomings in the competitive environment in the UK banking system. It notes that the UK banking system is heavily concentrated. Four largest banks have a 77% of market share in personal current accounts and 85% of market share in current accounts for small and medium enterprises. Switching between banks is difficult and the terms of offered bank services are rather opaque. In addition, during the global financial crisis, two large banks, Lloyds and HBOS, merged even though the competition authority (i.e., Office of Fair Trade) estimated that such a merger would hamper competition in personal current accounts, and mortgage and small and medium enterprise banking services.

---

48. Whether higher capital requirements will actually reduce lending and adversely impact GDP in a significant way is debatable. The evidence does not support large effects. See Mehran and Thakor (2011) and the discussion in Chapter 13.
49. See Vickers (2012).

The Vickers Report comes with recommendations to improve the odds of establishing another viable bank (building on the mandatory divestiture of Lloyds' branch network). It also proposes measures to ease switching among banks for individuals and small and medium enterprises (faster transfer of accounts between banks). This focus on competition in banking has been much more dominant in the UK than in continental Europe or even the US.

Liikanen report: As discussed in Chapter 15, the Liikanen proposals suggest that banks should transfer proprietary trading and other trading activities to a separate legal entity if these activities are significant in size (Liikanen (2012)). In effect, deposit-taking activities and the pending government safety network would then be separated from risky trading activities in banking. However, a separate legal entity where the trading activities would reside could be a part of the same banking group (see also Chapter 11). Consequently, the European universal banking model could be left intact. Table 16.4 summarizes the Liikanen, Volcker, and Vickers proposals.

The Volcker rule is possibly the most stringent, but narrower in scope because it only prohibits proprietary trading and allows for market making activities and contains several exemptions. The Liikanen Report and the Vickers Report are much broader in scope but less stringent in terms of what they prohibit. In particular, they require the separation of substantially more activities in separate legal entities but do not prohibit them completely.

Apart from the structural remedies, the Liikanen Report also emphasizes the importance of implementing of the new regulatory framework in the EU for capital regulation and resolution of weak banks, established by Capital Requirement Regulation and Directive (CRR/CRDIV) and Bank Recovery and Resolution Directive. Stronger capital regulation will strengthen banks and their resilience in the future systemic financial crises. The effective resolution process will limit the use of government resources to wind down failing banks even if they are large and systemically important.

The Liikanen Report supports the need that banks build credible recovery and resolution plans (i.e., the action plans in the case of failure for banks and regulators) as proposed by the Bank Recovery and Resolution Directive. The Liikanen Report also suggests that structural separation between the depository and trading entity could be widened within the banking group if this is perceived necessary, for example, due to unrealistic recovery and resolution plans.

The Liikanen Report proposes the use of bail-in debt to increase the loss-absorbing capacity of the EU banking system. The priority of repayment of bail-in debt in the resolution process should be clearly defined and known to investors in advance. The bail-in debt should be kept outside the banking system in order to limit the systemic implications of burden sharing in the case of a bank failure.

The Liikanen Report also suggests a reevaluation of risk-weights used within the capital regulation framework. It also proposes a reform of bank corporate governance aimed at: (i) improving the quality of board of directors and management

TABLE 16.4 Structural Remedies Compared – Volcker, Vickers, and Liikanen

Permitted Activities of the Depositary Institution	Volcker Rule (Institutional Separation of Commercial Banking and Trading Activities)	Liikanen Report (Subsidiarization: Higher Risk Trading Activities Need to be Placed in a Separate Entity, but can be Within the Same Banking Group)	Vickers Report (Ring-Fencing: Retail Banking Activities are Ring Fenced from the Rest within the Banking Group)
Act as principal in securities and derivatives	No	No	No
Market making	Yes	No	No
Underwriting	Yes	Yes	Restricted
Engage in non-trading exposures to other financial intermediaries	Yes	Yes	Restricted
Holding company with depositary and trading subsidiaries	Not permitted	Permitted	Permitted
Geographic restrictions	No	No	Yes, for ring-fenced banks to provide service to clients outside the European Economic Area

Source: Gombacorta and van Rixtel (2013).

boards; (ii) enhancing risk management within the bank; (iii) designing prudent compensation practices; (iv) enhancing disclosure of risks; and (v) empowering regulators with sanctioning powers.

All this is very much work in progress. The complexity in implementing the various proposals makes it difficult to assess their future impact.[50] Having said this, one intended purpose of all of these measures is to make the financial system simpler, that is, reduce complexity. We have yet not seen the implementation of the proposed measures, but if they reduce complexity, then more timely intervention ("prompt corrective action") might be facilitated. Also resolving financial distress might become easier. To this end, also "living will" requirements are imposed. These seek to provide for a more orderly dismantling/liquidation of failed institutions.

CONCLUSION

U.S. banking history was shaped by American populism and the frontier mentality. The result was a fragmented financial services industry and a similarly fragmented public regulation of financial services. The issuance of bank notes and the need for cash-asset reserves conditioned the focus on liquidity in banking. The pyramiding of liquidity reserves led to systemic risk in the national banking system of the nineteenth century and to periodic financial panics. This led to the creation of the Federal Reserve System. Federal deposit insurance was added in 1933 in response to a virtual collapse of the banking system.

Regulation of interest rates and controlled entry into banking created monopoly rents for banks and mitigated the moral hazard arising from deposit insurance. This provided stability that lasted until the late 1970s when higher and more volatile interest rates induced massive disintermediation. Regulators responded by lifting interest-rate ceilings, relaxing investment restrictions, and reducing regulatory scrutiny. Thrifts that were legally locked into fixed-rate mortgages sustained huge losses owing to the consequent interest-rate risk. These losses impelled thrifts to undertake greater credit risk, resulting in further losses. The implosion of the thrift industry eventually led to a series of legislative and regulatory initiatives including FIRREA (1989) and FDICIA (1991).

The 2007–2009 global financial crisis has led to the regulatory and supervisory overhaul. In the United States, the Dodd–Frank Act was passed. In Europe, several initiatives, including common capital regulation, common rules on deposit insurance and on bank recovery and resolution (Single Resolution Mechanism) and the SSM – conferring bank-supervisory powers on the ECB – were adopted. The crisis facilitated pan-European agreement that would not have been feasible in times that are more tranquil. As with the Volcker Rule in the Dodd Frank Act, further structural changes in banking might be imposed in the United Kingdom (following the Vickers Report) and the EU (the Liikanen Report).

Regulatory reform has almost always been a reflexive reaction to financial crises. Actions following the 2007–2009 global financial crisis were no different. The unanswered question is: what are the welfare effects of these legislative and regulatory actions? There is a dearth of cost-benefit analyses.

REVIEW QUESTIONS

1. What are the key milestones of bank regulation in the United States?
2. If deposit insurance is deemed necessary, what steps should be taken to reform the system?
3. What are the pros and cons of market value accounting?
4. What are the pros and cons of "expanded" banking powers?
5. Do regulators always maximize social welfare? Why or why not? Can anything be done about this?
6. Discuss the key elements of FDICIA and provide a critique of it.
7. What is the main objective of the Dodd Frank Act?
8. Which measures in the Dodd Frank Act directly address systemic risk?
9. How would you reform our banking system?
10. What are the main legislative initiatives in the EU?

APPENDIX

Liquidity Constraints, Capital Requirements, and Monetary Policy

The size and composition of banks' balance sheets are constrained by the legal reserve requirement, which establishes a minimum ratio of cash assets to deposit liabilities, and the capital requirement that establishes minimum ratios of bank

---

50. All three are not carved in stone, and particularly the Liikanen proposals are very much part of an open debate in the EU. See Liikanen (2012) for the Liikanen report.

capital to risky assets (loans, to a first approximation) and to total assets (the so-called leverage ratio). For most of U.S. history, and certainly for the half-century following the Great Depression, capital requirements tended to be without effect or not binding. Therefore, the operating constraint on banks' size was the legal cash-asset reserve requirement.[50] This changed in the late 1980s when increased credit risks of banks' on- and off-balance-sheet activities were recognized. At the same time, legal cash-asset reserve requirements were reduced in a series of steps, at least partly in response to the dismal record of bank earnings. For many banks, the position of reserve requirements and capital requirements was reversed, so that the capital requirement became binding. This affected the way monetary policy, especially the Federal Reserve's open-market operations, played out in the economy.

In the traditional setting, Federal Reserve purchases of government securities would expand the *excess* cash-asset reserves of the banking system, prompting the banks to expand lending and the asset size of their balance sheets. The initial Federal Reserve purchase would drive up U.S. government securities prices and depress interest rates. The secondary effect of the expansionary open-market operations would come from the banks' reactions to new deposits from those who sold their government securities to the Federal Reserve. These autonomous deposits increase the banks' cash-asset reserves. In an effort to dissipate the new excess reserves, the banks lend newly created deposits. This expands the asset (liability) size of the banks and exerts added downward pressure on interest rates.

All of this would take place without any interference or influence from capital requirements. Indeed, this traditional interpretation of monetary policy assumes that the capital requirement is not binding. If, however, the capital requirement is binding, a very different picture emerges. The initial effects on interest rates via the government securities markets remain unchanged, but bank reactions are conditioned by an altered constraint. To be sure, a capital constraint can be relaxed by reducing dividends or selling bank equity, or even by realizing capital gains by selling assets or liabilities that are being carried at understated historical values. But such adaptations often are costly in the short run. Thus, the bank's capital may be fixed in the short run as a practical matter, and in such cases, it is the other balance sheet accounts that must accommodate to the capital constraint.

Capital requirements are of two types: risk-based and leverage ratios. For simplicity, we can think of the former as a minimum ratio of capital to loans and the latter as a minimum ratio of capital to total assets (liabilities). Now suppose the bank can hold nonearning cash assets, credit risk-free, interest-bearing government securities, or risky loans. Assume further that the cash-asset reserve requirement is zero, but there is a binding capital requirement of either the risk-based or leverage type. Banks have one class of noninterest bearing deposits and one type of capital, equity.

If the capital requirement is of the risk-based variety, and the Federal Reserve undertakes an expansionary open-market operation, the bank will receive an autonomous deposit. Some small fraction of the deposit inflow may be held in the form of cash for liquidity purposes, but most will flow into government securities. We know the bank will *not* make loans because it is capital constrained. Thus, interest rates will fall, deposit expansion will ensue, *but loans will not be made.*

Binding capital requirements, therefore, can explain a *credit crunch* even though monetary policy retains its effectiveness in terms of influencing interest rates. Interest rates are lowered by the Fed's expansionary open-market operations, first as a result of the Federal Reserve's purchase of government securities, and then as a result of the bank's purchase of government securities. The drop in interest rates will presumably spur investors to borrow via the capital markets, but not all have easy access to these markets. Thus, the expansionary impact of a given open-market operation may well be weakened, and it will certainly be rechanneled with smaller firms more likely to be stifled.

Now consider a leverage-type capital ratio that fixes the maximum amount of total assets the bank can hold for any given amount of capital. In this case, the banks are totally out of the monetary policy loop. A purchase of government securities by the Federal Reserve cannot produce even an initial increase in bank deposits. Since the bank's size is constrained by the capital requirement, it cannot accept the deposit of the seller of government securities unless it simultaneously eliminates another deposit of equal amount. In this interesting case, the initial purchase of government securities by the Federal Reserve will put expansionary downward pressure on interest rates, but the banks will not be able to expand. An autonomous deposit will require the bank to sell loans or securities in order to extinguish an equivalent amount of deposits. This will put upward pressure on interest rates and force banks to hold excess reserves.[51]

Supplanting cash-asset reserve requirements with capital requirements inevitably alters the way in which monetary policy affects the economy at large, and this has special relevance for understanding the 1991–1992 *credit crunch*. Bank loans

---

50. Even today, most money and banking textbooks explain the deposit expansion process as if the capital requirement is without effect. See our earlier discussion of the fixed coefficient model.

51. To firm up your understanding of this analysis, consider the possibility of having the Federal Reserve do its open-market operations by buying and selling bank equity instead of U.S. government securities.

were said to be unavailable despite the Federal Reserve's efforts to stimulate the economy by lowering short-term interest rates.[52] The Federal Reserve actively purchased government securities, expanding the reserves of the banking system, and bank assets grew, but lending remained largely unaffected. Banks simply increased their holding of government securities, and the economy grew sluggishly until the end of 1993.

REFERENCES

ABA, American Bankers Association, 2010. Reg Reform Title Listing, Dodd-Frank Wall Street Reform and Consumer Protection Act, Title Summaries. Washington, July, 2010. http://www.aba.com/Issues/RegReform/Pages/RR_TitleMenu.aspx.

Acharya, V.V., Brownlees, C., Engle, R., Farazmand, F., Richardson, M.P., 2011a. Measuring systemic risk. In: Acharya, V.V., Cooley, T.F., Richardson, M.P., Walter, I. (Eds.), Regulating Wall Street: the Dodd–Frank Act and the New Architecture of Global Finance. Wiley, New York, pp. 443–467.

Acharya, V.V., Adler, B., Richardson, M.P., Roubini, N., 2011b. Resolution authority. In: Acharya, V.V., Cooley, T.F., Richardson, M.P., Walter, I. (Eds.), Regulating Wall Street: the Dodd–Frank Act and the New Architecture of Global Finance. Wiley, New York, pp. 443–467.

Acharya, V.V., Cooley, T.F., Richardson, M.P., Walter, I., 2011c. Regulating Wall Street: the Dodd–Frank Act and the New Architecture of Global Finance. Wiley, New York.

Allen, F., Gale, D., 1993. Measurement distortion and missing contingencies in optimal contracts. Econ. Theory 2, 1–26.

Altman, E.I., Öncü, T.S., Richardson, M.P., Schmeits, A., White, L.J., 2011. Regulation of rating agencies. In: Acharya, V.V., Cooley, T.F., Richardson, M.P., Walter, I. (Eds.), Regulating wall street: the Dodd–Frank act and the new architecture of global finance. Wiley, New York, pp. 443–467.

Balderstone, F.E., 1985. Thrifts in Crisis: Structural Transformation of the Savings and Loan Industry. Ballinger, Cambridge, MA.

Barth, J.R., Caprio, Jr., G., Levine, R., 2004. Bank regulation and supervision: what works best? J. Financ. Intermed. 13, 205–248.

Benston, G., 1990. The Separation of Commercial and Investment Banking: the Glass–Steagall Act Revisited and Reconsidered. Oxford University Press, New York.

Berger, A.N., King, K.K., O'Brien, J.M., 1991. The limitations of market value accounting and a more realistic alternative. J. Bank. Financ. 15.

Bhattacharya, S., Thakor, A.V., 1993. Contemporary banking theory. J. Financ. Intermed. 3, 2–50.

Boot, A.W.A., 2014. Financial sector in flux. J. Money Credit Bank. 46, 129–135.

Boot, A.W.A., Thakor, A.V., 1993. Self-interested bank regulation. Am. Econ. Rev. 83, 206–212.

Boot, A.W.A., Greenbaum, S., Thakor, A., 1993. Reputation and discretion in financial contracting. Am. Econ. Rev. 83, 1165–1183.

Booth, J.R., 1993. FDIC improvement act and corporate governance of commercial banks. Econ. Rev. 1, 14–22, Federal Reserve Bank of San Francisco.

Brunnermeier, M.A., Crockett, C., Goodhart, C., Persaud, A., Shin, H.S., 2009. The Fundamental Principles of Financial Regulation. Geneva Reports on the World Economy, 11, Geneva, Switzerland.

Caballero, R.J., Krishnamurthy, A., 2008. Collective risk management in a flight to quality episode. J. Finance. 63, 2195–2230.

Campbell, T.S., Chan, Y.-S., Marino, A., 1992. An incentive-based theory of bank regulation. J. Financ. Intermed. 2, 255–276.

Carnell, R.S., 1992. Implementing the FDIC Improvement Act of 1991. Paper presented at a Conference on Rebuilding Public Confidence Through Financial Reform, Ohio State University, Columbus, Ohio, 1992.

Chan, Y.-S., Greenbaum, S.I., Thakor, A.V., 1992. Is fairly priced deposit insurance possible? J. Financ. 47, 227–246.

Corrigan, G.F., 1990. Reforming the U.S. financial system: an international perspective. Q. Rev. Federal Reserve Bank New York 15, 1–14, Spring.

Cihak, M., Demirgüç-Kunt, A., Martinez Peria, M.S., Mohseni-Cheraghlou, A., 2013. Bank regulation and supervision in the context of the global crisis. J. Financ. Stabil. 9, 733–746.

de Larosière, J., 2009. "Report of the High-level Group on Financial Supervision in the EU," ('The Larosière Report') http://ec.europa.eu/internal_market/finances/docs/de_larosiere_report_en.pdf

DeYoung, R., Kowalik, M., Reidhill, J., 2013. A theory of failed bank resolution: technological change and political economics. J. Financ. Stabil. 9, 612–627.

Donaldson, R.G., 1992. Costly liquidation, interbank trade, bank runs and panics. J. Financ. Intermed. 2, 59–82.

Eisenbeis, R.A., Horvitz, P.A., 1993. The Role of Forbearance and Its Costs in Handling Troubled and Failed Depository Institutions. Paper Presented at the American Finance Association Meetings, Anaheim, CA.

European Commission, 2013. Capital Requirements - CRD IV/CRR – Frequently Asked Questions. Brussels. http://europa.eu/rapid/press-release_MEMO-13-690_en.htm?locale=en.

Farhi, E., Tirole, J., 2012. Collective moral hazard, maturity mismatch, and systemic bailouts. Am. Econ. Rev. 102, 60–93.

Fischer, G.C., 1986. The Modern Bank Holding Company: Development, Regulation, and Performance. Temple University, Philadelphia, PA.

Flannery, M.J., 1991. Pricing deposit insurance when the insurer measures bank risk with error. J. Bank. Financ. 15, 975–998.

Gertler, M., Kiyotaki, N., 2013. Banking, Liquidity and Bank Runs in an Infinite-Horizon Economy. NBER Working Papers 19129, National Bureau of Economic Research.

Gilchrist, S., Yankov, V., Zakrajšek, E., 2009. Credit market shocks and economic fluctuations: evidence from corporate bond and stock markets. J. Monetary Econ. 56, 471–493.

Gombacorta, L., van Rixtel, A., 2013. Structural bank regulation initiatives: approaches and implications. BIS Working Paper 412.

---

52. Most Federal Reserve open-market operations are in the short end of the government securities market. This is because the short end of the market is deeper and more liquid and, therefore, can accept the Federal Reserve's large transactions with relatively little disruption.

Greenspan, A., 1993. FDICIA and the Future of Banking Law and Regulation. Proceedings of the Twenty-Ninth Annual Conference on Bank Structure and Competition, Federal Reserve of Chicago, titled: FDICIA: An Appraisal, pp. 3–9.

Hammond, B., 1957. Banks and Politics in America From the Revolution to the Civil War. Princeton University Press, Princeton, NJ.

Huertas, T.A., 1988. Can banking and commerce mix? Cato J. 7, 743–762.

Independent Commission on Banking, 2011. Final Report: Recommendations (The Vickers Report). London. http://bankingcommission.independent.gov.uk/.

Kacperczyk, M., Schnabl, P., July 2013. How safe are money market funds? Q. J. Econ., 128, 1073–1122.

Kane, E.J., 1989a. Changing incentives facing financial services regulators. J. Financ. Services Res., 2, 265–274.

Kane, E.J., 1989b. The unending deposit insurance mess. Science 246, 451–456.

Kane, E.J., 1990a. Principal-Agent Problems in S&L Salvage. J. Financ. 45, 755–764.

Kane, E.J., 1990b. Market Forces and Financial Misregulation. Talk delivered at the *Third Annual Australasian Finance and Banking Conference*.

Kane, E.J., 2014. Regulation and supervision: an ethical perspective. In: Berger, A.N., Molyneux, P., Wilson, J. O.S. (Eds.), The Oxford Handbook of Banking. Second ed. Oxford University Press, London, Forthcoming.

Kane, E.J., Yu, M., 1993. How Much did Capital Forbearance Add to the Tab for the FSLIC Mess?. Working paper, Boston College.

Kareken, J.H., Spring 1983. Deposit insurance reform; or, deregulation is the cart, not the horse. Q. Rev. Federal Reserve Bank Minneapolis, 7, 3–11.

Keeton, W.R., May/June 1991. The treasury plan for banking reform. Econ. Rev. Federal Reserve Bank of Kansas City, 76, 5–25.

Krainer, R.E., 2012. Regulating wall street; The Dodd–Frank act and the new architecture of global finance, a review. J. Financ. Stabil. 8, 121–133.

Kroszner, R., Rajan, R., 1994. Is the Glass–Steagall act justified? A study of the U.S. experience with universal banking before 1993. Am. Econ. Rev. 84, 810–832.

Liikanen, E., 2012. High-level expert group on reforming the structure of the EU banking sector, (The Liikanen Report). Final Report, Brussels http://ec.europa.eu/internal_market/bank/docs/high-level_expert_group/report_en.pdf.

Loewy, M.B., 1991. The macroeconomic effects of bank runs: an equilibrium analysis. J. Financ. Intermed. 1, 242–256.

Lucas, Jr., R.E., 2013. Glass–Steagall: a requiem. Am. Econ. Rev. 103, 43–47.

Marinč, M., Rant, V., 2014. A Cross-country analysis of bank bankruptcy regimes. J. Financ. Stabil. 13, 134–150.

Mehran, H., Thakor, A.V., 2011. Bank capital and value in the Cross-section. Rev. Financ. Stud. 24, 1019–1067.

Mester, L.J., May/June 1992. Banking and commerce: a dangerous liaison? Business Review, Federal Reserve Bank of Philadelphia, 17–29.

Morrison, A.D., White, L., 2013. Reputational contagion and optimal regulatory forbearance. J. Financ. Econ. 110, 642–658.

Myers, S.C., Majluf, N.S., 1984. Corporate financing and investment decisions when firms have information that investors do not have. J. Financ. Econ. 13, 187–221.

O'Hara, M., 1993. Real bills revisited: market value accounting and loan maturity. J. Financ. Intermed. 3, 51–76.

Pennacchi, G., 2006. Deposit insurance, bank regulation, and financial system risks. J. Monetary Econ. 53, 1–30.

Sarbanes-Oxley Act (SOX). 2002.

Saunders, A., 1991. The Separation of Banking and Commerce. Working paper, New York University Salomon Center.

Saunders, A., July/August 1985. Securities activities of commercial banks: the problem of conflict of interests. Bus. Rev. Federal Reserve Bank of Philadelphia, 17–27.

SEC, 2006. Credit Agency Reform Act of 2006. Securities Exchange Commission.

Shin, H.S., 2009. Reflections on Northern Rock: the bank run that heralded the global financial crisis. J. Econ. Perspect. 23, 101–119.

Shull, B., 1983. The separation of banking and commerce: origin, development, and implications for antitrust. Antitrust Bull. 28, 255–279, Spring.

Vickers, J., 2012. Some Economics of Banking Reform. University of Oxford, Department of Economics, Discussion Paper Series, 632.

Wall, L.D., January/February 1993. Too-big-to-fail after FDICIA. Econ. Rev. Federal Reserve Bank of Atlanta, 1–14.

White, L., 1988. Market Value Accounting: An Important Part of the Reform of the Deposit Insurance System. In Capital Issues in Banking, Association of Reserve City Bankers and the Banking Research Center, Northwestern University.

White, L., 2010. Markets: the credit rating agencies. J. Econ. Perspect. 24, 211–226.

Part IX

Financial Innovation

Chapter 17

The Evolution of Banks and Markets and the Role of Financial Innovation

---

"Finance is wholly different from the rest of the economy."

Alan Greenspan

GLOSSARY OF TERMS

Bank-Based Economies Economies where funding (credit) comes primarily from banks in the form of loans, and investors allocate a large share of savings as deposits in banks.

Commercial Letter of Credit A payment guarantee conditional upon successful delivery of goods or services by a seller. A financial institution that issues a commercial letter of credit guarantees that the seller of the goods and services is paid even if the buyer fails to make payment.

Financial-Market-Based Economies Economies with a financial system that relies predominantly on the financial market for the allocation of credit. Compared to bank-based systems, corporations depend more on funding directly through the financial markets and investors allocate more of their savings to investments rather than bank deposits.

Relationship Banking The provision of financial services by a financial intermediary that invests in obtaining customer-specific information with the expectation that this information will be used over multiple transactions. The bank develops a relationship with the borrower that often generates proprietary and qualitative ("soft") information, and it leads the bank to evaluate the profitability of the customer across products and over time, as opposed to on a single product or transaction in a single time period.

Securitization A process of pooling assets and then selling differentiated liquid claims against the cash flows generated by the asset pool.

Soft Information Information that is more qualitative and based on judgment, hence difficult to quantify.

Transaction Banking The provision of financial services with a focus on individual transactions based on readily quantifiable (hard) information.

INTRODUCTION

In Chapter 3 we explained how a financial system fosters economic growth. This chapter further elaborates on the financial system and its links with the real economy focusing on the relationship between banks and markets. Financial innovations and the recent growth of the financial sector are central parts of this discussion. We also address the differences between the Anglo-Saxon market-based financial systems found in the United States and the United Kingdom and the bank-based financial system that is common in continental Europe.

FINANCIAL DEVELOPMENT

Why does financial development matter for economic growth? In a frictionless world in which there are no informational asymmetries or transaction costs, financial development is uninteresting in the sense that it has little effect on economic growth. In such a world, there are no impediments to optimal resource allocation, so real resources can be efficiently allocated without the assistance of financial institutions and financial markets. In a sense, this takes us all the way back to Chapter 3, where we discussed the conditions under which financial intermediaries add economic value. We need similar conditions for financial development to matter for economic growth. That is, financial development matters because of economic frictions, and financial development mitigates their effects by lowering the cost of capital and increasing access to capital for individuals and companies.

S. I. Greenbaum, A. V. Thakor & A. W. A. Boot: Contemporary Financial Intermediation, Third edition. http://dx.doi.org/10.1016/B978-0-12-405196-6.00017-3

Financial development and economic growth

The empirical evidence shows that there is a strong positive link between economic growth and financial development. For example, a landmark study based on data for 1860–1963 concludes that periods of more rapid economic growth go hand in hand with an above average rate of financial development.[1] An interesting question here is one of causality: does financial development drive economic growth, or does economic growth lead to better financial development, or do economic growth and financial development both tend to move in the same direction because they are both similarly affected by some other force such as climate, geographic location, the work ethic of its people or its sociopolitical system? Our interest in financial development is obviously greatest if financial development leads to economic growth. There has been some disagreement on this. Some have argued in favor of a causal relationship, meaning that financial development leads to economic growth,[2] whereas others have maintained that financial development is largely a consequence of economic development.[3]

Research leading up to the 2007–2009 financial crisis seemed to settle the issue, at least for the time being, in favor of financial market development causally affecting economic growth, with some nuances related to the causality running in both directions.[4] This conclusion implies that a slow adjustment and development in the financial sector will hinder economic growth as a sluggish financial system may not meet the changing needs of the real economy. From this perspective, it would seem obvious that financial development is generally beneficial. Recent evidence, however, has shown that it is not necessarily the case that greater financial development is always unambiguously beneficial for the economy.

"Too much" financial development?

Financial development is important for growth because financial instruments lubricate economic activity. For example, when banks reduced the availability of commercial letters of credit in 2007–2009, world trade shrank considerably.

Nonet heless, some have wondered whether the pursuit of self-interest in the financial sector hurts economic growth by providing excessive liquidity to some sectors and causing price bubbles or crowding out of desirable economic activities.[5] Recent decades, have seen a substantial increase in the percentage of GDP coming from financial services. The question then is whether this is crowding out other sectors or it is simply an inevitable consequence of economic growth.

Figure 17.1 shows a marked growth in the financial sector in the years leading up to the financial crisis.

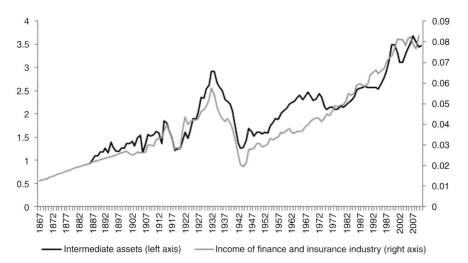

— Intermediate assets (left axis)   — Income of finance and insurance industry (right axis)

FIGURE 17.1   The Size of Intermediated Assets and Income in Finance and Insurance Industries over GDP. *(Source: Philippon (2015). Intermediated assets and Income of finance and insurance industry are both expressed in share of GDP).*

1. Goldsmith (1970).
2. See Hicks (1969) and Schumpeter (1912).
3. See Robinson (1952) and Lucas (1988).
4. Levine (1997) concludes that "A growing body of work would push even most skeptics towards the belief that the development of financial markets and institutions is a critical and inextricable part of the growth process and away from the view that the financial system is an inconsequential side show, responding passively to economic growth and industrialization."
5. Stiglitz (2010) states "the financial sector has become an end in itself rather than a means to an end."

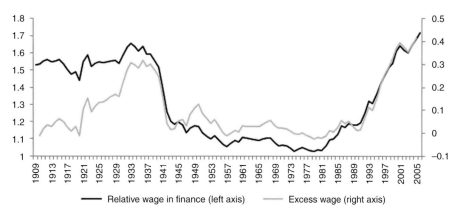

FIGURE 17.2 Relative Wage and Excess Wage in Finance in the United States. *(Source: Philippon and Reshef (2012); the relative wage in finance is computed as the ratio of the average wage in finance with respect to the average wage in the nonfarm private sector; excess wage denotes how much the relative wage in finance exceeds the average skill-adjusted average wage).*

If crowding out plays a role, then this growth in the financial sector may have come at the expense of other sectors of the economy. Also more indirect types of "crowding out" are possible. For example, talented MBA students as well as physicists and mathematicians increasingly chose careers in banking during 2003–2007, thereby diverting talent from other sectors. Even within the financial sector, resources might have been diverted from more to less valuable activities, for example, from relationship banking to trading activities.

Figure 17.2 shows that wages in the financial sector have outpaced those in other sectors. Figure 17.3 below shows the growth in credit intermediation in the United States.

Many countries came to see the financial sector as a growth engine of their economies and chose to allocate scarce public resources to subsidizing this sector. To the extent that these investments were at the expense of other sectors, another crowding out took place.

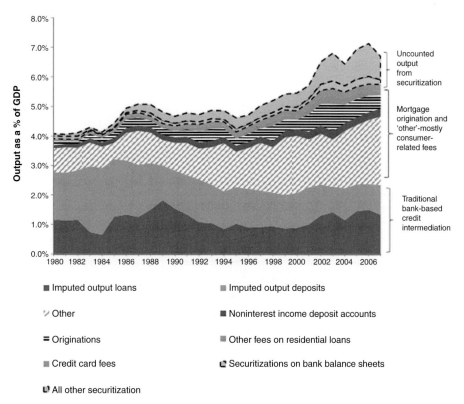

FIGURE 17.3 Credit Intermediation Output 1980–2007 in the United States. *(Source: Greenwood and Scharfstein (2013)).*

FINANCIAL INNOVATION

What is financial innovation? It is the creation of a new financial claim, institution, market, business practice, or process for distributing financial services. Securitization is an example. It is an alternative way of selling assets to investors. In contrast to other forms of innovation, most financial innovations are not patented.

The notion that financial innovation is good for economic growth is based on the idea that improvement in the allocation of capital or distribution of risk will follow. In the words of former Federal Reserve Chairman Ben Bernanke, "The increasing sophistication and depth of financial markets promote economic growth by allocating capital where it can be most productive."[6] Hence, the growth in debt, equity. and derivatives markets should not be surprising. See Figure 17.4.

Financial Innovation and Risk Sharing

Financial innovations – like the introduction of interest rate futures or credit default swaps – make it easier for investors to fine-tune their risk exposures, that is, better match risk and return to preferences.[7] This improved risk-management ability facilitates investment.

Similarly, the tradability of debt and equity allows investors to liquefy their holdings and helps in diversifying risks. Firms therefore might improve their access to financing. The desire to liquefy claims also helps explain the introduction of limited liability contracts like equity – an innovation in itself. Limited liability facilitates trading, and therefore promotes the liquidity of claims.

Lemons Problem

New types of securities are sometimes introduced to overcome information asymmetries. An ordinary debt claim might offer financing at lower cost than equity because it is less information sensitive. An equity claim might suffer from a "lemons problem" in that firms might have an incentive to sell overvalued equity to exploit less informed investors, and recognizing this, investors may price the equity accordingly that could then lead to a market failure.[8] Note that this problem can be avoided if the true value of a firm can be verified at a reasonable cost, in which case low-cost equity financing might be available. The costly-state-verification literature has focused on *ex-post* verification in the presence of sizable verification costs. A debt claim may help since with debt (contrary to equity) verification is not always needed. That is, if debt is repaid, there is no need to verify. If not, one needs to verify whether there is indeed a lack of resources. Having a debt

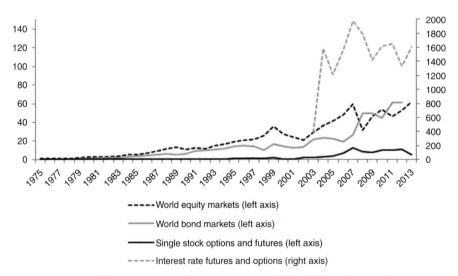

----- World equity markets (left axis)

——— World bond markets (left axis)

——— Single stock options and futures (left axis)

- - - - Interest rate futures and options (right axis)

FIGURE 17.4   Nominal Amounts of World Equity, Bonds, and Derivatives Markets in USD Trillion. *(Source: World Federation of Exchanges, http://www.world-exchanges.org/statistics).*

6. See Bernanke (2007).

7. More technically: financial innovations tend to complete the market. A complete set of Arrow–Debreu securities permits investors to acquire a portfolio of state-dependent securities that optimally matches state-dependent pay-offs to individual preferences.

8. This was the insight provided by Akerlof (1970). See Chapter 1.

contract in conjunction with a third party, for example, a bankruptcy court that can impose a severe penalty on the firm if it falsely claims insufficiency of funds, can solve the misrepresentation problem. Note that in the case of external equity, there is no fixed payment and verification is always needed. The upshot of this is that a debt security can be seen as a value-enhancing financial innovation to help facilitate access to funding in an environment in which it is costly for investors to verify the firm's actual cash flows.[9]

Various other approaches to mitigate problems of information asymmetry are available. For example, a rights issue could help solve the lemons problem. With a rights offering, existing shareholders get the right to buy newly issued shares, which are typically offered at a discount relative to the market price. If only existing shareholders buy the new shares, pricing is not that important. Why? Observe that in a nonrights secondary offering, when shares are publicly issued at a price that is too low, new shareholders get a windfall at the expense of existing shareholders. With a rights issue, the new shares are reserved for purchase by the existing shareholders, so it cannot trigger a wealth transfer. A rights issue may therefore allow the firm to raise new equity in circumstances in which a public equity issue would be subject to a lemons problem and may therefore have been infeasible.

Still other financial innovations can resolve agency- and asymmetric information problems. For example, convertible bonds give bondholders protection against risk-seeking behavior by shareholders. The idea is that when a lot of debt exists, new debt financing might not be available because it might induce shareholders to favor excessive risk at the expense of the bondholders (see Chapter 1 for a discussion of moral hazard). That is, shareholders' leveraged claim provides them an expanded upside potential if risks work out, while the downside is borne by the debtholders. Thus, debt may result in risk-shifting moral hazard. With convertible debt, bondholders share in the upside if risks work out (because they can convert to equity). As a consequence, incentives are better aligned.

Regulatory Arbitrage

Financial innovations are often motivated by regulatory and transaction costs. Regulatory arbitrage refers to innovations designed to circumvent the costs of public regulation. Innovations could also be aimed at reducing other transaction costs that impede trade. For example, credit default swaps (CDS) may improve the allocation of capital by improving the distribution of credit risk. However, from 2003 to 2008, the growth in OTC derivatives outpaced real investment by a factor of twelve.[10] And after 2006, real investments stagnated while OTC derivatives continued to grow faster than ever (see Figures 17.5 and 17.6). While the outsized growth of OTC derivatives, especially credit default swaps, in the period preceding the 2007–2009 crisis (the Great Recession) may have continued to serve a useful risk sharing purpose, the growth of this market also contributed to the financial system's fragility.

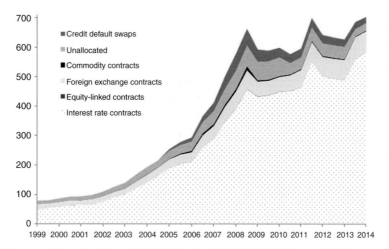

FIGURE 17.5   The Nominal Amounts of Over-the-Counter (OTC) Derivatives (in USD trillion). *(Source: BIS, Derivatives statistics, http://www.bis.org/statistics/derstats.htm).*

9. See Gale and Hellwig (1984).
10. See Posen and Hinterschweiger (2009).

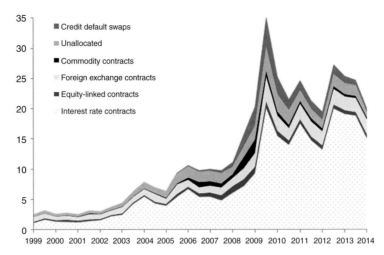

FIGURE 17.6 The Gross Amounts of Over-the-Counter (OTC) Derivatives (in USD trillion). *(Source: BIS, Derivatives statistics, http://www.bis.org/statistics/derstats.htm).*

THE DARK SIDE OF FINANCIAL INNOVATION

Financial innovation, although mightily useful, has a dark side as well. For example, financial institutions have been known to introduce exploitatively complex products with obscure cost structures, and it is not clear that the buyers of these products fully understand their costs and benefits. For example, in the Netherlands and the United Kingdom, life insurance companies offered policies with high profit margins for the insurance companies that had tax advantages for the buyers of the policies and low initial prices as inducements for purchase, but with complex cost-benefit tradeoffs that many retail buyers failed to understand. In such cases, financial innovations worsen the allocation of capital. The more recent innovations in securitization could possibly be interpreted in that way. As indicated in Chapter 11, securitization provides diversification benefits, reduces funding costs, and hence produces benefits for originating banks, borrowers, and investors. As long as originators retain some exposure, they have an incentive to screen and monitor loan applicants. However, if the loan originators do not retain a portion of the risk associated with making loans, lending standards may suffer, as we saw during the 2007–2009 crisis.[11] (The housing boom in the United States created a large number of mortgages that were securitized, creating complex mortgage-backed securities that obscured the risk and enabled originators and those who sold the securities to distribute over-priced securities.)

The most noteworthy innovations associated with the 2007–2009 financial crisis, for example, CDOs, SIVs, and CDS, enhanced marketability. Private benefits were striking, but so were abuses that increased market fragility (see Chapter 14). Moreover, banks, became more enmeshed with financial markets, and therefore got caught up in the boom-and-bust cycles that often afflict financial markets.[12] Table 17.1 summarizes the costs and benefits of financial innovation.

TABLE 17.1 The Benefits and Dark Side of Financial Innovation

Benefits of Financial Innovations	Dark Side of Financial Innovations

Financial innovations might improve the allocation of capital via
• better risk sharing
• diversification
• lower transaction costs
Financial innovations may also help mitigate information asymmetries among companies and investors
	Financial innovations might
	• mislead market participants
	• add complexity
	• induce excessive risk-taking
	• intertwine banks with financial markets, which might result in:
	  • greater complexity
	  • lower stability

11. See Keys et al. (2010) and the discussion in Chapter 14.
12. Special Report on Financial Innovation, *The Economist*, February 25, 2012, and Shleifer and Vishny (2010).

BANKS AND FINANCIAL MARKETS

The theory of financial intermediation emphasizes the role of banks in screening and monitoring borrowers in the process of lending. Bank lending is typically contrasted with direct funding via the financial markets. Banks are thought to be better than markets at resolving informational problems. By screening, banks weed out the less creditworthy borrowers. Without screening, lenders might demand higher interest rates to compensate for the presence of these less creditworthy borrowers, but this can induce adverse selection (see Chapter 1). In particular, the high interest rate would eventually attract only the riskiest borrowers and discourage the safest.[13] Lenders would then predominantly fund risky borrowers, precisely what the lemons problem predicts. In contrast, banks that carefully screen potential borrowers can tailor their credit contracts to borrower characteristics as discussed in Chapter 2. Banks also monitor their borrowers *after* loans have been granted. Without monitoring, borrowers might be tempted toward risk taking, especially if the risk can be shifted to the lender. Monitoring of borrowers by lending banks mitigates a moral hazard.

Relationship Banking

The intricate involvement of banks in lending is often referred to as relationship banking. Relationship banking is defined as the provision of financial services by a financial intermediary that invests in obtaining customer-specific information, often proprietary (meaning that it is not available to competing lenders) and more qualitative ("soft information") in the context of a long-term interaction with its customers. There are thus three key aspects of relationship lending: a more direct value-enhancing involvement of the bank with its customers, repeated interactions, and the bank's assessment of the profitability of the relationship over a long time horizon rather than in a single transaction. This contrasts with transaction banking – and/or deal making in the financial market – that focuses on individual transactions.

As discussed in Chapters 7 and 8, relationship banking provides several benefits.[14] Intertemporal smoothing of contract terms that would entail lender losses in the short term can be recouped later in the relationship. Credit subsidies to young companies may reduce moral hazards and informational frictions that banks face in lending to such borrowers. Banks may be willing to provide subsidized funding if they can expect to offset the initial losses through the long-term. Without access to subsidized credit early in their business lives, borrowers might forgo worthwhile projects. Relationship lending makes these loans feasible because the proprietary information generated ties the borrower to the bank and enables the bank to recoup its early subsidies to the borrower through higher profits later in the relationship.[15]

A second benefit of relationship lending is contractual flexibility unobtainable in the financial market. The proximity to customers that characterizes relationship banking generates and also allows the use of soft information. The intimate involvement with its customers gives the bank the ability to adjust contractual terms with the arrival of new information and hence encourages more fine-tuned contracts *ex ante* that also leave room for *ex-post* adjustments.

Value of Soft Information

Soft information can be seen as more qualitative and nuanced and noncontractible information (e.g., information about "character" – see Chapter 7). Because it is costly, proprietary soft information is the bedrock or glue of the durable relationship between the bank and its borrower. Moreover, because soft information is not readily transferable, shifting banks can prove costly for the borrower. This allows for implicit – nonenforceable – long-term contracting. Proprietary information is thought to be more readily protectable in a bank–borrower relationship. Therefore, both the bank and the borrower may realize the added value of their relationship.

The borrower–lender proximity and mutual dependence may also have a dark side. An important one is the hold-up problem that stems from the information monopoly the bank may develop due to the generation of proprietary borrower information during the relationship. Such an informational monopoly may permit the bank to exploit borrowers. The threat

13. The reason is that the risky borrowers – who have a lower probability of actually repaying the loan at the high interest rate – are less averse to paying the high interest rate than the less risky borrowers. See the credit rationing theories discussed in Chapter 8.
14. The discussion below follows Boot and Thakor (2014).
15. See Petersen and Rajan (1995), and Allen and Gale (1997) for a general characterization of intertemporal smoothing within a bank-based system.

of being "locked in," or informationally captured by the bank, may dampen loan demand *ex ante*, causing a loss of potentially valuable investment opportunities. Alternatively, firms may opt for multiple bank relationships. This may reduce the informational monopoly of any individual bank, but possibly at a cost in terms of the availability and cost of credit. Essentially, this introduces competition in the bank-borrower relationship. In the "Insight box", we expand on the potential effects that competition has on relationship banking.

Insight: *impact of competition on relationship versus transaction banking*

Since relationship banking is often profitable, it also invites competitive entry. This potential competition should impact the incentives for relationship banking. Two conflicting points of view have emerged. One is that competition among financiers encourages borrowers to switch to other banks or to the financial market. The consequent shortening of the expected "life-span" of bank–borrower relationships may induce banks to reduce their relationship-specific (informational) investments. It then becomes more difficult for banks to "subsidize" borrowers in earlier periods in return for a share of the rents in the future. Thus, the funding role for banks in the case of young corporations may no longer be sustainable in the face of competition.

Alternatively, competition may actually elevate the importance of a relationship-orientation because it puts the bank in a stronger competitive position. Since competition pressures profit margins on existing products it increases the importance of differentiation. More intense relationship lending may be one way for the bank to differentiate. A more competitive environment may then encourage banks to become more client-driven and customize services, thus generating a stronger focus on relationship banking.[16]

The impact of competition on relationship banking is complex; several effects need to be disentangled. However, empirical evidence seems to support the prediction that the nature of relationship banking adapts to increasing interbank competition, so higher competition does *not* drive out relationship lending.[17] There is also evidence that in recent years, the geographic distance between borrowers and lenders has increased, and this has been accompanied by higher loan defaults.[18]

The other dimension is related to the structure of the explicit contracts that banks can write. Because banks write more discretionary contracts, bank loans are more flexible and generally easier to renegotiate than bond issues or other public capital market contracts. This has obvious benefits in an environment in which information is changing rapidly. However, renegotiability may be a mixed blessing because it creates what has been called the "soft budget constraint" problem. This problem refers to the fact that the borrower, rationally anticipating that its loan will be renegotiated if it is financially distressed, has a weaker incentive to avoid excessive risk or take the hard and costly steps to reduce the probability of such states of financial distress. This worsens the moral hazard in the bank–borrower relationship and increases the bank's credit risk *ex ante*.[19]

Seniority and Bargaining Power

If the bank has priority/seniority over other lenders, its bargaining position is enhanced. The bank can therefore more credibly intervene in the decision process of the borrower. For example, the bank might believe that the firm's strategy is flawed, or a restructuring is long overdue. Without bank priority, the borrower may choose to ignore the bank's wishes. To see this, note that the bank could threaten to call the loan, but such a threat may lack credibility if the bank has low priority because the benefits of liquidating the borrower's assets are greater for higher-priority lenders and the costs from the termination of the borrower's business are higher for lower-priority lenders. The borrower will therefore understand that without priority, the bank's costs may outweigh the benefits of calling back the loan. When the bank loan has sufficiently high priority, the bank can credibly threaten to call the loan, and this may mitigate the negative effects of lender discretion in calling back the loan.

This identifies a potential advantage of bank financing: timely intervention. Of course, one could ask whether bondholders could be given priority and allocated the task of timely intervention. However, bondholders typically have less borrower information than banks and relatedly hold smaller stakes. This makes them ill-suited for timely intervention.

In Table 17.2, we have summarized the various arguments forced against relationship banking.

---

16. See Boot and Thakor (2000) on the latter, that is, the positive effects of competition on the intensity of relationship banking, and Petersen and Rajan (1995) on the negative effects of competition (via the effect that the increased possibility for the borrower to switch banks in a more competitive system reduces the scope for intertemporal subsidies).

17. See Degryse and Ongena (2007) whose evidence supports this prediction of Book and Thakor (2000).

18. See DeYoung et al. (2008).

19. The experience of the European Union in restructuring Greek debt could be seen as an example of that.

TABLE 17.2 Advantage and Drawbacks of Relationship Banking Relative to Financial Markets Funding

Advantages	Drawbacks	Solutions
Intensive information acquisition: • Monitoring contains moral hazard problem • Screening mitigates adverse selection problem	Soft budget constraint problem	Priority of claims (higher seniority for the bank) enables banks to intervene in a more timely (and credible) manner in case of financial distress
Long-term relationship allows for • Intertemporal smoothing • Flexibility • Confidentiality and proprietary information	Hold-up problem	Choose relationships with multiple banks and obtain easier access to alternative financing sources

BANK VERSUS MARKET: COMPLEMENTARITIES AND SHADOW BANKING

In contrast to the standard view that banks and financial markets compete, the previous section suggests that there are also complementarities between bank lending and capital market funding. We argued that prioritized bank debt may facilitate timely intervention. This feature of bank lending is valuable to the firm's bondholders as well. They might find it optimal to have bank debt take priority over their own claims because this efficiently delegates the timely intervention task to the bank. The bondholders will obviously ask to be compensated for their subordinated status. In other words, the priority and subordination features will be priced. Consequently, the borrower may reduce its total funding cost by accessing both the bank-credit market and the financial market.[20]

Banks and markets compete to be sure, but the view now is that they exhibit two other forms of interaction: they complement each other, and they coevolve. We discussed competition and complementarity above. Coevolution occurs because a more developed financial market makes it cheaper for the bank to fund itself. Banks then have stronger incentives and resources to invest in intermediation technologies that then helps them evolve.[21]

Securitization Connects Banks and Markets

Securitization connects banks and markets in various ways. A bank originates loans against which asset-backed securities are issued and sold in the market, so that market-based financing replaces deposit funding of the bank's loans. The bank thus relies on the market to get these loans "off its books." The market in turn relies on the bank to originate loans against which asset-backed securities are created to satisfy the demand for these securities from investors. This way, securitization fosters an interaction between banks and markets.

Fragility and Securitization

Before the 2007–2009 financial crisis, securitization was rapidly gaining in importance. Securitization became prevalent for ever-wider types of credits including business credits which were previously thought to be difficult to securitize because of their opacity. Also, a new market for securitization involving asset-backed commercial paper (ABCP) conduits emerged as a significant force. But the subprime crisis of 2007–2009 and the accompanying Great Recession exposed some of the most striking vulnerabilities of securitizations. One of the major vulnerabilities that securitization exposed was how much fragility maturity mismatching can generate, especially when opaque assets are financed with very short-maturity market-based funding. Nonrenewal of short-term funding due to solvency concerns about opaque and risky assets creates liquidity risk. While this liquidity risk was mitigated to some extent by liquidity guarantees (standby letters of credit and refinancing commitments), the underwriting institutions often underestimated the risks involved and overstretched themselves.[22] Unfortunately, a useful technology was seriously impugned because risks were underestimated and there were also incentive

---

20. See Berglof and Von Thadden (1994) and Holmstrom and Tirole (1997). Datta et al. (1999) show empirically that the monitoring associated with bank loans *facilitates* borrowers' access to the public debt market.

21. See Song and Thakor (2010) for a theory of dynamic financial system architecture in which banks and markets compete, complement, and evolve.

22. Gennaioli et al. (2015) and Thakor (2015) develop theories in which a long period of successful outcomes can lead to an underestimation of risk due to behavioral biases--departures from economically rational behavior that have been documented by psychologists.

TABLE 17.3 Comparison of Credit Rating Grades Given by the Three Biggest Credit Rating Agencies

Moody's	S&P	Fitch	Rating Description
Aaa	AAA	AAA	Prime
Aa1	AA+	AA+	High grade
Aa2	AA	AA	
Aa3	AA-	AA-	
A1	A+	A+	Upper medium grade
A2	A	A	
A3	A-	A-	
Baa1	BBB+	BBB+	Lower medium grade
Baa2	BBB	BBB	
Baa3	BBB-	BBB-	
Ba1	BB+	BB+	Non-investment grade Speculative
Ba2	BB	BB	
Ba3	BB-	BB-	
B1	B+	B+	Highly speculative
B2	B	B	
B3	B-	B-	
Caa1	CCC+	CCC	Substantial risks
Caa2	CCC		Extremely speculative
Caa3	CCC-		Default imminent with little prospect for recovery
Ca	CC	CC	
C		C	
	SD/D		In default

Source: SEC (2012).

conflicts and abuses. In retrospect, it is clear that financial contracts needed to be better designed and incentive conflicts at virtually every stage in the securitization process needed to be better handled.[23]

The 2007–2009 financial crisis significantly impaired the market for securitization. However, the risk diversification that securitization can accomplish remains. Thus, we expect securitization to re-emerge, albeit in a form that entails lower levels of liquidity risk, as well as reduced moral hazard in screening and monitoring.

ROLE OF CREDIT-RATING AGENCIES

In the intersecting world of banks and financial markets, credit-rating agencies have become indispensable. Credit-rating agencies assess the creditworthiness of debt instruments issued by companies, banks, nonbank financial institutions, and governments and sells this information (see Table 17.3 and our discussion in Chapter 2). The three main credit-rating agencies (CRAs) are Moody's Investors Service, Standard & Poor's (S&P), and Fitch Ratings.

To see why CRAs exist, we can revisit their roles as diversified information producers that we discussed in Chapter 2. Another role that rating agencies play is influencing the firm's future credit quality. For example, by putting a firm on a "watch list" (which indicates that a rating downgrade may occur in the near future) the CRA may induce the firm to undertake actions that arrest the possible deterioration in its credit quality.[24] This role of CRAs means that they serve a role similar to that of banks in affecting the credit risks of borrowers.[25] As CRAs become more sophisticated and reliable, their role as certifiers of credit quality is elevated, and the certification role of banks diminishes in relative importance, permitting

---

23. See Mian and Sufi (2009) and Keys et al. (2010).

24. For a theory along these lines, see Boot et al. (2006). See also Hirsch and Bannier (2007).

25. As shown in the theory developed by Holmstrom and Tirole (1997).

bank borrowers to migrate to the capital market. In this sense, CRAs intensify the competition between banks and markets. But CRAs also pull banks into the capital market. For example, banks originate loans that they securitize, and then seek ratings for the securitized pools from CRAs. The ratings, in turn, facilitate the sale of (securitized) asset-backed securities.

Credit-Rating Agencies under Fire

This rather positive interpretation of CRAs is clouded by events of the early twenty first century. In the 2001 crisis surrounding Enron, CRAs were accused of being strategically sluggish in downgrading. More recently, CRAs have been blamed for the 2007–2009 subprime crisis in which they were allegedly too lenient in rating mortgage-backed securities.[26] Standard and Poor's agreed to a $1.37 billion settlement in connection with alleged misdeeds in their ratings of various structured finance claims during the Great Recession. Allegedly, the CRAs have an incentive to overstate the qualities of asset-backed claims because of the "issuer-pays" model in which they are paid by the conduit/distributors who benefit from the exaggeration of the quality of their securities. Competition among CRAs for the rating assignments induces CRAs to overstate credit qualities, goes the argument.

Apart from concerns about conflicts of interest, the role of CRAs in securitization transactions has introduced financial stability concerns. Of particular concern are the so-called "rating triggers." For example, some debt contracts may dictate accelerated repayments when the rating is downgraded. The consequences of such accelerated debt repayments might, however, be so severe as to give pause to the rating agencies. Complications also arise from the role played by the so-called "monoliners." These are insurers that guarantee municipal bonds and also the lowest-risk tranches in securitizations. Monoline insurers are critical to the viability of many securitizations. However, the ability of the monoliners to issue credible guarantees depends on their having AAA ratings. This generates an interesting concatenation. In rating (and monitoring) the monoliners, CRAs affect the viability of the securitization market. Thus, the impact of CRAs is both direct (rating securitization tranches) and indirect (rating the monoliners). The potential failure of such monoliners has serious implications for the value of various structured finance products.

This further underscores the linkages and dependencies in the financial markets. Other concerns are the oligopolistic nature of both the rating and guarantee businesses, and their importance for structured finance markets.[27]

Under the Dodd–Frank Act, the legal liability of CRAs has been elevated. Whether this will result in more accurate credit ratings is an open question.

CONCLUSION

We have emphasized the three-dimensional interaction – competition, complementarity, and coevolution – between banks and financial markets. And the recent financial innovations have possibly strengthened these relationships. As a final observation, note that the financial systems are either bank-based (continental Europe) or financial market driven (US, UK). In the former, bank financing is dominant while direct funding from the financial market plays a more important role in the latter. The dichotomy between a bank-based system and a financial market-driven economy appears to have weakened in recent years. In particular, innovations like securitization have made banks' assets more marketable and increased the sensitivity of banks to financial market developments. Banks have thus become an extension of rather than a substitute for the financial markets.

REVIEW QUESTIONS

1. Explain the difference between bank-based and financial-based economies.
2. Compare recent trends in financial markets and banking systems across the world.
3. Describe the relationship between financial development and economic growth.
4. Compare relationship banking to transaction banking.
5. Describe the advantages and disadvantages of relationship banking.
6. Describe the benefits and drawbacks of financial innovations.
7. Explain how a financial innovation, such as a commercial letter of credit, helps facilitate trade.
8. Explain the role of CRAs in today's financial markets.

---

26. See Cantor (2004) and White (2010). An additional concern is that in their "new" structured business, rating agencies might have become compromised (or at the very least conflicted) because they essentially became "partners" in the business model of securitization.
27. See also U.S. Senate (2002).

REFERENCES

Akerlof, G.A., 1970. The market for lemons: quality uncertainty and the market mechanism. Q. J. Econ. 84, 488–500.

Allen, F., Gale, D., 1997. Financial markets, intermediaries and intertemporal smoothing. J. Polit. Econ. 105, 523–546.

Berglof, E., Von Thadden, E.-L., 1994. Short-term versus long-term interests: capital structure with multiple investors. Q. J. Econ. 109, 1055–1084.

Bernanke, B., 2007. Regulation and financial innovation, speech to the Federal Reserve Bank of Atlanta's 2007 Financial Markets Conference. Sea Island, Georgia. http://www.federalreserve.gov/newsevents/speech/bernanke20070515a.htm

Boot, A.W.A., Milbourn, T.T., Schmeits, A., 2006. Credit ratings as coordination mechanisms. Rev. Financ. Stud. 19, 81–118.

Boot, A.W.A., Thakor, A.V., 2014. Commercial banking and shadow banking: the accelerating integration of banks and markets and its implications for regulation. In: Berger, A.N., Molyneux, P., Wilson, J.O.S. (Eds.), Oxford Handbook of Banking, second ed., Oxford University Press, Oxford UK, pp. 47–76.

Boot, W.A., Thakor, A.V., 2000. Can relationship banking survive competition? J. Financ. 55, 679–713.

Cantor, R., 2004. An introduction to recent research on credit ratings. J. Bank. Financ. 28, 2565–2573.

Datta, S., Iskandar-Datta, M., Patel, A., 1999. Bank monitoring and the pricing of corporate public debt. J. Financ. Econ. 51, 435–449.

Degryse, H., Ongena, S., 2007. The impact of competition on bank orientation. J. Financ. Intermed. 16, 399–424.

DeYoung, R., Glennon, D., Nigro, P., 2008. Evidence from informational-opaque small business borrowers. J. Financ. Intermed. 17, 113–143.

Gale, D., Hellwig, M., 1984. Incentive-compatible debt contracts: the one-period problem. Rev. Econ. Stud. 52, 647–663.

Gennaioli, N., Shleifer, A., Vishny, R., 2015. Neglected risks: the psychology of financial crises. Am. Econ. Rev. 105, 310–314.

Greenwood, R., Scharfstein, D.S., 2013. The growth of finance. J. Econ. Perspect. 27, 3–28.

Goldsmith, R.W., 1970. Financial Structure and Development. Yale University Press, New Haven, CT.

Hicks, J.R., 1969. Automatists, Hawtreyans, and Keynesians. J. Money Credit Bank. 1, 307–317.

Hirsch, C., Bannier, C.E., 2007. The Economics of Rating Watchlists: Evidence From Rating Changes. Working Paper, Goethe University, Frankfurt.

Holmstrom, B., Tirole, J., 1997. Financial intermediation, loanable funds, and the real sector. Q. J. Economics 112, 663–691.

Keys, B.J., Mukherjee, T., Seru, A., Vig, V., 2010. Did securitization lead to lax screening: evidence from subprime loans. Q. J. Econ. 125, 307–362.

Levine, R., 1997. Financial development and economic growth: views and agenda. J. Econ. Lit. 35, 688–726.

Lucas, Jr., R.E., 1988. On the mechanics of economic development. J. Monetary Econ. 22, 3–42.

Mian, A.R., Sufi, A., 2009. The consequences of mortgage credit expansion: evidence from the US mortgage default crisis. Q. J. Econ. 124, 1449–1496.

Petersen, M.A., Rajan, R.G., 1995. The effect of credit market competition on lending relationships. Q. J. Econ. 110, 407–443.

Philippon, T., 2015. Has the U.S. finance industry become less efficient? On the theory and measurement of financial intermediation. Am. Econ. Rev., 105, 1408–1438.

Philippon, T., Reshef, A., 2012. Wages and human capital in the U.S. financial industry: 1909-2006. Q. J. Econ., 127, 1551–1609.

Posen, A.S., Hinterschweiger, M., 2009. How useful were recent financial innovations? There is reason to be skeptical, Real Time Economic Issues Watch, May 7th.

Robinson, J., 1952. The Generalization of the General History. The Rate of Interest, and Other Essays. Macmillan, London.

Schumpeter, J., 1912. Theorie der wirtschaftlichen Entwicklung. Dunker & Humblot, Leipzig, Germany.

SEC, 2012. Report to Congress Credit Rating Standardization Study, As Required by Section 939(h) of the Dodd-Frank Wall Street Reform and Consumer Protection Act. U.S. Securities and Exchange Commission, September. http://www.sec.gov/news/studies/2012/939h_credit_rating_standardization.pdf

Shleifer, A., Vishny, R.W., 2010. Unstable banking. J. Financ. Econ. 97, 306–318.

Song, F., Thakor, A.V., 2010. Financial system architecture and the co-evolution of banks and markets. Econ. J. 120, 1021–1255.

Stiglitz, J., 2010. Contribution to the *The Economist* Online Debate 'Financial Innovation'.

Thakor, A.V., 2015. Lending booms, smart bankers, and financial crises. Ame. Econ. Rev. 105, 305–309.

U.S. Senate, 2002. Hearings before the Senate Committee on Governmental Affairs: Rating the Raters: Enron and the Credit Rating Agencies.

White, L.J., 2010. Markets: the credit rating agencies. J. Econ. Perspect. 24, 211–226.

Part X

The Future

Chapter 18

The Future

"It is always wise to look ahead, but difficult to look further than you can see."

Winston Churchill

GLOSSARY OF TERMS

Conglomerate Discount The amount by which the price of a conglomerate trades at is lower than the sum of the prices at which its individual divisions would trade as stand-alone businesses.

Internal Capital Markets The availability of funds from within the firm to finance investments, thereby reducing dependence on external financing.

SIFI Systemically important financial institution. This refers to institutions whose failure is expected to have systemic consequences for the economy.

INTRODUCTION

Your intellectual curiosity and patience are rewarded. The closing chapter, one of conjecture and surmise, is at hand. Though predictions about the future of banking maybe unavoidable, they are also often fraught with drama. With provocative titles like, "The Banks of Tomorrow: Think Google and Facebook"[1] or "Banks Need to Take on Amazon and Google or Die,"[2] scribblers raise the specter of existential threats. Overlooked is the possibility that banks of the future may look neither like Google and Facebook nor like contemporary banks. New kinds of intermediaries may emerge with the capability to eclipse existing banks as well as extant social media paragons.

In this chapter, we begin with a discussion of the main drivers for change in the financial services industry. Three are especially compelling: governmental intervention/regulation, information technology, and customer preferences. As discussed in previous chapters, government regulation is ever-present in reshaping financial markets and institutions. Technology, however, may be even more powerful in driving change. It is indispensable for the deepening of financial markets, the emergence of new distribution channels, and for financial innovations, including those in payments systems. It may encourage disintermediation and disaggregation of the value chain. For example, specialized payments providers may emerge, and internet-based platforms may allow for open-source financial services like peer-to-peer (P-2-P) lending bypassing intermediaries. Changes in customer preferences play a key role as well. In part, technology is changing social attitudes and customer preferences. Witness how the development of hand-held mobile devices like smartphones (e.g., i-Phones and Blackberries) has transformed consumer purchase and payment practices. How will banks and other intermediaries in the value chain respond to these developments, and what future scenarios are likely to be generated?

While changes in customer preferences and payments technology may most directly affect retail banking, we will argue that major developments can be expected in corporate and investment banking as well.

CHANGE DRIVERS

Public regulation, technology, and customer preferences are perhaps most disruptive and can be seen as the primary forces of change. Chapters 15 and 16 explained how the Great Recession led to a major expansion of regulation. This trend toward more intrusive governmental regulation is likely to continue with structural implications for the banking industry. Information technology is reshaping the financial services industry too. Shifts from credit and debit cards to mobile and digital means of payment are already in evidence. Social media and the internet create new challenges for extant business models as they reduce the cost of information and encourage its dissemination in unpredictable ways. Technology disaggregates the value chain and introduces new players, processes, and products. As this happens, new externalities and risks are likely

---

1. See http://www.wired.com/2013/08/why-do-we-need-banks/; August 22, 2013, commentary by Marcus Wohlson.
2. Financial Times December 3, 2013, comments by Francisco Gonzalez.

S. I. Greenbaum, A. V. Thakor & A. W. A. Boot: Contemporary Financial Intermediation, Third edition. http://dx.doi.org/10.1016/B978-0-12-405196-6.00018-5

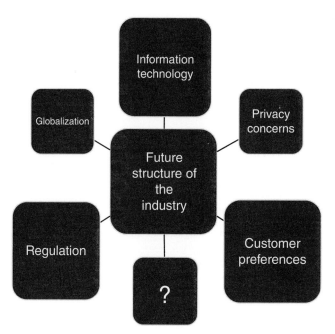

FIGURE 18.1 Forces Affecting the Industry.

to emerge, encouraging the development of new types of governmental regulations, for example, witness the recent push to regulate the internet in the United States and the discussion surrounding "net neutrality." There is thus a natural dynamic in the interaction between technology and regulation; one that is continuously evolving and not easily understood.

Apart from regulation and information technology, we see a third force for change in the financial landscape – evolving customer preferences. Consumers desire empowerment and more control over their finances. Social media affect the process by which customers are engaged, and want to be reached. A more detailed discussion of each of these forces follows. Figure 18.1 displays the various forces. While information technology, regulation and customer preferences are identified as the key forces driving change, Figure 18.1 also recognizes the importance of privacy concerns and globalization. We discuss privacy concerns – particularly surrounding the use of data – in the following section on regulation. Globalization is not a force that is discussed explicitly, but obviously has an impact on the structure of the industry and the effectiveness of nation-based regulation. Geo-political developments (from Russia, Middle-East to concerns about foreign ownership of domestic assets) may impact the degree of globalization in the years to come as well as cross-border financial flows and the international scope of financial institutions.

Regulation

Recent legislation in Europe, the United States and the rest of the world has empowered public regulators at the expense of shareholders and management (private interests). This incursion was responsive to:

- growth in global systemic risk with increasing integration of markets and institutions both within and across countries;
- social and political agendas assigned to banks and markets;
- growing complexity of the financial sector;
- regulatory arbitrage that undermined public regulation.

  Following is a discussion of each.

Global Systemic Risk and Interconnectedness

One aspect of the Great Recession that caught regulators by surprise was the violence with which shocks in one part of the financial system were transmitted to others. The subprime mortgage crisis in the United States – triggered a worldwide trauma. As we saw in Chapter 17, financial institutions and markets are increasingly integrated within and across national boundaries. Interconnectedness, globalization, and the proliferation of financial claims slowed a bit during the 2007–2009 financial crisis, but are likely to reassert their full force. Therefore, we expect financial system contagion to not only continue in the future, but possibly even become more pronounced.

Intrafinancial sector linkages can be expected to mushroom as well. The linkages of shadow banks – which mostly escaped regulatory oversight prior to the 2007–2009 crisis – to other parts of the financial system may have been motivated by the economic demands of the system (including regulatory arbitrage), have also promoted opacity and fragility. In particular, the regulatory costs faced by legacy depository institutions spur the development of the shadow financial system that, in turn, renders regulation less effective. Not only will central banks need to track more voluminous flows of information that involve both traditional financial institutions as well as shadow banking and other forms of market-based finance, but they will need a better understanding of what all of these information flows imply about systemic risk. The effectiveness of the regulatory response (see Chapters 15 and 16) is still unclear.

Complexity of Regulations

As global financial markets, institutions, and contracts become more complex, regulators strive to keep pace by enacting increasingly intrusive regulations. The Dodd–Frank Act weighed in at more than 2000 pages and it spawned many more thousands of pages of directives. However, more regulations lead to ever more circumventing innovation or regulatory arbitrage. Unintended consequences often engender costs that outweigh any conceivable benefits of the original regulation.

While some have advocated simpler approaches to regulation,[3] this dynamic of more regulations and innovative approaches to circumvent them is difficult to counter. Limiting the burden of regulation might encourage the industry to choose simpler and more transparent business models. But gaps in regulation are inevitable and there will always be the fringe players who exploit the public safety net. As these actions lead to visible problems and failures, regulators will step in with more intrusive regulation. The unintended consequences can be considerable. In particular, the resulting regulatory burden may deter entry into the industry and promote further activities "in the shadows."[4]

Social and Political Agendas

Politics has always played a role in the regulation of banks and financial markets. The allocation of credit is of enormous economic significance, so if it can be controlled by politicians, it can serve political and social agendas. As social movements – focusing on poverty, social discrimination, income and wealth inequality, diversity, global warming, etc. – or even sectoral preferences, such as housing and agriculture, gather momentum, the pressure on financial institutions grows.[5] The financial system thereby becomes an instrument of social planning and the efficient provision of financial services is sacrificed.

Other Social and Economic Concerns

A related social agenda seeks to strengthen the fiduciary responsibility of financial institutions. In several countries, financial intermediaries have been criticized for selling inappropriate products, providing misleading information, and/or failing to verify that their products meet the legitimate needs of customers. In the United Kingdom and The Netherlands, for example, major scandals involving insurance-related pension products are winding their way through the courts. In the United States, billions of dollars have been imposed on in fines banks for selling toxic investment products while allegedly misrepresenting information. The European watchdog for systemic risk – the ESRB (ESRB, 2014) – has declared that the "*mis-selling*" of products to customers is a financial stability concern and has recommended assessing business practices as an integral part of prudential supervision. For decades, investment advisers in the United States have been constrained by "suitability" requirements. The more recent Dodd–Frank Act has created a new consumer protection agency to further discourage misrepresentation of financial services.

Privacy is yet another public policy concern. Ongoing initiatives across the world put increasingly stringent restrictions on financial institutions' use of client data. Competition is another concern. Some countries – particularly the United Kingdom – have attacked monopolistic concentrations as banks have grown larger and fewer through mergers and acquisitions.

These various concerns suggest an evolving regulatory landscape that will have a major impact on the financial services industry of the future. The ultimate financial system design will depend upon how the tension between private and public interests is resolved. Will the struggle between Wall Street and Main Street abate, or will the public backlash against the financial services industry continue? The intrusiveness of public regulation will depend on how the industry is publicly perceived and on this score there is quite a bit of fence mending that lies ahead for the global financial services industry.

---

3. Haldane (2012) is a forceful exponent of this. He discusses how a dog that is trying to catch a Frisbee manages to deal with the complexities of dealing with the trajectory of the Frisbee, and asks whether the simplicity of a dog is not precisely what we need in regulation. In other words, is complexity of regulation as a response to the growing complexity of finance not counterproductive?

4. Large systemic institutions face extra requirements (the SIFI – systemically important financial institutions – category). Also controlling a sprawling international presence has not been easy, and institutions following the 2007–2009 financial crisis have been hit with heavy fines (primarily) by US regulators for failures in appropriately controlling behavior across their worldwide operations, e.g. fines for money laundering, Libor rigging, dealings with prohibited countries, etc. (see for example HSBC). This suggests that there is also a cost to being "super sized," a diseconomy of scale and/or scope.

5. Lucas (2014) shows how governments affect the allocation of credit via public guarantees.

Technology

Information technology is the great enabler. Markets and institutions have become more integrated, and financial innovations have proliferated, particularly those that enhance the tradability of assets and the transfer of risks that previously resided on the balance sheets of financial institutions. Also, distribution channels, payments systems, and more generally the way the financial services sector provides services and interacts with potential customers, are all affected by information technology. This more fluid landscape creates regulatory challenges and reshapes the business of banking. Several related questions follow:

- Will technology firms displace banks in the provision of payments services?
- Can banks retain their retail customers?
- Will P-2-P lending, crowdfunding, and other alternative credit arrangements circumscribe the market for traditional banks?
- Will nondeposit financial institutions and nonfinancial businesses make further inroads in the business of banking?
- Will traditional banks suffer disproportionally from rising costs owing to more intrusive public regulators giving rise to an ever-expanding shadow banking system?
- How will evolving debt and equity markets (both public and private) affect investment and commercial banks?

We will address these questions later in the chapter.

Customer Preferences

The rise of social media and the sought immediacy of consumer gratification will have implications for financial services firms. The digital and mobile economy alters customer service expectations and affects the way customers perceive their financial institution. The ability to effect transactions online instantaneously has not only made the multiday delays of traditional providers annoying anachronisms, but also made the interaction between bank and customers more anonymous. It also made it easier for customers to change providers and "shop around" for the best deal.

The vast branch of networks will either evolve or disappear. Bank branches, like coffee shops, may become social-exchanges and entertainment-driven marketing vehicles. Traditional branch services are likely to be digitized and delivered remotely via the cloud. Millennials take pride in never setting foot in a bank branch, and if this should change in the future, it will be for a yet undetermined motive. Security concerns in the digitized world are somehow going to be resolved. Biometrically based security might become standard practice and intelligent software that uses retinal recognition or venous identification might discourage fraud.

The connection between an increasingly digitized customer and the financial services provider of the future is yet to develop. What role will loyalty play? What kind of cross-selling will be obtained? Particularly in Europe, where the social welfare state retreats and distrust of financial institutions are widespread, consumers have a great desire for independence and empowerment. Trusted institutions do not hawk toxic financial products on their clientele, and if they do, serious consequences should ensue.

Banks feel the pressure to connect to society, and be responsive to environmentally conscious citizens. Customers want their banks to behave in a socially responsible fashion and to be accountable. Many banks have adopted mission statements emphasizing their commitment to the environment and the long-term well-being of people and society. Goldman Sachs emphasizes its "responsibility for environmental and social stewardship," and Deutsche Bank emphasizes its "commitment to long-term environmental sustainability." Some banks even have centered their whole business model and decision processes around sustainability, and chosen an ownership structure that safeguards their environmental mission. Triodos Bank of The Netherlands is an example of that. See Figure 18.2 for illustrative statements of these banks.

Building trust will be paramount. Transparency in the operations of financial institutions will be expected. To be successful, banks will need a better understanding of their customers and to tailor product offerings accordingly. To achieve this, banks will need a greater service ethic and show true commitment to their clientele. A profound change in banking culture and compensation practices will be required.

Interrelationships Between Drivers for Change

The drivers for change are interrelated. For example, parts of social media that play a role in shaping customer behavior (and possibly customer preferences) are products of information technology. And technology may facilitate regulatory arbitrage, evoking a regulatory response. Social media may also elevate systemic risks through herding behavior that leads

"We take seriously our responsibility for environmental and social stewardship and are committed to leveraging our people, capital and ideas to further effective market-based solutions that help address critical environmental issues."
See: http://www.goldmansachs.com/citizenship/environmental-stewardship-and-sustainability/

"Deutsche Bank has a commitment to long-term environmental sustainability. This includes reducing the Bank's own impact (e.g., reducing waste and working towards becoming more carbon neutral) and supporting innovative new technology."
See: https://www.db.com/unitedkingdom/content/en/sustainability.html

Triodos 🌀 Bank

Why we're different

"We only lend our customers' money to people and organisations working to make the world a better place, actively seeking out and promoting sustainable, entrepreneurial businesses driven by values and ideas - rather than just refusing to back businesses that do harm." See: https://www.triodos.com/en/about-triodos-bank/

FIGURE 18.2   Banks and Sustainability.

to bank runs, bubbles, and manias. Change drivers all have a level of unpredictability that elevates uncertainty about the future of banking.

INITIATIVES THAT ARE CHANGING THE LANDSCAPE

The proliferation of web-based services and data-processing capabilities is changing the financial services landscape. Major changes are evident in distribution systems and the way financial institutions interact with their clientele. In addition, there are new disruptive players on the periphery with business models that challenge existing practices and institutions.

Payments

This core area of banking is being coveted by technology firms and payment specialists like Google, Apple, and PayPal; Bitcoin as a more fundamental innovation affecting payments processes is discussed later. A much discussed example is

Apple Pay, announced as a payment system that will run on the iPhone obviating the need for debit or credit cards. (See Box 18.1.)

So far, banks have maintained their central role in payments because they control the infrastructure for settling payments, are perceived to be crucial for security, and have a strong hold on customers' clearing accounts. Also, the payments innovators are not typically independent of banks, but have developed in joint ventures or other types of alliances with traditional banks. In some countries, banks themselves have managed to offer the leading on-line payments solution. For example, the Scandinavian (Nordic European) banks are providing mobile banking with high-growth user bases, and in The Netherlands, the payment firm Currence, owned by the leading Dutch banks, has a market share of approximately 60% of online payments.[6]

Payments are a highly contested area that may trigger major changes in the financial services industry. Should the new payments solution providers undermine the banks direct interface with customers, cross-selling opportunities might be lost. In any case, online platforms will be developed that could disrupt existing financial institutions. We turn to this next.

Online Platforms and Disaggregation

Disaggregation of the value chain could follow from online platforms becoming the preferred customer interface. Online platforms could offer a supermarket type model facilitating access to various products and services of disparate providers along with record keeping. Technology firms such as Google, Facebook, Amazon, or Apple may use a payments solution such as Apple Pay as a platform and gain direct customer interface for related products and services. Legacy financial institutions then might be relegated to serving as the back office to the platform.

Desired empowerment and autonomy dictate that customers feel in control and do not view themselves as being steered to goods for the benefit of the platform owner. Customers' possible need for assistance in making informed decisions may provide an opportunity for existing financial institutions to adopt the role of financial advisors but possible conflicts arise when these institutions have their own products to sell. Conflicts of interest erode the credibility of institutions, but if financial institutions can find a way to maintain credibility as trusted advisors many new possibilities may emerge.

The competition between banks and alternative providers for the payments business will not spare purveyors. The weapons of this contest will be technology and marketing savvy. The disruptive forces affecting banking – technology, regulation, and customer preferences – may also offer new opportunities for other businesses that have tried to enter banking. For example, Tesco, a large UK supermarket chain provides banking services to its customers under its own brand. There is also no reason why a platform should be limited to offering only financial services. A lifestyle oriented focus could integrate financial and nonfinancial offerings. What does this imply for banks as stand-alone entities? Would this transform them in back-office service providers discussed above, or can they remain in the lead and safeguard their turf as financial services providers?

The ultimate outcome may well turn on how the government intervenes. Public regulation may differentially tax, subsidize, or judiciously ignore various players. Here we see the complicated interplay of customer preferences, technological disruptions, and the restraining hand of government seeking to control financial services. Would banks continue to be special and protected by bank licenses? For now, following the 2007–2009 financial crisis, governments seem keen to control their financial players and grant them special status (including providing them with implicit and explicit guarantees).

---

6. See Oliver Wyman (2014) on Scandinavia, and reports of the BIS contained in BIS (2014).

Direct Lending and Disintermediation

The financial services platform might act as a market place where people interact directly and financial institutions serve the limited role of an advisor or broker. P-2-P lending has parties transacting directly without the benefit of a financial intermediary (except possibly for back-office services). The platform would reduce search costs and therefore serve as a broker. However, issues inhibiting direct lending have been asymmetric information and moral hazard which financial intermediaries mitigate rather effectively.

New specialized lenders have arisen that seek to replace relationship lenders and traditional credit scoring with sophisticated algorithms based on Big Data mining. While still in its infancy, such analysis predicts creditworthiness by analyzing buying habits, memberships, reading proclivities, lifestyle choices, and all manner of opportunistic demographic correlates. Similarly, the growing availability of inexpensive information allows for public certification of creditworthiness similar to the trustworthiness scores on eBay, or the client satisfaction scores on TripAdvisor. One could envision similar developments enabling P-2-P lending as well. Whether society will accept the widespread use of these data is a different matter. In any event, more and more potentially sensitive personal information can already be obtained with a few mouse clicks. Big Data may also facilitate crowdfunding, another form of direct lending involving multiple lenders and a singular borrower.[7]

At the consumer level, we may see a (re)emergence of more community-oriented arrangements. As P-2-P lending and crowdfunding suggest, customers may take matters in their own hands; empowerment thus. Local arrangements may emerge where communities organize their financial affairs directly. Particularly in Europe, where social welfare states previously led to centralization, the trend is toward decentralization of services and private initiative. Whereas markets are becoming more global, people want more control over their own affairs and local initiatives and consumer empowerment may thrive.

Bitcoin

Bitcoin, a purely virtual currency, exists in a digital form exclusively.[8] There is disagreement as to whether Bitcoin represents an authentic currency in providing a stable store of value, but its potential as an alternative vehicle for transactions is less controversial. Bitcoin bypasses the existing institutional payments system, and is a P-2-P electronic cash that permits payment without the involvement of traditional financial institutions. A typical credit card transaction involves at least five parties (banks at both ends, a credit card company, a payment processor, and a clearing house) and takes days to settle. With Bitcoins, a transaction merely requires a transfer between Bitcoin accounts and an electronic verification process.

Bitcoin is unlikely to replace major currencies as a medium of exchange anytime soon. However, it has demonstrated the viability of an electronic currency, *absent government backing*. It is an early-stage innovation; the institutional structure is still developing. A key question is what regulatory framework will be developed for such *cryptocurrencies*? Bitcoin might be the most well known, but others are in the making as well – referred to as "altcoins" (alternative bitcoins). Also, the protocol dictating the procedures surrounding the management, record keeping, and supply of bitcoins will evolve over time. While having Bitcoin as a purely private-sector developed currency is its major attraction, concerns about security and safety are inescapable. Can the technology safeguard the ownership and transaction infrastructure without government guarantees? And how will the public react if Bitcoins become the preferred medium of exchange for illegal activities? Another uncertainty surrounding cryptocurrencies is the high volatility of Bitcoin's value relative to major currencies. For now, Bitcoin is a development in its infancy, yet showing progress. It has managed to be taken seriously. Few had expected that.

Investment Banking, Trading, and Exchanges

Much of the discussion thus far has involved commercial and retail banking. However, major changes in financial markets and investment banking are envisioned as well. Investment banks play an important role in bringing capital users and capital providers together. These banks are primarily engaged in public and private offerings of debt and equity claims and also maintain secondary markets in these securities thereby augmenting liquidity. In the run up to the Great Recession (the 2007–2009 financial crisis), investment banks were very active in securitizing home mortgages and in making a market for

---

7. "Crowdfunding refers to the efforts by entrepreneurial individuals and groups – cultural, social, and for-profit – to fund their ventures by drawing on relatively small contributions from a relatively large number of individuals using the internet, without standard financial intermediaries" (Mollick (2014), p.2).
8. For papers on bitcoin, see Nakamoto (2013) and Yermack (2013).

OTC derivatives, two of the financial instruments assigned greatest culpability. But this was not all: their trading activities across the board mushroomed.

Investment banks also are subject to disruption by advances in technology, changes in public regulation and customer preferences. Two of the most prominent investment banks in the United States – Lehman Brothers and Bear Stearns – failed in the Great Recession while others sustained embarrassing losses and severe devaluation of their equity. In retrospect, these banks processed too much risk and their losses had systemic implications. This latter observation prompted a major expansion in the public regulation of investment banks. Both Goldman Sachs and Morgan Stanley, the two bellwethers of U.S. investment banking, submitted to the regulation of the Federal Reserve in exchange for access to the discount window. Proprietary trading was curtailed and financial leverage was reduced from historically high levels. Regulatory strictures remain in flux, but the direction of change is clear. Major Wall Street institutions, previously relatively free of public regulation, came to be reigned in much like their cousins in commercial banking. Some believe the rigors of public regulation will be relaxed in time with incessant lobbying – the financial services industry is one of the best funded financial lobbies in both Washington, DC and state capitals – and especially with a protracted period of capital scarcity. However, this is an agenda for the future.

Technology affects investment banking and the capital markets by irreversibly lowering the costs of information, communication, and transportation.[9] We expect new entry among capital providers. Hedge funds, pension managers, insurance companies, and private equity firms can all be expected to encroach on the traditional domain of investment banks further advancing integration and augmenting competition.

Another uncertainty comes from the demand side for investment banking services. At the corporate level, firms may use variations on vehicles like trade finance to enhance capital availability to members of a production value chain without relying on commercial and investment banks. In industries with substantial investment needs involving deep uncertainties and dependence on a few customers, downstream and upstream financing for major investments (again circumventing banks and financial markets) may become more common. An example is Intel providing equity finance for ASML, a Dutch company that builds the machines that Intel uses for chip production. This may undermine the stronghold of investment banks in arranging securities offerings.

Investment banks' role in IPOs and secondary offerings also might be challenged by the internet-based platforms discussed earlier. If investors are easily reached and mobilized with targeted direct communication, one could envision a smaller role for investment banks, or at least one that makes them less indispensable and costly.[10] Historically, however, investment banks have been adroit in moving from one business opportunity to another. Hence, rumors of their demise may be premature, and the competitive dynamics of the banking industry in relation to nonbank competitors have yet to unfold.

ARE BANKS DOOMED?

What role will banks play in these developments? How will banks respond to payment solutions that Apple has enabled with its iPhones? Will we see an Apple Bank? These developments are not without risk for traditional banks. A major transition is going on in the industry, and the *status quo* may not be an option for incumbents.[11]

This does not mean that banks are doomed. In the past, banking institutions have shown remarkable resilience, despite questions about their viability. As far back as 1994, prominent economists John Boyd and Mark Gertler commented on the predicted demise of banks in a well-known study titled, "Are Banks Dead? Or Are The Reports Greatly Exaggerated?"[12] At that point, the discussion was about the banks' role in lending. In particular, the question was whether securitization would undermine the banks' lending franchise. They concluded that while securitization made banks less important for the actual funding of loans, the core functions of banks in the lending process – origination

---

9. A recent manifestation has been the emergence of high-frequency (algorithmic) trading whereby transactions are effected with a speed defying human sentience. While recognizing the promise of improving price discovery, potential abuses can be anticipated.

10. Information technology has spurred the proliferation of alternative trading platforms diminishing the centrality of traditional organized exchanges like the NYSE. Exchanges set rules to govern the trading and information flows. The mushrooming of exchanges has led to the need for separate clearing organizations. In addition, many banks have outsourced there custodian activities. All this has led to a further disaggregation of the value chain.

11. As a recent report by McKinsey & Co, a consultancy, puts it: "Digitization often lowers entry barriers, causing long-established boundaries between sectors to tumble. At the same time, the "plug and play" nature of digital assets causes value chains to disaggregate, creating openings for focused, fast-moving competitors. New market entrants often scale up rapidly at lower cost than legacy players can, and returns may grow rapidly as more customers join the network" (Hirt and Millmott, 2014). See also reports by other consultancies: "Building the bank of 2030 and beyond" E&Y, 2013; "Retail banking 2020: evolution or revolution?", PwC, 2014; and "Banking disrupted," Deloitte, 2014.

12. Boyd and Gertler (1994). See also the insightful historic account by Samolyk (2004).

(including screening), servicing, and monitoring – would be preserved, as would the centrality of banks. Also, banks would typically play a role in the securitization vehicles by providing back-up lines of credit and guarantees of the commercial paper that funds many of the vehicles.

The message of that article might still have some relevance today. With the mushrooming of the shadow banking sector, banks have not been entirely passive. They have broadened their scope and have successfully used the bank holding company structure to participate in the shadow banking system.[13]

Banks have Advantages

Compared with threatened incumbents in other industries, banks benefit from the anxiety of people about the safety of their liquid wealth. The financial crisis of 2007–2009 may have created anxiety about the stability of banks, but banks are still seen as the place where money is safe. "In banks we trust" is not an empty slogan.[14] The same cannot be said about all the new internet-based competitors. Whatever the popularity of Apple, will people trust technology companies in safeguarding their money? Being a bank with a license and an implicit guarantee from the government has value.

The perceived safety of banks and the special status that banks continue to have in the financial system allow banks to have funding-cost advantages and earn extra rents vis-à-vis competitors. Interestingly, during and after the 2007–2009 financial crisis, investment banks assigned such a high value to a commercial bank license and access to deposits that the largest among them converted to bank holding companies. Indeed, being a bank, particularly a large bank, offers (subsidized) safety net benefits in addition to more stable short-term funding via deposits. This means that as long as banks manage themselves efficiently, invest intelligently, and avoid being stifled by public regulation they are unlikely to disappear any time soon. However, they do face serious challenges, particularly on the retail side, where banks will need to connect to their social-media-focused customers.

Size of Banks and the Financial Sector

What about the scale and scope of financial institutions, and the size of the financial sector at large? Recent work suggests substantial scale economies in banking, particularly when it comes to back-office activities and payments.[15] The message on scope – the span of activities – is less convincing. Typically, research has documented a "conglomerate discount," which suggests that conglomeration is inefficient, but recent work shows that this discount largely disappears during crises, suggesting some benefits from "internal capital markets" during times of funding stress.[16] More integrated banks may therefore coexist with more specialized players.

A related question is what needs to be under one corporate roof, and to what extent will services be offered in networks, alliances or joint ventures? Information technology has facilitated more complicated, larger organizations and hence augmented scale and scope economies.[17] However, information technology has also facilitated smooth interfaces between independent firms, for example, insurance products could be offered through the distribution network of banks without banks owning the insurance company. Indeed, our earlier discussion on online platforms noted the ease with which products could be bundled in a distribution network.

Apart from technological forces, regulatory and political developments will have a substantial impact on concentration. One could interpret the SIFI classification within Basel III (with its capital surcharges) as a size penalty. Whether this has a real impact in influencing financial institutions size and complexity remains to be seen. Another unknown is the degree to which banks will engage in cross-border banking. The 2007–2009 financial crisis has led to a retreat by institutions to home markets, but whether this is a temporary development is unclear. National supervisors have sought to strengthen their control over institutions operating within their countries. While developments like the Banking Union initiative in the EU may counter this somewhat, the recent trend is toward fragmentation along national lines. Clearly, cross-border banking, except for capital market activities, has experienced limited success. Cultural differences between countries expressed in terms of a more favorable attitude toward home-based institutions may explain this.

---

13. See Cetorelli (2014) and Cetorelli et al. (2012).

14. Vatanasombut et al. (2008) highlight that trust plays a key role in the retention of customers with online banking. They also find that perceived security reinforces trust.

15. See Hughes and Mester (2014), Davies and Tracey (2012), and DeYoung (2010).

16. Consider, Schmid and Walter (2014). See also Laeven and Levine (2007). Note that this may also point to too-complex-to-fail issues, and increase the benefits of the government safety net.

17. Similarly, for Google and Facebook running larger networks and platforms may offer benefits that reinforce scale.

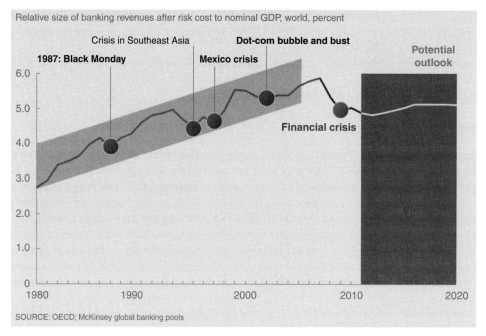

FIGURE 18.3 Financial Sector Share in GDP. *(Source: McKinsey (2012), The Triple Transformation: Achieving a Sustainable Business Model. 2nd McKinsey Annual Review on the Banking Industry, McKinsey & Company, October 2012, exhibit 13, page 27.)*

What will happen to the financial sector as a fraction of the economy at large? We have documented in Chapter 17 that the financial sector has grown substantially over the last decades. But what will the future bring? Figure 18.3 shows that various crises in the last 35 years have only temporarily halted the growth of the financial sector as percentage of GDP.

There are, however, reasons to envision a potential decline. The internet and information technology have resulted in declines in the number of bank branches. Together with an increasing automation of back offices, this may well reduce employment in the financial services industry. Investment banking may mirror what has already happened in the market for legal services where online research has reduced the demand for junior lawyers. A degree of commoditization can be expected as well in financial services which may reduce overall profitability.

CONCLUSION

The interaction of technology, public regulation, and customer preferences will radically reshape financial institutions of the future. While there is considerable uncertainty about details, few deny that the online digital revolution will revolutionize banking. The consequent reconfiguration of institutions will have implications for economic and financial stability, but the key issue is how society will be served.

Remember that the "real" economy is lubricated with elemental financial services. Thus, whatever the institutional arrangements, a growing and wealthier population will require liquidity (monetary services), credit, and risk redistribution services. These services will be produced with some combination of private and governmental inputs almost irrespective of institutional arrangements. However, the institutional arrangements will matter in so far as efficiency and the distribution of rents are concerned.

The bigger picture is foretold by a colorful history. Advances in finance have moved steadily, inexorably from the physical to the virtual and from the simple to the complex. Flux and intangibility have been the companions of progress permitting finance to remain close to the center of economic activity while earning a not-so-modest profit for financiers. Ask the Mellons, Morgans, and Rothschilds.

REFERENCES

BIS, 2014. Payment, Settlement and Clearing in Various Countries. Updated September 2014, www.bis.org/cpmi/paysysinfo.htm.

Boyd, J.H., Gertler, M., 1994. Are banks dead? Or are the reports greatly exaggerated? Federal Reserve Bank Minneapolis Q. Rev. 18, 2–23.

Cetorelli, N., 2014. Hybrid Intermediaries. Federal Reserve Bank of New York, Staff Report 705.

Cetorelli, N., Mandel, N., Mollineaux, L., 2012. The evolution of banks and financial intermediation: framing the analysis. Federal Reserve Bank NY Econ. Policy Rev. 18, 1–12.

Davies, R., Tracey, B., 2012. Too big to be efficient? The impact of implicit funding subsidies on scale economies in banking. Journal Money Credit Banking 46, 219–253.

DeYoung, R., 2010. Scale Economies are a Distraction. Federal Reserve Bank of Minneapolis, *The Region*, September 2010, pp. 14–16.

ESRB, 2014. 16th General Board Meeting on December 18th 2018. The General Board of the European Systemic Risk Board (ESRB), Press Release, see https://www.esrb.europa.eu/news/pr/2014/html/pr141223.en.html.

Haldane, A., 2012. The Dog and the Frisbee. Presented at the Federal Reserve Bank of Kansas City's Thirty-Sixth Economic Policy Symposium, *The Changing Policy Landscape*, Jackson Hole, Wyoming.

Hirt, M., Millmott, P., May 2014. Strategic principles for competing in the digital age. McKinsey Q., 1–14.

Hughes, J.P., Mester, L.J., 2014. Measuring the performance of banks: theory, practice, evidence, and some policy implications. In: Berger, A.N., Molyneux, P., Wilson, J. (Eds.), The Oxford handbook on banking, second ed., Chapter 10, pp. 247–281.

Laeven, L., Levine, R., 2007. Is there a diversification discount in financial conglomerates? J. Financ. Econ. 85, 331–367.

Lucas, D., 2014. Evaluating the government as a source of systemic risk. J. Financ. Perspect. 2, 45–58.

Mollick, E., 2014. The dynamics of crowdfunding: an exploratory study. J. Bus. Venturing 29, 1–16.

Nakamoto, S., 2013. Bitcoin: a Peer-to-Peer Electronic Cash System. Working Paper, www.bitcoin.org.

Samolyk, K., 2004. The future of banking in America: the evolving role of commercial banks in U.S. credit markets. FDIC Banking Rev. 16, 29–65.

Schmid, M., Walter, I., July 2014. Firm structure in banking and finance: is broader better? J. Financ. Perspect. 2, 65–74.

Vatanasombut, B., Igbaria, M., Stylianou, A.C., Rodgers, W., 2008. Information systems continuance intention of web-based applications customers: the case of online banking, 2008. Information Management 45, 419–428.

Wyman, O. Payments are Changing But How Prepared are Retail Banks? Oliver Wyman Financial Services Point of View, 2014.

Yermack, D., 2013. Is bitcoin a real currency? An economic appraisal. NBER Working Paper No. 19747.

Subject Index